Integrating Theory
and Practice in
Clinical Neuropsychology

Integrating Theory and Practice in Clinical Neuropsychology

Edited by

Ellen Perecman

Department of Neurology,
North Shore University Hospital
and
Department of Neurology,
Cornell University Medical College

 LAWRENCE ERLBAUM ASSOCIATES, PUBLISHERS
1989   Hillsdale, New Jersey   Hove and London

Copyright © 1989 by Lawrence Erlbaum Associates, Inc.
  All rights reserved. No part of this book may be reproduced in
any form, by photostat, microfilm, retrieval system, or any other
means, without the prior written permission of the publisher.

Lawrence Erlbaum Associates, Inc., Publishers
365 Broadway
Hillsdale, New Jersey 07642

Library of Congress Cataloging-in-Publication Data

Integrating theory and practice in clinical neuropsychology.

  Includes bibliographies and indexes.
  1. Clinical neuropsychology.   I. Perecman, Ellen.
RC341.I48   1988   152   88–33614
ISBN 0–8058–0285–1

Printed in the United States of America
10 9 8 7 6 5 4 3 2 1

To my son, Adam

Contents

13   Management of Neuropsychological Impairment After Severe Head Injury *337*
J. M. Mazaux, M. Gagnon, and M. Barat

14   Staying in the Community After a Head Injury *359*
Noemi F. Cohen

15   Assessment of Cognitive Disorders in the Elderly *381*
Wilma G. Rosen

Contributors

William Badecker, Ph.D. The Johns Hopkins University, Cognitive Science Center, Baltimore, MD 21218

Michel Barat, M.D. Université de Bordeaux II et Service de Réeducation Neurologique, Hôpital Péllégrin, 33076 Bordeaux Cedex, France

Joan C. Borod, Ph.D. Queens College, The City University of New York, Department of Psychology, New Science Building E318, Flushing, NY 11367 and Mount Sinai School of Medicine, Department of Neurology

Alfonso Caramazza, Ph.D. The Johns Hopkins University, Cognitive Science Center, Baltimore, MD 21218

Laird Cermak, Ph.D. Memory Disorders Research Center, Boston VA Medical Center, 150 South Huntington Avenue, Boston, MA 02130

Ilene Cohen, Ph.D. Bellevue Geriatric Clinic, Bellevue Hospital, First Avenue at 27th Street, New York, NY 10016

Noemi Fleischman-Cohen, M.S. Headways, One To One Community-Based Rehabilitation Program, 333 Marlboro Road, Englewood, NJ 07631

Terrence Deacon, Ph.D. Harvard University, Biological Anthropology, 11 Divinity Avenue, Cambridge, MA 02138

Todd E. Feinberg, M.D. Beth Israel Medical Center, Neurobehavior Center, Fierman 403, 317 East 17th Street, New York, NY 10003

Michele Gagnon, Ph.D. Université de Bordeaux II, Departement d'Informatique Medicalé, 33076 Bordeaux, France

Felicia C. Goldstein, Ph.D.   University of Texas Medical Branch, Department of Neurology E39, Neurology Laboratory, Galveston, TX 77550

Jordan Grafman, Ph.D.   Cognitive Neuroscience Unit, Medical Neurology Branch, NINCDS/Building 10, Room 5C422, Bethesda, MD 20892

Richard C. Katz, Ph.D.   Audiology and Speech Pathology Service, Veterans Administration, Outpatient Clinic, 425 South Hill Street, Los Angeles, CA 90013

Lucia Kellar, Ph.D.   Bellevue Geriatric Clinic, Bellevue Hospital, First Avenue at 27th Street, New York, NY 10016

Andrew Kertesz, M.D.   Department of Clinical Neurological Sciences, St. Joseph's Hospital, London, Ontario, Canada N6A 4V2

Elissa Koff, Ph.D.   Department of Psychology, Wellesley College, Wellesley, MA 02181

Anneliesse Kotten, Ph.D.   Fachklinik Bad Heilbrunn, Abteilung Neurologie, Wurnerweg 30, 8173 Bad Heilbrunn, West Germany

Harvey S. Levin, Ph.D.   University of Texas Medical Branch, Division of Neurosurgery E17, Neurology Laboratory, Galveston, TX 77550

Jean-Michel Mazaux, M.D.   Université de Bordeaux II et Service de Réeducation Neurologique, Hôpital Péllégrin, 33076 Bordeaux Cedex, France

Steven E. Mazlin, Ph.D.   Department of Neurology, Mount Sinai School of Medicine, 1 Gustav L. Levy Place, New York, NY 10029

Allan F. Mirsky, Ph.D.   Chief, Laboratory of Psychology and Psychopathology, NIMH, Bethesda, MD 20892

Wilma G. Rosen, Ph.D.   Columbia-Presbyterian Medical Center, Neurological Institute, 710 West 168th Street, New York, NY 10032-3784

Georgine Vroman, Ph.D.   Bellevue Geriatric Clinic, Bellevue Hospital, First Avenue at 27 Street, New York, NY 10016

Glen E. Waldman, M.D.   Department of Neurology, Mount Sinai School of Medicine, 1 Gustav L. Levy Place, New York, NY 10029

Barbara A. Wilson, Ph.D.   University of Southampton, West Wing—Level C, Southampton General Hospital, Tremona Road, Southampton S09 4XY, United Kingdom

Acknowledgments

My first debt of gratitude is to the authors whose contributions constitute this volume. I thank them for their efforts, for their cooperation, and for their patience. The theme of the volume is taken from a series of workshops I organized for the Institute for Research in Behavioral Neuroscience and the Ph.D. Program in Speech and Hearing Sciences at the Graduate Center, City University of New York in 1986–87. Many of the authors in this volume participated in those workshops.

Much of the work on this book was carried out while I held an appointment in the Department of Neurology at New York University School of Medicine. I would like to express my gratitude to that department for providing me with the space and services needed to bring this project to fruition.

Finally, I would like to thank Jason W. Brown for his advice, support and encouragement.

Introduction

Ellen Perecman

The extent to which a brain injured individual can resume premorbid functioning depends on factors ranging from the physiological to the psychological. From the physiological point of view, prognosis for recovery will depend on the potential for regeneration of the nervous system and an assumption of redundancy in the functional organization of the brain. According to Feinberg, Mazlin, and Waldman (Chapter 2), the traditional view that the adult mammalian central nervous system is incapable of regeneration led neurologists to hold a pessimistic attitude toward recovery and rehabilitation of the human central nervous system. Feinberg et al suggest, however, based on data from serial lesion studies in animals, that compensation by intact parts of the brain is possible but not automatic. Thus, although its generalizability to man remains a matter of speculation, evidence of some form of redundancy of function in mammals provides a hopeful future for brain injured members of our society.

From the psychological point of view the issues involved are not as straightforward. Presumably motivation plays a role in the rehabilitation process. But, why, one might ask, would a brain-injured person lack the motivation to recover? Perhaps because he or she has lost touch with his premorbid self—with the identity he or she is being asked to recover.

Hofstadter and Dennett (1981) argue that the Self—one's identity—is defined by "[t]hose things of which I am conscious, and the ways in which I am conscious of them" (p. 9).[1] Based on this definition, any change in the "ways in which I am conscious of them", will give rise to a change in—even loss of—one's sense of Self. Because damage to the brain can alter the instruments of consciousness, namely, perception and action, it is not unlikely that the brain-damaged person suffers a loss of identity, a loss of Self. In an age when "finding one's Self" is considered an ennobling goal, the tragedy of losing one's Self assumes even greater proportions.

---

[1]Hofstadter, D. R., & Dennett, D. C. (1981). *The mind's I*. New York: Basic Books, Inc.

Philosophers of mind and experimental neuropsychologists are perhaps too comfortable treating the self as an abstraction, and its demise as a theoretical manipulation. But for the clinician, the Self is so stark a reality and its loss has such concrete repercussions that he or she risks erring on the side of underestimating the value of theoretical formulation in clinical practice.

MODELING BRAIN FUNCTION

As argued throughout this volume, diagnosis and treatment of an impairment depend critically on a well-defined theory of normal function, because as Feinberg, Mazlin, and Waldman explain (Chapter 2), "it is difficult to state with precision what has been regained after injury if one cannot describe with certainty what normal brain functions have been lost." Similarly, if we are to attempt to improve an impaired performance, we must begin with a model of what constitutes normal, or at least, successful performance and a set of predictions about the ways in which a performance can deviate from normal. Yet Wilson (Chapter 6) reminds us that although therapy has much to gain from theoretical models, "[j]ust as bridges were built long before the discovery of Newtonian mechanics so remediation of deficits has taken place without recourse to theory."

In Chapter 3, Mirsky offers a theoretical framework for the assessment and treatment of attentional disorders. He presents a model in which attention is characterized ". . . not a unitary phenomenon but [as] comprised of a series of . . . stages", and in which each stage, that is, focus, execute, sustain, encode and shift, is mediated by a different part of the brain. Mirsky also speculates on how the various sources of information (e.g. neuroanatomical, neurophysiological and neuropsychological) combine in mediating attentional processes, increasing the predictive power of his model.

In Chapter 4, Grafman presents a model of the higher-order cognitive processes associated with the frontal lobes. After reviewing frontal lobe lesion studies, including psychosurgery studies, and recent models of knowledge representation, Grafman elaborates his own model, which is informed by the psychological disorders that accompany frontal lobe lesions in man and which describes the nature of cognition and mood representation in the frontal lobes, including the processing of temporal relations and order, planning and problem solving, memory, use of objects in the environment, learning, suppression of old habits, language, mood regulation, confabulation, and perseverative behavior. The model operates in terms of managerial knowledge units (MKU), which, Grafman suggests, are the predominant type of information unit in the frontal lobe, somewhat analogous to schemas, scripts, and frames. The MKUs form a hierarchical system ranging from the concrete to the abstract, and Grafman argues that "almost all aspects of human behavior will be under the control and guidance of a hierarchy of MKUs."

Addressing the issue of assessment and treatment of frontal lobe disorders, Grafman suggests that "the stumbling block preventing the development of effective management techniques and tools is the lack of a credible model of behavior to help practitioners describe the patient's deficits in a coherent manner."

One of the most critical (and interesting) issues raised by the problem of modeling brain function is *how* one defines the point at which a deviant response indicates impairment. That is, how does one distinguish (both from a practical and theoretical point of view) the deviant response that reflects impaired processing from the deviant response that reflects a preference for the creative alternative?

THE NEUROANATOMY AND NEUROPHYSIOLOGY OF BRAIN INJURY

After presenting a brief history of neuropsychology, Deacon (Chapter 1) reviews what is currently known about the connectional anatomy of the cerebral cortical circuits and contends that "if the 19th century 'diagram makers' were guilty of inventing, singling out, or oversimplifying neural connections to fit their psychological models of brain processes, neuropsychological theories at present are guilty of ignoring the growing body of 'diagrams' of empirically identified neural connections."

Deacon notes that the remarkable similarity in cellular and connectional anatomy in mammalian brains makes it possible to apply many of these general findings to humans and explores the anatomical implications of associationist and microgenetic models. He argues that associationist and holistic theories are "not so much alternative theories of mind as descriptions of complementary aspects of a single process" and that "one of the major biases that associationist theories have introduced is the assumption that sensory input and motor output are somehow opposite functions." Rather, Deacon maintains that "[t]he secret of the transformation of the signal from one level of processing to the next may lie in this interaction of centrifugal and centripetal signals."

Feinberg et al (Chapter 2) provide an overview of the neurological aspects of brain injury and recovery, which begins with a particularly striking reminder of the immediacy of the effects of brain injury: After a stroke, changes in cellular morphology can be seen within the first hour or two after interruption of blood flow. The authors then address anatomic, physiologic and biochemical mechanisms of injury and proceed to review theories of recovery and what is known about the potential of the CNS for reorganization after injury. Among the mechanisms of recovery they discuss are the resolution of acute effects, equipotentiality, redundancy, vicarious functioning, and behavioral substitution. Aspects of morphological and functional reorganization treated are regeneration, sprouting, reactive synaptogenesis, and neurochemical adaptation. For these authors, it seems clear that "we may be able to manipulate recovery long before we fully understand it".

MEMORY IMPAIRMENT

Too often in neuropsychology definition is mistaken for explanation. In Chapter 5, Cermak alludes to this problem in the context of research on memory when he points out that "[t]heories which separate memory from that which is not memory are important because they help to *define* amnesia. But they are relatively less important when it comes to *explaining* amnesia.", Cermak discusses three dichotomies in models of memory and how they relate to one another: a) procedural vs. declarative memory; b) episodic vs. semantic memory; and c) aware vs. unaware memory, arguing that ". . . disagreements between theorists ought not to center upon which model is the true description of amnesia but, rather, upon the functional loci of specific phenomena that have been discovered to be true about amnesia, such as encoding deficits, retrieval deficits, priming, etc."

In a critical analysis of the role of assessment in memory therapy, Wilson (Chapter 6) suggests that most current tests are not sufficiently "ecologically relevant." She describes the Rivermead Behavioral Memory Test which, in her view, meets this requirement in that "instead of asking people to remember strange drawings, lists of words, or paired-associates, it asks them to carry out everyday memory tasks, such as delivering a message or remembering an appointment . . ." Wilson reviews various theoretical approaches to treatment which she maintains are not mutually exclusive, but rather are most useful when applied in some combination over the course of treatment. Wilson suggests that memory therapy too must be "ecologically relevant" and argues that memory rehabilitation should include techniques for improving memory as well as assistance in social, emotional and environmental matters.

DISORDERS OF EMOTIONAL PROCESSING

Borod and Koff (Chapter 7) address the problem of the neuropsychology of emotion from the point of view of hemispheric specialization, reviewing the literature on perception and expression of emotion with respect to inter- as well as intrahemispheric factors in normal, brain-damaged, and psychiatric populations. They describe the evolution of their experimental work on the neuropsychological mechanisms underlying emotional expression and techniques for assessing emotional processing, emphasizing that the communication of emotion is a multidetermined behavior, involving a variety of modes or channels (e.g. face, intonation, lexical/speech context, gesture) that interact in complex ways and that disorders of emotional processing may be observed in any or all of these channels. They also provide data arguing for a dissociation between systems controlling emotional facial expression and non-emotional facial movement. Borod and Koff discuss the therapeutic implications of the hypothesis that right anterior areas mediate production while right posterior areas mediate comprehension of facial emotion and suggest ways in which preserved residual emotional capacity in aphasics can be used to prime language.

PERSONALITY CHANGES
IN CLOSED HEAD INJURY

Goldstein and Levin (Chapter 8) address the effect of psychiatric disturbance as a source of disability in head-injured patients, focusing on the importance of personality changes in the outcome of Closed Head Injury (CHI). Using the term 'personality' to refer to what has been called mental, psychosocial, behavioral, and emotional, these authors identify a number of overlapping dimensions within which personality sequelae may fall: affective (mood), cognitive (thought processes), behavioral (overt actions), and somatic (physical complaints). They discuss factors that may contribute to personality change such as premorbid personality, preexisting psychiatric disturbance, lateralization and location of brain injury, and responses of patient and family to the disability, and describe common patterns of personality change seen in acute and chronic stages of recovery. They conclude with suggestions for the treatment of personality disturbances.

APHASIA

Kertesz (Chapter 9) provides a comprehensive review of issues relating to assessment of aphasia, including the various clinical and theoretical rationales for testing aphasics and an historical survey of aphasia tests. He begins his chapter by pointing out that the optimal test must attempt to reconcile the needs of both clinical and research goals: "practicality and comprehensiveness, stability and flexibility, generalizability and specificity, wide-spread applicability and sensitivity." Kertesz suggests that such a test does not currently exist, perhaps because investigators do not agree on what a test for aphasia should measure. Stressing the need for a reproducible repeated measure in clinical and research settings, Kertesz offers a blueprint for the optimal assessment tool for aphasia.

In Chapter 11, Kotten confronts the controversial issue of the efficacy of aphasia therapy. In a critical review of studies of assessment and treatment of aphasia, she discusses test construction, comparability of tests, explanatory force of test results, and sensitivity of tests to changes over time. In an effort to explain the contradictory conclusions drawn from many of the studies, Kotten suggests that they stem from methodological problems inherent in comparing across studies and even across patients. Kotten cautions that comparisons across studies are difficult because different studies assume different approaches to the treatment question, and that comparing across patients requires consideration of what she refers to as the "human factor," the particular relation between the patient and the therapist. Kotten suggests that until the issue of interpretation is resolved, the question of the efficacy of aphasia therapy remains an open one.

While Kertesz and Kotten offer a clinical perspective on the place of theory in practice in the context of aphasia, Badecker and Caramazza (Chapter 10) speak to this issue from the point of view of the experimental neuropsychologist. These authors seek to demonstrate how studies of lexical processing impairments in aphasic "can inform our theories of normal language processing," and "that the nature of language pathology may be validly inferred only by reference to well-defined linguistic and cognitive theories." They begin with a discussion of methodological issues in the study of aphasic impairments, in particular the single-case versus group study approach, and then proceed to review studies of lexical processing in normals and in aphasics which bear on the representation of morphologically complex words and on the role of morphemic units in lexical processing. On the basis of these studies, they develop arguments that there are distinct processing mechanisms for words and non-words, that morphological decomposition is a constituent process in lexical access, and that lexical access procedures employ both whole-word and morpheme access units.

NEW TRENDS IN REHABILITATION

Although the high technologies of modern medicine have led to improvements in the rate of survival after a head injury, improving the quality of life of the survivor may present yet a greater challenge. Mazaux, Gagnon, and Barat (Chapter 13) contend that standard therapeutic intervention strategies are not applicable in cases of head injury because of the unique problems of the head injured, specifically the interplay of anatomical, physiological, psychopathological, and social factors. They suggest that a comprehensive therapeutic framework including "first aid and emergency care, neurosurgical procedures, rehabilitation of motor and cognitive functioning, reorganization of the patient's self-image, and late social adjustments . . . will optimize the efficacy of the rehabilitation" for these patients. The authors discuss management issues specific to each of the successive stages of rehabilitation, such as the impact of comforting nursing during coma, acceleration of arousal processes, and neuropsychological remediation, and then address rehabilitation procedures that focus on social adjustment, family life, and the return to work. Mazaux et al conclude that future rehabilitation efforts should focus on that which sets head injury apart from other conditions, and specifically on social reintegration.

Social reintegration is in fact the primary concern of Cohen's chapter (Chapter 14). Consistent with the arguments of Mazaux et al, Cohen contends that rehabilitation efforts rarely result in independence for the head-injured patient because of residual neuropsychological and psychiatric impairments "that dramatically alter the quality of their own lives as well as that of their significant others." In view of this, Cohen argues that to be most effective the rehabilitation process must not only involve the head-injured patient but must also direct its attention to educating and offering support to the patient's family and to cultivating channels of communication and outreach between the patient and society. Moreover, she maintains that the emotional burden is eased by including the professional community and society at large in the rehabilitation schema. With these principles of rehabilitation as her guidelines, Cohen established a "home- and community-based rehabilitation program designed to encourage patients to remain in society and which attempts to address the needs of the patient, family, and community." In this chapter, Cohen describes preliminary results of the program.

ETIOLOGY AND AGE AS FACTORS
IN THE REHABILITATION SETTING

Depending on the etiology and age of the patient population, one encounters a unique set of problems and concerns. As Goldstein and Levin (Chapter 8) point out, "[t]he heterogeneity of severity and location of damage in closed head injury (CHI) undoubtedly contributes to the range of sequelae in contrast to disease states such as stroke, which tend to produce well-defined focal lesions and specific lateralized deficits." They also note that this population offers a particularly complex problem because what you see is not necessarily what you get. They call attention to the fact that the lack of somatic complaints in severely head-injured patients is likely to be related to inaccurate self-appraisal, denial, or awareness of physical disability, and similarly that diminution in social contact may be related to poor memory and *not* to residual sensory and motor deficit. They indicate the importance of distinguishing between patients who are in fact unmotivated and those who may appear unmotivated but actually have neuropsychological deficits which compromise performance. Another problem peculiar to CHI patients is understanding the importance of providing structured contexts for the execution of a task. These authors point out that patients may have difficulty initiating a task because they are overwhelmed by the task demands. Yet, when provided with structure they show evidence of sustained effort and high drive. Goldstein and Levin also raise the issue of the effect of CHI on the family of the patient and note that in this population, the family's reaction to disability can reinforce and maintain maladaptive responses.

Cognitive rehabilitation of the elderly involves another set of issues. First, it is known that age influences rate and extent of recovery after brain injury; the brain tissue surrounding the lesion in younger patients is usually in better condition than is the case in the aging brain. This may account for why our society is often reluctant to consider rehabilitation a viable option for older patients, and why Vroman et al (Chapter 16) suggest that society holds that older patients do not "deserve" a chance at rehabilitation.

Diagnostic issues are also unique to the elderly in that not only are questions of a memory deficit complicated by a link to depression, but the elderly often have a sense of helplessness in facing the fact that they are aging and that younger people are prone to dismissing their complaints on the ground that they are inevitable consequences of aging.

Rosen (Chapter 15) points out that all patients do not initially show the total expected pattern of deficits and that cognitive abilities do not show the same pattern of decline across patients. As an example, she cites studies indicating that there are distinct clinical variants of Alzheimer's disease. According to Rosen, differentiation between an early dementia and normal aging is problematic primarily in persons who are quite intelligent and have or had a high level of occupational functioning. For Rosen, the issue is whether a "normal" test score actually reflects the patient's premorbid abilities or a decline from a still higher level of functioning, and she suggests a procedure for dealing with such a situation.

Rosen proposes that all of the disorders affecting the elderly are "time-locked," and that this feature is potentially the most useful in the resolution of a diagnostic dilemma in an elderly individual, because it predicts that different disorders are accompanied by different changes in cognitive function over time. She presents three cases, which initially presented problems in differential diagnosis, and discusses how the problem was resolved by taking into account the "time-locked" nature of the different disorders.

THE USE OF COMPUTERS
IN COGNITIVE REHABILITATION

Katz (Chapter 12) advocates the use of computers and treatment software in aphasia therapy as tools which extend the abilities of the clinician. "The clinician," he reminds us, "is responsible for treatment efficacy, not the microcomputer, software, programmer, designer, or publisher." Katz discusses treatment software in the context of theoretical concerns which he maintains are basic to any aphasia treatment whether it be computerized or not—models of rehabilitation, approaches to treatment, stages of recovery, structure and content of tasks. He reviews studies assessing the feasibility and effectiveness of microcomputers in treating aphasic adults and concludes that they can stimulate language and independent thinking, model compensatory strategies, optimize the learning situation by determining the appropriate level of task difficulty, as well as offer the opportunity for individualized intervention.

Vroman, Kellar, and Cohen (Chapter 16) present case reports from a pilot study of the use of microcomputers in treating geriatric patients with memory complaints. Results of the study indicated a consistent maintenance of gains over a period up to one year suggesting that, as a group, elderly patients had learned to apply newly acquired strategies on a regular basis. Vroman et al argue that for the elderly, computers are useful in fostering independence, increasing self confidence, and teaching effective strategies for overcoming cognitive failures. They also suggest that another advantage of computer-based rehabilitation for the elderly is the role it plays in helping to restore a sense of control over one's environment when a feeling of loss of that control can be a significant cause of depression. Vroman et al reason that because computerized tasks are adapted to the patient's level of capability, and the patient masters one goal before proceeding to the next, patients will eventually assume a sense of control over their environment. Vroman et al speculate that "this experience of control may generalize to other areas of life, thus alleviating some of the secondary depression associated with cognitive dysfunction."

The thesis of this volume is that atheoretical application of practical techniques in clinical neuropsychology is as ill-conceived as a neuropsychological theory that fails to acknowledge the role of historical or situational context in behavior or task performance. The chapters that follow address this thesis as experimental psychologists join clinicians in an effort to bridge the gap between theoretical abstraction and practical reality.

1

Holism and Associationism in Neuropsychology: An Anatomical Synthesis

Terrence W. Deacon

INTRODUCTION

Neuropsychological theories make implicit assumptions about brain organization and the relationships between structure and function. These include assumptions about the movement and representation of information within brain structures and neural circuits and about the phylogenesis and development of these substrates. Unfortunately, our knowledge of human neuroanatomy remains incomplete and is particularly lacking in detailed information about the patterns of axonal connections—the basic circuits of the brain. As a result, the anatomical assumptions of neuropsychological theories are often represented by no more than diagrams of logical relationships between operationally defined functions, where the relationships are attributed to connections and the functions are assigned to areas.

The last decades have seen remarkable advances in experimental neuroanatomy using nonhuman species. Since the discovery of autoradiographic and peroxidase axonal tracer techniques in the 1970s, the development of information concerning the connectional patterns of monkey, cat, and rat brains has proceeded at an explosive rate. It is probably not too ambitious to expect that the details of the connectional anatomy for the brains of these model laboratory species will be thoroughly catalogued well before the turn of the next century. Although we still lack the means to directly analyze human brain circuitry at a comparable level of detail, the remarkable similarity in cellular and connectional anatomy in mammalian brains makes it possible to apply many of these general findings to the problem of understanding human brain anatomy.

If the 19th century "diagram makers" were guilty of inventing, singling out, or oversimplifying neural connections to fit their psychological models of brain processes; neuropsychological theories at present are

1

guilty of ignoring the growing body of "diagrams" of empirically identified neural connections. Maps of the direct and indirect pathways through which information can be transmitted within the brain, and of the general patterns these pathways exhibit, can provide rigorous constraints within which to guide development of models of brain function. Perhaps for the first time in the study of the human brain it is possible to ask what sort of neuropsychological theories are suggested by the anatomy rather than the other way around.

Neuroanatomical evidence can provide us with a kind of information about mental processes not accessible through neuropsychological investigations alone. Ultimately the relationships between cognitive functions are a reflection of brain organization. But the human brain is not a computing device originally designed with the performance of these functions in mind. The neural architecture of the human brain was determined by the happenstance accumulation of successful evolutionary accidents over the hundreds of millions of years before the appearance of *Homo sapiens*. Consequently human neural systems carry within their architecture the imprint of past adaptations. Present functions that have inherited these systems are constrained by the logic of these past functions at least as much as by present demands. Even the neural logic of such a uniquely human activity as language is undoubtedly constrained by more ancient and unrelated neurological adaptations that have only recently become recruited to serve this new function (e.g., see Deacon, 1988). The evolutionary constraints within which human brain functions have had to develop are unlikely to be evident except through comparative neuroanatomical investigations.

In the discussion that follows I focus on two very general attributes of the connectional anatomy of cerebral cortical circuits: the reciprocality and the directionality of cortico-cortical connections. The existence of reciprocal connectivity for most cortical connections has been recognized for some time but has not been appreciated for its implications with respect to neuropsychological theories. The "directionality" of these connections is defined with respect to certain asymmetries in laminar organization. This systematic asymmetry of connections provides important clues for comparing directional or hierarchic patterns of cortical organization and may, therefore, help settle one of the oldest disputes in neuropsychology: that between localizationist-connectionist-associationist theories and anti-localizationist-microgenetic-holistic theories. These overly clumsy designations are meant to capture both the historical and theoretical sense of a long and changing debate between two major rival paradigms for modeling the organization of brain processes. The debate is of such general character that at times it has taken on an almost philosophical tone.

Nonetheless, the neurological implications of each of these alternative views are of more than historical interest. They have been translated into the paradigms of clinical practice and experimental design that have guided the treatment of neurological disorders and the investigation of neural processes.

TWO NEUROPSYCHOLOGIES: A BRIEF HISTORICAL REVIEW

Since the early part of the 19th century mainstream neurology and neuropsychology have embraced one of these general approaches at the expense of the other, and as is so often the case with major competing theoretical paradigms in science, the history of the field has seen a series of pendulum swings from associationism to holism, and from localizationism to antilocalizationism. Although the underlying ideas trace back to perennial philosophical debates over associationist theories of mind, the origins of these polar perspectives in neurology can be dated to the phrenological theories of Franz Josef Gall (1791; Gall & Spurzheim, 1810–1818) and the criticisms of this view by Pierre Flourens (1824/1943).

The associationist perspective begins from the underlying premise that each mental event and its corresponding underlying brain process can be analyzed into component mental events and neural processes. The idea that component processes are initially independent elements that may or may not enter into some higher-order process has further led to the view that different component processes may be carried out by different, relatively independent neural structures or circuits (localizationism). Higher-order functions are derived by linking together the functions of these separate structures and by collecting together the results of their activity in specialized centers whose specific functions are to integrate these diverse inputs. This analysis essentially models cognition as a sequential hierarchic process where the simplest component neural analyses must be completed before passing their results on to higher centers to be integrated into more complex analyses. Higher-order mental processes and lower-order processes are described by the same associational logic, but the content of the operations at each level differs. The resultant progression is from simple to complex, from simple component features to complex integrated wholes. The difference between the smallest sensory stimulus element and an abstract concept is treated as a difference in hierarchic complexity. Presumably, following the associationist logic, concepts can be analytically decomposed in a series of steps into relationships among minimal sensory elements. Correspondingly, brain processes in higher centers are seen as operating on the results of the calculations in the next lower centers in the hierarchy while brain processes at the lowest most primary levels are seen as operating directly on sense data.

In contrast, the holistic (or anti-associationistic) perspective begins from the premise that mental processes are not decomposable into subprocesses that can exist independent of the whole cognition in which they are involved. Holistic theories argue that cognitive processes are not more complex relationships among simpler perceptual or motor processes, but that these fractional units are artificially abstracted glimpses of aspects of an indecomposable whole. Often this has led to the further argument that localized brain structures cannot be treated as though they have functional autonomy. Rather, mental activities are processes of the whole brain and the functions of the parts reflect their relative positions within the entire network. Many holistic theorists have argued that perceptions, intentions, memories and other mental events cannot be localized to specific structures (anti-localizationism). Consequently, the function of the whole should not be deducible from an analysis of the functions of the parts. Where associationism views cognitions as built up piecemeal from smaller more basic units collected from different areas of the brain, holism views cognitions as emerging whole and integrated from the outset, with different aspects of the whole developing in parallel in all regions of the brain. Thus, the holistic model is more akin to a parallel processing model of neural function in which all parts of the system are simultaneously at work on a different aspect of the same integrated process.

The difference between the two approaches is most evident in the interpretation of behavioral changes after focal brain damage. From an associationist-localizationist perspective the loss of brain tissue is expected to be correlated with either the loss of a specific function or the interruption of the interactions between intact functions—disconnection. From a holistic-antilocalizationist point of view the total amount of damaged tissue is more critical than its exact location. The greater the loss of brain tissue the more disturbed all cognitive functions become. Because each cognitive act is the product of a process encompassing the whole brain, the coherence of every motor act and every perceptual process is expected to be degraded by the damage.

Associationism and localizationism have had a long theoretical partnership in neuropsychology. Critiques of these theories tend to treat them as interdependent, and the acceptance of one has historically implied acceptance of the other. The same can be said for alternative theories. Anti-associationism and antilocalizationism arguments seem to reoccur and support each other in most holistic theories. However the debates over associationism and localizationism can in part be separated and individual theorists have supported one and not the other in some contexts.

The Development of Localizationist-Connectionist Theories

The modern form of the debate between localizationist and antilocalizationist theorists began to take shape at the end of the 19th century when Paul Broca (1861, 1863, 1865, 1866) demonstrated that localized damage to the left inferior frontal lobe of the brain caused loss of speech. This appeared to vindicate the discrete localizaton of function proposed by Gall a half century before. The next major step in this direction was taken by Carl Wernicke (1874), who identified a posterior temporal locus of damage in cases with the amnesic form of language disturbance. Wernicke's impact on neuropsychology was not so much determined by his discovery of another form of aphasia as by his synthesis of clinicoanatomical findings with a conception of the nervous system composed of functional centers linked together by connections that relayed information from one center to the next like a telegraph system.

Wernicke's theory, an important advance over the preceding localizationist ideas, grew directly out of the anatomical studies of Theodore Meynert (1866, 1867). Meynert had traced fibers from the auditory nuclei in the brain stem to ultimate termination sites within the superior temporal lobe and had also recognized that the sensory/motor division between postcentral and anterior cortical areas might thus comprise part of a sensory-motor reflex arc. Wernicke saw the implications of emphasizing connectional patterns within the brain for the analysis of brain damage. The result was a synthesis of ideas about the localization of functions with an anatomical interpretation for the means by which separated functions became associated: *connectionism*. His connectionistic interpretation of the aphasias set the stage for most subsequent associationist-localizationist theories. He distinguished motor (Broca's) aphasia from sensory (Wernicke's) aphasia in terms of damage to two corresponding functionally specialized centers. He reasoned that Broca's (motor) aphasia resulted from damage to the motor memory area for speech production and that his own cases of sensory aphasia resulted from damage to the auditory memory area for the sound structure of words (it was at the time still thought that the cortex was not directly involved in sensory reception and motor production, but only in higher level cognitive and mnemonic processes). But Wernicke went beyond this localized centers approach by also suggesting that disconnection of either language area from the "subcortical" centers involved in direct sensory or motor processing would produce distinguishably different sorts of impairments than the two forms of cortical aphasia (termed subcortical sensory or motor aphasia). He also reasoned that disconnection of cortical areas from one another should also produce unique deficits. Disconnecting the sensory from the motor language areas would effectively sever the speech "reflex arc" and should produce repetition and speech production deficits, disconnecting visual areas and the temporal language area should produce reading deficits, and disconnecting the writing area in the frontal lobe from either the temporal or visual areas should result in writing or copying deficits. This approach provided a wealth of testable predictions, many of which were in some way vindicated by subsequent investigators (e.g., Lichtheim, 1885; Liepmann, 1912, 1913; Liepmann & Pappenheim, 1914).

The clinico-anatomical evidence for connectionism was supplemented by new neuroanatomical discoveries. Fritsch and Hitzig (1870) had electrically stimulated the cerebral cortex of animals and demonstrated both localization of function and a direct role for cortex in the production of movement. This was a serious blow to the view that the cerebral cortex was involved only in "higher" cognitive functions, and not directly involved in simple sensory reception or movement, and strongly supported the idea that functions could be localized in cortex. The development of new histological staining methods for neurons and myelin also contributed to the influence of connectionism. A number of neuroanatomists, using different techniques, began to recognize that the cerebral cortex could be subdivided into distinct areas on the basis of cellular organization. Campbell (1905) and Brodmann (1905; 1909) produced maps of cortical areas based on cellular architecture and Flechsig (1900; 1901) and Vogt and Vogt (1919) produced corresponding maps based on myelin patterns. The Vogts additionally analyzed the correspondence between their myeloarchitectonic divisions and the electrical excitability of motor areas. These studies led many to hypothesize that the architectural parcellation of cortex corresponded in a one-to-one manner with functional localization.

Out of these studies a new synthesis of neuroanatomical and neuropsychological theories developed. According to the classic model put forward by Campbell in his 1905 monograph, there were three major tiers of neocortical areas within the cortical hierarchy for each sensory/motor modality: primary areas with direct peripheral connections, secondary "belt" areas that were adjacent to and connected with a particular primary area, and association areas that were connected with adjacent belt areas and with each other but had no direct peripheral connections.

In posterior cortical areas, according to this view, each of the highly specialized sensory areas was presumed to be a passive recipient area for registering sensory inputs. The adjacent belt area, which received its input from this receptive area, served a perceptual-psychic function. The "output" of the perceptual-psychic area was a completed perception. The association area for each modality received as its input the completed perceptual information from the sensory-psychic area. Association areas were thought to be the center for storage of sensory memories, and by virtue of interconnections between different association areas, the substrate for sensory-motor integration and abstract conceptualization.

Motor areas appeared to be organized in a similar hierarchic triad, but with the direction of information flow reversed. Motor responses were assumed to be activated by particular stimulus associations relayed into the frontal lobes from posterior association areas. In prefrontal cortex these sensory associations are associated with motor associations and the intention to act is formulated. This behavioral plan is then relayed to the motor "belt" zone (premotor cortex) where the components of the movement are assembled together, then this region sends its output to primary motor cortex which executes the components of the movement.

These interpretations were further supported by ontogenetic and phylogenetic investigations of cortical parcellation. Flechsig (1901) demonstrated that during early childhood the primary sensory and motor areas reach adult levels of myelin development first among all cortical areas, the belt areas reach adult levels next, and the association areas reach adult levels last. In the prevailing recapitulationist atmosphere of the period, this progression was taken as strong evidence that "primary" areas served the most primitive and basic functions of the cortex—simple sensation and motor output—whereas association areas performed the most highly evolved and complex functions. Elliott-Smith (1910) further bolstered this interpretation by demonstrating that in phylogenetically "lower" brains (e.g., hedgehog) primary areas appeared to occupy most of the cortical surface, whereas in more "advanced" brains (e.g., primates and humans) most of the surface appeared to be occupied by association cortex. In recent research this phylogenetic hierarchy has been almost exactly reversed, with association areas considered to be most ancient and specialized primary sensory or motor areas most recent neocortical areas (Sanides, 1969; 1970). This finding has played an important role in the development of an alternative model (Brown, 1977); see the following discussion.

In sum, the connectionist model maintained its reflex arc pattern of organization through a three tiered cortical hierarchy, with information entering through primary sensory areas and exiting from primary motor cortex. Although the hierarchic schema has been elaborated and the distinctions between receptive and sensory-psychic functions has blurred, the broad outlines of this model can be found essentially intact in most modern texts on neurology or neuropsychology (e.g., Kolb & Whishaw, 1984; Mesulam, 1986).

The Development of Holistic Theories

Not long after Broca had presented his findings on the speech area this view was criticized in a discussion with the British neurologist John Hughlings Jackson (Luria, 1980). Although Jackson's prescient criticism (1869) was largely overshadowed by the success of the connectionist approach at the end of the 19th century, his theories and case studies would eventually play a central role in articulating an alternative (Jackson, 1932; 1958). His critiques were both antiassociationist and antilocalizationist. Although he was one of the early champions of localization of function in opposition to the tradition of Flourens, he nonetheless felt that the atomistic localizationism of Broca and Wernicke was equally in error. He particularly criticized the logic of identifying the symptoms that result from damage to a specific area of the brain with the function of that area. And he noted many cases where even total loss of a presumed functional center typically left some residual functionality. But more importantly, he criticized connectionism for its lack of attention to the "vertical" organization of mental functions.

According to Jackson, mental processes develop through a hierarchy of increasingly complex stages. Mental events develop through progressive levels of differentiation from "lower" spinal and brain stem structures, to simple sensory-motor systems, and finally to the "highest" cortical integration centers in a quasiphylogenetic hierarchy (Jackson, 1884). The earliest stages reflect primitive unarticulated mental content, the intermediate stages reflect superficial input-output relationships, and the highest stages represent the integrated development of conscious thought. Brain damage should alter the pattern of this developmental process, not just eliminate some specific functions. The loss of some function, a "negative sign," is then only part of the effect of the destruction of brain tissue. There should also be alteration of the products of cognition, "positive signs," that reflect the altered development of thoughts and intentions.

For example, with respect to aphasia, Jackson (1868, 1878) argued that the connectionist focus on the component parts of the speech act (e.g. sounds, words, movement of the vocal musculature) was limited to the merest surface aspects, the more easily localized input-output processes of speech. In contrast, he emphasized the dynamic and intentional aspects of language, the fact that speech is not just the stringing together of words, but rather an intentional act of conceptualizing and communicating a whole proposition. Jackson argued that the defining symptom of aphasia was not, strictly speaking, loss of language, but rather a disruption of the ability to propositionalize and comprehend propositional speech. He cited cases of paradoxical enhancement of emotional ejaculatory speech in many aphasic patients. This was, he presumed, an expression of the release of intact "lower" centers also involved in speech after higher language processes were compromised. True aphasia in Jackson's sense was a disorder of a central symbolizing function, which could not be understood on the model of a sensory-motor reflex arc.

Jackson envisioned a parallel between the hierarchic stages of developing action and the anatomical hierarchy of motor control. Jackson's hierarchical conception of neural organization was in sharp contrast to the simple reflex model proposed by connectionists. Subsequently, however, connectionist models began to emphasize hierarchic organization, whereas holistic models downplayed it. For example, Sherrington (1906) later translated Jackson's hierarchic model into a theory of motor functions based on a hierarchy of reflex arcs upon reflex arcs (a view also expressed in Russian neurology at that time by Pavlov). For Sherrington, reflex reaction and feedback was seen as the basis for the organization of action at higher levels. Jackson had focused instead on reflexes as positive signs of lower systems released from their integration with higher systems. Sherrington's "reflexology" approach to the origins and regulation of movement retained the hierarchic structure of Jackson's conception of motor function but sacrificed its developmental features. In contrast, many later holists were to sacrifice the anatomical-hierarchic features of Jackson's model but retain its integrated developmental view.

A number of articulate critics of localizationist-connectionist theories began to gain a wide audience in the beginning of the 20th century. Experimental studies by Goltz from 1876 to 1884, and insightful critiques by Freud (1891), Marie (1906), Pick (1913, 1931), Head (1926), and others began to expose both the oversimplification of the clinico-anatomical associations and the tenuousness of some of the claims for precise localization of functions (although localizationist claims continued, e.g., Henschen, 1920–1922; Kleist, 1934). The most devastating anti-localizationist critique of the new connectionism came from the work of Karl Lashley (e.g., 1929, 1931b, 1933, 1946, 1951, 1952). Though not a neurologist, his impact on neuropsychology was enormous both as a critic of accepted ideas and as an innovative experimentalist who endeavored to devise ways of testing many prevailing assumptions. Included among his critiques of the associationist-connectionist models of brain function are four central claims: (a) that the architectonic divisions of the cortex do not correspond with either connectional or functional divisions; (b) that association connections within the cortex are not necessary for the development of learned associations between the modalities thereby connected; (c) that specific memories and learned associations are diffusely represented within the cerebral cortex as a whole; and (d) that motor functions could not be controlled by sensory feedback via reflex arcs but instead have to be understood as unfolding from preset internally originating motor programs (Diamond, 1982).

Lashley's evidence came largely from maze-learning studies with rats. In the face of prevailing connectionist expectations his experiments demonstrated that extensive disruption of cortico-cortical connections (sensory-motor reflex arcs) did not eliminate previously learned sensory-motor associations nor destroy the ability to learn new associations. With respect to specificity of function, he found that the best predictor of functional deficit was the total size of the damaged cortical area rather than the specific location of the damage. Although, in hindsight, it might be argued that his choice of experimental animals and the non-specificity of his experimental paradigms may partially be responsible for the negative results, this research played an important role in pointing out the poverty of prevailing models of cortico-cortical association. Lashley's critique of cortical associationism was further underscored by the discovery that the so-called association areas of the cortex did not depend upon primary projection areas for all their input, as was assumed by the connectionist view, but also received extensive thalamic projections of their own (LeGros, Clark, & Northfield, 1939; Rose & Woolsey, 1949; Walker, 1938).

Henry Head (1926) and Kurt Goldstein (1926, 1927, 1948) best exemplify the subsequent translation of antilocalizationism and holism into the neuropsychology of the first half of this century. Although both recognized the localizability of brain damage in a wide range of syndromes they carefully distinguished between the effects of damage to peripheral input-output channels from the reorganizational effect that the same damage might have on central cognitive processes. For both, following Jackson, disruption of a central regulative feature of thought processes was always evident and proportional to the extent but not specific locale of damage. Head argued that this might be manifested as an impairment of intelligence, or, in aphasic cases, as a general disturbance of symbolic function. Goldstein termed this central reorganizing effect a disturbance or loss of "abstract attitude," characterized by a shift toward more "concrete" and stimulus-bound thought processes and behavior. He viewed this as a generalized disintegration of intellectual processes that always accompanied damage to the cerebral cortex (Goldstein, 1926, 1948).

By the early 1950s the influence of these holistic views began to fade with experimental demonstrations that many of the antilocalizationist anticonnectionist claims could not be supported to the extent suggested by Lashley's early rat experiments. Electrophysiological mapping of cortical areas demonstrated that multiple representations of topographic sensory and motor maps corresponded with architectonic boundaries (e.g., Rose & Woolsey, 1949). Cortical lesion experiments in animals (e.g., Lashley, 1948; Chow & Hutt, 1953; Harlow, 1953; Pribram, 1954, 1958) and focal brain damage cases in humans (e.g., Denny-Brown, 1951; Teuber, 1959;

Luria, 1980) accumulated as evidence that highly specific deficits could result from damage to distinct association areas, and disconnection experiments with animals (Myers & Sperry, 1953; Myers, 1955, 1956; Sperry, Stamm, & Miner, 1956; Sperry, 1958, 1961; Mishkin, 1979) and human commissurotomy patients (Bogen & Vogel, 1962; Gazzaniga, Bogen, & Sperry, 1962; Sperry, 1970; Sperry, Gazzaniga, & Bogen, 1969) demonstrated that long cortical connections did play important roles in the communication of information between cortical areas.

Although antilocalizationism has lost considerable ground since Lashley, the antiassociationism that was behind the holistic theories of Jackson, Goldstein, and others is not necessarily directly challenged by the demonstration of localized functional specialization nor by the importance of cortico-cortical association connections. The historical marriage of anti-associationism and antilocalizationism as a response to the connectionist doctrine was not intrinsic to either critique. One contemporary theory has incorporated both a role for functional specialization and a role for association connections and yet retains a holistic foundation. Jason Brown (1977, 1979) argued for a theory of brain function related to Jackson's (1884) model though Brown's theory incorporates considerably more information about functional localization and is influenced by a somewhat different theory of brain phylogeny (Sanides, 1969, 1970). Brown's theory incorporates the differential function of distinct cortical areas, correlated hierarchic differentiation of structure and function, and a major functional role for associational connections. Despite this rapprochement with localization, the theory is explicitly antiassociationist.

Brown, like Jackson, argued that developing perceptions and actions proceed through a hierarchy of stages that correspond to neural processes in a quasiphylogenetic hierarchy of brain structures. These cognitive events originate in primitive core brain structures then develop within limbic areas, then generalized cortex (association areas), then focal cortex (belt areas), and reach their culmination of development in specialized sensory and motor areas (note that Jackson's model places primary sensory-motor processes midway between "lower" and "higher" brain functions). The specific areas comprising each tier of cortex, from limbic to specialized areas, are assumed to be both structurally and functionally discrete (in contrast to Lashley's notion of mass action and equipotentiality). Brown used the term *microgenesis* to refer to this hierarchic unfolding of perception and action by direct analogy to developmental processes in embryology and evolution. Each momentary conscious event is the culmination of a microgenetic process extending through all levels of the central nervous system. Compared with associationist-connectionist models the direction of development is reversed, and primary sense data appear to play a terminal rather than initial role in the development of perceptions, thoughts, and actions.

Although association connections are important to Brown's theory, their functional role is quite different than for connectionist theories. In Brown's view the association connections that link adjacent cortical areas into a hierarchical series do not relay perceptions (or partially analyzed perceptions) from one area to the next. Rather, they provide areas at a subsequent level with information concerning the degree to which processing at the previous level is complete. Similarly, intermodal association connections are thought to coordinate the independent development of processes in different modalities rather than to carry sensory or motor information between them. This explanation of the function of cortical connections would not be incompatible either with the findings of Lashley or with disconnection experiments. In this way Brown retained the emphasis on global unity and parallelism of mental processes that has long characterized the holistic view without denying specific differentiation of local function.

Brown's interpretation of the effects of brain damage follows Jackson in its focus on the way that damage alters the developmental processes of thought. Because the function of each hierarchic level is, in a sense, complete in itself, damage to some structure midway in the hierarchy does not truncate the developmental process. The disruption of function in that structure, because it represents a level in a developmental process, will be manifested as a restructuring of performance in which the normally "buried" or "submerged" content of that level emerges into the foreground (Brown, 1977). The form that this takes has been variously described as "regression" (Brown, 1977), the expression of (pathological) content from a more "preliminary level" (Brown, 1979), "prematurely displayed" moments in a developmental "flow," desynchronization of processes at different levels, and retardation or slowing of a particular stage of a microgenetic process with respect to the others (Brown & Perecman, 1986). The pathological development of sensory processes may be expressed as sensory imagery, hallucination, or dreams (Brown, 1985b). The pathological development of action may be expressed as perseveration, disturbance of intention, or the inability to inhibit the insertion of irrelevant actions or emotional expressions within a behavioral sequence (Brown, 1985a).

ANATOMICAL IMPLICATIONS OF MICROGENETIC AND ASSOCIATIONIST MODELS

The importance of Brown's theory in the present context is that it makes explicit certain anatomical implications of a holistic perspective. By articulating a holistic developmental model of brain processes in anatomical terms, it allows some interesting comparisons with the alternative associationist models. Both models correlate functional levels with distinct cortical levels. They differ with respect to the developmental sequence and temporal order that hierarchical processes follow, and where (and how) these processes originate. This difference is most clearly evident in the explanation of perceptual processes.

Because associationist models consider sensory input as primary, the first stage of the perceptual hierarchy has its locus in "primary" sensory cortex. The basic building blocks of perception are extracted here from the incoming sense data as discrete disconnected bits of information. These primary sensory features are then conveyed by connections to secondary (belt) areas where they are combined into higher-order features, and finally through a series of such stages complex features are combined to form a complete sensory gestalt that is "recognized" in the highest level association areas (Hubel & Wiesel, 1962; 1965; Gross, Rocha-Miranda, & Bender, 1972). Figure 1.1 diagrams this hierarchic model with respect

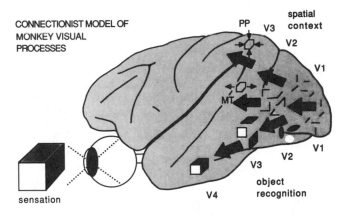

FIGURE 1.1.   Diagram of the monkey brain showing a highly schematic summary of a current connectionist interpretation of visual processes (elaborated from Mishkin and Appenzeller, 1987). Sensory stimuli enter the eye and are relayed to the primary visual area (V1) via the lateral geniculate nucleus of the thalamus. In V1 neurons respond to simple oriented line elements and relay these features and color information to the first "belt area" (V2) where color and more complex properties of the perceptual object are analyzed, depicted by shaded areas and convex angle-edges. In the next tier (V3) these previous properties are further assembled into more complete features, depicted as colored sides. In the final step of the ventral process (V4) the final gestalt is assembled, "recognized" and remembered. In a parallel dorsal pathway attributes of spatial context (indicated by arrows and an outline of the object) are analyzed in the posterior parietal area (PP). Association of V3 and V4 processes with information from adjacent limbic areas (L—hidden on the medial surface of the cortex) supplies affective associations to the perception.

to visual perception. Via connections between association areas and limbic areas these perceptions are also imbued with emotional significance and thereby capable of being paired with reward systems essential for learning and the consolidation of memories (Geschwind, 1965; Mishkin, 1979).

This is a sequential, or serial processing model, in which one stage depends on the completion of a previous stage for its raw materials. It can be compared to the operation of an assembly line, in which a small number of components are assembled into a subassembly at one stage in the sequence, and then this subassembly is passed on to a subsequent stage where it will become one of the basic components of a larger more complex subassembly. Only at the last stages does the product actually begin to take shape and become a recognizable whole.

In contrast, the microgenetic model of perception proceeds in exactly the reverse order (Brown, 1985b; see Fig. 1.2). A perception begins as an undifferentiated mental image, confounded with the body image and the state of affect, which is not at this stage differentiated from the self as an external object. According to Brown (1977), this earliest stage is realized within midbrain and limbic areas. The next stage in the differ-

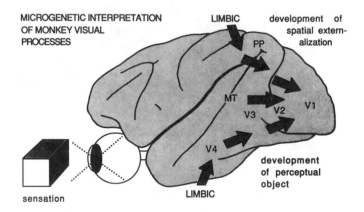

FIGURE 1.2.   Diagram of the monkey brain showing a schematized model of a microgenetic interpretation of visual processes. Abbreviations are the same as in figure 1.1. Note the reversal of direction with respect to the connectionist model. The development of a perceptual object or image begins in limbic structures, and through a series of stages, each successive level of cortex from V4 and PP to V1 contributes to the differentiation of this perceptual object. The arrows do not indicate the movement of perceptual content from one level to the next only the progressive direction of activation and development. To parallel the current evidence for independent analysis of spatial, movement and object-oriented features I have depicted dorsal and ventral visual processes as separate microgenetic pathways.

entiation of the perceptual object takes place in temporo-parietal association areas where it develops into a preperceptual image differentiated in spatiotemporal modality and externalized from the body image but as yet without explicit form. Finally, in focal and specialized sensory cortex the image becomes differentiated in its precise detail as an external physical object. Some aspect of perception and recognition occurs at all levels, but as the process develops into its final differentiated form, the lower-level processes recede into the unconscious. Only disruptions of the process cause these earlier moments in the development of perceptions to emerge. Two examples of such truncated processes are suggested: mental imagery, in which the final levels of the process are not constrained by an actual external object, and hallucination, where earlier stages of image development may intrude into consciousness as though they were completed perceptual objects (Brown, 1983 & 1985b). Cases of blindsight or deep dyslexia are also demonstrations of emergence of these early phases of perception.

Although the associationist model might be compared to an assembly-line process, the microgenetic view is best compared to the process of sculpting. What begins as a relatively formless mass at an early stage is progressively carved first by broad strokes into the crude shape of the model and then by more delicate and precise strokes as progressively more refined levels of detail become revealed. Only at the last stages do we come to recognize the specific expression of the object. Associationist models of cognition begin with the fine details, whereas the microgenetic model ends with them.

However, with respect to motor processes the distinction between the two theories is not so clear. In Sherrington's (1906) classic reflex theory of motor behavior and the views of subsequent behaviorist theorists, motor behavior could be understood as comprised of sequences of individual reflex movements compounded together into more complex movement patterns in the course of learning. Here again, in assembly line fashion, the process begins from the smallest units of behavior (sensory-motor reflexes) and hierarchically builds more complex wholes (see Fig. 1.3). Complex skilled behaviors were presumed to be built up and organized via multiple levels of sensory feedback triggering multileveled motor outputs.

This view was seriously challenged by Lashley's seminal paper on the problem of serial order in behavior (Lashley, 1951, but see also Lashley, 1931a) demonstrating that the unfolding of a complex skilled movement is too well integrated and happens too quickly for feedback to control the parts independently. Contemporary connectionist theories incorporate some degree of central preprogramming of motor acts into their models of motor function, although it is still a source of debate whether sensory

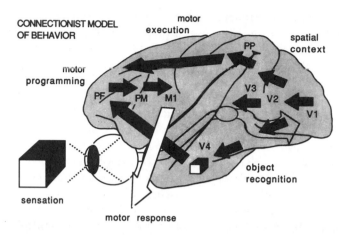

FIGURE 1.3.   Diagram of the monkey brain showing a schematized model of a connectionist interpretation of sensory-motor relations in the production of action. Abbreviations for visual areas are the same as for figure 1.1. Notice the continuity of the "forward" progression of the developing action from sensory association areas (V4, IP and PP) to prefrontal association cortex (PF) then to premotor cortex (PM) and finally to primary motor cortex (M1). This requires that the information progresses from specialized to association areas posteriorly and then from association areas to specialized motor cortex anteriorly.

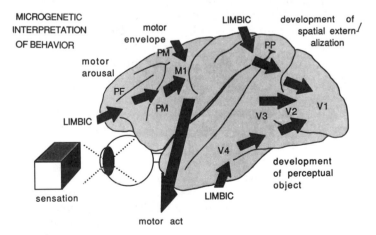

FIGURE 1.4.   Diagram of a monkey brain showing a schematized interpretation of the microgenetic view of the development of actions. Abbreviations are the same as for figure 1.3. Notice that both anterior and posterior systems develop in parallel from limbic origins with endstages in primary areas (M1 and V1). Long association connections have been depicted as bidirectional and are not presumed to be directly involved in the development of either the perceptual or motor act except insofar as they coordinate the parallel unfolding of these processes in the production of action.

information acts as a direct stimulus for initiating these programs or simply provides information to them after they have been more centrally initiated (Berman, 1982). In either case connectionist models presume that the long association fibers linking posterior to anterior association areas carry this sensory information forward into the motor system where it is necessary to activate motor activities. For example, the explanation for the role of inferior parietal damage in the production of apraxic disorders has often been described as disconnection between parietal and frontal areas (e.g., Geschwind, 1965). The connectionist hierarchy for the initiation of an action follows a multisynaptic pathway that originates in the lowest level of the sensory hierarchy, projects by stages to sensory association cortex, projects from sensory association cortex to polymodal prefrontal areas, projects from prefrontal areas to premotor cortex, which finally projects to the primary motor area, the lowest level and final common output pathway for behavior (Jones & Powell, 1970).

The microgenetic theory also views primary motor cortex as the final stage in motor processes (Fig. 1.4). However, due to its focus on a central origin for action it differs with regard to the role of sensory information and the sort of information that passes from one level to the next in this hierarchy. As in the development of a perception, this hierarchy begins from activation within the core midbrain followed by activation of anterior limbic cortex, then prefrontal cortex, then premotor cortex, and finally agranular motor cortex. The earliest stage involves the development of an integrated sensory–motor arousal in which the developing sensory object-to-be and action-to-be are not distinguished. This is followed by the differentiation of a "motor envelope" within mesial and prefrontal cortical areas that incorporates all of the constituents of the to-be–realized action and its object into an undifferentiated unity. Subsequent premotor and motor cortex processes comprise the final levels of this differentiation in which discrete motor elements begin to gain independence and serial order emerges.

Although sensory information is seen to play a role in the microgenesis of action it does not play an initiatory role as it does in many associationist theories. A complementary sensory image of the developing motor action develops simultaneously within each sensory modality and the long association connections are assumed to play a predominantly coordinating role synchronizing these parallel processes. Brown (1987) does not, however, replace the sensory activation model with a central role for volitional activation. The sense of volition develops with the unfolding action and is not a separate agency or stimulus for action. He argued that "the phase of initiation actually precedes that of awareness and the feeling of agency."

CONNECTIONAL ANATOMY AND THE HIERARCHICAL ORGANIZATION OF NEOCORTEX

The Classical Hierarchy

The development of the first axon degeneration tracing techniques in the 1940s marks the beginning of the modern field of comparative neuroanatomy. With such techniques it at last became possible to examine the patterns of long connections in the brain. By the beginning of the 1970s considerable evidence from these techniques pointed to the existence of major cortico-cortical connections that correspond to the predictions of the connectionist models of the cortical hierarchy. Jones and Powell (1970), in a classic paper on cortico-cortical connections in the monkey brain, demonstrated that axonal connections linked adjacent areas within a modality exactly as would be necessary for information to pass from primary sensory areas to secondary sensory areas, and from there to tertiary association areas. They also showed that the posterior association areas have long projections that terminate in the prefrontal cortex and that the prefrontal cortex projects onto the premotor area, which finally projects to primary motor cortex.

Newly developed electrophysiological techniques of the 1960s allowing single cell recording further supported this hierarchic model. For example, Hubel and Wiesel (1962) demonstrated that the primary visual area receives strictly retinotopic inputs and that many of its cells are fine tuned to respond to simple visual features. These include precisely oriented line elements in specific positions within the visual field. However, the precision of retinotopic representation decreases and the complexity of the features capable of driving cortical cells increases in extrastriate areas progressively distant from the occipital pole (Hubel & Wiesel, 1965). Most notably, in inferior temporal areas there is little evidence of retinotopy, cells have typically large visual receptive fields, and many cells appear to be preferentially driven by the presence of such specific and complex stimuli as hands and faces (Gross et al., 1972). Lesion experiments done with monkeys verified that removal of striate cortex results in cortical blindness, whereas removal of the inferotemporal visual areas disturbs visual learning processes but does not impair simple discrimination (Mishkin, 1966). Although, it has proven somewhat more difficult to characterize the functional hierarchies of non-visual modalities, distinctions between precise sensory or musculotopic maps in primary areas and more diffuse maps in association areas have been found in all other modalities, as has the more crucial role of association areas in the learning of complex discriminations (Mishkin, 1979; Pandya & Seltzer, 1982a).

Reciprocal Connections

The recent development of high-resolution tracing techniques (utilizing autoradiographic, peroxidase, and fluorescent tracers) has added yet more connectional information. Tigges, Spatz, & Tigges (1973) and Tigges, Tigges, & Perachio (1977) demonstrated the existence of reciprocal (not just unidirectional) projections between areas 17 and 18 in the squirrel monkey brain. They also noted that these reciprocal projections were asymmetric with respect to their laminar origin and termination patterns within each region. Parallel studies in parietal areas (Jones & Wise, 1977; Jones, Coulter, & Hendry, 1978) also demonstrated that connections between areas at different stages in the somatosensory hierarchy were reciprocal and exhibited distinct laminar patterns. Rockland and Pandya (1979), Tigges et al. (1981), and Maunsell and Van Essen (1983) subsequently analyzed connection data in the entire range of monkey visual areas and concluded that the connections of adjacent areas throughout the visual cortical hierarchy are generally reciprocated and exhibit the same systematic laminar pattern of terminations and origins as do areas 17 and 18. Connections originating in more caudal regions terminate most densely within middle cortical layers (iiic–iv) in their rostral targets whereas caudally directed reciprocal projections terminate most densely in the most superficial and deep cortical layers (i and vi) while avoiding middle layers. Cells from which rostral directed projections originate are predominantly supragranular in origin (e.g. layer iii) while the reciprocal projections arise more numerously from cells in infragranular layers (e.g., layer v). This relationship is diagrammed in Fig. 1.5 (but see next section for terminology). In hierarchic terms, projections directed away from primary visual cortex, up the hierarchy, toward association areas all share one set of laminar characteristics while projections directed toward primary visual cortex, down the hierarchy, all share another.

These reciprocal projections also exhibit systematic differences in the tangential as well as radial aspect of their termination patterns (see Fig. 1.5). Projections from primary to secondary areas (and from secondary to tertiary, etc.) terminate in discrete columnar fields within the middle cortical layers. In contrast, the reciprocal projections terminate in a sheet-like pattern that extends across the territories of many columns in cortical layer i (and to a lesser extent in vi). As a result, in one direction the termination pattern is relatively discrete and focused, whereas in the other it is relatively diffuse.

Subsequent investigations of laminar patterns in nonvisual sensory modalities (Deacon, 1985, 1988; Friedman, 1983; Friedman, Jones, & Burton, 1980; Galaburda & Pandya, 1983; Jones, Coulter, & Hendry, 1978; Pandya & Seltzer, 1982b) and non-primate species (Bullier, Kennedy, & Salinger,

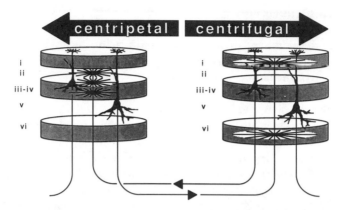

FIGURE 1.5.   Simplified diagram of the connectional and laminar relationships of intracortical reciprocal projections between adjacent cortical areas.
The roman numerals i–vi indicate cortical layers and the major termination
layers are depicted as disks. Neurons projecting centrifugally are shown in
gray, and neurons projecting centripetally are shown in black. Note that the
centrifugal axons fan out in layers i and vi, whereas the centripetal axons
terminate more focally in columns in middle layers iii–iv.

1984; and Sesma, Casagrande, & Kaas, 1984) have demonstrated this same
basic correlation between laminar termination patterns and the direction of projections with respect to cortical hierarchies. This correlation
has two significant implications for neuropsychological as well as neurophysiological models of cortical function. First, information is transmitted in both directions not just one; and second, there is a systematic
difference in the termination patterns of projections directed either toward, or away from, primary sensory areas. This difference likely correlates with a difference in the kind of information transmitted in either
direction.

An explanation of this relationship (for the visual system) that integrated it into the prevailing connectionist model of visual function was
proposed by Maunsell and Van Essen (1983; Van Essen & Maunsell, 1983)
although the idea was implicit in the terminology used by a number of
papers (e.g., Tigges et al., 1977). The basic idea was that projections from
primary to secondary and from secondary to tertiary areas (and so on)
relayed primary visual information up the visual hierarchy where at
each stage it became progressively more complex, analogous to the
way geniculo-cortical projections relayed visual information from the
thalamus (where it is presumed only simple analysis is performed) to
the striate cortex (where it is presumed that more complex analysis is
performed). These ascending projections were termed *forward* projections (also *orthograde*), whereas the reciprocal projections were termed

feedback projections (also *retrograde*). Although there was no functional role specified for these feedback projections in connectionist theories, they were presumed to relay information about the progress of the higher-order analysis of a visual input back to its previous source. These were compared to reciprocating cortico-geniculate projections. Despite the terminological integration into the connectionist model, evidence directly pertaining to the function of either cortico-cortical or cortico-geniculate feedback projections is still lacking.

Centripetal/Centrifugal Organization and Laminar Patterns

To avoid any confusion that might arise when using terminology that distinguishes different anatomical relationships but also connotes different theoretical positions regarding function, let me introduce some descriptive terms that define the patterns and directions of projections solely on the basis of anatomical features. I suggest that we use the terms *internal* and *external* termination patterns to distinguish between projections that terminate predominantly in middle cortical layers (internal) and those that terminate predominantly in the most superficial and/or deep layers (external). A majority of both cortico-cortical and thalamo-cortical connections can be distinguished on the basis of these criteria. The remaining forms can be treated as mixed or intermediate.

To describe the direction of a projection within some cortico-cortical gradient let me also introduce two terms that indicate the quasi-hierarchic relationship between primary sensory and motor areas, their association areas, and limbic areas. I have chosen these terms in order to avoid higher/lower analogies, which confuse anatomical designations with a theoretical interpretation of priority of functions in these areas. I propose identifying the direction of a projection with respect to a dichotomy posed between centrally organized systems (e.g. limbic cortex) and systems that more precisely reflect peripheral sensory or motor constraints in their organization (e.g. primary sensory and motor areas). Connections that originate from cells in a more centrally organized structure and terminate in a more peripherally organized structure are termed *centrifugal* projections, while connections that originate from cells in a more peripherally organized structure and project to a more centrally organized structure are termed *centripetal* projections (see Fig. 1.6). Thus, projections from primary visual cortex (area 17) that terminate in belt cortex (area 18) are termed centripetal projections and the reciprocal projections from belt cortex to primary cortex are termed centrifugal. Because of the close correlation between direction and laminar pattern many ambiguous cases may be resolved when both laminar pattern and direction are considered together.

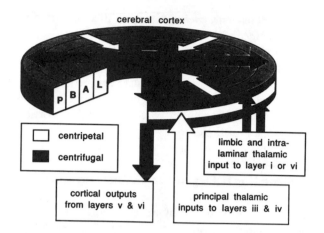

FIGURE 1.6.   A highly schematized diagram showing the relationship between centripetal and centrifugal pathways of the cerebral cortex, including some subcortical connections. Centrifugal projections are shown in black, and centripetal projections are shown in white. The letters P, B, A, and L refer to major tiers in the cortical hierarchy (P = peripherally specialized areas; B = belt areas; A = association areas; L = limbic areas). The cerebral cortex is depicted as a disk to emphasize the central-peripheral gradient of organization. Cortical inputs and outputs are also divided into centripetal (from peripheral to central) and centrifugal (from central to peripheral) projections. Centrifugal subcortical outputs from layer v project to striatal, brain stem, and spinal targets, and those from layer vi project to thalamic targets. The thalamic afferents to the cortex are subdivided into centrifugal and centripetal projections on the basis of principle layers of termination (centripetal = middle layers, depicted as a white band; versus centrifugal = deep or superficial layer) and with respect to the origin of the thalamic information (peripheral sensory-motor sources; versus central limbic or midbrain sources). This suggests that the centrifugal/centripetal pattern of organization can be generalized beyond cortical circuits.

With these terms it becomes relatively easy to summarize the findings regarding the laminar organization of cortico–cortical projections within the visual, auditory, and somatic modalities. In each system it appears that centripetal projections exhibit the internal termination pattern while centrifugal projections exhibit the external termination pattern. The interpretation of the functional role ascribed to these types of projections by current connectionist theories can be stated as follows: Centripetal, internally terminating projections are characteristic of the "forward" progress of sensory analysis as sensory information passes from areas where simple reception and feature extraction take place to a terminal area where higher-order perceptual recognition takes place. Centrifugal, externally terminating projections on the other hand, are serving a "feedback" function, and do not convey primary information.

Sensory–Motor Association Connections

The long association connections that link posterior cortical areas with prefrontal and motor areas are also reciprocal (Deacon, 1985; Pandya & Yeterian, 1985). Like the reciprocal connections within sensory modalities these association connections are also asymmetric with respect to laminar termination patterns. Projections from posterior association areas that terminate within the prefrontal cortex exhibit a slightly modified internal pattern. They project most heavily upon middle layers in a clearly columnar pattern. Unlike most internal termination patterns in posterior areas some of the sensory-prefrontal projections have an additional dense termination in layer ii. The reciprocal frontal-sensory projections appear to terminate in a fairly typical external pattern with most dense terminations in deep and superficial layers, extending well beyond columnar dimensions in a sheetlike pattern (Deacon, 1985; in press).

Although prefrontal cortex is not in any obvious sense included in the same cortical hierarchy as are any of the posterior association areas, its laminar interrelationships with these areas suggest that we treat sensory projections to prefrontal cortex as centripetal and prefrontal projections to sensory areas as centrifugal connections. This distinction agrees with connectionist expectations about the forward flow of information from sensory to frontal areas. However, it may be at odds with Brown's view that long association connections serve a coordinating role with respect to the parallel elaboration of processes in sensory and frontal areas. Coordination between symmetric frontal and posterior hierarchies might rather have suggested symmetrical termination patterns.

Frontal Lobe Organization
and the Failure of Forward/Feedback Theories

Both the forward/feedback terminology and the connectionist explanation of the role of reciprocal cortical connections run into difficulties when connections within the frontal lobes are considered. As in posterior cortical areas nearly all major frontal lobe projections are reciprocal and have distinct laminar organization. On the analogy with the projection patterns discerned in posterior systems we should be able to correlate the direction of forward information flow with internal termination patterns and the reciprocal feedback connections with external termination patterns. According to connectionist (as well as holist) theories of motor function, the forward flow of information is in the direction of motor outflow. In other words, projections from prefrontal, to premotor, to primary motor cortex (centrifugal projections) should exhibit internal termination patterns.

This expectation is the reverse of the association between direction and laminar patterning found in sensory areas because the direction of information flow is reversed in frontal areas.

Tracer studies in the frontal lobes do not support such a reversal of laminar patterning. The earliest reports of laminar findings that might have been interpreted as troublesome for this view come from the work of Künzle (1978). In an analysis of somatic, premotor, and motor cortex interconnections he noted that premotor projections to the motor cortex exhibit a predominantly superficial termination pattern, whereas projections from motor cortex to premotor and somatic areas are columnar and focused on middle layers. More recently, preliminary reports of monkey studies by Deacon (1984, 1985, in press) with respect to arcuate and prefrontal connections, and by Primrose and Strick (1985) with respect to supplementary motor and premotor connections, indicate that this termination pattern is characteristic of the major types of frontal connections. In general, the association between centripetal projections and internal terminations and centrifugal projections and external terminations is the same in the frontal lobes as in posterior areas. Within the prefrontal cortex this relationship is more complex, with intermediate patterns of termination (Deacon, in press). It is also unclear which prefrontal to prefrontal projections (if any) are to be considered centrifugal and which centripetal.

How do forward/feedback interpretations fare with respect to these connectional findings? According to the connectionist interpretation, where internal patterns are associated with forward and external patterns are associated with feedback processes, there is some difficulty interpreting the frontal projection patterns. There are two possible connectionist interpretations: (a) The forward direction within the frontal lobes is from primary motor to premotor to prefrontal areas (analogous to treating the primary motor area as koniocortex) and the premotor area is merely supplying feedback to motor cortex; or (b) the different laminae within the frontal lobes have exactly reversed their functional roles in frontal as opposed to posterior areas so that external terminations correlate with the forward flow of information and internal terminations correlate with the feedback flow. Both of these interpretations are problematic.

With respect to the first interpretation, considerable neurophysiological and neurological evidence can be cited that contradicts it. For example, motor cortex damage invariably produces paralysis, especially of distal musculature, whereas damage to premotor or prefrontal areas more typically results in praxic disorders where movement capability is intact but organization or initiation of movement may be disturbed (Stuss & Benson, 1986; Wise, 1985). Studies with monkeys have shown that prefrontal, supplementary motor and premotor areas are most active preceding an action, during preparatory or choice phases, rather than synchronized with the resultant movement (Gemba & Sasaki, 1984a, 1984b; Kurata & Tanji, 1986; Mauritz & Wise, 1986; Ono, Nishino, Fukuda, Sasaki, & Nishijo, 1984). The reverse appears to characterize motor cortex. This preparatory and initiatory role of supplementary motor and premotor areas cannot be described as feedback to the motor cortex, and even if we were to accept such an interpretation it still provides no account of a "forward" process from motor to premotor cortex.

The second interpretation is troubled by more basic considerations. If the forward/feedback interpretation of functional-connectional relationships does not hold for frontal lobe circuits, it must also put in doubt the corresponding functional interpretation of posterior cortical circuits. If we retain the forward/feedback interpretation for posterior cortical areas but not for frontal areas that exhibit the same connectional patterns we must be willing to give up an otherwise well-founded expectation that similar structure implies similar function within the nervous system. The widespread distribution and systematic nature of the correlation of centripetal pathways with internal layers and of centrifugal pathways with external layers strongly suggests that the same sorts of general neural calculations are being performed within these circuits throughout the cerebral cortex. Given the fact that posterior and frontal cortical circuits are organized in the same way, is there a single interpretation of this asymmetric cortical connectional pattern that applies to both sensory and motor processes?

In this regard the symmetry of Brown's microgenetic theory is much more promising (see Fig. 1.7). Both perceptual and motor functions are envisaged as unfolding in parallel along the same hierarchic trajectory, from central processes in primitive midbrain and limbic structures to highly differentiated processes in specialized sensory or motor areas of the cortex. In the anatomical terms introduced here these are centrifugal processes and immediately suggest that centrifugal pathways may be involved. In both perceptual and motor processes the microgenetic theory assumes that what passes from one level to the next in the cortical hierarchy is the product of processes affecting stimuli at that level, not (as might be suggested by associationist motor theories) some unfinished "content" produced at previous stages and passed on to the next stage to be further completed. When one stage of a sensory or motor act is differentiated it is complete *at that level* and although the subsequent levels of differentiation are constrained by this result they don't operate on the content of the previous stages. Motor and sensory processes are only distinguished by the end product of their development, otherwise the "act of perception" and a "motor act" are not differently organized.

In many ways the microgenetic theory treats all forms of mental process as motorlike. It emphasizes the similarity between the kinds of

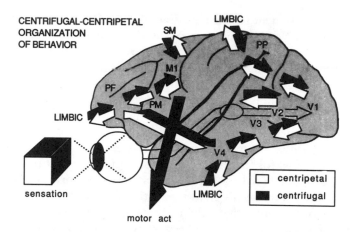

FIGURE 1.7.   Diagram of the monkey brain showing a schematized model of the centrifugal and centripetal organization of sensory-motor processes. Abbreviations are the same as in figures 1.1–1.4. Centrifugal projection pathways are indicated by dark arrows and centripetal projection pathways are indicated by white arrows. Note the symmetry between posterior and anterior "hierarchies" and the centrifugal/centripetal relationship between posterior and frontal areas, indicated by the projection from inferotemporal cortex (V4) and parietal cortex (IP and PP) to prefrontal cortex.

mental "efforts" necessary to focus sensory attention, elaborate a mental image, recall a past conversation, mentally plan a behavior, or control the execution of a difficult skilled behavior. And it seems to provide models for explaining a number of phenomena that are most difficult to explain in associationist terms. But like the alternative connectionist-associationist theories, microgenesis seems to systematically ignore at least half the cortico-cortical connections of the cerebral cortex (centripetal connections), and as a result provides insufficient explanations for a wide range of phenomena explained well by the connectionist alternative.

Despite his focus on centrifugal processes, Brown (1977) did in places describe a role for peripheral input at each level in the perceptual process. Brown's theory denies two assumptions of the associationist approach: (a) the idea that sense data are the content of perceptual experience and (b) the idea that information constituting one stage of the perceptual process is transmitted to the succeeding stages (in adjacent cortical areas) as a perception is analyzed or developed. Nonetheless, for his model to be complete and explicit it must still incorporate some account of the transmission of neural information from region to region and specify the form this information takes, if different than described by associationist theories. This must include the means by which information from the external objects of perception influences the developing mental image and some means for coordinating or synchronizing the activities of the

separate levels or stages of microgenetic processes. Both sorts of information must converge at every stage. With respect to the first requirement Brown (1977) said that "the perception-to-be, is shaped or determined by sensory information in the direction of the external object" and
that there is a "reiteration of sensory control [at each stage to] maintain
cognitive development in the direction of the object" (p. 95), although his
theory is not explicit about the neural substrates through which this sensory information is conveyed to each area. With respect to the second
requirement Brown (1979) referred to the role of association connections
between cortical areas in terms of the coordination and synchronization of
microgenetic processes in parallel cortical hierarchies. The implication is
apparently that these intracortical connections play some sort of activational or inhibitory role with respect to their target areas but do not
necessarily convey any perceptual or conceptual content from one area to
another.

Although anti-associationist theories have historically been associated
with holistic interpretations of neuroanatomical-neuropsychological relationships, Brown's approach demonstrates that the two aspects are sepa-
rable, and that anti-associationism and holism may not be incompatible
with regional specificity of function. The lack of explicit anatomical hypotheses regarding information transmission in microgenetic theory may
not so much be a necessary feature as it is an attempt to focus attention
away from associational relationships (between cortical areas) and focus
instead on developmental relationships in cognition (within cortical areas
and between cortical and subcortical systems).

THE ANATOMICAL BASIS
FOR A SYNTHETIC VIEW

Two Halves Don't Necessarily Make a Whole

The systematic laminar termination patterns of cerebral cortical connections have provided reasons to doubt the consistency and completeness of
either of these seemingly polar views of cognitive processes. Can these
data also provide guidance for either bringing these two views into har-
mony with one another or alternatively replacing both with a more general synthesis that overcomes the major weaknesses of each?

In order to begin sorting out the relationship between the connectional
anatomy and these two neuropsychological paradigms one must first recognize that each view effectively ignores a particular half of the neural
pathways linking cerebral cortical areas together. In sensory cortical
areas the associationist models focus only on centripetally directed information processes while in prefrontal and motor areas they focus only on

centrifugally directed information processes. The microgenetic approach does not suffer from the same anterior-posterior inconsistency but nonetheless focuses exclusively on centrifugal information processes in all cortical areas. Can the two approaches be integrated such that each will explain distinctly different processes within each sensory modality?

Because neither view has a place for frontal centripetal processes, a combined theory would still be somewhat incomplete. However, to a certain extent the complementarity of the two approaches does allow centrifugal and centripetal processes to be treated independently, at least with regard to sensory processes. For example, within sensory areas we can apply connectionist interpretations to centripetal processes and microgenetic interpretations to centrifugal processes. Beyond a mere juxtaposition of the two theories, this comparison suggests a number of structure-function relationships not implicit in either theory alone.

Centripetal projections terminate in precise cortical columns, interdigitated with columns receiving collosal terminations (callosal projections have a mixed termination pattern; e.g., see Goldman & Nauta, 1977). Consequently, they conserve the point-by-point, column-by-column *topography* of their area of origin and are well suited to convey complex spatially organized information from area to area. In contrast, centrifugal projections terminate in broad sheets that extend across the territories of many columns and probably do not conserve the topographic integrity of their place of origin. However, the more distributed termination pattern of a centrifugal projection system is likely capable of conveying the *temporal patterning* of the internally correlated neural activity of one area and conveying it in synchrony to a large sector of a recipient cortical area. In summary, there is a promising correspondence between the characteristics of centripetal pathways and the requirements of connectionist theory and between the characteristics of centrifugal pathways and the requirements of microgenetic theory. Centripetal pathways may preserve the topographic organization of peripherally originating information as it is conveyed from projection areas to association and limbic areas, whereas centrifugal pathways may preserve the temporal patterning and synchrony of distributed cortical activity as it is conveyed from limbic and association areas to specialized areas. In more general terms the centrifugal projections might be described as enhancing or inhibiting activity patterns that are intrinsic to the areas in which they terminate, whereas centripetal projections might be described as introducing extrinsic patterns of activity that selectively enhance or inhibit intrinsic tendencies.

With this dichotomy in mind a number of perceptual functions can be associated with each major pathway. For example, shifting and focusing sensory attention, the production of states of sensory anticipation and expectation, and the elicitation of sensory "imagery" or memories can be associated with progression along the centrifugal pathway, whereas the extraction of perceptual detail and abstraction of higher-order pattern can be associated with a progression along the centripetal pathway. Disorders of perception can likewise be associated with disturbances preferentially affecting a particular pathway.

Syndromes that result from damage to peripherally specialized sensory cortical areas (e.g. cortical blindness) should significantly impair perceptual abilities but, according to this view, should not impair "mental imagery" in that modality to the same degree. However, the retained mental imagery should lack a certain level of differentiation and detail—a feature that would not be predicted from traditional connectionist approaches. Recognition of sensory objects in the disturbed modality should persist only insofar as peripheral input is independently supplied via alternative thalamocortical routes and should also be limited to global stimulus attributes (e.g. as in blindsight). More intriguing is the possibility that the reduction of centripetal information might release typical constraints on centrifugal processes and result in a transient enhancement of relatively unregulated mental imagery in the form of hallucinations.

Syndromes that result from damage to cortical areas more centrally located (e.g., posterior parietal, inferior temporal, and prefrontal cortex) should exhibit aspects of attentional and/or volitional disturbance with intact perceptual and motor functions. These disturbances indicate the effects of depriving primary and secondary areas of limbically originating centrifugal information. A typical visual system example is Balint's syndrome, (Balint, 1909; Benton, 1979) likely due to damage to posterior parietal areas, where there is a particular difficulty shifting attention and gaze to different aspects of the visual stimulus and difficulty interpreting complex spatial relationships. Conversely, inappropriate activation of centrifugal visual circuits, such as originating from limbic disorders such as schizophrenia or epilepsy, tend to produce hallucination (Brown, 1985b).

A number of optical illusions exemplify the interplay between these two systems insofar as these illusions are based upon cases where global gestalt information and attentional expectations interfere with the "literal" perception of the stimulus. Typical examples include gestalt inversions of figure/background or three dimensionality (e.g. the "Necker Cube"), inappropriate judgments of linearity or length because of the proximity of other elements that differentially direct visual attention, and dynamic optical illusions such as the apparent expansion or contraction of visual objects following a period of staring at a rotating spiral. In dynamic optical illusions we see that the entire perceptual experience can be distorted in a dramatic and systematic way by attentional adaptation. The duration (up to 10 seconds) and progressive decrementing of dynamic optical illusions may provide some estimate of the temporal lability of centrifugal process effects.

The connectional symmetries between frontal and posterior cortical systems suggest that there may be similarities between the function of posterior centrifugal pathways and motor processes. One of the major biases that associationist theories have introduced is the assumption that sensory input and motor output are somehow opposite functions—that the brain's input and output systems are separated and linked by association areas and connections. The parallel organization of circuits in sensory and motor areas requires us to reevaluate this simple dichotomy between input and output areas.

Diamond (Diamond & Hall, 1969, Diamond, 1979, 1982) challenged this sensory-motor dichotomy on other grounds. The somatic sensory areas and motor areas of the monkey and human brain are organized so their most peripherally specialized areas (MI and SI) lie adjacent to each other forming parallel topographic body maps. Both areas contribute major projections to the pyramidal tracts, both can independently support motor functions (Sasaki & Gemba, 1982), and both receive subcortical afferents conveying somatosensory information (Jones, 1986). In a number of presumably primitive mammals (including opossum and hedgehog) there even appears extensive overlap in these areas (Diamond, 1979). For these (and other) reasons Diamond suggested that the somatosensory and motor areas be treated as a single somatic projection system.

These criticisms of the dichotomy between input and output areas of the cortex can be applied to all modalities. All cortical areas have subcortical outputs that arise from layers v and vi in sensory as well as motor cortex. These projections terminate in the thalamus, basal ganglia, and brainstem and spinal cord sites (see Fig. 1.6). The subcortical outputs from frontal and sensory areas have different output functions because they are differentiated by axon termination sites (Kuypers & Catsman-Berrevoets, 1984). For example, brainstem efferents from visual areas predominantly terminate in the superior colliculi, brainstem efferents from auditory areas predominantly terminate in the inferior colliculi, and the corresponding efferents from somatic and motor areas predominantly terminate within the spinal cord. In this sense the skeletal muscle projection cells are merely a special subclass of cortical efferent cells. As the skeletal muscle projections constitute the final common pathway of the frontal centrifugal projection system, so too, the brainstem projections of the sensory areas are the final common pathways of the posterior centrifugal projection systems.

In posterior systems the centrifugal pathways have been described as providing activational information from more centrally organized areas to more peripherally organized areas. The same logic can be applied to frontal areas. Both theories describe the development of motor output in terms of a series of stages along the centrifugal pathway from limbic and prefrontal to premotor to motor cortex. The connectionist view suggests that motor programs are somehow resident in prefrontal and premotor areas and executed by the motor cortex. If this were the case we should expect that complex spatially organized information must be passed centrifugally. But the centrifugal pathways are not organized in a way that would suggest that they preserve spatial information. Like their posterior counterparts they exhibit broad termination patterns rather than discrete columns (Deacon, in prep.). Brown's view that subsequent motor levels receive only activational information from previous levels is more consistent with the relatively more diffuse organization of centrifugal pathways.

The activational role of the motor centrifugal pathways is clearly evident in the progression of disorders associated with damage to progressively more centrifugal areas. At the centripetal end, damage to anterior limbic areas results in various degrees of akinesis and suppression of spontaneous behavior (Damasio & Van Hoesen, 1983). Damage to the supplementary motor area also results in reduced spontaneous behavior, difficulty in the initiation of movements, and a loss of volitional control of movement (Stuss & Benson, 1986). The "alien hand sign" has been attributed to supplementary motor damage (Goldberg, 1985; Goldberg, Mayer, & Toglia, 1981). In this syndrome volitional control of the hand appears lost but movement ability remains. The hand often exhibits spontaneous motor patterns (e.g., grasping objects, spontaneously manipulating touched objects, such as unbuttoning a button; moving the arm and hand in the direction of tactile stimuli), and the patient may attribute this to an alien volition somehow resident in the hand itself. In a sense, it is a pathological embodiment of the classic reflexology model of motor behavior. Damage to premotor areas is typically associated with limb-kinetic apraxia, some slight paralysis and the disorganization of complex skilled movements, though not with the same sense of a loss in volition that accompanies more central damage (Wise, 1985). Proximal musculature seems more affected in both supplementary motor and premotor damage and some degree of spasticity is also evident (Luria, 1980). Finally, damage to motor cortex is invariably associated with some degree of paralysis, particularly of distal musculature, but without signs of spasticity in spared movement abilities (Denny-Brown, 1951; Luria, 1980; Stuss & Benson, 1986). In summary, the centrifugal development proceeds from proximal to distal, whole behavior activation to individual movement execution, and from volitionally regulated to automatically released movement patterns. The role of prefrontal cortex in this hierarchy, via its additional centrifugal projections to supplementary motor and premotor areas is more complex and will be addressed after a brief discussion of frontal centripetal pathways.

Drawing on the analogy of sensory centripetal pathways, we are now in a position to provide a more general interpretation of frontal centripetal processes. The centripetal projections within the frontal areas are organized so as to preserve topographic detail from area to area. As in posterior areas, they likely carry complex patterned information from more peripheral sources. Two major classes of peripheral inputs enter the motor cortex, those relayed from the cerebellum and those relayed from somatosensory sources. By analogy to posterior systems, this peripheral information is conveyed via centripetal pathways to premotor, supplementary motor, prefrontal and eventually limbic areas. In this sense, following Luria (1980), the frontal complex can be described as a "motor analyzer." Information from discrete musculotopic motor programs and somatic tactile input (e.g., kinesthetic sense) is "analyzed" by the centrifugally developing action as sensory information is analyzed by the developing attentional activation of posterior systems. The centrifugal projections likely provide information that plays a selectional role in motor behavior, differentiating and biasing intrinsic activity patterns initiated by more central processes of the prefrontal and limbic cortex.

Although skilled motor behavior is centrally organized and activated, its final expression is "filtered" and biased by peripheral sensory information. In addition, complex movement sequences require both sustained activation and millisecond-by-millisecond gating of successive motor cortex activation patterns. Sensory feedback is too slow to account for this sequencing (Lashley, 1951). However, centripetal motor projections also provide premotor and supplementary cortex with topographically precise information about the just previously-activated motor event (including automatic cerebellar programs). This information may play a crucial role in "gating" the successive steps in a rapidly unfolding movement sequence. This interpretation of a dynamic interplay between the two pathways is explored more fully in the final section.

A parallel explanation also applies to the role of posterior projections to frontal areas. These inputs also arrive via centripetal projections, and so might be assumed to contribute to the centripetally developing analysis in frontal areas rather than the centrifugally developing motor activation. This interpretation differs slightly from that provided by either theory. Traditional connectionism would attribute more of an activational role to these projections, although Brown argues that they serve only a coordinating role. Only postcentral and parietal cortex posterior-frontal projections terminate in motor cortex, premotor cortex (Jones, 1986) and supplementary motor cortex (Jurgens, 1984), whereas projections from all modalities terminate in arcuate (Deacon, 1984) and prefrontal areas (Pandya & Yeterian, 1985) of monkeys. This multimodal aspect of the frontal hierarchy is not entirely unique. A number of posterior regions have multimodal input, specifically those at the far centripetal extreme of the hierarchy including inferior parietal cortex and superior temporal sulcus cortex in the monkey (Pandya & Yeterian, 1985). In general, the centrifugal development proceeds from multimodal to unimodal areas. These posterior multimodal areas send centripetal projections to prefrontal areas as do supplementary cortex and some premotor areas, and these are reciprocated. These findings suggest that the prefrontal cortex represents a stage prior to the centrifugal differentiation of muscular from perceptual components of action. All the centripetal inputs to prefrontal cortex likely play a role in the differentiation of the intention to act, and the centrifugal efferents from prefrontal cortex to all modalities influence the centrifugal development within each. The differentiation of action must be thought of as beginning with the coordinated and undifferentiated activation of all modalities. The developing intentional "motor" response is more than just a muscular output. It is comprised of the coordinated parallel activation of all centrifugal pathways. Here we have returned full circle to describe the motorlike function of sensory areas.

Not all mental processes developing through the cortical hierarchies are microgenetic in their time scale. There is reason to suspect that many aspects of learning may be described in the same terms as momentary actions or perceptions. The process of acquiring a skilled movement pattern is in many ways analogous to learning to distinguish between different complex sensory stimuli. The earliest stages of both processes lack peripheral specificity and both require considerable volitional control and mental exertion. The early stages of a developing skill are characterized by only crude similarity of the motor patterns from trial to trial with considerable variety in the details of movement, and the early stages of a developing sensory discrimination are characterized by distractability and attention to irrelevant sensory details. As each is learned, they become progressively unconscious, automatic, and constrained in the variance between different performances. This is clearly a centrifugal progression, not on a microgenetic time scale, but on a protracted time scale that may be measured in hours, days, or years. The fact that the final "overlearned" discrimination or behavior can become automatic and nearly unconscious suggests that at this stage centrifugal processes play a minimal role. Thus, the nearly automatic reflexlike response or sensory discrimination might well approach at its extreme limit the classic connectionist model.

The Counter-Current Analogy

By using the logic of connectionist theory to describe processes proceeding along centripetal pathways, and using the logic of microgenetic theory to describe the processes proceeding along centrifugal pathways a more comprehensive view of cortical processes has emerged. The constraint of having to consistently apply one model to a single type of projection pattern wherever it occurs has also helped to uncover hidden problems in both theories. For example, where connectionist interpretations appropriately describe the function of long sensory-frontal projections they probably do not appropriately describe the frontal centrifugal motor hierarchy. Where microgenetic interpretations appropriately describe the frontal centrifugal motor hierarchy they probably do not appropriately describe the function of long sensory-frontal projections. By the same logic it has been possible to describe the functional organization of two major neglected pathways: frontal centripetal projections and prefrontal-sensory projections. Finally, this synthesis has provided a more unified view of all cortical processes, by emphasizing the motor-like functions of sensory areas and sensory-like functions of motor areas. It is fair to say, then, that the synthesis of these two views, according to this anatomical constraint, has provided a result that is far more than just the sum of the two theories.

Despite these contributions there is still something missing in this synthesis. By treating the two processes in isolation there is no real theoretical integration. The result may be an enhancement of descriptive power over either theory alone, but it does not address the underlying problem of explaining why the brain is laid out this way in the first place. More importantly, it does not provide an explanation for the cognitive process itself—the mechanism responsible for the transformation of information from one stage to the next and from one area to another.

I think that the centripetal/centrifugal geometry itself holds the key to this question. The precisely opposed juxtaposition of these two pathways in all cortical systems indicates that the two corresponding developmental processes are also in some way interdependent. Every cortical area intermediate between primary and limbic regions receives and sends both centrifugal and centripetal projections, and signals from both pathways likely converge upon the same pyramidal cells within each cortical column. Presumably both pathways are often (if not usually) simultaneously active, and so their interaction within an area undoubtedly alters what is relayed to efferent areas in both directions. In other words, the secret of the transformation of the signal from one level of processing to the next may lie in this interaction. Peripheral information may be necessary to differentiate a developing perceptual object or motor envelope (as it develops centrifugally), and the activation of attentional constraints and preperceptual images may be necessary to selectively abstract certain local features and global spatial relationships from peripheral information (developing centripetally).

The means by which information developing in one direction can alter the development of information in the other direction is not immediately obvious. However, there are other systems that have a similar organization and may provide the essential clues to an answer. The first general feature of this connectional relationship is the precise complementarity of oppositely directed pathways. The second is the gradient that these pathways span, each in opposite directions. This gradient is defined by a number of polar attributes: from local independence of spatially segregated features to global integration of spatially distributed features; from highly differentiated representation of the periphery to diffuse representation of the periphery; from minimal influence of autonomic arousal state to central representation of autonomic arousal; from highly facile processes with minimal integration across time to processes that exhibit patterns that are predictable over relatively long periods (in neurological terms).

The combination of oppositely directed pathways and a gradient across which they extend has suggested to me an analogy with counter-current fluid diffusion systems (see Fig. 1.8). Counter-current flow, as it is also called, describes a general feature found in many biological as well as engineering systems. Examples of counter-current diffusion processes can be found in the flow of water and blood through a fish gill or the flow of coolants within a nuclear reactor. There are many different ways to describe the same basic principle. What they all share in common is an opposed flow of two separated but interacting media (e.g., water in a heat exchanger) such that their region of interaction forms a gradient along which some parameter (e.g., heat) of one decreases while the corresponding parameter in the other increases, as a result of their interaction (e.g., diffusion). The logic of the opposed direction of flow is that it enables the gradient of difference between the two media to be distributed equally along the interface, even when the values are far from the static equilibrium point for the two sources of the flow. Figure 1.8 demonstrates this in a schematic fashion. Because of the opposed flow each fluid only comes in contact with the other at points where their concentration values are closest and so one can be increased or decreased to very nearly the concentration of the other. As a result the exchange medium (e.g., a membrane) can function far more efficiently than if interposed between the two fluid media in a passive state. This is why counter-current flow is so widespread in biological adaptations and engineering applications.

The analogy between fluid systems and information transformation systems derives both from the geometric similarity between

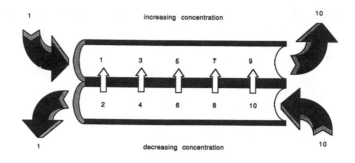

COUNTER-CURRENT DIFFUSION

FIGURE 1.8. Diagram of the principle of counter-current diffusion. The flow of two different fluids in opposite directions through adjacent tubes is indicated by the large shaded arrows. The concentration (or other parameter such as heat, etc.) of some component of each fluid is indicated by numbers, and the small white arrows depict the diffusion of this component from one fluid to the other across the permeable interface that separates them. Notice that the lower half of the system begins with a high concentration (10) and is reduced to a low value, whereas the upper half begins with a low concentration (1) and is increased to a high value by the diffusion process. Because the equilibrium value for static diffusion would be 5, the diffusion process is pushed well beyond static equilibrium in the vicinity of the tubes. Notice also that the gradient between any two adjacent regions of the two fluids in the tubes is the same. To compare this to an information diffusion system reinterpret the numbers to represent measures of some informational parameter such as the spatial complexity or temporal variety of a signal.

counter-directed neural pathways and oppositely flowing fluid diffusion systems, and from the similar alignment of both along some gradient. The concept of *diffusion* of some energetic or material quantity such as heat or dissolved oxygen across a permeable boundary between two fluids can be given more general formulation as follows: *Two media interact such that there is a decrease in some parameter describing one medium and a complementary increase in that parameter for the other medium.* In these general terms we can also describe the "diffusion" of information between two information carrying channels: *Two information carrying channels interact such that the information in each is used to transform the information in the other with the result that some parameter describing the information of one is increased while the corresponding parameter in the other is decreased in the process.* Appropriate informational parameters might be some measure of total variety/ redundancy or spatial/temporal complexity, or some measure of other pattern parameters of the signal. A counter-current information processing system can formally be described as *a set of interactions between channels*

whose inputs are from two sources of information with opposite extreme values of
some parameter, in which the first stage in the series of diffusion-interactions
involving that parameter for one is the last stage in the series for the other and vice
versa.

Once we recognize the formal correspondence of these two analogous
processes (diffusion in the chemical-thermodynamic and informational
senses, respectively), it is possible to see the corresponding enhancement
that counter-current organization can provide for an informational diffusion system such as the brain. As in fluid systems, counter-current organization maximizes diffusion (i.e., total assimilation of information) and
distributes the gradient of difference between centrally generated information and peripherally originating information uniformly throughout
the system. Relatively stable, integrated information representing internal
states and central programs, enters the network from one end, directed
centrifugally, whereas highly complex, fragmented and rapidly changing
information representing the sensory environment enters the network
from the opposite end, directed centripetally. As sensory information
passes by stages centripetally it progressively loses local complexity but
gains in global integration, and as limbic information passes by stages
centrifugally it progressively differentiates and decreases in integration
with other systems as well as becoming less constrained by internal states.
At each stage the two pathways bring together centripetal and centrifugal
patterns of information that have been transformed by preceding stages so
as to converge towards the same level of differentiation. The brain might
thus be described as being arranged so as to generate the closest possible
match to peripherally captured pattern information at every level of
central-peripheral interaction.

The incompleteness of both microgenetic and associationist models of
cortical processes is a consequence of their assumption of unidirectionality.
The arguments presented here suggest that centrifugal processes *require*
centripetal processes and that centripetal processes *require* centrifugal processes in order to function. There can be no development in one direction
without a complementary development in the other. Centrifugally developing perceptual images require centripetally flowing peripheral information to progressively differentiate them, and centripetally progressing
sensory stimulation patterns require centrifugally developing perceptual
images in order to organize sensory features and abstract their integrated
relationships. In this way it can be said that the developing *perceptual object*
(to use Brown's term) assimilates sensory information in order to differentiate. By a parallel process centrifugally elaborating motor programs
require centripetally directed peripheral motor-programming and somatosensory information to bias and gate the progressively differentiating
behavior sequence. Each stage in a sensory or motor process represents a

completed image (more generally, an attentional envelope) or action (more generally, an intentional envelope) at a particular level of differentiation and a completed registration and assimilation of peripheral features at the corresponding level of detail. The processes of "recognition" and "decision" are not localized to the "highest" cognitive centers (whatever this might mean) but are distributed throughout all levels.

Fundamental to this hierarchic interdependence between globally organized processes at one extreme and locally differentiated processes at the other is the fact that these processes also reflect different temporal scales (see also Brown, 1982). The primary sensory and motor areas are engaged in processing information that is both spatially complex and extremely short lived. The immediately previous pattern of activity must instantly make way for the next. There is no room for a long lasting stable pattern of activity. At the other extreme, limbic and association areas sustain activities whose duration may extend from many seconds to minutes. The more general or global attributes that guide perceptual attention or guide the execution of a skilled behavior are also highly redundant in time. Centrifugal projections, then, are conveying information from a slower more redundant process to a faster more variable one, whereas centripetal projections are conveying information from a more rapidly fluctuating process to a slower one. The time scales for the basic units of analysis at the two extremes of the cortical hierarchy may differ by as much as two to three orders of magnitude. This is not to say that neurons fire at a different rate at the two extremes, only that there is a great difference in the time period over which redundancy in neural activity patterns should be observed (analogous to cycle length in some rhythmic process; see Brown, 1982). This may help explain why association areas and limbic structures appear so involved in mnemonic processes: not because they are the locus of memory, or because they have some specialized mnemonic function, but because of their position at the slow end of cortical processes. They provide the stable centrifugal constraint that enables systems with far more facile and easily perturbed processes to achieve the level of redundancy necessary to consolidate memories.

This simple counter-current analogy needs to be augmented in a number of ways before it is adequate. With respect to anatomical details I have tended to downplay subcortical relationships, particularly the multiple thalamic inputs to and parallel subcortical outputs from each stage of cortical processing. These both link across modalities and provide independent sources of peripheral information (in addition to that entering the network from either the limbic or specialized cortex ends). It is interesting that thalamocortical projections also exhibit an internal/external termination pattern dichotomy (Frost & Caviness, 1980; Rausell & Avendano, 1985; Friedman, Bachevalier, Ungerlieder & Mishkin, 1987; Herkenham,

1980). These appear to have a similar centrifugal/centripetal relationship as well. Projections with internal patterns (e.g. principal projection nuclei) generally relay spatially organized peripherally specialized information, whereas those with external patterns (e.g. intralaminar and limbic nuclei) generally relay information from deep midbrain or limbic structures that are more centrally organized. As indicated in figure 6 (and discussed in the last section), cortical-subcortical efferents too must be considered in the total centrifugal scheme. So it appears that the logic of centripetal/centrifugal organization is probably not limited to cortical circuits. For these reasons the simple analogy of input at one end and output at the other of each pathway is insufficient. The basic logic of counter-current organization must be complicated to deal with a system with multiple inputs and outputs.

The counter-current concept provides a useful framework to help conceive of an information processing system laid out as are the circuits of the human cerebral cortex. But it also goes further than previous models. It provides a model, not just of the relationships between cognitive and neural stages, but of the mechanism underlying the transformations of information from one stage to another in the process of cognition. It is an attempt to outline the means by which processes of the brain are capable of assimilating information about the world and of differentiating actions with respect to it. As with any analogy, this model reflects only certain general features of this pattern of cortical organization. However, I believe it provides the first alternative to the one-directional, hierarchic models or undifferentiated parallel models of brain processes that we have explicitly or implicitly relied upon for insights, hypotheses, and explanations regarding the function of the brain and mind.

CONCLUSIONS

In hindsight it seems that associationist and holist theories of mental processes were not so much alternative theories of mind as descriptions of complementary aspects of a single process. The failure of each to provide more than just a descriptive account of the movement or change of information in cortical systems derives from a failure to recognize this complementarity. The reformulation of neuropsychological theory in terms of the interaction between centrifugal and centripetal processes breaks down many preconceptions about hierarchic organization that have been the source of contention and confusion since the beginnings of neuropsychology. Because the centrifugal/centripetal logic is reflected both in cortical organization and in cortical-subcortical relationships, attention to this pattern may well lead the way to a more comprehensive general model of brain function.

During the last century the evolution of associationist and holist theories of brain function has been powerfully influenced by neuroanatomy and neurophysiology as much as by the findings of neurologists. During different periods, experimental findings have been crucial to the rise or fall of one or the other paradigm. It now appears that new neuroanatomical findings may force a rapprochement between these two major paradigms of neuropsychology. The model presented here in answer to the contradictions between theories, and between theory and anatomy, shares much in common with the original connectionists' models. Like its 19th-century predecessors, the counter-current theory of cortical information processing has grown out of anatomical considerations, is based on a simple analogy, and suggests a wide range of new predictions concerning brain functions. However, the neurosciences have become unimaginably more complex since Wernicke's time, and it is likely true that any simple model will quickly be found to be inadequate in a number of ways. On the other hand, the survivability of this particular model is not as important as its capacity for generating new questions and providing new perspectives on old questions. In this regard, I feel that some version of a complementary, bidirectional model of cortical information processing will ultimately provide the best model of cortical processes.

The neurosciences are only just emerging from a long pretheoretical slumber. Up to this point in time theories of brain function have been little more than adaptations of philosophical arguments. Their elaboration has been limited by the complexity and relative inaccessibility of brain processes. The rapid growth of new information to fill this void has radically changed the scientific context in which our classic conceptions of brain function evolved. As a result many of the most basic assumptions we bring to the clinic and laboratory—what functions ought to be "higher" or "lower," what constitutes "input" or "output," and which direction is "forward" and which is "backward"—will all need to be reexamined.

ACKNOWLEDGMENTS

Thanks are due to Alan Sokoloff for his assistance in the editing of this paper and to Gary Goldberg for his comments and suggestions.

REFERENCES

Balint, R. (1909). Seelenlähmung des "Schauens," Optische Ataxia, raumliche Storung der Aufmerksamkeit [Mental disorders of gaze, optic ataxia, spatial disturbances of attention]. *Monatsschrift für Psychiatrie und Neurologie, 25,* 51–81.

Benton, A. L. (1979). Visuoperceptive, visuospatial, and visuoconstructive disorders. In K. Heilman & E. Valenstein (Eds.), *Clinical neuropsychology.* London & New York: Oxford University Press.

Berman, A. J. (1979). On sensory interactions with motor programs. In J. Orbach (Ed.), *Neuropsychology after Lashley* (pp. 419–435). Hillsdale, N. J.: Lawrence Erlbaum Associates.

Bogen, J., & Vogel, P. (1962). Cerebral commissurotomy in man: Preliminary case report. *Bulletin of the Los Angeles Neurological Association, 27,* 169.

Broca, P. (1861). Remarques sur le siège de la faculté du langage articulé, suivies d'une observation d'aphémie (perte de la parole) [Remarks on the seat of articulate language, followed by an observation of aphemia (loss of speech)]. *Bulletin de la Société Anatomique de Paris, 36,* 330–357.

Broca, P. (1863). Localisation des fonctions cerebral. Siège de la faculté du langage articulé [Localization of cerebral function. The seat of articulate language]. *Bulletin de la Société d'Anthropologie, 4,* 200–208.

Broca, P. (1865). Sur le siège de la faculté du langage articulé [The Seat of the faculty of articulate language]. *Bulletin de la Société d'Anthropologie de Paris, 6,* 337–393.

Broca, P. (1866) Sur la faculté generale du langage, dans ses rapports avec la faculté du langage articulé [On the general faculty of language, based on its relationship with the faculty of articulate language]. *Bulletin de la Société d'Anthropologie de Paris (Second Series), 1,* 377–382.

Brodmann, K. (1905). Beiträge zur histologichen Lokalisation der Grosshirnrinde [Contributions to the histological localization of the cerebral cortex]. *Journal für Psychologie und Neurologie, 4,* 177–226.

Brodmann, K. (1909). *Vergleichende Lokalisationslehre der Grosshirnrinde in ihren Prinzipien dargestellt auf Grund der Zellenbraus [Comparative study of localization of the cerebral cortex with its principles demonstrated on the basis of cell structure.]* Leipzig: A. Barth.

Brown, J. (1977). *Mind, brain, and consciousness.* New York, Academic Press.

Brown, J. (1979). Language representation in the brain. In H. Steklis & M. Raliegh (Eds.), *The neurobiology of social communication in primates* (pp. 133–195). New York: Academic Press.

Brown, J. (1982). Hierarchy and evolution in neurolinguistics. In M. Arbib, D. Caplan, & J. Marshall (Eds.), *Neural models of language processes* (pp. 447–467). New York: Academic Press.

Brown, J. (1983). Microstructure of perception: Physiology and patterns of breakdown. *Cognition and Brain Theory, 6,* 145–184.

Brown, J. (1985a). Frontal lobes and the microstructure of action. *Journal of Neurolinguistics, 1,* 31–77.

Brown, J. (1985b). Imagery and the microstructure of perception. *Journal of Neurolinguistics, 1,* 89–141.

Brown, J. (1987). The microstructure of action. In E. Perecman (Ed.), *The frontal lobes revisited* (pp. 251–272). New York: The IRBN Press.

Brown, J., & Perecman, E. (1986). The neurological basis of language processing. In R. Chapey (Ed.), *Language intervention strategies in adult aphasia* (pp. 12–27). Baltimore: Williams, and Wilkins.

Bullier, J., Kennedy, H., & Salinger, W. (1984). Branching and laminar origin of projections between visual cortical areas in the cat. *Journal of Comparative Neurology, 228,* 329–41.

Campbell, A. (1905). *Histological studies on the localization of cerebral function.* Cambridge: Cambridge University Press.

Chow, K. L., & Hutt, P. J. (1953). The association cortex of *Macaca mulatta:* A review of recent contributions to its anatomy and functions. *Brain, 76,* 625–677.

Damasio, A. R., & Van Hoesen, G. W. (1983). Emotional disturbances associated with focal lesions of the limbic frontal lobe. In K. Heilman & P. Satz (Eds.), *Neuropsychology of human emotion* (pp. 85–110). New York: Guilford Press.

Deacon, T. (1984). Connections of the inferior periarcuate area in the brain of *Macaca fascicularis*: An experimental and comparative investigation of language circuitry and its evolution. Ph.D. Thesis, Harvard University.

Deacon, T. (1985). "Counter-current flow" of cortico-cortical information processing through the laminar segregation of reciprocal connections. *Society for Neuroscience, Abstracts, 11*, 203.1.

Deacon, T. (1988). Human brain evolution: I. Evolution of language circuits. In H. Jerison & I. Jerison (Eds.), *Intelligence and evolutionary biology* (pp. 363–382). Berlin: Springer-Verlag.

Deacon, T. (in preparation). Laminar organization of frontal cortico-cortical connections in the monkey brain.

Denny-Brown, D. (1951). The frontal lobes and their functions. In A. Feiling (Ed.), *Modern trends in neurology* (pp. 13–89). London: Butterworth.

Diamond, I. T. (1979). The subdivisions of the neocortex: A proposal to revise the traditional view of sensory, motor and association areas. In J. Sprague & A. Epstein (Eds.), *Progress in psychobiology and physiological psychology, Vol. 8.* New York: Academic Press.

Diamond, I. T. (1982). The functional significance of architectonic divisions of the cortex: Lashley's criticism of the traditional view. In J. Orbach (Ed.), *Neuropsychology after Lashley,* (pp. 101–135). Hillsdale, N.J.: Lawrence Erlbaum Associates.

Diamond, I. T., & Hall, W. C. (1969). Evolution of neocortex. *Science, 164,* 251–262.

Elliott-Smith, G. (1910). Some problems related to the evolution of the brain. *Lancet, 1,* 1–6.

Flechsig, P. (1900). Über Projections und Associations Zentren des menschlichen Gehirns [On projection and association centers of the human brain]. *Neurologie Zentralblatt, 19.*

Flechsig, P. (1901). Developmental (myelogenetic) localization of the cerebral cortex in the human subject. *Lancet, 2,* 1027–1029.

Flourens, M. J. P. (1843). *Examen de phrénologie [Phrenology Examined].* Paris, Paulin. (English translation by C. de L. Meigs). Philadelphia: Hogan and Thompson, 1943.

Flourens, M. J. P. (1824). *Recherches expérimentales sur les propriétés et les fonctions du système nerveux dans les animaux vertébrés [Investigations of the properties and functions of the various parts which compose the cerebral mass].* Paris: Chez Crevot. (Partial english translation in G. von Bonin (Ed.), *The cerebral cortex* (pp. 3–21). Springfield, Ill.: Charles C. Thomas, 1960.)

Freud, S. (1891). *Zur Auffassung der Aphasien [On the Interpretation of Aphasia].* Vienna: Deuticke.

Friedman, D. (1983). Laminar patterns of termination of cortico-cortical afferents in the somatosensory system. *Brain Research, 273,* 147–151.

Friedman, D. P., Bachevalier, L. G., Ungerlieder, L. G., & Mishkin, M. (1987). Widespread thalamic projections to layer I of primate cortex. *Society for Neuroscience, Abstracts, 13,* 73.17.

Friedman, D., Jones, E. G., & Burton, H. (1960). Representation pattern in the second somatic sensory area of the monkey cerebral cortex. *Journal of Comparative Neurology, 192,* 21–41.

Fritsch, G. & Hitzig, E. (1870). Über die elektrische Erregbarkeit des Grosshirns [On the electrical excitability of the cerebrum]. *Arch. Anat. Physiol. Wiss. Med., 37,* 300–382.

Frost, D., & Caviness, V. Jr. (1980). Radial organization of thalamocortical projections. *Journal of Comparative Neurology, 194,* 369–394.

Galaburda A. M., & Pandya D. N. (1983). The intrinsic architectonic and connectional organization of the superior temporal region of the rhesus monkey. *Journal of Comparative Neurology, 221,* 169–84.

Gall, F. J. (1791). *Philosophisch-Medicinische Untersuchungen über Nature und Kunst im Kranken und Gesunden den Zustand des Menschen. [Philosophical Medical Investigations of Nature and Art in Man in Sickness and in Health.]* Vienna: Graffer.

Gall, F. J. & Spurzheim, C. (1810–1818). *Anatomie et physiologie du système nerveux en général et du cerveau en particulier avec des observations sur le possibilité de reconnaître plusieurs dispositions intellectuelles et morales de l'homme et des animaux, par la configuration de leurs têtes [Anatomy and physiology of the general nervous system, and the brain in particular, with observations on the possibility of recognizing many moral and intellectual dispositions of men and animals by the configurations of their heads.]* Vols. 1–5, Paris: Schoell.

Gazzaniga, M., Bogen, J., & Sperry, R. (1962). Some functional effects of sectioning the cerebral commissures in man. *Proceedings of the National Academy of Sciences USA, 48,* 1765–69.

Gazzaniga, M., Bogen, J., & Sperry, R. (1965). Observations of visual perception after disconnection of the cerebral hemispheres in man. *Brain, 88,* 221.

Gazzaniga, M., & Sperry, R. (1967). Language after section of the cerebral commissures. *Brain, 90,* 131–148.

Gemba, H., & Sasaki, K. (1984a). Compensatory motor function of the somatosensory cortex for the motor cortex temporarily impaired by cooling in the monkey. *Experimental Brain Research, 55,* 60–68.

Gemba, H., & Sasaki, K. (1984b). Distribution of potentials preceding visually initiated and self-paced hand movements in various cortical areas of the monkey. *Brain Research, 306,* 207–214.

Geschwind, N. (1965). Disconnection syndromes in animals and man. *Brain, 88,* 237–294, 585–644.

Goldberg, G. (1985). The supplementary motor area. *Behavioral and Brain Sciences, 8,* 567–616.

Goldberg, G. (1987). From intent to action: Evolution and functions of the premotor systems of the frontal lobe. In E. Perecman (Ed.), *The frontal lobes revisited* (pp. 273–306). New York: The IRBN Press.

Goldberg, G., Mayer, N., & Toglia, J. (1981). Medial frontal cortex infarction and the alien hand sign. *Archives of Neurology, 38,* 683–686.

Goldman, P., & Nauta, W. (1977). Columnar distribution of cortico-cortical fibers in the frontal association, limbic, and motor cortex of the developing rhesus monkey. *Brain Research, 122,* 393–413.

Goldstein, K. (1926). Über Aphasie. [On aphasia.] *Schweizer Archiv für Neurologie und Psychiatrie, 19.*

Goldstein, K. (1927). Die Lokalization in der Grosshirnrinde. [Localization in the cerebral cortex.] In A. Bethe & von Bergmann (Eds.), *Handbuch der normalen und pathologischen Physiologie, Vol. 10.* Berlin: Springer.

Goldstein, K. (1948). *Language and language disturbances.* New York: Grune and Stratten.

Goltz, F. (1876–1884). Über die Verrichtungen des Grosshirns [On the functions of the hemispheres]. *Pflüger's Arch. Ges. Physiol. 13, 14, 20, 26. (English translation in G. von Bonin (Ed.), The cerebral cortex.* Springfield, IL: Charles C. Thomas, 1960.)

Gross, C. (1973). Inferotemporal cortex in vision. In E. Stellar & J. Sprague (Eds.), *Progress in physiological psychology.* New York: Academic Press.

Gross, C. G., Rocha-Miranda, C. E., & Bender, D. B. (1972). Visual properties of neurons in inferotemporal cortex of the macaque. *Journal of Neurophysiology, 35,* 96–111.

Harlow, H. F. (1953). Higher functions of the nervous system. *Annual Review of Psychology*, *15*, 493–514.

Head, H. (1926). *Aphasia and kindred disorders of speech*. 2 Vols. London: Cambridge University Press.

Henschen, S. (1920–22). *Klinische und anatomische Beiträge zur Pathologie des Gehirns* [Clinical and anatomical contributions to the pathologies of the brain]. Stockholm: Nordiska Bokhandel.

Herkenham, M. (1980). Laminar organization of thalamic projections to the rat neocortex. *Science*, *207*, 532–534.

Hubel, D. H., & Wiesel, T. N. (1962). Receptive fields, binocular interaction and functional architecture in the cat's visual cortex. *Journal of Physiology*, *160*, 106–154.

Hubel, D. H., & Wiesel, T. N. (1965). Receptive fields and functional architecture in two nonstriate visual areas (18 and 19) of the cat. *Journal of Neurophysiology*, *28*, 229–289.

Jackson, J. H. (1868). Defect of intellectual expression (aphasia) with left hemiplegia. *Lancet*, *1*, 457.

Jackson, J. H. (1869). On Localization. [Reprinted in *Selected writings of John Hughlings Jackson*, Vol. 2. New York: Basic Books, 1958).

Jackson, J. H. (1878). On affections of speech from disease of the brain. *Brain*, *1*, 304–330.

Jackson, J. H. (1882). On some implications of dissolution of the nervous system. *Medical Press and Circular*, 7. [Reprinted in J. Taylor, (Ed.), *Selected writings of John Hughlings Jackson*. London: Hodder and Stoughton, 1932].

Jackson, J. H. (1884). Evolution and Dissolution of the Nervous System. [Reprinted in *Selected writings of John Hughlings Jackson, Vol. 2*. New York: Basic Books, 1958].

Jackson, J. H. (1932). In J. Taylor (Ed.), *Selected writings of John Hughlings Jackson*. London: Hodder and Stoughton, Ltd.

Jackson, J. H. (1958). *Selected writings of John Hughlings Jackson, Vol. 2*. New York: Basic Books.

Jones, E. G. (1986). Connectivity of primate sensory-motor cortex. In E. G. Jones & A. Peters (Eds.), *Cerebral cortex vol. 5, sensory-motor areas and aspects of cortical connectivity* (pp. 113–183). New York: Plenum Press.

Jones, E. G., Coulter, J. D., & Hendry, S. H. C. (1978). Intracortical connectivity of architectonic fields in the somatic sensory, motor and parietal cortex of monkeys. *Journal of Comparative Neurology*, *181*, 291–348.

Jones, E. G., & Powell, T. P. S. (1970). An anatomical study of sensory pathways within the cerebral cortex of the monkey. *Brain*, *93*, 793–820.

Jones, E. G., & Wise, S. P. (1977). Size laminar and columnar distribution of efferent cells in the sensory-motor cortex of monkeys. *Journal of Comparative Neurology*, *175*, 391–438.

Jurgens, U. (1984). The efferent and afferent connections of the supplementary motor area. *Brain Research*, *300*, 63–81.

Kleist, K. (1934). *Gehirnpathologie [Brain pathology]*. Leipzig: Barth.

Kolb, B., & Whishaw, I. (1984). *Fundamentals of human neuropsychology*. Second Edition. New York: W. H. Freeman.

Kornhuber, H., & Deeke, L. (1985). The starting function of the SMA. *Behavioral and Brain Sciences*, *8*, 591–592.

Kunzle, H. (1978). Autoradiographic analysis, efferent connections from premotor and adjacent prefrontal regions (areas 6 and 9) in *Macaca fascicularis*. *Brain Behavior and Evolution*, *15*, 185–234.

Kurata, K., & Tanji, J. (1986). Premotor cortex neurons in macaques: Activity before distal and proximal forelimb movements. *Journal of Neuroscience*, *6*, 403–411.

Kuypers, H. G. J. M., & Catsman-Berrevoets, C. E. (1984). Frontal cortico-subcortical projections and their cells of origin. In F. Reinoso-Suarez & C. Ajmone-Marsan (Eds.), *Cortical integration, basic, archicortical, and cortical association levels of neural integration* (pp. 171–193). IBRO Monograph Series. New York: Raven Press.

Lashley, K. (1929). *Brain mechanisms and intelligence.* Chicago: University of Chicago Press.

Lashley, K. (1931a). Cerebral control versus reflexology. *Journal of General Psychology, 5,* 3–19.

Lashley, K. (1931b). Mass action in cerebral function. *Science 73,* 245–254.

Lashley, K. (1933). Integrative functions of the cerebral cortex. *Physiological Review 13,* 1–42.

Lashley, K. (1948). The mechanism of vision: XVIII. Effects of destroying the visual "associative areas" of the monkey. *Genetic Psychology Monographs, 37,* 107–166.

Lashley, K., & Clark, G. (1946). The cytoarchitecture of the cerebral cortex of *Ateles:* A critical examination of architectonic studies. *Journal of Comparative Neurology, 85,* 223–305.

Lashley, K. (1951). The problem of serial order in behavior. In L. A. Jeffress (Ed.), *Cerebral mechanisms in behavior,* Hison Symposium (pp. 112–136). New York: Wiley.

Lashley, K. (1952). Functional interpretation of anatomic patterns. *Proceedings of the Association for Research on Nervous and Mental Diseases, 30,* 529–547.

LeGros Clark, W., & Northfield, D. (1939). The cortical projection of the pulvinar in the macaque monkey. *Brain, 60,* 126–142.

Lichtheim, L. (1885). On aphasia. *Brain, 7,* 433–484.

Liepmann, H. (1912). Anatomische Befunde bei Aphasischen und Apraktischen [Anatomical findings in aphasics and apraxics]. *Neurologisches Zentralblatt, 31,* 1524.

Liepmann, H. (1913). Motorische Aphasie und Apraxia. *Monatsschrift für Psychiatrie und Neurologie, 34.*

Liepmann, H., & Pappenheim, M. (1914). Über einen Fall von sogenannter Leitungsaphasie mit anatomischen Befund [On a case of so-called conduction aphasia with anatomical findings]. *Zeitschrift für Neurologie und Psychiatrie, 27,* 1–41.

Luria, A. R. (1980). *Higher cortical functions in man.* (Second edition, English translation). New York: Basic Books.

Marie, P. (1906). Revision de la question de l'aphasie [Reexamination of the aphasia question]. *Semaine Médicale, 26,* 241–247, 493–500, 565–571.

Maunsell, J. H. R., & Van Essen, D. C. (1983). The connections of the middle temporal visual area (MT) and their relationship to a cortical hierarchy in the macaque monkey. *Journal of Neuroscience, 3,* 2563–2586.

Mauritz, K. H., & Wise, S. P. (1986). Premotor cortex of the rhesus monkey: neuronal activity in anticipation of predictable environmental events. *Experimental Brain Research, 61,* 229–244.

Mesulam, M.-M. (1986). (Ed.) *Principles of behavioral neurology.* Philadelphia: F. A. Davis.

Meynert, T. (1866). Anatomische Begründung gewisser Arten von Sprachstörungen. [The anatomical foundation for determining the nature of speech disorders.] *Oesterreichische Zeitscrift für Heilkunde, 10.*

Meynert, T. (1867). Der Bau der Grosshirnrinde und seine ortlichen Verschiedenheiten, nebst einem pathologisch-anatomischen Corollarium [The structure of the cerebral cortex and its local variations, together with a pathological-anatomical corollarium]. *Vierteljahrschrift für Psychiatrie, 1,* 77–93.

Mishkin, M. (1966). Visual mechanisms beyond the striate cortex. In R. W. Russell (Ed.), *Frontiers in physiological psychology* (pp. 93–119). New York: Academic Press.

Mishkin, M. (1979). Analogous neural models for tactile and visual learning. *Neuropsychologia, 17,* 139–152.

Mishkin, M., & Appenzeller, T. (1987). The anatomy of memory. *Scientific American, 256,* 80–89.

Myers, R. E., & Sperry, R. W. (1953). Interocular transfer of a form discrimination habit in cats after section of the optic chiasm and corpus callosum. *Anatomical Record, 115,* 351.

Myers, R. E. (1955). Interocular transfer of pattern discrimination in cats following section of crossed optic fibers. *Journal of Comparative and Physiological Psychology, 48*, 470–473.

Myers, R. E. (1956). The function of the corpus callosum in interocular transfer. *Brain, 57*, 358–363.

Ojemann, G. A. (1983). Brain organization for language from the perspective of electrical stimulation mapping. *Behavioral and Brain Sciences, 2*, 189–230.

Ono, T., Nishino, H., Fukuda, M., Sasaki, K., & Nishijo, H. (1984). Single neuron activity in dorsolateral prefrontal cortex of monkey during operant behavior sustained by food reward. *Brain Research, 311*, 323–332.

Pandya, D., & Seltzer, B. (1982a). Association areas of the cerebral cortex. *Trends in Neuroscience, 5*, 386–390.

Pandya, D., & Seltzer, B. (1982b). Intrinsic connections and architectonics of posterior parietal cortex in the rhesus monkey. *Journal of Comparative Neurology, 204*, 196–210.

Pandya, D., & Yeterian, E. (1985). Architecture and connections of cortical association areas. In A. Peters & E. G. Jones (Eds.), *Cerebral Cortex Vol. 4, Association and auditory cortices* (pp. 3–61). New York: Plenum Press.

Petrides, M., & Pandya, D. (1984). Projection to the frontal cortex from the posterior parietal region in the rhesus monkey. *Journal of Comparative Neurology, 228*, 105–116.

Pick, A. (1913). *Die agrammatischen Sprachstörungen [Agrammatic Speech Disorders].* Berlin: Springer.

Pick, A. (1931). Aphasie [Aphasia.] In A. Bethe & von Bergmann (Eds.), *Handbuch der normalen und pathologischen Physiologie* Vol. 15, No. 2 (pp. 1416–1524). Berlin: Springer.

Pribram, K. H. (1954). Toward a science of neuropsychology (method and data). In R. A. Patton (Ed.), *Current trends in psychology and the behavioral sciences* (pp. 115–142). Pittsburg: University of Pittsburg Press.

Pribram, K. H. (1958). Neocortical function in behavior. In H. F. Harlow (Ed.), *Biological and Biochemical Bases of Behavior* (pp. 151–172). Madison: University of Wisconsin Press.

Primrose, D., & Strick, P. (1985). The organization of interconnections between the premotor areas of the primate frontal lobe and the arm area of primary motor cortex. *Society for Neurosciences Abstracts, 11*, 1274.

Rausell, E., & Avendano, C. (1985). Thalamocortical neurons projecting to superficial and to deep layers in parietal, frontal and prefrontal regions in the cat. *Brain Research, 347*, 159–165.

Rockland, K., & Pandya, D. (1979). Laminar origins and terminations of connections of the occipital lobe in the rhesus monkey. *Brain Research, 179*, 3–20.

Rose, J., & Woolsey, C. (1949). Organization of the mammalian thalamus and its relation to the cerebral cortex. *Electroencephalography and Clinical Neurophysiology, 1*, 391–404.

Sanides, F. (1969). Comparative architectonics of the cerebral cortex of mammals and their evolutionary interpretation. *Annals of the New York Academy of Science, 167*, 404–423.

Sanides, F. (1970). Functional architecture of motor and sensory cortices in primates in light of a new concept of neocortex evolution. In C. Noback & W. Montagna (Eds.), *The Primate Brain* (pp. 137–208). New York: Appleton-Century-Crofts.

Sasaki, K., & Gemba, H. (1982). Development of cortical field potentials during learning processes of visually initiated hand movements in the monkey. *Experimental Brain Research, 48*, 429–437.

Sesma, M., Casagrande, V.A, & Kaas, J. H. (1984). Cortical connections of area 17 in tree shrews. *Journal of Comparative Neurology, 230*, 337–351.

Sherrington, C. (1906). *The integrative action of the nervous system.* New Haven: Yale University Press.

Sperry, R. (1958). The corpus callosum and interhemispheric transfer in the monkey. *Anatomical Record, 131*, 297.

Sperry, R. (1961). Cerebral organization and behavior. *Science, 133,* 1749–57.

Sperry, R. (1970). Perception in the absence of neocortical commissures. *Research Association for Research on Nervous and Mental Diseases, 48,* 123–148.

Sperry, R., Gazzaniga, M., & Bogen, J. (1969). Interhemispheric relationships; the neocortical commissures. Syndromes of hemispheric disconnection. In P. Vinken & G. Bruyn (Eds.), *Handbook of clinical neurology Vol. 4.* Amsterdam, North-Holland.

Sperry, R. W., Stamm, J. S., & Miner, N. (1956). Relearning tests for interocular transfer following division of optic chiasma and corpus callosum in cats. *Journal of Comparative and Physiological Psychology, 49,* 529–533.

Stuss, D., & Benson, D. (1986). *The frontal lobes.* New York: Raven Press.

Teuber, H. L. (1959). Some alterations in behavior after cerebral lesions in man. In A. D. Bass (Ed.), *Evolution of Nervous Control from Primitive Organisms to Man* (pp. 157–194). Washington D.C.: American Association for the Advancement of Science.

Tigges, J., Spatz, W., & Tigges, M. (1973). Reciprocal point-to-point connections between parastriate and striate cortex in the squirrel monkey (*Saimiri*). *Journal of Comparative Neurology, 148,* 481–490.

Tigges, J., Tigges, M., & Perachio, A. (1977). Complementary laminar terminations of afferents to area 17 originating in area 18 and in the lateral geniculate nucleus in the squirrel monkey. *Journal of Comparative Neurology, 176,* 87–100.

Tigges, J., Tigges, M., Anschel, S., Cross, N., Letbetter, W., & McBride, R. (1981). Areal and laminar distribution of neurons connecting the central visual cortical areas 17, 18, 19 and MT in squirrel monkey (*Saimiri*). *Journal of Comparative Neurology, 202,* 539–560.

Van Essen, D. C., & Maunsell, J. H. R. (1983). Hierarchical organization and functional streams in the visual cortex. *Trends in Neuroscience, 6,* 345–350.

Vogt, C., & Vogt O.)1919–1920). Allgemeine Ergebnisse unserer Hirnforschung [General results of our brain research]. *Journal für Psychologie und Neurologie, 25.*

Walker, A. (1938). *The primate thalamus.* Chicago: University of Chicago Press.

Wernicke, C. (1874). *Der Aphasische Symptomenkomplex [The aphasic symptom complex].* Breslau: Cohn and Weigart.

Wise, S. (1985). The primate premotor cortex: Past, present and preparatory. *Annual Review of Neuroscience, 8,* 1–19.

2

Recovery from Brain Damage: Neurological Considerations

Todd E. Feinberg
Steven E. Mazlin
Glen E. Waldman

The purpose of this chapter is to provide an overview of the neurological aspects of brain damage and recovery. In the first section, we address the anatomic, physiologic and biochemical mechanisms of injury. This will be followed by a review of theories of recovery and what is known about the potential of the central nervous system (CNS) for reorganization after injury. We conclude with a discussion of the factors that influence outcome after CNS damage.

MECHANISMS OF DAMAGE

There are many factors that affect the particular course and outcome after brain injury. These factors include the extent and site of injury, the etiology of the damage, the rapidity of onset, the amount of associated edema, the state of the brain prior to injury and other factors too numerous to mention.

When stroke occurs as a result of cerebral vascular disease the site of damage and its configuration often conform to the vascular supply of a particular vessel or vessels. When the brain is examined after such a stroke, the infarct becomes grossly demarcated from the surrounding brain usually within 12 to 18 hours. The brain appears swollen and softened and may be discolored. Tissue breakdown occurs after 3 or 4 days and cavitation may result after nonviable debris is removed from the site of injury. This process may continue for months after a stroke. The resulting cavity and the scar that persist after the injury remain for the life of the patient (Escourolle & Poirier, 1973; Schochet & McCormick, 1979). When areas of damage are examined by light microscopy, changes in cellular morphology can be seen within the first hour or two after interruption of blood flow. These changes include shrinking of neurons and swelling of astrocytes and other cellular elements. Within the first 24 hours white cells can be seen to migrate into the areas of infarction and begin the process of removing the necrotic (dead) debris.

The damage that results after closed head injury (CHI) has certain unique features. In 1956, Strich described a series of patients with post-traumatic dementia who, at autopsy, demonstrated degenerative changes in cerebral white matter. This has come to be known as shear injury (Peerless & Rewcastle, 1967), or diffuse axonal injury (DAI) (Adams, Graham, Murray, & Scott, 1982).

Strich suggested that axonal damage occurred by mechanical forces acting upon the head at the time of impact. The characteristic features of DAI are focal lesions in the corpus callosum and in the dorsal lateral quadrant (or quadrants) of the rostral brainstem and microscopic evidence of diffuse damage to axons (Adams et al, 1982; Adams, Mitchell, Graham, & Doyle, 1977). Adams suggested that this particular type of injury is most likely to be produced by road traffic accidents. He attributed this to the peculiar type of rotatory acceleration that occurs during these injuries, because this particular type of injury affects predominately white matter. The damage may be subtle or only microscopically apparent. It has been suggested that Magnetic Resonance Imaging (MRI) may be a more effective imaging technique to demonstrate the pathological anatomy of this type of injury (Levin, Handel, Goldman, Eisenberg, & Guinto, 1985).

Metabolic factors have been found important in determining the outcome of cerebral hypoxia. For instance, Hossman and Kleihues (1973) have confirmed that animals subjected to total cerebral ischemia for as long as 1 hour exhibited at least partial recovery of tissue function, whereas animals subjected to incomplete ischemia with less than 10% of normal blood flow did not (Rehncrona, Rosen, & Siesjo, 1980). It has further been found that hypoglycemia (low serum glucose) favors a good outcome after cerebral hypoxia. For instance, fasted animals given an intravenous infusion of glucose prior to ischemia were severely affected after incomplete ischemia, whereas fasted animals subjected to incomplete ischemia or fed animals subjected to complete ischemia were able to restore their energy state to near normal after a 30 minute period of ischemia. Clinical corroboration came from a study where stroke admissions were reviewed comparing blood glucose on admission (Pulsinelli, Waldman, Sigsbee, Rawlinson, & Plum, 1980). A significant difference was found in stroke outcome when comparing age—matched hyperglycemic patients with euglycemic acute stroke patients (Plum, 1983). Patients with elevated serum glucose levels on admission did less well.

Diaschisis is a term derived from Greek meaning "shocked throughout" and describes a reversible suppression or dysfunction of neural elements that are remote from the areas of actual cerebral injury. This definition is meant to exclude those areas which are directly affected by an ischemic insult by mass effect, edema, vasospasm, or other local vascular or toxic effects. Since its original description by Von Monakow (1914), diaschisis has been found in animals and humans after lesions in the spinal cord, brainstem, subcortical nuclei, thalamus, white matter, cholinergic system, cerebellum, and cortex. Diaschisis is most commonly demonstrated by alteration of the EEG or evoked potentials, or changes in cerebral oxygen metabolic rate ($CMRO_2$), glucose utilization (CMR Glu), or blood flow (CBF) in areas remote from an area of infarction. Feeney and Baron (1986) provided an excellent summary of these experiments. The exact mechanism of diaschisis remains unknown. It is often invoked as an explanation for cerebral dysfunction in areas larger than those immediately damaged by injury. It is likely that some recovery in the postacute state is the result of a lessening of the effects of diaschisis.

MECHANISMS OF RECOVERY

Many theories have been proposed to explain the restitution of lost functions after brain injury. These accounts are as often complementary as contradictory. It is probably the case that multiple mechanisms are involved and no single explanation accounts for all recovery after a single lesion, and no single explanation applies to all lesions (Goldberger, 1974).

Theories of recovery have been linked historically to the controversy surrounding localizationist doctrine (Kertesz, 1985; Rosner, 1974). The early experiments of Flourens (1824), which demonstrated recovery from cortical lesions in pigeons, were used as evidence against cerebral localization. Although our knowledge of cerebral specialization and localization has advanced considerably since then, still modern theories of recovery inevitably reflect our current (and still incomplete) notions of normal brain functioning (Laurence & Stein, 1978). It is difficult to state with precision what has been regained after injury if one cannot describe with certainty what normal brain functions have been lost.

Resolution of Acute Effects

Depending on the nature and extent of a brain lesion, there is a variable period of time after injury when some improvement is attributable to the resolution of acute physiological derangements. Although there is evidence that the CNS can respond in a positive manner days or weeks after injury (see the following discussion) much early improvement probably occurs as a result of the subsidence of negative factors (i.e., resolution of edema and restitution of blood flow to partially ischemic areas).

As previously noted, diaschisis (Prince, 1910; Von Monakow, 1914) is another factor that contributes to potentially reversible early dysfunction. The central idea here is that areas of brain connected to damaged regions may show temporary dysfunction, which results in a greater degree of initial deficit than one would expect given the extent of primary damage. Diaschisis is actually a more specific explanation for loss of function than recovery (Laurence & Stein, 1978).

Equipotentiality, Redundancy, Vicarious Functioning, and Behavioral Substitution

These terms refer to closely related processes and are frequently found in classical explanations of recovery. Just as diaschisis is an explanation of functional impairment more than an explanation of functional recovery, equipotentiality, redundancy, and vicarious functioning are actually explanations of spared rather than recovered capacities (Rosner, 1970).

The theory of *equipotentiality* or mass action (Lashley, 1929) states that the neurons within individual cortical regions contribute in a homogeneous fashion to a particular function. Lashley observed that the degree of behavioral impairment after a brain lesion depended upon the amount, not the anatomical locus, of the damage. Recovery is mediated by the remaining tissue within a specified homogeneous region. It has been argued that this principle has less application in higher primates (Chow, 1967), but absolute lesion size (as well as location) has been found to be an important variable in determining recovery from aphasia after stroke (Knopman et al, 1983). Lesion location seems to be the critical variable in recovery from hemiparesis (Knopman & Rubens, 1986).

The theory of *redundant representation* is closely allied to that of equipotentiality (Goldberger, 1974; Rosner, 1970). Redundancy implies anatomical distinctness (as opposed to homogeneity) between the region damaged and that responsible for recovery (Laurence & Stein, 1978). Theories of redundant functioning imply parallelism between anatomically distinct substrates, with either region capable of subserving a particular function in the absence of the other. Jackson's (1873) theory of hierarchical representation in the nervous system is in effect a theory of redundant representation (Marshall, 1985). When higher centers are destroyed, lower centers remain to subserve a function. Laurence and Stein (1978) pointed out that many lesion studies that fail to find deficits (and support the redundancy hypothesis) may not have performed sufficiently refined behavioral analysis to detect a loss in quality of performance. They suggest, in addition, that studies that fail to find altered performance after damage, have not, in general, excluded as an explanation the animals capacity to function with reduced information, or to develop new strategies.

The theory of *vicarious functioning* can be traced back to Munk (1881) who proposed that certain "unoccupied" areas of the brain could assume the function of damaged regions. The brain regions substituting for the damaged areas would normally have played no role in the function in question had the damage not occurred. The theory differs in this regard from equipotentiality and redundancy. Vicarious functioning implies that the substituting region had a latent capacity to mediate the adopted function, but this region must alter the mode of functioning it possessed prior to injury. "Reverse ablation" (Bucy, 1934) of these secondary areas indicated that the regions necessary for recovery are not required for the function in question prior to injury of the primary regions.

Objections to this theory have been raised. It has been suggested that a vigorous definition of vicariousness would require that the secondary system perform its new function in a manner identical to the system it replaces. Goldberger (1974) noted that most investigators have failed to demonstrate this. For instance, monkeys subject to cerebellar lesions rely upon somatosensory input for recovery (Goldberger & Growden, 1973), and deficits can be reinstated with lesions in somatosensory systems (Goldberger, 1974). However, Goldberger suggests that the frequent compensatory adjustments the recovering animal makes during movement indicate compensation via alternative mechanisms more than replacement of lost functions per se.

In *behavior substitution* there is enhancement of the functioning of remaining neural systems which compensates for, rather than adopts, the functions of the damaged regions. These mechanisms are referred to as alternate strategies (Marshall, 1985) or "tricks" (Sperry, 1947). Gazzaniga and his coworkers suggest that much of the recovery experienced by split-brain patients and brain injured subjects is a function of alternative strategies discovered by the patient (Gazzaniga, 1978; Gazzaniga & Hillyard, 1971; LeDoux, Wilson, & Gazzaniga, 1978). In split-brain patients, mechanisms such as interhemispheric cross-cuing and enhancement of the remaining skills of either hemisphere would constitute strategic alterations.

The theory chosen to explain a given instance of recovery depends to some extent on the system one is studying. For instance, in explaining recovery from aphasia (a topic we return to later), it would seem imprudent to invoke mass action or redundancy as a sole explanation for recovery, given the differential effects of various lesions in different locations. Theories of vicarious functioning or unmasking (see the following text) are consistent with the suggestion that the nondominant hemisphere is compensating for lost language functions (Kinsbourne, 1971; Nielsen, 1946). Vicariousness would predict that the right hemisphere in normal right handers possesses some latent language capacity, an idea supported in part by data in split-brain patients (Gazzaniga & Hillyard, 1971).

Geschwind (1974) suggested that in childhood aphasia, recovery of speech occurred too rapidly for relearning to have occurred. Rather he suggested that the nondominant hemisphere begins to utilize capacities it already possesses.

Vicariousness would also predict that nondominant hemisphere lesions need not produce aphasia. The relative rarity of "crossed aphasias" bears out this prediction. (This would be the human analogue of Bucy's "reverse ablations.") Both vicariousness and unmasking would predict that damage or dysfunction of the right hemisphere would lead to loss of language in the recovered aphasic who has sustained a dominant hemisphere lesion. Mempel, Srebrzynskia, Sobczynska and Zarski (1963) and Kinsbourne (1971) demonstrated that a right carotid injection of amytal impaired speech in aphasics who had sustained left-hemisphere damage, and Kinsbourne showed that left carotid injections in the same patients did not affect speech. There is other data that suggest that in patients who have recovered from aphasia after unilateral left-hemisphere stroke, a second stroke in the contralateral hemisphere leads to loss of language functioning (Heilman, Rothi, Campanella, & Wolfson, 1979; Levine & Mohr, 1979). Thus, many of the predictions of a theory of vicarious functioning are relevant to recovery from aphasia. This, of course, does not preclude other possibilities.

Morphological and Functional Reorganization

Regeneration, Sprouting, and Reactive Synaptogenesis.   The traditional view-point that the adult mammalian central nervous system is incapable of regeneration (Cajal, 1928) led neurologists to a generally pessimistic attitude toward recovery and rehabilitation of the human nervous system. Current knowledge indicates, however, that both the normal and damaged CNS are capable of considerable morphological change.

Two types of neural regeneration are widely recognized (Bishop, 1982; Cotman & Nieto-Sampedro, 1985; Stenevi, Bjorklund, & Moore, 1974; Tsukahara & Murakami, 1983; Wall, 1980). The first is *regenerative sprouting* from damaged axons, a process well described in the peripheral nervous system (Edds, 1953). In regenerative sprouting a transected neuron develops a terminal sprout at its distal margins. If the developing growth cone contacts a target, synaptogenesis occurs. In the adult central nervous system the ability of transected neurons to spontaneously restore their original synaptic connections is limited (Bernstein & Bernstein, 1973). The glial scar that results from mechanical transection is probably a major obstacle to extended regrowth, but when the lesions are chemically induced with neurotoxins, considerable axonal regrowth does occur (Marshall, 1985).

The second form of regeneration is *collateral sprouting*. When only a portion of the innervation of a tissue is interrupted the remaining undamaged neurons may sprout new terminals and occupy vacated synaptic sites (reactive synaptogenesis). In 1958, Liu and Chambers demonstrated collateral sprouting in the cat spinal cord, the first demonstration of its kind in the CNS. Raisman (1969) and Raisman and Field (1973) showed that sprouting occurs in the rat septal nucleus after transection of its inputs from either fimbria or medial forebrain bundle (MFB). Transection of MFB results in axonal sprouting of fimbrial afferents upon synaptic sites vacated by MFB afferents. The opposite occurs after transection of fimbrial fibers. Collateral sprouting is now recognized as occurring in response to injury in numerous and diverse CNS structures including septum, interpeduncular nucleus, red nucleus, hippocampus, central adrenegic neurons, optic tract, lateral geniculate, and others (see Cotman & Nieto-Sampedro, 1985; Marshall, 1985; Moore, 1974; Tsukahara & Murakami, 1983). In many circumstances the new synapses have been proven to be functional (Cotman & Nieto-Sampedro, 1985) although the exact relationship of sprouting to recovery is not yet clear.

Recent research has demonstrated the possibility of transplanting fetal nervous tissue into mature CNS (see Cotman & Nieto-Sampedro, 1985, for a review). For instance, fetal rat septal, raphe and entorhinal neurons have been successfully transplanted into entorhinal cortex and have innervated recipient hippocampus (Cotman & Nieto-Sampedro, 1985). There is evidence that transplanted tissue also stimulates the growth of the recipient's remaining neurons as well. It is likely that research of this kind will greatly enhance our knowledge of recovery mechanisms and may yield practical techniques that facilitate repair. A full review of this field of research will not be undertaken here.

Neurochemical Adaptations. Neurons that remain after partial denervation of their targets may respond with several adaptations which serve to increase transmission along intact pathways. These mechanisms include increased rate of transmitter synthesis or release, decreased inactivation of released transmitter, or increased postsynaptic response to released transmitter (Marshall, 1985). All of these mechanisms have been documented in the CNS in response to injury.

When postsynaptic tissue is denervated, the membrane becomes supersensitive to chemical stimulation (Cannon & Rosenblueth, 1949). This phenomenon is known as denervation supersensitivity. It has been proposed as a mechanism of recovery of function after CNS damage (Cannon & Rosenblueth, 1949; Glick, 1974; Stavraky, 1961).

In a recent article, Marshall (1985) presented a compelling argument that neurochemical adaptations underlie the recovery of function demonstrated in a rat model of somatosensory inattention. Rats subject to 6-OHDA injections into the dopamine-containing cell bodies of the substantia nigra or their projections develop a syndrome of somatosensory inattention and will not orient to tactile stimuli applied to the contralateral body surface. The recovery of somatotopic localization (when it occurs) begins by the 4th day after surgery and is complete by the 28th day. Several features of this recovery suggest neurochemical adaptations (and especially postsynaptic supersensitivity) may be responsible for this return of function. Marshall noted that recovery depends upon survival of at least 5%–10% of neostriatal dopaminergic terminals. If there is greater than 95% depletion of the DA content of the neostriatum, recovery will not occur. In spontaneously recovering rats, impairments are reinstated by DA receptor blockade or DA synthesis inhibition, which suggests that the continued functioning of this population of residual DA neurons mediates recovery. There is no microscopic or biochemical evidence that the number of DA terminals in the neostriatum returns toward normal; it is therefore unlikely that regrowth or collateral sprouting is responsible for recovery. Further, the time course of behavioral recovery closely corresponds to the time course of postsynaptic supersensitivity to DA agonists. There is evidence that an increased density of D–2 receptors on neostriatal cells mediates the postsynaptic supersensitivity and recovery of somatotopic localization, although other mechanisms remain possible. Whatever the actual mechanism, the data suggest that at least in this model, neurochemical adaptations do indeed contribute to behavioral recovery.

Unmasking.   The concept of unmasking has been developed by Wall and associates (Basbaum and Wall, 1976; Merrill & Wall, 1978; Millar, Basbaum, & Wall, 1976; Wall, 1980; Wall & Egger, 1971). The fundamental hypothesis is that there are numerous synapses that are normally "silent" or "relatively inefficient" (Laurence & Stein, 1978) in the intact animal which may become activated should the normally active pathways be disrupted. This theory has in common with the theory of vicarious functioning the suggestion that latent pathways are activated in response to nervous-system damage.

It has been demonstrated in a number of experiments on different cell populations that when neurons lose their usual afferent input, they become responsive to novel input. After lesions are made in rat nucleus gracilis, which destroy afferent input from the leg, the somatotopic map of the thalamus changes such that the areas normally responsive to leg stimulation become responsive to stimulation of the arms. Similar alterations are noted in the receptive fields of the nucleus gracilius after deafferentation accomplished by selective dorsal-root sectioning. These changes have also been observed in cat spinal cord after partial and complete dorsal-root section.

Some cells altered their receptive properties immediately after deafferentation, but the majority took days or weeks to change. Although the exact mechanism of the unmasking phenomenon is still unknown, Wall suggests that the synaptic connections that mediate unmasking may exist prior to deafferentation. After damage to usual pathways these pathways become effective, possibly via sprouting of existing connections or disinhibition of these pathways.

FACTORS THAT INFLUENCE OUTCOME

In this section we consider the numerous variables that are assumed to determine outcome after brain injury. Because the most intensively studied question is which variables affect outcome in aphasia, we focus on this issue, although some of the principles have application to the issue of recovery in general.

Aphasia Subtype and Initial Severity

Outcome has been found to vary according to aphasia subtype. Kertesz and McCabe (1977) found that "complete" recovery occurred in 63% of the conduction aphasics, 50% of the transcortical aphasics, and 48% of the anomic aphasics. In none of the other aphasia subtypes did any patients recover completely; however, "excellent" ratings eventually were achieved by 33% of the Broca's aphasics, 14% of the Wernicke's aphasics, and 0% of the global aphasics. The data from Lendrem and Lincoln (1985) support these findings—Broca's, conduction, and anomic aphasics had higher scores than either Wernicke's aphasics or global aphasics on long-term follow-up. Mohr et al., (1980) studied aphasia after penetrating head injury and also concluded that motor aphasics did better than sensory aphasics.

On the other hand, though Demeurisse and coworkers (Demeurisse et al., 1980) agreed that global aphasics had the worst prognosis, they found that the final outcome was slightly, although not significantly, better in Wernicke's than in Broca's aphasics. In the Brust, Shafer, Richter, and Bruun (1976) study, 76% of fluent aphasics were considered either "mild" or "cleared" after 1 to 3 months, whereas the same could be said for only 34% of nonfluent aphasics. However, many globally aphasic patients were in the nonfluent group and were largely responsible for its poor performance.

The variation in results from one study to another can be partially understood if one takes into account the contribution of "initial severity," as well as the use of different language tests and different criteria for assigning patients to categories based upon severity. The initial severity of an aphasia is considered highly predictive of outcome (Kertesz & McCabe, 1977; Lendrem & Lincoln, 1985; Sands, Sarno, & Shankweiler, 1969; Sarno, Silverman, & Sands, 1970). This factor must always be considered when comparing outcome among different subtypes.

"Final outcome" is not the only measure of recovery—the "rate of improvement" has also been investigated. These terms are sometimes used interchangeably, but they are not synonymous. For example, it makes sense that the most severely affected aphasics—the ones with the worst final outcome—should have a low recovery rate. However, it is not obvious that the least severely affected aphasics—the ones with the best final outcome—should also have a low recovery rate. This is expected because their minimal initial deficits leave little room for improvement. The data from Kertesz and McCabe (1977) show that the highest recovery rates are among Broca's and conduction aphasics. On the other hand, Demeurisse et al. (1980) found that Wernicke's aphasics had slightly higher recovery rates than Broca's aphasics, but the difference was not significant. Finally, Lendrem and Lincoln (1985) found no difference in recovery rates among any of their patients, whether they were Broca's, Wernicke's, conduction, or anomic aphasics. Furthermore review of the literature does not settle the conflict (Butfield & Zangwill, 1946; Vignolo, 1964).

Etiology

Recovery has been treated in the literature as a function of etiology largely by comparing stroke and trauma cases. Kertesz and McCabe (1977) studied 7 patients who sustained closed head injury, as well as 47 patients with stable infarcts or hemorrhages. In the trauma group, initially 3 out of 7 patients had "aphasia quotients" that were "excellent." (The aphasia quotient is determined using the Western Aphasia Battery and is a measure of oral language performance; see Kerterz "Assessing Aphasic Disorders," this volume.) Eventually all 7 patients achieved an "excellent" rating. In the CVA group, initially 17% were "excellent," and long-term follow-up (average 28.6 months) revealed that only 40% ultimately reached that status.

The preceding data suggest that posttraumatic aphasics have a better prognosis than post-CVA aphasics. However, hard conclusions are difficult to draw for several reasons. The number of trauma cases in the Kertesz and McCabe study was quite small, and no data were available regarding lesion size and location in either group. Many of the less severely affected post-CVA aphasics (i.e., anomics) completely recovered soon after the insult and were not included in the analysis. Finally, the mean age of the trauma patients was 32, whereas that of the stroke patients was almost 60. Although most studies assessing recovery as a function of age do not demonstrate significant correlations, many authors still feel that an inverse relationship exists (this topic is addressed later in the chapter).

Despite the preceding data, other research also suggests that stroke patients are less likely to recover than trauma patients. For instance, Brust et al. (1976) evaluated 177 post-CVA aphasics—initially 47% were "severe," 28% were "moderate," and 25% were "mild." Testing 1 to 3 months later revealed that 19% had total resolution of their deficits. On the other hand, Mohr et al. (1980) followed 244 patients with aphasias secondary to penetrating head injuries. Complete recovery occurred within 10 years in 34%. Luria (1947; 1970) obtained similar data from a group of 139 posttraumatic aphasics. Initially 86% were "severe" and 14% were "mild." In the residual stage, however, 30% were free of aphasia. Caution should be exercised in the comparison of these 3 studies because follow-up intervals dramatically differed. We would expect to have seen further improvement in the CVA patients if repeat assessment had been done several months later.

Aside from CVA and trauma, comparisons of other etiologies of aphasia have not been formally addressed in the literature. For example, do differential recovery rates exist between patients with infarcts and intraparenchymal hemorrhages? There is a clinical impression that the latter sometimes have an advantage, because hemorrhage may distort tissue, rather than destroy it. Imaging techniques currently available should make such questions readily answerable.

Tumors, by virtue of their subacute to chronic course, cannot be quantitatively compared to the various forms of acute CNS pathology (i.e., infarcts, hemorrhages, trauma). The severity of deficits produced by a tumor is dependent upon the lesion's rate of growth. Slowly expanding tumors tend to create fewer deficits than acute lesions of comparable size. This phenomenon is known as the "serial lesion effect," and is discussed elsewhere in the chapter.

Lesion Size and Location

Kertesz, Harlock, and Coates (1979) found that severity of language disturbance significantly correlated with lesion size for their aphasic group taken as a whole. Among the various aphasia subtypes the anomics showed the highest, and the only significant correlation between severity and size. Naeser, Helm-Estabrooks, Haas, Auerbach, and Srinivasan (1987) found that the total temporoparietal lesion size in Wernicke's aphasics predicted the degree of naming dysfunction. Knopman, Selnes, Niccum, and Rubens (1984) found that normal naming scores were quite rare at 1 month post–CVA and eventually were achieved only by patients with lesions less than 60 cm³ on CAT Scan (CT); larger lesions always produced dysfunction, even at 6 months post–CVA. However, small lesions did not guarantee complete recovery of naming. There were several patients with lesions less than 60 cm³, or even less than 30 cm³, who had persistently poor naming. These smaller lesions affected either the posterior superior temporal/inferior parietal region, or the insula/putamen region. Thus it appears that large lesions predict poor recovery of naming, whereas small lesions usually, but not always, are associated with a better prognosis. Location of lesion is an important variable in both large and small lesions.

Selnes, Niccum, Knopman, and Rubens (1984) studied the recovery of single-word comprehension. Lesion size showed a strong correlation with the comprehension deficit at 1 month as well as 6 months post CVA. All patients with lesions less than 60 cm³ eventually achieved near-normal performance. Although damage to Wernicke's area was more frequent in patients with persistently poor single-word comprehension, such damage, even when severe, did not prevent full recovery. Related work by Selnes, Knopman, Niccum, and Ruben (1983) concluded that Wernicke's area played a major role in sentence comprehension. This was recently corroborated by Naeser et al. (1987), who found that Wernicke's aphasics with lesions of up to 50% of Wernicke's area had good auditory comprehension as early as 6 months post–CVA. If their lesions involved more than 50% of Wernicke's area, then comprehension remained poor more than 1 year later. Extension of the infarct into the middle temporal gyrus predicted an even worse prognosis, whereas extention into the supramarginal gyrus had no adverse effect. Overall, the total temporoparietal lesion size did not correlate significantly with the severity of the auditory comprehension deficit.

Another parameter that has been investigated with CT is language fluency. Knopman et al. (1983) found that lesions less than 25 cm³ were usually associated with normal fluency at 1 month post CVA. Only 1 out of 14 aphasics with such a lesion had persistent dysfunction at 6 months post CVA. On the other hand, no patients with lesions greater than 100 cm³ had normal fluency in the early stage, and 10 out of 12 patients still had severe deficits in the late stage. Thus, for very large or very small lesions, size was a good predictor of outcome. For moderately sized lesions, however, location becomes a more important factor. The crucial lesion for persistent nonfluency was felt to be in the left rolandic cortex and under-lying white matter, whereas damage to Broca's area was not necessary.

Other work had demonstrated that the evolution of aphasic syndromes can also be predicted on the basis of lesion location and size. For instance, Kertesz et al. (1979) reported that global aphasics who evolved into Broca's aphasics had more anterior lesions than the chronic global aphasics. The Broca's aphasics who evolved into anomics had smaller, although similarly placed lesions as compared to the chronic Broca's aphasics. Although the course of a given patient can never be predicted with certainty, CT is nevertheless a powerful tool. Its only shortcoming is that in the acute/subacute stages of an infarct, lesion boundaries and sulcal markings may be indistinct. It is still too soon to know whether MRI will increase the predictive power of the aphasiologist even further.

Age

Clinical observation suggests that there is an inverse correlation between age and recovery of function after brain damage, and children seem to have a greater capacity for recovery of language functions (Hecaen, 1976). In adults many studies have specifically assessed the role of age in the recovery from aphasia. Age, etiology, and type of aphasia can be con-founding variables. For instance, posttraumatic aphasias tend to occur in younger people more often than vascular aphasias. If the former etiology carries a better prognosis than the latter (Brust et al., 1976; Butfield & Zangwill, 1946; Kertesz & McCabe, 1977; Luria, 1970; Marks, Taylor, & Rusk, 1957; Mohr et al., 1980; Wepman, 1951), then we might pre-maturely assert that age rather than etiology was the critical variable. It has been reported that Broca's aphasics tend to be younger than either Wer-nicke's or global aphasics (Brown & Grober, 1983; Miceli et al., 1981; Obler, Albert, Goodglass, & Benson, 1978; Schechter, Schejter, Abar-banel, Groswasser, & Solzi, 1985; Steinvil, Ring, Luz, Schechter, & Solzi, 1985). If the former type has a better prognosis than the latter (Butfield & Zangwill, 1946; Kertesz & McCabe, 1977; Lendrem & Lincoln, 1985; Mohr et al., 1980), we might prematurely conclude that age is crucial in predicting recovery.

Wepman (1951) and Vignolo (1964) felt that age and recovery were negatively correlated. Sands et al. (1969) found that patients less than fifty years of age had a better prognosis than those more than sixty. The etiology of the aphasia was CVA in all 30 patients; however, a breakdown of aphasia type by age was not given.

Kertesz and McCabe (1977) also found an inverse relationship that persisted even when the authors eliminated the posttraumatic group from their analysis. In addition, their data showed no significant difference in the mean ages of the various types of aphasic patients. This study would be convincing but the negative correlation between age and recovery did not reach statistical significance. Other studies by Lendrem and Lincoln (1985), Pickersgill and Lincoln (1983), and Sarno and Levita (1971) also failed to corroborate the impression that younger adults recover better from aphasia.

Gender

The debate over whether gender affects recovery from aphasia has received renewed attention because of the hypothesis that gender may influence brain organization. McGlone (1977, 1980) suggested that because males may have stronger language lateralization than females, they therefore might develop more frequent and severe aphasias after left cerebral insults. She found that right-handed men were three times as likely as right-handed women to become aphasic after unilateral left hemisphere lesions.

Basso, Capitani, & Moraschini (1982) reported that the initial severity of aphasia in males was slightly greater than in females, but the difference was not significant. After controlling for this insignificant difference in initial severity, they found a significant difference in the recovery of oral expression—with females recovering more often than males. This differential response did not extend to auditory comprehension.

Pizzamiglio and Mammucari (1985) found no difference in the initial severity of aphasia between the sexes; however, 3 months later the female global aphasics had significantly more improvement relative to their male counterparts in tests of comprehension. Schechter et al. (1985) found that males had more severe aphasias associated with poorer prognoses, but the trend was not statistically significant.

Finally, Sarno, Buonaguro, and Levita (1985) found that in a moderately aphasic group the females had more initial impairment than the males. At the second exam 1 to 2½ years later, there were no differences between the sexes. The authors concluded that gender did not significantly affect recovery from aphasia. Other studies came to the same conclusion (Kertesz & McMabe, 1977; Lendrem & Lincoln, 1985).

Handedness

The role of handedness in aphasia is difficult to assess for two reasons. First, what most clinicians consider obvious left-handedness (i.e., writing with the left hand) occurs in only a relatively small fraction of the population. The real evaluation of handedness involves far more than just ascertaining which hand is used for writing. Laterality indices use questionnaires to elicit preference on a variety of motor skills, often in conjunction with actual performance tests and evaluation of family members. It turns out that many apparent right-handers actually have strong sinistral tendencies, whereas as Subirana (1969) pointed out, there are left-handers who have made concessions to the world of right-handers. In order to obtain true information regarding laterality, the individual's language and motor function must be relatively intact—often not the case in the aphasic, hemiparetic populations under study.

Nevertheless, there is a popular theory that sinistrality inversely correlates with left-hemisphere language lateralization; that is, the more left-handed a person is, the more bilateral is his or her language representation (Gloning & Quatember, 1966; Gloning, Gloning, Haub, & Quatember, 1969; Hécaen & Sauguet, 1971; Subirana, 1958, 1969). There are two corollaries to this theory. One states that left-handers have a higher incidence of aphasia than right-handers, because the former group should become aphasic regardless of which hemisphere is damaged (Gloning & Quatember, 1966, 1969; Hécaen & Sauguet, 1971). The second corollary states that aphasia in sinistrals is less severe and undergoes more rapid and complete recovery than in dextrals (Gloning & Quatember, 1966; Hécaen & Sauguet, 1971; Smith, 1971; Subirana, 1958, 1969; Zangwill, 1960). The intact functioning of the opposite language-bearing hemisphere is the proposed mechanism.

Pickersgill and Lincoln (1983) found that handedness was not a crucial factor in recovery from aphasia. However, only 1 patient out of 33 was predominantly left-handed on the basis of a formal inventory.

Subirana (1958, 1969) studied 108 stroke patients—65 pure right-handers, 37 right-handers with left-handed tendencies (or sinistrality in family members), and 6 predominant left-handers. Only 6% of the first group had transient aphasias, whereas 60% and 100% of the second and third groups, respectively, had transient aphasias. Zangwill (1960) replicated Luria's (1947, 1970) work, which produced similar results. Left cerebral trauma was the insult in all 160 patients—64 pure dextrals, 73 dextrals with sinistral tendencies, and 23 either sinistral or ambidextrous patients. Initially, 90% of the first group had severe aphasias, whereas only 60% and 65% of the second and third groups, respectively, had severe aphasias. In the residual stage 75% of the first group still had marked impairment, but less than 10% of the latter two groups had significant dysfunction.

One problem with Subirana's and Luria's work is the lack of detailed knowledge regarding lesion size and location. Two additional studies attempted to account for these variables. Gloning et al. (1969) studied 32 "non-right-handed" patients with left cerebral dysfunction who expired from 1 week to 3 months after admission. Based upon subsequent autopsy data, each patient's lesion was matched with that of a right-handed patient who had had left cerebral dysfunction of similar etiology. The matching took into account both lesion size and location. From language tests given during the first week of hospitalization, the authors concluded that there was no difference between the two groups. Naeser and Borod (1986) studied 8 sinistral aphasics in a manner similar to Gloning et al. (1969), except that CT scans were used to match their lesions to those of 8 dextral aphasics. All patients had sustained left CVAs, and all underwent language testing at about the same time after stroke onset. Again, no differences were found between the two groups.

Rapidity of the Insult—
Serial Lesion Phenomena

Neurologists have long recognized that patients with slowly developing CNS lesions often present with a relative paucity of signs and symptoms compared to those patients whose lesions are of similar size and location, but develop more rapidly. Riese (1950) dated the first mention of this empirical observation as far back as the 18th century, whereas in the 19th century Jackson (1879) coined the phrase "momentum of lesions" (mass × velocity) to describe it. Although this principle of clinical neurology is very difficult to evaluate quantitatively in human populations, this is not the case with animal models, where a substantial body of knowledge has accumulated.

In work done almost 50 years ago, Kennard (1938) found that recovery of motor function in the monkey after ablation of motor cortex was enhanced when the ablation was done in a multistage procedure. In other words, several operations were performed in which small amounts of tissue were successively removed, instead of removing the same total volume of tissue all at once. Ades (1946) reported similar findings after multistage ablations in other cortical areas. In fact, his initial discoveries regarding retention of visual discrimination following peristriate cortex ablations were made wholly by chance. Finger, Walbran and Stein (1973) designated this phenomenon the "serial lesion effect," a term which has achieved popularity in the literature.

Researchers have manipulated a host of experimental parameters and evaluated their influence on the serial lesion effect. For instance, too small an interlesion interval seems to negate the benefit of serial lesions. The amount of tissue destroyed in each operation appears important. In one experiment a four-stage ablation with a 3-week interlesion interval gave better results than a two-stage ablation with a 10-week interlesion interval

(Stein, Butters, & Rosen, 1977). The neurophysiological mechanisms underlying the serial lesion effect are as yet poorly understood. Diaschisis (neural shock) and denervation supersensitivity are among the suggested mechanisms (Finger, 1978). Of concern to clinicians is whether the serial lesion effect crosses phylogenetic boundaries and can be applied to man, for as Rosenzweig (1980) suggests, neurosurgical morbidity might be decreased in multistage operations.

Animal Models of Rehabilitation

Over 20 years ago Schwartz (1964) demonstrated that the effects of an occipital cortex lesion in a newborn rat were partially negated by placing the rat in an "enriched" environment postoperatively. When tested about 4 months later, such a rat solved mazes as well as an intact rat who had spent his youth in a "normal" environment. The enriched condition offered rats a larger cage with greater social interaction, as well as stimulation with inanimate objects. Subsequently, Rosenzweig (1980) showed that social stimulation alone was not as effective as the combination of social and inanimate stimulation in enhancing the recovery of lesioned rats. Also important was the finding that rats with lesions made in young adulthood still benefited from enrichment.

There are anatomic and biochemical correlates to the so-called enriched condition. The brains of animals reared under these conditions show increased cortical thickness that is greatest in occipital regions (Diamond, Krech, & Rosenzweig, 1964). This reflected larger neuronal cell bodies and nuclei (Diamond, 1967), greater complexity of dendritic structure (Greenough, 1976) and larger number of glial cells (Diamond et al., 1966). In addition, the enriched brains showed higher levels of cholinesterase, lower levels of acetylcholinesterase, and a greater RNA/DNA ratio (Rosenzweig & Bennett, 1978).

It is difficult to prove that these cerebral changes were directly responsible for the behavioral enhancement seen in enriched rats. As Rosenzweig (1980) pointed out, experiments with stimulant drugs have induced similar cerebral changes without any accompanying behavioral improvement. Thus, although the plasticity of the young animal brain is obvious, further research is needed to unravel the mechanisms underlying the enrichment phenomenon, and to apply this data to rehabilitation therapy in humans.

Miscellaneous Factors

Many other factors have been implicated in determining the recovery from aphasia. Jackson (1978) argued that hemiplegia must be considered in relation to impairments of speech. Indeed, Brust et al. (1976) thought that hemiparesis (as well as visual field cuts) predicted a worse prognosis. Smith (1971) also maintained that residual language functions were worse in hemiplegic patients. Tranel, Biller, Damasio, Adams, and Cornell (1987) discussed three cases of global aphasia without hemiparesis and concluded that it was associated with an unusually good prognosis. Kertesz (1984) found that recovery from nonfluency inversely correlated with severity of hemiparesis. This is what one would expect because a large lesion involving motor speech regions is likely to encroach upon the motor strip as well and result in hemiparesis. This relationship was not present with other language parameters, probably because posterior aphasics with prominant comprehension disturbance are less likely to have hemiparesis. Mohr et al. (1980) discovered that in penetrating head injury, aphasia could continue to improve years after the hemiparesis had stabilized. On the other hand, Boone (1961) did not find a significant relationship between recovery from aphasia and severity of the motor dysfunction.

Motivational factors are probably very important in influencing recovery from brain damage. The work of Franz and Odin (1917) showed that strong motivation could improve an apparently fixed motor deficit. Stoicheff (1960) related the performance of aphasics to positive and negative verbal feedback.

Individual differences may play a crucial role. This might help explain how seemingly identical lesions produce vastly different clinical syndromes. It is known that in humans the planum temporale of the left hemisphere tends to be larger than that on the right (Geschwind & Levitsky, 1968). This hemispheric asymmetry may be the anatomic basis for language dominance. The CAT Scan has proved useful in measuring these hemispheric asymmetries in vivo (LeMay 1977; LeMay & Kido, 1978). In one CAT Scan study, LeMay (1977) reported that in a group of right-handed males 78% had greater left than right occipital lengths and 67% had greater left than right occipital widths. Among left-handers, however, only 37% had greater left than right, 24% had left equal to right, and 39% had right greater than left occipital lengths. Subsequent studies confirmed these overall hemispheric asymmetries among right-handers but failed to find significant differences between this group and non-right-handers (Chui & Damasio, 1980; Naeser & Borod, 1986). These considerations suggest that aphasic patients with left hemisphere lesions who have reversed left-right asymmetries might have a better prognosis. It has been found that reversed asymmetry in right-handers does relate to recovery of some language functions in global aphasics (Pieniadz, Naeser, Koff, & Levine, 1983). Further data suggest that left handers with right occipital length asymmetry have a better prognosis after left-posterior infarcts as far as recovery of auditory comprehension is concerned (Naeser, 1984; Naeser & Borod, 1986). Naeser (1984) suggested that dominance for handedness, motor speech output, and posterior language functions may be distributed independently between the hemispheres and may vary across individuals. It may be the patient's particular anatomy, which determines the locus of these functions, that determines the pattern of spared or impaired abilities found after brain damage. Ojemann and Whitaker (1978) approached the same topic electrophysiologically. They showed variability among patients in language disruption during cortical stimulation studies.

CONCLUDING REMARKS

Many unanswered questions remain regarding how the nervous system recovers after injury. The relative contributions toward recovery made by various aforementioned mechanisms and factors remain to be elucidated. It is certain that recovery is a multifactorial process and there are probably many levels at which the clinician may intervene to facilitate the process. Animal data suggest that some pharmacologic agents may contribute to recovery (see Brailowsky, 1980, for a review) and hopefully some of the knowledge gained in animal trials will be tested in humans. We still need better pharmacologic therapies to minimize the damage that occurs immediately after stroke. And finally, although the notion of brain transplantation seems to some farfetched, its potential is only beginning to be explored. It is quite conceivable that we may be able to manipulate recovery long before we fully understand it.

ACKNOWLEDGMENTS

The authors wish to thank Ms. Norma Kamen for her help with the preparation of this manuscript.

REFERENCES

Adams, J. H., Graham, D. I., Murray, L. S., & Scott, G. (1982). Diffuse axonal injury due to nonmissile head injury in humans: An analysis of 45 cases. *Annals of Neurology, 12,* 557–563.

Adams, J. H., Mitchell, D. E., Graham, D. I., & Doyle, D. (1977). Diffuse brain damage of immediate impact type. Its relationship to "primary brainstem damage" in head injury. *Brain, 100,* 489–502.

Ades, H. W. (1946). Effects of extirpation of parastriate cortex on learned visual discrimination in monkeys. *Journal of Neuropathology and Experimental Neurology, 5,* 60–66.

Basbaum, A., & Wall, P. D. (1976). Chronic changes in the response of cells in adult cat dorsal horn following partial deafferentation. *Brain Research, 116,* 181–204.

Basso, A., Capitani, E., & Moraschini. S. (1982). Sex differences in recovery from aphasia. *Cortex, 18,* 469–475.

Bernstein, J. J., & Bernstein, M. E. (1973). Neuronal alteration and reinnervation following axonal regeneration and sprouting in mammalian spinal cord. *Brain Behavior and Evolution, 8,* 135–161.

Bishop, B. (1982). Neural plasticity: Responses to lesions in the peripheral nervous system. *Physical Therapy, 62,* 1275–1282.

Boone, R. (1961). Relationship of progress in speech therapy to progress in physical therapy. *Archives of Physical Medicine and Rehabilitation, 42,* 30–32.

Brailowsky, S. (1980). Neuropharmacological aspects of brain plasticity. In P. Bach-y-Rita (Ed.), *Recovery of function: Theoretical considerations for brain injury rehabilitation* (pp. 187–224). Baltimore: University Park Press.

Brown, J., & Grober, E. (1983). Age, sex, and aphasia type: Evidence for a regional cerebral growth process underlying lateralization. *The Journal of Nervous and Mental Disease, 171,* 431–434.

Brust, J. C., Shafer, S. Q., Richter, R. W., & Bruun, B. (1976). Aphasia in acute stroke. *Stroke, 7,* 167–174.

Bucy, P. C. (1934). The relation of the premotor cortex to motor activity. *Journal of Nervous and Mental Disease, 79,* 621–630.

Butfield, E., & Zangwill, O. L. (1946). Re-education in aphasia. A review of 70 cases. *Journal of Neurology, Neurosurgery and Psychiatry, 9,* 75–79.

Cajal, S. R. (1928). *Degeneration and regeneration of the nervous system.* London: Oxford University Press.

Cannon, W. B., & Rosenblueth, A. (1949). *Supersensitivity of denervated structures.* New York: Macmillan.

Chow, K. L. (1967). Effects of ablation. In G. C. Quarton, M. Melnechuk, & F. O. Schmitt (Eds.), *The neurosciences: First study program* (pp. 705–713). New York: Rockefeller University Press.

Chui, H. C., & Damasio, A. R. (1980). Human cerebral asymmetries evaluated by computerized tomography. *Journal of Neurology, Neurosurgery and Psychiatry, 43,* 873–878.

Cotman, C. W., & Nieto-Sampedro, M. (1985). Progress in facilitating the recovery of function after central nervous system trauma. In F. Nottebohm (Ed.), *Hope for a new neurology* (pp. 83–104). *Annals of the New York Academy of Sciences, 457.*

Demeurisse, G., Demol, O., Derouck, M., Beuckelaer, R., Coekaerts, M. J., & Capon, A. (1980). Quantitative study of the rate of recovery from aphasia due to ischemic stroke. *Stroke, 11,* 455–458.

Diamond, M. C. (2967). Extensive cortical depth measurements and neuron size increases in the cortex of environmentally enriched rats. *Journal of Comparative Neurology, 131,* 357–364.

Diamond, M. C., Krech, D., & Rosenzweig, M. R. (1964). The effects of an enriched environment on the histology of the rat cerebral cortex. *Journal of Comparative Neurology, 123,* 111–120.

Diamond, M. C., Law, F., Rhodes, H., Lindner, B., Rosenzweig, M. R., Krech, D., & Bennett, E. L. (1966). Increases in cortical depth and glia numbers in rats subjected to enriched environment. *Journal of Comparative Neurology, 128,* 117–126.

Edds, M. V. (1953). Collateral nerve regeneration. *Quarterly Review of Biology, 28,* 260–276.

Escourolle, R., & Poirier, J. (1973). *Manual of basic neuropathology.* Philadelphia: Saunders.

Feeney, D. M., & Baron, J. C. (1986): Diaschisis. *Stroke, 17,* 817–830.

Finger, S. (1978). Lesion momentum and behavior. In S. Finger (Ed.), *Recovery from brain damage: Research and theory* (pp. 135–164). New York: Plenum Press.

Finger, S., Walbran, B., & Stein, D. G. (1973). Brain damage and behavioral recovery: Serial lesion phenomena. *Brain Research, 63,* 1–18.

Flourens, P. (1824). *Experimental research on the properties and functions of the nervous system in vertebrate animals.* Paris: Crevot.

Franz, S. I., & Odin, R. (1917). On cerebral motor control: The recovery from experimentally produced hemiplegia. *Psychobiology, 1,* 3–18.

Gazzaniga, M. (1978). Is seeing believing: Notes on clinical recovery. In S. Finger (Ed.), *Recovery from brain damage: Research and theory.* New York: Plenum Press.

Gazzaniga, M. S., & Hillyard, S. A. (1971). Language and speech capacity of the right hemisphere. *Neuropsychologia, 9,* 273–280.

Geschwind, N. (1974). Late changes in the nervous system: An overview. In D. G. Stein, J. J. Rosen, & N. Butter (Eds.), *Plasticity and recovery of function in the central nervous system* (pp. 467–508). New York: Academic Press.

Geschwind, N., & Levitsky, W. (1968). Human brain: left–right asymmetry in temporal speech region. *Science, 161,* 186–187.

Glick, S. D. (1974). Changes in drug sensitivity and mechanisms of functional recovery following brain damage. In D. G. Stein, J. J. Rosen, & N. Butters (Eds.), *Plasticity and recovery of function in the central nervous system.* New York: Academic Press.

Gloning, I., Gloning, K., Haub, G., & Quatember, R. (1969). Comparison of verbal behavior in right-handed and non right-handed patients with anatomically verified lesion of one hemisphere, *Cortex, 5,* 43–52.

Gloning, K., & Quatember, R. (1966). Statistical evidence of neuropsychological syndromes in left-handed and ambidextrous patients. *Cortex, 2,* 484–488.

Goldberger, M. E. (1974). Recovery of movement after CNS lesions in monkeys. In D. G. Stein, J. J. Rosen, & N. Butters (Eds.), *Plasticity and recovery of function in the central nervous system* (pp. 265–337). New York: Academic Press.

Goldberger, M. E., & Growden, J. H. (1973). Pattern of recovery following cerebellar deep nuclear lesions in monkeys. *Experimental Neurology, 39,* 307–322.

Greenough, W. T. (1976). Enduring brain effects of differential experience and training. In M. R. Rosenzweig & E. L. Bennett (Eds.), *Neural mechanisms of learning and memory* (pp. 255–278). Cambridge: MIT Press.

Hecaen, H. (1976). Acquired aphasia in children and the ontogenesis of hemisphere functional specialization. *Brain and Language, 3,* 114–134.

Hecaen, H., and Sauguet, J. (1971). Cerebral dominance in left-handed subjects. *Cortex, 7,* 19–48.

Heilman, K. M., Rothi, L., Campanella, D., & Wolfson, S. (1979). Wernicke's and global aphasia without alexia. *Archives of Neurology, 36,* 129–133.

Hossman, K. A., & Kleihues, P. (1973). Reversibility of ischemic brain damage. *Archives of Neurology, 29,* 375–384.

Jackson, J. H. (1873). On the anatomical and physiological localization of movements in the brain. *Lancet, 1,* 84–85, 162–164, 232–234.

Jackson, J. H. (1878). On affections of speech from disease of the brain. *Brain, 1,* 304–330.

Jackson, J. H. (1879). On affections of speech from disease of the brain. *Brain, 2,* 323–356.

Kennard, M. A. (1938). Reorganization of motor function in the cerebral cortex of monkeys deprived of motor and premotor areas in infancy. *Journal of Neurophysiology, 1,* 477–496.

Kertesz, A. (1984). Recovery from aphasia. In F. C. Rose (Ed.), *Advances in neurology: Vol. 42, Progress in aphasiology* (pp. 23–39). New York: Raven Press.

Kertesz, A. (1985). Recovery and Treatment. In K. M. Heilman & E. Valenstein (Eds.), *Clinical neuropsychology* (pp. 481–505). New York: Oxford University Press.

Kertesz, A., Harlock, W., & Coates, R. 1979). Computed tomographic localization, lesion size, and prognosis in aphasia and nonverbal impairment. *Brain and Language, 8,* 34–50.

Kertesz, A., & McCabe, P. (1977). Recovery patterns and prognosis in aphasia. *Brain, 100,* 1–18.

Kinsbourne, M. (1971). The minor cerebral hemisphere as a source of aphasic speech. *Archives of Neurology, 25,* 302–306.

Knopman, D. S., & Rubens, A. B. (1986). The validity of computed tomographic scan findings for the localization of cerebral functions. *Archives of Neurology, 43,* 328–332.

Knopman, D. S., Selnes, O. A., Niccum, N., Rubens, A. B., Yock, D., & Larson, D. (1983). A longitudinal study of speech fluency in aphasia: CT correlates of recovery and persistent nonfluency. *Neurology, 33,* 1170–1178.

Knopman, D. S., Selnes, O. A., Niccum, N., & Rubens, A. B. (1984). Recovery of naming in aphasia: Relationship to fluency, comprehension and CT findings. *Neurology, 34,* 1461–1470.

Lashley, K. S. (1929). *Brain mechanisms and intelligence.* Chicago: University of Chicago Press.

Laurence, S., & Stein, D. G. (1978). Recovery after brain damage and the concept of localization of function. In S. Finger (Ed.), *Recovery from brain damage: Research and theory* (pp. 369–407). New York: Plenum Press.

LeDoux, J. E., Wilson, D. H., & Gazzaniga, M. S. (1978). Block design performance following callosal sectioning: Observations in functional recovery. *Archives of Neurology, 35,* 406–508.

LeMay, M. (1977). Assymmetries of the skull and handedness: Phrenology revisited. *Journal of Neurological Science, 32,* 243–253.

LeMay, M. & Kido, D. K. (1978). Asymmetries of the cerebral hemispheres on computed tomograms. *Journal of computer assisted tomography, 2,* 471–476.

Lendrem, W., & Lincoln, N. B. (1985). Spontaneous recovery of language in patients with aphasia between 4 and 34 weeks after stroke. *Journal of Neurology, Neurosurgery, and Psychiatry, 48,* 743–748.

Levin, H. S., Handel, S. F., Goldman, A. M., Eisenberg, H. M., & Guinto, F. C. (1985). Magnetic resonance imaging after "diffuse" nonmissile head injury. *Archives of Neurology, 42,* 963–968.

Levine, D. N., & Mohr, J. P. (1979). Language after bilateral cerebral infarctions: Role of the minor hemisphere. *Neurology, 29,* 927–938.

Liu, C. N., & Chambers, W. W. (1958). Intraspinal sprouting of dorsal root axons. *Archives of Neurology, 79,* 46–61.

Luria, A. R. (1970). *Traumatic aphasia.* The Hague: Mouton.

Luria, A. R. (1947). *Traumatic aphasia.* USSR: Press of the Academy of Medical Sciences.

Marks, M., Taylor, M., & Rusk, H. A. (1957). Rehabilitation of the aphasic patient: A survey of three years' experience in a rehabilitation setting. *Neurology, 7,* 837–843.

Marshall, J. F. (1985). Neural plasticity and recovery of function after brain injury. *International Review of Neurobiology, 26,* 201–247.

McGlone, J. (1977). Sex differences in the cerebral organization of verbal functions in patients with unilateral brain lesions. *Brain, 100,* 775–793.

McGlone, J. (1980). Sex differences in human brain asymmetry: A critical survey. *The Behavioral and Brain Sciences, 3,* 215–263.

Mempel, E., Srebrzynskia, J., Sobczynska, J., & Zarski, S. (1963). Compensation of speech disorders by nondominant cerebral hemisphere in adults. *Journal of Neurology, Neurosurgery and Psychiatry, 26,* 96.

Merrill, E. G., & Wall, P. S. (1978). Plasticity of connection in the adult nervous system. In C. W. Cotman (Ed.), *Neuronal plasticity* (pp. 97–111). New York: Raven Press.

Miceli, G., Caltagirone, C., Gainotti, G., Masullo, C., Silveri, M. C., & Villa, G. (1981). Influence of age, sex, literacy, and pathologic lesion on incidence, severity, and type of aphasia. *Acta Neurologica Scandinavica, 64,* 370–382.

Millar, J., Basbaum, A. I., & Wall, P. D. (1976). Restructuring of the somatotopic map and appearance of abnormal neuronal activity in the gracile nucleus after partial deafferentation. *Experimental Neurology, 50,* 658–672.

Mohr, J. P., Weiss, G. H., Caveness, W. F., Dillon, J. D., Kistler, J. P., Meirowsky, A. M., & Rish, B. L. (1980). Language and motor disorders after penetrating head injury in Viet Nam. *Neurology, 30,* 1273–1279.

Moore, R. Y. (1974). Central regeneration and recovery of function: The problem of collateral reinnervation. In D. G. Stein, J. J. Rosen, & N. Butters (Eds.), *Plasticity and recovery of function in the central nervous system.* New York: Academic Press.

Munk, H. (1881). *Verber die Funktionen der Grosshirnrinde, gesammelte Mitteilungen aus den Lahren 1877–1880,* Berlin: August Hirshwald.

Naeser, M. A. (1984). Relationship between hemispheric asymmetries on computed tomography scan and recovery from aphasia. *Seminars in Neurology, 4,* 136–150.

Naeser, M. A., & Borod, J. C. (1986). Aphasia in left-handers: Lesion site, lesion side, and hemispheric asymmetries on CT. *Neurology, 36,* 471–488.

Naeser, M. A. Helm-Estabrooks, N., Haas, G., Auerbach, S., & Srinivasan, M. (1987). Relationship between lesion extent in 'Wernicke's areas' on computed tomography, and predicting recovery of comprehension in Wernicke's aphasia. *Archives of Neurology, 44,* 73–82.

Nielson, J. M. (1946). *Agnosia, Apraxia, Aphasia: Their value in Cerebral Localization* (2nd ed.). New York: Hoeber.

Obler, L. K., Albert, M. L., Goodglass, H., & Benson, D. F. (1978). Aphasia type and aging. *Brain and Language, 6,* 318.

Ojemann, G. A., & Whitaker, H. A. (1978). Language localization and variability. *Brain and Language, 6,* 239–260.

Peerless, S. J., & Rewcastle, N. B. (1967). Shear injuries of the brain. *Canadian Medical Association Journal, 96,* 577–582.

Pickersgill, M. J., & Lincoln, N. B. (1983). Prognostic indicators and the pattern of recovery of communication in aphasic stroke patients. *Journal of Neurology, Neurosurgery, and Psychiatry, 46,* 130–139.

Pieniadz, J. M., Naeser, M. A., Koff, E., & Levine, H. L. (1983). CT Scan cerebral hemispheric asymmetry measurements in stroke cases with global aphasia: Atypical asymmetries associated with improved recovery. *Cortex, 19,* 371–391.

Pizzamiglio, L., & Mammucari, A. (1985). Evidence for sex differences in brain organization in recovery in aphasia. *Brain and Language, 25,* 213–223.

Plum, F. (1983). What causes infarction in ischemic brain?: The Robert Wartenberg lecture. *Neurology, 33,* 222–223.

Prince, M. (1910). Cerebral localization from the point of view of function and symptoms. *Journal of Nervous and Mental Diseases, 37,* 337–354.

Pulsinelli, W. A., Waldman, S., Sigsbee, B., Rawlinson, D., & Plum, F. (1980). Experimental hyperglycemia and diabetes mellitus worsen stroke outcome. In E. Betz (Ed.), *Pathophysiology and pharmacotherapy of cerebral vascular disorder* (pp. 196–199). Baden-Baden: Verlag Gerhard Witzstrock.

Raisman, G. (1969). Neuronal plasticity in the septal nuclei of the adult brain. *Brain Research, 18,* 25–48.

Raisman, G., & Field, P. M. (1973). A quantitative investigation of the development of collateral reinnervation of the septal nuclei. *Brain Research, 50,* 241–264.

Rehncrona, S., Rosen, I., & Siesjo, B. K. (1980). Excessive cellular acidosis: An important mechanism of neuronal damage in the brain. *Acta Physiologica Scandinavia, 110,* 425–437.

Riese, W. (1950). *Principles of neurology. Nervous and Mental Disease Monographs, 80,* 1–168.

Rosenzweig, M. R. (1980). Animal models for effects of brain lesions and for rehabilitation. In P. Bach-y-Rita (Ed.), *Recovery of function: Theoretical considerations for brain injury rehabilitation*. Baltimore: University Park Press.

Rosenzweig, M. R., & Bennett, E. L. (1978). Experimental influences on brain anatomy and chemistry in rodents. In G. Gottlieb (Ed.), *Studies on the development of behavior and the nervous system: Vol. 4, Early influences* (pp. 289–327). New York: Academic Press.

Rosner, B. S. (1970). Brain Functions. *Annual Review of Psychology, 21*, 555–594.

Rosner, G. (1974). Recovery of function and localization of function in historical perspective. In D. G. Stein, J. J. Rosens, & N. Butters (Eds.), *Plasticity and recovery of function in the central nervous system*. New York: Academic Press.

Sands, E., Sarno, M. T., & Shankweiler, D. (1969). Long-term assessment of language function in aphasia due to stroke. *Archives of Physical Medicine and Rehabilitation, 50*, 202–206.

Sarno, M. T., Buonaguro, A., & Levita, E. (1985). Gender and recovery from aphasia after stroke. *Journal of Nervous and Mental Disease, 173*, 605–609.

Sarno, M. T., & Levita, E. (1971). Natural course of recovery in severe aphasia. *Archives of Physical Medicine and Rehabilitation, 52*, 175–178.

Sarno, M. T., Silverman, M., & Sands, E. (1970). Speech therapy and language recovery in severe aphasia. *Journal of Speech and Hearing Research, 13*, 607–623.

Schechter, I., Schejter, J., Abarbanel, M., Grosswasser, Z., & Solzi, P. (1985). Age and aphasic syndromes. *Scandinavian Journal of Rehabilitation Medicine Supplement, 12*, 60–63.

Schechter, I., Schejter, J., Abarbanel, M., Kren, R., Mendelson, L., Ring, H., & Becker, E. (1985). Sex and aphasic syndromes. *Scandinavian Journal of Rehabilitation Medicine Supplement, 12*, 64–67.

Schochet, S. S., & McCormick, W. F. (1979). *Essentials of Neuropathology*. New York: Appleton.

Schwartz, S. (1964). Effect of neonatal cortical lesions and early environmental factors on adult rat behavior. *Journal of Comparative and Physiological Psychology, 57*, 72–77.

Selnes, O. A., Knopman, D. S., Niccum, N., & Rubens, A. B. (1983). Computed tomography scan correlates of auditory comprehension deficits in aphasia: A prospective recovery study. *Annals of Neurology, 13*, 558–566.

Selnes, O. A., Niccum, N., Knopman, D. S., & Rubens, A. B. (1984). Recovery of single word comprehension: CT Correlates. *Brain and Language, 21*, 72–84.

Smith, A. (1971). Objective indices of severity of chronic aphasia in stroke patients. *Journal of Speech and Hearing Disorders, 36*, 167–207.

Sperry, R. W. (1947). Effect of crossing nerves to antagonistic limb muscles in the monkey. *Archives of Neurology and Psychiatry, 58*, 452–473.

Stavraky, G. W. (1961). *Supersensitivity following lesions of the nervous system*. Toronto: University of Toronto Press.

Stein, D. G., Butters, N., & Rosen, J. (2977). A comparison of two and four-stage ablations of sulcus principalis on recovery of spatial performance in the rhesus monkey. *Neuropsychologia, 15*, 179–182.

Steinvil, Y., Ring, H., Luz, Y., Schechter, I., & Solzi, P. (1985). Type of aphasia: Relationship to age, sex, previous risk factors, and outcome of rehabilitation. *Scandinavian Journal of Rehabilitation Medicine Supplement, 12*, 68–71.

Stenevi, V., Bjorklund, A., & Moore, R. Y. (1973). Morphological plasticity of central adrenergic neurons. *Brain, Behavior and Evolution, 8*, 110–134.

Steward, O., Cotman, C. W., & Lynch, G. S. (1973). Re-establishment of electrophysiologically functional entorhinal cortical input to the dentate gyrus deafferented by ipsilateral entorhinal lesions: Innervation of the contralateral entorhinal cortex. *Experimental Brain Research: 18*, 396–414.

Stoicheff, M. L. (1960). Motivating instructions and language performance of dysphasic subjects. *Journal of Speech and Hearing Research, 3,* 75–85.

Strich, S. J. (1956). Diffuse degeneration of the cerebral white matter in severe dementia following head injury. *Journal of Neurology Neurosurgery and Psychiatry, 19,* 163–185.

Subirana, A. (1958). The prognosis in aphasia in relation to cerebral dominance and handedness. *Brain, 81,* 415–425.

Subirana, A. (1969). Handedness and cerebral dominance. In P. J. Vinken & G. W. Bruyn (Eds.), *Handbook of Clinical Neurology.* Amsterdam: North Holland.

Tranel, D., Biller, J., Damasio, H., Adams, H. P., & Cornell, S. H. (1987). Global aphasia without hemiparesis. *Archives of Neurology, 44,* 304–308.

Tsukahara, N., & Murakami, F. (1983). Axonal sprouting and recovery of function after brain damage. In J. E. Desmedt (Ed.), *Motor control mechanisms in health and disease.* New York: Raven Press.

Vignolo, L. A. (1964). Evolution of aphasia and language rehabilitation: A retrospective exploratory study. *Cortex, 1,* 344–367.

Von Monakow, C. (1914). Cerebral localization and dissolution of function resulting from cortical lesions. Wiesbaden: J. F. Bergmann.

Wall, P. D. (1980). Mechanisms of plasticity of connection following damage in adult mammalian nervous systems. In P. Bach-y-Rita (Ed.), *Recovery of function: Theoretical consideration for brain injury rehabilitation* (pp. 91–105). Baltimore: University Park Press.

Wall, P. D., & Egger, M. D. (1971). Formation of new connections in adult rat brains after partial deafferentation. *Nature, 232,* 542–545.

Wepman, J. M. (1951). *Recovery from Aphasia.* New York: Ronald Press.

Zangwill, O. L. (1960). *Cerebral dominance and its relation to psychological functioning.* Edinburgh and London: Oliver & Boyd.

3

The Neuropsychology of Attention: Elements of a Complex Behavior

Allan F. Mirsky

There is no satisfactory treatment of the assessment of attention, or of the neuropsychological basis of attention disturbance, in any current textbook of clinical neuropsychology. Perhaps the closest approximation to a satisfactory discussion of some of the clinical phenomena is provided by recent discussions of neglect or hemiinattention syndromes (e.g., Heilman, 1979). Heilman and Valenstein (1979) have proposed that the unilateral neglect or hemiinattention phenomenon is due to a localized failure of arousal and/or orienting and have adduced data from human and animal behavioral and neurophysiological studies in support of this view. Although unilateral neglect is a spectacular symptom when it occurs, it represents a relatively small part of the attention-related clinical problems with which the neuropsychologist clinician is faced. Moreover, a theoretical account of attention impairment that is limited to failure of arousal or incapacity to orient seems to capture relatively little of a complex behavior. In the present chapter, a relatively novel theoretical view of the elements of attention will be proposed. Although this proposal is based upon some of the same clinical data that led Heilman and coworkers to suggest a cortico–limbic–reticular loop to support attention, it extends the clinical base beyond cases of stroke to consider attention impairment such as is seen in epileptic disorders and schizophrenia. Aside from considering lesions and other conditions accompanied by a loss of function, the data also include information gathered from dynamic physiological studies in animal subjects performing on tasks designed to model elements of attention in humans.

MODELS OF ATTENTION

In recent years, cognitive psychologists have become interested in the problem of attention, and insightful and original analyses and models have been contributed by Kahneman (1973), Posner (1978), Shiffrin and Schneider (1977), and others.

The complexities of some of the models proposed by cognitive psychologists are beyond our current knowledge of the correspondence between function and structure in the brain. Moreover, it would be premature to attempt to achieve a complete synthesis of the neuropsychological and the cognitive approaches to attention and attention disorder. Nevertheless, there are some basic principles stemming from cognitive psychology that can guide the development of a neuropsychologically-based model of attention. These are: (a) Attention (or to use the more inclusive term, information processing) is not a unitary phenomenon but is comprised of a series of elements or stages. The notion of stages suggests that information processing occurs in sequential fashion. For the most part, we are unable at this point to speculate about information processing stages within a neuropsychological context, because we simply do not have sufficient information. However, the notion of individual components or elements of attention is one that we can apply; (b) Another insight that the cognitive psychologists have provided is the contrast between automatic and controlled processing (Posner, 1978; Shiffrin & Schneider, 1977). Each of these has different characteristics and different demands upon the information-processing system; we shall attempt to integrate this distinction in our treatment. (c) Also useful is the notion that attention is not an inexhaustible resource; allocations of this limited resource have to be made in part on the basis of the supply available to the individual and in part on the basis of motivational criteria.

The technique perfected by Evarts (1966) for studying the functions of individual nerve cells in behaving monkeys has stimulated a variety of behaviorally oriented studies. Some of this work suggests that there are individual neurons in which functions that support attention can be assessed (e.g., Bakay Pragay, Mirsky, Ray, Turner, & Mirsky, 1978). This research has helped to illuminate the brain regions involved in attention and the nature of that involvement. The data from some of these studies of particular relevance to this discussion are incorporated in the model developed here.

THE ELEMENTS OF ATTENTION

Elsewhere, Duncan and I (Mirsky & Duncan, in press) have written about two clinical entities that have generated more research on attention than any other psychopathological or neuropathological disorders: absence epilepsy and schizophrenia. The attention disturbance in schizophrenia, in particular, has been the subject of intense research interest, because it is the most persistent, and possibly the most salient, characteristic of the disorder that has been described (Mirsky & Duncan, 1986). It was within the context of attempting to analyze the nature of the disturbed attention in schizophrenia that Zubin (1975) proposed a view of the "elements" of attention that has proven useful in interpreting the results of our own research. According to Zubin's analysis, attention can be subdivided into a number of elements or aspects. These include (a) the capacity to *focus* upon or select some part of the environment, (b) the ability to *sustain* or maintain that focus for an appreciable period, and (c) the ability to *shift* adaptively from one aspect or element of the environment to another.

This analysis of the elements of attention accords well with some recent data obtained in the Laboratory of Psychology and Psychopathology of the National Institute of Mental Health. These data are derived from an analysis of an extensive series of neuropsychological tests administered to a variety of neuropsychiatric patients and normal controls, studied either as inpatients or outpatients under a variety of research protocols. The data of most interest for this discussion involve the factor analysis of 10 test scores commonly considered to be measures of attention which were, in turn, derived from eight frequently used tests of attention. The tests and the scores derived from each were as follows:

1. The Trail Making Test (Reitan & Tarshes, 1959)—time to complete.
2. Talland Letter Cancellation Test (Talland, 1965)—number correct.
3. Digit Symbol Substitution Test (DSST) (subtest of the Wechsler Adult Intelligence Scale-Revised [WAIS-R], Wechsler, 1955)— number correct.
4. Stroop Color-Word Interference Test (Stroop, 1935)—total time.
5. Continuous Performance Test (CPT) (Rosvold, Mirsky, Sarason, Bransome, & Beck, 1956; Mirsky & Van Buren, 1965)—mean number of correct responses, X and AX tasks combined.
6. CPT—mean number of errors of commission, A and AX tasks.
7. CPT—mean reaction time for correct responses, X and AX tasks combined.
8. Digit Span (subtest of the WAIS-R)—total score forward and backward.
9. Arithmetic (subtest of the WAIS-R)—highest score.
10. Wisconsin Card Sorting Test ([WCST] Grant & Berg, 1948)— number of errors.

A brief description of each of the tests follows. The *Trail Making Test,* part of the Halstead-Reitan neuropsychological battery, requires the subject to connect a series of numbers (in numerical order) by drawing pencil lines between them; then, the subject must connect an alternating series of numbers and letters in a similar task. The *Talland Letter Cancellation Test* requires the subject to cross out designated letters in an array of random letters. In the *DSST,* the subject is asked to write symbols below a series of digits in accordance with a specified digit-symbol code. The key feature of the *Stroop Color-Word Interference Test* is the requirement that subjects read a series of color names (red, green, blue) printed in inks of conflicting colors. Their scores on simpler tasks (reading color names printed in black ink, reading color names of Xs) are also obtained.

The *CPT* is essentially a visual vigilance task in which the subject is required, for a 10-minute period, to press a response key to a specified target letter and to withhold responses to nontarget letters. The *Digit Span* and *Arithmetic* tests assess the ability to hold numbers in short-term memory and either to repeat them immediately (Digit Span) or to solve a verbally presented arithmetic problem (Arithmetic). The *WCST* requires subjects to sort a set of test cards according to a set of sample cards. The test cards present stimulus material differing in color, form, or number, which usually do not match the sample cards and thus require some decision as to the category that defines the match. The correct sorting category is systematically changed by the examiner after the subject has made a series of 10 consecutive correct sorts.

The scores obtained by a group of 86 subjects (who received a complete battery of neuropsychological tests) were subjected to a factor analysis using an orthogonal rotation. The results of this factor analysis indicated that the 10 scores described above could be characterized by four factors that accounted for 71% of the variance.

Table 3.1 presents the rotated factor loadings derived from this factor analysis, together with a tentative identification of the component of attention represented by each of the factors. Four tests loaded heavily on Factor 1; they are Trail Making, Talland Letter Cancellation, DSST, and Stroop. They all appear to tap some aspect of perceptual-motor speed and could be designated as measuring the *focusing* aspect of attention. The phenomenon of neglect may develop when the capacity to focus on a particular aspect of attention fails. Because speed is in fact a key feature of performance on each of these four tests, the *execute* component of the task seems intertwined with *focus* in this factor. The CPT measures alone load heavily on Factor 2, which can unambiguously be designated a vigilance factor; therefore, it seems reasonable to label this as reflecting the *sustain* component of attention. Factor 3 is represented only by the Digit Span and Arithmetic tests. It seems to assess a numerical-mnemonic quality of attention; the *encode* aspect of attention/information processing seems to capture this. Finally, Factor 4 is represented by only one test, the WCST. As in the case of Factor 2, the identity of this factor seems readily apparent; it taps the flexibility aspect of attention—the capacity to *shift.*

FACTOR ANALYTIC STUDY OF ATTENTION MEASURES
10 Measures, 86 Subjects

Measure	Rotated Factor Loadings			
	Factor 1	Factor 2	Factor 3	Factor 4
Trail Making Test	−0.797	0	0	0
Talland Letter Cancel.	0.754	0	0	0
Digit Symbol Sub. Test	0.726	0	0	0
Stroop Test	0.678	0	0	0
CPT-Omission Errors	0	−0.881	0	0
CPT-Commission Errors	0	0.877	0	0
CPT-Response Time	0	0.651	0	0
Digit Span	0	0	0.835	0
Arithmetic	0	0	0.719	0
Wisconsin Card Sort Errors	0	0	0	0.826
Variance Explained	24%	21%	14%	12%
Identity of Factor	Perceptual-Motor Speed	Vigilance	Numerical-Mnemonic	Flexibility
Component of Attention	**FOCUS EXECUTE**	**SUSTAIN**	**ENCODE**	**SHIFT**

The zeros are not in fact zero factor loadings but stand for nonsignificant values.

LOCALIZATION OF THE ELEMENTS OF ATTENTION: NEUROANATOMY, NEUROLOGY, AND NEUROPSYCHOLOGY

We next review brain regions involved in attention to allow incorporation of these behavioral findings into a neuropsychological/neuroanatomical context. In Fig. 3.1 are presented a series of semischematic views of the human brain, designed both to illustrate and summarize those regions of the cerebrum that current research has identified as attention-related. Beginning with the most rostral depiction, at the lower right are represented the tectum and the mesopontine regions of the reticular formation. The work of Moruzzi and Magoun (1949) and Lindsley, Bowden, and Magoun (1949) established these areas as essential to the maintenance of consciousness and attention.

The mesial view of the right hemisphere (center of the figure) depicts the midline thalamic region (and the reticular nuclei) for which a role in attention is supported by the work of Ajmone Marsan (1965) and Jasper and coworkers (Jasper, 1958).

In phantom on this brain view are presented the corpus striatum and hippocampus, as well as those portions of the medial frontal lobe

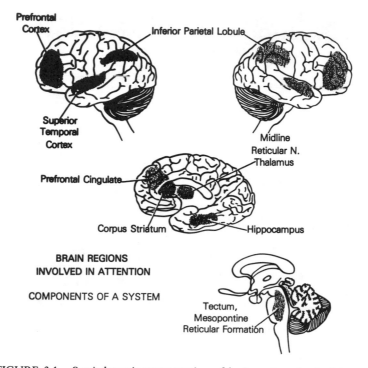

Prefrontal Cortex

Inferior Parietal Lobule

Superior Temporal Cortex

Midline Reticular N. Thalamus

Prefrontal Cingulate

Corpus Striatum

Hippocampus

BRAIN REGIONS INVOLVED IN ATTENTION

COMPONENTS OF A SYSTEM

Tectum, Mesopontine Reticular Formation

FIGURE 3.1.   Semischematic representation of brain regions involved in attention. *Note:* Figs. 3.1, 3.4, and 3.5 are taken from "Behavioral and Psychophysiological Markers of Disordered Attention" by A. F. Mirsky, *Environmental Health Perspectives,* 1987, *74,* 191–199.

heavily concerned with attention, including the anterior cingulate gyrus (Heilman, Watson, Valenstein, & Damasio, 1983). The corpus striatum has recently been implicated in the neglect phenomenon (Healton, Navarro, Bressman, & Brust, 1982, Heilman et al., 1983). The involvement of the hippocampus in attention is supported by both behavioral and electrophysiological measures; the classical hippocampal theta rhythm index of arousal has been well characterized (Adey, 1969).

The top two views provide a rough and tentative summary of current knowledge of cortical areas implicated in attention: the prefrontal cortex (Milner, 1963) and the inferior parietal lobe, lesions of which can lead to the neglect phenomenon. The inferior parietal lobule is shown of greater size in the right-hemisphere view because of the reported greater likelihood of neglect following right-hemisphere lesions (Heilman et al., 1983). The role of the superior temporal cortex or, more accurately, the superior temporal sulcus, as a multimodal sensory convergence area with a presumptive role in attention is perhaps best supported by the anatomical studies of Pandya and coworkers (e.g., Pandya & Yeterian, 1985).

LOCALIZATION OF THE ELEMENTS OF ATTENTION: SINGLE-UNIT BEHAVIORAL NEUROPHYSIOLOGY

The behaviorally oriented single-unit neurophysiological studies of Bakay Pragay and coworkers have described some portions of a map of those parts of the monkey brain that apparently support attention. Their initial investigation of the mesopontine reticular formation (Bakay Pragay et al., 1978) led to the identification of neurons that appeared active (i.e., "task-related") in the context of a visual attention task. This task, which was designed to be analogous to the CPT (Rosvold et al., 1956) required the monkey to attend to a visual display. Animals were trained to perform for liquid reinforcement. The task requires the animal to keep a "hold" key depressed for 2 seconds in order to elicit the next stimulus. Go (target) and no-go (nontarget) stimuli appear interspersed in quasirandom order. In the event a go stimulus appears, the animal must move his hand briskly from the hold key to a response key in order to obtain the reward; when a no-go stimulus appears, the animal must maintain his hand on the hold key for an additional interval in order to be rewarded. Extracellular recordings were made from the monkey's brain while he performed this task. Bakay Pragay and colleagues identified two basic types of task-related neurons: Type I cells, which fired only on go trials and seemed to be related to the execution of the motor response; Type II cells, which increased their firing on both go *and* no-go trials. Type II cells ceased responding to the task stimuli when they were no longer associated with reinforcement. Moreover, in some instances, Type II cells began firing hundreds of milliseconds before the occurrence of task stimuli—as though in anticipation of the appearance of the reinforced stimuli in this repetitive, predictable task. Fig. 3.2 presents examples of frequency histograms of spike potentials recorded from a Type I cell and two Type II cells, one asymmetric and one symmetric. The latter shows evidence of anticipatory firing in advance of stimulus onset. Figure 3.3 illustrates another characteristic of many of the anticipatory Type II cells, one that supports the interpretation that they are involved in attention. In this cell, isolated in the medial aspect of the prefrontal cortex of the monkey (see bottom of figure), several variations in the usual CPT parameters were tried. When the hold period is altered unexpectedly, from 2 to 1, 3 or 4 seconds, the pattern of cell firing is changed significantly. Three- and 4-second hold periods (seen in the middle and lower portions of the figure) produce a considerable increase in cell firing and a decrease in reaction time—as though heightened arousal and increased attention were produced by the change in task parameters. However, if the hold time is shortened to 1 second (top of the figure) resulting in a task that is very difficult for the

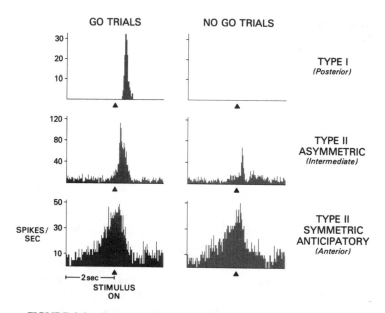

FIGURE 3.2.   Frequency histograms based on numbers of spike potentials recorded during go (left side of figure) and no-go (right side of figure) trials in three task-related cells in the frontal cortex of the monkey. Each histogram summarizes, usually, 15–20 or more trials. The interval used for summating spikes was 32 msec. The Type I cell (which shows no responses during no-go trials) was recorded from the motor cortex, the Type II Asymmetric cell from the premotor cortex and the Type II Symmetric Anticipatory cell from the prefrontal cortex. The dark triangle indicates the point at which the stimulus came on. *Note:* From "Attention Related Unit Activity in Frontal Association Cortex During a Go/No-Go Visual Discrimination Task" by E. Bakay Pragay, A. F. Mirsky, and R. Nakamura, 1987, *Experimental Neurology, 96,* 481–500. Reprinted by permission.

animal (too arousing?), then the firing of the cell becomes disorganized and the reaction time increases significantly. The cells illustrated in Figs. 3.2 and 3.3 were obtained in a study of the frontal lobes of the monkey by Bakay Pragay, Mirsky, and Nakamura (1987); however, they are quite representative of Type I and II cells, wherever they have been recorded. Bakay Pragay et al. (1987) found Type II cells in regions of the monkey prefrontal cortex extending from the midprincipal sulcus to the central sulcus, although the frequency with which they were encountered diminished in the more caudal (and thus more purely motor) locations. Type II cells were also identified in the medial prefrontal regions (Fig. 3.3) and in the cingulate gyrus. Moreover, Bakay Pragay, Mirsky, and Nakamura (1988) also found Type II cells in the inferior parietal lobule (Area 7) and the prestriate cortex (Area V4). Every region of the monkey brain that

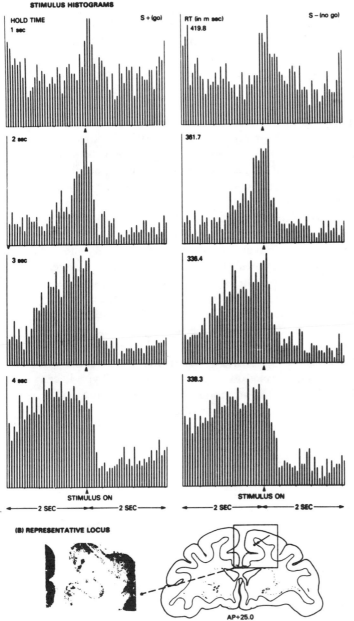

STIMULUS HISTOGRAMS

HOLD TIME
1 sec

S + (go)

RT (in m sec)
419.8

S − (no go)

2 sec

361.7

3 sec

336.4

4 sec

338.3

STIMULUS ON

STIMULUS ON

◄— 2 SEC —►◄— 2 SEC —►

◄— 2 SEC —►◄— 2 SEC —►

(B) REPRESENTATIVE LOCUS

AP+25.0

FIGURE 3.3. Frequency (stimulus) histograms, of the same type illustrated in Fig. 3.2, for a Type II Symmetric Anticipatory cell under varying hold conditions. The location of the cell (medial, prefrontal cortex) is illustrated at the bottom of the figure at (B). The second pair of histograms from the top shows the cell's response with the customary hold period of 2 sec; average Reaction Time (RT) for go trials was 361.7 msec. The third and fourth pairs of histograms from the top show change in cellular response when the hold time was unexpectedly lengthened, respectively, to 3 and 4 seconds. Note increase in cell firing to this task change, presumably reflecting increased attention on the part of the animal. The mean RT decreased to 336.4 and 338.3 msec., respectively, during these manipulations. Top histograms illustrate the cell's response to decreasing the hold time to 1 sec.: The pattern of firing becomes disorganized; the mean RT increased to 419.8 msec. Stimulus on at dark triangles; go trials on left, no go on right.

83

has been explored by Bakay Pragay and coworkers on the basis of a presumptive role in attention (i.e., mesopontine reticular formation, medial thalamus, prefrontal and frontal association cortex, inferior parietal and prestriate cortex) has been found to contain attention-related Type II cells. There are no contradictions with the map of the human brain depicted in Fig. 3.1.

Certainly, the characteristics of Type II cells could be construed as essential to the function of *focusing* on some aspect of the environment. Both go and no-go stimuli elicit increased firing and remain potent as long as the stimuli are associated with reinforcement. And the Type II cells can *sustain* task-related firing over hundreds of trials. Furthermore, the cell almost immediately ceases task-related firing as the task stimuli are dissociated from reinforcement. Such a disconnection implies the capacity for rapid *shifting* to other aspects of the environment that may hold more promise as reinforcers.

The data are not sufficient to say whether the Type II cells in different attention-related regions of the monkey brain are differentiated in function. The prefrontal cells in the Bakay Pragay et al. (1987) study showed great flexibility in response to changes in task parameters and contingencies; however, because these experimental maneuvers were not tried in most of the mesopontine cells, it is not clear whether this flexibility is unique to the prefrontal cortex. Other characteristics by which Type II cells differ include the degree of symmetry between go and no-go trials (as for example in the two Type II cells in Fig. 3.2), the latency at which the cell fires in "anticipation" of stimulus onset and whether the cell increases or decreases firing in relation to the stimuli. The Type II cell may represent a kind of primordial attention cell that, depending on the network in which it is embedded, can support the functions necessary for attention that are postulated here.

AN ATTENTION SYSTEM

There is little doubt that the brain structures presented in Fig. 3.1 could be construed to form a system; anatomical connections among the various areas have been described and are represented schematically in Fig. 3.4. These pathways have been well described (e.g., Jones & Peters, 1986) and are not documented further here. The question now arises as to whether there can be tentative assignment of the attention functions described in Table 3.1 to the components of the attention system depicted in Fig. 3.1. The bulk of evidence indicates that performance on tests of attention may be impaired selectively by different brain lesions. This could imply that separate aspects of attention (focus, sustain, shift, etc.) are supported by different brain regions. In Fig. 3.5 is presented a speculative effort to

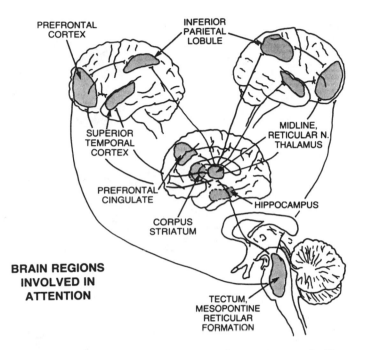

FIGURE 3.4.   Semischematic representation of brain regions involved in attention; some interconnections among the regions are shown. The connections are conceivably sufficient to support the concept of an attention "system."

combine the various sources of information: the neuroanatomical, the neurophysiological and the neuropsychological (with special emphasis on the data of Table 3.1).

It should be noted at the outset that this effort to assign functional specialization of components of attention to different brain regions is not meant to be absolute, and the possibility exists that some brain regions may share more than one attentional function. Caveats aside, what is suggested by the model can be summarized by the following statements:

1. Attention can be subdivided into a number of separate functions, including *focus, execute, sustain, encode,* and *shift.*
2. These functions are supported by different brain regions, which have become specialized for this purpose but which nevertheless are organized into a system.
3. The function of *focusing* on environmental events is shared by superior-temporal and inferior-parietal cortices as well as by structures that comprise the corpus striatum, including caudate, putamen, and globus pallidus.

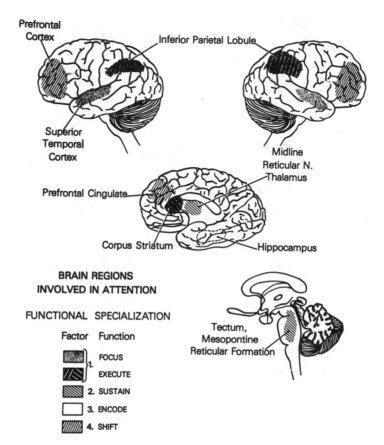

FIGURE 3.5. Semischematic representation of brain regions involved in attention, with tentative assignment of functional specializations to the regions.

4. The inferior-parietal and corpus-striatal regions have a strong motor-*execute* function.

5. *Sustaining* a focus on some environmental event is the major responsibility of rostral midbrain structures including the tectum, mesopontine reticular formation, and midline and reticular thalamic nuclei.

6. Considerable amounts of *encoding* of stimuli are accomplished by the hippocampus—an essential mnemonic function that seems to be required for some aspects of attention.

7. The capacity to *shift* from one salient aspect of the environment to another is supported by the prefrontal cortex.

8. Damage or dysfunction in one of these brain regions can lead to circumscribed or specific deficits in a particular attention function.

APPLICATION OF PRINCIPLES
FROM COGNITIVE PSYCHOLOGY

The possibility was suggested earlier that three of the principles derived from the cognitive psychological approach to attention are of relevance to the current model. The principle of attentional stages or *elements* has obviously been central to the development of this model. The elements identified here could ultimately be arranged into a sequential model. The other most direct application, conceivably, is to the concept of attention as a limited resource; thus, as lesions, disease, or "functional" disorders (e.g., petit mal epilepsy, schizophrenia) damage one or more parts of the attention system, there may be impairment of specific elements of attention (as previously indicated); however, there may also simply be less of the total attentional resource available to allocate to various demands. Nevertheless, to the extent that the remaining, intact portions of the system can substitute for the lesioned portions, the capacity for at least some attention remains, despite the loss of considerable amounts of tissue.

The least certainty lies in the application of the concept of automatic vs. controlled aspects of information processing to the present model. The qualities of automatic information processing, namely, that it occurs without conscious awareness and is not capacity limited, do not seem readily assignable to any specific part of this system. There are two possibilities: One is that automatic processing involves a low demand on the system, but that it is a system characteristic rather than one dependent on a specific element, such as are proposed here. The second possibility, as suggested by Nuechterlein, Parasuraman, and Qiyuan (1983), is that vigilance tasks that require detection of highly practiced stimulus material can occur virtually automatically. This would be compatible with classifying the *sustain* aspects of the model as concerned with automatic processing. More demanding vigilance tasks would, however, be classified as controlled processing. In terms of the present discussion, the balance of the attention system (i.e., elements concerned with *focusing, execution,* and *shifting*) is necessary for controlled information processing.

SOME APPLICATIONS OF THE MODEL

The goal of presenting this model is to assess each of the elements of attention that have been described (by the use of specific tests), and thereby to assess the integrity of the putative cerebral regions that support those elements. However, it is premature to assume that the model is sufficiently robust at present to withstand that sort of practical usage. Until sufficient empirical data have been accumulated, circumspection and caution must guide the practical clinical applications of this model. There are, however, sufficient data (as presented in this chapter) to commend this approach for further research in attention, because it represents a more rational view of the behaviors comprising attention than can be achieved by merely multiplying tests of attention that have been used in previous studies.

Two major large-scale investigations of attention, currently underway, are making use of the empirical findings and the theoretical schema presented here. One (being conducted jointly with the Department of Mental Hygiene of the Johns Hopkins University) involves a study of approximately 500 second-grade public school children; all subjects are being administered a battery of tests that include at least one of the tests from each of the clusters in Table 3.1. For Factor 1 (*Focus, Execute*), the tests include letter cancellation and the DSST; for Factor 2 (*Sustain*), the test is the CPT; Factor 3 (*Encode*) is assessed by the Digit Span and Arithmetic subtests of the Wechsler Intelligence Scale for Children; Factor 4 (*Shift*) is measured by performance on the Wisconsin Card Sorting Test. Preliminary analysis of scores from a subset of the subjects suggests that the factor structure seen in adults (Table 3.1) can also be discerned in these 8-year-olds. The data gathered will be intercorrelated with classroom observations of the same children, in the hope of learning more about the antecedents of deviant behaviors in this population. Another goal is to use the scores from the "Attention Battery" to aid in the prediction of future disordered behaviors (Kellam, Branch, Agrawal, and Ensminger, 1975). There are data that indicate that among certain types of high-risk populations (e.g., children at genetic risk for schizophrenia), poor attention scores will predict those individuals who will actually develop schizophrenia spectrum disorders (Mirsky, 1988). Figure 3.6 illustrates the relation between attention scores in a group of high-risk subjects (and controls) at age 11 in terms of the psychiatric diagnoses of the same subjects at age 26. The attention test used was a cancellation task, so presumably the functions being assessed, and on which the subjects who developed the schizophrenia spectrum disorder were impaired, were *Focus, Execute*. These data, in turn, might suggest that early in life there was damage to the brain regions supporting these functions (parietal cortex, corpus striatum) in these subjects. Although low scores on the arithmetic subtest of the WISC (the *Encode* Factor) characterized all high-risk subjects, they did not distinguish the schizophrenia spectrum cases from those with other diagnoses. The use of more rationally derived attention scores than those currently employed should add to the precision of the prediction in high-risk studies.

This point is illustrated in the second current major use of the test battery; we are continuing (in conjunction with colleagues from Hebrew University and Haifa University) to study a population of Israeli high-risk

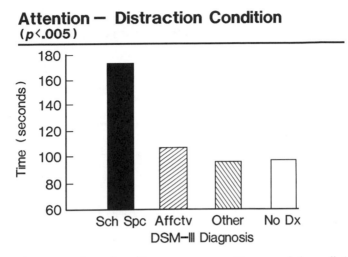

FIGURE 3.6.   Scores by subjects at average age 11 on a symbol cancellation task under conditions of distraction; data from the Israeli high-risk study. The DSM-III diagnoses were based on a SADS-L interview administered when the subjects were, on the average, 26 years old. Sch Spc = schizophrenia spectrum disorders ($n = 9$); Affctv = affective disorders ($n = 11$); Other = other diagnoses ($n = 7$); No Dx = no diagnosis ($n = 63$). The difference among groups was significant at $p < .005$. *Note:* From "Research on Schizophrenia in the NIMH Laboratory of Psychology and Psychopathology 1954–1987" by A. F. Mirsky, 1988, *Schizophrenia Bulletin, 14,*151–156.

subjects (and normal controls) that have been followed for over 20 years (Mirsky, Silberman, Latz, & Nagler, 1985). Some of these subjects have already developed schizophrenia spectrum disorders (Fig. 3.6); others remain at risk. The goal in this study is to administer the full attention battery, suitably modified for this population, to determine the relationship between attention test scores and a number of variables. These include: current diagnoses, "soft" neurological signs, as measured at ages 11 and 17 in these subjects, and other biological measures such as those derived from CT scans.

CONCLUSION

Because this is an early articulation of this theoretical view of attention, it is imperfect and necessarily will be subject to revision. Nevertheless, as I have tried to illustrate here, it may provide a heuristic device for testing neuropsychological hypotheses about disorders of attention. Elsewhere, Duncan and I have speculated about the relevance of such a model to the pathophysiology of schizophrenia and petit mal epilepsy. The analysis may be a unique way of viewing the pathophysiological bases of disorders of attention and it seems to capture some of the complexities of a complex behavior. Additional research will attest to the usefulness or wisdom of the approach.

ACKNOWLEDGMENTS

Some of the material here appears in similar form in Mirsky (in press, 1988) and in Mirsky and Duncan (in press).

REFERENCES

Adey, W. R. (1969). Spectral analysis of EEG data from animals and man during alerting, orienting and discriminative responses. In C. R. Evans & T. B. Mulholland, (Eds.), *Attention in neurophysiology: An international conference* (pp. 194–229). London: Butterworths.

Ajmone Marsan, C. (1965). The thalamus. Data on its functional anatomy and on some aspects of thalamo-cortical integration. *Archives Italiennes de Biologie, 103,* 847–882.

Bakay Pragay, E., Mirsky, A. F., & Nakamura, R. (1987). Attention-related unit activity in frontal association cortex during a go/no-go visual discrimination task. *Experimental Neurology, 96,* 481–500.

Bakay Pragay, E., Mirsky, A. F., & Nakamura, F. K. (1988). Attention-related unit activity in the inferior parietal and prestriate cortex of the monkey during a go/no-go visual discrimination task. Unpublished manuscript.

Bakay Pragay, E., Mirsky, A. F., Ray, C. L., Turner, D. F., & Mirsky, C. V. (1978). Neuronal activity in the brainstem reticular formation during performance of a "go/no-go" visual attention task in the monkey. *Experimental Neurology, 60,* 83–95.

Evarts, E. (1966). A technique for recording activity in subcortical neurons in moving animals. *Electroencephalography and Clinical Neurophysiology, 29,* 1011–1027.

Grant, D. A., & Berg, E. A. (1948). A behavioral analysis of degree of reinforcement and ease of shifting two new responses in a Weigl-type card sorting problem. *Journal of Experimental Psychology, 38,* 404–411.

Healton, E. B., Navarro, C., Bressman, S., & Brust, J. C. M. (1982). Subcortical neglect. *Neurology, 32,* 776–778.

Heilman, K. M. (1979). Neglect and related disorders. In K. M. Heilman, E. Valenstein, (Eds.), *Clinical Neuropsychology* (pp. 268–307). New York: Oxford University Press.

Heilman, K. M., & Valenstein, E. (1979). Mechanisms underlying hemispatial neglect. *Annals of Neurology, 5,* 166–170.

Heilman, K. M., Watson, R. T., Valenstein, E., & Damasio, A. R. (1983). Localization of lesions in neglect. In A. Kertesz (Ed.), *Localization in neuropsychology* (pp. 471–492). New York: Academic Press.

Jasper, H. H. (1958). Recent advances in our understanding of ascending activities of the reticular system. In H. H. Jasper (Ed.), *Reticular formation of the brain* (pp. 319–331). Boston: Little, Brown.

Jones, E. G., & Peters, A. (1986). *Cerebral cortex: Sensory-motor areas and aspects of cortical connectivity* (Vol. 5). New York: Plenum.

Kahneman, D. (1973). *Attention and effort.* Englewood Cliffs, NJ: Prentice-Hall.

Kellam, S. G., Branch, J. D., Agrawal, K. C., & Ensminger, M. E. (1975). *Mental Health and Going to School.* Chicago: University of Chicago Press.

Lindsley, D. B., Bowden, J. W., & Magoun, H. W. (1949). Effect upon the EEG of acute injury to the brain stem activating system. *Electroencephalography and Clinical Neurophysiology, 1*, 475–486.

Milner, B. (1963). Effects of different brain lesions on card sorting. *Archives of Neurology, 9*, 90–100.

Mirsky, A. F. (in press). Behavioral and psychophysiological effects of petit mal epilepsy in the light of a neuropsychologically based theory of attention. In M. S. Myslobodsky & A. F. Mirsky (Eds.), *Elements of petit mal epilepsy*. New York: Peter Lang.

Mirsky, A. F. (1987). Behavioral and psychophysiological markers of disordered attention. *Environmental Health Perspectives, 74*, 191–199.

Mirsky, A. F. (1988). Research on schizophrenia in the NIMH Laboratory of Psychology and Psychopathology 1954–1987. *Schizophrenia Bulletin,14,*151–156.

Mirsky, A. F., & Duncan, C. C. (in press). Attention impairment in human clinical disorders: Schizophrenia and petit mal epilepsy. In D. E. Sheer & K. H. Pribram (Eds.), *Attention: Theory, brain functions and clinical applications*. Hillsdale, NJ: Lawrence Erlbaum Associates.

Mirsky, A. F., & Duncan, C. C. (1986). Etiology and expression of schizophrenia: Neurobiological and psychosocial factors. *Annual Review of Psychology, 37*, 291–319.

Mirsky, A. F., Silberman, E. K., Latz, A., & Nagler, S. (1985). Adult outcomes of high-risk children. *Schizophrenia Bulletin, 11*, 150–154.

Mirsky, A. F., & Van Buren, J. M. (1965). On the nature of the "absence" in centrencephalic epilepsy: A study of some behavioral, electroencephalographic and autonomic factors. *Electroencephalography and Clinical Neurophysiology, 18*, 334–348.

Moruzzi, G., & Magoun, H. W. (1949). Brain stem reticular formation and activation of the EEG. *Electroencephalography and Clinical Neurophysiology, 1*, 455–473.

Neuchterlein, K. H., Parasuraman, R., & Qiyuan, J. (1983). Visual sustained attention: Image degradation produces rapid sensitivity decrement over time. *Science, 220*, 327–329.

Pandya, D. N., & Yeterian, E. H. (1985). Architecture and connections of cortical association areas. In A. Peters, E. G. Jones (Eds.), *Cerebral cortex: Association and auditory cortices* (Vol. 4, pp. 3–61). New York: Plenum.

Posner, M. I. (1978). *Chronometric explorations of mind*. Hillsdale, NJ: Lawrence Erlbaum Associates.

Reitan, R. M., & Tarshes, E. L. (1959). Differential effects of lateralized brain lesions on the Trail Making Test. *Journal of Nervous and Mental Disease, 129*, 257–262.

Rosvold, H. E., Mirsky, A. F., Sarason, I., Bransome, E. D., Jr., & Beck, L. H. (1956). A continuous performance test of brain damage. *Journal of Consulting Psychology, 20*, 343–350.

Shiffrin, R. M., & Schneider, W. (1977). Controlled and automatic human information processing. II: Perceptual learning, automatic attending, and a general theory. *Psychological Review, 84*, 127–190.

Stroop, J. R. (1935). Studies of interference in serial verbal reactions. *Journal of Experimental Psychology, 18*, 643–662.

Talland, G. A. (1965). *Deranged memory*. New York: Academic Press.

Wechsler, D. (1955). *Wechsler adult intelligence scale manual*. New York: Psychological Corporation.

Zubin, J. (1975). Problem of attention in schizophrenia. In M. L. Kietzman, S. Sutton, & J. Zubin (Eds.), *Experimental approaches to psychopathology*, (pp. 139–166). New York: Academic Press.

4

Plans, Actions, and Mental Sets: Managerial Knowledge Units in the Frontal Lobes

Jordan Grafman

INTRODUCTION

Imagine a bank manager sitting at his desk. In front of him he sees books, ledgers, pens and pencils, an appointment calendar, a writing tablet, and notes from his most recent staff meeting. In the background, classical music is playing on the radio; hallway, lobby, and street noises are heard intermittently. What can this imagined scene tell us about the requirements of human information processing?

When he focuses attention, the bank manager may need to recognize individual objects (e.g., a pen or a notebook). He may look at his calendar, note an appointment, and try to remember the reason for the meeting tomorrow morning. He may turn to his writing tablet next to try and continue writing a memorandum on the new tax laws. Perhaps his thoughts drift when he fails to retrieve a critical piece of legislation, and he begins to attend to the radio music and hallway noises before returning to his memorandum. A little later he may lean back in his chair and wonder whether "it's all worth it."

What this little vignette illustrates in a microcosm are the *obvious* demands of information processing: recognition of objects, sounds, and words as well as the retrieval of information from context-sensitive and context-free stores and from long–term and working memory. However, there are other less-obvious aspects of cognitive processing that are required in this scenario. What about the context of the bank manager's acts? Why does one act follow another? A simple explanation might posit a "spreading activation" of related activities with an associated lowering of activity thresholds. These characterizations are not enough to explain the bank manager's behavior at his desk. We need also to consider the following questions that cannot be answered by resorting to the foregoing explanation: How does the bank manager know where he is? How does he know what he is supposed to be doing during the day? How does he know what is appropriate behavior at work? How does he know how to use analogies? All these questions and more refer to knowledge that is routinely unavailable in working memory. In other words, much of this knowledge is processed in the background of focused cognition or mood. Conceivably, a bank manager could function quite adequately under certain conditions without the cognitive processes that insure a stable background. How crucial are these cognitive processes to the functioning of the individual? What are the characteristics of their mental representations and attached computational procedures? What happens if these background cognitive structures and procedures become impaired?

Our argument is that such an impairment exists following damage to the frontal lobes of the human brain. This chapter focuses on the frontal lobe patient, his psychological disorders and competency in day-to-day functioning. The symptom pictures provided by patients with frontal lobe lesions will motivate a model of higher-order cognitive processing that can generate testable hypotheses and is compatible with recent theories of induction, problem solving, action, and knowledge representation. Although Grafman (1985) recently proposed such a model, it was vague in many of its predictions. The purpose of this chapter is to make the model more precise and to adapt a theoretically neutral lexicon in describing it's parts and processes.

An important point about our effort to describe a framework for understanding the psychological disorders that follow lesions to the frontal lobe in humans needs to be made. That is, despite a very active neurobehavioral interest in studying the cognitive and mood disorders that emerge subsequent to frontal lobe lesions (for an early paper, see Bianchi, 1895), no *testable* model of cognition or mood has yet emerged that addresses the "nature" of the frontal lobe deficit(s) (Teuber, 1972). The chapter begins with a review of a series of studies of humans with frontal lobe lesions to illustrate the pattern of deficits that is typically seen (Goldstein, 1944; Hecean & Albert, 1975; Lhermitte, Derouesne, & Signoret, 1972; Milner, 1982; Milner & Petrides, 1984) and also discuss the problems in interpreting such deficits. Next, we briefly review recent models of knowledge representation (in particular, representation of large units of knowledge such as "schemas and scripts"). We then outline a neuropsychological model (or perhaps better stated, a framework) that we believe captures the essence of the frontal lobe deficit pattern. We then conclude the chapter by suggesting some strategies for the evaluation of patients with frontal lobe lesions.

SAMPLE DEFICITS FOLLOWING
FRONTAL-LOBE LESIONS IN HUMANS

Impaired Processing of Temporal Relations and Order

The perception and memory of temporal variables like order and time are often fleeting and quite difficult for psychologists to define and evaluate (e.g., see Friedman & Wilkins, 1985). Nevertheless, patients with frontal lobe lesions are occasionally characterized as having temporal processing deficits (Duncan, 1986). For example, Milner, Petrides, and Smith (1985) claimed that dorsolateral frontal lesions affect recency discrimination when contrasted with other memory functions. On both picture and word-learning tasks, subjects had to occasionally decide which of two paired stimuli was shown most recently. Frontal patients performed well on item recognition tests, but performed poorly on recency discrimination tasks. Thus, they knew that they had seen an item before but couldn't say when. The opposite finding occurred in patients with temporal lobe lesions.

On another task, Milner, Petrides and Smith (1985) attempted to disambiguate item recognition from estimates of frequency of item presentation. Again, they found that patients with frontal lobe lesions performed poorly, discriminating the frequency with which they were shown stimuli (this appeared most prominently when items had to be discriminated at the higher frequencies). For both the frequency and recency estimation tasks, there was a modality specific finding with patients who had left frontal lesions impaired on verbal tasks and patients with right frontal lesions impaired on nonverbal tasks.

Fuster (1985), on the basis of research with monkeys, also supported the notion that frontal lobe lesions affect the "temporal" organization of goal-directed behavioral sequences. He was especially interested in the timing of responses to environmentally and temporally distinct events. Petrides (1985) examined this idea with patients who had either frontal or temporal lobe lesions by administering conditional associative-learning tasks. He found that patients with frontal lobe lesions could remember the items in the tasks, but had difficulty establishing which items were associated.

It is sometimes noted that patients with frontal lobe lesions have a tendency to become inattentive during questioning or task performance (Duncan, 1986). Salmaso and Denes (1982) showed this formally on a simple detection task. They found that patients with frontal lesions had a diminished capacity to discriminate between old and new signals and also had a lower confidence in the accuracy of their responses on the task than normals. Perhaps patients with frontal lobe lesions lose their concentration partially because they can't link related contexts and thus events tend to appear with no apparent cause-effect relationship. If true, then the frontal lobes would play an important role in *mediating the organization of certain kinds of knowledge (Warrington, 1985)*.

Impairments in Planning and Problem Solving

Observations on patients with frontal lobe lesions have revealed that they have difficulty in developing concepts and being able to respond to the shifting demands of a situation. Milner (1963, 1964) decided to use the Wisconsin Card Sorting Test developed by Grant and Berg (1948) to evaluate patients with cortical surgical excisions for the relief of intractable epilepsy. Postoperative findings were of particular interest. Milner found that patients with dorsofrontal excisions were particularly impaired on this task achieving an average of only 1.4 categories (out of 6). The errors they made on this task were perseverative in nature. That is, they continually chose a category as appropriate long after it had "ceased to be appropriate." Milner argued that size of lesion alone could not account for these findings. Orbitofrontal excisions did not effect performance on this task. Stuss et al. (1983) found that leucotomized schizophrenics with presumed orbitofrontal disconnection performed poorly on the Wisconsin Card Sorting Test (WCST) if explicit verbal instructions were given before the last 64 cards were administered. They argued that a dissociation between knowing and doing contributed to the poor performance of the patients with orbitofrontal lesions. Drewe (1974) found that medial frontal lobe lesions affected performance on the WCST most severely. Like Milner (1964) and Stuss et al. (1983), she found no relationship between performance on the WCST and intelligence level.

Robinson, Heaton, Lehman, and Stilson (1980) attempted to assess the utility of the WCST for discriminating patients with frontal lobe lesions from other patients for clinical purposes. Forty-six out of 69 focal lesion patients had frontal lobe involvement. A diffuse group was also included. Their results indicated that patients with frontal lobe involvement performed significantly worse on the WCST than patients with nonfrontal focal involvement. However, no difference between the diffuse and focal frontal groups emerged. In addition, despite the unusually high base rate of focal frontal cases in their focal groups, discriminant analyses were not particularly encouraging in the use of the WCST as a "test for frontal lobe disease." Pendleton and Heaton (1982) also looked at the utility of the WCST for diagnostic purposes when compared to the Category Test developed by Halstead (1947). Both are routinely used clinically to detect impaired concept formation ability. Error scores on both tests were only modestly correlated after administration to a heterogeneous brain-damaged group. The WCST proved slightly better in detecting patients with frontal lobe lesions whereas the Category Test proved more sensitive to detecting patients with nonfrontal or diffuse lesions.

Nelson (1976) modified the WCST by using cards that shared only one attribute with the three target cards, avoiding the ambiguity of the standard set where a card can share more than one attribute with a target card. As with the standard WCST, on the modified version patients with frontal lobe lesions continued to perform worse than patients with lesions to other regions of the brain. No right-left differences were noted.

Golding (1981) used another version of the card sorting problem, the Wason four-card problem, to evaluate the performance of brain-injured patients on a concept formation task. The four-card problem requires subjects to make inferences as to the nature of the card that is face down given the cards that are shown. These inferences are in the form of "Whenever there is a circle on one-half of the card there is yellow on the other half"—true or false? Subject performance was analyzed for levels of insight: complete, partial, or none. Patients with left-hemisphere lesions performed worse than controls, whereas patients with right-hemisphere lesions demonstrated superior verbal problem solving on this task! Unfortunately, patients with frontal lobe lesions were not separately analyzed on this task. Cicerone, Lazar, and Shapiro (1983) used a version of Levine's concept formation card task to assess its sensitivity to patients with frontal lobe lesions. Patients with frontal lobe lesions performed more poorly than those patients with lesions to other areas of the brain. Patients with frontal lobe lesions also offered fewer hypotheses as the task progressed. Cicerone, Lazar, and Shapiro suggested that subjects had difficulty with the number of alternative stimulus attributes on which they could focus. Thus they had trouble "segregating relevant from irrelevant stimuli."

The ability to form and shift concepts allows humans to be flexible in planning and estimating. Because patients with frontal lobe lesions have historically been impaired on tasks measuring flexibility, some researchers have begun to directly test patients' performance on planning and estimating tasks. Shallice and Evans (1978) asked patients to estimate answers to factual questions, such as "What is the height of a double-decker bus?". They point out that while the answer is 14 and ½ feet high any estimate falling between 12 and 18 feet is reasonable. No hemisphere effect was found, but patients with frontal lesions did significantly worse than nonfrontal patients on this task. This finding was independent of intelligence level or arithmetic ability. Shallice and Evans interpreted this finding as a deficit in planning functions (also see Smith & Milner, 1984) for a discussion on "estimation problems" in patients with frontal lesions.) Shallice (1982) then went on to directly test frontal patients for planning deficits by using the "Tower of London" Test. This task requires subjects to plan out a series of moves in order to achieve a goal. The goal is to move three beads from one stick to another by following constraining rules. Left-anterior patients were particularly impaired on this task. Other reasons for the deficit performance besides planning were ruled out by control tasks. Shallice developed a theory to explain these planning deficits which is discussed in the following section.

Shallice used other tests to assess frontal lobe patient performance based on reports of their sensitivity and specificity, but found that only 1 of 10 tests—a Card-Sorting Test—could discriminate between patients with anterior and posterior lesions (Shallice, 1982). Shallice (1982) and others (e.g., Duncan, 1986) have argued that a cognitive processing explanation should be able to resolve why patients fail on such tests, but some investigators (e.g., Mesulam, 1986) still believe that "perseveration" and "premature closure" are sufficient explanations for the failure of frontal-lobe patients on card-sorting tasks.

Lezak (1982) has stressed that clinical evaluation of the patient with initiation, planning, and executive capacity deficits is in need of better instruments. These deficits are seen as tremendously disabling for the patient as he or she tries to continue interpersonal relationships and work responsibilities. Lezak herself has used the Tinker Toy game as a novel clinical approach to assess the ability of patients to plan out and create constructions. Functionally "dependent" patients were impaired "across the board" on this task (unfortunately, no frontal group was used).

Craine (1982) attempted to develop a retraining program for patients suffering from frontal lobe lesions. He used a case-example to highlight the difficulties in retraining such patients. Despite his attempts, no generally effective methods are available for assisting frontal-lobe patients with their planning deficits. This is not a functionally trivial problem as Lezak pointed out (Lezak, 1982). In fact, Locke, Shaw, Saari and Latham (1981) illustrated nicely how goal setting affects task performance under diverse conditions from work to learning how to drive. It plays a major role in tasks requiring directed attention, controlled effort, and motivation (Kahneman, Slovic, & Tversky, 1982). It should be clear that when frontal-lobe lesions result in cognitive problems such as impaired planning, the effects of such problems on day-to-day living can be dramatic.

Memory Deficits Associated with Frontal-Lobe Disorders

Because we have already identified temporal ordering, contextual association, and planning deficits as resulting from frontal-lobe lesions, it would be likely that such patients would appear to have memory problems (Vilkki, 1985). How restrictive are these memory deficits? Do they also appear if the above information processing deficits described earlier are controlled for in an experimental investigation? Ghent, Mishkin, and Teuber (1962) studied patients with penetrating missile wound injury and found that frontal-lobe patients did not show impairment on tasks such as memory span or spatial location—even when a delay was added. Butters, Samuels, Goodglass, & Brody (1970) tested patients with frontal- and parietal-lobe lesions on visual and auditory Peterson and Peterson type tasks using verbal and nonverbal stimuli. Their left frontal group demonstrated no memory disorder although their right frontal group showed an abnormally steep decay in retention under delay conditions. Given that these were group comparisons, their small numbers ($n = 4$) and the possibility that their lesions encroached upon the parietal area limited the inferences that could be made from patient performance in this study. Stuss, Kaplan, Benson, et al. (1982) examined schizophrenics who had undergone prefrontal leucotomy on memory tests, including the Wechsler Memory Scale, the Bender-Gestalt, word lists, Recurring Figures and Word Tests, consonant trigram–Peterson and Peterson task, the Rey Figure, a test of retrograde amnesia, and memory for designs. These patients were compared to unoperated schizophrenics who were chronically hospitalized. Patients with the frontal leucotomy were particularly at risk for proactive interference on multitrial tasks using various delays. However, on most other tasks, patients with frontal-lobe lesions performed within the range of the study control groups. This is a rather dramatic finding and tended to overshadow the poor frontal group performance on the consonant trigram task.

Freedman and Cermak (1986) studied patients with frontal lobe lesions and Korsakoff's disease on Wicken's test of proactive inhibition. They found that initially, both Korsakoff and frontal patients who previously were determined to have poor memory ability, also did not show release from proactive inhibition on the fifth trial (although having normal interference rate over the first four trials of the five-trial task). Experience on this task benefited the Korsakoff patients who eventually demonstrated release on the fifth trial, but did not benefit the "poor memory" frontal group. The "good memory" frontal group (whose lesions were not necessarily in distinct locations from the poor memory group) also showed appropriate release on this task. Freedman and Cermak (1986) speculated that disruption of thalamic and/or basal forebrain projections to the frontal lobe (Nauta, 1962) could account for the impaired release from proactive inhibition in the "poor memory" frontal group. Thus, at least some frontal patients appear to be quite sensitive to interference. Moscovitch (1976) also found this effect for left frontal patients in particular.

Rocchetta (1986) had subjects classify object pictures into categories. Tests of immediate and delayed recall of objects were also administered. Subsequent to the memory tests, subjects were asked to reclassify the objects, name the categories and point to the items contained in each category. Various error types were scored. Left and right frontal patients had a deficit in categorizing the pictures. Temporal patients had normal performance. Many items remained unclassified by frontal patients or they had numerous subcategories such as birds in addition to animals. Both frontal groups had diminished immediate recall but only left frontals were impaired on delayed recall (category recall). On item recall, left temporal groups were particularly impaired. Left temporal patients were found to make some use of the categorical structure of the information for recall whereas frontal patients could not (right frontal only).

Moscovitch (1982) later reviewed the spectrum of memory disorders seen in patients with frontal lobe lesions and found a pattern quite similar to that seen in Korsakoff patients (the pattern included increased susceptibility to interference, difficulty in using mnemonics, poor release from proactive interference, and poor memory for temporal order). These findings led Moscovitch to suggest that the failure of Korsakoff patients on certain cognitive tasks (e.g., release from proactive inhibition) was due to frontal-lobe involvement in these patients. Kanareikin and Volkov (1981) felt that memory deficits that followed frontal-lobe lesions might be at least partially due to an impaired mediational system that was not sufficiently linked to the to-be-remembered information. Schacter (1987) has suggested that frontal patients have trouble remembering the spatiotemporal contexts of episodic and/or declarative information.

Utilization Behavior and the Dependency Syndrome

Recently Lhermitte (Lhermitte, 1983, 1986; Lhermitte, Pillon, & Serdaru, 1986) and coworkers described a set of patients with lesions of the frontal lobes who exhibit a disinhibition of the "working memory" system in that such patients appear completely dependent upon stimuli in their environment. That is, they appear to "automatically utilize" objects in their environment without instruction, almost compulsively. This behavior appeared dissociated from context in a very obvious and dramatic way. These types of behaviors had been amply documented previously by Luria (1980), and Lhermitte's theoretical accounts, although somewhat murky, nevertheless stand as striking examples of the effects of frontal-lobe lesions on contextual behavior.

Miscellaneous Cognitive Deficits

Besides the aforementioned cognitive deficits that often follow lesions to the frontal lobe in humans, a variety of other impairments have also been observed. These include impairments in learning, suppression of old habits, confabulations, perseverative behaviors, impairments in language (Miller & Milner, 1985) and impaired motor learning. A review of some of these findings follows.

Drewe (1975) examined patients with frontal-lobe lesions on a go/ no-go learning task. She found that patients with frontal-lobe lesions were markedly impaired on this task; they committed more errors, took more trials to reach criterion, and fewer patients achieved criterion. Right frontals did not differ from left frontals on this task. Patients with medial frontal lesions were particularly impaired. Using variants of this task (the delayed alternation and delayed response paradigms), Freedman and Oscar-Berman (1986) found that bilateral frontal-lobe damage dramatically impaired performance on delayed alternation and response and that performance on these tasks was independent from that on standardized tests of memory (i.e., they were not sensitive to patients with anterograde amnesia). Performance on these tasks was, however, correlated with number of perseverative errors (for the previous category) on the Wisconsin Card Sorting Test. Both the perseverative explanation and the fact that these tasks were originally developed for testing of monkeys makes them useful as instruments in "comparative neuropsychology."

Some reports in the literature indicate that patients with frontal-lobe lesions are impaired on tasks requiring visuospatial analysis (Miller, 1985). Butters, Soeldner, and Fedio (1972) examined patients on the Money Map Test of Directional Sense and the Stick Test (that required both matching and reversal of stick constructions) and found that patients with left frontal-lobe lesions were particularly impaired on the segment of the Money Map Test that involved an imagined rotation of their own body. This impairment of performance on spatial tasks had been previously reported by Teuber (1964). Stuss, Benson, Kaplan, Della Malva, & Weir (1984) administered a set of visuospatial and visuoconstructive tasks to leucotomized patients (with presumed orbitofrontal white-matter lesions). Except for the Picture Arrangement subtest of the Wechsler Adult Intelligence Scale, leucotomized patients did not show evidence of either spatial or constructional deficits (including tests requiring copying, figure-ground discrimination, construction, right-left orientation, and recognition). Recently, Lang, Lang, Kornhuber, & Kornhuber (1986) reported right frontal-lobe dominance for learning a visuomotor tracking task based on CNV recordings during task performance. Finally, Guitton, Buchtel, and Douglas (1982) reported that frontal-lobe lesions in humans cause impaired generation of goal-directed saccades and suppression of reflexive glances. Dorsolateral lesions were particularly suspect in this regard and the deficits appeared even when the goal of the movement was known but the stimulus had not appeared.

Black (1976) has reported that unilateral penetrating missile wound injury to the frontal lobes did not result in any cognitive deficits on the WAIS, Wechsler Memory Scale or Shipley-Hartford Scale when compared with patients with posterior lesions or control generated standardized scores. This would not necessarily have surprised Bolton (1903) who saw frontal-lobe lesions as primarily causing mental disease but not simple intellectual deficits. Zangwill (1966) felt that frontal-lobe lesions particularly affected "divergent" thinking, which would be related to problems in regulation of speech and thought. Benton (1968) found that verbal fluency and temporal orientation were impaired in patients with frontal-lobe lesions. Perret (1974) thought that at least part of the reasons for problems with verbal cognition could be that patients with frontal-lobe lesions had enormous problems suppressing "verbal habitual responses" as seen on fluency or stroop tests (see Logan & Cowan, 1984, for a theoretical perspective). Several studies (Kapur & Coughlan, 1980; Mercer, Wapner, Gardner, & Benson, 1977; Shapiro, Alexander, Gardner, & Mercer, 1981; Stuss, Alexander, Lieberman, & Levine, 1978) have tried to link confabulation and frontal lesions claiming that deficits in inhibition, self-monitoring, and perseveration contributed to confabulation.

Goldberg and Tucker (1979) observed motor perseverations in frontal-lobe patients and were able to break down the deficits into executive, motor, and semantic. Executive processes were also distinguished from the analysis of units for visual encoding. Copying tasks were used for these studies. Goldberg and Costa (1985) elaborated on the preceding observations. They found that some drawings by frontal-lobe damaged patients contained elements of previous drawings, other drawings followed the form of the previous drawing, whereas others contained semantic substitutions which utilized objects/forms that were generated on previous drawings. These findings indicated that, even in copying, a multiple levels approach to perseveration could be a useful heuristic.

The dramatic cognitive deficits just reported are somewhat similar to those originally described by Luria (1969). Drewe (1975) attempted to replicate Luria's finding in an experiment with frontal-lobe patients. Drewe found general support for Luria's clinical descriptions (Luria, 1966, 1973) in her results although she could not exactly replicate Luria's clinical-anatomical correlations (the tasks were of the go/no-go variety). Despite Drewe's replication, Canavan, Janota, and Schurr (1985) cautioned that at least some of the deficits Luria found in patients with frontal-lobe lesions, such as disinhibition and impulsive behavior, could be the result of very large lesions that infringed upon nonfrontal structures. We discuss this issue in more detail in a later section.

LOBOTOMY, LEUCOTOMY, AND PSYCHOSURGERY

There is a highly charged literature on the effects of psychosurgery in patients with psychiatric disorders who are nonresponsive to conventional treatments (Kucharski, 1984). These studies, despite their methodological problems, have provided much of the data concerning the effects of orbitofrontal white-matter lesions upon cognition and mood (Landis, Zubin, & Mettler, 1950; Petrie, 1949; Stuss, Kaplan, & Benson, 1982; Stuss, Kaplan et al., 1981). Psychosurgery's supporters (e.g., Fulton, 1952) have extolled its virtues despite limited theoretical rational for its use. Benson et al. (1981) reported that the larger the frontal lesion, particularly if asymmetric, the better the psychiatric outcome and the better the performance on neuropsychological testing. Stuss, Benson, Kaplan, Weir, & Della Malva (1981) found that leucotomized patients in their Northhampton, VA series performed well when compared to controls on tests of attention. Other findings from this group are reviewed elsewhere in this chapter and in a recent monograph (Stuss & Benson, 1986). These studies generally involve small numbers of subjects with lifelong histories of psychopathology so severe that leucotomy was indicated. Caution is advised when generalizing from such data to other patient groups with frontal involvement.

MOOD REGULATION

As noted by Stuss and Benson (1984), some patients with frontal-lobe lesions also demonstrate marked dysregulation of mood state. Robinson, Kubos, Starr, Rao, & Price (1984) and Robinson, Lipsey, Rao, & Price (1986) have extensively documented a population of stroke patients with frontal-lobe lesions who, with remarkable consistency, demonstrate post-stroke depression. This depression appears most severe and persistent in those patients with left-anterior lesions. Grafman, Vance, Weingartner, Salazar, & Amin (1986) reported elevated levels of self-reported and observed anxiety symptomatology in patients with right-frontal penetrating brain wounds. This expression of anxiety was noted some 15 years postinjury indicating the persistence of such disorders. It would of course be interesting if elevated levels of anxiety could be found to be associated with specific cognitive deficits. Although no definitive study has yet emerged, we speculate about such relationships in the theoretical discussion in the last part of this chapter.

Behar et al. (1984) reported that performance of obsessive-compulsive patients on neuropsychological tasks resembled the performance of frontal lobe patients. Performance patterns of schizophrenic patients have also been reported to resemble those of patients with frontal-lobe lesions (Nasrallah & Weinberger, 1986). Powell (1981) reviewed many of the similarities between patients with frontal-lobe lesions and patients with psychiatric disorders and reported that after frontal-lobe lesions or operations, symptoms of anxiety, fearfulness, depression, and neuroticism all increased compared to controls. It is not clear from these reports that the symptomatology determining the diagnosis of a psychiatric disorder in non-brain-injured patients is mimicked following brain injury. Another interesting point made by Powell (1981) is that there is a dearth of research on positive affect (humor, laughter, "feeling optimistic or good") and whether that affect is reduced or altered in patients with frontal-lobe lesions.

Andy, Webster, & Carraniza (1981) noted a similarity between patients with frontal-lobe lesions and patients with psychotic disorders. Carlson (1977) claimed that frontal-lobe patients are frequently initially seen by psychiatric services due to a masking depression or schizophrenic like symptomatology. His patients' outcome following psychosurgery was viewed as positive. Cakuls and Finlayson (1978) agreed with Carlson that frontal-lobe lesions often masquerade as psychiatric disorders but denied that their own patients had such good postsurgical outcome. As previously noted, the effectiveness of psychosurgery as a treatment for psychiatric disorders is questionable as are the theoretical underpinnings for the procedure itself.

Kolb and Taylor (1981) noted a striking impoverishment of spontaneous narrative speech produced by patients with left-frontal lesions, whereas patients with right frontal-lobe lesions frequently interrupted testing by spontaneous conversation despite infrequent changes in facial expression. Deutsch, Kling & Steklis (1979) observed patients with frontal-lobe lesions in a social situation. None of the frontal-lobe patients scanned the waiting room before sitting down. They would just directly go to a chair (unlike other patients and controls). Frontal-lobe patients only attended to a new person entering the room if they (frontal-lobe patients) were engaged in a task (e.g., reading). Frontal-lobe patients often used expressions whose sense was autobiographical and not decipherable by the listener. They appeared emotionally labile and would often draw a conversation back to their own interest. Deutsch et al. (1979) suggested that one reason frontal-lobe patients are socially inappropriate may be that such patients cannot use their own body as a spatial referent or, perhaps, a social referent. Lhermitte (1983, see preceding discussion) may have observed this in another context.

Eslinger and Damasio (1985) observed a single case with bifrontal lesions and demonstrated how orbital and mesial lesions could result in markedly impaired social and personal motivation and behavior. Their patient was unable to "analyze or integrate the premises of a real-life problem. He seemed not to have available automatically, programs of action capable of driving him to motion." They found that real-life situations failed to evoke normal patterns of social behavior although the patients cooperation in testing was adequate and his cognitive and concept formation skills were above average. Their patient appeared unable to be spontaneously motivated for action. This patient's orbital and mesial frontal lobe were partially destroyed and the remaining orbital-mesial cortex was dissociated from dorsolateral and other association cortex. Damasio and Van Hoesen (1983) had earlier delineated this orbitofrontal group by claiming such patients showed a form of social dysinhibition, lack of appropriate judgment, and a lack of concern for previously acquired rules of social behavior. Fuster (1980) has warned us about the over-reliance on spectacular but methodologically suspect single cases such as that of Gage (Harlow, 1848). The suspicion, often documented, is that cases such as Gage often include lesions outside of the frontal cortex.

Recently, Stuss and Benson (1983) concluded that two distinct subgroups of personality disorders emerged with frontal-lobe brain damage. Following dorsolateral frontal-lobe lesions, pseudodepression is observed, whereas orbitofrontal lesions result in a pseudopsychopathy. Despite the best efforts of Stuss and Benson (1983), it is still difficult to disentangle the various disorders of emotion seen following frontal lobe lesions. In addition, many of the studies referred to are repetitious in their observed results but rather vague in theoretical explanation and prediction.

Thus, as a group, patients with frontal-lobe brain damage tend to demonstrate impaired processing of temporal order, contextual relations, planning, reasoning, memory, and mood regulation. Despite well-documented neural regions and pathways, both the management of these patients, as well as a comprehensive understanding of their deficits is lacking a programmatic effort.

MANAGEMENT

It is quite evident after reviewing the cognitive and mood changes that follow frontal-lobe lesions in man that these deficits are frequently profound and result in a "socially disabled" person (Ackerly, 1964). Eslinger and Damasio's (1985) account of their patient B. V. indicates that the

full impact of the frontal-lobe patient's behavioral problem may not be-
apparent on routine neuropsychological evaluation. Thus, it is critical that
a complete and detailed interview and questionnaire be administered to a
"significant other" who may often describe a series of vignettes when the
patient was embarrassing, agitated, difficult, or just puzzled and confused.

Craine (1982) discussed several case studies in which he developed
behavioral management programs for patients with frontal-lobe lesions.
Unfortunately, there is at this time no consistently successful approach to
managing the cognitive, and especially behavioral, deficits shown by these
patients (but see Goldstein & Levin, 1987). Reward or punishment contingencies have been tried with little success. Pharmacological intervention has also been attempted with occasional success at subduing agitated
or aroused behavior while sacrificing what little appropriate spontaneity
was available to the patient. Perhaps, the stumbling block preventing the
development of effective management techniques and tools is the lack of a
creditable model of behavior to help practitioners describe the patient's
deficits in a coherent manner. An analogy to this state of affairs might
exist if professionals interested in improving the memory processing of
amnesic patients were unable to characterize the stages or processes of
memory that were impaired.

NEUROANATOMY

Neuroanatomical studies have indicated that the frontal lobes receive afferents and sent efferents to all other major regions of the cortex, basal
ganglia, and limbic system (Nauta & Fiertag, 1986). Within frontal-lobe
cortex, Goldman-Rakic and Porrino (1985) have shown in a series of
elegant studies that the cellular organization of the frontal lobes has a
columnar appearance and that these columns are differentially innervated
by specific transmitter containing neurons. Fuster (1985) documented that
the frontal lobe has shown remarkable growth relative to the rest of the
brain with phylogenetic development. In particular, the prefrontal cortex,
which includes all areas anterior to the major motor regions including the
frontal eye fields, has shown the most dramatic increase in cortical mass.
In addition, Goldman-Rakic (1984, 1987) has pointed out that this region
develops rather late ontogenetically compared to other brain regions (ma-
turing by the early teenage years).

Thus, we can briefly summarize the neuroanatomy of the frontal lobes
by indicating that it is a slowly developing region with modular characteristics that integrates information from all major neural systems in the
brain and that is only fully developed in man. For further neuroanatomical
information, we refer the interested reader to Nauta and Fiertag (1986).

THEORETICAL MODELS

Convergent evidence from anatomical, neuropsychological, observational, and affective studies all indicate that if viewed as a homogenous region, the frontal lobes are the final point of representation for modular and domain-referenced processes before a response is made to an environmental or self-generated stimulus. Unfortunately, the level of explicitness of neuropsychological models of frontal-lobe cognitive processes has been, for the most part, shallow. There are some important exceptions. Brown (1985a, 1985b) has offered an explanation of frontal-lobe functioning within the context of his microgenetic theory, but it is heavily biased toward motor behavior (in particular, the apraxias) and cannot predict the variety of deficits seen after prefrontal lobe lesions. In their book, Stuss and Benson (1986) summarized aptly the other competitive theories of frontal-lobe functioning including those of Milner and Fuster. The one theory that begins to bridge the gap between purely descriptive observations of behavior and a theoretical model is the one proposed by Shallice.

Shallice (1982) tried to interpret the functions of the frontal lobes within two broad models. One addresses the nature of the representation of information in the frontal lobe, and the other addresses how these representations are activated and retrieved. Shallice has worked out the later model more clearly. He has argued for the existence of two major activation processes: a supervisory attention system and a contention scheduling system. The contention scheduling system activates overlearned representations relatively automatically based on sensory information or activation of temporarily dated memories. The supervisory attention system takes priority and dictates episodic reaction when nonroutine information is perceived or when there is a mismatch between an activated routine and sensory information. The routines or schemas that are activated are only weakly determined and defined within this system although the models proposed by Abbott, Black, & Smith (1985) or Barsalou and Sewell (1985) could fit nicely into this context.

What is intuitively comforting about Shallice's conceptual framework is that it gets close to the heart of the behavioral observations of patients with frontal-lobe lesions. That is, patients with localized frontal-lobe lesions typically do quite well on conventional psychological tasks. They tend to appear abnormal when required to maintain a behavioral or cognitive set. For example, in the middle of a meal in a public restaurant, a frontal-lobe patient might get up and begin conversing about personal matters with people he has never met before who are sitting at an adjacent table. Although access to specific information such as language (appropriate expression and comprehension), visuospatial skills (identifying places), recognition of events and objects are intact (identification of food), the ability to "run" through an overlearned event such as eating in a restaurant (i.e., a restaurant schema) is impaired. In this example, the act of talking to a stranger is clearly intact and in another circumstance (or schema) is appropriate. However, it is not typically appropriate in a restaurant in the presence of personal friends and without regard to explanations for the unusual (i.e., inappropriate) behavior.

Although we believe that Shallice's attentional model has pointed us in the correct *direction* for explaining a host of deficits that follow frontal-lobe lesions in humans, it is still lacking a clear structural description of the information actually represented—the so-called schema. The description of the schema is crucial because it may define the situations most likely to trouble the patient with frontal-lobe lesions.

SCRIPTS, SCHEMAS, AND FRAMES

The framework next proposed to account for the deficits found in patients with frontal-lobe lesions descends from recent work in cognitive science that proposes the existence of large-scale conceptual units sometimes called **frames** (Minsky, 1975, 1983), **scripts** (Schank, 1982), or **schemas** (Mandler, 1984). All of these theories argue that information to be remembered and expressed often comes in large units such as stories, routine activities, or problem-solving rules. This information must be represented in large stereotyped memory units with their own functional architecture (i.e., psychological organization) distinct from that seen in proposed lexical-semantic systems that focus on category structures or single word/object representation. The functional architecture tends to be hierarchical in these "schema" models with informational themes broken down into their constituent parts (e.g., see Mandler, 1984).

The grammar (or syntax) of these large-scale representations varies depending on the author and stimulus material used, whether it be stories (Mandler, 1984), visual scenes (Minsky, 1975), or events (Schank, 1982). Regardless of the idiosyncrasy of representation, each representational model has primary and minor nodes which locate event, story, or thematic content by actors, objects, actions, time, and sequence. This literature, along with that devoted to problem solving and reasoning (Ericsson & Simon, 1984; Wilensky, 1983) was the inspiration that led to the development of our own model. In order to fully appreciate the debt we owe to prior investigators, we encourage the reader to obtain some of the articles (also see Galambos, Abelson, & Black, 1986; Thorndyke, 1984; Thorndyke & Hayes-Roth, 1979) referred to in this chapter.

MANAGERIAL KNOWLEDGE UNITS (MKUs)

The preceding literature review, although rich with description, is weak in theoretical modeling. This makes it difficult to develop predictions and to test hypotheses regarding the behavior of patients with frontal-lobe lesions. In order to account for the deficits in reasoning, memory, and interpersonal behavior noted in patients with frontal-lobe lesions, we have developed a model of frontal-lobe knowledge representation that we believe will provide broad explanatory power.

As used in this chapter, **managerial knowledge units** (MKUs) are meant to represent large-scale knowledge units that are somewhat analogous to schemas, scripts, and frames. The choice of the term MKU is meant to minimize comparisons between this model and those developed in the context of artificial intelligence research. Grafman (1985) has argued that the MKU is not only "psychologically real" but is the predominant type of information unit represented in the human frontal lobes.

The MKU differs from word, propositional, factual, rule, visual-object, spatial-location, and other "small-scale" representations not only by virtue of the amount of information stored (or coordinated), but by an explicit chronological sequential structure. MKUs would be activated by a system similar to that proposed by Norman and Shallice (1986) who described both implicit automatic/primed processes as well as explicit and focal attentional mechanisms that control actions (see Fig. 4.1).

An archtype MKU would be an overlearned sequence of events, real or imaginary, that is retrieved automatically and has a beginning and an end. For example, engaging in appropriate social communication, eating at a restaurant, or the "steps" required to bathe oneself could all be considered examples of MKUs. Working memory processes (Baddeley, 1986) concerned with processing events that occur within explicit attentional windows cannot stretch their resources to attend to such large-scale memories as MKUs and, therefore, are more responsive to the episodic events that are encoded as nodes within the MKU (see the following). Thus, in parallel with word and sentence recognition involved in reading a menu, with working memory processes that are occupied with activating and maintaining favorite food category representations, and so forth, there is activation of MKUs that represent the event that will occur next in the restaurant (despite the person not being consciously aware of such activation).

Properties of the MKU

The preceding brief discussion of the MKU does not do justice to the complex representation we envision the MKU to have. Therefore, we

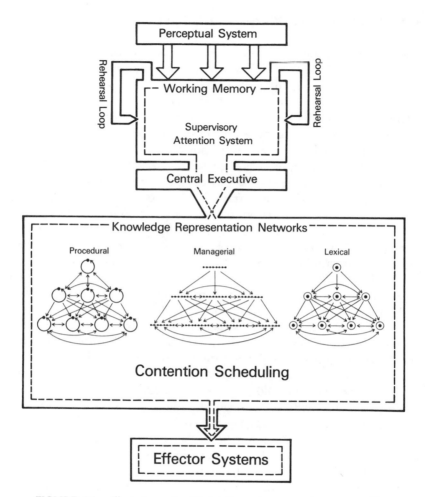

FIGURE 4.1. Illustrates a simplified information-processing system. The Knowledge Representation Networks are in long-term store. A Managerial Knowledge Unit can, for example, be activated by environmental stimuli via the Supervisory Attention System or it can be activated by priming via the Contention Scheduling System, which relies on "internally generated" stimuli, which are activated as part of other Managerial Knowledge Units.

would like to devote some space to mapping out some typical MKUs and describing their infrastructure as well as describing a possible hierarchy of MKUs. The advantage of being more precise is that the model being developed can then be experimentally challenged. This step alone would represent an advance in thinking about the kind of information subserved by the frontal lobes.

MKU Hierarchy

We conceive the MKU system to be organized in parallel with many other representational systems such as the lexical and syntactic memory systems (see Fig. 4.2). As such, we propose that the MKU system has a hierarchy of MKUs that range from the concrete to the abstract (see Fig. 4.3). Attentional activation processes may activate all MKU levels simultaneously although we suggest that the context dependent units will have more phasic activations, whereas the context-free units will have more tonic activations setting the "tone" of behavior.

The context-free semantic MKU corresponds to a set of context-dependent MKUs that have in common an abstract set of required actions and/or representations that take place in a specified temporal frame. For example, such an MKU might include the following nodes: a beginning and end, an object and subject, a goal(s), a goal attempt, and a resolution (see Fig. 4.4). These descriptors might be common to a set of context-dependent semantic MKUs such as eating in a restaurant, buying a gift, meeting a new person, and so forth. Although quite abstract, we also see the context-free MKU as providing a primitive and minimal behavioral structure within which a set of more specific MKUs may operate in parallel. The context–dependent semantic MKU corresponds to an abstract representation of a set of varying episodes, which can all be categorized under a specific "heading" such as eating in a restaurant. Each of the varying episodes (see the following) would be a representation of eating in a specific restaurant under varying circumstances. We see the context-dependent semantic MKU as providing a contextual behavioral structure within which a set of specific episodic MKUs may operate.

In our model, the episodic MKU corresponds to the representation of an activity that occurs in a certain environment, in a certain amount of time, and in a certain way, very often. For example, every Friday evening you eat a fish dinner at Sea World restaurant and you are served by the same familiar hostess and waitress who offer you the same menu that is always offered in the reliable old restaurant. The MKU is episodic because the context-specificity has a specific referent: Sea World restaurant and its characteristics. A set of episodic MKUs would force the creation of a context-dependent semantic MKU, an abstract representation of, for example, eating at a restaurant (see Fig. 4.5).

Embedded in this hierarchy of knowledge units are rules, conditions, procedures, and skill. Procedures and skills correspond to a variety of behaviors produced and observed in real time including skills such as typewriting, detecting signals, bicycle riding, and so forth, and procedures such as learning how to solve a class of limited problems or learning

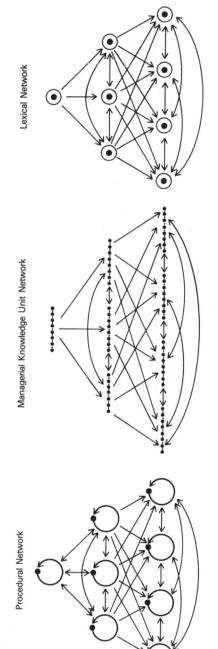

Representational Networks

Procedural Network

Managerial Knowledge Unit Network

Lexical Network

FIGURE 4.2. This figure suggests that the structure of a managerial knowledge unit network is theoretically similar to that of other knowledge networks.

A KNOWLEDGE UNIT HIERARCHY

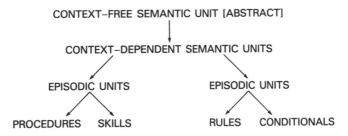

CONTEXT–FREE SEMANTIC UNIT [ABSTRACT]

CONTEXT–DEPENDENT SEMANTIC UNITS

EPISODIC UNITS   EPISODIC UNITS

PROCEDURES   SKILLS   RULES   CONDITIONALS

FIGURE 4.3.   A proposed Knowledge Unit hierarchy that is independent of lexical-type networks.

to decode perceptually distorted language/objects. Rules and conditions describe a variety of behavioral structures such as syntactic expression and understanding, limited behavioral rules such as, "if you touch a hot plate you will burn your hand," and arguments such as, "look both ways before you cross a busy traffic intersection."

The more abstract the MKU, the later its ontological representation. Events and behaviors need repetition and reliability for the more abstract representations to be constructed and activated. As important as a hierarchical conception is to our model, the intra-MKU environment also needs to be explicated, especially our conception of the "node-network."

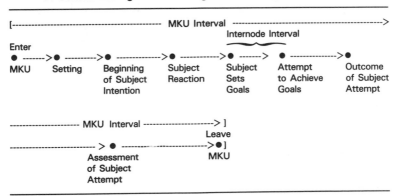

FIGURE 4.4.   The figure shows a suggested structure for a General Managerial Knowledge Unit. The nodes in this unit are relatively abstract. Note that the entire MKU interval, as well as the internode interval will have estimated time duration windows.

General Semantic MKU
(For Sequential Events)

● ------ >● --------- >● ------------ >● --------- >● -------- >● ------------- >● ------------ >●
MKU   Setting   Beginning   Subject   Subject   Subject   Outcome   MKU
Beginning   of Subject   Reaction   Goal   Attempt   of Subject   Ending
                        Intention   to Achieve   Attempt
                                                                Goal

Specific Semantic MKU
(For Cafe Eating)

● ------->● --------->● ------------->● ----------->● --------->● --------------->● ------------->●
Going   Arriving   Greeted   Seated   Orders   Eating   Reaction   Leave
to a   at the   by Host   & Menu   Food   to Food &   Cafe
Cafe   Cafe   Received   Payment
                                                                                 of Bill

Specific Episodic MKU
(For Visiting Paris, France)

● ------->● --------->● ------------->● ----------->● --------->● --------------->● ------------->●
Going   Arriving   Greeted   Brought to   Visit Paris Purchase   Acquired   Leave
to Paris   at C.   by Friend   Left Bank   neighbor-   Clothing   more   Paris
           DeGaulle   Hotel   hoods   knowledge
           Airport   of Paris
           near Paris   and New
                                                                                 Clothing

FIGURE 4.5.   The figure illustrates the varying specificity of the MKU representation. Note that some MKUs may be category specific (e.g., appropriate behavior for eating at any cafe) or episode specific (e.g., events during a specific trip to Paris, France.)

Node Network

The node within an MKU represents a critical property that gives definition to the MKU identity. Internodal linkage provides the structure, both temporal and semantic, for the MKU. The data that is linked to a particular node (see Fig. 4.6) can be abstract (e.g., data that represent the beginning of a sequence of events) or quite concrete (e.g., eating procedures that specify a knife and fork used to cut a sirloin steak). As part of an MKU, the node is activated in parallel with other cognitive representations and processes, such as word retrieval, visuospatial recognition, and even an independent representation of knife-and-fork skill to insure redundancy in the system and to create a massively parallel cognitive network (see Fig. 4.7).

Although there are numerous MKUs, we believe that node structures are organized much like hypothesized story grammars. For the purpose of example, we would claim that the general semantic MKU must contain the following nodes: (a) Setting node—a prototypical setting within which the MKU is activated; (b) Beginning of Subject Intention node—the initiation of cognitive and action processes; (c) Subject Reaction node—based on prototypical environmental events associated with MKU activation, the subject is required to make a cognitive or physiological response; (d) Subject Goal node—what the subject wants to achieve by the conclusion of the MKU suprathreshold activation; (e) Subject Attempt to Achieve Goal node—means-end analyses and actions; (f) Outcome of Subject Attempt node—success or failure to attain MKU goal is evaluated with success deactivating the MKU and failure reactivating it. MKUs are bordered by entry and terminal nodes that serve no meaningful purpose within the MKU structure except as points of activation and deactivation.

In our model, MKUs are almost always entered through an entry node and proceed while activated in a left-to-right grammar. Either the MKU is deactivated because a terminal node is reached, contention scheduling occurs, or the supervisory attention system activates other MKUs which may inhibit the currently active MKU below a threshold (see p. 107 for an introduction to these terms). Additional properties of the MKU include temporal coding for both the entire MKU running time as well as for internode intervals. This temporal coding feature may well be an emergent property of the MKU representation or could be a separate and real cognitive "clock."

Other Issues

Before arguing the relevance of our model for a conceptualization of frontal-lobe functions, we need to further describe some aspects of the MKU as currently conceived.

FIGURE 4.6.   Some nodes require procedural instantiation. In the case of the "eat food" node, both the motor components and the utensils required are specified. At the same time that the procedure is instantiated in the context of the MKU, we also propose that it would be activated as an independent action in a separately stored procedural network allowing for redundancy in action and representation.

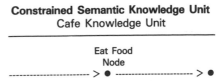

Constrained Semantic Knowledge Unit
Cafe Knowledge Unit

Eat Food
Node

Procedural Constraints

1 = Eat Chinese food with chopsticks
1A = Chopstick procedure

2 = Eat steak with knife and fork
2A = Knife and fork procedure

N = Contextural eating situation
NA = Contextual eating procedure

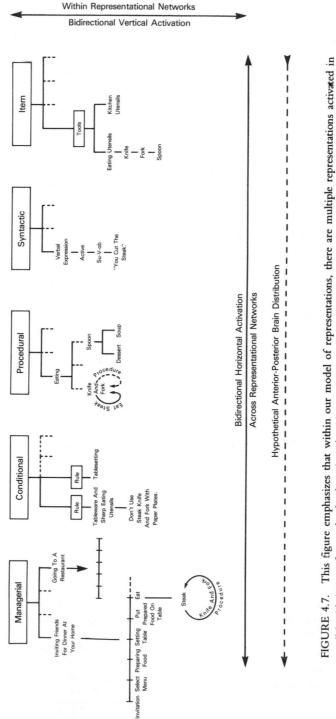

FIGURE 4.7. This figure emphasizes that within our model of representations, there are multiple representations activated in parallel with items often redundantly activated within each level of representation. In our model, the managerial representation is the most complex with item/lexical representations the most elemental. Activation proceeds vertically within networks and horizontally across networks. We speculate that the managerial knowledge unit is represented in the prefrontal regions of the brain, whereas the item/lexical units are represented in the posterior regions of the brain and are the endpoints on a continuum of higher-order knowledge representations.

Managerial Knowledge Unit Activation States

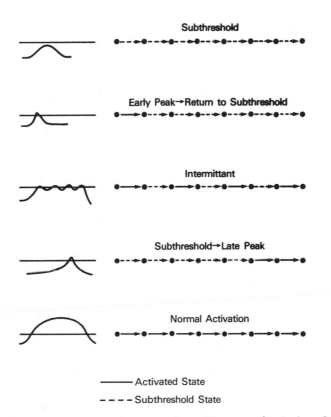

FIGURE 4.8. MKUs can have several possible states of activation. Our model would predict at least four possible abnormal activation states of an MKU, which are illustrated in the figure.

Properties

Each MKU has several possible states of activation in our model (see Fig. 4.8). Normally MKUs are either inactive, active but with undetermined time for execution, active with deadline, active with specified future time, being executed, and blocked/inhibited. In our model, MKUs have varying thresholds of activation depending on the frequency of their use and meaningfulness of interaction with environmental trigger-stimuli. Temporal properties of the MKU determine the execution parameters. In particular, internode interval temporal properties result in a "time" probability window within which varying time durations are more or less acceptable. For example, an MKU could exist that represents the requirements of taking a trip. Even though the beginning node of such an MKU could represent "trip planning" and the end node "trip debriefing," it would be unlikely that a long duration between two such nodes would be as alarming as between two adjacent or neighborhood nodes such as a node representing "packing" and one representing "departing."

MKU hierarchies also have a general-to-specific property. That is, the MKU "Going on a Trip" could be further specified as a more particular MKU, which presumably could have lower activation thresholds relative to the parent MKU. These further specified MKUs might include "A Holiday" or "A Conference" or even "Visit In-Law."

Associated with each MKU are specific arguments whose detail depends on the MKUs hierarchical level. For example, "Going on a Trip" arguments need to be specified for where? When? With whom? What is needed? For how long? What activities will be carried out during the trip? And so on. Fillers for such arguments could be attached to a specific episodic MKU. For context-dependent or context-free MKUs, it might be necessary to activate and attend to less "sophisticated" knowledge units such as semantic category networks to come up with fillers such as types of clothing, types of bags, types of medicine, types of books, types of maps, and so forth, from which to make the appropriate selections.

According to this conception of the properties of an MKU, the "unpacking" of an MKU can lead to the "formulation" of an intention. In our model, an intention is not a "willed act" as much as the activation of MKU Temporal processes that lead to a subsequent MKU node. Some of this activity occurs within the structure of working memory. If an argument for an MKU cannot be "specified," for example, "have no available travel bag," then a search for an appropriate bag will occur in parallel with activation of "buy" MKUs or "borrow" MKUs or "steal" MKUs. This search process can also be under the control of more than one independent MKU.

Many MKUs will be activated (in some states to be specified) as a consequence of the formulation of an intention. Provisional formulation of a new intention may give rise to MKU conflicts and so be referred to a hierarchical MKU representation for resolution.

A major point of our model is that almost all aspects of human behavior will be under the control and guidance of a hierarchy of MKUs. The "Going on a Trip" MKU supervises planning activity, the "Replace Item" MKU supervises inspection and discrimination activity, the "Buy" MKU supervises buying activity, the "City Navigation" MKU supervises going to the store, and the internode interval temporal window supervises our speed in catching a bus to go downtown. This concept clearly requires a massive parallel processing system capability (see Fig. 4.9).

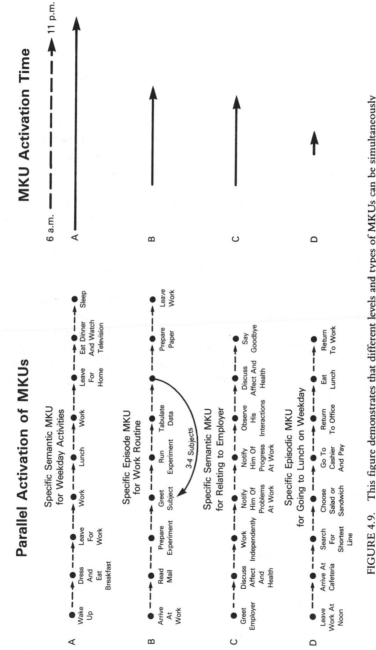

FIGURE 4.9. This figure demonstrates that different levels and types of MKUs can be simultaneously activated during the day with each MKU having a specific activation duration.

119

GENERAL IMPLICATIONS
OF THE MKU MODEL

Emotion, Mood, and the MKU

Affect can be associated with specific events. For example, humans can judge whether an event or stimulus is happy or sad, pleasant or unpleasant, noxious or enticing, and so forth. These associations may reflect conditioned responses or subject-specific impressions and have limited generality. We suspect that MKUs have a role to play in the modulation of emotion by "attaching" affective states to the more abstract units of behavior. One effect of this attachment would be the creation of an environmental "security measure." That is, if a series of actions or events are linked within a representation (as we define the MKU), and thus predictable, then a person's affective state (e.g., anxiety) could be better modulated given the activation of knowledge units that determine the probability of occurrence of a series of events. It is the linkage of that series of events (sic MKU) that helps modulate a particular affective status. Our model of an MKU hierarchy also suggests differing levels of modulation of affect.

MKUs include general (i.e., cultural) and specific (i.e., interpersonal) representations of modes of social behaviors that would be linked with an affective status. This would include behaviors such as mating, bonding, following guidelines about social constraints, and so on. If this can be experimentally tested, then we would be able to offer an explanation of how social behaviors provide control over emotions above and beyond episodic reactions.

Conscious Awareness and Activation of MKUs

How consciously aware could we be of knowledge units the size of the hypothetical MKU? Most information that can be captured within the time frame defined by working memory could be consciously accessed. Recognition of objects, faces, places, words, and so forth, are all events that can be consciously attended. Sentences, rules, conditions, and simple procedures are also generally accessible as a unit within the domain of working memory. However, certain procedures, skills, and of course, MKUs are likely to make conscious accessibility problematic.

Focused or local attentive processes predictably acquire information in a parallel and/or serial event-by-event manner whether the information is present in the environment or retrieved from memory stores. This type of recollection seems dependent upon a level of representation more akin to the semantic association networks than to an MKU. In addition, procedures and skills may be carried out so rapidly that focused attention would have difficulty capturing their essential features (i.e., a failure of intro-spection). This may partly be a limitation of the auditory-verbal linguistic mediative systems. On the other hand, imagery may be able to provide a parallel and global representation that suffices for conscious representa-tion of certain MKU activations. In sum, because of the structural and temporal limitations placed upon information processing by the working-memory system (Baddeley, 1986), conscious awareness of large knowl-edge representation units as we conceive the MKU to be would be im-possible. Given some of our previous examples, there are plenty of engineering reasons to have automatic activation of MKUs while at the same time consciously activating separately stored and informationally smaller, knowledge units so that we can function optimally within the constraints of working memory. Of course that makes the modeling of larger knowledge units such as the MKU challenging and elusive.

Explaining the Relationship of Functional Skills

The definition of expertise includes both the ability to be very skilled/proficient at performing an activity and the ability to explain this skill/proficiency to someone else. An expert is not only able to perform a procedure or skill better than most others but must have developed governing MKUs if his or her level of expertise pertains to larger knowl-edge units.

Insight into such expertise requires not only a general insight-specific MKU (which defines the expression of insight) but an all purpose cognitive-mediative MKU (which defines how to think about a problem). Reasoning can be defined as using the insight MKU to guide working memory processes such as analogy or logic in order to appreciate the resemblance of specific problems. In our model, analogies depend on MKU similarity as assessed by MKU structural comparisons through parallel activation. Logic is simply dependent upon the development of rules (i.e., lower-order knowledge units). Of course, reasoning also re-quires coordinated episodic long-term storage and retrieval processes to retain previously successful rules and to eliminate unsuccessful ones.

Problem solving by itself requires a strategy that must be represented by an MKU. The first step is to recognize that a problem exists. This recognition may occur via supervisory attentional mechanisms or by con-tention scheduling (mechanisms hypothesized by Shallice—see previous discussion) if the schedule routinely encounters problems within a certain time period. Instantiating specific routines (i.e., MKUs) such as analogies to solve a specific problem are required to help cope with the unique attributes of any problem. Sufficient exposure to a variety of stimuli that activate similar MKUs should lead to the development of a "concept" MKU.

Intelligence

In our model, MKUs represent mental models (Johnson-Laird, 1983) of complex behaviors. As such, they provide the user (i.e., the self) with a guide to action and are the basis of formal (e.g., logic or analogy) and informal (e.g., fantasy and imagination) modes of thought. As just described, MKUs can be considered similar to scripts (Schank, 1982), schemas (Mandler, 1984), or inductions (Holland, Holyoak, Nisbett, & Thogard, 1986) which have been used as grammars to analyze the representational macrostructure of stories, pictures, and actions and their recall. This macroapproach attempts to analyze and explain the coherence of a series of events or stimuli. Naturally, the more abstract the macrostructure, the less specified individual events have to be.

Does our conceptualization of a high-level unit of knowledge like the MKU assist in explaining what is described as "intelligent behavior"? No matter how intelligence may be defined, we think that the MKU has a role to play in its description. Most theorists would contend that those processes briefly touched upon in the preceding sections like reasoning, logic, and problem solving, form the basis of intelligent behavior. In that case, intelligence must be separated from expertise because an idiot savant would be considered unintelligent while at the same time maintaining an incredible expertise (or skilled procedure) such as calendar calculations.

The MKU would have to be invented to help account for intelligent activity. It is crucial in the case where coherence of seemingly independent events is required. For the analysis of specific events, MKUs are merely redundant with other semantic systems such as those utilized in object recognition.

Yet the existence of MKUs as memorial units (i.e., a "higher-order" semantic memory) cannot alone fully account for intelligent behavior because such behavior is also influenced by consciousness (Mandler, 1985). In this context, it is not so critical to define consciousness as to determine what cognitive processes can be consciously penetrated. The phenomena of consciously thinking about a problem has all the trappings of an executive "overseer." Alternatives to this formulation exist. For example, a strong MKU position would argue that how we think about a problem, whether it be retrieving information, computing analogies, or deciding on a variant of a procedure, is "MKU-driven." That is, we develop MKUs that are activated to steer thinking. For example, an MKU concerned with general thinking might look like Fig. 4.10. Compare this thinking MKU to the case MKU shown earlier.

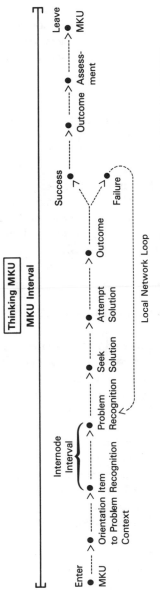

Thinking MKU

MKU Interval

Enter MKU

Orientation Item to Problem Recognition Context

Internode Interval

Problem Recognition

Seek Solution

Attempt Solution

Outcome

Local Network Loop

Success

Failure

Outcome

Assessment

Leave MKU

FIGURE 4.10. Within our model, even the act of thinking is guided by activation of a "Thinking" MKU.

123

This concept of MKU further diminishes the reality of "G" or similar global measures of intelligence, which could be replaced by the theoretical existence of the MKU hierarchy. Thus, intelligence could be thought of as a composite of storage capacity, speed of processing, and development and activation of skills or MKUs that are not only problem specific but also pertain to how to be intelligent, how to problem solve, when to problem solve, and so on. This also makes intelligent behavior partially influenced by environmental exposure and requirements (as regards the MKU component).

THE BREAKDOWN OF THE MKU SYSTEM: ANATOMY AND NEUROBEHAVIOR

In this last section of the chapter, we argue that lesions to the frontal lobe in humans specifically affect and impair the kind of representations and processes that compose the Managerial Knowledge Unit hierarchy presented in this chapter. Below we outline the kinds of deficits that could be expected when a particular component of the hierarchy of MKUs is lesioned. Then we list the tasks most sensitive for demonstrating the effects of MKU dysfunction. Finally, we suggest future approaches to the study of patients with lesions in the frontal lobes.

Damage to the Managerial Knowledge Hierarchy

The MKU hierarchy as conceived in this chapter is composed of multiple representations that can have parallel activation. This hierarchy of representation would include redundant information at each level with the highest levels containing the most abstract information. We propose that it is the very redundancy inherent in our model that masks potential cognitive deficits and mood disorders in patients with frontal-lobe lesions. Because space permits only a brief description of the possible functional deficits, we highlight those that we hope illustrate our points most succinctly.

Sustained and consistent attention should be affected by lesions to the frontal lobe, and thus the MKU system, for at least two reasons. Sustaining attention to a task requires that automatic processing of nonrelevant information is adequate (i.e., the background processing described in the example that began the chapter). This processing includes being oriented to time and place, environmental demands, and so on. This type of processing should occur in parallel to sustained attention in our model. Damage to the MKU system could impair automatic and parallel processing of information because specific MKUs that should be activated to process background details would not be activated, retrieved, and so forth. Sustained attention may also be MKU linked (i.e., linked to task expectations and rewards) and perhaps either decoupled from the MKU or damaged along with a particular MKU representation following frontal-lobe brain damage. In our model, focused attention (which we see involved in detection and identification) should be minimally affected because it can hypothetically be maintained independent of MKU activation in working memory.

Time duration/estimation could be effected by MKU damage on the following basis (see Fig. 4.11). Either impaired sustained attention processes would affect the encoding of stimuli that have the role of anchoring time duration estimates for the cognitive processing system or stored MKUs have as a property temporal markers that allow for *automatic* estimates of time durations (undoubtedly estimated within broad confidence ranges) that would be impaired without any damage to the knowledge contained in the MKU.

Transformation of information (as in mental transformation of objects or rearrangement of order) could also be affected by damage to the MKU since the MKU is by its very nature organized around the transformation of events or scenes via action. At its most primitive level, it could be organized to allow humans to operationally transform an object to recognize different views or configurations if those views or configurations were not currently present in the environment or in thought.

These three deficits would occur no matter the level in the MKU hierarchy that the damage occurred. However, we expect that certain MKU levels would be dissociatively damaged depending on the location of the brain damage (e.g., right dorsolateral frontal lobe or left orbitomedial frontal lobe). The effects of damage to specific levels of the MKU hierarchy are now discussed:

Rules and Conditions

Conditional learning is a rudimentary form of the MKU and can be directly impaired by damage to the frontal lobes. Conditional-learning deficits can occur independently of list-learning deficits or problems in story retrieval (that depend on MKU activation). However, if specific conditioned learning is a component of an MKU such as driving (e.g., stop at a red light when driving), it is possible that the driving MKU, although activated following frontal-lobe damage, would be subject to a default conflict with a conditional learning deficit (i.e., "I just felt like driving through a red light").

Procedures and Skills

Production systems (including procedures and skills) can be impaired independent of the representation of such actions (for a theoretical account

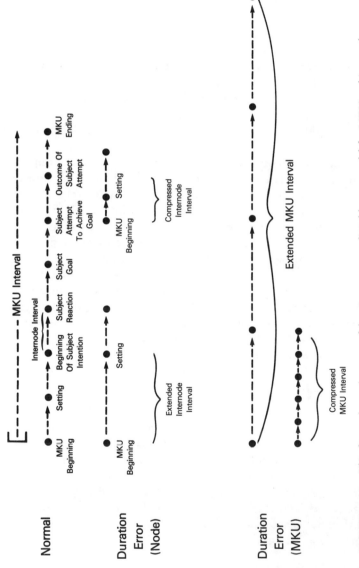

FIGURE 4.11. This figure shows the types of duration errors predicted by our model for MKU and internode activation. As shown, duration errors can either be extension or compression of the time allotted for activities.

see Foss & Bower, 1986). For example, a patient with a frontal-lobe lesion might be able to tell you how to solve a motor task but be unable to accurately perform it motorically. Individual components of a procedure or skill can be performed intact relative to the inability to perform the entire procedure as a unit. It is likely that sensory and motor feedback loops that ordinarily help self-correct procedural skills would also be impaired by damage to this system.

Episodic MKUs

This knowledge unit may be most susceptible to dysfunctions because of its low frequency activation status within the MKU hierarchy. Damage to the frontal lobe may impair access to old MKUs as well as the encoding of new ones. Attentional and time duration processes linked to the damaged MKUs may also be impaired. For example, a patient may have a specific semantic MKU available that denotes eating in a restaurant without being able to access an episodic MKU that would denote fast-food versus gourmet restaurant. Besides not having access to automatic behaviors that would guide the patient's appropriateness depending on which establishment they were in, additional automatic behaviors such as sustained attention, temporal order, and estimation of duration of the eating MKU would be disturbed and unreliable (see Fig. 4.12).

Specific Semantic MKUs

The semantic MKUs tend to be more abstract or context-free representations and are less susceptible to damage than context-dependent MKUs because context-dependent MKUs such as eating in a specific restaurant would be activated less frequently than a context-free MKU such as eating out (which would be activated when eating at any restaurant). We suspect that impaired semantic MKUs would drastically affect the ability of an individual to orient to time and place as well as to access the meaning of a series of events. People experiencing this deficit would require assistance in day-to-day functioning. For example, damage to this system alone would disturb the patient's ability to retrieve knowledge or restaurant behaviors although the patient might retain the conditional behavior of eating if food were placed in front of him or her. If episodic MKUs were still accessible, eating at a particularly frequented restaurant might override the loss of the semantic MKU.

General Semantic MKU

Damage to this system would require widespread frontal-lobe dysfunction. Patients would appear to be disoriented under most circumstances.

Breakdown in Temporal Order

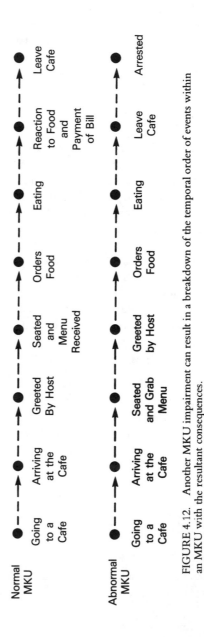

FIGURE 4.12. Another MKU impairment can result in a breakdown of the temporal order of events within an MKU with the resultant consequences.

This condition is typically seen as the last stage in a dementing process. It is unlikely that at this level the MKU hierarchy could be independently disturbed but that remains a target of investigation. For example, it is possible that a deficit to this MKU hierarchical level could result in a patient that would be frame-bound or rule-bound. Deficits would only occur in the most novel of circumstances when the person had to utilize the most abstract frame for orientation purposes (arriving in, and living in, an unusual culture).

Although we haven't addressed hemispheric differences, it is conceivable that the propositional elements of an MKU would be more affected by left-hemisphere lesions, whereas the analogue elements of an MKU, such as attention and time duration, would be affected more by right-hemisphere lesions. The available data is only suggestive of this hypothesis.

HOW DOES THE NEUROPSYCHOLOGICAL LITERATURE FIT INTO THE MKU MODEL PROPOSED HERE?

At least some support for the MKU model can be gained by studying patients with brain lesions. Patients have been reported who retain the ability to learn rules (based on improved performance) but not to recall ever learning the task in question. Other patients show an inability to learn and obey rules despite remembering the task. This dissociation has been described as providing supportive evidence for the distinction between declarative and procedural episodic memory processes. Some patients are reported to have good declarative memory for story events but are unable to say what makes the story coherent. Other patients are reported to retain what makes a story coherent without remembering the individual elements of a story. Although some of these studies are anecdotal, they nevertheless indicate a rich source of data for conceptualizing the breakdown and dissociation of MKUs from other knowledge domains.

One of the most disturbing consequences of orbitomedial frontal-lobe lesions is mood and personality disorder. The exact symptom cluster is dependent upon the side and size of the lesion, premorbid functioning, and cultural factors. These disorders can be dissociated from impairments seen in cognitive tasks where subjects may have difficulty forming a conceptual understanding of the task, showing consistent performance on a task, or understanding the relationship of individual stimuli/events to the overall task purpose. In the case of the orbitomedial lesions, an argument could be made that what is impaired in these patients are "social rule" MKUs. These knowledge units represent overlearned social schemas that allow for appropriate contextual interpersonal behaviors. As with cognitive MKUs, the social MKUs have subordinate social rules whose expression and modulating characteristics are dissociable from the MKU itself. For example, a person could have a social MKU that represents the sequence of behaviors acted out when someone attends a funeral. A specific social rule might be that "you don't laugh loudly at funerals." Injury to the frontal lobes could dissociate these components of behavior such that a person could function at a funeral except for inappropriately laughing loudly (or vice-versa).

An MKU breakdown characterized by an inability to express routine behaviors normally can be seen in patients with psychiatric disorders such as obsessive-compulsive disorder (Malloy, 1987) and schizophrenia (McAllister & Price, 1987), both of which have been associated with frontal-lobe dysfunction. Additional supportive evidence has been provided by the poor performance of subgroups of psychiatric patients on tasks sensitive to frontal lobe dysfunction although their performance on other tasks appears normal.

MANAGERIAL KNOWLEDGE UNITS: A PROPOSAL FOR TESTING A THEORY

What type of design or task would lend itself to testing the MKU model? Broadly defined, at last six kinds of issues need to be addressed by these tasks. These issues include retaining the order of a set of events or items; estimation of the duration of events; the interval length between initially learning about events and their later retrieval; the type of representations (i.e., conceptual unit size) stored in, and accessible from, long-term memory; the ability to generate and maintain a "line" of reasoning; and the ability to generate and store metaphors and analogies. These issues are relevant for both the architecture *and* function of the MKU model and are easily evaluated by current experimental psychology methods.

Both clinical symptomatology and the MKU model place importance on retaining the order of a set of events or items. Frontal-lobe patients frequently have problems accomplishing this. In our model, event order is critical for the accurate encoding, representation, and instantiation of an MKU. This function could be tested by requiring the patient to generate a list of events or items that have a known sequence, learn a particular sequence of events, or recall a story or sequence of events in the correct order. Frontal-lobe patients should make errors in providing or recalling the actual order of events while sparing their recall for the number of events. Because an MKU is posited to have a typical duration for both unit activation, node activation, and internode interval, fractionating the MKU system would also be likely to affect the estimation of how long it took (or would take) to complete a set of events. This could be tested by asking patients to estimate the duration of previous events (e.g., a set of tests, stimuli that appear with varying frequency, etc.). The MKU model would also predict that the longer the interval between event or story learning and retrieval, the more likely an MKU would be needed to account for "difficult to retrieve" episodic facts (in order to "set the gist"). An impaired MKU system would make MKU instantiation difficult requiring that the patient remember verbatim what was said or use cues provided by nonrelevant MKUs or environmental events captured by working memory.

The MKU, as just described, has a specific structure. We would expect this structure to be fractionated occasionally as a result of frontal-lobe brain injury so that only parts of an MKU could be retrieved and acted upon. Thus, a patient could begin an activity but be easily distracted into irrelevant (to the originally initiated MKU) activity by events in working memory.

Maintaining a "line" of reasoning involves the activation of abstract MKUs that have problem-solving routines. We recommend using a "game" task method such as 20 questions to reveal both a faulty line of question production and memory for previous probes in patients with frontal lesions. Finally, analogy and metaphor deficits directly imply the loss of abstract MKUs and can be tested by using tasks requiring analogical and metaphorical thinking.

We have developed a framework that we believe comprehensively describes the nature of cognitive and mood representations in the frontal lobes (see Fig. 4.13) and we have also made some initial predictions about expected deficits in the MKU system given frontal-lobe lesions. Perhaps parts of the model, or even the model in its entirety, will require revisions given new experimental evidence and theories with greater predictive power and face validity. Until this occurs, we offer our model as a challenge to others to test or falsify. If nothing else, debates over a cognitively based model of frontal-lobe information processing represents a step forward for human neuropsychological study.

ACKNOWLEDGMENTS

The author expresses his gratitude to Mrs. Ruth O'Reilly and Ms. Barbara King for their administrative expertise and their assistance in preparing the manuscript, and Alex Martin, Andres Salazar, and Francois Lalonde for their suggestions for improving the manuscript. I thank the National Institute of Neurological and Communicative Disorders and Stroke, and Medical Neurology Branch for providing the facilities which allowed me to prepare the manuscript.

Some MKU Markers

---

1. Temporal encoding (unit or internodal)
   A. Emergent property or representation
2. Intention (means-end analysis)
   A. Goal
   B. Subject/object
3. Sequential coding (is a prototypical left to right grammar)
4. Resolution of intention
   A. Interference versus unit completion
5. Action sequence: real or imagined
6. Setting

FIGURE 4.13.   This figure lists some of the proposed critical components of the archtype managerial knowledge unit. Each unit is encoded temporally, represents an intention, is sequentially coded, requires a resolution of the initial intention, and is usually composed of actions which occur in a typical setting.

The opinions and assertions contained here are the private views of the author and are not to be construed as official or necessarily reflecting the views of the National Institutes of Health, the United States Public Health Service, the Department of Health and Human Services, the Uniformed Services University of the Health Sciences, or the Department of Defense.

I would especially like to thank Tim Shallice for discussing and debating the idea of the managerial knowledge unit with me in Cambridge and Washington. He helped clarify many of the issues raised in this chapter but should not be held responsible for its faults.

REFERENCES

Abbott, V., Black, J. B., & Smith, E. E. (1985). The representation of scripts in memory. *Journal of Memory and Language, 24,* 179–199.

Ackerly, S. S. (1964). A case of paranatal bilateral frontal lobe defect observed for thirty years. In J. M. Warren & K. Akert (Eds.), *The frontal granular cortex and behavior* (pp. 192–218). New York: McGraw-Hill.

Andy, O. J., Webster, J. S., & Carraniza, J. (1981). Frontal lobe lesions and behavior. *Southern Medical Journal, 74,* 968–972.

Baddeley, A. (1986). *Working memory.* New York: Oxford University Press.

Barsalou, L. W., & Sewell, D. R. (1985). Contrasting the representation of scripts and categories. *Journal of Memory and Language, 24,* 646–665.

Behar, D., Rappaport, J. L., Berg, C. J., Denckla, M. B., Mann, L., Cox, D., Fedio, P., Zahn, T., & Wolfman, M. G. (1984). Computerized tomograhy and neuropsychological test measures in adolescents with obsessive-compulsive disorder. *American Journal of Psychiatry, 141,* 363–369.

Benson, D. F., Stuss, D. T., Naeser, M. A., Weir, W. S., Kaplan, E. F., & Levine, H. (1981). The long-term effects of prefrontal leucotomy. *Archives of Neurology, 38,* 165–169.

Benton, A. L. (1968). Differential behavioral effects in frontal lobe disease. *Neuropsychologia,* *6,* 53–60.

Bianchi, L. (1895). The functions of the frontal lobes. *Brain, 18,* 497–522.

Black, F. W. (1976). Cognitive deficits in patients with unilateral war-related frontal lobe lesions. *Journal of Clinical Psychology, 32,* 366–372.

Bolton, J. S. (1903). The functions of the frontal lobes. *Brain, 26,* 215–241.

Brown, J. W. (1985). Frontal lobe syndromes. *Journal of Neurolinguistics, 1,* 31–77.

Brown, J. W. (1985). Frontal lobe syndromes. In J. A. M. Frederiks (Ed.), *Handbook of clinical neurology: Vol. 1(45), Clinical neuropsychology* (pp. 23–42). New York: Elsevier.

Butters, N., Samuels, I., Goodglass, H., & Brody, B. (1970). Short-term visual and auditory memory disorders after parietal and frontal lobe damage. *Cortex, 6,* 440–459.

Butters, N., Soeldner, C., & Fedio, P. (1972). Comparison of parietal and frontal lobe spatial deficits in man: Extra personal vs. personal (egocentric) space. *Perceptual and Motor Skills, 34,* 27–34.

Cakuls, P., & Finlayson, R. (1978). Frontal lobe lesions. *Canadian Psychiatric Association Journal, 23,* 70.

Canavan, A. G. M., Janota, I., & Schurr, P. H. (1985). Luria's frontal lobe syndrome: Psychological and anatomical considerations. *Journal of Neurology, Neurosurgery, and Psychiatry, 48,* 1049–1053.

Carlson, R. J. (1977). Frontal lobe lesions masquerading as psychiatric disturbances. *Canadian Psychiatric Association Journal, 22,* 315–318.

Cicerone, K. D., Lazar, R. M., & Shapiro, W. R. (1983). Effects of frontal lobe lesions on hypothesis sampling during concept formation. *Neuropsychologia, 21,* 513–524.

Craine, J. F. (1982). The retraining of frontal lobe dysfunction. In L. E. Trexler (Ed.), *Cognitive rehabilitation: Conceptualization and intervention* (pp. 239–262). New York: Plenum Press.

Damasio, A. R., & Van Hoesen, G. W. (1983). Emotional disturbances associated with focal lesions of the limbic frontal lobe. In K. M. Heilman & P. Satz (Eds.), *Neuropsychology of human emotion* (pp. 85–110). New York: Guilford Press.

Deutsch, R. D., Kling, A., & Steklis, H. D. (1979). Influence of frontal lobe lesions on behavioral interactions in man. *Research Communications in Psychology, Psychiatry, and Behavior, 4,* 415–431.

Drewe, E. A. (1974). The effect of type and area of brain lesions on Wisconsin Card Sorting Test performance. *Cortex, 10,* 159–170.

Drewe, E. A. (1975). Go-no-go learning after frontal lobe lesions in humans. *Cortex, 11,* 8–16.

Drewe, E. A. (1975). An experimental investigation of Luria's theory on the effects of frontal lobe lesions in man. *Neuropsychologia, 13,* 421–429.

Duncan, J. (1986). Disorganization of behavior after frontal lobe damage. *Cognitive Neuropsychology, 3,* 271–290.

Ericsson, K. A., & Simon, H. A. (1984). *Protocol analysis: Verbal reports as data.* Cambridge, MA: MIT Press.

Eslinger, P. J., & Damasio, A. R. (1985). Severe disturbance of higher cognition after bilateral frontal lobe ablation: Patient EVR. *Neurology, 35,* 1731–1741.

Foss, C. L., & Bower, G. H. (1986). Understanding action in relation to goals. In N. E. Sharkey (Ed.), *Advances in cognitive science,* (Vol. 1, pp. 94–124). Chichester, U.K.: Ellis Horwood Limited.

Freedman, M., & Cermak, L. S. (1986). Semantic encoding deficits in frontal lobe disease and amnesia. *Brain and Cognition, 5,* 108–114.

Freedman, M., & Oscar-Berman, M. (1985). Bilateral frontal lobe disease and selective delay and response deficits in humans. *Behavioral Neuroscience, 100,* 337–342.

Friedman, W. J., & Wilkins, A. J. (1985). Scale effects in memory for the time of events. *Memory and Cognition, 13,* 168–175.

Fulton, J. F. (1952). *The frontal lobes and human behavior.* Springfield, IL: Charles C. Thomas.

Fuster, J. M. (1980). *The prefrontal cortex: Anatomy, physiology, and neuropsychology of the frontal lobe.* New York: Raven Press.

Fuster, J. M. (1985). The pre-frontal cortex, mediator of cross-temporal contingencies. *Human Neurobiology, 4,* 169–179.

Galambos, J. A., Abelson, R. P., & Black, J. B. (Eds.) (1986). *Knowledge structures.* Hillsdale, NJ: Lawrence Erlbaum Associates.

Ghent, L., Mishkin, J., & Teuber, H. L. (1962). Short-term memory after frontal lobe injury in man. *Journal of Comparative and Physiological Psychology, 55,* 705–709.

Goldberg, E., & Costa, L. D. (1985). Qualitative indices in neuropsychological assessment: An extension of Luria's approach to executive deficit following prefrontal lesions. In I. Grant & K. Adams (Eds.), *Neurological assessment of neuropsychiatric disorders* (pp. 48–64). New York: Oxford University Press.

Goldberg, E., & Tucker, D. (1979). Motor perseveration and long-term memory for visual forms. *Journal of Clinical Neuropsychology, 1,* 273–288.

Golding, E. (1981). The effects of unilateral brain lesions on reasoning. *Cortex, 17,* 31–40.

Goldman-Rakic, P. S. (1984). Modular organization of prefrontal cortex. *Trends in Neurosciences, 7,* 419–424.

Goldman-Rakic, P. S. (1987). Development of cortical circuitry and cognitive function. *Child Development, 58,* 601–622.

Goldman-Rakic, P. S., & Porrino, L. J. (1985). The primate mediodorsal (MD) nucleus and its projection to the frontal lobe. *The Journal of Comparative Neurology, 242,* 535–560.

Goldstein, K. (1944). The mental changes due to frontal lobe damage. *Journal of Psychology, 17,* 187–208.

Goldstein, F. C., & Levin, H. S. (1987). Disorders of reasoning and problem-solving ability. In M. J. Meier, A. L. Benton, & L. Diller (Eds.), *Neuropsychological rehabilitation* (pp. 327–354). New York: Guilford Press.

Grafman, J. (1985). Preserved memory processes following frontal lobe lesions. *Preserved Learning in Patients with organic memory disorders.* In J. Grafman & D. Schacter (chair), symposium conducted at the International Neuropsychological Society meeting, February 6–9, San Diego, California.

Grafman, J. Vance, S. C., Weingartner, H., Salazar, A. M., & Amin, D. (1986). The effects of lateralized frontal lesions on mood regulation. *Brain, 109,* 1127–1148.

Grant, D. A., & Berg, E. A. (1948). A behavioral analysis of degree of reinforcement and ease of shifting to new responses in a Weigl-type card-sorting problem. *Journal of Experimental Psychology, 38,* 404–411.

Guitton, D., Buchtel, H. A., & Douglas, R. M. (1982). Disturbances of voluntary saccadic eye-movement mechanisms following discrete unilateral frontal-lobe removals. In G. Lennerstrand, D. S. Zee, & E. L. Keller (Eds.), *Functional basis of ocular motility disorders* (pp. 497–500). Oxford: Pergammon Press.

Halstead, W. C. (1947). *Brain and intelligence: A quantative study of the frontal lobes.* Chicago: University of Chicago Press.

Harlow, J. (1848). Passage of an iron rod through the head. *Boston Medical and Surgical Journal, 39,* 389–393.

Hecaen, H., & Albert, M. L. (1975). Disorders of mental functioning related to frontal lobe pathology. In D. F. Benson & D. Blumer (Eds.), *Psychiatric aspects of neurologic disease* (pp. 137–149). New York: Grune & Stratton.

Holland, J. H., Holyoak, K. J., Nisbett, R. E., & Thogard, P. R. (1986). *Induction: Processes of inference, learning, and discovery.* Cambridge, MA: MIT Press.

Johnson-Laird, P. N. (1983). *Mental models: Towards a cognitive science of language, inference, and consciousness*. Cambridge, MA: Harvard University Press.

Kahneman, D., Slovic, P., & Tversky, A. (1982). *Judgment under uncertainty: Heuristics and biases*. Cambridge, MA: Cambridge University Press.

Kanareikin, K. F., & Volkov, V. N. (1981). Memory disorders in cerebrovascular lesions. *Soviet Neurology and Psychiatry*, winter, 17–26.

Kapur, N., & Coughlan, A. K. (1980). Confabulation and frontal lobe dysfunction. *Journal of Neurology, Neurosurgery, and Psychiatry, 43*, 461–463.

Kolb, B., & Taylor, L. (1981). Affective behavior in patients with localized cortical excisions: Role of lesion site and side. *Science, 214*, 89–91.

Kucharski, A. (1984). History of frontal lobotomy in the United States, 1935–1955. *Neurosurgery, 14*, 765–772.

Landis, C., Zubin, J., & Mettler, F. A. (1950). The functions of the human frontal lobe. *Journal of Psychology, 30*, 123–138.

Lang, W., Lang, M., Kornhuber, A., & Kornhuber, H. H. (1986). Electrophysiological evidence for right frontal lobe dominance in spatial visuomotor learning. *Archives Italiennes de Biologie, 124*, 1–13.

Lezak, M. D. (1982). The problem of assessing executive functions. *International Journal of Psychology, 17*, 281–297.

Lhermitte, F. (1983). "Utilization Behaviour" and its relation to lesions of the frontal lobes. *Brain, 106*, 217–255.

Lhermitte, F., Derouesne, J., & Signoret, J. L. (1972). Analyse neuropsychologique du syndrome frontal. [A neuropsychological analysis of the frontal syndrome]. *Revue Neurologique, 127*, 415–440.

Lhermitte, F. (1986). Human autonomy and the frontal lobes. Part II: Patient behavior in complex and social situations: The "Environmental Dependency Syndrome." *Annals of Neurology, 19*, 335–343.

Lhermitte, F., Pillon, B., & Serdaru, M. (1986). Human autonomy and the frontal lobes. Part I: Imitation and utilization behavior: A neuropsychological study of 75 patients. *Annals of Neurology, 19*, 326–334.

Locke, E. A., Shaw, K. N., Saari, L. M., & Latham, G. P. (1981). Goal setting and task performance: 1969–1980. *Psychological Bulletin, 90*, 125–152.

Logan, G. D., & Cowan, W. B. (1984). On the ability to inhibit thought and action: A theory of an act of control. *Psychological Review, 91*, 295–327.

Luria, A. R. (1966). *Human brain and psychological processes*. New York: Harper & Row.

Luria, A. R. (1969). Frontal lobe syndromes. In P. J. Vinken & G. W. Bruyn (Eds.), *Handbook of clinical neurology: Vol. 2. Localization in clinical neurology* (pp. 725–757). Amsterdam: North Holland.

Luria, A. R. (1973). *The working brain*. New York: Basic Books.

Luria, A. R. (1980). *Higher cortical functions in man* (2nd ed.). New York: Basic Books.

Malloy, P. (1987). Frontal lobe dysfunction in obsessive-compulsive disorder. In E. Perecman (Ed.), *The frontal lobes revisited* (pp. 207–223). New York: IRBN Press.

Mandler, J. M. (1984). *Stories, scripts, and scenes: Aspects of schema theory*. Hillsdale, NJ: Lawrence Erlbaum Associates.

Mandler, G. (1985). *Cognitive psychology: An essay in cognitive science*. Hillsdale, NJ: Lawrence Erlbaum Associates.

McAllister, T. W., & Price, T. R. P. (1987). Aspects of the behavior of psychiatric patients with frontal lobe damage: Some implications for diagnosis and treatment. *Comprehensive Psychiatry, 28*, 14–21.

Mercer, B., Wapner, W., Gardner, H., & Benson, D. F. (1977). A study of confabulation. *Archives of Neurology, 34*, 429–433.

Mesulam, M. M. (1986). Frontal cortex and behavior. *Annals of Neurology, 19,* 320–325.

Miller, L. (1985). Cognitive risk-taking after frontal or temporal lobectomy-I. The synthesis of fragmented visual information. *Neuropsychologia, 23,* 359–369.

Miller, L., & Milner, B. (1985). Cognitive risk-taking after frontal or temporal lobectomy-II. The synthesis of phonemic and semantic information. *Neuropsychologia, 23,* 371–379.

Milner, B. (1963). Effects of different brain lesions on card sorting. *Archives of Neurology, 9,* 90–100.

Milner, B. (1964). Some effects of frontal lobectomy in man. In J. M. Warren & K. Akert (Eds.), *The frontal granular cortex and behavior* (pp. 313–334). New York: McGraw-Hill.

Milner, B. (1982). Some cognitive effects of frontal lobe lesions in man. In D. E. Broadbent & L. Weiskrantz (Eds.), *The neuropsychology of cognitive function* (pp. 211–226). London: The Royal Society.

Milner, B., & Petrides, M. (1984). Behavioral effects of frontal lobe lesions in man. *Trends in Neurosciences, 7,* 403–407.

Milner, B., Petrides, M., & Smith, M. L. (1985). Frontal lobes and the temporal organization of memory. *Human Neurobiology, 4,* 137–142.

Minsky, M. (1975). A framework for representing knowledge. In P. Winston (Ed.), *The psychology of computer vision.* New York: McGraw-Hill.

Minsky, M. (1983). K-Lines: A theory of memory. In D. A. Norman (Ed.), *Perspectives on cognitive science.* Hillsdale, NJ: Lawrence Erlbaum Associates.

Moscovitch, M. (1976). Differential effects of unilateral temporal and frontal lobe damage on memory performance. Paper presented at the International Neuropsychological Society Meeting, Toronto, Canada.

Moscovitch, M. (1982). Multiple dissociations of function in amnesia. In L. S. Cermak (Ed.), *Human memory and amnesia* (pp. 337–370). Hillsdale, NJ: Lawrence Erlbaum Associates.

Nasrallah, H. A., & Weinberger, D. R. (1986). *The neurology of schizophrenia.* Amsterdam: Elsevier.

Nauta, W. J. H. (19672). Neural associates of the amygdaloid complex in the monkey. *Brain, 85,* 505–520.

Nauta, W. J. H., & Feirtag, M. (1986). *Fundamental neuroanatomy.* New York: W. H. Freeman.

Nelson, H. E. (1976). A modified card sorting test sensitive to frontal lobe defects. *Cortex, 12,* 313–324.

Norman, D. A., & Shallice, T. (1986). Attention to action: Willed and automatic control of behavior. In R. J. Davidson, G. E. Schwartz, & D. Shapiro (Eds.), *Consciousness and self-regulation: Advances in research* (Vol. 4, pp. 1–18). New York: Plenum Press.

Pendleton, M. G., & Heaton, R. K. (1982). A comparison of the Wisconsin card sorting test and the category test. *Journal of Clinical Psychology, 38,* 392–396.

Perret, E. (1974). The left frontal lobe of man and the suppression of habitual responses in verbal categorical behaviour. *Neuropsychologia, 12,* 323–330.

Petrides, M. (1985). Deficits on conditional associative-learning tasks after frontal and temporal lobe lesions in man. *Neuropsychologia, 23,* 601–614.

Petrie, A. (1949). Preliminary report of changes after prefrontal leucotomy. *Journal of Mental Sciences, 95,* 449–455.

Petrie, A. (1952). A comparison of the psychological effects of different types of operation on the frontal lobes. *Journal of Mental Sciences, 98,* 326–329.

Powell, G. E. (1981). Survey of the effects of brain lesions upon personality. In H. J. Eysenck (Ed.), *A model for personality* (pp. 65–87). New York: Springer-Verlag.

Robinson, A. L., Heaton, R. K., Lehman, R. A. W., & Stilson, D. W. (1980). The utility of the Wisconsin card sorting test in detecting and localizing frontal lobe lesions. *Journal of Consulting and Clinical Psychology, 48,* 605–614.

Robinson, R. G., Kubos, K. L., Starr, L. B., Rao, K., & Price, T. R. (1984). Mood disorders in stroke patients: Importance of location of lesion. *Brain, 107,* 81–93.

Robinson, R. G., Lipsey, J. R., Rao, K., & Price, T. R. (1986). Two year longitudinal study of post-stroke mood disorders: Comparison of acute onset with delayed-onset depression. *American Journal of Psychiatry, 143,* 1238–1244.

Rocchetta, A. I. D. (1986). Classification and recall of pictures after unilateral frontal or temporal lobectomy. *Cortex, 22,* 189–212.

Salmaso, D., & Denes, G. (1982). Role of the frontal lobes on an attention task: A signal detection analysis. *Perceptual and Motor Skills, 54,* 1147–1150.

Schacter, D. L. (1987). Memory, amnesia, and frontal lobe dysfunctions *Psychobiology, 15,* 21–36.

Schank, R. (1982). *Dynamic memory: A theory of reminding and learning in computers and people.* Cambridge, MA: Cambridge University Press.

Shallice, T. (1982). Specific impairments of planning. *Philosophical Transactions of the Royal Society of London, B298,* 199–209.

Shallice, T., & Evans, M. E. (1978). The involvement of the frontal lobes in cognitive estimation. *Cortex, 14,* 294–303.

Shapiro, B. E., Alexander, M. P., Gardner, H., & Mercer, B. (1981). Mechanisms of confabulation. *Neurology, 31,* 1070–1076.

Smith, M. L., & Milner, B. (1984). Differential effects of frontal lobe lesions on cognitive estimation and spatial memory. *Neuropsychologia, 22,* 697–705.

Stuss, D. T., Alexander, M. P., Liberman, A., & Levine, H. (1978). An extraordinary form of confabulation. *Neurology, 28,* 1166–1172.

Stuss, D. T., & Benson, D. F. (1983). Frontal lobe lesions and behavior. In A. Kertesz (Ed.), *Localization in Neuropsychology* (pp. 429–454). New York: Academic Press.

Stuss, D., & Benson, D. F. (1984). Neuropsychological studies of the frontal lobes. *Psychological Bulletin, 95,* 3–28.

Stuss, D. T., & Benson, D. F. (1986). *The frontal lobes.* New York: Raven Press.

Stuss, D. T., Benson, D. F., Kaplan, E. F., Della Malva, C., & Weir, W. S. (1984). The effects of prefrontal leucotomy on visuoperceptive and visuoconstructive tests. *Bulletin of Clinical Neurosciences, 49,* 43–51.

Stuss, D. T., Benson, D. F., Kaplan, E. F., Weir, W. S., & Della Malva, C. (1981). Leucotomized and non-leucotomized schizophrenics: Comparison on tests of attention. *Biological psychiatry, 16,* 1085–1100.

Stuss, D. T., Benson, D. F., Kaplan, E. F., Weir, W. S., Naeser, M. A., Lieberman, I., & Ferrill, D. (1983). The involvement of orbitofrontal cerebrum in cognitive tasks. *Neuropsychologia, 21,* 235–248.

Stuss, D. T., Kaplan, E,. F., & Benson, D. F. (1982). Long-term effects of prefrontal leucotomy: Cognitive functions. In R. N. Malatesha & L. C. Hartlage (Eds.), *Neuropsychology and cognition* (Vol. 2, pp. 252–271). The Hague: Martinus Nijhoff.

Stuss, D. T., Kaplan, E. F., Benson, D. F., Weir, W. S., Chiulli, S., & Sarazin, F. F. (1982). Evidence for the involvement of orbitofrontal cortex in memory functions: An interference effect. *Journal of Comparative and Physiological Psychology, 6,* 913–925.

Stuss, D. T., Kaplan, E. F., Benson, D. F., Weir, W. S., Naeser, M. A., & Levine, H. (1981). Long-term effects of prefrontal leukotomy: an overview of neuropsychological residuals. *Journal of Clinical Neuropsychology, 3,* 13–32.

Teuber, H. L. (1964). The riddle of frontal lobe function in man. In J. M. Warren & K. Akert (Eds.), *The frontal granular cortex and behavior* (pp. 410–477). New York: McGraw-Hill.

Teuber, H. L. (1972). Unity and diversity of frontal lobe functions. *Acta Neurobiologiae Experimentalis, 32,* 615–656.

Thorndyke, P. W. (1984). Applications of schema theory in cognitive research. In J. R. Anderson & S. M. Kosslyn (Eds.), *Tutorials in learning and memory* (pp. 167–191). San Francisco: W. H. Freeman.

Thorndyke, P. W., & Hayes-Roth, B. (1979). The use of schemas in the acquisition and transfer of knowledge. *Cognitive Psychology, 11,* 82–106.

Vilkki, J. (1985). Amnestic syndromes after surgery of anterior communicating artery aneurysms. *Cortex, 21,* 431–444.

Warrington, E. K. (1985). A disconnection analysis of amnesia. In D. S. Olton, E. Gamzu, & S. Corkin (Eds.), *Memory dysfunctions: An integration of animal and human research from preclinical and clinical perspectives.* (Vol. 44, pp. 72–77). New York: Annals of the New York Academy of Sciences.

Wilensky, R. (1983). *Planning and understanding: A computational approach to human reasoning.* Reading, MA: Addison-Wesley.

Winograd, T. (1975). Frame representations and the declarative-procedural controversy. In D. G. Bobrow & A. Collins (Eds.), *Representation and understanding: Studies in cognitive science* (pp. 185–210). New York: Academic Press.

Zangwill, O. L. (1966). Psychological deficits associated with frontal lobe lesions. *International Journal of Neurology, 5,* 395–402.

5

Encoding and Retrieval Deficits of Amnesic Patients

Laird S. Cermak

The recent surge of interest in amnesia research has produced a wealth of new and creative theories advanced to distinguish between those tasks that amnesics can do and those they cannot do. These theories have produced a number of sophisticated cognitive and neuropsychological investigations, which are both theoretically intriguing and clinically useful. One consequence of this new interest has, however, been a temporary delay in the exploration of issues that initially gave rise to research in amnesia. The underlying processing deficits that could explain why amnesics cannot learn new information have received little attention from researchers of late. Theories that separate memory from that which is not memory are important because they help to *define* amnesia. But they are relatively less important when it comes to *explaining* amnesia.

In the past, researchers vigorously debated the relative contribution of encoding versus retrieval deficits to the amnestic syndrome. Agreement between two major theories (one emphasizing encoding, the other emphasizing retrieval) seemed close, and investigators began to understand the interaction between these factors in the late 1970s. Because a premature end to this debate may cause us to lose sight of the significance of this agreement, the present review has been undertaken both to revitalize this important topic and to view it within the perspective of contemporary theories.

RETRIEVAL DEFICITS IN AMNESIA

The theory that amnesia may be due to a deficit in retrieval is based on the concept of associative interference. McGeoch (1932) introduced this concept by proposing that forgetting is caused by recently learned material blocking the retrieval of previously learned information. He felt that once learned, information is never really lost, but it might be blocked from retrieval by other material in memory competing at recall. Melton and Irwin (1940) later demonstrated that this blocking, or "interference," is actually due to both competition and unlearning. Competition entails blocking access to material; whereas unlearning refers to the active deletion of material from memory in order to learn new information.

Warrington and Weiskrantz (1970, 1973) were the first major proponents of an associative interference model of amnesia. They felt that amnesics could learn new material but had an inordinate amount of difficulty retrieving it due to interference. This interference occurred because the patient was unable to inhibit competition from irrelevant material in memory. Paradoxically, the amnesic's problem was not forgetting too much but forgetting too little.

Warrington and Weiskrantz initially supported their thesis with studies (1968, 1970) involving the partial exposure of pictures or words. Patients were presented with increasingly less fragmented stimuli across five learning trials on each of two successive days. They found that the amnesic patients were able to identify the stimuli more rapidly on Day 2, which implied that something had to have been retained. A comparison of the partial information technique with free recall and recognition revealed that retention could only be demonstrated in the partial information (i.e., cueing) condition. Based on this evidence, Warrington and Weiskrantz concluded that retention in amnesics depended more on the method of retrieval than upon the method of acquisition. Free recall was impossible for these patients, because they could not inhibit or reject incorrect responses. Cued recall was possible because it limited the choices for the patient.

In order to further test this hypothesis, Warrington and Weiskrantz (1974) reported a series of cueing experiments designed to limit the range of potentially interfering responses present at recall. Reducing the number of alternative responses enhanced the amnesics' ability to learn a list because they were less vulnerable to false positive responses. However, learning a second list using the same stimuli became more difficult under these conditions of reduced alternative responses because the well-learned items from the first list had greater potential to intrude during recall of the second list. Warrington and Weiskrantz's interpretation of these results was that amnesics had difficulty during the acquisition stage of List 2 due to their inability to eliminate or "unlearn" List 1 responses. This was a departure from their original view that interference had its effect solely on retrieval. In a subsequent experiment, Warrington and Weiskrantz (1978) demonstrated that this interference does not dissipate across learning trials. In fact, unlike normal control patients, the amnesics failed to improve across all four learning-recall trials of List 2. When asked to generate words from both lists to each three-letter response cue, the amnesics produced more List 1 responses than List 2 responses. The normal control subjects showed precisely the reverse outcome. Warrington and Weis-krantz viewed this as evidence that List 1 responses were so domineering to the amnesics that they actually impeded "learning" of List 2 responses. In this way retrieval-deficits theorists began to acknowledge an acquisition impairment as part of the amnesic's disorder.

ENCODING DEFICITS IN AMNESIA

Proponents of encoding deficit theories of amnesia (Cermak, 1972, 1979; Kinsbourne & Wood, 1975) have also had to adopt a less extreme position than that originally proposed. Initially, these theorists argued that the amnesic patients' memory disorder was directly related to an impairment in the way they analyzed information. Several experiments (Cermak & Butters, 1972; Cermak, Butters, & Gerrein, 1973; Cermak, Butters, & Moreines, 1974; Cermak, Naus, & Reale, 1976) demonstrated that am-nesic Korsakoff patients spontaneously analyzed only features represented at superficial levels of processing ("shallow" features such as those at the phonemic level) as opposed to those associated with deeper levels of pro-cessing (such as those on a semantic level). These deficits were easily documented, but their relationship to failures in retrieval was more dif-ficult to establish. Two possibilities existed: One was that the two deficits were totally independent of one another. The other was that the patients' poor analysis during input resulted in their confusion during retrieval. The latter notion was favored by encoding deficit theories when it was tested using Wickens' (1970) release from proactive inhibition technique (Cermak et al., 1974). This technique demonstrated that amnesic Korsa-koff patients' increased sensitivity to interference during retrieval was related to a lack of semantic encoding as exemplified by the fact that the amount of proactive interference reduction (PI release) demonstrated by these patients varied with the encoding requirements of the verbal mate-rials. Korsakoff patients demonstrated normal PI release when the verbal materials involved only rudimentary categorizations (e.g., letters vs. num-bers), but showed absolutely no release when the stimulus materials in-volved a semantic category distinction such as that between animals and vegetables. Thus, these amnesics' retrieval deficit was seen as a direct result of their inability to spontaneously analyze material on the basis of its semantic features.

Cermak and Reale (1978) subsequently investigated whether instruc-tions designed to improve semantic analysis would lead to improvements in amnesic Korsakoffs' retention. The examiner influenced the patients' analysis of incoming information by asking questions relating to either orthographic (Is this word printed in capital letters?); phonemic (Does this word rhyme with "ring"?); or semantic (Does this word fit into the sentence, "The man stooped down and picked up the _____"?) content. The rationale was that the deeper levels of analysis would result in more durable memories thus increasing the probability that the item could be recognized (Craik & Lockhart, 1972; Craik & Tulving, 1975). Cermak and Reale found that their amnesics performed in a pattern similar to, *but still far below,* normals. Appropriate semantic analysis of information did not automatically produce normal retrieval ability for these amnesics. In fact, it seemed that the patients forgot the "frame" into which the critical item had been analyzed as well as the item itself. Without either, the patient had no means of access to the desired information. Normal individuals probably remember both the act of performing the analysis and the end product of their analysis. They can, therefore, reenact their initial processing to facilitate retrieval of the desired verbal information.

In order to circumvent the necessity of retaining both the desired word and the "frame" into which it was analyzed, Cermak, Uhly, and Reale (1980) used a modified version of a Fisher and Craik (1977) paradigm. The procedure was similar to that just described except that the amnesic patients were cued either with the same question that had been used during the study phase (i.e., the same analytic set) or with new questions from the same level (i.e., semantic question during study and a semantic cue at the time of retrieval) or with questions from different levels of processing (i.e., semantic question and a phonemic cue). On this task, the only condition that benefitted Korsakoff patients was the one in which the same semantic set was provided at input and output. It appeared that Tulving's (1970) encoding specificity principle (that the best performance during retrieval occurs when retrieval conditions match study conditions) held for Korsakoff patients on the semantic level, but not for lower levels of analysis.

In order to more directly investigate the interaction of semantic analysis with semantic cueing in amnesia, an encoding-specificity procedure developed by Thomson and Tulving (1970) was used. Korsakoff patients were given a list of 12 word pairs consisting of a capitalized to-be-remembered (TBR) word and an associated cue word printed in lower case letters above it. The patient was instructed to memorize each TBR word and to pay attention to the small related cue word as it could be used to help him remember the critical word. Following this presentation, the patient was given 12 cue words and told to write down a TBR word the cue brought to mind in the blank space next to each cue. Five different input-output relationships were investigated: (a) S–S, in which a strongly associated cue word occurred at input and again at output; (b) W–W, in which the same weakly associated cue word occurred at input and output; (c) S–W, in which a strong associate was presented at input, but a weak associate at output; (d) W–S, in which a weak associate was presented at input, but a strong one at output and (e) O–O, in which no cues were given. The outcome (Table 5.1; Cermak, Uhly, & Reale, 1980) revealed that Korsakoff patients profited by strong associate encoding and retrieval cues (as evidenced by S–S recall above both O–O and W–S), but that they failed to show the same effect in the weak encoding and retrieval cue condition (W–W). This sensitization to strong associates suggests that some effect occurred during the encoding stage and this effect persisted through retrieval. Encoding specificity occurred only when previously established semantic associations were reinforced and subsequently cued. However, encoding specificity did not occur when a new association had to be formed. In other words, when the semantic context simply reestablished remote learning it enhanced retrieval, but when it required that the patient cognitively reorganize his semantic network for purposes of retaining an episode the outcome was abysmal.

TABLE 5.1
Percentage of Target Words Correctly Recalled

	Condition				
	S–S	W–W	W–S	O–O	S–W
Patient Group					
Korsakoff	57	14	33	29	7
Alcoholic	91	75	63	57	24

This finding of effective cueing of Korsakoff patients' retrieval only when previously established semantic associates are activated had actually been anticipated by Warrington and Weiskrantz (1978). These investigators noted that whenever amnesic patients were given a cue that normally produced the experimentally desired response, the patient tended to declare that the response was appropriate. However, when such regeneration did not lead directly to the desired response (as with weak cues), a correct answer was rarely elicited from the patients. This meant that amnesic patients might be cued successfully under conditions that automatically regenerated a correct response but that they then might fail to produce that same word immediately afterward when given a cue that did not automatically generate the desired response. These patients demonstrated correct retrieval only in the presence of appropriate generating cues and not when the cues were removed or weaker cues (even those present during input) were given.

To directly test this converging hypothesis between encoding and retrieval deficit theories, Cermak and Stiassny (1982) conducted a generation-recognition experiment. The procedure was the same as the encoding specificity paradigm except that after two lists utilizing a W–W condition, the retention test changed. At this point each patient was given 12 "strong" associates of each TBR words that had appeared in a third list presented with weak cues (W–S condition). This time, however, the patient was given four blank spaces in which to write down the first four words that the cue brought to mind. Then, the patient was asked to circle those words that he thought might have appeared on the most recent list that had been presented. As expected, the amnesic Korsakoff patients' performance was significantly below normal on the W–W cueing task. However, their performance on the generation–recognition phase of the experiment exceeded expectations in two ways: First, Korsakoff patients generated as many critical TBR words as did normal and alcoholic controls. Second, they recognized as many of these critical words as did the controls (Table 5.2).

TABLE 5.2
Generation-Recognition of Critical (List 3) Words

Patient Group	Total Words Generated	Number Critical Words Generated	Number Generated as Primary Response	Number Recognized as Correct Response	Number False Positives
Korsakoff	42.7	7.2	5.4	3.1	3.6
Alcoholic	47.4	6.8	4.6	3.2	2.0
Normal	48.0	8.3	6.0	4.4	1.9

Although this outcome was dramatic, it was obvious that the Korsakoff patients' impressive generation-recognition performance could have been due to activation of their semantic memory systems (Cermak, Reale, & Baker, 1978; Kinsbourne & Wood, 1975). These patients may have generated the critical words to the strong associative cues independently of the experimental events preceding such generation. Then they circled the strongest associate of each cue word on the basis of associative familiarity. To test this possibility, the same Korsakoff patients were given a form 2 months later that contained precisely the same strong-associate cues received previously. They were also given the same generation/recognition instructions as before. The number of critical (TBR) words that the Korsakoff patients generated in response to the strong associates at this time was the same as it had been on the initial task. In addition, they "recognized" as many of these critical words as they had previously. The only difference between the initial generation-recognition task and the one performed months later was that the critical word was more frequently generated as the first word on the initial task. It often occurred later in the word generation series following the 1 month delay. Apparently the recent presentation of an item temporarily strengthened that item's representation in the semantic memory hierarchy sufficiently enough to produce it sooner than ordinarily would be the case.

This finding of a temporary strengthening of an item's representation in semantic memory was previously demonstrated by Gardner, Boller, Moreines, and Butters (1973) who dubbed the elicitation of this response the "out of the blue" phenomena. Their patients had been asked to give examples of a particular category (e.g., cars) moments after viewing a serial list of to-be-retained unrelated items that had contained at least one car. They found that the patients provided the category exemplars that had occurred within the test list even though these items were not ordinarily strong associates of a particular category. This same effect has recently been replicated by Graf, Shimamura, and Squire (1985). Thus, it can be concluded that even unconscious activation of an amnesic patients' semantic memory hierarchy can temporarily alter the hierarchy and give the appearance of retention.

CONVERGENCE OF ENCODING AND RETRIEVAL DEFICITS THEORIES

The reasons why amnesic patients fail to utilize temporarily activated, weak associates as retrieval cues still remains an important issue in amnesia. Interestingly, it concerns the same issue that always surfaces in discussions of amnesics' inability to retain new information. It could be that these patients do not utilize weak associations between words because the relationship is not established at the time of input. Or it could be that the patient does realize the association at input but is not able to reconstruct the association at retrieval because more primary associates to the cue compete and appear to be more familiar to the patient. It is also entirely possible that the amnesic Korsakoff patient suffers from both deficits.

Warrington and Weiskrantz (1982) arrived at a similar conclusion in their final revision of the retrieval deficit theory. They had observed that amnesic patients are normal in their retention of highly related word pairs when the first member of the pair is given as a cue for the second but they are substantially impaired when the association between the two words is distant. Warrington and Weiskrantz concluded that the amnesic subject is impaired on those memory tasks in which the stored benefits of cognitive mediation are important, but are unimpaired when cognitive mediation is unnecessary for retention as in instances where previously acquired associations are activated. This conclusion is remarkably similar to that reached by encoding theorists.

Encoding and retrieval deficit theories converge even closer when encoding is redefined as a "product" of analysis in which the subject must cognitively manipulate those features of the information he has just analyzed to permit differential storage. The encoding deficit theory then views amnesia as an inability on the part of the patient to *profit* from his analysis of information. Some amnesics may not profit because analysis is faulty, whereas others, as Cermak (1976) has shown, may not profit because they fail to cognitively manipulate their analysis for purposes of storage. This concept of encoding deficits has received unexpected support from Graf, Shimamura, and Squire (1985) who stated that even though activation of previously acquired material can occur for amnesic patients "they lack the ability to elaborate, organize and consciously recollect information learned since the onset of amnesia" (p. 394).

All of these recent proposals suggest that anterograde amnesia results from the patient's inability to "encode" the products of his analysis. This view of encoding as manipulation and organization of features of information into a more permanent memory integrates theories of amnesia that focus on encoding, consolidation, and retrieval deficits. Common to all these theories is the opinion that amnesics cannot store new material because they cannot cognitively manipulate the features of the material to permit assimilation into a general knowledge system. Encoding deficit theory suggests that this inability occurs after the analysis of incoming information at the point where the patient attempts to organize the material into a form amenable to later retrieval. Amnesics are capable of analyzing the features of new information. Their failure is in manipulating the products of this analysis. Most criticisms of the encoding deficit theory have focused on the previous definition of encoding, which postulated a more direct relationship between analysis and retrieval. These criticisms are now explored in light of this new formulation of encoding deficits theory to determine if it meets their challenges.

CRITICISMS OF ENCODING DEFICIT THEORY

Over the years, two criticisms of the encoding deficit theory of amnesia have recurred. First, it has frequently been suggested that encoding difficulties are not obligatory to the occurrence of amnesia. Some patients seem to have *no* encoding deficits yet are amnesic; other patients who do have encoding difficulties appear to have normal memory abilities. Second, it has been noted that instructions designed to facilitate encoding of semantic features do not seem to lead to improved retention for amnesics. Based on these criticisms, a number of investigators have concluded that encoding deficits are of minor consequence to our understanding of amnesia (Baddeley, 1982; Hirst, 1982; Morton, 1985; Moscovitch, 1984; Squire & Cohen, 1984; Stern, 1981).

The first criticism that an encoding deficit is not an essential feature of the amnesic syndrome was directed toward the interchangeability of the terms *analysis* and *encoding* in the original encoding deficit theory. The revised encoding deficit theory acknowledges that all amnesic patients do not necessarily have deficiencies in their initial *analysis* of the features of verbal information but that they do all have difficulty in the cognitive manipulation of these features and the storage of the material on the basis of these features. Warrington and Weiskrantz' amnesic patients had normal analytic abilities, yet they did not profit from these analyses. Cermak (1976), and Cermak and O'Connor (1983) also reported a case of a densely amnesic postencephalitic patient who was able to analyze sophisticated semantic features of verbal information (as indicated by PI release and chunking abilities), yet has no memory for the desired material nor for how he had initially analyzed it. Lhermitte and Signoret (1972) presented similar findings for a group of postencephalitic patients and Squire (1982) proposed that his ECT patients had no analytic deficits yet did not consolidate new material into memory. Thus, if an encoding deficit is defined as the inability to perform the cognitive manipulations necessary for storage of information, it can be concluded that though analytic deficits are not critical to all amnestic disorders, encoding disorders are.

Quite possibly, the only patients who display pure analytic deficits as described in the preceding pages of this chapter are alcoholic Korsakoff patients. For this particular set of patients, the existence of these deficits is a well documented phenomenon. It has been reported for verbal processing (Cermak et al., 1974), pictorial processing (Huppert & Piercy, 1977), visual processing (Oscar-Berman, Goodglass, & Cherlow, 1973), and contextual processing (Hirst, 1982; Winocur & Kinsbourne, 1978). Thus, analytic deficiencies may exist for some amnesics and, when they do, can be invoked to explain the encoding problems that follow from these deficits. However, not all amnesics necessarily demonstrate analytic deficits, and when they do not, other factors ought to be investigated to explain their encoding disability.

Moscovitch (1982) recently suggested that the "analytic" deficits displayed by Korsakoff patients may not even contribute to their memory disorder but may be part of a more general cognitive disability correlated with frontal-lobe involvement. Evidence for his position comes from a study in which frontal patients demonstrated a failure to release from PI on a distractor memory task similar to that used with Korsakoff patients (Moscovitch, 1982).

Moscovitch's belief that Korsakoff patient's analytic deficits are independent from their memory disorder rests on the premise that frontal-lobe patients are free of memory disorders. However, frontal patients whose injury includes areas communicating with diencephalic regions do show significant memory loss (Freedman & Cermak, 1986). Furthermore, data showing that frontal patients with memory problems fail to release from PI, whereas frontal patients with no evidence of memory problems show normal release, underscores the relationship between analytic difficulties and memory disorders (Freedman & Cermak, 1986). Rather than disputing the relationship between encoding and memory deficits, this evidence extends it to what may be another class of patients.

A second criticism leveled against the original encoding deficits theory is that instructions or training designed to facilitate analysis do not seem to lead to improved retention. Paradoxically, the evidence supporting this criticism has come from our own studies showing that alcoholic Korsakoff patients are shown to profit very little from instructions to analyze the semantic features of verbal information (Cermak & Reale, 1978; Cermak et al., 1980). Because this outcome also occurred for our postencephalitic patient (S.S.), it seems to be true that analytic instructions, even when adequately accomplished by an amnesic patient, have little to no impact on retention. However, the fact that analysis can be improved does not necessarily imply that encoding has occurred. The fact that amnesic patients cannot encode the material into memory even when the features are appropriately analyzed for them is strong evidence that cognitive manipulation is necessary for storage. Once analysis and encoding are separated theoretically the suggestion that analytic improvements necessarily lead to memory improvements no longer follows. Thus, both major criticisms leveled against encoding theory can be addressed favorably by the present redefinition of encoding.

RELATIONSHIP OF THE REVISED ENCODING DEFICIT THEORY TO OTHER RECENT THEORIES OF AMNESIA

The integration of encoding and retrieval deficit theories into a common theory is by no means the only new approach to amnesia that has emerged during the last decade. Other theories have been proposed by a growing number of cognitive psychologists who have become interested in amnesia. As mentioned previously, many of these theories focus on a distinction between tasks amnesics can perform and those they cannot. The question that remains to be explored in this chapter concerns how the current encoding deficit theory interfaces with these more contemporary dichotomies.

A theoretical division (see Figure 5.1) that has been highly visiblerecently is one which divides memory into procedural and declarative memory (Cohen & Squire, 1980). Procedural memory necessitates retention of the process involved in performing a task rather than the specific

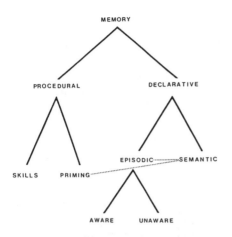

FIGURE 5.1.   Diagrammatic representation of the relationship of existing models of amnesia to one another. All models represented tend to dichotomize memory into those tasks amnesics can perform and those they cannot.

material learned. Laboratory experiments such as maze learning, mirror writing, and mirror reading have been used as examples of procedural memory. Declarative memory involves tasks in which the patient must demonstrate that he or she knows that a particular stimulus has been presented for learning. Recall, recognition, and relearning tasks all fall in this category. Cohen and Squire proposed that amnesic patients can perform procedural tasks normally but fail on declarative tasks. The amnesic patient seems to "know how" to perform a particular task, but does not "know that" he or she has learned it.

The most impressive demonstration of the procedural/declarative distinction has been the report of H.M.'s performance on the Tower of Hanoi task. This task involves learning how to move donut-shaped disks from one peg to another following a particular set of rules. Cohen (1984) reported that H.M. not only learned this task at a normal rate but he retained it as well as normals. Unfortunately, Butters, Wolf, Martone, Granholm, & Cermak (1985) found that other amnesics including Korsakoff patients, patients with Huntington's Disease, and our postencephalitic patient (who has an IQ over 130) could not learn or retain this task. Kim (1985) also reported a failure to replicate this ability with amnesics. Although the discrepancy in these results is troublesome, the distinction between Procedural and Declarative Memory does not depend on this specific task. The Tower of Hanoi task probably involves more than just procedural learning because it requires retention of previously made errors in order to correct them.

Another theory that has been proposed to differentiate amnesics' preserved memory abilities from their deficiencies is the Episodic/Semantic Memory distinction. Tulving (1972, 1983) has defined episodic memory as memory for specific, personally experienced events, whereas semantic memory pertains to the retention of general principles, associations, and rules. Kinsbourne and Wood (1975) have proposed that amnesics have an intact semantic memory in the presence of impaired episodic memory. Their proposal stemmed from the clinical observation that patients could describe an object, such as a railroad ticket but could not describe a single instance or episode in which they had used that object. Cermak, Reale, and Baker (1978) made a further assessment of amnesics' semantic memory organization using a search time paradigm. They reported that Korsakoff patients showed little to no impairment in lexical search rate (e.g., finding an animal beginning with the letter s), but they did show an impaired conceptual search rate (finding an animal with stripes). However, because only the *rate* of conceptual search was impaired and not the final selection of an answer, it was concluded that amnesics' semantic memory probably does retain its normal organization even though the ease with which certain features can be assessed is affected.

Cermak (1984, 1985) and Tulving (1985) have independently suggested that the episodic/semantic and the procedural/declarative models of amnesia need not be viewed in opposition to one another because the episodic/semantic distinction might represent a subdivision of the procedural/declarative distinction. Both episodic and semantic memory tasks seem to require that the patient "declare" that he or she knows about specific information. Procedural variables are not involved in either memory system because neither retrieval of contextual material (episodic) nor of general knowledge (semantic) is required to learn procedural tasks. Consequently, disagreements between theorists ought not to center upon which model is the true description of amnesia but, rather, upon the functional loci of specific phenomena that have been discovered to be true about amnesia, such as encoding deficits, retrieval deficits, priming, and so forth.

Still another distinction between amnesics' abilities and inabilities concerns memory with versus memory without awareness (Jacoby & Witherspoon, 1982). These investigators found that amnesics could be biased toward a particular spelling of an ambiguous word even when they could not recognize that word. Based on this outcome, Jacoby and Witherspoon proposed that a form of episodic memory, which they called "unaware memory," might be available to amnesics. In contrast, these patient's "aware memory" as measured by their recognition that a word had been presented on the prior list was deficient. Jacoby (1984) suggested that though memory with awareness is involved in the recognition of an episode, memory without awareness can be demonstrated by the effect that a specific episode has on subsequent behavior. Accordingly, this distinction between amnesics intact and deficient memory abilities can be subsumed entirely within the area of episodic memory. Interestingly, proponents of each of the three dichotomies thus far presented (procedural/declarative, episodic/semantic, and aware/unaware) cite Jacoby's experiments as support for their point of view. Cohen and Squire feel that biasing or priming is an example of procedural learning. Cermak feels it represents an "activation" of semantic memory, and Jacoby believes it is memory without awareness.

Cermak, Talbot, Chandler, and Wolbarst (1985) attempted to untangle these various explanations by devising a priming procedure that used pseudowords in contrast to real words. These investigators proposed that if semantic activation alone produced a priming phenomenon for amnesics, then the presentation of pseudowords would not enhance their perceptual identification of these stimuli on a subsequent threshold task, because pseudowords would not be represented in semantic memory. The results confirmed this prediction because exposure to pseudowords did not prime Korsakoff patients' identification on a subsequent threshold task This finding is similar to one presented by Diamond and Rozin (1984). Thus, Jacoby's two types of episodic memory do not seem to exist for Korsakoff patients because both types of episodic retention are impaired.

It is possible, however, that some patients with other types of memory disorders may be capable of "unaware" episodic retention of new material. Graf and Schacter (1985) have reported that head injured patients with memory problems were primed on a word completion task in the presence of a previously paired associate word more successfully than when no associative cue was present. These investigators took this to mean that their patients had been capable of some implicit associative learning of a new episode. This effect was not found in an investigation with Korsakoff patients (Cermak, 1985), but it did occur with our post-encephalitic patient (S.S.). Thus, temporary new associative learning may exist for some amnesics but not others. Schacter and Graf (1986) felt that density of amnesia determines which patients can or cannot perform this task. However, our results suggest etiology may be the determining factor. Furthermore, it may be the case that patients who suffer deficits in their analysis of information (Korsakoff patients) may have no ability to learn on an unaware level, whereas patients with other than diencephalic lesions who can perform analysis but not encoding of incoming information may obtain sufficient learning to support a temporary unaware memory of the episode.

Now we can return to the question of integrating the revised encoding deficit theory of amnesia with the dichotomous theories of amnesia. It has been seen that amnesics have normal processing abilities within both procedural and semantic memory but not within episodic memory. Their failure to retain specific experiences is the very essence of their anterograde amnesia. When these specific experiences represent information that occurred after the patient suffered his brain injury, the patient's inefficient "encoding" of the material is the factor that explains his inability to reconstruct that episode. Some patients may fleetingly retain the episode on an unaware level but never on an explicit, aware, level because they cannot cognitively incorporate the episode into their aware, permanent memory. Thus, encoding deficits can still be proposed to underlie the one area of impairment that has consistently been demonstrated in amnesia; namely, episodic memory.

ACKNOWLEDGMENTS

The author's research reported in this chapter was supported by a National Institute of Alcohol and Alcohol Abuse Grant AA–00187 to Boston University School of Medicine and by the Medical Research Service of the Veterans Administration. The comments and criticisms of Margaret O'Connor, James Becker, Hiram Brownell, Nelson Butters, and Dean Delis on an earlier version of this chapter are gratefully acknowledged.

REFERENCES

Baddeley, A. D. (1975). Theories of amnesia. In A. Kennedy & A. Wilkes (Eds.), *Studies in long term memory*. New York: Wiley.
Baddeley, A. D. (1982) Amnesia: A minimal model and an interpretation. In L. S. Cermak (Ed.), *Human memory and amnesia*. (pp. 305–336). Hillsdale, NJ: Lawrence Erlbaum Associates.
Butters, N., Wolfe, J., Martone, M., Granholm, E. & Cermak, L. S. (1985). Memory disorders associated with Huntington's disease: Verbal recall, verbal recognition and procedural memory. *Neuropsychologia, 23,* 729–743.
Cermak, L. S. (1972) *Human memory: Research and theory.* New York: Ronald Press.
Cermak, L. S. (1976) The encoding capacity of a patient with amnesia due to encephalitis. *Neuropsychologia, 14,* 311–326.
Cermak, L. S. (1979). Amnesic patients' level of processing. In L. S. Cermak & F. I. M. Craik (Eds.), *Levels of processing in human memory* (pp. 119–139). Hillsdale, NJ: Lawrence Erlbaum Associates.
Cermak, L. S. (1984). The episodic/semantic distinction in amnesia. In L. R. Squire & N. Butters (Eds.), *The neuropsychology of memory*. New York: The Guilford Press.
Cermak, L. S. (1985). *The extent of semantic priming in amnesics.* Paper presented at the Psychonomic Society Meetings, Boston.
Cermak, L. S., & Butters, N. (1972). The role of interference and encoding in the short-term memory deficits of Korsakoff patients. *Neuropsychologia, 10,* 89–96.
Cermak, L. S., Butters, N., & Gerrein, J. (1973). The extent of the verbal encoding ability of Korsakoff patients. *Neuropsychologia, 11,* 85–94.
Cermak, L. S., Butters, N., & Moreines, J. (1974). Some analyses of the verbal encoding deficit of alcoholic Korsakoff patients. *Brain and Language, 1,* 141–150.
Cermak, L. S., Naus, M. J., & Reale, L. (1976). Rehearsal and organizational strategies of alcoholic Korsakoff patients. *Brain and Language, 3,* 375–385.
Cermak, L. S., & O'Connor, M. (1983). The anterograde and retrograde retrieval ability of a patient with amnesia due to encephalitis. *Neuropsychologia, 21,* 213–234.
Cermak, L. S., & Reale, L. (1978). Depth of processing and retention of words by alcoholic

Korsakoff patients. *Journal of Experimental Psychology: Human Learning and Memory, 4*, 165–174.

Cermak, L. S., Reale, L., & Baker, E. (1978). Alcoholic Korsakoff patients' retrieval from semantic memory. *Brain and Language, 5*, 215–226.

Cermak, L. S., & Stiassny, D. (1982). Recall failure following successful generation and recognition of responses by alcoholic Korsakoff patients. *Brain and Cognition, 1*, 165–176.

Cermak, L. S., Talbot, N., Chandler, K., & Wolbarst, L. R. (1985). The perceptual priming phenomenon in amnesia. *Neuropsychologia, 23*, 615–622.

Cermak, L. S., Uhly, B., & Reale, L. (1980). Encoding specificity in the alcoholic Korsakoff patient. *Brain and Language, 11*, 119–127.

Cohen, N. J. (1984). Preserved learning capacity in amnesia: Evidence for multiple memory systems. In L. R. Squire & N. Butters, (Eds.), *The neuropsychology of memory* (pp. 83–103). New York: Guilford Press.

Cohen, N. J. & Squire, L. R. (1980). Preserved learning and retention of pattern analyzing skill in amnesia: Dissociation of knowing how and knowing that. *Science, 210*, 207–209.

Craik, F. I. M., & Lockhart, R. S. (1972). Levels of processing: A framework for memory research. *Journal of Verbal Learning and Verbal Behavior, 11*, 671–684.

Craik, F. I. M., & Tulving, E. (1975). Depth of processing and retention of words in episodic memory. *Journal of Experimental Psychology: General, 104*, 268–294.

Diamond, R., & Rozin, P. (1984). Activation of existing memories in anterograde amnesia. *Journal of Abnormal Psychology, 93*, 98–105.

Fisher, R. P., & Craik, F. I. M. (1977). The interaction between encoding and retrieval operations in cued recall. *Journal of Experimental Psychology: Human Learning and Memory, 3*, 701–711.

Freedman, M., & Cermak, L. S. (1985). Semantic encoding deficits in frontal lobe disease and amnesia. *Brain and Cognition, 5*, 108–114.

Gardner, H., Boller, F., Moreines, J., & Butters, N. (1973). Retrieving information from Korsakoff patients: Effects of categorical cues and reference to the task. *Cortex, 9*, 165–175.

Graf, P., & Schacter, D. L. (1985). Implicit and explicit memory for new associations in normal and amnesic subjects. *Journal of Experimental Psychology: Learning, Memory and Cognition, 11*, 501–518.

Graf, P., Shimamura, A. P., & Squire, L. R. (1985) Priming across modalities and priming across category levels: Extending the domain of preserved function in amnesia. *Journal of Experimental Psychology: Learning, Memory and Cognition, 11*, 386–396.

Hirst, W. (1982). The amnesic syndrome: Descriptions and explanations. *Psychological Bulletin, 91*, 435–460.

Huppert, F. A., & Piercy, M. (1977). Recognition memory in amnesic patients: A defect of acquisition? *Neuropsychologia, 15*, 654–662.

Jacoby, L. L. (1984). Incidental vs. intentional retrieval: Remembering and awareness as separate issues. In L. R. Squire & N. Butters (Eds.), *The neuropsychology of memory*. New York: The Guilford Press.

Jacoby, L. L., & Witherspoon, D. (1982). Remembering without awareness. *Canadian Journal of Psychology, 36*, 300–324.

Kim, J. K. (1985). *Problem solving in alcoholic Korsakoff patients*. Unpublished doctoral dissertation, State University of New York at Stony Brook.

Kinsbourne, M., & Wood, F. (1975). Short-term memory processes and the amnesic syndrome. In D. Deutsch & J. A. Deutsch (Eds.), *Short-term memory* (pp. 257–291). New York: Academic Press.

Lhermitte, F., & Signoret, J. L. (1972). Neurological analysis and differentiation of amnesic syndromes. *Revue Neurologique, 126*, 161–178.

McGeoch, J. A. (1932). Forgetting and the law of disuse. *Psychological Review, 39*, 352–370.

Melton, A. W., & Irwin, J. (1940). The influence of degree of interpolated learning on retroactive inhibition and the over-transfer of specific responses. *American Journal of Psychology, 53,* 173–302.

Morton, J. (1985). The problem with amnesia: The problem with human memory, a review of "Human Memory and Amnesia." *Cognitive Neuropsychology, 2,* 281–290.

Moscovitch, M. (1982). Multiple dissociations of function in amnesia. In L. S. Cermak (Ed.), *Human memory and amnesia* (pp. 337–370). Hillsdale, NJ: Lawrence Erlbaum Associates.

Moscovitch, M. (1984). The sufficient conditions for demonstrating preserved memory in amnesia: A task analysis. In L. R. Squire & N. Butters (Eds.), *Neuropsychology of memory* (pp. 104–114). New York: The Guilford Press.

Oscar-Berman, M., Goodglass, H., & Cherlow, D. G. (1973). Perceptual laterality and iconic recognition of visual materials by Korsakoff patients and normal adults. *Journal of Comparative and Physiological Psychology, 82,* 316–321.

Schacter, D. L., & Graf, P. (1986). Preserved learning in amnesic patients: Perspectives from research on direct priming. *Journal of Clinical and Experimental Neuropsychology, 8,* 727–743.

Squire, L. R. (1982). Comparisons between forms of amnesia: Some deficits are unique to Korsakoff's syndrome. *Journal of Experimental Psychology, 8,* 560–571.

Squire, L. R., & Cohen, N. J. (1984). Human memory and amnesia. In G. Lynch, J. L. McGaugh, & N. M. Weinberger (Eds.), *Neurobiology of learning and memory* (pp. 3–64). New York: The Guilford Press.

Stern, L. D. (1981). A review of the theories of human amnesia. *Memory and Cognition, 9,* 247–262.

Thomson, D. M., & Tulving, E. (1970). Associative encoding and retrieval: Weak and strong cues. *Journal of Experimental Psychology, 86,* 255–262.

Tulving, E. (1970). Short- and long-term memory: Different retrieval mechanisms. In K. H. Pribram & D. Broadbent (Eds.), *Biology of memory* (pp. 7–9). New York: Academic Press.

Tulving, E. (1972). Episodic and semantic memory. In E. Tulving and W. Donaldson (Eds.), *Organization of memory* (pp. 382–403). New York: Academic Press.

Tulving, E. (1983). *Elements of episodic memory.* Oxford: Clarendon Press.

Tulving, E. (1985). How many memory systems are there? *American Psychologist, 40,* 385–398.

Warrington, E. K., & Weiskrantz, L. (1968). A new method of testing long-term retention with special reference to the amnesic patient. *Nature, 217,* 972–974.

Warrington, E. K., & Weiskrantz, L. (1970). Amnesic syndrome: Consolidation or retrieval? *Nature, 228,* 628–630.

Warrington, E. K., & Weiskrantz, L. (1973). An analysis of short-term and long-term memory defects in man. In J. A. Deutsch (Ed.), *The physiological basis of memory.* New York: Academic Press.

Warrington, E. K., & Weiskrantz, L. (1974). The effect of prior learning on subsequent retention in amnesic patients. *Neuropsychologia, 12,* 419–428.

Warrington, E. K., & Weiskrantz, L. (1978). Further analysis of the prior learning effect in amnesic patients. *Neuropsychologia, 16,* 169–177.

Warrington, E. K., & Weiskrantz, L. (1982). Amnesia: A disconnection syndrome? *Neuropsychologia, 20,* 233–248.

Wickens, D. D. (1970). Encoding strategies of words: An empirical approach to meaning. *Psychological Review, 22,* 1–15.

Winocur, G., & Kinsbourne, M. (1978). Contextual cueing as an aid to Korsakoff amnesics. *Neuropsychologia, 16,* 671–682.

6

Coping Strategies for Memory Dysfunction

Barbara Wilson

INTRODUCTION

Suppose you were asked to learn the name of the following Welsh railway station: "Llanfairpwllgwyngyllgogerychwyrndrobwllllantysiliogogogoch"? You might start by breaking the name down into small sections, such as "Llan/fair/pwll," and so on. The problem here is that it is not always clear where a "section" ends and another begins. Some sections are easier for an English-speaking person to hold in the mind than others. "Gogogoch" is one of these, and is possibly so because parts of it have meaning for you, the sounds are familiar, and it has a rhythm which lends itself to memory. It is also placed at the end of the whole name so you can round off the name with a confident flourish of familiar sounds. Would you be helped if you knew the meaning of the name? It is "The church of St. Mary in a hollow of white hazel, near a rapid whirlpool and St. Tysilio's church, near a red cave." You could work out that "Llan" means "church" and that "tysilio" is a complete name in itself. However, your task would remain difficult—far more so than learning the translation in English. If your difficulties were compounded by a bout of toothache or a hangover, or a degree of emotional stress, learning such a name would be even more arduous, particularly if you could see no purpose in learning it in the first place!

This kind of problem is faced by memory-impaired people every day of their lives. Memory impaired people are constantly being asked to remember new and apparently meaningless or irrelevant information while having to cope with a barrage of problems brought on by their impairment. These problems may well include poor concentration, inability to organize behavior, lack of reasoning power, and incomprehension of one kind or another. Memory impaired people are also likely to be distracted or fatigued more quickly than others.

THEORY AND TREATMENT

Behind every good treatment lies a good theory. We can extend this maxim by suggesting that treatment is improved when the therapist is aware of the theory that informs the treatment. What do we mean when we use the term *theory*? One definition suggests that theory is "contemplation or speculation" as distinct from practice. What we want is a definition of theory that establishes a relationship between theory and practice; we want theory to *inform* practice. A more acceptable definition describes theory as a set of premises or principles put forward to explain a group of phenomena or which underlies a body of facts. Such a definition on its own will not help us much because it remains too broad and could encompass anything from Darwin's theory of evolution to a specific and complex explanation of the workings of a computer. However, under the umbrella of such a definition we can offer different sets of analogues to explain different sets of relatively complex phenomena. Many theories in cognitive psychology are of this kind. For example, Baddeley and Hitch (1974) used the analogy of a central executive system served by several slave systems to explain the nature of working memory. Baddeley (1984a) suggested that a theory is like a map, it helps us to understand where we are and guides us in our efforts to get from one position to another.

Theories, regarded in this way, can enable therapists to hypothesize about the effects of treatment and conceptualize outcomes. Take, for example, the levels-of-processing theory offered by Craik and Lockhart (1972). Regarded as one of the most influential theories in cognitive psychology, it suggests that the deeper we process information the more likely we are to remember it. In treatment we can use such a theory to hypothesize that the problems of a memory-impaired patient are caused by shallow processing; and if this should be the case we might improve matters by encouraging the patient to achieve deeper levels of processing. The patient can be encouraged to answer questions about the material to be remembered, and should success be achieved as a result of this, it will support our adherence to a strategy that has been informed by Craik and Lockhart's theory.

Similarly, the working memory analogue or model offered by Baddeley and Hitch (1974) can be invoked to help understand the secondary memory deficits associated with a patient who has sustained frontal-lobe damage. The analogue states that the central executive controls or coordinates attention and planning. In the classic amnesic syndrome, the central executive performs normally, as do the other components involved in working memory, but problems are experienced in long-term memory.

With a patient who has suffered damage to the frontal lobes, however, the central executive itself is faulty. In this patient's case, the memory failures that occur will be due to poor attention and planning rather than to poor memory per se. In treating this patient we might, therefore, attempt to improve attention and planning skills through certain exercises, or we might try to adapt the patient's particular environment so that an external structure reduces the patient's need to plan and organize activities. (We return to the discussion about restoration of function versus alternative solutions later in the chapter.) The point that needs stressing here is that therapists involved in treating this patient can be informed by theory. More specifically, therapists can learn from Baddeley and Hitch's model that the part of their patient's brain that controls behavior is damaged and that, although it might be working reasonably well on some occasions, there will be other times when it is not, and at these times the patient will be distractable and unable to take in information or block out irrelevant messages. The effect of being informed by such theories during practice is, I would argue, to make our practice more effective and less time consuming.

Theoretical models or analogues used in rehabilitation have come from many fields and are not limited to cognitive psychology. Some of the most fruitful approaches to treatment have been informed by theories arising from the work of behavioral psychologists. Treatments that are based on behavioral studies have, for the most part, come from learning theory and many successful programs have been employed with the neurologically impaired (see, e.g., Goldstein & Ruthven, 1983; Wilson, 1984, 1987a; Wood, 1984).

Therapists in rehabilitation can draw theoretical support from many fields, and we should be ready to apply theories from a wide spectrum of disciplines. At the same time we should recognize that not all clinical advances come from a theoretical base. Obviously, successful treatments can be found with little or no reference to theory. Just as bridges were built long before the discovery of Newtonian mechanics so remediation of deficits has taken place without recourse to theory. A young man who became totally alexic following a gunshot wound (Wilson, 1987a) was taught to read again by an untrained helper working at a training center for the mentally handicapped. Once the man had learned to read we were able to explain his progress by applying the dual route model of reading (Morton & Patterson, 1980). This has helped us formulate ideas about future treatments of similar cases. In this way references are made forward and backward between theory and practice, connections are formed, and our work is pursued within a context of informed debate rather than closed silence.

ASSESSMENT FOR REHABILITATION

It is unlikely that a successful behavioral treatment program could be designed without a dependable and accurate behavioral assessment and task analysis being performed initially. Indeed, it has been argued that assessment and treatment cannot be conceived in isolation from each other in behavior modification or therapy programs. One of the most influential assessment models in the behavioral approach is the SORC designed by Kanfer and Saslow (1969). SORC stands for Stimulus-Organism-Response-Consequence. This model assumes that human behavior is determined by the four "events" or "variables." In order to explain the processes involved in SORC, let us assume that we have a patient who cannot remember the steps involved in transferring from a wheelchair to a bed.

Stimulus events may be physical, social, or internal. Our patient finds herself in a situation where she is required to transfer from wheelchair to bed (physical event). Her husband is watching her and expresses irritation because she cannot remember the correct sequence (social event). The patient herself feels anxious (internal event). Organismic variables refer to the biological condition of the person involved: Our patient has a hemiplegia and a hemianopia as well as a large left-hemisphere lesion.

Responses are observable or measurable behaviors. In our patient we can observe (a) motor behaviors (she grimaces and grips the left armrest of the wheelchair); (b) affective behavior (she describes herself as frightened); and (c) physiological behavior (her heart rate increases and her palm becomes sweaty).

Consequences follow from responses. In the case of our patient, she starts to transfer but forgets to put on the brakes. Her husband jumps up, shouts, and puts on the brake himself. He then talks and pushes his wife through the rest of the sequence.

We know quite a bit about this woman's transferring behavior but if we want to teach her how to transfer we need a neuropsychological assessment too. We need to know more about her level of intellectual functioning: whether she has problems judging depth, distance, angles, and orientation; whether she has comprehension problems; can she retain information over a period of time; how does she perform on verbal and nonverbal tasks?

Equipped with all the information gathered from a combination of neuropsychological and behavioral assessments we are in a position to plan treatment. We might decide to (a) counsel the husband on the nature of his wife's problems; (b) teach the patient anxiety reduction techniques; and (c) use a chaining procedure to teach the patient the steps involved in transferring.

As far as remediation of organic memory impairment is concerned, too much emphasis has been placed in the past on neuropsychological assessment and too little on assessment of everyday memory problems. The behavioral aspects of memory failures have, to a large extent, been ignored. Conventional tests have concentrated attention on goals associated with improvements on laboratory tests themselves, and there has been little if any carry-over into real-life situations. Neuropsychological tests have not provided patients, relatives, or therapists with information that informs rehabilitation. Although psychologists may be intrigued by a patient's inability to remember "hard" paired associates, or absorbed by the fact that a patient is two standard deviations below the mean for a recognition memory test, such information holds little interest for those nonpsychologists who are concerned for the patient's well being in the community outside the laboratory. Of course neuropsychological tests are important for research purposes, they can increase our understanding of the workings of the brain, but other tests that are perhaps more ecologically relevant are needed if we are to alleviate some of the difficulties and frustrations experienced by memory-impaired people and their immediate communities. One such test, which attempts to bridge the gap between conventional, neuropsychological tests, and behavioral assessment procedures, is the Rivermead Behavioral Memory Test (Wilson, Cockburn, & Baddeley, 1985).

THE RIVERMEAD BEHAVIORAL MEMORY TEST (RBMT)

This test is administered and scored like any standardized test but instead of asking people to remember strange drawings, lists of words, or paired associates, it asks them to carry out everyday memory tasks, such as delivering a message or remembering an appointment or retaining the type of information needed for adequate everyday functioning, such as the contents of a brief newspaper article or the stages in a new short route. The test has been influenced by behavioral theories and grew out of direct observation of everyday memory failures. Behavioral assessment techniques were used in the validation study. Theories from cognitive psychology have also influenced the design: Items include immediate and delayed recall, visual, verbal, spatial, and prospective memory tasks. The last named has been the subject of much interest in recent years and is being researched (see, e.g., Harris, 1984), yet the RBMT appears to be the only test that formally assesses this important function of memory. Neuropsychological theories of localization also influenced the development of the test as attempts are made to tap a range of left- and right-hemisphere skills. Performance of dysphasic patients on the RBMT has been investigated recently (Wilson, Cockburn, & Baddeley, 1987). Findings suggest this group is impaired in remembering a new name and in remembering a newspaper story but performance on other memory tasks is not significantly different from other brain-damaged controls.

Originally standardized and validated with 176 brain-damaged subjects and 118 normal controls aged between 16 and 69 years, with IQs ranging from 68 to 136, the test has since been given to several other groups of subjects including elderly normal, elderly depressed, and early Alzheimer patients (L. W. Poon, personal communication, August 1986), patients with multiple sclerosis, Parkinson's disease, AIDS sufferers, psychogeriatric day patients, and children. Most of these studies are not yet published but some interesting findings are reported. In the Poon study, for example, 60 normal elderly subjects took part along with 25 elderly depressed patients and 33 early Alzheimer patients. The Alzheimer patients scored a mean of 2.47 items correct out of a possible 12 (S.D. = 2.03). The elderly depressed scored a mean of 8.28 (S.D. = 2.28) and were not significantly different from the elderly normals who scored a mean of 9.16 (S.D. = 1.87). Thus, the test seems sensitive to organic but not emotional impairment.

Cockburn and Collins (in press) compared 20 normal elderly living in the community with 20 psychogeriatric patients attending a day hospital. All were between the ages of 69 and 90 years. There was a highly significant ($p < .001$) difference between the groups. In another unpublished study Cockburn compared a "young" elderly group (55–70 years) with an "old" elderly group (71–90 years) on several memory tests. The RBMT discriminated best between the two groups, mainly because of the prospective memory items. The "old" elderly were significantly poorer than the "young" elderly on all three of the prospective memory tasks but not on the remaining items.

In the original validation study the mean score of normal controls was 10.60 (S.D. = 1.41). This was used to determine the cut-off points to maximize the discrimination between the controls and the patients. Interrater reliability (up to six testers tested 40 patients simultaneously but independently) was 100%. Parallel-form reliability (there are four parallel versions of the test) was 0.85. Validity was established through correlations with (a) other memory tests and (b) therapists' observations of everyday memory failures. In the case of memory tests, correlations ranged from 0.26 (digit span) to 0.60 (recognition memory words, Warrington, 1984), and 0.60 (Paired-associate learning, Randt, Brown, & Osborne, 1980). The correlation with therapists' observations was 0.75. These findings indicate that the RBMT is a valid and reliable test of everyday memory skills.

As was hoped at the early design stages of the test, the RBMT can help identify areas for treatment, particularly with patients who are not severely amnesic. Thus, patients who fail the immediate and delayed route memory tasks but pass most of the other items in the battery are almost certainly going to have difficulty finding their way around, although their verbal memory skills will remain reasonably intact. It would, therefore, make sense for therapists to devise strategies to help such a patient find his or her way around certain locations. In this particular case, given the more intact verbal ability, it might help if route learning was achieved by concentrating on the patient's verbal strengths: Topographical tasks would have to be changed into verbal ones.

TREATMENT OF EVERYDAY MEMORY PROBLEMS

Treatment is another term which can be interpreted in several ways. It can be thought of narrowly as pertaining to attempts to restore functioning, or it can include any intervention strategy or technique that aims to assist clients (patients) and their carers to manage, bypass, reduce, or come to terms with a particular impairment. Given this latter interpretation, memory rehabilitation will not only offer a patient memory techniques but will also give a wide range of assistance in social, emotional, and environmental matters.

There are several ways we might approach treatment. We might attempt to improve or restore general memory functioning for our memory-impaired patient; we might consider strategies that encourage anatomical reorganization; we might try to bypass or avoid problem areas; we might consider alternative ways to help the memory-impaired person remember information, or we might teach the person ways to use residual skills more efficiently. Let us consider each of these in turn.

Improvement and/or Restoration of Function

In 1981, Harris and Sunderland carried out a survey of the management of memory disorders in rehabilitation units in Great Britain. They found that games and exercises were the most widely used treatment techniques. Presumably, these games and exercises were employed in attempts to improve impaired memory. The authors suggest that the theoretical principle behind this approach is the "mental muscle theory," which suggests that memory is like a muscle, which can be improved or strengthened by exercise. However, there is no evidence to support such a proposition. Miller (1978) has suggested that it is not possible to restore memory following neurological damage. Wilson (1982) described efforts to improve the general ability to remember of a man with classic amnesic syndrome. These efforts proved to be fruitless, although some successes were achieved when treatment focused on specific problem areas of behavior.

There is very little evidence to support the notion that exercising memory, even among non-brain-damaged subjects, will improve general memory functioning. Chase, Lyon, and Ericsson (1981) trained one student to increase his digit span from the normal 7–8 digits to a phenomenal 80 digits but when tested on span for letters, the student reverted to an average span of 7–8 words. There was in fact no generalization to other areas in this student's case.

Although the outlook for achieving general improvement in memory remains fairly pessimistic, there are some studies that seem to suggest that, in certain circumstances, improvement might take place—at least within the head injured population. Grafman and Matthews (1978) gave 75 memory impaired, head injured patients 3 months training in memory tasks. Patients were seen three times a week and after 3 months, they had improved their performance on memory tests by 50%. Wilson (1987b) also reported small but meaningful improvements in general memory functioning in a group of patients, most of whom had sustained head injuries. They appeared to benefit from group training sessions held each day for 3 weeks. Such results, however, remain problematic because improvement may have been due to natural recovery. Miller (1984) refered to this dilemma, noting that it is particularly difficult to separate out treatment effectiveness from spontaneous recovery when treating a head-injured population, because such a group may not reach its maximum level of recovery for a lengthy period after the injury.

We have to conclude that the case for improvement of memory functioning after brain damage through practice, exercise, or stimulation remains doubtful. Obviously, practice is required in any treatment regime as a support for learning, but practice on its own is unlikely to advance steps toward recovery of brain functioning. Where such steps are observed it would be more sensible to consider that natural recovery has been operating. It is conceivable, however, that there will be a critical stage following brain damage when practice or exercise will play a crucial role as a therapeutic technique.

Anatomical Reorganization

This is an approach to treatment that is based upon the belief that undamaged areas of the brain can take on the skills or functions of damaged areas

The theory of cerebral plasticity points to the possibility of reorganization of neural tissues, and clear evidence is available that such reorganization can occur in immature organisms (Finger & Stein, 1982). It would appear that in such cases, as far as human beings are concerned, there is a price to pay. For example, infants who have undergone left hemispherectomy develop language in the right hemisphere but subtle language deficits can be detected in adulthood (Dennis & Whitaker, 1977). Furthermore, the visuospatial abilities of these individuals are compromised.

Anatomical reorganization in adults seems very unlikely. LeVere (1975) stated categorically that mature biological systems cannot change their fundamental methods of operation. Nevertheless, Buffery (1976), in an attempt to develop (or increase) the language ability of the right hemisphere in a dysphasic man, stimulated the right cerebral-hemisphere of his patient. Buffery used tachistoscopically presented stimuli, together with auditory and tactile stimulation. Improvements in the man's language skills were noted by Buffery who suggested that this resulted from language development in the right hemisphere. However, it is equally possible that the stimuli transmitted to the right hemisphere were transferred across the corpus callosum and processed by the [albeit faulty] left hemisphere. Improvement in language could therefore be attributed to partial recovery of the left hemisphere.

As far as memory impairment is concerned, there are no studies claiming anatomical reorganization in mature humans (see Feinberg et al, this volume). Despite this absence of evidence, belief that large areas of the brain are not used (and presumably up for grabs) is widespread among relatives of memory-impaired people. In a recent book by a journalist, for example, we are told: "We make use of only 10% of our brains" (MccGwire, 1986, p. 85). Unfortunately, the spread of such myths can encourage false optimism in relatives, who might become impatient with the painstakingly objective work of therapists. However, given our current knowledge, we must insist that anatomical reorganization remains, at least, open to question.

Bypassing or Avoiding Problem Areas

Accepting the argument that, as far as our present state of knowledge allows, anatomical reorganization and restoration of function are not achievable to any great degree in humans, then what options remain open to us? A method that appears to bring some success in terms of coping better with everyday memory problems, is that which encourages clients to bypass or avoid situations in which their present weaknesses put them at a disadvantage. Just as people who are deaf avoid using telephones, and people who cannot read try to avoid situations where reading skills are required, so memory-impaired people can possibly be helped by therapists who structure situations where powers of retrieval and new learning are avoided. One way rehabilitationists might aid their clients in this way is to design structured environments that do not call upon the necessity to remember. Examples of this approach can be seen in some reality orientation programs where signposts, noticeboards, and labels are used to help patients orient themselves in time and place (see Holden & Woods, 1982, for further examples).

The rationale or set of principles guiding treatment of this nature is to be found in the field of behavior therapy where stimulus control is a recognized way of altering behavior. We have already seen, in the section on assessment, that behavior is partly determined by stimulus events, which might be physical, social, or internal. Changing the stimulus events can change the behavior that they precipitate. For example, if Mr. Smith always goes to the wrong bed on the ward because he cannot remember which is his bed, then the ward can be seen as the physical event that triggers bed-forgetting behavior. By making Mr. Smith's bed noticeable and easily discriminable—by putting a large notice above the bed—we have changed part of the physical environment and Mr. Smith may not need to remember which is his bed because it has been made to appear very obvious. Harris (1980) described a geriatric unit that had a high rate of incontinence until all the lavatory doors were painted a distinctive color. The rate of incontinence dropped, presumably because the need to remember lavatory doors was no longer there. Wilson (1987a) described a young man undergoing memory therapy. In order to get his attention before beginning any activity he was asked, "Are you ready M? . . ." He invariably replied, "Ready, willing and disabled." Mildly amusing at first, this response became annoying and even infuriating to those who had to hear it hundreds of times! A solution was reached when therapists stopped asking the question, "Are you ready?" and substituted, "We're going to start now, M . . . ." As most memory impaired people repeat the same questions or tell the same stories over and over again it is worth asking whether such repetition can be avoided by bypassing the situation that triggers the behavior.

Although restructuring the environment in this way can lead to quick solutions, the problems to which such behavior modification can apply are limited in scope and number. It looks as though environmental adaptations have a limited role to play in memory therapy. However, we should not underestimate their relevance because of their somewhat simplistic appearance: For people who have considerable intellectual handicaps as well as memory difficulties, *and for their carers,* such adaptation, or avoidance of a problem, may make life a lot easier!

Alternative Ways of Remembering

This approach is in some ways similar to the previous one but instead of avoiding or reducing the patient's need to remember, we are now trying to encourage her or him to remember in a different way. Attempts are made to find alternative ways of completing a task that can no longer be achieved in the preferred or habitual manner. Luria, Naydin, Tsvetkova, & Vinarskaya's (1969) theory of functional adaptation, which states that there is more than one way to complete a cognitive activity, has influenced the development of this approach. Luria et al. claim that when irreversible destruction of nerve cells has occurred, restoration of function in its original form is impossible, and rehabilitation should, therefore, attempt to reconstruct the disturbed function. Luria also believed that functional restoration can take place "even in cases where the duration of the disease is measured in years" (p. 72).

An interesting study reporting functional reorganization is that of Kashiwagi, Kashiwagi, and Hasegawa (1987). They were working with Japanese aphasics who had difficulties learning their multiplication tables. The Japanese learn their tables by means of mnemonic rhymes called "Kuky." They learn, therefore, through an auditory-speaking route. Although the aphasics failed to make progress using the auditory-speaking route, they made good progress when persuaded to use a visual-writing route.

Functional adaptation is widely accepted in many areas of rehabilitation and is recognized as one of the most successful approaches. There is a range of equipment, for example, to enable hemiplegic patients to complete tasks with one hand. People who cannot bend down to pick up a dropped object may be supplied with a long-handled retrieving stick. Quadriplegics can press computer keys with equipment attached to their heads. People who can no longer read through vision may do so through touch. Similarly, in memory therapy people can use tape recorders, computers, log books, and other aids to help them remember. Harris (1978, 1984) described the desirable characteristics of such external memory aids. Some of the features that will enhance their efficacy include active, rather than passive cues; cues should be given as close as possible to the time when action is required; and information should supply a specific reminder for each particular action.

It is likely that functional adaptation by using external aids is the most beneficial treatment approach for amnesic patients. Most people without organic impairment will use an external aid of some kind on some occasions. Unfortunately, many neurologically impaired patients are unable or unwilling to place a similar reliance on such aids. Workers in the field often hear statements such as "I don't want to rely on such things. It's cheating." Other patients simply forget to record the relevant information or forget to refer to what has been recorded. On the other hand, it sometimes happens that a patient relies too heavily on an external aid. A severely amnesic, postencephalitic patient, for example, keeps a journal as a matter of compulsion. A new entry is made every few minutes and this patient usually records that he has just woken up. With each new entry he is likely to cross out the previous one, and might add, "ignore previous claims." Here is an extract from one page of this man's journal:

> 5:45 p.m.   perfectly awake (first time)
> 5:48 p.m.   completely awake (first time)
> 6:04 p.m.   immaculately awake (first time)
> 6:12 p.m.   universally awake (first time)
> 6:15 p.m.   totally awake (first time)
>
> (These entries have continued unchanged for over 2 years.)

However, it is more common to meet patients who will not or cannot refer to external aids. Some of these patients can be persuaded that it is not cheating to use such devices. They will eventually listen to arguments that point out that most "normal" people use such devices and that dependence on them will not retard any recovery of function (Harris, 1980a). On other occasions it may be necessary to try out a selection of external aids in order to discover which is the most useful and acceptable to the patient. On other occasions the best strategy may be to teach the patient to use the aids, perhaps by implementing a behavior program or by combining an alarm with a notebook. Fowler, Hart, and Sheehan (1982) used alarms to remind patients to consult their daily schedules.

Given the potential importance of these functional adaptations, it is perhaps surprising how little their use in rehabilitation has been reported. Fowler et al. (1979) and Gouvier (1982) discussed their work in this area, and Wilson and Moffat (1984) reported the use of timers to remind dysarthric patients to swallow. They also describe the responses of some patients to the use of electronic memory aids. Klein and Fowler (1981) used an electronic timer to remind paraplegic patients to lift regularly in order to reduce the risk of pressure sores. Jones and Adam (1979) described a potential prosthetic memory aid, and Davies and Binks (1983) used a particular aid to help a Korsakoff patient. The field remains wide open for systematic work with amnesic patients and their use of memory aids.

Using Existing Skills More Efficiently

It must be recognized that even severely amnesic patients do not forget everything. Few people lose all their memory functioning, and one approach we can take in memory therapy is to help our patients use whatever skills they still possess more efficiently. It is here that theories from cognitive psychology have potential influence. For example, the levels-of-processing model referred to earlier, and the ensuing deeper processing, can inform therapeutic strategies aimed at helping some memory-impaired people (particularly those whose memory problems are mild to moderate) improve their recall of verbal information. Principles relating to distributed rather than massed practice, organization, chunking, and encoding specificity can guide therapists when they design memory-therapy programs (see Baddeley, 1984b, for further discussion of these principles).

Theoretical explanations of the amnesic syndrome (encoding deficit, storage deficit, and retrieval deficit) may be inadequate as explanations of the amnesic syndrome but they can, nevertheless, assist our thinking about methods of treatment. Some memory-impaired people are very likely to have problems connected with encoding, storage, or retrieval. Wilson (1987a) discussed theoretical and practical issues involved in the development of treatment programs aimed at improving coding, storage, and retrieval.

In recent years considerable efforts have been made to teach brain damaged people to use mnemonics to improve recall or learn new information. See for examples, Lewinsohn et al. (1977), Glasgow, Zeiss, Barrera, & Lewinsohn (1977), and Wilson and Moffat (1984b). Bower (1972) suggested that mnemonics probably work because they allow previously isolated items to become integrated with one another. They may also require deeper levels of processing and provide retrieval cues. There have been some critics who question the value of employing mnemonics with organically impaired people (e.g., O'Connor & Cermak, 1987), whereas others (Wilson, 1987a) believe they can make a valuable contribution as long as their role is strictly limited to certain specific areas. Of course mnemonics will be seen to fail if therapists expect patients to use them in novel situations or employ them to improve general memory functioning. Amnesic patients are rarely able to achieve such goals. If, on the other hand, mnemonics are treated as useful teaching aids that can be employed to assist brain damaged people in the learning of limited bits of information then the chances are that they will indeed provide that kind of assistance.

From a series of studies carried out with brain damaged people, Wilson (1987a) came to the following conclusions about the use of mnemonics in rehabilitation.

1. Mnemonics are usually more effective than rote rehearsal in teaching new information.
2. It is usually better to employ dual coding (i.e., use more than one strategy when teaching information).
3. Teach the information one step at a time. (Several earlier investigations have expected brain-damaged people to employ mnemonics in lists of 10 or 15 words!)
4. Drawn images are better than mental ones.
5. Take into account individual preferences and styles.
6. Teach information that the patient wants/needs to remember. (Avoid the use of experimental material.)

Behavior therapy techniques can also be employed to help patients make better use of residual abilities. Some very interesting work has been conducted recently by Schacter and his colleagues (see, e.g., Glisky, Schacter, & Tulving, 1986) whereby amnesic patients are taught to use computers. Schacter described his teaching as the "Method of Vanishing Cues." In fact the teaching method is not new in itself but is an interesting application of "backward chaining," a shaping procedure used successfully for decades by behavior modifiers, including those working in the field of memory rehabilitation. The point that this example illustrates, however, is that the application of cognitive and behavioral techniques to the field of memory therapy is likely to be an expanding development in the foreseeable future.

Combining Methods

An important point to stress here is that the preceding approaches described are not mutually exclusive. Different methods can be applied during different stages of recovery. For example, when a patient first suffers a stroke, physical therapists and speech pathologists will probably try to restore lost functioning, but after 6 months or so they may well need to implement functional adaptations. Thus, instead of trying to teach the patient to walk and talk again, they may be required to shift emphasis toward creating wheelchair independence and an alternative communication system.

Conversely, a combination of approaches may be employed at any one time. Therapists might design a program that looks like the following:

1. Try to improve memory functioning in general by giving exercises and practice in memory tasks.

2. Help the patient find his or her way around the rehabilitation unit by adapting the environment to suit his or her needs.
3. Give the patient external aids to help him or her remember when to go to an appointment.
4. Use mnemonics to teach the patient the names of therapists.

Eventually, we may combine psychological and pharmaceutical treatments to produce more unified memory-therapy programs. Where such an amalgamation occurs we might expect more successful outcomes (see, e.g., Durand, 1982, who combined behavioral and drug treatments for children who exhibited severe self-injurious behavior).

GENERALIZATION

Questions relating to generalization are constantly asked in rehabilitation. When, in Shakespeare's "Henry IV, Part One," Glendower boasts, "I can call spirits from the vasty deep," Hotspure replies, "But will they come when you do call for them?" Similarly, we may provide patients with memory aids but we cannot guarantee that they will use them. We can teach patients strategies to learn more efficiently but many patients will not use these strategies. Others will use the strategies for one problem but not for others, or in one situation only.

We should not, however, condemn the strategy itself if there is no ensuing generalization. After all, antibiotics are effective in killing bacteria but only if we remember to take the antibiotics. Failure to generalize means that some action has to take place; there is no point in sitting around hoping that generalization will occur. It might be possible to avoid the need to generalize. Let us consider, for example, a patient whose memory impairments are due largely to attention difficulties. We observe him for a few days and find his poor attention means he is unable to remember his exercises in physiotherapy, he cannot remember what has been said to him, and he cannot find his way around the unit. We consider doing some attention-training tasks on the computer but realize that although this is likely to lead to improvement on the computer tasks, it will probably fail to generalize to the problems experienced in physiotherapy and elsewhere. If we work *directly* on the patient's physical exercises, on his ability to remember instructions, and on his capacity for finding his way around the unit, then any success we obtain in these areas means we do not have to concern ourselves with the question of generalization.

It is possible in some instances to teach generalization. Take the case of a patient who is willing to use her notebook in occupational therapy but

will not use it at home or in other situations. This problem could be
tackled by means of a behavioral program as set out below:

1. Define problem behavior.	K does not refer to her notebook at home.
2. State goal.	Teach K to check notebook after every meal.
3. Observe and record (baseline).	Referred to book once only during 7 days observation.
4. Plan treatment.	(a) set timer to sound when K has coffee at end of meal;
	(b) each time timer bleeps, remind K to look at her book;
	(c) If K asks question and you know the information is in the notebook, ask her to find out by looking in her book;
	(d) when K has learned to pair timer with notebook, fade out. Coffee should act as cue to check book.
5. Begin treatment.	
6. Monitor and evaluate progress.	Begun 1-12-87.
7. Change procedure if necessary.	By 1-30-87 checking after every meal. Start fading timer.

The next stage in K's program would be to use a similar procedure in
other situations. Teaching generalization is an accepted part of treatment
programs with the mentally handicapped (Carr, 1980), but it does not seem
to be recognized to the same extent in neuropsychological rehabilitation.

If it is not possible to teach generalization we may have to decide that
the next best strategy is to teach relatives, carers, or other staff involved
how to guide the patient through the procedure or to prompt the patient
to use the aid. The method of expanding rehearsal (Landauer & Bjork,
1978) is useful for teaching some limited information to even severely
amnesic people, although one would not expect amnesics to remember to
test themselves at gradually increasing intervals. Nevertheless, we can
readily explain to those in daily contact with the patient the principles
behind the method of expanding rehearsal. Similarly, databank wrist-
watches are potentially useful external aids for some memory impaired
people, although many will be unable to learn how to program them.
Relatives can help set the watches, however, without removing the ser-
viceability of the instruments, which fulfill most, if not all, of the criteria

described by Harris (1978, 1984).

SUPPORTING THE RELATIVES
AND CARERS OF THE MEMORY IMPAIRED

It is nearly always the family who bears the greatest burden and responsibility for memory-impaired people, and it is for this reason that, irrespective of whether therapy is available to the patient, support and advice for relatives and carers is likely to prove to be the most effective strategy at the end of the day. Moffat (in press) reported several investigations into home-based cognitive rehabilitation with the elderly. He described a relatives' support group aimed at reducing stress among carers. Information on dementia and advice on coping with memory problems were the carers most frequently expressed needs. Moffat is also concerned with involving carers in treatment and he described some ingenious solutions to such problems as losing things around the house.

Memory impairment is not only a problem experienced by the elderly. Indeed, it is one of the most common sequelae of many neurological conditions. In an attempt to help the relatives of the young memory impaired, Deborah Wearing and Barbara Wilson launched the Amnesia Association in September 1986. This association was formed to work for the relief of amnesic people and their relatives, to coordinate and initiate research into memory impairment, and to disseminate information about amnesia to those directly affected, to those involved in diagnosis, and to care agencies.

Primarily, the Amnesia Association is an action group committed to the provision of appropriate long-term care facilities for memory impaired people. One of the important projects for the near future is the establishment of a pilot center for people with amnesia. We want to establish a unit for long-term residential and day care where the memory impaired can live in a comfortable home environment with specially trained staff, and where therapeutic techniques and regimes can be evaluated. In addition, we are establishing a network of regional support groups so that carers, psychologists, doctors, social workers, speech therapists, occupational therapists and other interested parties can work together and pool their resources.[1]

As a final twist to this chapter the reader might like to return to the question set at the beginning: How would you set about learning the longest named railway station in the world? Does your answer differ from ideas you may have considered initially?

---

[1]Further information about the Amnesia Association can be obtained from The Amnesia Association, 25 Prebend Gardens, Chiswick, London W4 ITN, England.

REFERENCES

Baddeley, A. D. (1984a). Memory theory and memory therapy. In B. Wilson & N. Moffat (Eds.), *Clinical management of memory problems* (pp. 5–27). London: Croom Helm.

Baddeley, A. D. (1984b). *Your memory: A user's guide.* Harmondsworth: Penguin.

Baddeley, A. D., & Hitch, G. J. (1974). Working memory. In G. A. Bower (Ed.), *The psychology of learning and motivation* (Vol. 8, pp. 47–90). New York: Academic Press.

Bower, G. H. (1972). A selective review of organizational factors in memory. In E. Tulving & W. Donaldson (Eds.), *Organization of memory.* New York: Academic Press.

Buffery, A. W. H. (1976). Clinical neuropsychology: A review and preview. In S. Rachman (Ed.), *Contributions to medical psychology* (pp. 115–136). Oxford: Pergamon Press.

Carr, J. (1980). Imitation, discrimination and generalisation. In W. Yule & J. Carr (Eds.), *Behaviour modification for the mentally handicapped* (pp. 79–89). London: Croom Helm.

Chase, W. G., Lyon, D. R., & Ericsson, K. A. (1981). Individual differences in memory span. In J. P. Das & N. O'Connor (Eds.), *Intelligence and learning* (pp. 157–162). New York: Plenum Press.

Cockburn, J., & Collins, C. (in press). Assessment of everyday memory in the elderly. *Age & Aging.*

Craik, F. I. M., & Lockhart, R. S. (1972). Levels of processing: A framework for memory research. *Journal of Verbal Learning and Verbal Behaviour, 11,* 671–684.

Davies, A. D. M., & Binks, M. G. (1983). Supporting the residual memory of a Korsakoff patient. *Behavioural Psychotherapy, 11,* 62–74.

Dennis, M., & Whitaker, H. A. (1977). Hemispheric equipotentiality and language acquisition. In S. J. Segalowitz & F. Gruber (Eds.), *Language development and neurological theory* (pp. 93–106). New York: Academic Press.

Durand, V. M. (1982). A behavioral/pharmacological intervention for the treatment of severe self-injurious behavior. *Journal of Autism and Developmental Disorders, 12,* 243–251.

Finger, S., & Stein, D. (1982). *Brain damage and recovery.* New York: Academic Press.

Fowler, R., Hart, J., & Sheehan, M. (1972). A prosthetic memory: An application of the prosthetic environment concept. *Rehabilitation Counselling Bulletin, 15,* 80–85.

Glasgow, R. E., Zeiss, R. A., Barrera, M., & Lewinsohn, P. M. (1977). Case studies on remediating memory deficits in brain damaged individuals. *Journal of Clinical Psychology, 33,* 1049–1054.

Glisky, E. L., Schacter, D. L., & Tulving, E. (1986). Computer learning by memory impaired patients: Acquisition and retention of complex knowledge. *Neuropsychologia, 24,* 313–328.

Goldstein, G., & Ruthven, L. (1983). *Rehabilitation of the brain damaged adult.* New York: Plenum Press.

Gouvier, W. (1982). Using the digital alarm chronograph in memory retraining. *Behavioral Engineering, 7,* 134.

Grafman, J., & Matthews, C. G. (1978). Assessment and remediation of memory deficits in brain injured patients. In M. M. Gruneberg, P. E. Morris, & R. N. Sykes (Eds.), *Practical aspects of memory* (pp. 720–728). London: Academic Press.

Harris, J. E. (1978). External Memory Aids. In M. M. Gruneberg, P. E. Morris, & R. N. Sykes (Eds.), *Practical aspects of memory* (pp. 172–179). London: Academic Press.

Harris, J. E. (1980a). Memory aids people use: Two interview studies. *Memory and Cognition, 8,* 31–38.

Harris, J. E. (1980b). We have ways of helping you remember. *Concord. The Journal of the British Association for Service to the Elderly, No. 17,* 21–27.

Harris, J. E. (1984). Remembering to do things: A forgotten topic. In J. E. Harris & P. Morris (Eds.), *Everyday memory, actions and absentmindedness (pp. 71–92). London: Academic Press.*

Harris, J. E., & Sunderland, A. (1981). A brief survey of the management of memory disorders in rehabilitation units in Britain. *International Rehabilitation Medicine, 3,* 206–209.

Holden, U. P., & Woods, R. T. (1982). *Reality orientation: Psychological approaches to the confused elderly.* London: Chuchill Livingstone.

Jones, G., & Adam, J. (1979). Towards a prosthetic memory. *Bulletin of the British Psychological Society, 32,* 165–167.

Kanfer, F. H., & Saslow, G. (1969). Behavioural diagnosis. In C. Franks (Ed.), *Behaviour therapy: Appraisal and status* (pp. 404–445). New York: McGraw-Hill.

Kashiwagi, A., Kashiwagi, T., & Hasegawa, T. (1987). Improvement of deficits in mnemonic rhyme for multiplication in Japanese aphasics. *Neuropsychologia, 25,* 443–447.

Klein, R. M., & Fowler, R. S. (1981). Pressure relief training device: The microcalculator. *Archives of Physical and Medical Rehabilitation, 62,* 500–501.

Landauer, T. K., & Bjork, R. A. (1978). Optimum rehearsal patterns and name learning. In M. M. Gruneberg, P. E. Morris, & R. N. Sykes (Eds.), *Practical aspects of memory* (pp. 625–632). London: Academic Press.

LeVere, T. E. (1975). Neural stability, sparing and behavioral recovery following brain damage. *Psychological Review, 82,* 344–358.

Lewinsohn, P. M., Danaher, B. G., & Kikel, S. (1977). Visual imagery as a mnemonic aid for brain injured persons. *Journal of Consulting and Clinical Psychology, 45,* 717–723.

Luria, A. R., Naydin, V. L., Tsvetkova, L. S., & Vinarskaya, E. N. (1969). Restoration of higher cortical function following local brain damage. In P. J. Vinken & G. W. Bruyn (Eds.), *Handbook of clinical neurology* (Vol. 3, pp. 368–433). North Holland: Amsterdam.

McGwire, S. (1986). *Kim story. A fight for life.* London: Harrap.

Miller, E. (1978). Is amnesia remedial? In M. M. Gruneberg, P. E. Morris, & R. N. Sykes (Eds.), *Practical aspects of memory* (pp. 705–711). New York: Academic Press.

Miller, E. (1984). *Recovery and management of neuropsychological impairments.* Chichester: Wiley.

Moffat, N. (in press). Home based rehabilitation programmes for the elderly. In L. Poon, D. Rubin, & B. Wilson (Eds.), *Everyday cognition in adult and later life.* New York: Cambridge University Press.

Morton, J., & Patterson, K. E. (1980). A new attempt at an interpretation or, an attempt at a new interpretation. In M. Coltheart, K. Patterson, & J. C. Marshall (Eds.), *Deep dyslexia* (pp. 91–118). London: Routledge & Kegan Paul.

O'Connor, M., & Cermak, L. (1987). Rehabilitation of organic memory disorders. In M. J. Meier, A. L. Benton, & L. Diller (Eds.), *Neuropsychological rehabilitation* (pp. 260–279). London: Churchill Livingstone.

Randt, C. T., Brown, E. R., & Osborne, D. P. (1980). A memory test for longitudinal measurement of mild to moderate deficits. *Clinical Neuropsychologia, 2,* 184–194.

Warrington, E. K. (1984). The Recognition Memory Test: Windsor NFER-Nelson.

Wilson, B. A. (1982). Success and failure in memory training following a cerebral vascular accident. *Cortex, 18,* 581–594.

Wilson, B. A. (1984). Memory therapy in practice. In B. A. Wilson & N. Moffat (Eds.), *Clinical management of memory problems* (pp. 89–111). London: Croom Helm.

Wilson, B. A. (1987a). *Rehabilitation of memory.* New York: Guilford Press.

Wilson, B. A. (1987b). Identification and remediation of everyday problems in memory impaired adults. In P. Nathan, N. Butters, & O. Parsons *Neuropsychology of alcoholism: Implications for diagnosis and treatment.* New York: Guilford Press.

Wilson, B. A., Cockburn, J., & Baddeley, A. D. (1985). *The Rivermead Behavioural Memory Test manual*. Thames Valley Test Co., 22 Bulmershe Rd., Reading, Berkshire, England.

Wilson, B. A., Cockburn, J., & Baddeley, A. D. (1987). *The Rivermead Behavioural Memory Test: Second supplement*. Thames Valley Test Co., 22 Bulmershe Rd., Reading, Berkshire, England.

Wilson, B. A., & Moffat, N. (Eds.). (1984a). *Clinical management of memory problems*. London: Croom Helm.

Wilson, B. A., & Moffat, N. (1984b). Rehabilitation of memory for everyday life. In J. E. Harris & P. Morris (Eds.), *Everyday memory: Actions and absentmindedness* (pp. 207–233). London: Academic Press.

Wood, R. L. (1984). Behaviour disorders: Their presentation and management. In D. N. Brooks (Ed.), *Closed head injury: Social, psychological and family consequences* (pp. 195–219). Oxford: Oxford University Press.

7

The Neuropsychology of Emotion: Evidence from Normal, Neurological, and Psychiatric Populations

Joan C. Borod
Elissa Koff

NEUROPSYCHOLOGY OF EMOTION

Hemispheric Specialization

Introduction

The right hemisphere and emotion have been linked since at least 1912, when Mills (1912a, 1912b) observed that right-hemisphere pathology was associated with deficits in emotional processing. Since that time, anecdotal evidence, case studies, and a scattering of more systematic reports (e.g., Goldstein, 1952; Hecaen, 1962) have confirmed this relationship in impaired individuals. Stimulated by these observations, a substantial number of recent studies have examined the role of the intact right hemisphere in the processing of emotion. This literature has been extensively reviewed by Borod, Koff, and Caron (1983), Ley and Bryden (1981), and Tucker (1981). Most of these studies involve normal adults subjected to procedures designed to reflect hemispheric lateralization (e.g., tachistoscopic viewing). Another recent line of research addresses, in systematic fashion, emotional processing in brain-damaged patients. The logic applied to these studies is predicated on the following notion: If dominance of the right hemisphere for emotional processing in normal subjects reflects actual cerebral mechanisms, then patients with right-hemisphere lesions should exhibit more impairment in emotional processing than those with left-hemisphere lesions.

In the first section of the chapter ("Neuropsychology of Emotion"), the neuropsychology of emotion is discussed with respect to hemispheric specialization (Part I), factors affecting lateralization (Part II), and intrahemispheric factors (Part III). Part I raises theoretical issues regarding communication channel and processing mode and then reviews the extant literature involving the perception and expression of emotion. Within this review, studies using facial, prosodic, or lexical procedures in normal or brain-damaged subjects are presented. Part II discusses some of the factors affecting hemispheric specialization for emotion, including valence, gender, and handedness. Finally, Part III discusses the findings regarding intrahemispheric factors (e.g., caudality of lesion site) among brain-damaged patients with right- or left-sided lesions. In the second section of this chapter ("Description of Experiments"), the following sets of experiments are described: facial asymmetry studies of normal subjects and facial emotional expression studies of brain-damaged subjects. In the third section ("Summary and Discussion"), the experiments are summarized and the results interpreted. Finally, in the last section of the chapter ("Implications"), implications of this work are suggested in both a clinical (Part I) and theoretical vein (Part II). In Part I, rehabilitation possibilities with stroke patients are discussed. In Part II, the application of the procedures described in this chapter is discussed as relevant to unraveling the neuropsychological mechanisms underlying psychiatric disorders. Also in Part II, our own experiments with depressed and schizophrenic subjects are described.

To aid the reader in interpreting the data described in the experimental sections of this chapter, three tables are included with details and information relevant to our experiments with normal (Table 7.1), brain-damaged (Table 7.2), and psychiatric (Table 7.3) subjects.

Communication Channels. Communication of emotion is a multi-determined behavior involving several different modes or channels (e.g., facial, intonational, lexical/speech content, gestural) that interact in complex ways. Clinical disorders of emotional processing may be observed in any or all of these channels. Early work with normal populations (e.g., LoCastro, 1972; Mehrabian & Weiner, 1967) suggested that facial and intonational channels are more effective than speech content in communicating emotion, but more recent data indicate that the channel that contributes the most information varies according to the particular subject characteristics and situations under examination (Ekman, Friesen, O'Sullivan, & Scherer, 1980).

Although some studies of neurologically normal subjects have simultaneously examined multiple channels of emotional communication (e.g., Ekman et al., 1980), studies of neurological subjects typically have examined a single channel of communication, such as facial expression (Borod, Koff, Perlman Lorch, & Nicholas, 1986a; Bruyer, 1981; Buck & Duffy, 1980; Kolb & Milner, 1981), prosody (Danly, Shapiro, & Gardner, 1982; Ross, 1981; Ross, Harney, de Lacoste, & Purdy, 1981; Tucker,

Watson, & Heilman, 1977; Weintraub, Mesulam, & Kramer, 1981), or speech content (Foldi, Cicone, & Gardner, 1983; Weinstein & Kahn, 1955; Weisenberg & McBride, 1935). To our knowledge, there have been very few systematic experimental studies of multiple channels of emotional processing in brain-damaged populations. In a case study of two right brain-damaged (RBD) subjects, Ross and Mesulam (1979) observed the loss of affective prosody, facial expression, and gesturing. In two recent experimental studies, Benowitz et al., (1983) examined three channels of affective perception (face, voice, gesture) and Borod, Koff, Perlman Lorch, & Nicholas (1985) examined three channels of affective expression (face, intonation, speech content) in subjects with unilateral brain damage and in normal controls. In both studies, RBDs had deficits in processing facial and vocal affect relative to left brain-damaged (LBD) subjects. In addition, the Borod et al. study explored the relationship among the three channels. Although the utilization of facial and intonational channels was significantly correlated for all subjects, both channels were related to the speech channel only for the normal control (NC) subjects.

Processing Modes. Although a substantial number of studies concerning hemispheric specialization for the expression and perception of emotion have been conducted with normal subjects, relatively fewer investigations have been carried out with brain-damaged patients. Among the studies of brain-damaged subjects (for review, see Ruckdeschel-Hibbard, Gordon, & Diller, 1986), most are concerned with deficits in the perception of emotion. Studies of expressive emotional deficits in brain-damaged patients have been much less common. The relationship between expression and perception is of general interest and is stimulated by the debate in neurolinguistics concerning the comprehension and production of speech.

Although there has been a sizeable body of research concerning speech production and perception in left brain-damaged patients (e.g., Goodglass & Kaplan, 1983), only two studies to date have addressed the relationship between expression and perception of emotion in right brain-damaged patients. In an examination of the prosodic channel, Ross (1981) described 10 subjects with lesions of the right hemisphere in whom dissociations between expressive and perceptual deficits occurred: Subjects with exclusively anterior pathology showed expressive deficits but no comprehension deficits; those with posterior pathology showed only comprehension deficits. In an examination of the facial channel, Borod et al. (1986a) studied expression and perception in RBD, LBD, and NC subjects. When correlations between these two modes were computed, no systematic relationships emerged for any of the individual subject groups or for the total group. The lack of significant correlations between expression and perception variables suggests that these two types of performance may be tapping relatively separate aspects of affective processing.

Perception Studies

A variety of studies, employing diverse methodologies and stimuli, have supported a right-hemisphere advantage for the perception of emotional information in normal subjects. Dependent variables in these studies are of two major types—ear differences during dichotic listening and visual-field differences during tachistoscopic viewing. As a function of the primarily contralateral innervation of the central nervous system (E. Gardner, 1975), superiority of the left side (e.g., left ear, left visual-field) implies relatively greater activation or involvement of the right hemisphere. For the facial channel, tachistoscopic studies have demonstrated a left visual-field advantage for perceiving emotional facial expressions in stimuli ranging from line drawings to photographs (Buchtel, Campari, DeRisio, & Rota, 1978; Hansch & Pirozzolo, 1980; Ley & Bryden, 1979; McKeever & Dixon, 1981; Strauss & Moscovitch, 1981; Suberi & Mc-Keever, 1977). This left visual-field superiority for processing emotional faces appears to be independent of the left visual-field superiority for face recognition (Ley & Bryden, 1979; Suberi & McKeever, 1977) and for visuospatial perception (McKeever & Dixon, 1981). For the prosodic channel, dichotic listening experiments have produced a left-ear advantage for processing the emotional tone of natural speech (Haggard & Parkinson, 1971; Safer & Leventhal, 1977), nonverbal vocalizations (Carmon & Nachson, 1973; King & Kimura, 1972), and musical passages (Bryden, Ley, & Sugarman, 1982). For the lexical channel, Graves, Landis, & Goodglass (1981) reported that male subjects processed emotional words more accurately than nonemotional words in the left visual field, whereas neither males nor females showed differences between the two types of words in the right visual field.

In studies of the perception of emotion in brain-damaged subjects, subjects typically are required to discriminate between two emotionally toned stimuli (same-difference judgments) or to identify the emotion being expressed in the stimulus. For the facial channel, clinical studies have demonstrated that deficits in the perception of emotional facial expressions are associated more frequently with pathology of the right, rather than the left, hemisphere (Benowitz, 1980; Borod et al., 1986a; Bowers, Bauer, Coslett, & Heilman, 1985; Cicone, Wapner, & Gardner, 1980; DeKosky, Heilman, Bowers, & Valenstein, 1980; Etcoff, 1984). For the prosodic channel, patients with right hemisphere lesions have been shown to be impaired in making judgments about the emotional tone of spoken sentences (Heilman, Scholes, & Watson, 1975; Tucker et al., 1977). For the lexical channel, Wechsler (1973) reported that right brain-damaged patients showed greater impairment of recall for emotionally charged prose than left brain-damaged patients. In related studies, emotionally loaded lexical materials have been shown to facilitate the performance of aphasic patients on tasks involving auditory comprehension (Boller, Cole, Vrtunski, Patterson, & Kim, 1979), writing, oral reading (Landis, Graves, & Goodglass, 1982), praxis (Borod, Perlman Lorch, Koff, & Nicholas, 1987), and speech output (Hughlings-Jackson, 1874). Such findings have been interpreted as supporting a dominant role for the right hemisphere in the perception of emotionally toned lexical stimuli. Because these aphasic patients have left-hemisphere damage, the argument is that the right hemisphere is somehow able to take over these functions or possibly is able to facilitate the performance of the compromised left hemisphere.

Expression Studies

When expression has been studied in normals, subjects are typically instructed to produce expressions upon command; in brain-damaged subjects, conclusions about emotional expression often are based on clinical observations or on experimental paradigms utilizing spontaneous elicitation procedures. By definition, deliberate, or posed, movements are those that are clearly intended by the individual or requested of him or her; involuntary, or spontaneous, movements are those unintended movements that arise as part of an instinctual reaction to an appropriately evocative situation (Myers, 1976). Although it is relatively simple to elicit posed expressions (e.g., by using oral command), it is considerably more difficult to devise elicitation procedures for spontaneous expressions. Further, the techniques for eliciting spontaneous emotion tend to be cumbersome (e.g., slide-viewing [Borod et al., 1985; Buck & Duffy, 1980]), indirect (e.g., observed while the patient is undergoing neuropsychological testing [Kolb & Milner, 1981]), and not always amenable for use in clinical settings. The distinction between posed and spontaneous expression is believed to be important because of neuroanatomical evidence that voluntary (posed) behavior is contralaterally innervated by cortical structures through the pyramidal system; involuntary (spontaneous) behavior is presumed to be bilaterally innervated by subcortical structures (Kahn, 1964; Kuypers, 1958; Tschiassny, 1953) through the extrapyramidal system.

To study expression in normal subjects, the communication channel that lends itself most readily to laterality paradigms is the facial one. In normal right-handed adults, studies have documented that the left side of the face or "hemiface" moves more extensively (Borod & Caron, 1980; Borod, Caron, & Koff, 1981a; Borod, Koff, & White, 1983) and appears more intense (Campbell, 1978; Heller & Levy, 1981; Rubin & Rubin, 1980; Sackeim & Gur, 1978) than the right hemiface during emotional expression. This appears to be the case during both posed and spontaneous expression (Borod, Koff, & White, 1983; Dopson, Beckwith, Tucker, & Bullard-Bates, 1984; Moscovitch & Olds, 1982; cf. Ekman, Hager & Friesen, 1981; Hager & Ekman, 1985). The greater involvement of the left hemiface in emotional expression is consistent with the dominant role for the right cerebral hemisphere observed in emotional perception. This conclusion follows from the belief that the face, and particularly its lower portion, is predominantly innervated by the contralateral hemisphere. The findings for facial asymmetry are independent of hemiface size (Jaeger, 1984; Koff, Borod, & White, 1981; Sackeim & Gur, 1980) and hemiface mobility (Borod & Koff, 1983). (For reviews of this literature, see Borod & Koff [1983], Campbell [1986], Hager [1983], Rinn [1984], Sackeim & Gur [1983]).

In brain-damaged populations, there are fewer studies of emotional expression than there are of perception, and many of these have been case studies or anecdotal reports. For the facial channel, subjects with unilateral right-hemisphere pathology have shown impairments in the expression of spontaneous (Borod et al., 1985, 1986a; Buck & Duffy, 1980; Ross & Mesulam, 1979) and posed (Borod et al., 1986a) emotion relative to patients with unilateral left-hemisphere pathology or normal controls (cf. Heilman & Valenstein, 1979). For the prosodic channel, the majority of studies have demonstrated deficits in emotional expression in patients with right-hemisphere lesions, when compared to those with left-hemisphere damage, under spontaneous (Borod et al., 1985; Ross & Mesulam, 1979) and posed (Danly et al., 1982; Ross, 1981; Ross et al., 1981; Tucker et al., 1977; Weintraub et al., 1981) conditions. Using the case study approach, Ross and Mesulam (1979) described two subjects who lost the ability to spontaneously express emotion through speech after right-hemisphere damage; their voices became monotonous and colorless and lacked emotional inflection. For the lexical channel, a special role for the right hemisphere in the mediation of emotional speech was suggested as early as 1874, with Hughlings-Jackson's observation (1874) that emotional words, for example, curses, could be selectively spared in aphasics who had lost the ability to use propositional speech. In a more recent study (Borod et al., 1985), oral expression of emotion in right brain-damaged patients was more inappropriate, propositional, and descriptive (as opposed to feeling oriented) than in left brain-damaged patients.

Factors Affecting
Lateralization of Emotion

Emotional Valence

Although there appears to be strong empirical support for right–hemisphere dominance for emotion, there is also some evidence (e.g., Borod, Caron, & Koff, 1981b; Reuter-Lorenz & Davidson, 1981; Sackeim et al., 1982) to suggest differential hemispheric specialization for emotion as a function of valence or pleasantness level. This has been termed *the valence hypothesis*. In these studies, based on observations of patients with unilateral lesions (e.g., Gainotti, 1972) and clinical observations following unilateral carotid artery injections of sodium amytal (e.g., Perria, Rosadini, & Rossi, 1961; Terzian, 1964), negative emotion is primarily associated with the right hemisphere and positive emotion with the left or both hemispheres (Dimond & Farrington, 1977; Sackeim et al., 1982; Tucker, 1981). Using heart rate (Dimond & Farrington, 1977), electromyographic (EMG) (Schwartz, Ahern, & Brown, 1979), and lateral eye movement (Ahern & Schwartz, 1979) indices, some researchers have concluded that the right hemisphere may be more engaged by negative than positive emotions and the left hemisphere by positive emotions. In studies of EEG activation, valence appears to be more salient for the frontal than for the parietal region, such that there is greater right frontal involvement in negative emotion (Davidson, Schwartz, Saron, Bennett, & Goleman, 1978; Karlin, Weinapple, Rochford, & Goldstein, 1979; Tucker, Stenslie, Roth, & Shearer, 1981) and greater left frontal involvement in positive emotion (Davidson & Fox, 1982; Davidson et al., 1978); see Davidson (1985) for review of this literature. One variant of the valence hypothesis holds that negative affect is associated with the right hemisphere and positive affect with both hemispheres (Borod & Caron, 1980; Borod, Koff, & White, 1983; Sackeim & Gur, 1978). A review of a number of studies concerned with the effect of valence on facial asymmetry in normals (Borod & Koff, 1984) supports this hypothesis; most of these studies showed the left hemiface (and by implication, the right cerebral hemisphere) to be involved more frequently than the right hemiface in the expression of negative emotion. For the expression of positive emotion, however, the majority of studies found that the left and right hemifaces were involved with relatively equal frequency (implying bilateral mediation of positive emotions). A second variant of the valence hypothesis is that there is right–hemisphere specialization for affect perception and differential hemispheric specialization for affect expression (Davidson, 1985; Hirschmann & Safer, 1982).

Researchers have speculated about the way in which these differential effects of valence might operate. Kinsbourne (1980) and Davidson (1985) have made an argument for right-hemisphere involvement in withdrawal (i.e., negative) behaviors and left-hemisphere involvement in approach (i.e., positive) behaviors. Borod, Koff, and Buck (1986) suggested that the quality of the decision one has to make in the case of negative emotions is different than for positive ones. If negative emotions are linked with survival—that is, if they promote retreat from a dangerous situation—then a system would be required that is receptive to multimodal information, only a portion of which would be necessary in order that a decision to retreat be made. Resolution of fine detail would not be necessary in order to respond; rather, one would need to be able to quickly scan and evaluate the situation. This type of behavior seems to be linked more to Gestalt, synthetic processing than to discrete, focused analysis. Gestalt processing is associated more closely with the right than the left hemisphere.

Although many studies with normals have been concerned with valence, valence has received little attention in studies of brain-damaged patients (but see Borod et al., 1985, 1986a; Buck & Duffy, 1980). Such studies might in fact provide us with a way to test the alternative hypotheses concerning the effect of valence on the processing of emotion. If the valence hypothesis were operative, then RBDs might show a selective deficit for negative emotion and LBDs for positive emotion.

Gender Differences

Another factor that has been purported to affect hemispheric specialization for emotion is the gender of the subject. Although there is some controversy about the role of gender as a mediating variable in laterality experiments (e.g., Safer, 1981; Schweitzer & Chacko, 1980), there is evidence that males and females exhibit different patterns of lateralization. Studies of linguistic processing, for example, have suggested that females have more bilateral representation than males (Inglis & Lawson, 1981; McGlone, 1980). Studies of emotional processing, however, have suggested that females may be more lateralized than males (Davidson, Schwartz, Pugash, & Bromfield, 1976; Ladavas, Umilta, & Ricci-Bitti, 1980; McKeever & Dixon, 1981; Strauss & Moscovitch, 1981; but see Graves et al., 1981). Also, gender differences as a function of emotional valence have been reported. In some studies (Borod, Koff, & White, 1983; Strauss & Kaplan, 1980), females were less lateralized for positive than negative emotions; in another study (Borod & Caron, 1980), males were less lateralized. Finally, there is evidence to suggest that females are better "senders" (i.e., communicators) of emotion (Buck, Miller, & Caul, 1974) and are more expressive nonverbally (Argyle, Salter, Nicholson, Williams, & Burgess, 1970) than males. Although we do not understand what these gender differences reflect (e.g., they could be a function of anatomical structural differences, interpersonal factors, or display rules), they must be taken into account in studies of emotional processing.

Handedness

Considerable evidence exists that left-handers are less lateralized for linguistic functions than are right-handers (for review, see Borod & Goodglass, 1980), but the relationship between handedness and lateralization for emotion is not yet clear. At this point, a number of studies of right hemisphere processes, for instance, face perception (Gilbert, 1973), emotional tone perception (Safer & Leventhal, 1977), and conversion reactions (Stern, 1977), find that behavioral laterality is unrelated to handedness. It may be the case that certain nonverbal functions are based in the right hemisphere, regardless of the localization of other lateralized functions, such as hand preference.

To date, the literature on facial expression of emotion seems to support this finding. No relationship to handedness has been demonstrated for spontaneous emotional expression (Lynn & Lynn, 1938, 1943; Strauss, Wada, & Kosaka, 1983), posed emotional expression (Borod, et al., 1981a; Borod, Koff, & Caron, 1983; Campbell, 1979; Heller & Levy, 1981), nonemotional unilateral facial movement (Koff, et al., 1981), resting face asymmetries (Rappaport & Friendly, 1978), side of trigeminal neuralgia (i.e., facial pain) (Rothman & Wepsic, 1974), and the perceived similarity of each hemiface to the full face (Lindzey, Prince, & Wright, 1952). Though there are findings to the contrary (e.g., Rubin & Rubin, 1980; Moscovitch & Olds, 1982; Chaurasia & Goswami, 1975), the bulk of the evidence suggests that lateralization for facial affective expression functions is not related to handedness and is probably functionally independent of language and handedness.

Intrahemispheric Factors

In addition to supporting interhemispheric differences (right vs. left hemisphere) in emotional processing, the literature also suggests some intrahemispheric (anterior vs. posterior) differences. There has been speculation about the existence of an "emotional processor" in the right hemisphere analogous to the one proposed for language processing in the left hemisphere (e.g., Goodglass & Kaplan, 1983). Such a model would hold that expression/production is associated with anterior (i.e., pre–Rolandic) structures and that perception/comprehension is related to posterior (i.e., post–Rolandic) structures. Data from some studies with brain–damaged subjects are consistent with the notion that perception and expression are separate dimensions of affective processing. Most of these data come from studies of subjects with right-hemisphere pathology, although there also is support from studies with left brain-damaged patients.

Right-Hemisphere Pathology

For the facial channel, Borod et al. (1985) found that spontaneous expression of facial emotion was more impaired in patients with right anterior (i.e., frontal) than right posterior lesions. In contrast, perception of facial emotion has been reported to be impaired with right posterior (i.e., temporal or parietal) pathology (Benowitz et al., 1983; Etcoff, 1984). For the prosodic channel, Ross (1981) reported that the expression of prosody is impaired with right frontal lesions. In parallel with the findings for the facial channel, Ross (1981) and Heilman et al. (1975) found that the comprehension of prosody is associated with right posterior (i.e., temporal or parietal) structures. Studies bearing on the lexical channel have not yet been carried out. If differential organization for expressive versus perceptual behaviors exists, such information might be very useful in the diagnosis of clinical syndromes, working with cerebrovascular patients and designing rehabilitation and treatment studies.

Left-Hemisphere Pathology

Although most studies of emotional processing deficits have implicated the right hemisphere, emotional processing deficits also have been found in aphasics as a function of lesion site (e.g., Robinson, Kubos, Starr, Rao, & Thomas, 1984). Careful observations of emotional behavior in aphasics indicate that anterior aphasics often display illness-appropriate (though often extreme) emotional reactions, whereas posterior aphasics appear unconcerned with, or unaware of, their illness (Benson, 1973; Brown, 1984; Gainotti, 1972; Robinson & Benson, 1981). For the facial channel, Borod et al. (1986a) reported that patients with left posterior lesions (four Wernickes, two Conduction aphasics) were more impaired in expressing facial emotion than patients with left anterior, or anterior plus posterior, lesions. Although it might be argued that auditory comprehension difficulties underlie the emotional deficits observed in posterior aphasics, there actually was a significant inverse correlation between auditory comprehension and facial expression accuracy; that is, the poorer the comprehension, the more accurate the facial expression. For the prosodic channel, aphasic patients with posterior lesions (i.e., Wernicke's) show aberrant patterns of speech prosody in comparison to aphasics with more anterior lesions (i.e., Broca's) (Danly et al., 1982; Foldi, Cicone, & Gardner, 1983; Heilman et al., 1975; Packard, 1980; Ross & Mesulam, 1979; Schlanger, Schlanger, & Gerstman, 1976). As was the case for the right hemisphere, the lexical channel has not been studied within the context of intrahemispheric differences.

DESCRIPTION OF EXPERIMENTS

In this section, we review our studies on facial asymmetry in normal subjects and on facial emotional expression in brain-damaged patients with unilateral lesions. As we proceed, neuropsychological mechanisms underlying emotional processing are suggested. In addition, techniques for the assessment of emotional processing in normal subjects and in neurological populations are described. Summaries of these studies are presented in Tables 7.1 (Normal) and 7.2 (Brain-Damaged). As each study is presented, the reader should consult the appropriate table.

Studies of Facial Asymmetry in Normal Subjects

Our own work began with the observation that the two sides of the face, or hemifaces, often demonstrate striking asymmetries for extent of movement and for intensity of expression. We wondered whether these asymmetries were systematic, and, if so, what their relationship to other lateralized functions might be. We wished to pursue the implication of such asymmetries for the neuropsychological study of facial emotional expression, particularly in light of the fact that the lower portion of the face is predominantly innervated by the contralateral cerebral hemisphere (Kuypers, 1958). Because voluntary facial expression presumably involves cortical control, we reasoned that facial asymmetry might provide another window onto brain/behavior relationships. Also, if facial asymmetry proved to be a reliable phenomenon, we believed that it would provide a method for the neuropsychological study of emotional expression in the normal subject.

We begin by reviewing a series of studies we have been conducting on facial asymmetry in normal subjects utilizing a range of methodological techniques: (a) whole faces rated from videotapes in motion (Borod & Caron, 1980; Borod & Koff, 1983); (b) hemifaces rated from videotape stills (Borod, Kent, Koff, Martin, & Alpert, 1988); and (c) hemifaces rated from photographic composites (Moreno, Borod, Welkowitz, & Alpert, 1988). Studies controlling for peripheral factors that could possibly influence facial asymmetry findings are also described. (See Table 7.1.)

TABLE 7.1

Results from Experiments on Normal Adult Subjects

	Study	Characteristics[a] of		Elicitation Condition		Facial Stimuli			Emotion Type[b]		
No.	Authors & Year	Posers	Judges	Posed	Spontaneous	Part of Face	Type of Face	Medium	Positive	Negative	Neutral
1.	Borod & Caron (1980); Borod, Caron, & Koff (1981a)	19 RHF 12 RHM 12 LHF 8 LHM	2 RHF 1 LHF	✔	—[c]	Whole	Natural	Video	H,M,X	A,C,D,F,S	—
2.	Borod, Koff, & White (1983)	19 RHF 18 RHM	3 RHF	✔	✔	Whole	Natural	Video	H,X	D,S	—
3.	Borod, Kent et al. (1988)	16 RHM	1 RHM 1 RHF	✔	—	Hemi	Natural	Video[d]	H,P,X	A,C,D,F,S	N
4.	Moreno et al. (1988)	90 RHF	3 RHF	✔	—	Hemi	Composite	Photo	H,P	D,S	N

	Scoring System			Are individual expressions significantly different from each other?	Are positive emotions significantly different from negative emotions?	Significantly Left-Sided		
Study No.	Nature	Range Low	Range High			All Expressions	Positive Emotions	Negative Emotions
1.	Asymmetry	−7(left)	+7(right)	No	—	Yes	—	—
2.	Asymmetry	−7(left)	+7(right)	—	Males: No Females: Yes	Yes	Yes	Yes
3.	Intensity	+1(min.)	+7(max.)	No	No	Yes	No	Yes
4.	Intensity	+1(min.)	+7(max.)	No	—	Yes	—	—

[a]RH = right-hand, LH = left-handed, F = female, and M = male.

[b]A = anger, C = confusion, D = disgust, F = fear, H = happiness, M = amusement, N = neutral, P = pleasant surprise, S = sadness, and X = sexual arousal.

[c]not done, included, tested, or applicable.

[d]Static video.

Whole Face Ratings from Videotapes in Motion

In our first study (Borod & Caron, 1980; Borod et al., 1981a), facial asymmetry was examined during posed expression of emotion and related to traditional measures of lateral dominance. Fifty-one right- and left-handed normal adults were coached with verbal imagery and visual examples to deliberately produce eight different facial emotional expressions (three positive, five negative). Subjects were videotaped while posing each expression. Later, judges rated each expression for extent of muscular involvement in the lower face from extreme left-sided (a score of −7) to extreme right-sided (a score of +7), with 0 for symmetry. Slow motion replay was used to locate the film frame that demonstrated maximum or peak expression. Overall, the left hemiface was significantly more involved in facial expression than the right hemiface. There were no differences as a function of handedness (70% of both handedness groups were left-sided), and there were no differences among expressions. The finding of greater left hemiface involvement supported the notion of a special role for the right hemisphere in emotional expression.

In light of the possibility that the two hemispheres might be differentially specialized as a function of emotional valence, asymmetry findings for individual expressions were examined on a post hoc basis. All negative expressions (disapproval, confusion, disgust, grief) but one (horror) were significantly left-sided, but the more positive ones (happiness, flirtation, clowning) were not significantly lateralized. When factor analytic techniques were applied to these asymmetry data (Borod, Caron, & Koff, 1981b), one of the primary factors reflected a positive/negative dimension.

Our second study (Borod, Koff, & White, 1983; Borod & Koff, 1983) was designed to directly examine the relationship between emotional valence and facial asymmetry and to compare facial asymmetry during posed and spontaneous conditions. Thirty-seven right-handed normal adults were videotaped while producing five emotional expressions. In the posed condition, subjects were requested to deliberately produce facial expressions to verbal command and to visual imagery. In the spontaneous condition, subjects responded to emotionally laden slides (Buck, 1978). Expressions were later rated for asymmetry. Once again the left hemiface was significantly more involved in facial expression than the right hemiface, regardless of condition. Although there were no significant differences in asymmetry among the five expressions, analyses by valence produced differences. As in the previous study, negative expressions were consistently and significantly left-sided, whereas positive expressions were not systematically lateralized.

These studies suggested that the right hemisphere was dominant for emotional expression, especially when the emotion was negatively toned. Our review of the facial asymmetry literature (Borod & Koff, 1984), which paid special attention to valence and elicitation conditions, found 13 studies examining posed and seven studies examining spontaneous expression. When considering the findings for negative emotions, the left hemiface (and by implication, the right cerebral hemisphere) was involved more frequently than the right hemiface in the production of negative emotion. For positive emotion, the left and right hemifaces were involved with relatively equal frequency, suggesting bilateral involvement in the expression of positive emotion. Taken together, these findings provide support for that variant of the valence hypothesis that suggests right hemisphere involvement in negative emotion and bilateral control of positive emotion.

Hemiface Ratings from Videotape Stills

Our third study (Borod et al., 1988) also was designed to examine facial asymmetry during the expression of positive and negative emotions. In addition, several key methodological factors in the study of facial asymmetry were considered. These were (a) the nature of the elicitation condition, (b) the character of the facial stimuli, and (c) the orientation in which the stimuli are viewed for ratings. Subjects were 16 neurologically healthy right-handed adult males. Subjects were videotaped individually while posing nine facial expressions (happiness, pleasant surprise, sexual arousal, sadness, anger, fear, disgust, confusion, indifference) under two separate conditions (verbal command and visual imitation). Asymmetry ratings were made of videotape stills of left and right hemifaces viewed separately, using a 7-point intensity scale from minimal to maximal. The vertical midline of each face was determined from four facial markers: the midpoint between the eyes, the center of the upper lip, the midpoint of the chin, and the center of the nose. The hemifaces of eight posers were rated in the normal orientation; those of the other eight posers were rated in the mirror-reversed orientation. There were no effects on the asymmetry ratings of valence, elicitation condition, or orientation. Overall, expressions were produced significantly more intensely on the left than the right side of the face. This finding is consistent with the hypothesis that the right cerebral hemisphere is dominant for the expression of facial emotion, regardless of valence.

Hemiface Ratings from Photographic Stills

The fourth study (Moreno et al., 1988) was designed to examine changes in facial asymmetry as a function of age using the composite photograph technique. Subjects were 30 young adult (ages 25–39), 30 middle-aged adult (ages 45–59), and 30 older adult (ages 65–79) right-handed females. Subjects were photographed while posing four facial emotional expressions (happiness, pleasant surprise, sadness, disgust). Composite facial stimuli were made from right hemifaces (original, mirror reversed) and from left hemifaces (original, mirror reversed). In order to create the composites, the vertical midline was determined by four markers (Weber, 1983); these were: (a) midpoint of the distance between external canthi of the eyes, (b) midpoint of the indentation above the upper lip, (c) the intersection of two arcs drawn above the face from the external canthi, and (d) the intersection of two arcs drawn below the face from the external canthi. Three judges rated the composite photos for intensity from 1 (minimal) to 7 (maximal). The left hemiface was rated as significantly more intense than the right hemiface, regardless of the valence of the emotion or the age of the posers. Because the left hemiface is associated with the right hemisphere, this finding again suggests the overall dominance of the right hemisphere for emotion, regardless of valence.

Controlling for Peripheral Factors

Although the finding of left-sided facial asymmetry was generally ascribed to central (i.e., cerebral) mechanisms, the possibility existed that it could be a function of more peripheral factors. For example, were the two sides of the face to differ in degree of muscular activity, the side with the greater mobility might be perceived as more expressive. Also, were the hemifaces to differ in size, the expression mapped on the smaller side might be perceived as more extensive. To rule out such confounds, three studies have been carried out in our laboratory.

In the first study (Borod & Koff, 1983), 37 normal adults were videotaped while producing emotional facial expressions and while executing nonemotional unilateral facial movements. Although the left, relative to the right, hemiface was rated as moving more extensively during emotional expression and as being more facile during nonemotional movement, these two asymmetry ratings were not correlated. In the second study (Jaeger, 1984), facial emotional expressions were rated for asymmetry and for size from composite photographs in 30 normal adults. There was no significant relationship between the two measures. In the third study (Koff, Borod, & White, 1983), hemiface size and mobility were examined in 42 right- and left-handed normal adults. Size was measured from photographs of the full face, and mobility from videotapes of unilateral facial movements. Although the right hemiface was measured as larger and the left hemiface judged to be more facile, again, the two asymmetry ratings were not related to each other. These findings suggested that it could be coincidental rather than causal that emotional expression distributed over the generally smaller and more mobile left hemiface appeared to be more extensive and/or intense.

Studies of Facial Emotional Expression in Brain-Damaged Patients

To provide neuroanatomical verification for the findings in normal subjects, the following set of studies examined facial emotional expression in focal lesion patients with right- or left-hemisphere pathology and in matched normal controls. Five aspects of these studies are described: (a) evaluation of general performance (Borod et al., 1986a; Kent, Borod, Koff, Welkowitz, & Alpert, 1988), (b) qualitative performance (Borod et al., 1986a), (c) specific dimensions of performance (Borod, Koff, Perlman Lorch, & Nicholas, 1988), (d) controls for deficits of facial movement (Borod et al., 1988), and (e) facial asymmetry (Borod, Koff, Perlman Lorch, & Nicholas, 1986b). (See Table 7.2.)

Fifteen males with unilateral left (LBD) and 12 males with unilateral right (RBD) brain damage served as subjects; 16 normal males (NC) served as controls. Patients were from the neurology wards of the Boston V.A. Medical Center. All subjects were right-handed by self- or family report; the three groups did not differ on formal assessment of lateral dominance (Coren, Porac, & Duncan, 1979).

The three groups were similar on demographic variables, with an overall mean age of 57 years (S.D. = 8.1), 13 years of education (S.D. = 2.8), and an occupational level of 3.9 (S.D. = 1.5) as measured by the Hollingshead-Redlich Scale (Hollingshead & Redlich, 1958). On this scale, 1 represents the highest level and 7, the lowest level; thus, the typical socioeconomic occupational level was that of a middle-class white-collar worker. For age, the mean ($\overline{X}$) years and standard deviation (S.D.) were 55.0 ± 8.7 for RBDs, 55.7 ± 7.5 for LBDs, and 59.1 ± 8.1 for NCs. For education, the $\overline{X}$ years and S.D. were 11.8 ± 2.9 for RBDs, 12.5 ± 2.9 for LBDs, and 14.1 ± 2.3 for NCs. For occupation, the $\overline{X}$ level and S.D. were 4.0 ± 1.2 for RBDs, 3.6 ± 1.7 for LBDs, and 4.2 ± 1.6 for NCs. For time since illness onset, the $\overline{X}$ months and S.D. were 21.7 ± 31.4 for RBDs and 35.7 ± 46.5 for LBDs. When one-way analyses of variance for Subject Group (RBD, LBD, and/or NC) were performed on each of these demographic variables, none of the group differences were significant. Because there were group differences, though not significant, demographic variables were correlated with facial expression variables (Kent et al., 1988). Several correlations for education were significant, whereas those for age, occupation, and months post onset were not. Holding education constant through analysis of covariance, the results for the facial emotional expression variables remained the same.

Patients were tested at least 1 month after the onset of illness (median = 9 months); the two groups of brain-damaged subjects did not differ significantly in number of months post onset. Patients were eligible for the study if their lesions were the result of a single episode cerebrovascular accident (e.g., occlusion, embolism, thrombosis, hemorrhagic infarct) and if there was a negative history of psychiatric disorder, psychotropic drug treatment, or secondary neurological disorder (e.g., epilepsy, dementia). Evidence of the unilateral and focal nature of the lesion was confirmed by CT scan in all but two cases, where clinical data from neurological examination were used. Fourteen (63%) of the patients had lesions restricted to the cortex and/or subcortical white matter, whereas the remainder had cortical lesions extending to subcortical grey matter structures (e.g., basal ganglia, thalamus). The percentages of patients with lesions in a particular region, for RBDs and LBDs, respectively, were: frontal–58%, 60%; parietal–92%, 67%; temporal–58%, 67%; occipital–17%, 7%; subcortical white matter–83%, 60%; and subcortical grey structures–50%, 27%. At the time of testing, the majority of each patient group had clinically-determined deficits on the side contralateral to their lesion. These deficits were hemiplegia (58% of RBDs, 60% of LBDs), facial paralysis (75% of RBDs, 80% of LBDs), and visual-field loss (58% of RBDs, 47% of LBDs). Using the Fisher exact probability test to examine the number of RBDs and LBDs with or without a lesion in each brain region *and* with or without each motor-sensory deficit, none of the comparisons were significant.

Although all of the LBDs were aphasic (three Brocas, two Mixed Nonfluents, two Globals, two Conductions, four Wernickes, two Unclassifieds), all had adequate auditory comprehension (mean Boston Diagnostic Aphasia Examination [Goodglass & Kaplan, 1983] z-score = −0.88, S.D. = 0.7) and cognitive functioning (mean WAIS Performance IQ [Wechsler, 1958] = 94, S.D. = 16) to perform the experimental tasks. All subjects had sufficient visuoperceptual skill, as assessed by ability to correctly describe two practice slides, Thematic Apperception Test Card 3GF (Murray, 1958) and a scene from a kindergarten classroom (Buck, 1978).

General Performance

To study the expression of emotion, subjects were videotaped as they viewed positive and negative emotionally toned slides (spontaneous condition) and as they deliberately produced positive (happiness, sexual

TABLE 7.2
Results from Experiments on Brain-Damaged Patients

No.	Study Authors & Year	Characteristics[a] of Posers[b]	Characteristics[a] of Judges	Elicitation Condition Posed	Elicitation Condition Spontaneous	Facial Stimuli Part of Face	Facial Stimuli Type of Face	Facial Stimuli Medium	Emotion Type[c] Positive	Emotion Type[c] Negative
1.	Borod et al. (1986a)	*RHM* 12 RBDs 15 LBDs 16 NCs	2 RHF	✔	✔	Whole	Natural	Video	*Posed* H,P,X *Spontaneous* H,X	*Posed* A,C,D, F,S C,D,S
2.	Borod, Koff et al. (1988)	same as above	2 RHF	✔	✔	Whole	Natural	Video	Same as above	Same as above
3.	Kent et al. (in press)	same as above	1 RHM 3 RHF	✔	—[e]	Whole	Natural	Video[f]	Same as above for posed	
4.	Borod et al. (1986b)	*RHM* 12 RBDs 15 LBDs	2 RHF	✔	✔	Whole	Natural	Video	*Posed* H *Spontaneous* H	

TABLE 7.2
(continued)

Study No.	Scoring System — Nature	Range — Low	Range — High	Significant Differences Among Groups	Group Comparisons via Post Hoc Tests	Group by Condition Interaction	Group by Valence Interaction	Group Comparisons — Positive Emotions	Group Comparisons — Negative Emotions
1.	Accuracy	0 (unsuccessful)	1 (successful)	Yes	NCs > RBDs, LBDs > RBDs	No	Yes[d]	NCs > RBDs, LBDs > RBDs	NCs > RBDs
2.	Responsivity	0 (no response)	1 (response)	Yes	NCs > RBDs, LBDs > RBDs	No	No	—	—
	Appropriateness	0 (inappropriate)	1 (appropriate)	Yes	NCs > RBDs	No	Yes	NCs > RBDs, LBDs > RBDs	None
	Intensity	1 (minimal)	7 (maximal)	No	—	No	No	—	—
3.	Category accuracy	0 (inaccurate)	1 (accurate)	Yes	NCs > RBDs	—	Yes*	NCs > RBDs, LBDs > RBDs	None
	Valence accuracy	0 (incorrect)	2 (correct)	Yes	NCs > RBDs, LBDs > RBDs	—	Yes	NCs > RBDs, LBDs > RBDs	None
	Intensity	1 (minimal)	7 (maximal)	No	—	—	Yes	LBDs > RBDs, LBDs > NCs	None
4.	Asymmetry	1 (left)	7 (right)	Yes	RBDs > LBDs	No	—	—	—
	Intensity	1 (minimal)	7 (maximal)	Yes	LBDs > RBDs	No	—	—	—

[a] RH = right-handed, F = female, and M = male.
[b] RBD = right brain-damaged, LBD = left brain-damaged, and NC = normal control.
[c] A = anger, C = confusion, D = disgust, F = fear, H = happiness, P = pleasant surprise, S = sadness, and X = sexual arousal.
[d] Although the Group × Condition × Valence interaction was not significant, exploratory post hoc analyses revealed that RBDs were significantly more impaired than LBDs and NCs for posed positive, spontaneous positive, *and* spontaneous negative emotions.
[e] Not done, included, tested, or applicable.
[f] Static video.
* $p < .10$.

arousal, pleasant surprise) and negative (sadness, anger, fear, disgust, confusion) expressions (posed condition) (Borod et al., 1986a). Expressions were posed both to verbal command and visual imitation. Two judges viewed the videotapes and rated each expression as successful (a score of 1) or unsuccessful (a score of 0). To be rated as successful, an expression had to occur and had to be appropriate for the particular stimulus. Overall, RBDs were significantly more impaired in expressing emotion than either LBDs or NCs. This was especially striking for posed positive, spontaneous positive, and spontaneous negative emotions. In general, these findings are consistent with right-hemisphere dominance for emotion, but when the data were further broken down by valence, the result for posed negative emotions was discrepant with this hypothesis.

Because of the unexpected finding for posed negative emotions, the expression data from the posed conditions (verbal, visual) have been rerated using improved techniques (Kent et al., 1988). Again, RBDs were significantly less successful (i.e., less accurate) than LBDs and NCs in producing positive emotions, and there were no group differences for negative emotions. This finding held whether the accuracy of a particular expression was determined according to emotion type (e.g., sadness) or valence type (e.g., unpleasant).

Qualitative Performance

In addition to assessing the basic performance of brain-damaged patients on tasks of facial emotional expression, we conducted qualitative analyses on those unsuccessful responses in the posed condition (Borod et al., 1986a). We observed what we have termed *paramotias* (i.e., a part of the Gestalt facial expression was inaccurate), unrecognizable expressions, and facial groping (i.e., a disorganized performance of multiple facial movements without production of any one specific expression configuration). RBDs demonstrated more of these errors than NCs and LBDs. LBDs produced significantly more vocalizations (e.g., saying "sad" when requested to look sad) than either RBDs or NCs. These error categories can be viewed as grossly analogous to deficits associated with speech output in aphasics: paramotias—literal paraphasias; unrecognizable facial expressions—neologisms; and facial groping—articulatory groping.

Dimensions of Performance

The main purpose of this study was to elucidate aspects of facial emotional expression that previously had been associated with unilateral brain damage (Borod et al., 1988). The facial expressions previously assessed for general performance (success/failure) were reexamined, and three aspects of facial behavior were analyzed: appropriateness, intensity, and responsivity. These aspects were selected because of observations in the clinical literature that right-hemisphere pathology is associated with inappropriate affect (H. Gardner, 1975), flattened or constricted affect (Gainotti, 1972), and low levels of arousal (Heilman, Schwartz, & Watson, 1978). Two judges viewed the videotapes and rated each facial expression for appropriateness (0 = inappropriate, 1 = appropriate), responsivity (0 = no response, 1 = the occurrence of a response), and intensity (1 [minimal] to 7 [maximal]). When ratings of the posed and spontaneous facial expressions were examined, RBDs were less responsive and less appropriate than NCs or LBDs. These differences were significant for responsivity ratings for both positive and negative emotions and for a appropriateness ratings for positive emotions only. There were no significant differences among the groups for intensity.

When examining the relationship among the three aspects of emotional expression for all subjects, there was a significant correlation between responsivity and intensity (rho = .63, $p < .01$) but no relationship between responsivity and appropriateness (rho = −.06) or between intensity and appropriateness (rho = .01). The relationship between responsivity and intensity may indicate that both are reflecting an underlying dimension such as arousal. Further, the fact that responsivity was the only aspect on which RBDs were consistently impaired seems to argue for a relationship between deficits in arousal and right-hemisphere dysfunction. There is a growing body of literature demonstrating that arousal deficits are critical to the right-hemisphere syndrome. Right-hemisphere pathology has been associated with abnormal patterns of autonomic nervous system responding, as measured, for example, by skin conductance (Heilman et al., 1978; Morrow, Vrtunski, Kim, & Boller, 1981).

Controlling for Nonemotional Facial Movement

Although results of facial emotional expression studies have typically been ascribed to central (i.e., cerebral) processing mechanisms, the possibility that these findings could reflect either peripheral characteristics of the face or nonemotional facial behaviors has to be ruled out empirically. It is conceivable that impairments in facial motor behavior could affect the brain–damaged subject's ability to execute tasks involving facial emotion and also influence the perceiver/rater's judgments about behaviors associated with such tasks. For example, the face of a patient with a dense central facial paralysis may appear so distorted or unusual that any emotional expression would look inappropriate. Also, a patient with restricted mobility of the facial musculature might produce emotional expressions of limited intensity, creating the impression of flattened affect. Finally, a patient with bucco-facial apraxia may be unable to respond to a command to use his or her facial muscles to express an emotion. To address this issue, we correlated our measures of emotional facial expression (appropriateness, intensity, responsivity) with measures of nonemotional facial movement (facial paralysis, hemiface mobility, bucco-facial apraxia) (Borod et al., 1988). Nonemotional facial movements were videotaped for each subject; paralysis was rated for asymmetry, mobility was rated for adequacy, and apraxia was rated for execution (facility) and accuracy. Both RBDs and LBDs had substantial facial paralysis and impairment in muscular mobility on the hemiface contralateral to their lesion site; LBDs had significant deficits in bucco-facial praxis.

When we correlated the emotional parameters with the nonemotional measures, correlations were nonsignificant. These data argue for a dissociation between systems controlling emotional facial expression and nonemotional facial movement.

Facial Asymmetry During Posed and Spontaneous Conditions

In this study (Borod et al., 1986b), patterns of facial asymmetry in posed and spontaneous facial expression were examined in the LBDs and RBDs. The study was undertaken to explore the observation in the clinical literature that patients with central facial paralysis exhibit decreased mobility on the hemiface contralateral to their lesion during posed (i.e., voluntary), but not spontaneous, movement. For patients with cortical lesions and facial paralysis, one would predict the occurrence of facial asymmetry during posed, and the absence of (or a less striking) asymmetry during spontaneous expression. In this study, the smile was observed in three conditions—posed to command, elicited during spontaneous slide viewing, and spontaneously occurring. Expressions were rated for asymmetry (1 [extreme left-sided] to 7 [extreme right-sided], with 4 representing symmetry). Intensity ratings (1 [minimal] to 7 [maximal]) also were made. For asymmetry, RBDs and LBDs differed significantly but there were no differences as a function of condition. For intensity, LBDs produced significantly more intense expressions than RBDs. When the posed expression data were rerated in the study by Kent et al. (1988), again, the LBDs were judged to produce more intense positive (but not negative) emotions than NCs and RBDs.

In view of clinical reports concerning central facial paralysis among brain-damaged patients, an effect of condition had been anticipated. The fact that condition did not affect facial asymmetry is in accord with two recent experimental studies (Borod, Koff, & White, 1983; Dopson et al., 1984; but see also Ekman et al., 1981). In these two studies, in which facial expressions were elicited from the same subjects (normal adults) under posed and spontaneous conditions, patterns of facial asymmetry were consistent across conditions. Although the clinical evidence suggests a distinction between posed and spontaneous facial behavior, it is important to note that the anatomical evidence regarding the origins and courses of the neural pathways for spontaneous emotional expression has not been clearly delineated (Barr & Kiernan, 1983; Miehlke, 1973; Peele, 1961).

SUMMARY AND DISCUSSION

To summarize the findings from the studies of normal subjects, facial asymmetry during the posed (and spontaneous) expression of emotion was significantly left-sided whether the measurements were made from whole faces or hemifaces using either videotapes or photographic stills. These findings support the hypothesis that the right hemisphere is dominant in the expression of facial emotion. Although we did not find overall support for the hypothesis that positive and negative emotions are differentially associated with the left and right hemispheres, respectively, we did find that positive emotions were less lateralized to the left side of the face than were negative emotions (suggesting right hemisphere involvement in negative expressions), but this was only the case for the whole-face ratings made from videotapes. In the ratings made from hemifaces, the expressions were left-sided regardless of valence. Whether the inconsistent findings for valence result from the use of whole face rather than hemiface stimuli, are due to the observation of dynamic rather than static faces, or are a function of other factors, for example, sex of subjects (Borod, Koff, & Buck, 1986), remains to be explored in future research studies. Among the most obvious differences between these two types of facial stimuli is that the whole face is more ecologically valid than the hemiface.

To summarize the studies of brain–damaged patients, the findings suggest that the right hemisphere is dominant for the expression of facial emotion and that deficits in emotional facial expression are not associated with deficits in nonemotional facial movement. Among the brain–damaged patients, the deficits in facial emotional expression were more marked when assessed by responsivity and appropriateness measures than by intensity measures.

When emotional valence was considered, the studies of brain–damaged patients demonstrated differences as a function of elicitation condition. For spontaneous expression, RBDs were significantly more impaired than LBDs for both positive and negative emotions; this is consistent with the hypothesis that the right hemisphere is dominant for emotion in general. For posed expression, however, RBDs were significantly more impaired than LBDs for positive emotions but equivalent to LBDs for negative emotions. Because the data for posed expression contrast with both the right hemisphere and the valence hypotheses, we reexamined the posed data with an improved rating technique (Kent et al., 1988); the finding held. This finding of a selective deficit in RBDs for positive emotion may be related to findings by Gardner and his colleagues (Bihrle, Brownell, Powelson, & Gardner, 1986) concerning the deficit of right-hemisphere patients for the appreciation of humorous materials. Of further note for perception of facial emotion, but not discussed in this chapter, these same RBDs were impaired relative to the LBDs in identifying negative but not positive emotions (Borod et al., 1986a). The finding for perception is consistent with data from the normal literature (i.e., the valence hypothesis) arguing that the right hemisphere is specialized for negative but not for positive emotions.

In our studies of normal, as well as brain-damaged subjects, we have been careful to control for peripheral factors that could influence judgments made about facial expressions. In our studies with normals, we examined the possible artifactual effects of nonemotional hemiface mobility and hemiface size (Borod & Koff, 1983; Koff, Borod, & White, 1983). Although hemiface mobility was left-sided and hemiface size larger on the right side, these peripheral factors were not related to the direction of facial asymmetries. In our studies of brain-damaged patients, it is conceivable that deficits in facial motor behavior could affect a patient's ability to execute tasks of facial emotion, as well as affect a perceiver's ability to make judgments about facial expressions. Both the RBDs and the LBDs had paralysis and restricted mobility on the hemiface contralateral to the lesion; LBDs had bucco-facial apraxia. There were, however, no significant relationships between measures of emotional expression and those of nonemotional movement. Taken together, the findings from normal and brain-damaged subjects argue for the dissociation between systems controlling facial emotional expression and nonemotional facial movement.

Another source of potential confound in studies of facial expression in brain-damaged patients is perceptual deficit. It could be argued that individuals with deficits in classifying or perceiving a particular emotional expression would have difficulty in producing or modeling that same expression. To that end, we have examined the perception of facial emotion in the same group of RBDs and LBDs. Overall, these RBDs were significantly impaired relative to the LBDs and NCs in identifying facial emotional expressions (Borod et al., 1986a). There was, however, no relationship between perception and expression. Ross (1981, 1985) has postulated a dissociation between these two functions for voice; our data suggest that the same may be true for face.

In speculating about the neuropsychological mechanisms underlying the system for facial emotional expression, the findings from the brain-damaged population raise several issues. The only measure for which RBDs were significantly impaired, relative to LBDs and NCs, across all emotions was responsivity. Impaired responsivity may be reflecting an underlying deficit in arousal; that arousal may be a relevant variable is consistent with Heilman et al.'s research (1978) on hypoarousal in RBDs. Further, facial gropings and paramotias suggest a deficit in motor programming of the facial musculature. The intimate relationship between frontal structures and motor programming has been well established (Carpenter, 1972) and is reinforced by findings regarding an association between emotional expression and frontal lobe pathology. Another speculation is that the right hemisphere lends itself to emotional processing due to its synthetic and Gestalt processing features (Van Lancker, 1987).

IMPLICATIONS

Rehabilitation of Stroke Patients

These clinical studies have implications for rehabilitation of brain-damaged patients. If right-hemisphere pathology is associated with affective deficits, then the findings we have described are relevant for diagnosis and treatment. For example, if left-hemisphere pathology, typically associated with depressed language function, is accompanied by relatively preserved emotional functioning, speech pathologists may be able to utilize this phenomenon in speech rehabilitation. In a somewhat fanciful vein, perhaps a therapy could be developed for aphasics which primes the impaired language system through perceptual strategies (e.g., audiorecordings of people emoting via laughter or crying) or expressive strategies (e.g., producing exaggerated facial expressions of emotion). Melodic Intonation Therapy (Sparks, Helm, & Albert, 1974) is a technique that exploits the aphasic's preserved intonational capacity; Visual Communication Therapy (Gardner, Zurif, Berry, & Baker, 1976) taps into the ability of some aphasics to utilize visual elements for communication; and Visual Action Therapy (Helm-Estabrooks, Fitzpatrick, & Barresi, 1982) takes advantage of the preserved gestural capacity of some aphasic patients. There have been reports in the clinical (Chester & Egolf, 1974) and experimental (Buck & Duffy, 1980) literature that aphasics can communicate nonverbally (e.g., via facial expression, emotional vocalizations, body movements, pantomime), even in the face of severe language disturbance.

Although the major focus of our work has been on the right hemisphere's role in emotional processing, we also have learned a great deal about the left hemisphere. In the study just described on the expression of facial emotion (Borod et al., 1986a), there was a significant inverse correlation between facial expression performance and auditory comprehension. That is, the more impaired the patient's comprehension, the more emotionally expressive he or she was. Further, these aphasics (LBDs) produced pleasant facial expressions with significantly greater intensity than RBDs or NCs (Borod et al., 1986b; Kent et al., 1988). These data provide experimental evidence that aphasics may use compensatory behaviors, for example, intense facial expressions, for nonverbal communication. Whether these behaviors are voluntary or unconscious and what the nature of the mechanisms underlying the use of these compensatory behaviors is remain unknown. One possibility is that aphasics, deprived of language and the facility for interacting with the external environment, develop more sensitivity to their inner experience and feeling states (Perecman, 1987, personal communication). A second possibility is that some sort of anatomical change due to the brain damage promotes disinhibition of the typical social display rules (Buck, 1984). Finally, these "nonverbal" behaviors may be all that remain intact in aphasics and therefore are utilized more frequently and are more available for access.

In related work (Borod, Fitzpatrick, Helm-Estabrooks, & Goodglass, 1984; in press) addressing this issue, we developed a scale to assess nonvocal communication of aphasics within naturalistic settings. This seven-item scale rates communicative behaviors including pointing, leading, gesturing, and pantomiming. Analysis of ratings by speech/language pathologists, nurses, neurologists, hospital personnel, and family members showed the scale to have substantial internal consistency, interrater reliability, and construct validity. Neither patient variables (e.g., age, education, lesion site, months post onset) nor cognitive variables (e.g., comprehension, general intellectual functioning) appeared to influence nonvocal communication. Of interest in this study was a significant negative correlation (rho = −.51) between the aphasia severity rating from the BDAE and nonvocal communication ratings made by family members. In a similar vein, Helmick, Watamori, and Palmer (1976) found significant negative correlations between the aphasia severity rating from the Porch Index of Communicative Ability (Porch, 1971) and ratings on the Functional Communication Profile (Sarno, 1969) made by spouses. It appears that the more impaired the patient is in terms of verbal communication, the more nonvocal communication takes place. Although the preservation of nonvocal communication may be related to biological factors (e.g., neuroanatomical changes), social forces may also be operating.

For example, family members may become especially facile at decoding nonverbal communication. Another possibility is that family members may know each other so well that less speech is necessary for comprehension to take place.

Finally, in a study on bucco-facial apraxia (Borod et al., 1987), we addressed the role of emotional context in facilitating practic performance. Patients with left- and right-hemisphere cerebrovascular pathology and normal adult controls were videotaped while executing tasks of bucco-facial praxis in emotional and nonemotional conditions. Each practic movement was assessed for target attainment (0 = inaccurate, 1 = accurate) and motor execution (1 = clumsy, to 3 = smooth [with finesse.]). LBD aphasics were significantly impaired, relative to NCs and RBDs, in both accuracy and execution on tasks of bucco-facial apraxia. Emotional context facilitated performance for all subjects. The performance of LBDs improved the most with cueing and approached the levels obtained by NCs and RBDs. In light of evidence supporting a special role for the right hemisphere in emotional processing, this could be an instance of right-hemisphere (or subcortical/limbic) compensation for a behavioral deficit typically arising from left-hemisphere pathology. The effect of facilitation could be analogous to the mechanism postulated to account for the improvement of speech fluency in aphasics treated with Melodic Intonation Therapy (Sparks et al., 1974).

Neuropsychological Mechanisms Underlying Psychiatric Disorders

There is a growing body of literature suggesting hemispheric dysfunction in psychiatric disorders (Flor-Henry, 1979; Seidman, 1983; Tucker, 1981; Wexler, 1981). The bulk of the research implicates right hemispheric dysfunction in depression and left hemispheric dysfunction in schizophrenia. In this section, we briefly review the literature regarding neuropsychological mechanisms underlying psychiatric disorders and present findings from several new studies of unipolar depressives and schizophrenics. Summaries of these studies are presented in Table 7.3 (Psychiatric). As each study is presented, the reader should consult the table. Note that the findings with respect to depression appear fairly consistent and compelling, whereas evidence regarding schizophrenia has been less reliable.

Unipolar Depression

Data for right hemisphere dysfunction in depression come from studies employing EEG (Abrams & Taylor, 1979; Flor-Henry & Koles, 1980; Karlin, Weinapple, Rochford, & Goldstein, 1979; Tucker, Stenslie, Roth,

& Shearer, 1981), skin conductance (Gruzelier & Venables, 1974), auditory tests of dichotic perception (Yozawitz et al., 1979), and quantitative (Flor-Henry, 1976; Kronfol, Hamsher, Digre, & Waziri, 1978) and qualitative (Kinsbourne, 1981) analyses of neuropsychological test data. The majority of these studies have utilized cognitive stimuli and perceptual procedures. There also are recent reports of neuropharmacological asymmetries in catecholaminergic (Oke, Keller, Mefford, & Adams, 1978; Robinson & Bloom, 1977) and serotonergic (Mandell & Knapp, 1979) systems. The animal and human clinical literature has implicated both noradrenergic and serotonergic systems in affective disorders (Mandell & Knapp, 1979; Schildkraut & Kety, 1967). The possibility of right-sided cortical (or subcortical) involvement in depression has been suggested by findings of subcortical diminution in ipsilateral norepinephrine concentration and behavioral hyperactivity following right but not left cortical ablation in the rat (Robinson, 1979). Further support for this notion comes from demonstrations that unilateral right-sided ECT may be superior to left-sided ECT in its antidepressant effects (Cronin et al., 1970) and from studies showing that altered patterns of hemispheric lateralization observed in depressed patients on dichotic listening tasks (Moscovitch, Strauss, & Olds, 1981) and on neuropsychological tests (Kronfol et al., 1978) reverted to the typical patterns following successful ECT administration.

Schizophrenia

The bulk of the literature concerned with the neuropsychology of schizophrenia points to some degree of left-hemisphere dysfunction (for reviews, see Seidman, 1983; Wexler, 1981). There are, however, a number of studies where the performance of schizophrenics does not differ from that of normal controls (Fennel, Moskowitz, & Backus, 1982; Templer & Connolly, 1976; Wexler & Heninger, 1979), where patients have shown over rather than underactivation of the left hemisphere (Gur, 1978), or where right- rather than left-hemisphere dysfunction has been implicated (Nelson, Maxwell, & Townes, 1986; Schweitzer, 1982).

Experimental Design Issues

The literature on the neuropsychology of psychiatric disorders, in parallel with the literature on the neuropsychology of normal functioning, is confounded by a number of experimental design issues. With respect to methodology, the majority of the studies in this area have presented cognitive stimuli (e.g., digits, geometric shapes) and have demanded perceptual strategies (e.g., identification, recognition, discrimination). Utilization of such stimuli and strategies may have obscured underlying brain-behavior relationships, because major psychiatric disorders also involve disturbances in affect which perhaps are more manifest in expressive behaviors. Thus, cognitive tasks and perceptual strategies may be less likely to elicit differences among subject groups because the affected dimensions are more likely to be emotional than cognitive, and expressive rather than perceptual. Neuropsychological investigations of psychiatric disorders may be better served by examining affective functions and utilizing expressive tasks.

With respect to subject sampling issues, there are profound problems with diagnostic categorization of subjects. Inclusion of different diagnostic subtypes under the rubric of "schizophrenia" or "depression" may obscure important differences and preclude precise characterization of the underlying brain-behavior relationships. For example, unipolar and bipolar patients are sometimes combined in depressed groups, and negative-symptom and positive-symptom schizophrenics can be combined in schizophrenic groups. Several recent studies highlight the importance of subject classification. Studies on depression (e.g., Vingiano, 1984) suggest that bipolar depressives display reversed patterns of laterality compared to unipolar depressives and that successful ECT treatment of unipolar depressives produces a temporary diminution in performance on tasks involving the right hemisphere. Recent literature on schizophrenia has identified two sets of clinical distinctions: (a) productive ("Type I" or positive-symptom) versus deficit ("Type II" or negative-symptom) (Crow, 1980) and (b) lexically deficient versus spatially deficient (Alpert & Martz, 1977). These distinctions suggest that some schizophrenics have deficits similar to those observed in patients with left-hemisphere pathology (Type I, lexically-deficient), whereas others have deficits that parallel those in right-hemisphere pathology (Type II, spatially deficient). In fact, two studies have demonstrated that negative-symptom schizophrenics, especially those showing affective flattening, manifest specific right hemisphere deficits; schizophrenics with minimal negative symptoms and less affective flattening do not show this pattern to the same degree (Gruzelier & Manchanda, 1982; Mayer, Alpert, Stastney, Perlock, & Empfield, 1985) (see Table 7.3).

Experimental Studies

To examine neuropsychological mechanisms underlying unipolar depression, two studies of affective responses were undertaken, using expressive (Jaeger, Borod, & Peselow, 1986), as well as perceptual (Jaeger, Borod, & Peselow, 1987), procedures. Posed facial expressions of two positive (happiness, pleasant surprise) and two negative (sadness, disgust) emotions were photographed in 30 unipolar depressive ($\overline{X}$ age = 51.8) and 30 normal control ($\overline{X}$ age = 52.0) right-handed adult males (Jaeger,

TABLE 7.3
Results from Experiments Focusing on Psychiatric Patients

	Study	Characteristics[a] of		Processing	Communication Channel		Facial Stimuli			Emotion Type[c]		
No.	Authors & Year	Posers[b]	Judges	Mode	Facial	Prosodic	Part of Face	Type of Face	Medium	Positive	Negative	Neutral
1.	Jaeger et al. (1986)	RHMs 30 UDs 30 NCs	2 RHMs 1 RHF	Expression	✓	—[d]	Whole	Natural	Photo	H,P	D,S	—
2.	Jaeger et al. (1987)	Same as above	—	Perception	✓	—	Hemi	Composite	Photo	H	—	—
3a.	Borod, Alpert et al. (in press)	RHMs 6 SZs 5 RBDs	2 RHMs 1 RHF	Expression	✓	✓	Whole	Natural	Video[e]	H,I,P	A,D,F,S	
b.		6 PDs 4 NCs		Perception	✓	✓	Whole	Natural	Photo	*Facial* H	*Facial* A,D, F,S	R
										Prosodic H	*Prosodic* A,S	N

TABLE 7.3
(continued)

Study No.	Nature	Scoring System Range Low	Scoring System Range High	Significant Differences Among Groups	Significant Group Comparisons via Post Hoc Tests	Significant Group by Expression Interaction	Significant Group Comparisons Positive	Significant Group Comparisons Negative
1.	Accuracy	0 (incorrect)	1 (correct)	Yes	NCs > UDs	Yes	P:NCs > UDs	D:NCs > UDs*
	Intensity	1 (minimal)	7 (maximal)	No	—	Yes	H:NCs > UDs P:NCs > UDs	S:UDs > NCs
2.	Laterality ratio	-1.00 (left)	+1.00 (right)	Yes	UDs > NCs	—	—	—
3a.	Accuracy	0 (incorrect)	1 (correct)	Yes	NCs > SZs NCs > RBDs* PDs > SZs*	—	—	—
	Intensity	1 (minimal)	7 (maximal)	Yes[f]	NCs > SZs	—	—	—
b.	Accuracy	0 (incorrect)	1 (correct)	Yes	NCs > SZs NCs > RBDs* PDs > SZs	—	—	—

[a]RH = right handed, F = female, and M = male.
[b]NC = normal control, PD = Parkinson's Disease, RBD = right brain-damaged, SZ = schizophrenic, and UD = unipolar depressive.
[c]A = anger, D = disgust, F = fear, H = happiness, I = interest/excitement, N = neutral/indifference, P = pleasant surprise, R = surprise, and S = sadness.
[d]Not done, included, tested, or applicable.
[e]Video static.
[f]There was a significant Group × Channel interaction. Using post tests, for the facial channel, NCs and RBDs were more intense ($p < .05$) than SZs and PDs. For the prosodic channel, NCs and PDs were more intense ($p < .05$) than SZs and RBDs, and RBDs were more intense ($p < .05$) than SZs.
* $p < .10$.

Borod, & Peselow, 1986). These whole-face photographs were rated by three naive judges for accuracy (using a four-option multiple choice format) and for intensity (using a 7-point Likert scale from 1 [minimal] to 7 [maximal]). Depressed patients were rated as significantly impaired relative to normals in the intensity and accuracy with which they produced facial emotional expressions, especially positive ones. In light of our earlier findings of a selective deficit in RBDs for posing positive emotions, these data raise the possibility of right hemispheric disorganization in patients with unipolar depression.

In the second study of unipolar depression (Jaeger, Borod, & Peselow, 1987), the same 30 unipolar depressives and 30 controls performed a perception task requiring affective judgments of chimeric faces during free-field viewing, a task which has been shown to produce a laterality index of hemispace bias (Levy, Heller, Banich, & Burton, 1983). Although both groups showed a significant left-hemispace bias, which is typically observed in this task, the depressed patients were significantly less lateralized than the controls. As with the perceptual data just described, these data for expression are also consistent with the literature indicating atypical patterns of lateralization among unipolar depressives on tasks involving right-hemisphere functions.

To examine neuropsychological mechanisms underlying flat-affect schizophrenia, schizophrenics with flat affect were compared with right brain-damaged patients on affective measures of expression and perception using both facial and vocal stimuli (Borod, Alpert et al., in press). A range of emotions, as defined by Ekman (1982) and Izard (1977), were used. On both expressive and perceptual tasks, schizophrenics performed significantly less accurately than normal controls and nonlateralized brain-damaged (i.e., Parkinson's Disease) patients but did not differ from right brain-damaged patients. This was the case for both face and voice. This finding supports the speculation that right-hemisphere mechanisms may be compromised in schizophrenics with flat affect.

Conclusion

Using experimental measures of affective processing, these data corroborate the notion in the literature that right-hemisphere dysfunction is involved in unipolar depression and flat-affect (negative-symptom) schizophrenia. Although the findings for schizophrenia are suggestive, the number of subjects studied to date is small, and we await the results of a larger investigation currently being conducted by Borod and Alpert. The findings for unipolar depression appear more robust and require interpretation. The right hemisphere's presumed mediation of autonomic arousal (e.g., Heilman et al., 1978), considered together with the widely reported examples of autonomic dysfunction in unipolar depression (e.g., Bruno, Myers, & Glassman, 1983), provide a possible mechanism for the association of right hemisphere dysfunction and depression. Thus, our findings may not necessarily point to localized involvement of the right cerebral hemisphere in depression but may reflect impairment of other systems, for example, those involving subcortical systems related to arousal. Whatever the underlying mechanism, it appears that the affective tasks and procedures which we have developed for normal and brain-damaged populations are applicable to psychiatric populations as well.

ACKNOWLEDGMENTS

This work was supported, in part, by USPHS Grants Nos. MH37952 and MH35976 to the Psychiatry Department of the New York University School of Medicine and by USPHS Grant No. NS06209 to the Aphasia Research Center of the Boston University School of Medicine. A portion of this chapter was presented as part of a symposium, "Facial Asymmetry: Expression and Paralysis," at the International Neuropsychology Society meeting in Barcelona, Spain, July 3, 1987. We are grateful to the Medical Research Services of the Boston, Cleveland, and Manhattan V.A. Medical Centers. Finally, the contributions of colleagues, such as M. Alpert, R. Buck, L. Obler, and J. Welkowitz, are greatly appreciated.

REFERENCES

Abrams, R., & Taylor, M. A. (1979). Differential EEG patterns in affective disorder and schizophrenia. *Archives of General Psychiatry, 36,* 1355–1358.

Ahern, G. L., & Schwartz, G. E. (1979). Differential lateralization for positive versus negative emotion. *Neuropsychologia, 17,* 693–698.

Alpert, M., & Martz, M. J. (1977). Cognitive views of schizophrenia in light of recent studies of brain asymmetry. In C. Shagass, S. Gershon, & A. J. Friedhoff (Eds.), *Psychopathology and brain dysfunction* (pp. 1–13). New York: Raven Press.

Argyle, M., Salter, V., Nicholson, H., Williams, M., & Burgess, P. (1970). The communication of inferior and superior attitudes of verbal and nonverbal signals. *British Journal of Social and Clinical Psychology, 9,* 222–231.

Barr, M. L., & Kiernan, J. A. (1983). *The human nervous system: An anatomical viewpoint.* Philadelphia: Harper & Row.

Benowitz, L. (1980). Cerebral lateralization in the perception of nonverbal emotional cues. *McLean Hospital Journal, 5,* 146–167.

Benowitz, L., Bear, D. M., Rosenthal, R., Mesulam, M., Zaidel, E., & Sperry, R. W. (1983). Hemispheric specialization in nonverbal communication. *Cortex, 19,* 5–11.

Benson, D. F. (1973). Psychiatric aspects of aphasia. *British Journal of Psychiatry, 123,* 555–566.

Bihrle, A. M., Brownell, H. H., Powelson, J. A., & Gardner, H. (1986). Comprehension of humorous and nonhumorous materials by left and right brain-damaged patients. *Brain and Cognition, 5,* 399–411.

Boller, F., Cole, M., Vrtunski, P. B., Patterson, M., & Kim, Y. (1979). Paralinguistic aspects of auditory comprehension in aphasia. *Brain and Language, 7,* 164–174.

Borod, J., Alpert, M., Brozgold, A., Martin, C., Welkowitz, J., Diller, L., Peselow, E., Angrist, B., & Lieberman, A. (in press). A preliminary comparison of flat affect schizophrenics and brain-damaged patients on measures of affective processing. *Journal of Communication Disorders.*

Borod, J., & Caron, H. S. (1980). Facedness and emotion related to lateral dominance, sex, and expression type. *Neuropsychologia, 18,* 237–242.

Borod, J., Caron, H. S., & Koff, E. (1981a). Asymmetry of facial expression related to handedness, footedness, and eyedness: A quantitative study. *Cortex, 17,* 381–390.

Borod, J., Caron, H. S., & Koff, E. (1981b). Asymmetries in positive and negative facial expressions: Sex differences. *Neuropsychologia, 19,* 819–824.

Borod, J., Fitzpatrick, P., Helm-Estabrooks, N., & Goodglass, H. (1984, October). *A scale for the evaluation of nonvocal communication in aphasic patients.* Paper presented at the meeting of the Academy of Aphasia, Los Angeles, CA.

Borod, J., Fitzpatrick, P., Helm-Estabrooks, N., & Goodglass, H. (in press). The relationship between limb apraxia and the spontaneous use of communicative gesture in aphasia. *Brain and Cognition.*

Borod, J., & Goodglass, H. (1980). Hemispheric specialization and development. In L. Obler & M. Albert (Eds.), *Language and communication in the elderly* (pp. 91–103). Lexington, MA: D. C. Heath.

Borod, J., Kent, J., Koff, E., Martin, C., & Alpert, M. (1988). Facial asymmetry while posing positive and negative emotions: Support for the right hemisphere hypothesis. *Neuropsychologia, 26,* 759–764.

Borod, J., & Koff, E. (1983). Hemiface mobility and facial expression asymmetry. *Cortex, 19,* 355–361.

Borod, J., & Koff, E. (1984). Asymmetries in affective facial expression: Anatomy and behavior. In N. Fox & R. Davidson (Eds.), *The Psychobiology of affective development* (pp. 293–323). Hillsdale, NJ: Lawrence Erlbaum.

Borod, J., Koff, E., & Buck, R. (1986). The neuropsychology of facial expression in normal and brain-damaged subjects. In P. Blanck, R. Buck, & R. Rosenthal (Eds.), *Nonverbal communication in the clinical context.* University Park, PA: Pennsylvania State University Press.

Borod, J., Koff, E., & Caron, H. (1983). Right hemispheric specialization for the expression and appreciation of emotion: A focus on the face. In E. Perecman (Ed.), *Cognitive processes in the right hemisphere* (pp. 83–110). New York: Academic Press.

Borod, J., Koff, E., Perlman Lorch, M., & Nicholas, M. (1985). Channels of emotional expression in patients with unilateral brain damage. *Archives of Neurology, 42,* 345–348.

Borod, J., Koff, E., Perlman Lorch, M., & Nicholas, M. (1986a). Expression and perception of facial emotion in brain-damaged patients. *Neuropsychologia, 24,* 169–180.

Borod, J., Koff, E., Perlman Lorch, M., & Nicholas, M. (1986b, February). *Facial asymmetry during posed and spontaneous expression in patients with unilateral cortical lesions.* Paper presented at the meeting of the International Neuropsychology Society, Denver, CO.

Borod, J., Koff, E., Perlman Lorch, M., & Nicholas, M. (1988). Emotional and nonemotional facial behaviour in patients with unilateral brain damage. *Journal of Neurology, Neurosurgery and Psychiatry, 51,* 826–832.

Borod, J., Koff, E., & White, B. (1983). Facial asymmetry in posed and spontaneous expressions of emotion. *Brain and Cognition, 2,* 165–175.

Borod, J., Perlman Lorch, M., Koff, E., & Nicholas, M. (1987). The effect of emotional context on bucco-facial apraxia. *Journal of Clinical and Experimental Neuropsychology, 9,* 155–161.

Bowers, D., Bauer, R. M., Coslett, H. B., & Heilman, K. (1985). Processing of faces by patients with unilateral hemisphere lesions. I. Dissociation between judgments of facial affect and facial identity. *Brain and Cognition, 4,* 258–272.

Brown, J. (1984). Book review. *Journal of Nervous and Mental Disorders, 172,* 232–234.

Bruno, R. L., Myers, S. J., & Glassman, A. H. (1983). A correlational study of cardiovascular autonomic functioning and unipolar depression. *Biological Psychiatry, 18,* 227–235.

Bruyer, R. (1981). Asymmetry of facial expression in brain-damaged subjects. *Neuropsychologia, 19,* 615–624.

Bryden, M. P., Ley, R. G., & Sugarman, J. H. (1982). A left ear advantage for identifying the emotional quality of tonal sequences. *Neuropsychologia, 20,* 83–87.

Buchtel, H., Campari, F., DeRisio, C., & Rota, R. (1978). Hemispheric differences in discriminative reaction time to facial expressions. *Italian Journal of Psychology, 5,* 159–169.

Buck, R. (1978). The slide viewing technique for measuring nonverbal sending accuracy: A guide for replication. *Catalog of Selected Documents in Psychology, 8,* 63.

Buck, R. (1984). *The communication of emotion.* New York: Guilford Press.

Buck, R., & Duffy, R. J. (1980). Nonverbal communication of affect in brain-damaged patients. *Cortex, 16,* 351–361.

Buck, R., Miller, R. E., & Caul, W. F. (1974). Sex, personality, and physiological variables in the communication of affect via facial expression. *Journal of Personality and Social Psychology, 30,* 587–596.

Campbell, R. (1978). Asymmetries in interpreting and expressing a posed facial expression. *Cortex, 14,* 327–342.

Campbell, R. (1979). Left-handers' smiles: Asymmetries in the projection of a posed expression. *Cortex, 15,* 571–579.

Campbell, R. (1986). Asymmetries of facial action: Some facts and fancies of normal face movement. In R. Bruyer (Ed.), *The neuropsychology of facial perception and facial expression* (pp. 247–267). Hillsdale, NJ: Lawrence Erlbaum Associates.

Carmon, A., & Nachson, I. (1973). Ear asymmetry in perception of emotional nonverbal stimuli. *Acta Psychologia, 37,* 351–357.

Carpenter, M. B. (1972). *Core text of neuroanatomy.* Baltimore: Williams & Wilkins.

Chaurasia, B. D., & Goswami, H. K. (1975). Functional asymmetry in the face. *Acta Anatomica, 91,* 154–160.

Chester, S., & Egolf, D. (1974). Nonverbal communication and aphasia therapy. *Rehabilitation Literature, 35,* 231–233.

Cicone, M., Wapner, W., & Gardner, H. (1980). Sensitivity to emotional expressions and situations in organic patients. *Cortex, 16,* 145–158.

Coren, S., Porac, C., & Duncan, P. (1979). A behaviorally validated self-report inventory to assess four types of lateral preferences. *Journal of Clinical Neuropsychology, 1,* 55–64.

Cronin, D., Bodley, L., Potts, M., Mather, M. D., Gardner, R. K., & Tobin, J. C. (1970). Unilateral and bilateral ECT: A study of memory disturbances and relief from depression. *Journal of Neurology, Neurosurgery, and Psychiatry, 33,* 705–713.

Crow, T. J. (1980). Molecular pathology of schizophrenia. More than one disease process? *British Medical Journal, 280,* 66–68.

Danly, M., Shapiro, B., & Gardner, H. (1982, October). *Dysprosody in right brain-damaged patients: Linguistic and emotional components.* Paper presented at the meeting of the Academy of Aphasia, Lake Mohonk, NY.

Davidson, R. (1985). Affect, cognition, and hemispheric specialization. In C. E. Izard, J. Kagan, & R. Zajonc (Eds.), *Emotion, cognition, and behavior* (pp. 320–365). New York: Cambridge University Press.

Davidson, R., & Fox, N. (1982). Asymmetrical brain activity discriminates between positive and negative affective stimuli in human infants. *Science, 218,* 1235–1237.

Davidson, R., Schwartz, G. E., Pugash, E., & Bromfield, E. (1976). Sex differences in patterns in EEG asymmetry. *Biological Psychology, 4*, 119–138.

Davidson, R., Schwartz, G. E., Saron, C., Bennett, J., & Goleman, D. (1978). *Frontal versus parietal EEG asymmetry during positive and negative affect*. Paper presented at the Society for Psychophysiological Research, Madison, WI.

DeKosky, S. T., Heilman, K. M., Bowers, D., & Valenstein, E. (1980). Recognition and discrimination of emotional faces and pictures. *Brain and Language, 9*, 206–214.

Dimond, S. J., & Farrington, L. (1977). Emotional response to films shown to the right and left hemisphere of the brain measured by heart rate. *Acta Psychologia, 41*, 255–260.

Dopson, W. G., Beckwith, B. E., Tucker, D. M., & Bullard-Bates, P. C. (1984). Asymmetry of facial expression in spontaneous emotion. *Cortex, 20*, 243–252.

Ekman, P. (1982). *Emotion in the human face*. Cambridge: Cambridge University Press.

Ekman, P., Friesen, W., O'Sullivan, M., & Scherer, K. (1980). Relative importance of face, body, and speech in judgments of personality and affect. *Journal of Personality and Social Psychology, 38*, 270–277.

Ekman, P., Hager, E., & Friesen, W. V. (1981). The symmetry of emotional and deliberate facial actions. *Psychophysiology, 18*, 101–106.

Etcoff, N. L. (1984). Selective attention to facial identity and facial emotion. *Neuropsychologia, 22*, 281–295.

Fennel, E. B., Moskowitz, R., & Backus, D. (1982, February). *Dichotic listening in schizophrenic and depressed patients*. Paper presented at the meeting of the International Neuropsychology Society, Pittsburgh, PA.

Flor-Henry, P. (1976). Lateralized temporal-limbic dysfunction and psychopathology. *Annals of the NY Academy of Sciences, 280*, 777–797.

Flor-Henry, P. (1979). On certain aspects of the localization of the cerebral systems regulating and determining emotion. *Biological Psychiatry, 14*, 677–698.

Flor-Henry, P., & Koles, Z. J. (1980). EEG studies in depression, mania, and normals: Evidence for partial shifts of laterality in the affective psychoses. *Advances in Biological Psychiatry, 4*, 21–43.

Foldi, N., Cicone, M., Gardner, H. (1983). Pragmatic aspects of communication in brain-damaged patients. In S. J. Segalowitz (Ed.), *Language function and brain organization* (pp. 51–86). New York: Academic Press.

Gainotti, G. (1972). Emotional behavior and hemispheric side of lesion. *Cortex, 8*, 41–55.

Gardner, E. (1975). *Fundamentals of neurology*. Philadelphia: W. B. Saunders.

Gardner, H. (1975). *The shattered mind: The person after brain damage*. New York: Alfred A. Knopf.

Gardner, H., Zurif, E. B., Berry, T., & Baker, E. (1976). Visual communication in aphasia. *Neuropsychologia, 14*, 275–292.

Gilbert, C. (1973). Strength of left-handedness and facial recognition ability. *Cortex, 9*, 145–151.

Goldstein, K. (1952). The effect of brain damage on the personality. *Psychiatry, 15*, 245–260.

Goodglass, H., & Kaplan, E. (1983). *The assessment of aphasia and related disorders* (2nd ed.). Philadelphia: Lea & Febiger.

Graves, R., Landis, T., & Goodglass, H. (1981). Laterality and sex differences for visual recognition of emotional and nonemotional words. *Neuropsychologia, 19*, 95–102.

Gruzelier, J., & Manchanda, R. (1982). The syndrome of schizophrenia: Relations between electrodermal response, lateral asymmetries and clinical ratings. *British Journal of Psychiatry, 141*, 488–495.

Gruzelier, J., & Venables, P. (1974). Bimodality and lateral asymmetry of skin conductance orienting activity of schizophrenics: Replication and evidence of lateral asymmetry in patients with depression and disorders of personality. *Biological Psychiatry, 8*, 55–73.

Gur, R. E. (1978). Left hemisphere dysfunction and left hemisphere overactivation in schizophrenia. *Journal of Abnormal Psychology, 87,* 226–238.

Hager, J. C. (1982). Asymmetries in facial expression. In P. Ekman (Ed.), *Emotion in the human face* (pp. 318–352). Cambridge, MA: Cambridge University Press.

Hager, J. C., & Ekman, P. (1985). The asymmetry of facial actions is inconsistent with models of hemispheric specialization. *Psychophysiology, 22,* 307–318.

Haggard, M. P., & Parkinson, A. M. (1971). Stimulus task factors as determinants of ear advantages. *Quarterly Journal of Experimental Psychology, 23,* 168–177.

Hansch, E. C., & Pirozzolo, F. J. (1980). Task relevant effects on the assessment of cerebral specialization for facial emotion. *Brain and Language, 10,* 51–59.

Hecaen, H. (1962). Clinical symptomatology in right and left hemisphere lesions. In V. B. Mountcastle (Ed.), *Interhemispheric relations and cerebral dominance* (pp. 215–243). Baltimore: John Hopkins Press.

Heilman, K. M., Scholes, R., & Watson, R. T. (1975). Auditory affective agnosia: Disturbed comprehension of affective speech. *Journal of Neurology, Neurosurgery, and Psychiatry, 38,* 69–72.

Heilman, K. M., Schwartz, H., & Watson, R. T. (1978). Hypoarousal in patients with the neglect syndrome and emotional indifference. *Neurology, 28,* 229–232.

Heilman, K. M., & Valenstein, E. (1979). *Clinical neuropsychology.* New York: Oxford University Press.

Heller, W., & Levy, J. (1981). Perception and expression of emotion in right-handers and left-handers. *Neuropsychologia, 19,* 263–272.

Helm-Estabrooks, N., Fitzpatrick, P., & Barresi, B. (1982). Visual action therapy for global aphasia. *Journal of Speech and Hearing Disorders, 47,* 385–389.

Helmick, J. W., Watamori, T. S., & Palmer, J. M. (1976). Spouses' understanding of the communication disabilities of aphasic patients. *Journal of Speech and Hearing Disorders, 41,* 238–243.

Hirschmann, R. S., & Safer, M. A. (1982). Hemispheric differences in perceiving positive and negative emotions. *Cortex, 18,* 569–580.

Hollingshead, A. B., & Redlich, F. C. (1958). *Social class and mental illness.* New York: Wiley.

Hughlings-Jackson, J. (1874). On the nature of duality of the brain. *Medical Press and Circular, 1,* 19, 41, 63.

Inglis, J., & Lawson, J. S. (1981). Sex differences in the effects of unilateral brain damage on intelligence. *Science, 212,* 693–695.

Izard, C. E. (1977). *Human emotions.* New York: Plenum Press.

Jaeger, J. (1984). *The neuropsychology of emotion in major depressive disorder.* Unpublished doctoral dissertation, Yeshiva University, New York.

Jaeger, J., Borod, J., & Peselow, E. (1986). Facial expression of positive and negative emotions in patients with unipolar depression. *Journal of Affective Disorders, 11,* 43–50.

Jaeger, J., Borod, J., & Peselow, E. (1987). Depressed patients have atypical hemispace biases in the perception of emotional chimeric faces. *Journal of Abnormal Psychology, 96,* 321–324.

Kahn, E. A. (1964). Facial expression. *Clinical Neurosurgery, 12,* 9–22.

Karlin, R., Weinapple, M., Rochford, J., & Goldstein, L. (1979). Quantitative features of negative affective states: Report of some hypnotic studies. *Research Communications in Psychology, Psychiatry, and Behavior, 4,* 397–413.

Kent, J., Borod, J., Koff, E., Welkowitz, J., & Alpert, M. A. (1988). Posed facial emotional expression in brain-damaged patients. *International Journal of Neuroscience, 43,* 81–87.

King, F. L., & Kimura, D. (1972). Left-ear superiority in dichotic perception of vocal nonverbal sounds. *Canadian Journal of Psychology, 26,* 111–116.

Kinsbourne, M. (1980, October). *The attempt to find an organizing principle for the specialized function of each hemisphere.* Paper presented at the Society for Research in Child Development Symposium, "The Development of Emotion and Cerebral Asymmetry," Tarrytown, N.Y.

Kinsbourne, M. (1981, June). *Hemispheric specialization and neuropsychology*. Paper presented at the Neurology Colloquium, Boston V.A. Medical Center.

Koff, E., Borod, J., & White, B. (1981). Asymmetries in hemiface size and mobility. *Neuropsychologia, 19,* 825–830.

Koff, E., Borod, J., & White, B. (1983). A left hemispace bias for visualizing emotional situations. *Neuropsychologia, 21,* 273–276.

Kolb, B., & Milner, B. (1981). Observations on spontaneous facial expression after focal cerebral excisions and after intracarotid injection of sodium amytal. *Neuropsychologia, 19,* 505–514.

Kronfol, Z., Hamsher, deS., Digre, K., & Waziri, R. (1978). Depression and hemispheric functions: Changes associated with unilateral ECT. *British Journal of Psychiatry, 132,* 560–567.

Kuypers, H. G. J. M. (1958). Corticobulbar connections to the pons and lower brainstem in man. *Brain, 81,* 364–390.

Ladavas, E., Umilta, C., & Ricci-Bitti, P. E. (1980). Evidence for sex differences in right-hemisphere dominance for emotions. *Neuropsychologia, 18,* 361–366.

Landis, T., Graves, R., & Goodglass, H. (1982). Aphasic reading and writing: Possible evidence for right hemisphere participation. *Cortex, 18,* 105–112.

Levy, J., Heller, W., Banich, M. T., & Burton, L. A. (1983). Asymmetry of perception in free viewing of chimeric faces. *Brain and Cognition, 2,* 404–419.

Ley, R. G., & Bryden, M. P. (1979). Hemispheric differences in processing emotions and faces. *Brain and Language, 7,* 127–138.

Ley, R. G., & Bryden, M. P. (1981). Consciousness, emotion, and the right hemisphere. In R. Stevens & G. Underwood (Eds.), *Aspects of consciousness* (pp. 215–240). New York: Academic Press.

Lindzey, G., Prince, B., & Wright, H. K. (1952). A study of facial asymmetry. *Journal of Personality, 21,* 68–84.

LoCastro, J. (1972). *Judgment of emotional communication in the facial-vocal-verbal channels*. Unpublished doctoral dissertation, University of Maryland, College Park, MD.

Lynn, J. G., & Lynn, D. R. (1938). Face-hand laterality in relation to personality. *Journal of Abnormal and Social Psychology, 33,* 291–322.

Lynn, J. G., & Lynn, D. R. (1943). Smile and hand dominance in relation to basic modes of adaptation. *Journal of Abnormal and Social Psychology, 38,* 250–276.

Mandell, A., & Knapp, S. (1979). Asymmetry and mood, emergent properties of serotonin regulation. *Archives of General Psychiatry, 36,* 909–916.

Mayer, M., Alpert, M., Stastney, P., Perlick, D., & Empfield, M. (1985). Multiple contributions to the clinical presentation of flat affect in schizophrenic population. *Schizophrenic Bulletin, 11,* 420–426.

McGlone, J. (1980). Sex differences in human brain asymmetry: A critical survey. *The Behavioral and Brain Sciences, 3,* 215–263.

McKeever, W. F., & Dixon, M. F. (1981). Right hemisphere superiority for discriminating memorized from nonmemorized faces. *Brain and Language, 12,* 246–260.

Mehrabian, A., & Weiner, M. (1967). Decoding of inconsistent communications. *Journal of Personality and Social Psychology, 6,* 109–114.

Miehlke, A. (1973). *Surgery of the facial nerve*. Philadelphia: W. B. Saunders.

Mills, C. K. (1912a). The cerebral mechanism of emotional expression. *Transactions of the College of Physicians of Philadelphia, 34,* 381–390.

Mills, C. K. (1912b). The cortical representation of emotion, with a discussion of some points in the general nervous mechanism of expression in its relations to organic nervous disease and insanity. *Proceedings of the American Medico-Psychological Association, 19,* 297–300.

Moreno, C., Borod, J., Welkowitz, J., & Alpert, M. (1988, January). *Lateralization for the expression and perception of facial emotion as a function of age.* Paper presented at the meeting of the International Neuropsychology Society, New Orleans, LA.

Morrow, L., Vrtunski, B., Kim, Y., & Boller, F. (1981). Arousal responses to emotional stimuli and laterality of lesion. *Neuropsychologia, 19,* 65–71.

Moscovitch, M., & Olds, J. (1982). Asymmetries in spontaneous facial expression and their possible relation to hemispheric specialization. *Neuropsychologia, 20,* 71–81.

Moscovitch, M., Strauss, E., & Olds, J. (1981). Handedness and dichotic listening performance in patients with unipolar endogenous depression who received ECT. *American Journal of Psychiatry, 138,* 988–990.

Murray, H. A. (1958). *Explorations in personality.* New York: Oxford University Press.

Myers, R. F. (1976). Comparative neurology of vocalization and speech: Proof of a dichotomy. *Annals of the New York Academy of Sciences, 280,* 745–757.

Nelson, D. V., Maxwell, J. K., & Townes, B. D. (1986, February). *Cerebral laterality and interhemispheric relations in schizophrenia and affective disorders.* Paper presented at the meeting of the International Neuropsychology Society, Denver, CO.

Oke, A., Keller, R., Mefford, I., & Adams, R. V. (1978). Lateralization of norepinephrine in the human thalamus. *Science, 200,* 1411–1413.

Packard, J. L. (1980). *Intonation in aphasia: A preliminary report.* Unpublished manuscript, Cornell University, Ithaca, NY.

Peele, T. L. (1961). *The neuroanatomic basis for clinical neurology.* New York: McGraw-Hill.

Perria, L., Rosadini, G., & Rossi, G. F. (1961). Determination of side of cerebral dominance with amobarbital. *Archives of Neurology, 4,* 173–181.

Porch, B. (1971). *Porch index of communicative ability.* Palo Alto, CA: Consulting Psychologists Press.

Rappeport, M., & Friendly, M. (1978). *Facial asymmetry in emotion: Observer and stimulus differences.* Paper presented at the meeting of the Canadian Psychological Association, Ottawa.

Reuter-Lorenz, P., & Davidson, R. (1981). Differential contributions of the two cerebral hemispheres to the perception of happy and sad faces. *Neuropsychologia, 19,* 609–613.

Rinn, W. B. (1984). The neuropsychology of facial expression: A review of the neurological and psychological mechanisms for producing facial expression. *Psychological Bulletin, 95,* 52–77.

Robinson, R. G. (1979). Differential behavioral and biochemical effects of right and left hemispheric cerebral infarction in the rat. *Science, 205,* 707–710.

Robinson, R. G., & Benson, D. F. (1981). Depression in aphasic patients: Frequency, severity, and clinical pathological correlation. *Brain and Language, 14,* 282–291.

Robinson, R. G., & Bloom, F. (1977). Pharmacological treatment following experimental cerebral infarction: Implications for understanding psychological symptoms of human stroke. *Biological Psychiatry, 12,* 669–679.

Robinson, R. G., Kubos, K. L., Starr, L. B., Rao, K., & Thomas, P. R. (1984). Mood disorders in stroke patients. Importance of location of lesion. *Brain, 107,* 81–93.

Ross, E. (1981). The aprosodias. *Archives of Neurology, 38,* 561–569.

Ross, E. (1985). Modulation of affect and nonverbal communication by the right hemisphere. In M.-M. Mesulaum (Ed.), *Principles of behavioral neurology* (pp. 239–257). Philadelphia: F. A. Davis.

Ross, E., Harney, J. H., de Lacoste, C., & Purdy, P. (1981). How the brain integrates affective and propositional language into a unified behavioral function. Hypothesis based on clinicoanatomic evidence. *Archives of Neurology, 38,* 745–748.

Ross, E., & Mesulam, M.-M. (1979). Dominant language functions of the right hemi-sphere? Prosody and emotional gesturing. *Archives of Neurology, 36,* 144–148.

Rothman, K. J., & Wepsic, J. G. (1974). Side of facial pain in trigeminal neuralgia. *Journal of Neurosurgery, 40,* 514–516.

Rubin, D. A., & Rubin, R. T. (1980). Differences in asymmetry of facial expression be-tween left- and right-handed children. *Neuropsychologia, 18,* 373–377.

Ruckdeschel-Hibbard, M., Gordon, W., & Diller, L. (1986). Affective disturbances associ-ated with brain-damage. In S. Filskov & T. Boll (Eds.), *Handbook of clinical neuropsy-chology* (Vol. 2, pp. 306–337). New York: John Wiley & Sons.

Sackeim, H., Greenberg, M., Weiman, A., Gur, R., Hungerbuhler, J., & Geschwind, N. (1982). Functional brain asymmetry in the expression of positive and negative emotions: Lateralization of insult in cases of uncontrollable emotional outbursts. *Archives of Neu-rology, 19,* 210–218.

Sackeim, H., & Gur, R. C. (1978). Lateral asymmetry in intensity of emotional expression. *Neuropsychologia, 16,* 473–481.

Sackeim, H., & Gur, R. C. (1980). Asymmetry in facial expression. *Science, 209,* 834–836.

Sackeim, H., & Gur, R. C. (1983). Facial asymmetry and communication of emotion. In J. T. Cacioppo & R. E. Petty (Eds.), *Social psychophysiology* (pp. 307–352). New York: Guilford Press.

Safer, M. (1981). Sex and hemisphere differences in access to codes for processing emotional expressions and faces. *Journal of Experimental Psychology: General, 110,* 86–100.

Safer, M., & Leventhal, H. (1977). Ear differences in evaluating emotional tones of voice and verbal content. *Journal of Experimental Psychology: Human Perception and Performance, 3,* 75–82.

Sarno, M. T. (1969). *The functional communication profile manual of directions.* Rehabilitation Monograph 42. New York Institute of Rehabilitation Medicine, New York University Medical Center.

Schildkraut, J. J., & Kety, S. S. (1967). Biogenic amines and emotion. *Science, 156,* 21–24.

Schlanger, B., Schlanger, P., & Gerstman, L. J. (1976). The perception of emotionally toned sentences by right hemisphere damaged and aphasic subjects. *Brain and Language, 3,* 396–403.

Schwartz, G. E., Ahern, G. L., & Brown, S. L. (1979). Lateralized facial muscle response to positive and negative emotional stimuli. *Psychophysiology, 16,* 561–571.

Schweitzer, L. (1982). Evidence for right hemisphere dysfunction in schizophrenic patients with left hemisphere overactivation. *Biological Psychiatry, 17,* 655–673.

Schweitzer, L., & Chacko, R. (1980). Cerebral lateralization: Relation to subject's sex. *Cor-tex, 16,* 559–566.

Seidman, L. J. (1983). Schizophrenia and brain dysfunction: An integration of recent neu-rodiagnostic findings. *Psychological Bulletin, 94,* 195–238.

Sparks, R., Helm, N., & Albert, M. (1974). Aphasia rehabilitation resulting from melodic intonation therapy. *Cortex, 10,* 303–316.

Stern, D. (1977). Handedness and the lateral distribution of conversion reactions. *Journal of Nervous and Mental Diseases, 164,* 122–128.

Strauss, E., & Kaplan, E. (1980). Lateralized asymmetries in self-perception. *Cortex, 6,* 283–293.

Strauss, E., & Moscovitch, M. (1981). Perception of facial expressions. *Brain and Language, 13,* 308–332.

Strauss, E., Wada, J., & Kosaka, B. (1983). Spontaneous facial expressions occurring at onset of focal seizure activity. *Archives of Neurology, 40,* 545–547.

Suberi, M., & McKeever, W. F. (1977). Differential right hemisphere memory storage of emotional and nonemotional faces. *Neuropsychologia, 15,* 757–768.

Templer, D. I., & Connolly, W. (1976). Affective vs. thinking disturbance related to left- vs. right-sided brain functioning. *Psychological Reports, 38*, 141–142.

Terzian, H. (1964). Behavioral and EEG effects of intracarotid sodium amytal injection. *Acta Neurochirurgica, 12*, 230–239.

Tschiassny, K. (1953). Eight syndromes of facial paralysis and their significance in locating the lesion. *Annals of Otology, Rhinology, and Laryngology, 62*, 677–691.

Tucker, D., Watson, R. T., & Heilman, K. M. (1977). Discrimination and evocation of affective intoned speech in patients with right parietal disease. *Neurology, 27*, 947–950.

Tucker, D. M. (1981). Lateral brain function, emotion, and conceptualization. *Psychological Bulletin, 89*, 19–46.

Tucker, D. M., Stenslie, C. E., Roth, R. S., & Shearer, S. L. (1981). Right frontal lobe activation and right hemisphere performance: Decrement during a depressed mood. *Archives of General Psychiatry, 38*, 169–174.

Van Lancker, D. (1987, February). *Prosodic perception and the cerebral hemispheres.* Paper presented at the meeting of the International Neuropsychology Society, Washington, DC.

Vingiano, W. (1984). *Perceptual asymmetry in depressed patients before and after treatment with electroconvulsive therapy: A tachistoscopic study.* Unpublished doctoral dissertation, New York University, NY.

Weber, S. (1983). *Facial asymmetry in the expression of emotion in infants.* Unpublished doctoral dissertation, New York University, NY.

Wechsler, A. F. (1973). The effect of organic brain disease on recall of emotionally charged versus neutral narrative texts. *Neurology, 23*, 130–135.

Wechsler, D. (1958). *The measurement and appraisal of adult intelligence.* Baltimore: Williams & Wilkins.

Weinstein, E., & Kahn, R. (1955). *Denial of illness.* Springfield, IL: Charles C. Thomas.

Weintraub, S., Mesulam, M.-M., & Kramer, L. (1981). Disturbances in prosody. *Archives of Neurology, 38*, 742–744.

Weisenberg, T. H., & McBride, K. E. (1935). *Aphasia: A clinical and psychological study.* New York: Commonwealth Fund.

Wexler, B. E. (1981). Cerebral laterality and psychiatry: A review of the literature. *American Journal of Psychiatry, 137*, 279–291.

Wexler, B. E., & Heninger, G. R. (1979). Alterations in cerebral laterality during acute psychotic illness. *Archives of General Psychiatry, 36*, 278–284.

Yozawitz, A., Bruder, G., Sutton, S., Sharpe, L., Gurland, B., Fleiss, J., & Costa, L. (1979). Dichotic perception: Evidence for right hemispheric dysfunction in affective psychosis. *British Journal of Psychiatry, 135*, 224–237.

8

Manifestations of Personality Change After Closed Head Injury

Felicia C. Goldstein
Harvey S. Levin

Disturbances in "personality" following closed head injury (CHI), that is, alterations in typical ways of interpreting and expressing emotions, thoughts and behaviors, have major implications for the quality of life of the patient and family. Personality changes after severe head injury produce considerable stress in family members (McKinlay, Brooks, Bond, Martinage, & Marshall, 1981; Oddy, Humphrey, & Uttley, 1978) and adversely affect the patient's work performance and social relationships (Oddy & Humphrey, 1980; Weddell, Oddy, & Jenkins, 1980). Moreover, these disturbances of mood, cognition, and behavior often interfere with the rehabilitation of physical, interpersonal, and occupational skills (Eames & Wood, 1985; Muir et al., 1983). Personality deficits may either exacerbate neuropsychological impairment (e.g., a lack of interest in problem solving and the use of strategies) or may themselves stem from neuropsychological impairment (e.g., an apparent loss of motivation, which is actually caused by distractibility) (Goldstein & Levin, 1987; Prigatano, 1987). Clearly, an understanding of difficulties in responding to the environment is crucial to both the neuropsychologist attempting to assess disorders and to the rehabilitation team working with patients and families. Mental health professionals are being increasingly consulted concerning the management of psychiatric disturbances in head injured patients as a result of the realization that these problems constitute a major source of disability (Goethe & Levin, 1984).

Although personality changes contribute immensely to the outcome of CHI, they are generally difficult to define, conceptualize, and measure objectively (Prigatano, 1987). Nomenclature from the Diagnostic and Statistical Manual for Mental Disorders (DSM-III, American Psychiatric Association, 1980) is not readily adapted to the characterization and range of deficits seen after head injury (Levin, Benton, & Grossman, 1982). At present, there is no classification scheme for the "personality" changes that occur or agreement that these alterations are equivalent to those in psychiatric groups without structural brain damage (Jennett & Teasdale, 1981; Prigatano, 1987). Moreover, health-care providers may tend to view the descriptor "personality" as fraught with characterological implications, permanency and lack of systematized breakdown for treatment purposes. A number of terms are currently used to describe these changes including "mental" (Jennett & Teasdale, 1981), "psychosocial" (McLean, Dikmen, Temkin, Wyler, & Gale, 1984), "behavioral" (Rosenthal, 1983), and "emotional" (Dikmen & Reitan, 1977).

Despite these difficulties, a review of the literature suggests a consensus that personality sequelae actually fall within a number of overlapping dimensions including affective (mood), cognitive (thought processes), behavioral (overt actions) and somatic (physical complaints). In addition, specific disturbances may be relatively prominent depending on the stage of recovery (e.g., agitation in the acute phase) and type of injury (e.g., somatic complaints following mild head injury). We use the term *personality* to refer to transient or permanent alterations in these underlying dimensions. We first discuss potential factors that contribute to the clinical picture including the roles of premorbid personality, brain injury, and responses of the patient and family to disability. Next, common patterns seen in the acute and chronic stages of recovery are described. Finally, we discuss current treatment directions for remediation of personality disturbances.

FACTORS CONTRIBUTING
TO PERSONALITY CHANGE

An understanding of the factors contributing to outcome after CHI leads to an appreciation of the wide range of sequelae that may occur. Lishman (1968, 1973) noted the inappropriateness of a simple neurologic model that attempts to relate psychiatric disturbance solely to brain damage. In recognition of this caveat, most discussions have emphasized the role of three variables in determining responses of the patient (Lishman, 1973; Rosenthal, 1983). As seen in Table 8.1, these factors include preinjury characteristics, the extent and location of brain damage, and adaptation to the consequences of injury. In this section, we follow this approach in considering the potential influences of each variable.

Preinjury Factors

Preinjury factors, such as the emotional and psychosocial stability of the patient as well as the cohesion and support of the family system, have been

TABLE 8.1
Etiological Factors in Psychiatric Disturbance
After Head Injury

Premorbid personality and mental constitution
Amount of brain damage
Location of brain damage
Development of epilepsy
Environmental factors
Compensation and litigation
Response to intellectual impairment
Emotional impact and emotional repercussions of injury

Note: Adapted from Lishman, W. A. (1973). The psychiatric sequelae of head injury: A review. *Psychological Medicine, 3,* 304–318. Reprinted with permission of the author and publisher.

proposed to play a role in the expression of posttraumatic disturbance (Bond, 1984; Lishman, 1968, 1973; Rosenthal, 1983). There have been suggestions from the epidemiological literature that head injured patients may possess personal and social characteristics that predispose them toward injury (See Tsuang, Boor, & Fleming, 1985, for a review). However, the contribution of these patterns to enduring changes after trauma remains controversial.

Personality characteristics including low frustration tolerance, poor control of anger and hostility, and a tendency to engage in risk-taking behaviors have been described as more typical of individuals involved in traffic accidents (Tsuang et al., 1985). Adolescent and young adult males in particular appear to be in motor vehicle accidents related to the use of alcohol (Kraus, 1987). In addition, a higher preinjury divorce rate in comparison with the general population has been reported (Kerr, Kay, & Lassman, 1971). Although preexisting psychiatric disturbance has been posited to contribute to head injury, investigators have not typically considered incidence rates for specific psychiatric disturbance nor have they used uniform criteria for assessment (Levin et al., 1982). Moreover, information is sparse concerning the role of social support and family cohesion as determinants of outcome after CHI.

The notion that preinjury characteristics interact with the response to illness makes clinical sense. It has been hypothesized that a more stable premorbid personality may be better adapted to cope with the consequences of disability (Bond & Brooks, 1976; Lishman, 1973). In addition, premorbid personality may contribute to the way in which personality changes are expressed (Lishman, 1973). Yet, it is extremely difficult to predict the association between specific traits and their manifestations (Jennett & Teasdale, 1981). Some patients may show an exaggeration of behaviors such as aggressiveness, egocentricity, and impulsivity. On the other hand, these characteristics (e.g., aggressiveness) could also become less prominent with the cessation of such activities as drinking (Bond, 1984) or possibly an atypical pattern of brain injury which might have a "calming effect."

Prigatano (1987) suggested that the role of premorbid personality may be relatively more important in cases of mild head injury than in severe head injury where other factors such as severity of tissue damage and disability are the chief determinants of disturbance. The work of Rutter and colleagues with children demonstrates the importance of showing a "dose-response" relationship between severity of injury and behavior (Brown, Chadwick, Schaffer, Rutter, & Traub, 1981; Rutter, 1981). Using a control group and studying change over time, Brown et al. found that their mild head-injury group exhibited a higher rate of behavioral disturbance prior to the injury (assessed by screening the family shortly after injury) in contrast to severely injured children and controls. Moreover, this pattern did not change over serial assessments. Their finding points to potential preexisting factors in subgroups of the CHI pediatric population. Research by McLean, Temkin, Dikmen, & Wyler (1983) with adults suggests the benefits in using controls who are friends of the patients and are therefore similar not only in demographic features such as age and education but also in terms of social/personality characteristics. It is also plausible that premorbid factors are more critical in the later phases of recovery as patients and families begin to confront the impact of the injury. Levin and Grossman (1978) observed agitated behavior associated with such symptoms as hallucinations and aggression in patients who had no previous history of neuropsychiatric disorder or drug/alcohol abuse, thus pointing to the role of other factors (e.g., severity of brain injury, alterations of neurotransmitters) in maintaining the behavior.

Studies need to use carefully selected control groups to rule out the impact of premorbid personality if the interest is to establish a relationship between clinical variables and posttraumatic behavioral disorder. On the other hand, an understanding of premorbid factors in contributing to emotional disorder can be enhanced by a thorough investigation of pre-injury personality. In the absence of information obtained prior to the head trauma, this is best accomplished through an interview with a relative soon after injury and before repercussions have colored his or her perception of the patient (Jennett & Teasdale, 1981).

Effects of Brain Injury

Research has demonstrated compelling evidence for the relationship between severity of brain injury and certain manifestations. Head injury can produce a variety of focal lesions as well as widespread diffuse damage. The most frequent neuroanatomic sites for cortical contusions and intracranial hematomas are the orbitofrontal and temporal regions (Adams, Mitchell, Graham, & Doyle, 1977; Adams, Graham, Murray, & Scott, 1982), whereas in very severe injuries, damage to the mid-brain and rostral brain stem may be implicated (Bond, 1984). In addition, diffuse axonal injury may occur immediately on impact, resulting in later degeneration of nerve fibers with reduced bulk of the cerebral white matter (Adams et al., 1977, 1982; Strich, 1956). Cerebral swelling reflected by early compression of the ventricular system (slitlike ventricles, compressed basal cisterns) has been linked to acute psychiatric manifestations (Levin & Grossman, 1978).

The heterogeneity of severity and location of damage undoubtedly contributes to the range of sequelae in CHI as opposed to disease states such as stroke which tend to produce well-defined focal lesions and specific, lateralized deficits (Thomas & Trexler, 1982). Although a review of the role of brain damage in producing these changes is beyond the scope of this chapter (see excellent reviews by Bear, 1983; Borod, this volume; Heilman, Bowers, & Valenstein, 1985), investigators typically consider both the lateralization (e.g., left versus right hemisphere) and localization (e.g., frontal, temporal) of injury to be important.

Lateralization and Localization of Injury

Damage to the right hemisphere (in right-handed patients) has been linked to disturbances in the comprehension and expression of emotion. Difficulty in processing emotional content with damage to the right hemisphere is illustrated by the case of a severely impaired closed head-injured patient whom we followed up to 10 years postinjury. A right frontoparietal depressed skull fracture and areas of hemorrhagic contusions involving the frontoparietal and temporal regions were associated with subfalcine herniation to the left (see Figs. 8.1 and 8.2). Neglect of the left visual field partially resolved over a 10-year period. At followup, the patient demonstrated impoverished affective expression and defective prosody of speech that paralleled the course of her visual neglect. Her identification of the affect of tape recorded sentences (Heilman, Scholes, & Watson, 1975) was impaired (four errors in 16 sentences) in contrast to perfect performance by control subjects.

Anosognosia, or denial of illness, another feature of nondominant hemisphere damage that may also be seen after dominant damage (i.e., Wernicke's aphasia), is characterized by failure to acknowledge deficits or their severity (Bear, 1983). For example, a patient may report that a paralyzed limb will not move because it is "tired" (Prigatano, 1987).

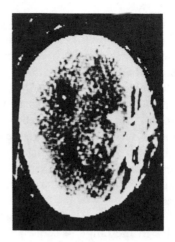

FIGURE 8.1. CT scan on day of injury showing a depressed fracture of the right-frontal and parietal bones. Areas of high density under the fracture represent intra- and extracerebral hematomas (confirmed at surgery), whereas scattered areas of mixed intensity are contusions. There is a 16 to 18 mm shift of the septum pellucidum.

Damage to the dominant hemisphere (often the left), on the other hand, has been linked to such features as depression and anxiety. K. Goldstein (1948) reported that left-hemisphere damaged patients showed a "catastrophic reaction" characterized by impulsivity and anxiety in response to difficulty in performing everyday tasks. However, there is controversy concerning whether left-hemisphere damage is primarily responsible for these changes (Prigatano, 1987).

Site of lesion may also determine patterns of change. Damage to the frontal lobes, particularly to the orbitofrontal region, may result in alterations of personality characterized by disinhibition, emotional lability, impaired impulse control, and agitation, whereas lesions to the frontal convexities can lead to behaviors consisting of indifference, apathy and loss of initiative (Massey & Coffey, 1983). Patients with frontal-lobe damage may recover to a normal range of intelligence (at least on standardized IQ tests), although evidencing marked disability in social/occupational functioning (Eslinger & Damasio, 1985; Stuss & Benson, 1986). Ross and Stewart (1987) recently commented on the presence of pathological crying in two patients with damage to the right-inferior frontal region. Both patients had a history of major depression prior to their illnesses. The results suggest that structural brain damage as well as premorbid psychiatric disturbance combine to produce behavior that is not typical of either process alone.

Lishman (1968) commented on the presence of lesions in the left temporal lobe and the association of psychiatric disturbance in his series of penetrating head injuries. He also described a relationship between early onset of epilepsy and later disability and cited results of other investigators supporting the role of temporal lobe seizures in producing psychiatric manifestations (e.g., aggression). As Rosenthal (1983) noted, however, a direct correlation between aggressive behavior and temporal-lobe seizures may not be particularly strong because posttraumatic epilepsy occurs in about 5% of survivors and does not always involve the temporal lobes. Hypothalamic and basilar branch injuries may also produce disturbances characterized by apathy, irritability, and alteration in drive states related to appetite, sleep, and sexual activity (Bond, 1984; Rosenthal, 1983). A "Basal Syndrome" was identified by Kretschmer (cited in Rosenthal, 1983) incorporating these behaviors and also involving damage to the orbitofrontal region.

Finally, there are cases in which neuroradiologic and neurologic findings are normal (e.g., mild head injury) and patients still report a variety of complaints. Postconcussional symptoms including irritability, anxiety, depression, insomnia, and fatigue can persist despite apparent recovery on neuropsychological tests (Binder, 1986). In a recent three-center study of outcome of minor head injury, Levin and associates (1987b) reported that subjective complaints (e.g., depression) persisted at 1 and even 3 months postinjury despite recovery of neuropsychological functioning to the level of a matched control group. The presence of intracranial lesions undetected by CT, alteration in neurotransmitters, and effects of extracerebral injury (e.g., labyrinth disturbance producing vertigo) may contribute to the clinical profile.

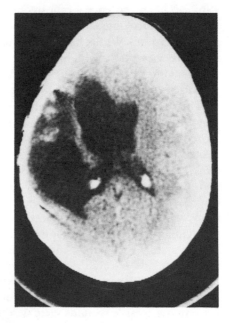

FIGURE 8.2. Axial noncontrast CT at level of frontal, temporal, and parietal opercula at 10 years postinjury. Massive right-hemisphere porencephaly (shown on left side of figure) involves large portions of frontal and temporal lobes with a smaller degree of parietal involvement. Small areas of basal ganglia and thalamus are spared.

Responses to Injury

Personality changes can also reflect an interplay of both the patient's reactions to disability and the response of family members and friends. K. Goldstein (1948) saw the "catastrophic reaction" as a response by the patient to cognitive confusion and loss of abstract reasoning which created a state of anxiety. This anxiety, in turn, led to socially inappropriate behavior. Leftoff (1983) described an association between cognitive deficits and psychiatric sequelae in a 39-year-old man who developed paranoid ideation following a cerebrovascular accident. Detailed neuropsychological testing disclosed cognitive deficits in problem-solving abilities and abstraction. Leftoff postulated that paranoid thinking was related to the patient's inability to interpret interpersonal relationships and served the purpose of imposing organization.

Apart from a response to cognitive impairment, sequelae may reflect attempts to cope with disability. Lezak (1983) noted that personality changes frequently arise as a result of loss, frustration, and life difficulties. Depression is one of the most common emotional characteristics of brain-injured patients and may be a healthy sign that signals awareness of deficits. On the other hand, patients may fail to acknowledge their problems and be extremely resistant to therapy (Prigatano, 1987).

Litigation has been described as a factor that can serve to maintain maladaptive behavior, particularly in cases of mild head injury (Miller, 1961). The persistence of postconcussional symptoms without corresponding neurologic sequelae and in patients with mild head injuries who are involved in lawsuits has suggested a potential for malingering. However, this viewpoint is highly controversial with several studies showing minimal links between persisting symptoms and current attempts at compensation (See Binder, 1986, for a review).

The families' reaction to disability and their subsequent behaviors can serve to reinforce and maintain maladaptive responses. McKinlay and Brooks (1984) observed that the level of complaints voiced by relatives was related to their own personality traits (higher scores on the Neuroticism Scale of the Eysenck Personality Inventory indicating anxiety, depression, and overreaction). Stress in family members appears to be related to perceived changes in the patients behavior, with relatives who display higher levels of stress reporting more inappropriate behaviors in patients (McKinlay et al., 1981). Figure 8.3 shows the potential relationships among stress, personality, and perceived changes. Although not necessarily causal, this research does suggest that family characteristics may be related to their own ability to cope with the patient's altered personality.

Rosenbaum and Najenson (1976) observed that patients who sustained penetrating missile wounds were described by their spouses as displaying

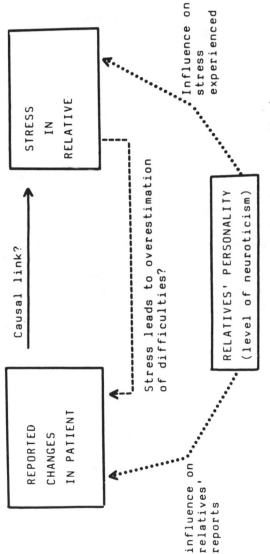

FIGURE 8.3. Possible relationships between relatives' reports, stress in relatives, and personality. From McKinlay, W. W., & Brooks, D. N. (1984). Methodological problems in assessing psychosocial recovery following severe head injury. *Journal of Clinical Neuropsychology, 6,* 82–99. Reprinted with permission of the author and publisher.

"childlike dependent" behaviors. This pattern was not totally attributable to brain injury because a group of paraplegic patients also showed the same trend in contrast to control subjects. The researchers noted that these behaviors were most likely related to the effects of a long hospitalization. In addition, parents became increasingly involved with the patients and their wives and displayed an overprotective attitude. Tarsh and Royston (1985) suggested that the postconcussional syndrome is maintained when family members perceive the patient as disabled. Such research may indicate that following head injury, factors in the environment can reinforce patient behaviors.

In summary, a number of factors including premorbid personality, location and severity of brain damage, as well as responses to disability contribute to the clinical picture after CHI. In the following sections, we describe the typical patterns of change that are reported in the acute and chronic phases of recovery.

CHARACTERISTICS OF PERSONALITY CHANGE

As noted earlier, a schema for classifying personality changes after CHI has not appeared in the literature. Yet, many investigators agree that personality reflects a number of interacting dimensions involving emotion, motivation, translation of behavior into action, and the ability to perceive internal and external stimuli. Prigatano's (1987) model of personality emphasizes the impact of brain damage on feelings, emotions, and motivations. In his framework, feelings refer to sensations of internal bodily states (e.g., hunger, thirst), emotions characterize interpretations of these feeling states and their appropriate interruption, whereas motivations serve to energize goal-directed activities. Brain injury may interfere with basic arousal components (e.g., brainstem), whereas damage to higher cerebral centers (e.g., frontal lobes) may produce deficits in the ability to perceive and interpret feelings. Lezak's (1978) characterization of changes after head injury also tends to emphasize alterations in emotional and motivational responses. These include an impaired capacity for self-control and regulation, lack of social perceptiveness, stimulus-bound behavior, and inability to profit from experience.

Recently, Levin et al. (1987a) developed the Neurobehavioral Rating Scale to characterize neurobehavioral changes after CHI (see Fig. 8.4). The scale, which is an adaptation of the Brief Psychiatric Rating Scale (Overall & Gorham, 1962), includes 27 dimensions rated by the clinician following a structured interview and a brief mental status examination. In a study involving 101 survivors of CHI, a principal components analysis of the Scale identified a number of factors underlying neurobehavioral sequelae such as cognition/energy (coherence of cognition, efficiency of memory, behavioral slowing), metacognition (inaccurate self-appraisal, unrealistic planning, and disinhibition), somatic concern/anxiety (physical complaints, anxiety, depression, and irritability) and language (expressive and receptive language deficits).

In the following sections, we characterize "personality" changes observed in patients in both the acute and chronic stages of recovery (see Table 8.2). As seen in Table 8.2, our discussion emphasizes the most commonly encountered alterations in affect (mood), cognition (ability to perceive and interpret experience), behavior (translation of motives into goal-directed activity), and somatic (perception of bodily changes) components.

TABLE 8.2
Common Features of Personality Change

Acute Stages			
Agitation			
Disinhibition			
Confabulation			
PTA			

Chronic Stages			
Affective	*Cognition*	*Behavior*	*Somatic*
Hypomania	Conceptual disorganization	Anergia	Headaches
Depression	Paranoid ideation	Social withdrawal	Dizziness
Emotional blunting	Disturbances in self-appraisal and planning	Disinhibition	Hypersensitivity Photophobia Decreased energy

Acute Stages of Recovery

Transient changes in dimensions of behavior and cognition are commonly associated with the initial injury. Patients may exhibit acute manifestations including agitation, inappropriate speech, disinhibition, and emotional lability. Confabulation (e.g., distorted reasons for being in the hospital), paranoid ideation, and, less frequently, visual and auditory hallucinations may exist (Bond, 1984; Levin & Grossman, 1978). Table 8.3 shows typical patterns of disturbance in selected patients exhibiting posttraumatic psychosis who were followed at the University of Texas Medical Branch in Galveston. Patients evidenced agitation as well as confabulatory and delusional speech that lacked a systematized quality (as seen, for example, in

NEUROBEHAVIORAL RATING SCALE

H.S. Levin, J.E. Overall, K.E. Goethe, W. High, R.A. Sisson

DIRECTIONS: Place an X in the appropriate box to represent level of severity of each symptom.

	Not Present	Very Mild	Mild	Moderate	Mod. Severe	Severe	Extremely Severe
1. **INATTENTION/REDUCED ALERTNESS**—fails to sustain attention, easily distracted; fails to notice aspects of environment, difficulty directing attention, decreased alertness.	☐	☐	☐	☐	☐	☐	☐
2. **SOMATIC CONCERN**—volunteers complaints or elaborates about somatic symptoms (e.g., headache, dizziness, blurred vision), and about physical health in general.	☐	☐	☐	☐	☐	☐	☐
3. **DISORIENTATION**—confusion or lack of proper association for person, place, or time.	☐	☐	☐	☐	☐	☐	☐
4. **ANXIETY**—worry, fear, overconcern for present or future.	☐	☐	☐	☐	☐	☐	☐
5. **EXPRESSIVE DEFICIT**—word-finding disturbance, anomia, pauses in speech, effortful and agrammatic speech, circumlocution.	☐	☐	☐	☐	☐	☐	☐
6. **EMOTIONAL WITHDRAWAL**—lack of spontaneous interaction, isolation, deficiency in relating to others.	☐	☐	☐	☐	☐	☐	☐
7. **CONCEPTUAL DISORGANIZATION**—thought processes confused, disconnected, disorganized, disrupted; tangential social communication; perseverative.	☐	☐	☐	☐	☐	☐	☐
8. **DISINHIBITION**—socially inappropriate comments and/or actions, including aggressive/sexual content, or inappropriate to the situation, outbursts of temper.	☐	☐	☐	☐	☐	☐	☐
9. **GUILT FEELINGS**—self-blame, shame, remorse for past behavior.	☐	☐	☐	☐	☐	☐	☐
10. **MEMORY DEFICIT**—difficulty learning new information, rapidly forgets recent events, although immediate recall (forward digit span) may be intact.	☐	☐	☐	☐	☐	☐	☐
11. **AGITATION**—motor manifestations of overactivity (e.g., kicking, arm flailing, picking, roaming, restlessness, talkativeness.)	☐	☐	☐	☐	☐	☐	☐
12. **INACCURATE INSIGHT AND SELF-APPRAISAL**—poor insight, exaggerated self-opinion, overrates level of ability and underrates personality change in comparison with evaluation by clinicians and family.	☐	☐	☐	☐	☐	☐	☐
13. **DEPRESSIVE MOOD**—sorrow, sadness, despondency, pessimism.	☐	☐	☐	☐	☐	☐	☐
14. **HOSTILITY/UNCOOPERATIVENESS**—animosity, irritability, belligerence, disdain for others, defiance of authority.	☐	☐	☐	☐	☐	☐	☐
15. **DECREASED INITIATIVE/MOTIVATION**—lacks normal initiative in work or leisure, fails to persist in tasks, is reluctant to accept new challenges.	☐	☐	☐	☐	☐	☐	☐
16. **SUSPICIOUSNESS**—mistrust, belief that others harbor malicious or discriminatory intent.	☐	☐	☐	☐	☐	☐	☐
17. **FATIGABILITY**—rapidly fatigues on challenging cognitive tasks or complex activities, lethargic.	☐	☐	☐	☐	☐	☐	☐
18. **HALLUCINATORY BEHAVIOR**—perceptions without normal external stimulus correspondence.	☐	☐	☐	☐	☐	☐	☐
19. **MOTOR RETARDATION**—slowed movements or speech (excluding primary weakness).	☐	☐	☐	☐	☐	☐	☐
20. **UNUSUAL THOUGHT CONTENT**—unusual, odd, strange, bizarre thought content.	☐	☐	☐	☐	☐	☐	☐
21. **BLUNTED AFFECT**—reduced emotional tone, reduction in normal intensity of feelings, flatness.	☐	☐	☐	☐	☐	☐	☐
22. **EXCITEMENT**—heightened emotional tone, increased reactivity.	☐	☐	☐	☐	☐	☐	☐
23. **POOR PLANNING**—unrealistic goals, poorly formulated plans for the future, disregards prerequisites (e.g., training), fails to take disability into account.	☐	☐	☐	☐	☐	☐	☐
24. **LABILITY OF MOOD**—sudden change in mood which is disproportionate to the situation.	☐	☐	☐	☐	☐	☐	☐
25. **TENSION**—postural and facial expression of heightened tension, without the necessity of excessive activity involving the limbs or trunk.	☐	☐	☐	☐	☐	☐	☐
26. **COMPREHENSION DEFICIT**—difficulty in understanding oral instructions on single or multistage commands.	☐	☐	☐	☐	☐	☐	☐
27. **SPEECH ARTICULATION DEFECT**—misarticulation, slurring or substitution of sounds which affect intelligibility (rating is independent of linguistic content.)	☐	☐	☐	☐	☐	☐	☐

FIGURE 8.4. Neurobehavioral Rating Scale. From H. S. Levin, et al. (1987). The Neurobehavioural Rating Scale: Assessment of the behavioural sequelae of head injury by the clinician. *Journal of Neurology, Neurosurgery, and Psychiatry, 50*, 183–193. Reprinted with permission of the publisher.

schizophrenia). There was an impressive range of coma durations in these patients. Neuroradiologic findings were typically abnormal and were characterized by diffuse cerebral swelling and intracranial hematomas.

Inappropriate behavior following emergence from coma is frequently accompanied by disorientation, difficulty in sustaining attention, and inability to remember daily activities (posttraumatic amnesia or PTA) (Russell & Smith, 1961). The presence and duration of PTA has been measured by serial interviews with the patient and clinical ratings of behavior. The Galveston Orientation and Amnesia Test (GOAT) developed by Levin, O'Donnell, and Grossman (1979) requests information concerning person, place, and time and memory for events preceding and following the injury. Scores below 75 (75 to 100 reflects normal functioning) are indicative of disorientation and memory impairments. Figure 8.5 shows the performance on the GOAT of a severely head injured patient who was involved in a motorcycle accident on August 15, 1984. The patient's Glasgow Coma Scale score on admission was 7 (no eye opening, localized to pain, trached). CT scans on the day of admission revealed a left-frontal contusion. He began obeying commands on August 17. The patient exhibited marked temporal disorientation, confabulated information concerning geographic location, and showed retrograde and anterograde amnesia. Serial administration of the GOAT indicated reorientation to a stable level by September 19, although the patient was unable to recall events leading up to and following his accident (GOAT score = 73 on October 3, 1984). Clinician ratings such as the Rancho Los Amigos Scale (1972) consist of observations by the staff in eight categories of behavior ranging from "no response" (patient unresponsive to stimuli) to "purposeful and appropriate" (alert, oriented, can transfer new learning, etc.).

These early manifestations of behavioral/cognitive disturbances are frequently related to both the severity of injury and later deficits. Levin and Grossman (1978) observed that agitation was associated with the presence of an initial language disturbance (aphasia) and was more common in patients with severe (loss of consciousness for more than 24 hours) versus mild head injuries. Agitation was predictive of residual anxiety and depression, thinking disturbance and greater psychopathology as measured by the Brief Psychiatric Rating Scale (Overall & Gorham, 1962). Lishman (1968) observed that PTA duration was related to later patterns of impaired cognition and affective/behavioral disorders, somatic complaints and psychiatric illness. Whereas Levin and Grossman (1978) did not observe a relationship between posttraumatic agitation and focal lesions on CT, a report (Gandy, Snow, Zimmerman, & Deck, 1984) using MRI technology found evidence for intracerebral lesions that were not detected by CT in three head-injured patients. One patient who was agitated, combative, and mute had findings on MRI of multiple areas of edema or contusion (bifrontal, biocipital, biparietal, and right temporal).

TABLE 8.3

Psychotic Behavior During the Early Stage of Recovery from Closed Head Injury

	Initial Glasgow Scale[a]				Coma[b] (days)	Initial CT	Manifestations Observed During Initial Hospitalization				
Age	Sex	V	E	M			Redupl	Confab/ delusions	Halluc	Agitation	Disinhib
20	F	4	4	6	0	WNL		Paranoid fear	Visual	Extreme hypoact	R
21	M	4	4	6	0	WNL		Having baby		Screaming; out of bed	R
19	M	2	4	6	0	WNL		Delusions of grandeur; paranoid		Thrushing; pacing	R
25	M	4	4	6	0	Right sylvian SAH; vertex EH				Motor restlessness	R; exhib
27	F	1	1	5	<1	Diffuse swelling		Having baby	Visual; audit	Motor restlessness	R; exhib
24	M	T	1	5	2	Right insula IH	Geogr	In prison for crime	Audit	Thrashing; screaming	R
18	M	3	1	5	4	Bifront IH	Geogr; context	In army		Motor restlessness	R
24	F	1	1	5	4	Diffuse swelling	Geogr; persons	Having baby, paranoid	Visual	Screaming; restlessness	R; exhib
19	M	1	1	4	20	Bifront SH	Geogr	Extraordinary confab of injury; paranoid		Screaming; restlessness	
21	M	1	1	2	36	Right temp EH		Circumstances of injury		Screaming; empty excitement	R

[a] Glasgow Scale scores obtained on admission to hospital. Abbreviations: T, tracheostomy; V, verbal; E, eye opening; M, motor.

[b] Coma duration refers to the period during which patient could not respond to commands.

Note: Abbreviations: CT, computed tomography; Redupl, reduplication; Confab, confabulation; SAH, subarachnoid hemorrhage; EH, epidural hematoma; IH, intracerebral hematoma; bifront, bifrontal; temp, temporal; geogr, geography; R, restraints required; Disinhib, disinhibition; Exhib, exhibitionistic behavior.

Adapted from Levin, H. S., Benton, A. L., & Grossman, R. G. (1982). Neurobehavioral consequences of closed head injury. New York: Oxford University Press.

Reprinted with permission of the publisher.

Name ___D.B.___

Age __28__ Sex __M__ F

Date of Birth __2 , 4 , 56__
mo day yr

Diagnosis ___CHI with Multiple Trauma___

Date of Test __9 , 5 , 84__
mo day yr

Day of the week s m t <u>w</u> th f s

Time __AM__ __PM__

Date of injury __8 , 15 , 84__
mo day yr

GALVESTON ORIENTATION & AMNESIA TEST (GOAT)

Harvey S. Levin, Ph.D., Vincent M. O'Donnell, M.A., & Robert G. Grossman, M.D.

INSTRUCTIONS: Error points (shown in parentheses after each question) are scored for incorrect answers and are entered in the two columns on the extreme right side of the test form. Enter the total error points accrued for the 10 items in the lower right hand corner of the test form. The GOAT score equals 100 minus the total error points. Recovery of orientation is depicted by plotting serial GOAT scores on at least a daily basis.

Error Points

1. What is your name? (2) ___D.B.___   When were you born? (4) ___Feb 4, 1956___ [__4__]

   Where do you live? (4) ___Around Abilene___

2. Where are you now? (5) city ___UTMB (Salt Lake City)___   (5) hospital ___Small church-type school___ [1 , 0]

   (unnecessary to state name of hospital)

3. On what date were you admitted to this hospital? (5) ___Couple of months—month so far___ [1 , 0]

   How did you get here? (5) ___I went and checked in myself___

4. What is the first event you can remember after the injury? (5) ___Going hunting___ [1 , 0]

   Can you describe in detail (e.g., date, time, companions) the first event you can recall after injury? (5)

5. Can you describe the last event you recall before the accident? (5) ___I guess going around and checking some [1 , 0]
   doctors___

   Can you describe in detail (e.g., date, time, companions)

   the first event you can recall before the injury? (5)

6. What time is it now? ___2:00 p.m.___ 1 for each ½ hour removed from correct time to maximum of 5) [__5__]

7. What day of the week is it? ___Wed.___ 1 for each day removed from correct one) [1 , 5]

8. What day of the month is it? ___28___ 1 for each day removed from correct date to maximum of 5) [1 , 5]

9. What is the month? ___March___ 5 for each month removed from correct one to maximum of 15)

10. What is the year? ___1984___ 10 for each year removed from correct one to maximum of 30)

Total Error Points [6 , 9]

Total GOAT Score (100-total error points) [3 , 1]

FIGURE 8.5. GOAT performance of severe CHI patient 20 days post injury.

Management of patients in the acute phase typically incorporates safety features (side rails, restraints), external structure (scheduled activities, maintenance of location of items in the room), and orientation (calendar in room, pictures of family members). When the patient recovers from PTA, concern about the inability to recall events concerning the accident is common. Patients are frequently transferred to a rehabilitation facility or home where more chronic effects on personality may be seen.

Chronic Stages of Recovery

Affective Changes

A number of affective changes have been observed after CHI including hypomania, depression, and emotional blunting. Following emergence from PTA, a patient may demonstrate a euphoric or elevated mood similar to, but less severe than, a manic episode (American Psychiatric Association, 1980). Such behavior may be accompanied by excited speech, paranoid ideation, disinhibition, and aggressiveness. Frequently, there is a lack of insight concerning the injury (Levin et al., 1982). Bond (1984) noted that hypomania is more common in the early stages of recovery when the patient is still confused and has difficulty integrating information although it may also be seen months to years after injury.

Depression is a more common affective feature following closed head injury and includes a constellation of symptoms involving changes in appetite and sleep, loss of energy, psychomotor agitation or retardation, difficulty in concentration, feelings of worthlessness or guilt, and suicidal ideation (American Psychiatric Association, 1980). Depression typically evolves as an appropriate reaction to the effects of trauma and may appear after acute hospitalization when the patient returns home and confronts the impact of the injury on daily functioning (Rosenthal, 1983). The presence of depressive symptoms is typical after both mild and severe CHI and appears unrelated to severity (Levin, 1987). This pattern may indicate the relative importance of premorbid features and environmental reactions. Other factors, such as altered levels of brain catecholamines and cholinergic metabolism, may also serve to maintain the response (Levin et al., 1982).

Although Dikmen and Reitan (1977) reported an improvement in emotional sequelae based on serial administration of the MMPI, more recent studies have not supported this finding. McKinlay et al. (1981) found that relatives described depression in patients as a frequent and enduring change both at three (57% of cases), six (52%) and 12 (57%) months postinjury. Levin and coworkers (1987a) administered the Neurobehavioral Rating Scale to patients during acute hospitalization (mean = 23.9

days) and at follow-up (mean = 139 days). Although factor scores related to unusual thought content, cognitive efficiency and behavioral slowing, and language abilities showed significant improvements over serial assessments, a factor measuring qualities including somatic complaints, anxiety, and depression was unchanged. Fordyce, Roueche, and Prigatano (1983) noted an intensification of emotional distress in patients tested 6 months or later after injury as compared to cases assessed earlier. Using a cross-sectional design, findings from the MMPI administered to patients and the Katz Adjustment Scale completed by relatives indicated that depression, anger, anxiety, thinking disturbance, and social withdrawal were more prevalent in the later stages of recovery.

Although depression may occur in the absence of neuropsychological impairment (Fordyce et al., 1983; Prigatano, 1987), it may also be related to the degree of deficit. Dikmen and Reitan (1977) observed a relationship between items on the MMPI measuring somatic preoccupation, depression and anxiety and the presence of cognitive deficit. Patients with moderate or severe deficits evidenced more emotional sequelae than those showing no or mild dysfunction. These results point to the importance of concurrently examining personality and neuropsychological dimensions.

Finally, a blunting of affect following CHI can reflect a basic arousal deficit characterized by lethargy, slow thought processes, and passivity or a motivational disturbance representing a lack of hedonic responses (Wood, 1984). Levin and Grossman (1978) noted that constriction of affective expression on the Brief Psychiatric Rating Scale was related to such behaviors as social withdrawal, solitary activities and cognitive impairment. Patients may appear unconcerned (anosodiaphoria) even in the absence of denial concerning their illness. Bilateral lesions of the frontal convexities can induce a "pseudodepressed" syndrome in which indifference, apathy, loss of initiative, and bradykinesia are the chief features. Right-hemisphere damage is frequently associated with these emotional changes in stroke patients (Heilman et al., 1985).

Levin and colleagues (1987a) identified a factor on the Neurobehavioral Rating Scale termed *cognition/energy* which consisted of items measuring cognitive efficiency, motor retardation, and emotional withdrawal. Scores on this factor showed greater patterns of disturbance as severity of injury increased (mild versus moderate versus severe injuries), which basically represented the contribution of conceptual disorganization rather than a direct relationship between severity and emotional blunting.

Cognitive Changes

Along with changes in affect, patients frequently demonstrate difficulties in organizing thoughts and interpreting experiences. One may observe unusual thought content, paranoid ideation, as well as inaccurate self-appraisal and insight. Conceptual disorganization is a prominent feature of head injury and has been found to be related to severity (Levin, Grossman, Rose, & Teasdale, 1979; Levin et al., 1987a). It is frequently characterized by confused and disconnected thought processes, tangential social communication, and perseveration.

Paranoid ideation may result from the patient's inability to interpret interpersonal situations, resulting in suspiciousness and misunderstanding of intentions. In addition, neuropsychological impairments involving perceptual dysfunction may lead to an impairment in the ability to analyze visual inputs, thereby enhancing paranoid interpretations (Prigatano, 1987). Delusions of grandeur and of persecution were observed in a severely closed head injured patient tested in our laboratory. On admission to the hospital, the patient had a GCS score of 4 (no eye opening, no verbalizations, decerebrate movements). CT scans showed areas of hemorrhage in the left-frontal and left parietal-occipital lobes. During the clinical interview 2 years post injury, the patient explained that he was more cooperative in the current testing session than in an earlier one because he realized that the examiner was not part of a "conspiracy." When questioned about his accident, he stated that he could not talk about it until he had determined whether it was a "wreck or an accident." In addition, when asked whether he believed that someone was responsible for the accident, he accused the examiner of trying to induce him to make false accusations. The patient had no known previous history of psychiatric disorder or substance abuse.

Temporal-lobe pathology as well as premorbid personality have been suggested to play a role in the development of paranoid ideation (Prigatano, 1987). The Organic Personality Syndrome (American Psychiatric Association, 1980) is often applied as a label for patients in whom emotional lability, impaired impulse control, apathy, and suspiciousness or paranoid ideation are the marked clinical features. However, this label does not include the associated intellectual deficits that are also frequently present in these patients.

Another characteristic of patients is their failure to acknowledge deficits produced by injury. McKinlay and Brooks (1984) found that patients and relatives expressed agreement concerning sensory and motor impairments but were less likely to concur on emotional and behavioral changes such as poor temper and anxiety. Patients tended to minimize the severity of these alterations. A failure to appreciate deficits may result in an impaired capacity for formulating goals and realistic plans. Levin et al. (1987a) found that a factor measuring "metacognition" or knowledge of one's cognitive processes was related to severity of injury. As seen in Fig. 8.6, disturbances involving self-appraisal (e.g., exaggerated self-opinion, overrating ability or underrating personality change in comparison to family and clinicians) and planning (e.g., poor formulation of future goals) were characteristic of patients sustaining severe injuries (GCS ≤ 8). Such deficits are typically associated with frontal-lobe lesions (Stuss & Benson, 1986). Levin and colleagues found suggestions for the notion that disturbances in metacognition were common in patients with frontal-lobe damage. However, a strict test relating impairments in planning and self-evaluation to frontal lesions in the CHI population has not yet been undertaken.

Behavioral Changes

Coupled with disturbances in affect and cognition, a common feature of many brain-injured patients is their loss of goal-directed activity which can manifest itself as a problem in initiating behaviors and sustaining effort on tasks. Anergia (decreased or absent motivation) may reflect an underlying depression or result from denial or minimization of deficits, leading to a failure to appreciate the importance of self-motivation for performance. Brain injury may also alter environmental responses to reinforcing stimuli. As a result, patients who would normally work hard to achieve a particular reward may not find the incentive as reinforcing as prior to the injury (Wood, 1984). Finally, patients may appear unmotivated but actually have neuropsychological deficits that compromise performance. Prigatano (1987) noted that distractible patients may be overwhelmed by task demands and, therefore, have difficulty initiating actions. When provided with structure, however, they show evidence of sustained effort and high drive. Rehabilitation efforts frequently incorporate treatment aimed at awareness of deficits and an understanding of emotional/motivational disturbances (Prigatano et al., 1984). In addition, behavior modification approaches incorporating positive reinforcement, time out, and a token economy system to shape behaviors such as goal setting may be beneficial (Newcombe, 1982).

Social withdrawal, another prevalent behavioral consequence, typically involves lessened social interactions and a relinquishment of recreational activities. Withdrawal may reflect a response to repeated failure and frustration from environmental interactions (Prigatano, 1987). There is some evidence that social withdrawal intensifies over time as indicated by relatives' ratings at 3, 6, and 12 months postinjury (McKinlay & Brooks, 1984). As a result of decreased interaction with others and self-absorption, the quality of family communications may change. Dependency, "childlike behaviors," egocentricity and increased attentional demands are characteristic of many patients (Rosenbaum & Najenson, 1976; Rosenthal, 1983).

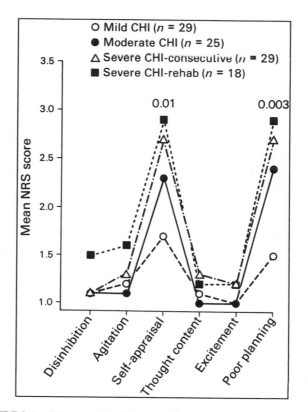

FIGURE 8.6. "Metacognition" factor of the Neurobehavioral Rating Scale. From Levin, H. S. et al (1987). The Neurobehavioural Rating Scale: Assessment of the behavioural sequelae of head injury by the clinician. *Journal of Neurology, Neurosurgery, and Psychiatry, 50,* 183–193. Reprinted with permission of the publisher.

Oddy and Humphrey (1980) examined psychosocial functioning in closed head injured patients within 4 weeks, 6 months, 12 months, and 2 years of their injuries. Patients and relatives were interviewed concerning changes in leisure activities, social contacts, and family relationships. At 1 and 2 years, 50% of the patients were engaged in fewer activities than prior to their injuries. Similarly, patients reported fewer friends and social visits which, though uncorrelated with residual sensory or motor deficits, was related to impaired performance on memory tests. Patients with long PTA durations generally had lessened interactions. Poor family relationships, particularly between the patient and a sibling, were characteristic of those patients judged by their relatives to have more personality changes and a greater number of subjective symptoms as reported by the relative.

Behaviors involving disinhibition or difficulty in the normal regulation of emotional states may occur after head injury. As a result of a defective ability to control and regulate behaviors into socially appropriate channels, patients often appear impulsive, restless, and impatient (Lezak, 1978). On the basis of interviews with relatives of severely (PTA of at least 2 days) injured patients, McKinlay et al. (1981) derived a category of disturbed behaviors consisting of such changes as violent and inappropriate social behavior, excessive talking, and childishness. Although violent behaviors were reported in fewer than 20% of the cases, there were indications that these actions posed serious stress to family members. Lezak (1978) also noted the high incidence of abuse encompassing sarcasm, rejection, and accusations of infidelity. Disturbances of the medial temporal lobes and limbic system and premorbid personality have been suggested to play a role in the appearance of such behaviors.

Somatic Changes

A final category of change observed after head injury involves the patient's perception of physical sensations and their expression. Typical somatic complaints include headaches, dizziness, hypersensitivity (e.g., to noise), and photophobia. These symptoms, along with reports of fatigue, irritability, depression, anxiety, decreased concentration and poor memory, are characteristic of the postconcussional syndrome following mild head injury (Binder, 1986; Levin et al., 1982). Levin and colleagues (1987b) recently conducted a three-center study to examine changes in sequelae of mild head-injured patients at baseline, 1 month, and 3 months postinjury. These patients had none or brief loss of consciousness, GCS scores of 13–15 implying the ability to follow commands, normal neurologic signs, and neuroradiologic findings, and did not require intracranial surgery. In addition, patients were free of an antecedent history of head injury and neuropsychiatric disturbance. The three most salient complaints at baseline across all centers were headaches, decreased energy, and dizziness which, although declining in frequency by 1 month, were still reported. These complaints (especially headaches) were present at 3 months even in patients demonstrating cognitive recovery (e.g., memory, concentration) to the level of control performance.

Levin et al. (1987a) observed greater somatic concern (i.e., physical complaints, depression, and irritability) in patients sustaining mild versus severe injuries and noted that the lack of complaints from these severe patients who were enrolled in rehabilitation was most likely related to inaccurate self-appraisal, denial, or unawareness of physical disability. However, such complaints also occur in other severity groups. Van Zomeren and Van Den Burg (1985) studied 61 severely closed head-injured patients 2 years postinjury. Complaints were evaluated through a questionnaire asking patients to rate whether particular characteristics (e.g., forgetfulness) were absent or present as compared to before the injury. A principal components analysis performed on these items in relationship to length of PTA and whether or not the patient had returned to work (RTW) revealed two factors. As seen in Table 8.4, PTA and RTW loaded most highly on a factor labelled *severity,* which consisted of other items including forgetfulness, slowness, inability to divide attention, and depression. A factor labelled *complaining* was unrelated to PTA and RTW. This dimension was correlated with symptoms including irritability, fatigue, dizziness, intolerance of light and noise, headaches, and emotional lability. Van Zomeren and Van Den Burg suggested that this later category of behaviors or "intolerances" may be more prevalent in patients without obvious deficits (e.g., physical handicaps) that would normally prevent them from resuming daily activities. Intolerances may develop as a result of stress produced by cognitive deficits and societal and personal expectations.

TREATMENT DIRECTIONS

As reviewed in the previous sections, a number of underlying dimensions to personality are altered following closed head injury. In line with suggestions from the research literature (e.g., Oddy & Humphrey, 1980), rehabilitation efforts have progressively moved away from an emphasis based solely on physical impairments to treatment of these longstanding disturbances. In addition, therapies have been aimed toward a more holistic approach involving not only the patient but significant others as well.

One technique for managing personality changes has been to utilize individual or group psychotherapy sessions. Such approaches may be useful in directing patients toward an understanding of impairments and the impact on daily activities (Prigatano, 1987). Psychotherapy is typically an effective adjunct to cognitive retraining. As Prigatano (1987) noted, patients may manifest a catastrophic reaction characterized by severe anxiety when dealing with cognitive tasks. Helping the patient to understand this reaction and developing techniques such as stress reduction are critical in maintaining patient interest and motivation. Individual therapy sessions may work on patient acceptance of the ramifications of disability and engagement in activities that are likely to generate success (e.g., to capitalize on strengths rather than weaknesses). Therapy can also focus on exploring interpersonal issues such as marital relations (Rosenbaum, Lipsitz, Abraham, & Najenson, 1978). Group sessions can be particularly

TABLE 8.4

Principal Components of PTA, RTW, and Residual Complaints as Indicated by
52 Patients. The factors are quartimax rotated.

	"Complaining" Factor 1	"Severity" Factor 2
PTA	−0.13	0.80
RTW	0.14	0.70
Forgetfulness	0.19	0.63
Irritability	0.59	−0.03
Slowness	0.25	0.66
Poor concentration	0.61	0.42
Fatigue	0.68	0.31
Dizziness	0.52	−0.03
Increased need of sleep	0.51	−0.24
Intolerance of light	0.72	−0.07
Intolerance of noise	0.61	0.33
Loss of initiative	0.51	0.38
Headache	0.57	−0.17
Crying more readily	0.60	0.16
Inability to do two things simul.	0.44	0.62
Intolerance of bustle	0.61	0.12
Depressed mood	0.32	0.53
More anxious	0.33	−0.05
Indifference	0.24	0.13

Note: PTA, posttraumatic amnesia; RTW, return to work.

Adapted from Van Zomeren, A. H., & Van Den Burg, W. (1985). Residual complaints of patients two years after severe head injury. *Journal of Neurology, Neurosurgery, and Psychiatry, 48,* 21–28. Reprinted with permission of the author and publisher.

beneficial to patients needing social skills training or help dealing with problems of social withdrawal and depression.

Behavior modification techniques are frequently more appropriate than insight training for severely injured patients whose cognitive deficits compromise the efficacy of traditional psychotherapy. In addition, such methods may help to motivate patients through the establishment of short (e.g., strengthening exercises) rather than long-term goals (e.g., to walk), the use of measurable and observable behaviors, and incentives that are defined by the patient. Eames and Wood (1985) have described the application of a token economy system at the Kemsley Unit of St. Andrew's Hospital (United Kingdom) to 24 severely closed head-injured patients whose extreme behaviors prevented placement in traditional rehabilitation and care facilities. At follow-up a number of patients were in higher level placements (e.g., at home, in supervised facilities) than prior to treatment and were engaged in hobbies and premorbid activities. The generalization of such techniques and their maintenance over time needs to be established, however.

Family therapy techniques also appear important to the treatment of disturbances. Lezak (1978) described typical reactions including isolation, depression, and frustration. Family stress tends to intensify over time and appears more related to the patient's personality and cognitive changes than to physical deficits (McKinlay et al., 1981). Families often complain that they lack information concerning the patient's condition and future (Lezak, 1978; Oddy et al., 1978). Although it is difficult to establish long-term prognosis, explanation of current behaviors and reassurance can aid families in understanding these alterations. Moreover, family members need to comprehend the impact of their own behavior in potentially maintaining patient responses.

Appreciation of personality changes after closed head injury has greatly increased due to systematic research efforts. Application of long-term follow-ups and an understanding of the impact of premorbid features, brain injury, and environmental correlates will ultimately add to our ability to manage and to treat these disturbances.

ACKNOWLEDGMENTS

Preparation of this chapter was supported in part by grant NS-21889, Javits Neuroscience Investigator Award (HSL). We are indebted to Liz Zindler for assistance in manuscript preparation.

REFERENCES

Adams, J. H., Mitchell, D. E., Graham, D. I., & Doyle, D. (1977). Diffuse brain damage of immediate impact type. *Brain, 100,* 489–502.

Adams, J. H., Graham, D. I., Murray, L. S., & Scott, G. (1982). Diffuse axonal injury due to nomissile head injury in humans: An analysis of 45 cases. *Annals of Neurology, 12,* 557–563.

American Psychiatric Association. (1980). *Diagnostic and statistical manual of mental disorders (3rd ed).* Washington, D.C.: American Psychological Association.

Bear, D. M. (1983). Hemispheric specialization and the neurology of emotion. *Archives of Neurology, 40,* 195–202.

Binder, L. M. (1986). Persisting symptoms after mild head injury: A review of the post-concussive syndrome. *Journal of Clinical and Experimental Neuropsychology, 8,* 323–346.

Bond, M. R. (1984). The psychiatry of closed head injury. In N. Brooks (Ed.), *Closed head injury: Psychological, social and family consequences* (pp. 148–178). New York: Oxford University Press.

Bond, M. R., & Brooks, D. N. (1976). Understanding the process of recovery as a basis for the investigation of rehabilitation for the brain injured. *Scandanavian Journal of Rehabilitation Medicine, 8,* 127–133.

Brown, G., Chadwick, D., Schaffer, D., Rutter, M., & Traub, M. (1981). A prospective study of children with head injuries: III. Psychiatric sequelae. *Psychological Medicine, 11,* 63–78.

Dikmen, S., & Reitan, R. M. (1977). Emotional sequelae of head injury. *Annals of Neurology, 2,* 492–494.

Eames, P., & Wood, R. (1985). Rehabilitation after severe brain injury: A follow-up study of a behaviour modification approach. *Journal of Neurology, Neurosurgery, and Psychiatry, 48,* 613–619.

Eslinger, P. J., & Damasio, A. R. (1985). Severe disturbance of higher cognition following bilateral frontal lobe ablation: Patient EVR. *Neurology, 38,* 1731–1741.

Fordyce, D. J., Roueche, J. R., & Prigatano, G. P. (1983). Enhanced emotional reactions in chronic head trauma patients. *Journal of Neurology, Neurosurgery, and Psychiatry, 46,* 620–624.

Gandy, S. E., Snow, R. B., Zimmerman, R. D., & Deck, M. D. (1984). Cranial nuclear magnetic resonance imaging in head trauma. *Annals of Neurology, 16,* 254–257.

Goethe, K. E., & Levin, H. S. (1984). Behavioral manifestations during the early and long-term stages of recovery after closed head injury. *Psychiatric Annals, 14,* 540–546.

Goldstein, F. C., & Levin, H. S. (1987). Disorders of reasoning and problem-solving ability. In M. J. Meier, A. L. Benton, & L. Diller (Eds.), *Neuropsychological rehabilitation* (pp. 327–354). New York: Churchill Livingstone.

Goldstein, K. (1948). *Aftereffects of brain injuries in war.* New York: Grune and Stratton.

Hagen, C., Malkmus, D., & Durham, P. (1972). Rancho Los Amigos Levels of Cognitive Functioning Scale. Rancho Los Amigos Hospital.

Heilman, K. M., Bowers, D., & Valenstein, E. (1985). Emotional disorders associated with neurological diseases. In K. M. Heilman & E. Valenstein (Eds.), *Clinical neuropsychology* (pp. 377–402). New York: Oxford University Press.

Heilman, K. M., Scholes, R., & Watson, R. T. (1975). Auditory affective agnosia: Disturbed comprehension of affective speech. *Journal of Neurology, Neurosurgery, and Psychiatry, 38,* 69–72.

Jennett, B., & Teasdale, G. (1981). *Management of head injuries.* Philadelphia: F. A. Davis Company.

Kerr, T. A., Kay, D. W., & Lassman, L. P. (1971). Characteristics of patients, type of accident, and mortality in a consecutive series of head injuries admitted to a neurosurgical unit. *British Journal of Preventive Social Medicine, 25,* 179–185.

Kraus, J. F. (1987). Epidemiology of head injury. In P. R. Cooper (Ed.), *Head injury* (pp. 1–19). Baltimore: Williams & Wilkins.

Leftoff, S. (1983). Psychopathology in the light of brain injury: A case study. *Journal of Clinical Neuropsychology, 5,* 51–63.

Levin, H. S. (1987). Neurobehavioral sequelae of head injury. In P. R. Cooper (Ed.), *Head injury* (pp. 442–463). Baltimore: Williams & Wilkins.

Levin, H. S., Benton, A. L., & Grossman, R. G. (1982). *Neurobehavioral consequences of closed head injury.* New York: Oxford University Press.

Levin, H. S., & Grossman, R. G. (1978). Behavioral sequelae of closed head injury. *Archives of Neurology, 35,* 720–727.

Levin, H. S., Grossman, R. G., Rose, J. E., & Teasdale, G. (1979). Long-term neuropsychological outcome of closed head injury. *Journal of Neurosurgery, 50,* 412–422.

Levin, H. S., High, Jr., W. M., Goethe, K. E., Sisson, R. A., Overall, J. E., Rhoades, H. M., Eisenberg, H. M., Kalisky, Z., & Gary, Jr., H. E. (1987a). The Neurobehavioural Rating Scale: Assessment of the behavioural sequelae of head injury by the clinician. *Journal of Neurology, Neurosurgery, and Psychiatry, 50,* 183–193.

Levin, H. S., Mattis, S., Ruff, R. M., Eisenberg, H. M., Marshall, L. F., Trabaddor, K., High, Jr., W. M., & Frankowski, R. F. (1987b). Neurobehavioral outcome following minor head injury: A three-center study. *Journal of Neurosurgery, 66,* 234–243.

Levin, H. S., O'Donnell, V. M., & Grossman, R. G. (1979). The Galveston orientation and amnesia test: A practical scale to assess cognition after head injury. *Journal of Nervous and Mental Disease, 167,* 675–684.

Lezak, M. D. (1978). Living with the characterologically altered brain injured patient. *Journal of Clinical Psychiatry, 39,* 592–598.

Lezak, M. D. (1983). *Neuropsychological assessment.* New York: Oxford Press.

Lishman, W. A. (1968). Brain damage in relation to psychiatric disability after head injury. *British Journal of Psychiatry, 114,* 373–410.

Lishman, W. A. (1973). The psychiatric sequelae of head injury: A review. *Psychological Medicine, 3,* 304–318.

Massey, E. W., & Coffey, C. E. (1983). Frontal lobe personality syndromes: Ominous sequelae of head trauma. *Postgraduate Medicine, 73,* 99–106.

McKinlay, W. W., & Brooks, D. N. (1984). Methodological problems in assessing psychosocial recovery following severe head injury. *Journal of Clinical Neuropsychology, 6,* 87–99.

McKinlay, W. W., Brooks, D. N., Bond, M. R., Martinage, D. P., & Marshall, M. M. (1981). The short-term outcome of severe blunt head injury as reported by relatives of the injured persons. *Journal of Neurology, Neurosurgery, and Psychiatry, 44,* 527–533.

McLean, A., Dikmen, S., Temkin, N., Wyler, A. R., & Gale, J. (1984). Psychosocial functioning at 1 month after head injury. *Neurosurgery, 14,* 393–399.

McLean, A., Temkin, N. R., Dikmen, S., & Wyler, A. R. (1983). The behavioral sequelae of head injury. *Journal of Clinical Neuropsychology, 5,* 361–376.

Miller, H. (1961). Accident neurosis. *British Medical Journal, 1,* 919–925, 992–998.

Muir, C. A., Haffey, W. J., Ott, K. J., Karaica, D., Muir, J. H., & Sutko, M. (1983). Treatment of behavioral deficits. In M. Rosenthal, E. R. Griffith, M. A. Bond, & J. D. Miller (Eds.), *Rehabilitation of the head injured adult* (pp. 381–393). Philadelphia: F. A. Davis Company.

Newcombe, F. (1982). The psychological consequences of closed head injury: Assessment and rehabilitation. *Injury: The British Journal of Accident Surgery, 14,* 111–136.

Oddy, M., & Humphrey, M. (1980). Social recovery during the year following severe head injury. *Journal of Neurology, Neurosurgery, and Psychiatry, 43,* 798–802.

Oddy, M., Humphrey, M., & Uttley, D. (1978). Stresses upon the relatives of head-injured patients. *British Journal of Psychiatry, 133,* 507–513.

Overall, J. E., & Gorham, D. R. (1962). The brief psychiatric rating scale. *Psychological Reports, 10,* 799–812.

Prigatano, G. P. (1987). Personality and psychosocial consequences after brain injury. In M. J. Meier, A. L. Benton, & L. Diller (Eds.), *Neuropsychological Rehabilitation* (pp. 355–378). New York: Churchill Livingstone.

Prigatano, G. P., Fordyce, D. J., Zeiner, H. K., Roueche, J. R., Pepping, M., & Wood, B. C. (1984). Neuropsychological rehabilitation after closed head injury in young adults. *Journal of Neurology, Neurosurgery, and Psychiatry, 47,* 505–513.

Rosenbaum, M., Lipsitz, N., Abraham, J., & Najenson, T. (1978). A description of an intensive treatment project for the rehabilitation of severely brain-injured soldiers. *Scandanavian Journal of Rehabilitation Medicine, 10,* 1–6.

Rosenbaum, M., & Najenson, T. (1976). Changes in life patterns and symptoms of low mood as reported by wives of severely brain-injured soldiers. *Journal of Consulting and Clinical Psychology, 44,* 881–888.

Rosenthal, M. (1983). Behavioral sequelae. In M. Rosenthal, E. R. Griffith, M. B. Bond, & J. D. Miller (Eds.), *Rehabilitation of the head injured adult* (pp. 197–208). Philadelphia: F. A. Davis Company.

Ross, E. D., & Stewart, R. S. (1987). Pathological display of affect in patients with depression and right frontal brain damage: An alternative mechanism. *The Journal of Nervous and Mental Disease, 175,* 165–172.

Russell, W. R., & Smith, A. (1961). Post-traumatic amnesia in closed head injury. *Archives of Neurology, 5,* 4–17.

Rutter, M. (1981). Psychological sequelae of brain damage in children. *The American Journal of Psychiatry, 138,* 1535–1544.

Strich, S. J. (1956). Diffuse degeneration of the cerebral white matter in severe dementia following head injury. *Journal of Neurology, Neurosurgery, and Psychiatry, 19,* 163–185.

Stuss, D. T., & Benson, D. F. (1986). *The frontal lobes.* New York: Raven Press.

Tarsh, M. J., & Royston, C. (1985). A follow-up study of accident neurosis. *British Journal of Psychiatry, 146,* 18–25.

Thomas, J. D., & Trexler, L. E. (1982). Behavioral and cognitive deficits in cerebrovascular accident and closed head injury: Implications for cognitive rehabilitation. In L. E. Trexler (Ed.), *Cognitive rehabilitation: Conceptualization and intervention* (pp. 27–81). New York: Plenum Press.

Tsuang, M. T., Boor, M., & Fleming, J. A. (1985). Psychiatric aspects of traffic accidents. *American Journal of Psychiatry, 142,* 538–546.

Van Zomeren, A. H., & Van Den Burg, W. (1985). Residual complaints of patients two years after severe head injury. *Journal of Neurology, Neurosurgery, and Psychiatry, 48,* 21–28.

Weddell, R., Oddy, M., & Jenkins, D. (1980). Social adjustment after rehabilitation: A two year follow-up of patients with severe head injury. *Psychological Medicine, 10,* 257–263.

Wood, R. L. (1984). Behaviour disorders following severe brain injury: Their presentation and psychological management. In N. Brooks (Ed.), *Closed head injury: Psychological, social, and family consequences* (pp. 195–219). New York: Oxford University Press.

9

Assessing Aphasic Disorders

Andrew Kertesz

INTRODUCTION

The reason for aphasia testing is variable and the assessment of aphasic disorders reflects the differing rationale and needs for testing. The primary goal of the clinician is often to diagnose the type of aphasic disorder and to compare it to similar clinical patterns that will allow prognosis and therapeutic planning. Secondly, the clinician wants to establish an objective baseline upon which improvement or the effect of therapy can be measured. Unless a reproducible repeated measure is used, the evaluation of recovery and treatment remains nebulous.

In addition, there are important theoretical reasons to assess aphasics. Language deficit contributes to the analysis of normal language function, even though the objection has been raised that aphasia does not directly reflect the normal functional organization of language. The dissociation of language components, such as the loss of comprehension without the loss of articulation, the preservation of repetition while losing comprehension or the ability to initiate speech, the dissociation of written from oral language, and the specific loss of processing for closed-class words are a few examples of the contribution of aphasiology to linguistics.

The objective assessment of aphasia also enables investigators to group comparable patients on the basis of lesion location, lesion size, or associated neurological deficits. This is essential for understanding the structure and physiological organization of the brain or parts of the brain that subserve language.

The assessment of aphasia also contributes to issues of cerebral dominance, laterality and interhemispheric organization of cognitive abilities. Studies of childhood aphasia are very important in learning about language development, the issue of hemispheric capacity for language, and the changes in brain plasticity with age.

Language studies and aging have illustrated some of the complex relationships of language and memory, semantic access, and semantic memory in Alzheimer's disease. Using standardized aphasia tests, language dissolution can be measured to follow Alzheimer patients through stages of deterioration where memory or cognitive tests are no longer useful.

Aphasia testing has contributed to the important issues of language and intelligence, language and short-term memory, and the overall relationship of verbal and nonverbal cognitive operations in the brain (Table 9.1).

As our knowledge of linguistics and aphasiology expands, testing also undergoes change. Researchers devise special tests to probe a certain phenomena and, if these become important theoretically or clinically, they are incorporated into general tests. Tests that are modern today may soon become obsolete. Frequent changes in assessment techniques, however, preclude useful standardization. Therefore, a few standardized, yet comprehensive aphasia batteries remain in use, because of the great clinical need, as well as the need for stability in comparisons of research data between investigators. The development of aphasia tests reflects the diversity of goals and rationale for aphasia testing. In conjunction with the development of psychometric standardization in the 1950s and 1960s, a similar development has taken place in establishing specific tests for aphasia that would conform to the psychometric standards of intelligence tests.

It is very difficult to satisfy the needs of both clinical and research goals, such as practicality and comprehensiveness, stability and flexibility, generalizability and specificity, wide-spread applicability and sensitivity.

TABLE 9.1
Rationale of Assessment

Clinical
Diagnosis, prognosis, therapeutic plan
Objective baseline to study recovery and intervention
Language dissolution in degenerative or neoplastic disease

Linguistic Theory
Phonemic, syntactic, semantic, pragmatic
Modularity, information processing, A.I. modelling

Neurological Theory
Structure, physiology, pharmacology, pathology
Neurobiology of recovery and reorganization

Neuropsychology Theory
Laterality, cerebral dominance
Interhemispheric organization
Development of language
Language and intelligence
Language and memory
Language and aging

These seemingly contradictory aims of aphasia assessment need to be reconciled if an optimal test is to be constructed.

From clinical experience with aphasics and standards derived from intelligence testing, as well as the construction of other psychological tests, one can summarize what an ideal aphasia test should do:

1. Explore all potentially disturbed language modalities.
2. Discriminate between clinically relevant aphasia types.
3. Include a range of difficulty in order to examine a representative range of severity of deficit (construct validity).
4. Include enough items to eliminate most of the day-to-day and test-to-test variability (internal consistency).
5. Include test items that measure the same factor (subtest internal consistency).
6. Include standardized administration and scoring (intertester and intrarater reliability).
7. Minimize the effect of intelligence, education and memory, to achieve, as specifically as possible, a test of language (content validity).
8. Discriminate between normals, aphasics, and nonaphasic brain-damaged individuals (criterion validity).
9. Be practical in length.
10. Measure the efficiency of communication (functional validity).

It is desirable to systematically test the input modality used in receiving the instructions, the input modality of the actual stimulus, and the output modality of the response. However, sampling these modalities in a mechanical and rigid fashion obscures the goals of testing. Lengthy, rigid, pedantic scoring, and compulsive testing of modalities actually decreases both the clinical utility and the attractiveness of the test. It is very difficult to achieve a compromise between inadequate sampling and excessive testing that will satisfy most people. Tests of excessive length will rarely be used in their entirety and, although they aim at comprehensiveness, this goal will be infrequently achieved. Short screening tests confirm diagnostic impressions and allow some prognostication. Unfortunately, they almost invariably fail to satisfy the need for subsequent research analysis or a reliable baseline level.

The requirements of standardization of psychological tests have been defined by Nunnally (1967) and further summarized in a booklet by the American Psychological Association (1974). The administration and scoring of a test have to be standardized in various ways to ensure that it measures what it claims to measure and that it does so reliably.

The *construct validity* of a test depends somewhat on the aim of a particular instrument. The theoretical construct of a test is defined by its developer and may be studied subsequently by factor analysis to determine if the subtests contribute to certain common factors that underlie in this instance, language function. It is generally felt to be important to have the test items of a subtest measure the same factor consistently. This internal consistency can be measured by comparing alternate items of the test (split-half reliability).

The grading of the level of difficulty of the test items, in order to sample a range of severity, is an important component of construct validity. It is necessary, for instance, to include relatively easy items to be able to measure the behavior of severely affected aphasics. This increases the range of severity measured and avoids the "floor effect" of the severely affected patients uniformly failing on difficult items. The "easy items" also eliminate the effect of intelligence and memory, thereby increasing specificity. "Difficult items" are used to diagnose the mildly affected patients (increased sensitivity). This decreases the "ceiling effect" or the lack of difference between the patients in the top of the range of deficit. Difficult items, however, introduce factors of memory and intelligence, therefore, decreasing the specificity of the test for language deficit and its ability to distinguish aphasic from nonaphasic impairment. The range of difficulty is not easy to quantify, but rating scales by several judges can be used.

The *predictive* or the *criterion validity* of a test is related to the level of difficulty of the test items, as well as what they measure. The test is given to various populations to determine the degree of overlap or its power to discriminate between the normals, aphasics, and nonaphasic brain-damaged individuals. The degree of distinction among populations is called *specificity* and the degree of inclusiveness of members of a population is *sensitivity*. It is difficult to achieve both with the same test. Some tests are more specific than others but few aphasia tests have reliable criterion validity measures. The screening of aphasics from nonaphasics is not a major clinical issue, although it can be important in patient selection for group studies.

Interrater reliability refers to the reproducibility of results of an assessment between examiners. A manual of test administration, describing the testing conditions and the methods of scoring in a clear and unequivocal fashion is essential. Some test manuals are too brief and imprecise, whereas others are too lengthy and complicated to use. Complex manuals, rigid scoring systems, or difficult-to-apply test conditions are not acceptable for clinical use. Yet, other tests leave the method of administration so poorly defined that the scores obtained are not comparable between testers. Some flexibility is desirable for clinicians who may cue or prompt the patient in an attempt to bring out the best potential of a certain function. Some tests do not allow this, whereas others attempt to standardize the extent of the cueing. In the scoring of a patient's response a great deal of latitude is given in some tests, which is desirable for certain clinical purposes. Nevertheless, this makes the comparison of patients difficult and introduces examiner bias. Tests that score only results may disregard communicative intent or strategy. There has not been an entirely satisfactory way to find a compromise between a subjective or qualitative rating of the patient's communication and an objective scoring that attempts to eliminate bias. Recently, tests to measure functional communication were developed in order to test language function in context. The scoring system of these tests is much less structured and relies on the examiner's subjective assessment of the overall communicative efficiency rather than item-by-item responses.

An important advance in standardization procedures has been the increasing use of video equipment. This way several clinicians can rate the same patient, without repeated examinations, achieving higher interrater reliability measures. Some of the difficulties experienced by clinicians attempting to test the same patients consecutively (e.g., patient reluctance, day-to-day fluctuation of function) can also be eliminated this way.

Intrarater consistency examines the level of variation within each examiner; in other words, consistency with one's self. In order to quantify this, the same recorded examination is rescored by the same examiner after a certain interval, which is dependent on both the length and the difficulty of the test.

Another source of variability is the patient himself. To assess this quality, the same test should be readministered to a number of stable patients. *Test–retest reliability* assesses the variation in responses by the same patient on different occasions.

Content validity or *face validity* refers to what the test measures. Clinicians and investigators can usually form an opinion after a careful examination of the test items (*face validity*). Content validity can be measured by comparing the test to another aphasia test that is acknowledged by a substantial number of authorities in the field to measure aphasic deficit. Equivalent subtests should be carefully paired when such an *intertest* reliability is carried out.

What one should measure is both one of the least agreed upon and most crucial issues in aphasia testing. Some aphasia tests permit a more comprehensive examination of cognitive functions than others. In order to be comprehensive, items are occasionally included that are beyond language function, such as general intelligence and memory. The overlap between intelligence, memory, and language is considerable. Therefore, if one is to investigate language alone or the association of these functions, distinctions are desirable. The items should measure language by sampling linguistic behavior. Items that are too long, requiring memory and complex cognitive processing, are more in the realm of problem-solving intelligence and should be avoided. These complex items are often intended to assess slightly altered behavior and many normals or non-aphasic individuals fail on them. Although the test gains sensitivity it loses specificity.

A consensus among aphasiologists is reflected by the subtests that are most commonly used. The following items are considered important by the majority of investigators:

*1. **Spontaneous speech*** (also called expository speech), speech output, and fluency can be measured by rating various aspects of a corpus of speech obtained by a standard interview, a picture description, or a description of a familiar activity, such as shaving or making spaghetti (as in an Italian test). Fluency, rate of speech, phrase length, grammaticality, articulation, "melodic line," and paraphasias are the most often rated factors. Even though the rating of speech production is more difficult than other speech parameters, Goodglass, Quadfasel, & Timberlake (1964) emphasized its importance, in addition to the usual input–output dichotomy, in differentiating aphasic patients. The importance of the fluency–nonfluency dimension has been generally accepted, although there is much less agreement on how it should be measured (Benson, 1967; Goodglass & Kaplan, 1972; Howes & Geschwind, 1964; Kerschensteiner, Poeck, & Brunner, 1972; Wagenaar, Snow, & Prins, 1975). Some scales are very extensive but too lengthy for practical use (Wagenaar et al., 1975). Multiple ratings scales use fractionated categories, such as word finding in spontaneous speech and number of utterances per minute that may be dissociated in the same patient. Some ambiguities reflect the complexities of speech production but create difficulties in classification. Other tests (e.g., the WAB) use a rating scale that incorporates various aspects of speech production into a list of definitions to be matched to certain clinical behaviors.

Recently the emphasis on agrammatism has increased the discussions of spontaneous speech rating. Agrammatical output is closely related to decreased fluency, although they are not synonymous. Problems arise when a relatively recovered nonfluent patient, who is now considered fluent by some rating scale is still somewhat agrammatic. The other side of the coin is the severely affected patient who is so nonfluent that there is not enough speech output to rate agrammatism unless the patient is rated agrammatic by default. Adequate, clinically relevant speech production rating is essential. Tests that do not have it, or have not placed emphasis on it, cannot be used for classification, and are, therefore, reduced in their clinical and research applicability.

2. Information content of spontaneous speech may be included into rating scales of speech production. It is usually close to the estimation of functional communication and to scales of severity. It may be specifically scored on a corpus of elicited speech, because it is difficult, if not impossible, to obtain entirely spontaneous speech. Elicited speech should be standardized so the content can be compared. Picture description constrains thematic output and vocabulary, and provides a standard stimulus for the comparison of linguistic features. Reply to specific questions tends to be more variable and it is influenced by premorbid intelligence, personality, education, and verbal ability.

3. Comprehension testing is the cornerstone of aphasia batteries. Verbal comprehension is related to many cognitive operations in the brain and any assessment has to take this into consideration. It is difficult to assess comprehension entirely independently of speech production or apraxia as the patient indicates comprehension by signalling the answer, i.e., pointing to one among a set of items or cards, or even shaking his head. Some comprehension tests that rely only on visual material may occasionally have false positive results if visual recognition is impaired. Even though auditory comprehension may be good, the patient may not visually recognize differences between the target item and the foils. Hemianopic patients may fail on a horizontal array of stimuli because they cannot see half of the items. A similar source of errors occurs in right-hemisphere damaged patients with visuospatial neglect. This is a common reason why some of these patients will be misclassified as "aphasic" by a rigid application of the scoring criteria for a test.

Verbal comprehension overlaps with verbal intelligence and some tests using complex ideation are, in fact, tapping a problem-solving ability that goes beyond verbal comprehension (Goodglass & Kaplan, 1983). Some of the longer items also test auditory short-term memory. Therefore, it is wise to use short items, under 8 to 10 lexical units, in order to measure comprehension independent of the influence of memory factors.

The difficulty level of comprehension items has to be wide enough to sample an entire aphasic population. Most aphasia tests fail to examine low-level comprehension, and therefore, cannot distinguish between severe global patients, who have a poor prognosis, and severe Broca's aphasics, who have recovered useful comprehension. For example, the "Token Test" is too difficult for severely affected aphasics who will score poorly even though they may have a significant amount of residual comprehension (Boller & Dennis, 1979). Similarly, the complex manipulation of syntax in some auditory tests of comprehension is not useful, except for moderately or mildly affected aphasics. Along with these constraints, the "on and off" nature of auditory verbal comprehension and the variability of a patient's responsiveness in some types of aphasia require a large number of test items. Because yes–no questions require only nodding or one word replies, they are powerful in discriminating between those who are globally affected and those with residual comprehension and a better prognosis. These questions, however, must be short and personally relevant to the patient to be the most effective (Kertesz, 1979). Moderately or mildly affected patients, on the other hand, must be tested with items varying in syntactic complexity, vocabulary, and the number of items in one sentence (auditory comprehension span). Multistep sequential commands or pointing to items that are varied in grammatical and semantic features in a systemic fashion are suitable to uncover mild deficits of comprehension.

The comprehension of grammar has recently received wide attention from linguistic studies, and the number of specific tests that explore one or more aspects of "receptive agrammatism" have increased greatly (Friederici, 1981; Goodglass et al., 1979; Heeschen, 1980; Parisi & Pizzamiglio, 1970). Comprehension of syntactic morphemes, especially relational and locative prepositions, is difficult even for Broca's aphasics as pointed out by Ombredane (1951), Luria (1966), and Goodglass, Gleason, & Hyde (1970). Most modern aphasia tests contain items of comprehension that assess these features. However, these tasks may not differentiate between various aphasic types and may even decrease the specificity of differential diagnosis if other features are not considered. Performance on these tasks may be abnormal in right-hemisphere damaged patients or even in normal subjects of different educational and cultural backgrounds. Tests of phonemic discrimination are less crucial for assessing comprehension than tests of semantic and syntactic competence (Blumstein, Baker, & Goodglass, 1977). Schuell and Jenkins (1961) emphasized the role of word frequency in comprehension, and Goodglass, Klein, Carey and Jones (1966) noted the differences between semantic categories, although this was subsequently questioned by Poeck, Hartje, Kerschensteiner, & Orgass (1973).

Changing the conditions of presentation and context, such as speaking more slowly and providing redundant but semantically related information, can facilitate comprehension (Gardner, Albert, & Weintraub, 1975). Low-level, residual comprehension can be detected in severely affected aphasics when gestures of refusal or quizzical expressions are taken into consideration as responses (Boller & Green, 1972). Some of these "appropriate" responses are subject to the examiner's interpretation and a standardized scoring procedure is necessary if they are to be useful.

4. *Repetition* is often neglected in aphasia tests because it is not considered a "natural" language function. However, it has significant theoretical and practical consequences for the analysis of aphasic disorders. Repetition is important in differentiating between conduction and transcortical aphasias, and without such a subtest these entities cannot be diagnosed. Repetition testing may include items that also test oral agility or articulatory competence. It is usual to include words, numbers, and sentences of increasing complexity and articulatory difficulty. Tongue twisters and repetitive phonemic structures are useful to assess verbal apraxia. Goodglass and Kaplan (1972) added high- and low-probability sentences to their repetition tasks noting that aphasics did poorly on the latter. Some tests include the repetition of nonsense words, semantically anomalous sentences or grammatically incorrect sentences to study phonological or syntactic processing but these usually are not standard. Sentences consisting of only closed-class or grammatical words, such as "no ifs, ands, or buts" have also been used and have been found to be particularly difficult for mildly affected aphasics.

5. *Naming* is universally tested at various levels of complexity. A visual presentation of objects is termed *confrontation naming*. The test items can be controlled for stimulus frequency, imageability, level of abstraction, manipulability, and word length. Some of these may have more effect than others, but extensive studies on the semantic structure of language and the lexicon have yielded relatively little clinical consistency as yet. Names of words from the various semantic categories of objects are generally lost to the same extent in aphasia, although there are occasional reports to the contrary. When words from a specific semantic category are lost, one refers to category specific anomias (Dennis, 1976; Goodglass et al., 1966; Hart, Berndt, & Caramazza, 1985; Warrington & McCarthy, 1983).

Using different modalities for presentation, the examiner may uncover a dissociation between naming to tactile stimulation and naming to visual stimulation, leading to a diagnosis of visual agnosia. Some tests incorporate a tactile naming task, whereas others use it as a control task if visual naming fails. Color anomia, often associated with pure alexia without agraphia, is probably better classified with the visual agnosias (Geschwind & Fusillo, 1966). Response modality may also be differentially affected. At times, written naming may be superior to oral naming (Bub & Kertesz, 1982; Hier & Mohr, 1977) but these are not often tested separately.

There are various methods for the administration of naming tasks. Some tests allow the patient to look at the stimulus without time restrictions. Others specify the duration of exposure and measure response time.

These time restrictions create difficulties for aphasics. Although they increase the sensitivity of the test at the upper level of functioning, they lower the score of the more severely affected patients and may even mask residual ability. Nevertheless, some limitation on the time permitted for each item is practical. Supplying of cues is not allowed by some tests and encouraged by others. If residual functioning is important, cueing may help bring it out. However, very few tests standardize the procedure or incorporate it into the scoring. Phonemic cues usually provide the initial sound of a word, whereas semantic cues use the first half of composite words to elicit the target word. Naming is fairly consistent for a given patient at a given time, and the number of items need not be as large as is necessary for the comprehension task.

Word finding in spontaneous speech is different from word finding in confrontation naming, but it too probes semantic and lexical access. Related tests are sentence completion, responsive speech (the context facilitates word retrieval), and word fluency, a task that is used in many intelligence tests and "frontal lobe" batteries. In the word-fluency task, the patient is asked to produce as many words as possible belonging to a semantic category, such as animals (contextual association) or words beginning with a certain letter (phonemic association), within one minute. Although problems in word fluency frequently persist even after other functions have recovered, it is not specific to aphasia and appears to be indicative of brain damage in general. It is often the earliest sign in Alzheimer's disease (Appell, Kertesz, & Fisman, 1982). Standardized versions of word fluency tasks were incorporated in several tests (Spreen and Benton, 1977; Goodglass and Kaplan, 1972; Kertesz, 1982). Automatized, overlearned sequences, such as the days of the week or months, nursery rhymes, and so on, represent word retrieval at a different level. At times, these tasks are performed surprisingly well in nonfluent aphasics, but their diagnostic value is not high.

6. Reading and writing have been a traditional part of aphasia examinations, and lately they have received special attention from cognitive psychologists who have been responsible for an infusion of terminology from linguistic and information processing models. The previous divisions of pure alexia, alexia without agraphia, verbal, literal, and sentence alexia are supplemented by deep and surface dyslexia, phonological alexia, and word-form alexia (letter-by-letter reading). Most aphasia tests include the reading of words and sentences. Some also include the identification of letters and numbers, the matching of words to a choice of pictures, and the reverse, and the matching of auditory input to a choice of written words, which may include visual, semantic, and phonological foils. Some tasks involve a psycholinguistic analysis of reading strategies: lexical or whole word reading versus the phonological, or grapheme-phoneme conversion route. Reading strategies are tested by using nonwords (read only by the grapheme-phoneme conversion route), matching orthographically different homophones or contrasting orthographically regular and irregular words. This area is in continuous development and extensive supplementary alexia and agraphia tests are being used in many laboratories including our own. The clinical value of these tests needs to be further investigated.

Reading and writing are greatly influenced by educational and other premorbid factors, and are, therefore, more difficult to standardize. The motor output for written language can be affected independently from oral language, although most of the time the extent of involvement appears to be related. Similarly, central processing may be independent of modality specific output, even though they are analogous and their deficits are related. Reading can also be dissociated from writing in various combinations of linguistic dimensions. One such linguistic dimension is the grapheme-phoneme conversion, which may be affected only in writing but not in reading (Bub & Kertesz, 1982). Alexia and agraphia can be residual disturbances even after an aphasia has resolved and this is a major source of evidence for a dissociation. In pure alexia, there are often signs of other visual involvement such as a color-naming defect or visual agnosia. There are also cases of transcortical alexia (reading aloud without reading comprehension) usually in association with transcortical sensory aphasia or recovering Wernicke's aphasia. Therefore, it is important to test reading comprehension as well as reading aloud. Reading and writing may be impaired as a result of right-hemisphere lesions: In reading, the left side of a word or sentence is neglected; in writing, patients produce perseverative loops. Motoric aspects of writing account for a substantial portion of the failure to write, even more than the motor impairment in speech. Similarly, visual confusions in reading at a perceptual level can be impaired at early stages of processing.

There is some question as to whether reading and writing deficits should be considered part of a total aphasic impairment for the purposes of scoring and recovery studies. There is, of course, evidence that illiterates develop aphasic syndromes that are definable without reading or writing (Lecours, Mehler, & Parente, 1987). Some aphasia tests incorporate the findings of written tests into their system of evaluation and diagnosis, whereas others keep them separate. There are arguments for both, depending on the intent and the theoretical model being tested. Recently there has been a trend toward treating oral and written language separately, and too often the possible interactions between them are disregarded.

7. Supplementary tests include the testing of functions that are associated with language mechanisms or may be impaired with them. Calculation and gesture are clearly related to language and tend to be specifically affected by left-hemisphere lesions. Calculation is education-dependent, but, along with reading and writing, it can be affected at various stages of processing (e.g., spatial, perceptual, specific computational, or linguistic levels). Lengthy tests that explore each of the stages in the process exist, but are rarely used clinically.

Gesture, pantomime, and skilled practiced, and symbolic movements are closely related to language. Impairment of praxis, which is usually tested by intransitive limb gestures, transitive movements that involve objects, bucco-facial movements, and complex sequential action, is closely associated with aphasia. Dissociations often occur that have an anatomical and functional basis (Kertesz, Ferro, & Shewan, 1984). If praxis is tested with imitation and object use in addition to verbal commands, the distinction of ideomotor and ideational apraxia can be made. Ideational apraxia is best defined as object-use apraxia, but there is no universal agreement concerning this distinction and others consider it an apraxia of complex sequential movements (Poeck & Lehmkuhl, 1980). It is also important, if not more so, to determine the overall severity and the differential severity among oral, limb, and body praxis impairment.

APHASIA TESTS

Formal aphasia tests are relatively recent, but unstandardized descriptions of detailed testing have appeared since the early aphasiologists. Broca (1861) described a testing procedure that was probably commonly used by clinicians at that time. In fact, much of his interview with Lalonde, his second patient, is similar to what most clinicians would do today. Broca asked his patient conversational questions, commented on the patient's speech output and comprehension, and then went on to describe his gestures, tongue movements, writing, and arithmetic. Hughlings-Jackson (1878) included sign making, writing, comprehension, repetition, reading and tongue movements, as well as a description of spontaneous speech, as regular features of the aphasia examination. Pierre Marie (1906) tested a comprehension deficit with the "Three Paper Test," a precursor of all tests of comprehension for a complex sentence with sequential commands. In this test, which is still used in some aphasia examinations, the patient is asked to do various things, in sequence, with three pieces of paper. The test sentence contains many prepositions and relational words, indicating a clinical awareness of the difficulties with linguistically complex sentence structure.

The first systematic aphasia examination in English appeared in two large volumes by Henry Head (1926). He examined mainly head-injured soldiers and tailored the test to their deficits. Head emphasized flexibility. He did not standardize the test administration and used few anecdotal controls. Many of Head's ideas on testing were subsequently adopted. His Coin-Bowl Test and Hand-Eye-Ear Test can be considered precursors of the Token Test (DeRenzi & Vignolo, 1962). They involve sequential tasks with elements of right-left orientation and praxis in the latter.

Weisenberg and McBride (1935) constructed a standardized test battery from various existing intelligence tests. They applied Pierre Marie's "Three Paper Test," the complex commands from the Stanford-Binet comprehension test, and Abelson's geometrical figures with commands, such as "point inside the circle and the triangle, but not in the square" (very much like the Token Test). They obtained normative data although their standardization was rudimentary.

Eisenson's Examination for Aphasia (1954) is a clinical instrument with informal instructions to be administered in 30 to 90 minutes. A simple scoring system estimates the various levels of ability for each language function. Although the test has not been standardized and the scoring system is on an informal five-point scale, it has been widely used by clinicians as a guide for treatment goals. With the recent appearance of comprehensive and standardized tests, its use has considerably diminished.

The Language Modalities Test for Aphasia (LMTA) by Wepman and Jones (1961) uses a film strip to present visual stimuli, and auditory stimuli are presented by the examiner. There is a screening section consisting of 11 items and, if necessary, this is followed by an additional 46 items. A corpus of speech is elicited by asking the patient to compose a story based on four pictures. Examples of the categorical scoring are included in the manual.

The Minnesota Test for Differential Diagnosis of Aphasia (MTDDA) by Schuell (1965) consists of 69 tests with 606 items. This well-known aphasia examination is a major, standardized, detailed test battery. However, because of its size it is rarely, if ever, used in its entirety. Despite its name, the MTDDA does not define the criteria for the differential diagnosis of aphasic syndromes nor does it make an attempt to distinguish aphasia from other disorders which may include some form of language disturbance.

Testing is started at an estimated difficulty level, yet the length of the test remains excessive, requiring 2–5 hours. A short version of the test (Schuell, 1957) consists of subtests selected for their high diagnostic and prognostic value, but this test remains unstandardized. Eventually, it was withdrawn by the author who felt that the complete test was more desirable. Another short version of the test is used in England. Thompson and Enderby (1979) found that the majority of the items were too easy for most aphasics and lacked discriminating power. They obtained a significant correlation between a reduced number of subtests and the standard version. Although parts of the test remain in fairly wide use, it has not been used very much in recent published research, and its prognostic value is limited. As a consequence of the frequent revision of this battery, the original standardization is not always applicable.

The Neurosensory Center Comprehensive Examination for Aphasia (NCCEA) by Spreen and Benton (1968) consists of 20 language tests and 4 control tests of visual and tactile functions. Test interpretation requires considerable experience. An age and education correction is available for the scores. The scores may then be plotted on one of three profile sheets for percentile ranks in either an adult aphasic, nonaphasic brain damaged, or normal population. There is considerable overlap between the nonaphasic brain damaged and aphasic populations because some of the test items are relatively difficult for nonaphasics as well. The test is intended for use in its entirety and several subtests provide a second set of items if errors occur in the first set. It should be noted that the NCCEA does not provide for the sampling and scoring of spontaneous speech. Repetition sampling is also limited.

The Porch Index of Communicative Abilities (PICA) by Porch (1967, 1971) uses the same 10 common objects as stimuli in 18 subtests. These are subdivided into response modalities: four verbal, eight gestural and six graphic.

The scoring system is complex as it tries to account for all possible responses and it requires extensive training to master. A 40-hour workshop is recommended by the author.

The PICA does not distinguish between aphasia types other than: (a) severe verbal formulation difficulty, (b) severe dysarthria, and (c) inadequate verbal monitoring. In addition, bilateral damage has a special pattern. The test does not include the assessment of conversational speech or picture description, and its scope is limited by the use of only 10 test items.

The PICA has also been criticized for not assessing spontaneous speech and auditory comprehension in sufficient detail (Boone, 1972). Although the PICA samples the same modalities as other aphasia tests, the test does not distinguish between various cognitive processes or make linguistic and behavioral distinctions. The effectiveness of communication is not fully tested, and there is no opportunity for any supportive feedback. The

PICA requires approximately 1 hour to administer and another 30 minutes to score. Procedures for administration of the test are quite rigid, and include instructions on the seating of the patient and the speed and rhythm of the testing.

The Appraisal of Language Disturbance (ALD) by Emerick (1971) is an example of a mechanistic modality matrix. Such a matrix combines all possible stimulus and response modalities regardless of their clinical importance. Some of the subtests are aimed at a central nonlinguistic processor. The test is rather long and takes from 1–2 hours.

The Boston Diagnostic Aphasia Examination (BDAE) by Goodglass and Kaplan (1972, 1983) is a comprehensive, modern aphasia test designed, according to its authors, for: (a) diagnosis of presence and type of aphasic syndromes leading to differences concerning cerebral localization; (b) measurements of levels of performance over a wide range for both initial evaluation and detection of change over time; (c) comprehensive assessment of the assets and liabilities of the patients in all areas as a guide to therapy.

The scoring system is complex and some of it is based on subjective rating scales, but detailed instructions are provided in the manual. The rating scale for grammatical form is difficult because only three levels are defined on the seven-point scale. The paraphasia rating in running speech is also quite subjective with the middle range representing only a very slight deficit of "once per minute of conversation." The scoring of repetition does not allow for the occurrence of paraphasias and sentence reading is also scored all or nothing, which is somewhat unrealistic. The low interrater correlation on the word finding scale, even among experienced raters, is related to the difficulty in judging the categories of information proportional to fluency. This rating scale also differs from the others in that the normal score is in the middle. Severity ratings are based on definitions.

The type or category of aphasia is no longer determined by the patient's Z score profile but rather by their percentile ranking on the subtests. The formulas for assigning patients to categories are contained in the manual. An estimated 60% of patients is left in the mixed or undiagnosed category. A new subtest summary profile is in the test booklet.

The test is lengthy and it is rarely used in its entirety because administration of all the subtests may take 6 to 8 hours.

The Western Aphasia Battery (WAB) by Kertesz and Poole (1974) and the revised version by Kertesz (1982) incorporates many of the psycholinguistic principles of the BDAE. It attempts to be a comprehensive examination for both clinical and research use, yet remains practical in length.

The rationale and considerable clinical and research experience with the test have been detailed in a monograph (Kertesz, 1979). The scoring system is simple, requiring no transformations, but described in sufficient detail in the manual to achieve high interrater reliabilities, even in the scoring of spontaneous speech fluency where subjective scoring categories are used. High intrarater correlations were noted on repeated scoring of the same test and there is high test–retest reliability with stable aphasics (Kertesz, 1979). The internal consistency of test items was high using Cronbach's alpha (0.90) and Bentler's theta (0.97) coefficients (Shewan & Kertesz, 1980).

The classification system is based on the scores for spontaneous speech, fluency, comprehension, and naming. The limits for each of the categories were established after assessment of the first 150 patients (Kertesz & Poole, 1974). Subsequently, numerical taxonomic studies showed the cohesiveness of 10 groups, with acute and chronic populations analyzed separately (Kertesz, 1979).

The Aphasia Quotient (AQ) is the sum of verbal subtest scores, expressed as a percentage of "normal" performance. The AQ can be easily calculated simply by adding the verbal subtest scores and then multiplying by two. For a "Cortical Quotient" (CQ), a simple addition of all subscores is used. Recently the "Language Quotient" (LQ), containing oral and written language scores, was used to follow recovery (Shewan & Kertesz, 1984). The oral language tasks take about 45 minutes. Another 45 to 60 minutes are needed for reading, writing, and supplementary tasks.

TESTS OF FUNCTIONAL COMMUNICATION

These tests rate the communicative abilities of aphasics on an informal basis without structured questions. Such tests identify language behavior in natural interactions, but they are less objective and are based on unstandardized impressions of behavior. Examples are the Functional Communication Profile (FCP) by Taylor (1965) and the Communicative Abilities in Daily Living (CADL) by Holland (1980).

SHORT SCREENING TESTS IN APHASIA

These tests have limited accuracy but are practical in a busy clinic where more comprehensive, in-depth assessment is impossible. There are many clinicians who use their own individual screening tests, but only two are standardized or available as a publication: The Sklar Aphasia Scale (SAS) by Sklar (1973) and the Aphasia Language Performance Scales (ALPS) by Keenan and Brassell (1975).

APHASIA EXAMINATIONS FOR POLYGLOTS, AND IN OTHER LANGUAGES

Many of the aphasia tests reviewed above have been translated into several other languages. Attempts have been made to design functionally equivalent examinations in several languages, especially for polyglots or for the comparison of linguistic characteristics of aphasics in different language areas. Benton originated this effort in English, French, German, Italian, and Spanish. The English version of the Multilingual Aphasia Examination (MAE) is published by Benton and Hamsher (1976). Paradis (1987), with the help of his graduate students from as many as 24 countries, has also developed a linguistically oriented examination specifically for polyglots. This test is called the Bilingual Aphasia Examination (Paradis, 1987). Comprehensive aphasia tests have been developed at French, Italian, Dutch, and German centers. The Aachener Aphasie Test (Huber, Poeck, Weniger, & Willmes, 1983) is well standardized and widely used in Germany. Italian and English versions are in preparation.

TESTS OF SINGLE MODALITIES

DeRenzi and Vignolo (1962) developed the Token Test for the mild auditory comprehension disturbance that may occur in expressive syndromes. An expressive equivalent, the Reporter Test was constructed by DeRenzi and Ferrari (1978).

The Boston Naming Test (BNT) by Kaplan, Goodglass, and Weintraub (1978) is an extended picture-naming task. Normative data for it, along with the BDAE, have been published by Borod, Goodglass, & Kaplan (1980).

CONCLUSION

Most, but not all, aphasia tests examine speech output or expressive function, comprehension, naming, repetition, reading, and writing. Some add arithmetic, praxis, and drawing as regular complementary subtests, whereas others have a more extensive supplementary section that may alter the examination such that it becomes a more general test of intelligence. The increasing number of special items, added for the sake of comprehensiveness, yields a diminishing return in information, and decreases the practicality of full administration. Aphasia testing remains important to most clinicians, and treating a patient without testing is like trying to navigate an uncharted sea. Not only the severity of impairment, but the pattern of deficits can be determined by the better tests, and both are helpful in formulating prognosis and treatment goals. Researchers need general aphasia tests in addition to the specifically constructed experimental tests in order to quantify change and define groups of patients with differing behavior. Few tests satisfy the needs of both research, and clinical practice, and only experience can determine which test is most suitable for which purpose.

REFERENCES

Appell, J., Kertesz, A., & Fisman, A. (1982). A study of language functioning in Alzheimer patients. *Brain and Language, 17*, 73–91.

American Psychological Association. (1974). *Standards for educational and psychological tests.* Washington, DC: Author.

Benson, D. F. (1967). Fluency in aphasia: Correlation with radioactive scan localization. *Cortex, 3*, 373–394.

Benton, A. L., & Hamsher, K. (1976). *Multilingual aphasia examination.* Iowa City, Department of Neurology, University Hospitals.

Blumstein, S. E., Baker, E., & Goodglass, H. (1977). Phonological factors in auditory comprehension in aphasia. *Neuropsychologia, 15*, 19–30.

Boller, F., & Dennis, M. (Eds.). (1979). *Auditory comprehension: Clinical and experimental studies with the Token Test.* New York: Academic Press.

Boller, F., & Green, E. (1972). Comprehension in severe aphasia. *Cortex, 8*, 382–394.

Boone, D. R. (1972). Porch index of communicative ability. In O. K. Buros (Ed.), *Seventh mental measurement yearbook* (Vol. 2, pp. 1354–1355). Highland Park, NY: Gryphon Press.

Borod, J. C., Goodglass, H., & Kaplan, E. (1980). Normative data on the Boston Diagnostic Aphasia Examination, Parietal Lobe Battery and the Boston Naming Test. *Journal of Clinical Neuropsychology, 2*, 209–215.

Broca, P. (1861), Remarques sur le siège de la faculté du langage articulé, suivies d'une observation d'aphémie (perte de la parole). *Bulletin de la Société Anatomique (Paris), 36*, 330–357.

Bub, D., & Kertesz, A. (1982). Deep agraphia. *Brain and Language, 17*, 146–165.

Dennis, M. (1976). Dissociated naming and locating of body parts after left anterior temporal lobe resection: An experimental case study. *Brain and Language, 3*, 147–163.

DeRenzi, E., & Ferrari, P. (1978). The Reporter's Test: A sensitive test to detect expressive disturbances in aphasics. *Cortex, 14*, 279–293.

DeRenzi, E., & Vignolo, L. (1962). The Token Test: A sensitive test to detect receptive disturbance in aphasics. *Brain, 85*, 665–678.

Eisenson, J. (1954). *Examining for aphasia: A manual for the examination of aphasia and related disturbances.* New York: Psychological Corporation.

Emerick, L. L. (1971). *The appraisal of language disturbance, manual.* Marquette: Northern Michigan University.

Friederici, A. D. (1981). Production and comprehension of prepositions in aphasia. *Neuropsychologia, 18*, 11–20.

Gardner, H., Albert, M. L., & Weintraub, S. (1975). Comprehending a word: The influence of speed and redundancy on auditory comprehension in aphasia. *Cortex, 11*, 155–162.

Geschwind, N., & Fusillo, M. (1966). Color naming defects in association with alexia. *Archives of Neurology, 15*, 137–146.

Goodglass, H., Blumstein, S. E., Gleason, J. B., Hyde, M. R., Green, E., & Statlender,

S. (1979). The effect of syntactic encoding on sentence comprehension in aphasia. *Brain and Language*, 7, 201–209.

Goodglass, H., Gleason, J., & Hyde, M. (1970). Some dimensions of auditory language comprehension in aphasia. *Journal of Speech and Hearing Research*, 13, 595–606.

Goodglass, H., & Kaplan, E. (1972). *Boston diagnostic aphasia examination (BDAE)*. Philadelphia: Lea & Febiger.

Goodglass, H., & Kaplan, E. (1983). *Boston diagnostic aphasia examination (BDAE)* (rev. ed.). Philadelphia: Lea & Febiger.

Goodglass, H., Klein, B., Carey, P., & Jones, K. (1966). Specific semantic word categories in aphasia. *Cortex*, 2, 74–89.

Goodglass, H., Quadfasel, F. A., & Timberlake, W. H. (1964). Phrase length and the type and severity of aphasia. *Cortex*, 1, 133–153.

Hart, J., Berndt, R. S., & Caramazza, A. (1985). Category specific naming deficit following cerebral infarction. *Nature*, 316, 439–440.

Head, H. (1926). *Aphasia and kindred disorders of speech*. Cambridge: Cambridge University Press.

Heeschen, C. (1980). Strategies of decoding actor-object-relations by aphasic patients. *Cortex*, 16, 5–20.

Hier, D. B., & Mohr, J. (1977). Incongruous oral and written naming. *Brain and Language*, 4, 115–126.

Holland, A. L. (1980). *Communicative abilities in daily living: Manual*. Baltimore: University Park Press.

Howes, D., & Geschwind, N. (1964). Quantitative studies of aphasic language. *Association for Research in Neurology and Mental Disease*, 42, 229–244.

Huber, W., Poeck, K., Weniger, D., & Willmes, K. (1983). *Aachener-aphasie test*. Verlag für Psychologie Toronto: Gottingen.

Hughlings-Jackson, (1878). On affections of speech from disease of the brain. *Brain*, 1, 304–330.

Kaplan, E., Goodglass, H., & Weintraub, S. (1978). *The Boston naming test*. Available from the authors at the Boston Aphasia Research Center. Boston, MA.

Keenan, S. S., & Brassell, E. G. (1975). *Aphasia language performance scales (ALPS)*. Murfreesboro, TN: Pinnacle Press.

Kerschensteiner, M., Poeck, K., & Brunner, E. (1972). The fluency-nonfluency dimension in the classification of aphasic speech. *Cortex*, 8, 233–247.

Kertesz, A. (1979). *Aphasia and associated disorders: Taxonomy, localization and recovery*. New York: Grune & Stratton.

Kertesz, A. (1982). *The western aphasia battery*. New York: Grune & Stratton.

Kertesz, A., & Poole, E. (1974). The aphasia quotient: The taxonomic approach to measurement of aphasic disability. *Canadian Journal of Neurological Sciences*, 1, 7–16.

Kertesz, A., Ferro, J., & Shewan, C. M. (1984). Apraxia and aphasia: The functional anatomical basis for their dissociation. *Neurology*, 34, 40–47.

Lecours, R. A., Mehler, J., Parente, M. A., et al. (1987). Illiteracy and Brain Damage. 2. Manifestations of unilateral neglect in testing "auditory comprehension" with iconographic materials. *Brain and Cognition*, 6, 243–265.

Luria, A. R. (1966). *Human brain and psychological processes*. New York: Harper.

Marie, P. (1906). Révision de la question de l'aphasie: La troisième circonvolution frontale gauche ne joue aucun rôle spécial dans la fonction du langage. *Seminaires de Médecin*, 21, 241–247.

Nunnally, J. (1967). *Psychometric theory*. New York: McGraw-Hill.

Ombredane, A. (1951). *L'aphasie et l'élaboration de la pensée explicite* [Aphasia and the elaboration of explicit thought]. Presse Universitaire de France.

Paradis, M. (1987). *The assessment of bilingual aphasia.* Hillsdale, NJ: Lawrence Erlbaum Associates.

Parisi, D., & Pizzamiglio, L. (1970). Syntactic comprehension in aphasia. *Cortex, 6,* 204–215.

Poeck, K., Jartje, W., Kerschensteiner, M., & Orgass, B. (1973). Sprachverstandnisstörungen bei aphasischen und nicht-aphasischen Hirnkranken [Language comprehension errors in aphasics and non-aphasics]. *Deutsche Medizinische Wochenschrift, 98,* 139–147.

Poeck, K., & Lehmkuhl, G. (1980). Das syndrom der ideatorischen apraxie und seine lokalisation [The syndrome of ideational apraxia and its localization]. *Nervenarzt, 51,* 217–225.

Porch, B. E. (1967). *Porch index of communicative ability: Theory and development.* Palo Alto, CA: Consulting Psychologists Press.

Porch, B. E. (1971). *Porch index of communicative ability: Administration, scoring, and interpretation,* (Rev. Ed.). Palo Alto, CA: Consulting Psychologists Press.

Schuell, H. (1965). *The Minnesota test for differential diagnosis of aphasia.* Minneapolis: University of Minnesota Press.

Schuell, H. (1957). A short examination for aphasia. *Neurology, 7,* 625–634.

Schuell, H., & Jenkins, J. J. (1961). Reduction of vocabulary in aphasia. *Brain, 84,* 243–261.

Shewan, C. M., & Kertesz, A. (1980). Reliability and validity characteristics of the Western Aphasia Battery (WAB). *Journal of Speech and Hearing Disorders, 45,* 308–324.

Shewan, C. M., & Kertesz, A. (1984). Effects of speech and language treatment on recovery from aphasia. *Brain and Language, 23,* 272–299.

Sklar, M. (1973). *Sklar aphasia scale: Protocol booklet.* Beverly Hills, CA: Western Psychological Services.

Spreen, O., & Benton, A. L. (1968). *Neurosensory center comprehensive examination for aphasia.* Victoria, B.C.: University of Victoria Press.

Spreen, O., & Benton, A. L. (1977). *Neurosensory center comprehensive examination for aphasia* (Rev.). Victoria, B.C.: Neuropsychology Laboratory, Department of Psychology, University of Victoria.

Taylor, M. L. (1965). A measurement of functional communication in aphasia. *Archives of Physical Medicine and Rehabilitation, 46,* 101–107.

Thompson, J., & Enderby, P. (1979). Is all your Schuell really necessary? *British Journal of Disorders of Communication, 14,* 195–201.

Wagenaar, E., Snow, C., & Prins, R. (1975). Spontaneous speech of aphasia patients: A psycholinguistic analysis. *Brain and Language, 2,* 281–303.

Warrington, E. K., & McCarthy, R. (1983). Category specific access dysphasia. *Brain, 106,* 859–878.

Weisenburg, T. H., & McBride, K. E. (1935). *Aphasia.* New York: Commonwealth Fund.

Wepman, J. M., & Jones, L. V. (1961). *Studies in aphasia: An approach to testing.* Chicago: Education-Industry Service.

10

Neurolinguistic Studies of Morphological Processing: Toward a Theory-Based Assessment of Language Deficit

William Badecker
Alfonso Caramazza

INTRODUCTION

Among the many patterns of impaired performance that appear with relative frequency in cases of language deficit are a variety of impairments reflecting the processing of morphologically complex words. Our interest in phenomena such as these—phenomena that, at first, may seem to be of limited scope—is engendered by the fact that they provide good examples of how studies of impairment can inform our theories of normal language processing, and of why it is necessary that explanations of these impairments be informed by these very same processing theories. Our goal is to demonstrate these two points.

To begin, it might be helpful to consider the relationship between neurolinguistics (or cognitive neuropsychology) and psycholinguistics in general. In many respects, the goals and methodology in these two domains of research are alike. They may differ in one obvious way—the performance of individuals with impaired or disrupted linguistic abilities consequent to brain damage constitutes the primary source of data for neurolinguistic research, whereas the typical subject in a psycholinguistic experiment is a college sophomore who exhibits no evidence of linguistic abnormality—but this difference in experimental population should not obscure the more fundamental similarities in subject matter and methods of study. Research in both of these domains addresses the task of determining (a) the kind of knowledge that underlies our various linguistic abilities and (b) the nature of the cognitive mechanisms that instantiate this linguistic competence in the production and comprehension of speech. More importantly, though, the theoretical frameworks for interpreting experimental research are also identical in nature.

For example, consider what many would characterize as the immediate task of neurolinguistics: to explain particular patterns of impaired performance on specific linguistic tasks. In order to explain any such pattern, one must begin by formulating hypotheses concerning the nature of the normal cognitive systems engaged in the execution of these tasks. Such models provide the basis for an explanation in that the hypothesized normal system must be constructed so that under nature's experimental condition it predicts an observed pattern of impaired performance on the relevant tasks. Because any such condition must be of a rather circumscribed sort, involving the loss or diminution of processing capacity of individual components of the system, the observed pattern of impaired performance must represent the transparent operation of the remaining intact system in interaction with the damaged components of processing. Hence, a prerequisite for developing an explanatory account of impaired performance on a set of linguistic tasks is a model of the processing system that can adequately serve as the basis for normal performance. The interpretation of linguistic deficit, as in any scientific enterprise, must be theory driven.

Similarly, the logic for relating data to models of normal performance in the psycholinguistic and neurolinguistic paradigms will also be of this theory-driven form (Caramazza, 1986); the only difference between reasoning from impaired and normal processing will be in the sorts of conditions imposed on the processing system. A measurement in a psycholinguistic study is interpretable only in terms of a hypothesized cognitive system and a set of assumptions about the conditions of the experiment (e.g., assumptions regarding the stimulus properties and task demands that are relevant to the computations of the proposed system). If tasks are imposed that the experimenter supposes will compete for specific processing resources of the system, the predicted effects of this competition on the performance to be measured provide (part of) the basis for expectations regarding the performance of the overall system. So too in the case of studies with aphasic subjects: The set of experimental conditions includes a disruption in one or more of the components of the normal system, but in principle this is little different from the imposition of special conditions on a normal subject. Because the special conditions in the case of an aphasic are restricted to disruptions to or loss of component mechanisms (as opposed to reorganization or creation of new mechanisms), they pose no special problem with regard to the interpretation of performance (Caramazza, 1986).

Nevertheless, one important difference imposed on experimental design by the aphasic's deficit condition concerns the (interpretable) groupings of data. For many well-known reasons, it is found expedient in psycholinguistic studies to group data from several subjects, using the average performance on different stimulus types to test the combined assumptions about the cognitive system and experimental conditions. However, the practice of averaging over normal subjects is justifiable only under the assumption that the normal system being studied is (in some sense) universal,[1] and that variation among individuals will not compromise this working hypothesis. The situation in the case of aphasic subjects does not sustain this assumption. One cannot assume that similar patterns of impaired performance on a particular set of tasks (e.g., those used for clinical classification) will ensure that a group so determined will be homogeneous with respect to intact cognitive systems that subserve language processing. Hence, the averaging method levels differences in performance which, in the case of clinical subjects, are potentially significant with respect to the evaluation of the proposed processing model (and of the processing account of their deficits). As a result, group studies in neurolinguistics are simply not valid. The single-case method, on the other hand, does not rely on the homogeneity of such groups, and so does not admit a theoretically arbitrary leveling of performance differences across subjects. As in the group–study approach, each subject is tested on a wide range of tasks, each invoking various processing mechanisms or components. By selecting sets of tasks that converge on particular processing mechanisms, we should be able to deduce the loci of deficit to the functional system from the patterns of impaired performance. The restriction to single cases insulates this mode of inference from the (often unrecognized) presuppositions and theoretical biases inherent in clinical groupings: By definition, the unit "group" of the single-case study is guaranteed to be homogeneous with respect to the impaired system. Of course, as one would require elsewhere, an important constraint on this approach is that, regardless of the number of patients observed, and no matter how varied their performance on different tasks, one must assume the same normal model to account for each subject. Thus, the single-case method does not imply that a single subject alone could serve as the basis for all of our hypotheses regarding the normal system. Rather, it is required that each subject be treated as an instance of a potentially distinct deficit, which must be explained in terms of restricted sorts of modifications to the same normal system. For further discussion of these issues, we refer the reader to Badecker and Caramazza (1985, 1986), Caramazza (1984, 1986), and Caramazza and McCloskey (1988).

LEXICAL PROCESSING: PSYCHOLINGUISTIC EVIDENCE

Having discussed some of the methodological issues concerning neurolinguistic research, we present an overview of results from psycholinguistic

---

[1]Minimally, averaging across subjects requires that speakers of the same language have at their disposal the same performance system.

studies of lexical processing in the hope that it will provide an adequate picture of the processing mechanisms that are hypothesized to underly normal performance. The two issues that are of greatest interest to us here are whether morphologically complex words are parsed into their component parts in the course of lexical access from written stimuli and how word naming (reading words aloud) differs from nonword naming.[2]

Early evidence that lexical access procedures include mechanisms for morphemic decomposition was derived from results indicating interference at the morphemic level. In a lexical decision task, Taft and Forster (1975) found that, among words matched for surface frequency and length, lexical decisions for items that were homographic with bound morphemes were affected by the cumulative frequency of these bound morphemes. For example, the word *vent,* which is less frequent than the bound unit *-vent* (occurring in *prevent, advent, invent,* etc.), took longer to accept than *card,* whose frequency is greater than that of its corresponding bound morpheme (*-card* in *discard*). At issue is whether this interference reflects aspects of pre- or postaccess processing, because decisions for both *vent* and *card* could be affected by factors internal to the lexicon (e.g., structural relations among morphologically related items). However, if a lexicon–internal account of this apparent morpheme conditioned interference were correct, then morpheme effects should not be found for nonwords (because, by hypothesis, nonwords do not access lexical representations). Taft and Forster also found that real stem nonwords (such as *juvenate* and *vive*) were rejected more slowly than nonwords that are fragments of words but which do not constitute morphemes (e.g., *lish,* of *relish*), and that nonwords comprised of legal stems and affixes (e.g., *dejuvenate*) took longer to reject and induced more errors than nonwords made up of legal affixes and pseudostems (e.g., *depertoire*).

There are two plausible accounts of the latter results. One is that the morphemes are parsed in nonwords like *dejuvenate,* and the activation of morpheme representations in the input lexicon interferes with the nonword decision. However, Manelis and Tharp (1977) noted that the average frequency of the lexical stems in the Taft and Forster study exceeded that of their pseudostems, and similarity between nonwords and actual words was not controlled for. Thus, though Taft and Forster's results may indeed reflect asymmetries in the access process, the effects may not be due to the morphological compositionality of the stimuli. They might instead be a consequence of the interference of familiar (within word)

---

[2]For a discussion of related issues, such as the role of morphemic structure in the perception of spoken words, or in spoken or written production, we refer the reader to Garrett (1980, 1982), Kempley and Morton (1982), and Jarvella and Meijers (1983). For a dissenting view of the evidence for morphological decomposition, see Butterworth (1983).

orthographic sequences. In order to rule out this possibility, Laudanna and Caramazza (1984; see also Caramazza, Laudanna, & Romani, 1988) created nonword lists that controlled for letter-sequence frequency and real word similarity. These nonwords were constructed from real and pseudo-Italian roots and affixes. Nonwords composed of legal roots and affixes took longest to reject, followed by the mixed cases, and then nonwords composed of pseudoroots and pseudoaffixes. A similar ranking of stimulus types was obtained when error rate was taken as the index of processing difficulty. Clearly, then, the effect is attributable to morphological decomposability.

A complementary finding is reported in Taft (1981). Lexical decisions were performed on prefixed and pseudoprefixed words (e.g., *receive* and *relish,* respectively), which were matched for surface frequency, length, and stress pattern. (The stems of the prefixed words appear in no other forms, so the possible influence of morphological paradigms was avoided.) Recognition was faster, and the error rate was lower, for the prefixed items. Taft (1981) also showed that these and the results of Taft and Forster (1975) were not artifacts of the experimental format. Ruben, Becker, and Freeman (1979) argued that the effects reported in Taft and Forster (1975) were the result of a list property—that morphological decomposition was a special strategy induced by the "overpresentation" of multimorphemic stimuli. Prefix stripping, on this account, was simply an efficient means for identifying nonwords in the context of so many prefixed words, but morpheme parsing is not otherwise normally performed. Note, though, that this task-specific account predicts that, in the absence of a lexical decision component of the task and the consequent advantage that prefix-stripping would provide for identifying nonwords, pseudoprefixed words should not induce any additional processing complexity.

Taft (1981) carried out two word naming studies to rebut Ruben et al.'s (1979) account. In the first, subjects were presented with a list comprised of prefixed (50%) and pseudoprefixed (50%) words matched for frequency, length, and stress pattern. Prefixed words were named faster and with fewer errors than pseudoprefixed words. Taft then showed that the effect attributed to the interference of parsing pseudoprefixed words was not induced by the presence of prefixed words. The same reading task was administered, this time with a list comprised solely of pseudoprefixed and other nonprefixed words (matched as in the preceding experiment). Again, the results reflected the predictions of the morphological decomposition hypothesis: pseudoprefixed words took longer to read and induced more errors than nonprefixed items.

One stimulus property that has been shown by lexical decision latencies to have a robust effect on lexical access is frequency of occurrence

(Gordon, 1983; but see also Balota & Chumbley, 1984, for criticisms). Taft (1979) showed that when surface frequency was held constant, the decision times for affixed words was affected by stem frequency: Prefixed or inflectionally suffixed English words with high frequency stems were recognized more quickly than matched items with lower stem frequency. Bradley (1980) reported similar findings for derivationally suffixed words with Level II endings (-*ness*, -*er*, and -*ment*), although the effects for stem frequency were not found for words with the (nonproductive) Level I ending -*ion*.[3] However, in lexical decision experiments in which the stem frequency of morphologically decomposable forms was controlled, surface frequency had a facilitatory effect comparable to that found for nondecomposable words (Burani & Caramazza, 1987; Burani, Salmaso, & Caramazza, 1984; Taft, 1979). From these studies it appears that lexical access procedures involve both whole-word recognition and morphological parsing. This picture is further supported by Stanners, Neiser, Hernon, and Hall (1979). They found that regular inflected forms (e.g., *sailed* and *helped*) prime their stems as effectively as the stems (*sail*, *help*) themselves do, but that irregular inflected forms do not (i.e., *shook* is not as good a prime for *shake* as *shake* itself is). Irregular forms do have some priming effects, but these would be expected on the basis of semantic relatedness; thus, the priming provides no evidence that morphologically irregular words are parsed during access.

It is also worth mentioning that the lexical access procedures described so far do not involve the mapping of graphemic representations into phonological ones in the service of recognition. Seidenberg, Waters, Barnes, and Tanenhaus (1984) found that reaction-time effects of irregular spelling-to-sound correspondences were limited to lower frequency words and were much more reliably found in word naming than in lexical decision experiments. Parkin (1984) found similar slowing of response time for exception words (words with a unique or very unusual spelling-to-sound correspondence such as *threat, pint,* and *soul*) in comparison with mildly irregular words (e.g., *wasp, palm,* and *swarm*) and regular words in a single-word reading experiment, but this effect was not found when subjects were required to delay their responses by 1500 msec. There have been several attempts to explain such phenomena. We argue that any adequate explanation must be cast in terms of the dual-route model of

---

[3]There are, in fact, two stimulus properties of the morphologically complex words with the Level I suffix that Bradley employed which ought to be distinguished: productivity and phonological transparency. For a discussion of the relevance of these properties to psychological models of language processing, see Anshen and Aronoff (1981), Aronoff (1980), Aronoff and Schvaneveldt (1978), and Cutler (1980).

reading.[4] According to this model, there are two available processing routes for reading. Along one route, known as the lexical route, (visual) orthographic information is mapped onto lexical representations, which serve as the locus of the information that guides the correct pronunciation of stimuli.[5] Alternatively, orthographic sequences can be mapped onto pronunciations by means of grapheme-to-phoneme correspondence rules. According to the dual route hypothesis, these mappings do not employ lexical information, therefore, the set of mechanisms that perform these particular transformations is referred to as the nonlexical (or grapheme-phoneme) route.

The motivation for this apparent violation of the rule of parsimony can be understood in part if one considers reading tasks in terms of stimulus characteristics. Words such as *yacht* and *hiccough* have highly irregular grapheme-to-phoneme mappings, so it is reasonable to expect that reading these words will require access to idiosyncratic lexical information. Reading nonwords (or novel, monomorphemic words), on the other hand, requires that there be some mechanism that is able to use regular spelling-to-sound correspondences. Given this dual-route model, Seidenberg et al.'s (1984) and Parkin's (1984) findings may be interpreted as follows: The operation of the grapheme-to-phoneme mechanisms will not have an effect on naming latencies except when, because of the low-item frequency, the address procedures are slowed enough to significantly shorten the lag between the output of both routes. In this circumstance,

---

[4]For opposing views, see Glushko (1979), Marcel (1980), Kay & Marcel (1981), and McClelland and Rumelhart (1981). We should hasten to add, however, that none of these authors has provided an adequate account of language deficits that selectively affect words or nonwords—deficits that constitute primary evidence for the dual-route account. We now discuss such deficits in greater detail. (Parkin, 1984, also discusses the problems with the interpretation of spelling-regularity effects within a single route model of word and nonword reading.)

One common objection that these authors make is that no adequate model of the nonlexical leg of the dual-route model has ever been advanced. We disagree. One such model of these mechanisms—though it certainly was not proposed as such by the authors—may be found in Sejnowski and Rosenberg (1985).

[5]More specifically according to the model of the lexical route we assume here, visual stimuli activate entries in the Lexical Address Component, which includes whole-word address procedures and morphological parsing address procedures. (These subcomponents operate independently and in parallel by means of passive activation.) Entries in these subcomponents specify (for regularly inflected words, at least) morphologically decomposed stem + affix representations in the Orthographic Input Lexicon, and these entries serve in turn as the points of entry into the Lexical Semantic System. In reading tasks, items in the Lexical Semantic System activate entries in a Phonemic Output Lexicon, whose output is passed on to the articulatory system. For further discussion of this model, see Caramazza, et al. (1985).

however, word naming would be slowed for items with irregular spelling-to-sound correspondences as a result of the conflict between the output of the lexical system and the output of the grapheme-to-phoneme component. For more frequent words, the lexical route will be much more efficient in accessing entries: Hence, the lag between access and the completion of the nonlexical processes will allow subsequent production processes to operate on as yet nonconflicting input. Within this dual route framework, an obligatory response delay would also be expected to give the system time to overcome such conflicts, thereby reducing the measurable effects of spelling regularity on naming latencies.

NEUROLINGUISTIC STUDIES

The question of whether visually presented words must be recoded into phonological forms prior to accessing representations in the lexicon has also been decided in the negative in order to account for the behavior of dyslexic subjects[6] who could read words (including words with irregular spelling-to-sound correspondences) but not nonwords, and whose performance on nonword lists is not affected by the inclusion of pseudohomophones, such as *brane, burd,* and so forth (Patterson & Marcel, 1977). This deficit can be explained within the framework of a dual-route model of reading by positing an impairment to the nonlexical, grapheme-to-phoneme component while the lexical route remains intact. Further evidence for the computational distinction between the visual-lexical mechanisms that remain intact in such subjects and the nonlexical (grapheme-phoneme) conversion procedures comes from a complementary deficit described by Marshall and Newcombe (1973), Shallice and Warrington (1980), and Patterson (1982). In this second variety of deficit, reading performance on pronounceable nonwords and some words with regular spelling-to-sound relationships is not affected, whereas reading performance on words with irregular spellings is generally impaired. Thus, the double dissociation exhibited by such cases provides neurolinguistic grounds for the gross distinction between processing routes (Coltheart, 1978; Shallice, 1981). Additional inferences about specific processing mechanisms may be drawn when patterns of impaired performance are examined in more detail. We focus on the components of the lexical route.

---

[6]We refer here to acquired dyslexia, as opposed to developmental dyslexia: Only in the case of the acquired deficits is it appropriate to assume that the intact system bears the sort of transparent relationship to the normal processing system that would enable us to reason from impaired performance to characteristics of the normal system.

Caramazza, Miceli, Silveri, & Laudanna (1984) presented two case studies of Italian subjects with selective disruptions in nonword reading. In the first of these, the case of LB, the ability to read nonwords depended on whether or not they could be parsed into legal-root and affix morphemes, even though this subject's ability to read words of all grammatical classes, and with varying degrees of morphological complexity, was virtually unimpaired. His performance on morphologically "legal" nonwords (forms corresponding to the "English nonword" *walkest*) was significantly better than on morphologically illegal nonwords (i.e., forms composed of a real stem and pseudoaffix, like *walkent*, or a pseudostem plus true affix, as in *wolkest*). LB's pattern of errors was also noteworthy: 79% of the erroneous responses to morphologically legal nonword stimuli were either words or (other) morphologically legal nonwords, whereas these kinds of errors occurred in only 24% of the responses to morphologically illegal nonword stimuli (compared to 4% for other nonword stimuli). This pattern of performance is interpretable only under the following assumptions: (a) the dual-route model best characterizes normal reading, (b) visual-lexical recognition involves morphological parsing, though not phonological recoding, in a lexical address component, and (c) LB's performance is a consequence of a disruption in the nonlexical conversion system, which has left intact only the visual-lexical system to subserve nonword reading. As a result, only nonwords that can be parsed into morphemic components will be processed by the unimpaired mechanisms.

The performance on word-reading tasks of AG, the other subject presented in Caramazza et al. (1985), is informative with respect to morphological processing in another regard. Several recent studies of acquired dyslexics have focused on the relationship between the production of morphological paralexias and phonological processing. Beauvois and Dérouesné (1979), Patterson (1982), and Job and Sartori (1984) reported subjects with nonword reading deficits who also have difficulties processing function words and morphologically complex words. Patterson (1982) argued that this association should be construed as evidence for the hypothesis that (some subcomponent of) the nonlexical route is implicated in the normal processing of written affixed words. However, both AG and WB (Funnell, 1983) exhibited impairments in processing nonwords but did not produce morphological paralexias—a dissociation that seriously undermines Patterson's proposal.

Evidence from other patients has been argued to show that the lexical address system involves morphological decomposition and whole-word recognition, and that it accesses morphologically, though not semantically, decomposed items in an orthographic input lexicon. Moody (1984) presents four case studies of acquired dyslexia with selective deficits in nonword reading *and* in reading morphologically complex words.[7] For example, these subjects made morphological deletion errors (*walking* → *walk*) when asked to read inflected verbs aloud. In a grammaticality judgment task in which the sole variety of syntactic deviance was the use of morphologically inappropriate forms, these subjects performed perfectly when stimuli were presented auditorily, but at chance levels on visual presentation. From such evidence it was argued that in all four subjects the deficit in reading morphologically complex words was an input deficit. Moody (1984) and Coltheart (1985) made the additional assumption that it is a morphological processing component that is impaired, an assumption to which we return shortly. Coltheart (1985) noted that if the morphological parsing of orthographic input is accomplished by affix stripping processes that precede whole-word recognition in a serial fashion, then pseudosuffixed words (such as *corner*) would be read incorrectly (as *corn*) by these subjects as often as words with true suffixes (i.e., as often as *caller* is read as *call*, *called*, etc.). However, this effect was not found; Moody's subjects performed variably on morphologically complex forms (90%, 45%, 35%, and 55% correct on true suffixed items), but all performed perfectly on the pseudosuffixed items. Such performance indicates that the morphological deletion errors do not arise simply because the affixes are irretrievably separated from the stem of the stimulus before any whole-word processing takes place (as would appear to be mandated by the model of morphological processing advocated by Taft, 1979; Taft & Forster, 1975). Instead, some whole-word processing can be accomplished independently of (or in parallel with) morphemic parsing of a written stimulus (Caramazza et al., 1985).

If we assume along with Coltheart that the subjects in Moody's study had impairments to input components devoted to morphological processing, then their performance may also be construed as evidence regarding the nature of the output of the lexical access parsing procedures. If the output for items such as *called* are semantic forms (or addresses of semantic forms) such as CALL + ⟨Past Tense⟩, then performance on suppletive forms such as *went* or irregular forms like *bought* should also be disrupted (because the expected output of the address procedures, under this analysis, would be GO + ⟨Past Tense⟩ and BUY + ⟨Past Tense⟩, respectively). If, on the other hand, morphemic parsing only mapped the segmental forms of orthographic representations of words into corresponding morphemic forms (i.e., into other orthographic representations) in an orthographic input lexicon, then the output for *called*, *went* and *bought* would be *call* + *ed*, *went*, and *bought*, respectively. In this case, one would expect that performance on these two types of stimuli would differ.

---

[7]Coltheart reported that these subjects were clinically classified as phonological dyslexics.

Moody reports the latter pattern of performance for her four subjects: Poor (45%, 35%, 25%, and 45% correct) on regular past-tense forms, but nearly perfect (100%, 95%, 90%, and 90% correct, respectively) on irregular past-tense forms that were matched to the regular forms for frequency. Thus, it would appear that the input components differentiate regular units of form, such as stems and regular affixes, and not lexical units that are determined strictly by the meaning of words.[8] These results, and the results concerning these subjects' performance with pseudosuffixed words, are consistent with the addressed morphology model discussed previously (Caramazza et al., 1985, 1988).

However, we must inject a word of caution because the conclusions we have drawn from Moody's study are contingent on our acceptance of the assumption that the morphological errors produced by her subjects were the result of an impairment to a morphological processing component. This may in fact be true, in which case the conclusions that we drew from these patterns of performance stand unchanged. Unfortunately, though, Moody's (and Coltheart's) hypothesis concerning the locus of deficit has not been supported with sufficient argument. One cannot conclude from the production of morphological paraphasias alone that the impairment responsible for these errors is morphological in nature. To explain why this is so, we describe a relevant single-case study that we reported in greater detail elsewhere (Badecker & Caramazza, 1987).

FM is a right-handed, 38-year-old male high-school graduate who suffered a stroke in 1981. His injury left him with moderate right-hemiparesis and language impairments. At the time of this study (4 years postonset), FM's speech was considered nonfluent with reduced phrase length, and his performance on sentence processing tasks (sentence–picture matching) revealed asyntactic comprehension. His speech was labored, and he produced literal paraphasias and some morphological errors. FM's reading performance included visual (*threat → thread*), semantic (*discover → Magellan*), inflectional (*sew → sewing; decayed → decays;* or *walks → walk*), derivational (*achieve → achievement; disconnect → connection* or *worker → work*), and other types of errors, in addition to correct responses.[9] FM's visual and semantic error responses were reliably more frequent, less abstract, and shorter (in letter length) than their corresponding stimuli (Gordon, Goodman-Schulman, & Caramazza, 1987). Morphological errors were the most common error type for morphologically complex stimuli; and these tended to be affix deletions and substitutions, although FM's reading errors also included a

---

[8]To our knowledge, these are not the inferences drawn by either Moody or Coltheart.

[9]This general pattern of reading performance is discussed at great length by Coltheart, Patterson, and Marshall (1980).

substantial number of affix insertions for monomorphemic stimuli. An analysis of the morphological errors in a large corpus of his reading responses revealed two interesting contrasts: FM performed better on words with the agentive -er suffix than with the comparative -er suffix (54% vs. 2% correct responses), and was more likely to mistakenly insert or substitute the agentive suffix (21 insertions, 5 substitutions) than the comparative suffix (zero insertions or substitutions).[10] Similarly, the plural morpheme -s was read correctly more often than the third person singular suffix -s (75/240 correct vs. 2/28 correct), and the plural morpheme was also inserted more often than the verbal inflection (103 vs. 2 insertions).[11] Although it is entirely possible that some of these contrasts only reflect a disparity in the relative proportions of nouns, verbs, and adjectives in the corpus[12] (especially in the case of morphological insertion and substitution errors), this could not be the whole story (e.g., as with the correct responses and deletions). Furthermore, there were some interesting contrasts between the visual and semantic errors that FM produced. For example, when he produced a visual or semantic error, the response was consistently more frequent than the stimulus. This was also the case when FM produced a morphological deletion error on the agentive and comparative stimuli (e.g., *dancer* → *dance* and *smaller* → *small*). However, when the agentive -er was either inserted or substituted for another suffix, the response was less frequent than the stimulus in 21 of the 26 cases. Given that the comparative -er was never inserted or substituted for another suffix, we have a strong candidate for a dissociation defined along a morphological dimension. From these response patterns, it might appear that some of the errors FM produced were the result of a deficit in a morphological processing component. To test this hypothesis, FM was given a series of reading tests with new controlled lists. For reasons of space, we limit our attention to the arguments made by Badecker

---

[10]These figures are based on the assumption that when the -er suffix is added to a verb, it is the agentive ending and not the comparative (which only attaches to adjectives). Because there are only three instances in which FM produced a morphologically illegal nonword response, in comparison to the hundreds of morphologically legal complex words he has produced as a morpheme insertion or substitution error, this would appear to be a rather safe assumption.

In a task using a controlled list that matched agentive nominals with (regular) comparative adjectives for surface frequency and length in letters, this pattern was replicated: 68% of FM's responses to the nominals were correct and 26% were morphological paralexias, whereas none of the adjectives were read correctly and 85% of his reading responses to these items were morphological paralexias.

[11]Another suffix, -y, was also mistakenly inserted often in comparison with the other affixes in the corpus: 13 insertions, 18 deletions, and 10 correct responses.

[12]There were 2987 nouns, 936 verbs, and 783 adjectives in the corpus (see Gordon et al., 1987).

and Caramazza (1987) for distinguishing visual from morphological paralexias.

Since FM produced visual errors on reading tasks, it was important to demonstrate that the morphological paralexias he produced were not simply a special case of visual paralexia. Three lists of test items containing pseudostems (like *earn* in *earnest*) were composed, and these words were matched with affixed and unaffixed controls in length in letters and in surface frequency.[13] It was reasoned that if morphological errors result from a visual processing deficit simply because the stem of an affixed stimulus competes with the whole stimulus item for activation, then lexical items with embedded words (the pseudostems) should induce analogous, pseudomorphological errors (i.e., where the pseudostem is preserved in the response, but the "affix" has either been deleted or replaced with an actual prefix or suffix). FM performed identically on the items with pseudostems and monomorphemic controls, but produced significantly more morphological errors on the affixed controls from each list. However, though this pattern is generally taken to be prima facie evidence that morphological errors do not arise from a visual processing deficit, we should also recall some of the other factors that we have reason to believe affect FM's visual error responses: frequency and concreteness.[14] For example, for several of the items with pseudostems that appeared in this test, the stimulus word (e.g., *flower*) is both more frequent and more concrete than its pseudostem (*flow*). An analysis of FM's errors on two of the pseudostem lists (lists containing word-initial pseudostems), broken down according to the relative frequency of the surface form and pseudostem, was carried out to determine the proportion of errors that were scored as pseudomorphological in the different frequency categories. FM's errors were more likely to be pseudomorphological errors on items for which the pseudostem frequency exceeded their surface frequency than on items for which the surface frequency was greater than their pseudostem frequency.

The interpretation of FM's morphological paralexias is also confounded by a grammatical category effect: in controlled tasks, FM read nouns better than adjectives or verbs. When FM's visual errors were analyzed, a similar pattern emerged: Visual and semantic error responses tended to be nouns more often than verbs or adjectives. If we consider those factors known to affect the probability of a visual error response, one might then

---

[13]There were a total of 179 pseudostem items, 52 of which had pseudostems in word final position and were matched to prefixed controls, and 127 of which contained a word-initial pseudostem and were matched to suffixed controls.

[14]For evidence that semantic concreteness versus abstractness affects normal lexical processing, see Kroll and Merves (1986).

conclude that the fact that FM produced fewer pseudomorphological errors on items like *flower* and *wicker* than morphological errors on truly affixed words might also be a function of these lexical characteristics: stimulus frequency, category, and concreteness. This account would also undermine the morphological deficit interpretation of the results cited earlier concerning agentive nominals like *singer,* which are deverbal, and comparative adjectives like *smaller,* which are inflected adjectives.

Badecker and Caramazza (1987) tried to circumvent this problem with a bootstrap approach to the comparisons needed to rule out an input processing explanation of FM's morphological errors. A sublist from two of the pseudosuffix lists was analyzed, taking all of the stimuli that met the following criteria: (a) the item's surface frequency is lower than that of the corresponding pseudostem; (b) the embedded word is a noun, and the surface form is either a verb or an adjective; (c) the pseudostem is more concrete than the item it is embedded in. (All of these words would also meet the requirement of having a pseudostem that is visually similar to the entire test item.) FM's performance on these words was then compared with his performance on matched agentive nominals and comparative adjectives. The pseudostem words (e.g., *listen*) were read correctly significantly more often than the comparative *-er* items (e.g., *taller*): 43% vs. 0% respectively. The comparison of the agentive *-er* list (containing items like *reader*) with the pseudostem words also revealed a statistically reliable difference when morphological errors and other errors are separated, but not when the error types are collapsed.[15] It would appear, then, that the differences between the agentive and comparative *-er* lists cannot be attributed to the effect of these various factors at the input (visual) level of lexical processing. This, of course, does not mean that none of the morphological errors that FM produces are actually visual in nature, but it does indicate that *some* of these errors are not visually based.

Unfortunately, in many studies of subjects who produce both visual and morphological paralexias (e.g., Job & Sartori, 1982; Patterson, 1978, 1980), no such effort has been made to distinguish these error types. As a result, it is not possible to evaluate the implications of their reading performance with regard to morphological processing mechanisms. The analysis of FM's pattern of performance is instructive if only because it reveals the complexity of the process whereby one may reason validly from observable patterns of performance to the nature of the impairments responsible for them. In order to provide a reasonable interpretation of

---

[15]If the morphological errors (operationally defined) are actually visual, then it is the latter comparison, with error types collapsed, that is most relevant to the discussion: that is, if morphological errors are in fact visual errors, then they should be grouped as such in the comparisons.

FM's performance, for example, it is necessary to consider how various factors in a richly articulated model of lexical processing could interact to produce particular patterns of performance that have been observed. Where it can be argued that nonmorphological features of the lexical system converge to produce observed patterns of morphological paralexias, it would be imprudent to posit a morphological processing deficit to account for these paralexias.

The foregoing discussion may give the impression that if the theory of lexical processing is so complex, then it may be impossible to identify true instances of morphological processing deficits. Were this the case, our ability to learn about the processing of morphologically complex words on the basis of neurolinguistic studies would be severely limited. Fortunately, we have reason to believe that both of these conclusions are unwarranted. In the pages that follow, we discuss cases where morphological processing deficits can inform our theories about the representation of morphologically complex words in the lexicon, in addition to cases which provide evidence concerning the role of morphemic units in lexical processing.

On the Representation of Morphological Relations: Inflection Versus Derivation

One set of issues regarding the representation of morphologically complex words that has been submitted to linguistic (e.g., Anderson, 1982; Aronoff, 1976; Lieber, 1981; Selkirk, 1982), psycholinguistic (e.g., Fowler, Napps, & Feldman, 1985; Garrett, 1982; Stanners et al., 1979), and neurolinguistic analysis (e.g., De Bleser & Bayer, 1985) concerns the relation between the representation of inflected (like English *walks, walking,* and *walked*) and derived words (such as English *farmer, darkness,* and *sanity*). For example, although some linguists argue that derivation is represented in the lexicon but inflection is controlled by syntactic (and/or phonological) rules or mechanisms (e.g., Anderson, 1982; Aronoff, 1976), others who place inflection in the lexicon disagree among themselves as to whether there is any need to distinguish the two varieties of affixation within the lexicon. Neurolinguistic arguments for placing inflection in the lexicon have been proposed by De Bleser and Bayer (1985) to account for the preservation of inflection in a case that they contend demonstrates intact lexical knowledge in the absence of syntactic and semantic processing mechanisms. Many studies of impairments characterized by inflectional omissions (e.g., Goodglass, Berko-Gleason, Alkerman Bernholtz, & Hyde, 1972) or substitutions (e.g., Miceli, Mazzuchi, Menn, & Goodglass, 1983) have clearly documented a dissociation between processing of inflectional affixes (impaired) and processing of word stems ("intact"), whereas the complement of this dissociation has also been reported (e.g., Buckingham, 1981; Butterworth, 1979; Caplan, Kellar, & Locke, 1972). In the latter case, subjects who produce neologisms in content word positions in spontaneous speech often inflect the neologisms using a regular suffix, but the inflections are not always syntactically appropriate (Buckingham, 1981). However, these data are ambiguous with respect to the locus of impairment. A subject could fail to produce correct inflections because the inflectional component of a morphologically decomposed lexical representation is degraded, or because of impairment in the mechanism computing the syntactic frames in the course of sentence production. However, direct evidence that inflectional morphology is represented in the lexicon and that it is distinguished there from derivational morphology has come from the case study of an aphasic subject, FS, described by Miceli and Caramazza (1987).

FS is a 60-year-old, right-handed male native speaker of Italian who, in 1978, suffered language deficits as the result of an acute intracerebral hematoma. (For a detailed discussion of FS's lesion sites, see Miceli & Caramazza, 1987.) The feature of FS's linguistic abilities that is of relevance here concerns the processing of morphologically complex words. For example, FS's spontaneous speech contains numerous morphological substitutions, as the italicized portions of the following passage illustrate:

> poi ancora spesso *andare* [allo] studio.   [In] via C. [a] *il Pariolo*
> then still often *go* (inf.) [to the] office. On C. street, i Parioli,
> (target = . . . vado (1st per. sg. present) . . . i Parioli)

> c'e   *la*   *mia*   *studia*   ancora aperto
> there's the (f.sg.) my (f.sg.) office (f.sg.) still open
> (target = . . . il (m.sg.) mio (m.sg.) studio (m.sg.) . . .)

A quantitative analysis of a corpus of his spontaneous speech indicated that, in addition to omitting or misselecting free-standing grammatical morphemes (22.3% and 19.8%, respectively), FS made a significant number of subject/verb agreement errors (55.9%) and determiner/noun and noun/adjective agreement errors (13.8% and 20%, respectively). In other respects, his sentence production capacity appears normal: for example, when measured in terms of the ratio of main to subordinate clauses or the number of prepositional phrases employed; and though FS's mean phrase length was somewhat reduced compared to normal controls, this appears to be due simply to the omission of free-standing grammatical markers or the misselection of both free and bound grammatical markers. In comparison with the inflectional errors that FS produced, though, the number of derivational errors was negligible. What must be ascertained is whether this pattern represents an impairment in the lexicon, or whether some other aspect of processing is implicated (e.g., an impairment affecting the syntactic specification of sentences). One hypothesized level of sentence processing, which includes a specification of the inflections of lexical items, is described by Garrett (1980, 1982) as the positional level. Thus, in terms of the hypothesized processing mechanisms, the most reasonable accounts of FS's impairment are as follows:

1. The representation of relations at the positional level misidentifies (wrongly or by underspecification) the inflectional form that is to be employed in a particular syntactic frame, and these representations are compromised; or
2. The mechanism(s) that would ordinarily select (access) a form on the basis of its (positional level) inflectional specification is disrupted (e.g., as modeled by Lapointe, 1985); or
3. Some "words" are represented in the lexicon as sequences of independent morphemes, the lexicon includes mechanisms for composing these words from their constituent morphemes, and either these mechanisms are impaired or the corresponding inflectional representations are compromised.

An attempt was made to distinguish these accounts on the basis of single-word repetition tasks employing lists of items controlled for form class, frequency, length, morphological complexity, type of suffix (inflectional vs. derivational), and presence of prefix versus pseudo prefix. Clearly, if the errors in FS's spontaneous speech were the result of a sentence processing deficit (1, 2), analogous errors should not appear in a single-word processing task. Likewise, morphological errors in this task would indicate a lexical (as opposed to syntactic) deficit such as proposed in (3). In fact, FS made a substantial number of repetition errors of this sort: 637 errors (96.5% of the incorrect word–responses, or 71% of the total corpus of errors) were morphological in nature. Even more strikingly, 615 (96.7%) of these errors were inflectional (substitution) errors.

Miceli and Caramazza (1987) presented a series of arguments that the substitution errors could not be attributed to any nonlexical factors (such as frequency, articulatory, or phonological complexity, etc.); here we simply discuss one such argument concerning FS's repetition performance with adjectives. FS was asked to repeat a list of adjectives inflected for number and person. (Items were matched for length in syllables and letters, for stem frequency, and for surface frequency.) FS's tendency to produce the citation form for these items (masc.sg.) induced a higher error rate for the masc.pl., fem.sg., and fem.pl stimuli than for the masc.sg. items: Of the 45 inflectional errors, 36 were substitution of the masc.sg. suffix for other inflectional endings (80.0%). Because the citation form of an adjective is usually the more frequent of its inflected variants, however, it is important to establish that the probability of producing a response is not determined predominantly by the relative frequencies of the inflected forms of a stimulus (i.e., by a nonlexical factor). FS repeated another set of inflected adjectives composed of (a) masc.sg and non–masc.sg. inflected adjectives whose masc.sg. form was the most frequent of the inflected forms, and (b) matched forms of adjectives whose masc.sg. form was less frequent than the non–masc.sg. forms. FS showed the same tendency to produce the masc.sg. form for each category of item. In particular, the masc.sg. form was repeated correctly for both categories (41/50 and 40/50), whereas the number of correct responses for the non–masc.sg. forms was much lower (5/50 and 11/50). Similar means were employed to establish that it was not the phonological form of the adjectival inflection that determined the pattern of responses. Though some adjectives exhibit a four-way inflectional contrast (e.g., *car-o*–masc.sg.; *car-i*–masc.pl.; *car-a*–fem.sg.; and *car-e*–fem.pl.), there are also a number of adjectives taking gender-neutral inflections (e.g., *fort-e*–masc./fem. sg. and *fort-i*–masc./fem. pl.). Again, performance favored the citation forms: FS repeated 81.2% of the singular forms correctly, but only 34.5% of the plural items. These and other results reported in Miceli and Caramazza (1987) provide strong evidence that the inflectional errors that FS produced are predominantly governed by factors pertaining to the morphological status of a word.

Returning to the overall nature of the morphological processing deficit, recall that FS's performance shows a marked distinction between inflectional and derivational morphology. At the current level of theorizing, the three hypotheses listed previously appear equally plausible as accounts of FS's sentence production impairment; yet only the third can offer a plausible explanation for FS's single-word performance as well. Thus, this case provides clear evidence that inflectional and derivational processes or representations are distinguished in the "cognitive lexicon."

Morphemes as Controlling Units in Writing

In addition to informing us about the kinds of properties that organize the lexicon, studies of impairment have also begun to reveal which roles morphological units play in governing the operation of output mechanisms. The case that we describe here provides evidence that certain stages of writing performance are controlled by morphemic representations (as opposed to representations of whole words regardless of the morphological complexity of the word). In particular, patterns of spelling performance that result from an impairment to a graphemic buffer indicate that the representations of the orthographic output lexicon that are passed on to the allographic/letter-name conversion mechanisms[16] are passed along in morphemic units.

The function of a buffer in the architecture of an information processing system is to hold, temporarily, representations that do not correspond to the units of analysis at a given point in the flow of information (Caramazza, Miceli, & Villa, 1986). One such buffer receives information from a phoneme-to-grapheme conversion system (for writing or spelling novel words and non-words) and from the orthographic output lexicon (for writing or spelling familiar words). In an attempt to characterize a variety of normal spelling errors that are hypothesized to arise at the level of this buffer,[17] Wing and Baddeley (1980) distinguished letter-interference effects from the effects of temporal degradation—effects that will be distributed differently throughout the word. According to their account, errors that arise from letter-interference tend to appear in the medial portion of a word (producing a bow-shaped distribution of errors), whereas errors that arise as a result of the decay of a memory trace appear more frequently at the end of a word. In the event of impairment to the graphemic buffer mechanism, an accentuation of one or both of these effects might be expected. Furthermore, in the absence of additional deficits, such an impairment should result in similar performance on words and nonwords, whereas lexical effects (such as concreteness or category effects) would not be expected (Caramazza, Miceli, Villa, & Romani, 1987).

Evidence that the representations of the orthographic output lexicon are passed along to the allographic/letter-name conversion mechanisms in morphemic units comes from a subject, DH, who exhibited a graphemic buffer deficit (Badecker, Hillis, & Caramazza, 1987). DH, a 49-year-old, high school educated male, suffered a stroke resulting in dyslexia, dysgraphia and mild anomia. DH's auditory comprehension is unimpaired, and his speech is grammatical and predominantly fluent: normal articulation and normal sentence and phrase length, with occasional hesitations for word retrieval. He produced morphological errors in reading and writing tasks, but not in spontaneous speech or in repetition tasks. The aspect of his performance that is of interest concerns the patterns of spelling errors in writing tasks.

---

[16]For a discussion of the lexical and post lexical components of the writing system, see Goodman and Caramazza (1986).

[17]Omissions, substitutions, insertions and transpositions of letters are the kinds of errors thought to arise at this level.

In writing from dictation and oral spelling from dictation tasks, DH produced spelling errors (substitutions, omissions, insertions, and transpositions), which tended to increase in frequency toward the end of a word. Spelling errors were more likely to occur in longer words: On controlled lists of 4-, 5-, 6-, 7-, and 8-letter, monomorphemic words, the correct response rate was 100%, 86%, 71%, 43%, and 14%, respectively. A representative distribution of spelling errors on monomorphemic words in writing to dictation is shown in Fig. 10.1. Omissions were scored as one full error at the position of the omitted item; insertions were scored as one half error at each of the two surrounding positions for word medial insertions, and one full error for the position preceding the insertion in the case of word final insertions (word initial insertions did not occur). Transpositions were scored as one full error at both of the affected positions. Positions were determined simply by counting letter positions in the target words. These positions were relativized by means of an algorithm presented in Wing and Baddeley (1980). DH's spelling performance showed no effect for grammatical category or abstractness/concreteness in either controlled written or oral spelling tasks. This pattern of performance is strongly indicative of a buffer deficit. In terms of Wing and Baddeley's (1980) account of the buffer, the letters of a (monomorphemic) word are registered virtually simultaneously in the buffer, but due to the temporal constraints of the writing task buffered letters at the end of a word are more likely to decay than word initial letters. DH's deficit appears to have accentuated this decay.

When the positions of spelling errors in morphologically complex words are analyzed in the same fashion, however, a different pattern emerges. DH produced fewer errors on suffixed words than on monomorphemic words matched for frequency and length. More importantly, however, the probability of producing a spelling error in one position or another differed from the error distribution in monomorphemic items. For example, DH wrote from dictation a list of items with word-initial embedded words (e.g., *dogma* and *agent*) and a matched list of suffixed items. To score spelling errors, letter positions were relativized within morphemes for the suffixed items (e.g., *walk-ed*) and within pseudomorphemes for the embedded-words items (e.g., *dog-ma*). The mean (pseudo-) suffix length (in letters) for the misspelled suffixed and pseudosuffixed words was 1.7 and 1.9, respectively; the position of DH's spelling errors on these lists is indicated in Fig. 10.2. This pattern is most interpretable if the controlling unit of representation for the graphemic buffer is not the word (as Wing & Baddeley, 1980, suggested), but the morpheme. That is, error distribution contrasts such as those in Fig. 10.2 suggest a reinterpretation of the word-length effect as a control-unit-length effect. Given that the suffixes correspond to short units in the

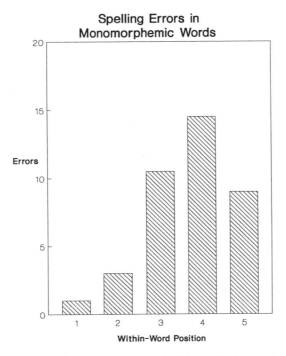

FIGURE 10.1.   DH's spelling errors as a function of relative position within target word.

buffer, whereas pseudosuffixes correspond to the ends of longer (whole word) units on this analysis, the fact that fewer spelling errors were produced in suffix positions than in pseudosuffix positions follows rather straightforwardly.

This analysis finds strong support when DH's spelling performance on words with productive, Level II suffixes (e.g., *sadness*) is compared with his performance on words containing relatively nonproductive, Level I suffixes (e.g., *active*) matched for length and frequency.[18] In both sets of stimuli, the addition of the suffix did not effect the orthographic form of the stem. However, whereas the meanings of the morphologically derived words with Level II suffixes were predictable from the meanings of the corresponding stems and suffixes, the semantic relations between the derived words and their components in the Level I suffix set were comparatively opaque. Normal processing evidence (such as Bradley's, 1980, results discussed previously) suggests that (certain) words with Level I

---

[18]For a discussion of these two types of affix, see Selkirk (1982) and Scalise (1984).

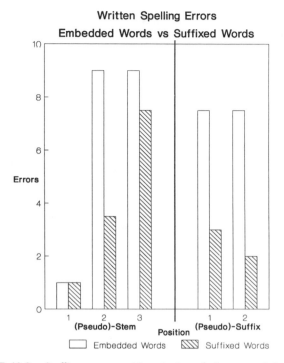

FIGURE 10.2.   Spelling error positions in (pseudo-)stems and (pseudo-)suffixes.

suffixes are not represented in morphologically decomposed form.[19] That is, under certain conditions (i.e., when the semantic and/or phonological relation between a derived word and its base is opaque) a polymorphemic word will be represented as one complete unit instead of being decomposed into its morphemic constituents. Figure 10.3 presents the distribution of DH's spelling errors for these contrasting varieties of suffixed words. DH produced more spelling errors on the Level I items than on the Level II words. Crucially, though, the greatest increase in error rate is in

---

[19]Bybee (1985) suggested that two lexical characteristics of affixed forms, the semantic and phonological transparency of the relation between these forms and their morphological base, determines whether derived words are morphologically independent of the words (or stems) from which they are derived. Although her account is cast in a framework more closely aligned with the satelite theory of morphological relations (as presented in Gurjanov, Lukatela, Moskovljevic, Savic, & Turvey, 1985; Lukatela, Kostic, Feldman, & Turvey, 1983); the arguments she presented for such a distinction seem to us also to apply to the distinction between decomposed and undecomposed representations of derived words. (See also Aronoff, 1976, for his discussion of morphological productivity and the nature of lexical representations.)

the suffix region of the Level I words. If morphological productivity is the factor that determines whether a word will be represented in decomposed form, then the degree of semantic opacity for some of the Level I items will be expected to have exceeded the allowable limits for decomposition. That is, we would anticipate that some of the words in the Level I list would be lexically represented in undecomposed form in the orthographic output lexicon, and that the output lexicon would, therefore, pass on control units corresponding to the whole word instead of the stem and suffix components from which the word is historically derived. On the basis of DH's performance, this appears to be the case. The patterns of errors in DH's writing thus provide evidence that the orthographic output lexicon passes on to the graphemic buffer representations that correspond to productive morphological units.

SUMMARY

In the preceding pages we have presented a number of case studies of normal and impaired language processing in order to motivate a particu-

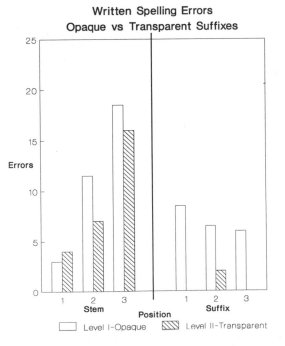

FIGURE 10.3. Stem and suffix spelling errors for Level I (semantically opaque) and Level II (semantically transparent) derived words.

ular view of normal lexical processing, and to demonstrate the role of such a model in the description and explanation of language impairment. With respect to normal lexical processing, we have cited evidence for distinct processing mechanisms for words and nonwords (the dual route model of reading), for morphological decomposition as a constituent process in lexical access, and for a lexical access procedure that employs both whole-word and morpheme access units. Furthermore, we have discussed studies (e.g., the cases of FM and DH) that shed light on how the morphological structure of words interacts with lexical and nonlexical factors in various components of the processing system. Our interest, however, has not been only to demonstrate how analyses of normal and impaired performance reveal the properties of psycholinguistic representations and cognitive mechanisms. We have also tried to demonstrate that the nature of language pathology may be validly inferred only by reference to well-defined linguistic and cognitive theories. DH's dysgraphic impairment is a case in point. In order to develop an explanation of the pattern of spelling errors in his performance, one must appeal to formal aspects of word structure (such as the different levels of derivational morphology) as well as the properties of buffer mechanisms in cognitive linguistic systems. Similarly, an explanation of FS's inflectional paraphasias compels one to differentiate among those cognitive components that might distinguish inflectional and derivational morphology (either representationally or in terms of the computations carried out in these components). Satisfactory accounts of these cases require a framework of description that is informed by linguistic and psychological theory.

ACKNOWLEDGMENTS

This research was supported by NIH grants NS23836 and NS22201 to The Johns Hopkins University. We would like to thank Kathleen Straub and Ellen Perecman for helpful comments on earlier drafts of this paper.

REFERENCES

Anderson, S. (1982). Where's morphology? *Linguistic Inquiry, 13,* 571–612.

Anshen, F., & Aronoff, M. (1981). Morphological productivity and phonological transparency. *Canadian Journal of Linguistics, 26,* 63–72.

Aronoff, M. (1976). *Word formation in generative grammar.* Cambridge, MA: MIT Press.

Aronoff, M. (1980). The relevance of productivity in a synchronic description of word formation. In J. Fisiak (Ed.), *Historical morphology* (pp. 71–82). The Hague: Mouton.

Aronoff, M., & Schvaneveldt, R. (1978). Testing morphological productivity. In M. Ebihara & G. Gianutsos (Eds.), *Papers in anthropology and linguistics* (pp. 106–114). New York: New York Academy of Sciences.

Badecker, W., & Caramazza, A. (1985). On considerations of method and theory governing the use of clinical categories in neurolinguistics and cognitive neuropsychology: The case against Agrammatism. *Cognition, 20,* 97–125.

Badecker, W., & Caramazza, A. (1986a). A final brief in the case against Agrammatism: The role of theory in the selection of data. *Cognition, 24,* 277–282.

Badecker, W., & Caramazza, A. (1987). The analysis of morphological errors in a case of acquired dyslexia. *Brain and Language, 32,* 278–305.

Badecker, W., Hillis, E., & Caramazza, A. (1987). Lexical morphology and its role in the writing system: Evidence from a case of acquired dysgraphia. Unpublished manuscript, Johns Hopkins University, Baltimore.

Balota, D., & Chumbley, J. (1984). Are lexical decisions a good measure of lexical access? The role of word frequency in the neglected decision stage. *Journal of Experimental Psychology: Human Perception and Performance, 10,* 340–357.

Beauvois, M. F., & Dérouesné, J. (1979). Phonological alexia: Three dissociations. *Journal of Neurology, Neurosurgery, and Psychiatry, 42,* 1111–1124.

Bradley, D. (1980). Lexical representation of derivational relation. In M. Aronoff & M.-L. Kean (Eds.), *Juncture* (pp. 37–55). Saratoga, CA: Anma Libri.

Buckingham, H. (1981). Where do neologisms come from? In J. W. Brown (Ed.), *Jargonaphasia* (pp. 39–62). New York: Academic Press.

Burani, C., & Caramazza, A. (1987). Representation and processing of derived words. *Reports of the cognitive neuropsychology laboratory, #25.* Johns Hopkins University, Baltimore. (In press, *Language and Cognitive Processes.*)

Burani, C., Salmaso, D., & Caramazza, A. (1984). Morphological structure and lexical access. *Visible Language, 18,* 342–358.

Butterworth, B. (1979). Hesitation and the production of verbal paraphasias and neologisms in jargon aphasia. *Brain and Language, 8,* 133–161.

Butterworth, B. (1983). Lexical representation. In B. Butterworth (Ed.), *Language Production* (Vol. 2, pp. 257–294). New York: Academic Press.

Bybee, J. (1985). *Morphology: A study in the relation between meaning and form.* Amsterdam: Benjamins.

Caplan, D., Kellar, L., & Locke, S. (1972). Inflection of neologisms in aphasia. *Brain, 95,* 169–172.

Caramazza, A. (1984). The logic of neuropsychological research and the problem of patient classification in aphasia. *Brain and Language, 21,* 9–20.

Caramazza, A. (1986). On drawing inferences about the structure of normal cognitive systems from the analysis of patterns of impaired performance: The case for single-patient studies. *Brain and Cognition, 5,* 41–66.

Caramazza, A., Laudanna, A., & Romani, C. (1988). Lexical access and inflectional morphology. *Cognition, 28,* 297–332.

Caramazza, A., & McCloskey, M. (1988). The case for single-patient studies. *Cognitive Neuropsychology, 5,* 517–528.

Caramazza, A., Miceli, G., Silveri, M., & Laudanna, A. (1985). Reading mechanisms and the organization of the lexicon: Evidence from acquired dyslexia. *Cognitive Neuropsychology, 2,* 81–114.

Caramazza, A., Miceli, G., & Villa, G. (1986). The role of the (output) phonological buffer in reading, writing, and repetition. *Cognitive Neuropsychology, 3,* 37–76.

Caramazza, A., Miceli, G., Villa, G., & Romani, C. (1987). The role of the graphemic buffer in spelling: Evidence from a case of acquired dysgraphia. *Cognition, 26,* 59–85.

Coltheart, M. (1978). Lexical access in simple reading tasks. In G. Underwood (Ed.), *Strategies of information-processing* (pp. 151–216). London: Academic Press.

Coltheart, M. (1985). Cognitive neuropsychology and the study of reading. In M. I. Posner

& O. S. M. Marin (Eds.), *Attention and performance, XI* (pp. 3–37). Hillsdale, NJ: Lawrence Erlbaum Associates.

Cutler, A. (1980). Productivity in word formation. Papers from the Sixteenth Regional Meeting, Chicago Linguistic Society, 45–51.

De Bleser, R., & Bayer, J. (1985). Inflectional morphology and aphasia. Unpublished manuscript, Aachen.

Dérouesné, J., & Beauvois, M.-F. (1979). Phonological processing in reading: Data from alexia. *Journal of Neurology, Neurosurgery and Psychiatry, 42,* 1125–1132.

Fowler, C., Napps, S., & Feldman, L. (1985). Relations among regular and irregular morphologically related words in the lexicon as revealed by repetition priming. *Memory and Cognition, 13,* 241–255.

Funnell, E. (1983). Phonological processes in reading: New evidence from acquired dyslexia. *British Journal of Psychology, 74,* 159–180.

Garrett, M. (1980). Levels of processing in sentence production. In B. Butterworth (Ed.), *Language production* (Vol. 1, pp. 177–220). New York: Academic Press.

Garrett, M. (1982). Production of speech: Observations from normal and pathological language use. In A. Ellis (Ed.), *Normality and pathology in cognitive functions* (pp. 19–76). London: Academic Press.

Glushko, R. (1979). The organization and activation of orthographic information in reading aloud. *Journal of Experimental Psychology: Human Perception and Performance, 5,* 674–691.

Goodglass, H., Berko-Gleason, J., Ackerman Bernholtz, N., & Hyde, M. R. (1972). Some linguistic structures in the speech of a Broca's aphasic. *Cortex, 8,* 191–212.

Goodman, R., & Caramazza, A. (1986). Dissociation of spelling errors in written and oral spelling: The role of allographic conversion in writing. *Cognitive Neuropsychology, 3,* 179–206.

Gordon, B. (1983). Lexical access and lexical decision: Mechanisms of frequency sensitivity. *Journal of Verbal Learning and Verbal Behavior, 22,* 24–44.

Gordon, B., Goodman-Schulman, R., & Caramazza, A. (1987). Separating the stages of reading errors. *Reports of the cognitive neuropsychology laboratory, #28.* Johns Hopkins University, Baltimore.

Gurjanov, M., Lukatella, G., Moskovljevic, J., Savic, M., & Turvey, M. (1985). Grammatical priming of inflected nouns by inflected adjectives. *Cognition, 19,* 55–71.

Jarvella, R. & Meijers, G. (1983). Recognizing morphemes in spoken words: Some evidence for a stem-organized mental lexicon. In G. Flores d'Arcais & R. Jarvella (Eds.) *The process of language understanding* (pp. 81–112). London: John Wiley & Sons.

Job, R., & Sartori, G. (1984). Morphological decomposition: Evidence from crossed phonological dyslexia. *The Quarterly Journal of Experimental Psychology, 36A,* 435–458.

Kay, J., & Marcel, A. (1981). One process, not two, in reading aloud: Lexical analogies do the work of nonlexical rules. *Quarterly Journal of Experimental Psychology, 33A,* 397–413.

Kempley, S., & Morton, J. (1982). The effects of priming with irregularly related words in auditory word recognition. *British Journal of Psychology, 73,* 441–454.

Kroll, J., & Merves, J. (1986). Lexical access for concrete and abstract words. *Journal of Experimental Psychology: Learning, Memory and Cognition, 12,* 92–107.

Lapointe, S. (1985). A theory of verb form use in the speech of agrammatic aphasics. *Brain and Language, 24,* 100–155.

Laudanna, A., & Caramazza, A. (1984). Morphological parsing and lexical access. Unpublished manuscript, Johns Hopkins University, Baltimore.

Lieber, R. (1981). *On the organization of the lexicon.* Bloomington, IN: IULC Publications.

Lukatela, G., & Kostic, A., Feldman, L., & Turvey, M. (1983). Grammatical priming of inflected nouns. *Memory and Cognition, 11,* 59–63.

Manelis, L., & Tharp, D. (1977). The processing of affixed words. *Memory & Cognition, 5,* 690–695.

Marcel, T. (1980). Surface dyslexia and beginning reading: A revised hypothesis of the pronunciation of print and its impairments. In M. Coltheart, K. Patterson, & J. Marshall (Eds.), *Deep dyslexia* (pp. 227–258). London: Routledge & Kegan-Paul.

Marshall, J., & Newcombe, F. (1973). Patterns of paralexia: A psycholinguistic approach. *Journal of Psycholinguistic Research, 2,* 175–199.

McClelland, J., & Rumelhart, D. (1981). An interactive activation model of context effects in letter perception: Part 1. An account of basic findings. *Psychological Review, 88,* 375–407.

Miceli, G., & Caramazza, A. (1987). Dissociation in inflectional and derivational morphology. *Reports of the cognitive neuropsychology laboratory, #23.* Johns Hopkins University, Baltimore. (In press, *Brain & Language.*)

Miceli, G., Mazzucchi, A., Menn, L., & Goodglass, H. (1983). Contrasting cases of Italian agrammatic aphasia without comprehension disorder. *Brain and Language, 19,* 65–97.

Moody, S. (1984). *Agrammatic reading in phonological dyslexia.* PhD thesis, University of London.

Parkin, A. (1984). Redefining the regularity effect. *Memory and Cognition, 12,* 287–292.

Patterson, K. (1978). Phonemic Dyslexia: Errors of meaning and the meaning of errors. *Quarterly Journal of Experimental Psychology, 30,* 587–601.

Patterson, K. (1980). Derivational Errors. In M. Coltheart, K. Patterson, & J. Marshall (Eds.), *Deep dyslexia* (pp. 286–306). London: Routledge & Kegan Paul.

Patterson, K. (1982). The relation between reading and phonological coding: Further neuropsychological observations. In A. Ellis (Ed.), *Normality and pathology in cognitive functions* (pp. 77–111). London: Academic Press.

Patterson, K., & Marcel, A. (1977). Aphasia, dyslexia and the phonological coding of written words. *Quarterly Journal of Experimental Psychology, 29,* 307–318.

Rubin, G., Becker, C., & Freeman, R. (1979). Morphological structure and its effect on visual word recognition. *Journal of Verbal Learning and Verbal Behavior, 18,* 757–767.

Scalise, S. (1984). *Generative morphology.* Dordrecht: Foris.

Seidenberg, M., Waters, G., Barnes, M., & Tanenhaus, M. (1984). When does irregular spelling or pronunciation influence word recognition? *Journal of Verbal Learning and Verbal Behavior, 23,* 383–404.

Sejnowski, T., & Rosenberg, C. R. (1985). NETalk: A parallel network that learns to read aloud. *Reports of the cognitive neuropsychology laboratory, #13.* Johns Hopkins University, Baltimore.

Selkirk, E. (1982). *The syntax of words.* Cambridge, MA: MIT Press.

Shallice, T. (1981). Neurological impairment of cognitive processes. *British Medical Bulletin, 37,* 187–192.

Shallice, T., & Warrington, E. (1980). Single and multiple component central dyslexic syndromes. In M. Coltheart, K. Patterson, & J. Marshall (Eds.), *Deep dyslexia.* (pp. 119–145). London: Routledge and Kegan Paul.

Stanners, R., Neiser, U., Hernon, J., & Hall, R. (1979). Memory representation for morphologically related words. *Journal of Verbal Learning and Verbal Behavior, 18,* 399–412.

Taft, M. (1979). Recognition of affixed words and the word frequency effect. *Memory and Cognition, 7,* 263–272.

Taft, M. (1981). Prefix stripping revisited. *Journal of Verbal Learning and Verbal Behavior, 20,* 289–297.

Taft, M., & Forster, K. (1975). Lexical storage and retrieval of prefixed words. *Journal of Verbal Learning and Verbal Behavior, 14,* 638–647.

Wing, A., & Baddeley, A. (1980). Spelling errors in handwriting: A corpus and distributional analysis. In U. Frith (Ed.), *Cognitive processes in spelling* (pp. 251–285). London: Academic Press.

11

Aphasia Therapy:
A Multidimensional Process

Anneliese Kotten

INTRODUCTION

Let us begin with a simple question: Does the outcome of aphasia therapy justify the cost? Such a question is rather controversial, and, as can easily be demonstrated, research on the efficacy of aphasia therapy has led to contradictory answers. As the number of aphasics increases the question of efficacy of speech therapy assumes greater interest for the public at large, and therapy studies have an audience beyond a small group of specialists. When the results are negative, the preexisting bias against therapy is reinforced, and, as a consequence, the opportunities for an individual aphasic to receive therapy (or the necessary amount of therapy) may diminish.

To illustrate these general remarks, consider the impact of a single recent study. On the basis of a randomized controlled trial, Lincoln et al. (1984) investigated the effects of "conventional" aphasia therapy under normal clinical conditions. A careful analysis of this study (e.g., Howard, 1986) yielded serious shortcomings concerning the selection and matching of patients, the statistical tests applied, the unspecified training methods, and so forth. Consequently, this study cannot be the basis for objective statements about the efficacy of therapy. Nevertheless, this study generated a series of articles in medical journals as well as local newspapers in Switzerland. These articles had a direct influence on the Swiss parliament's ongoing debate about the efficacy of aphasia therapy and on the debate over the need for an additional speech therapist at the rehabilitation department of a hospital in Luzern.

This incident brings to bear the fact that researchers have an important responsibility and, at the same time, it illustrates the problems that plague studies on aphasia therapy in general. Students of aphasia and therapists as well, may feel frustrated by the contradictory results of therapy research not only in the older investigations but also in more recent ones (e.g., Aten, Caligiuri, & Holland, 1982; Basso, Capitani, & Vignolo, 1979; David, Enderby, & Bainton, 1982; Lincoln, 1985; Lincoln et al., 1984; Marshall, Tompkins, & Phillips, 1982; Pickersgill & Lincoln, 1983; Shewan & Kertesz, 1984). Closer inspection of these studies reveals the dissimilarity of their research methods: The studies differ greatly with respect to selection and evaluation of patients, time of initiation, duration and frequency of therapy, and therapeutic methods. Moreover, most studies do not specify the training methods. Thus, the need for comparable research design and methodology is obvious. In order to achieve interpretable results of therapy studies, several authors have recently suggested rather sophisticated designs for single-case as well as group studies (e.g., Coltheart, 1983; Byng & Coltheart, 1986; Fitzgibbon, 1986; Hesketh, 1986; Howard, 1986; Pring, 1986). The last part of this chapter addresses the practical application of some of these designs.

APPROACHES TO APHASIA THERAPY

To fully understand the complexity involved in conducting and comparing therapy studies, one has to take into account the different approaches to aphasia therapy. Because I address only a few major points, I refer the reader to a number of other sources for fuller discussion of these issues (e.g., Chapey, 1981; Code & Müller, 1983; Davis & Wilcox, 1985; Kotten, 1981, in press; L. L. La Pointe, 1977, 1978, 1984; Lesser, 1985; Weniger, Huber, Stachowiak, & Poeck, 1980).

Therapeutic models/methods are usually based on one of three major theories of recovery: reactivation of language, reorganization of brain functions, and compensatory strategies.

Reactivation of Language

According to this theory, language is not lost, but access to language is reduced. Stimulation strategies are therefore used to lower the threshhold for language. The most elaborate model of stimulation therapy was developed by Schuell (1974). Auditory stimuli can be combined with visual (pictures/written words) stimuli and physical properties of stimuli, for example, loudness and duration can be varied. Stimulation therapy is based on the assumption that the effectiveness of a stimulus differs among individual patients. If a patient's response to a given stimulus is wrong, the patient will not be corrected; the therapist will either reissue or change the stimulus. Stimulation techniques are widely used as facilitation procedures, regardless of the theoretical approach. Another technique of equal importance is "deblocking" (Weigl, 1979), a cross-modal strategy that uses processing in a relatively intact modality to deblock the same language unit in a disturbed modality. According to Weigl the deblocking procedure can be used only if there is a modality in which functioning is up to 70% normal.

A quite different approach to stimulation therapy uses normal communication strategies to stimulate all means of conveying and understanding new messages. Within this therapeutic model, the therapist and the patient are free to choose their modality of communication but the therapist must apply certain rules of communication and carefully model a patient's behavior to achieve the best strategies for conveying a message (see Davis & Wilcox, 1985).

The combination of different strategies and the highly individual nature of each of these models make it very difficult to test and compare their effectiveness in groups of patients.

Reorganization of Brain Functions

Another theory postulates that recovery is due to a certain "plasticity" of the brain. Functions can be retrained directly or via functional subsystems.

In this category are models that rely explicitly on linguistic theory (Engl, Kotten, Ohlendorf & Poser, 1982; Hatfield, 1979; Hatfield & Shewell, 1983; Kotten, 1985; Weniger et al., 1980) or combine a linguistic and a nonlinguistic, cognitive approach (Salonen, 1980). The advantage of a linguistic approach is that tasks can be defined according to linguistic levels, and that with respect to modern psycholinguistic theories, the processing stages involved in a given task can be defined and controlled. This approach is, therefore, better suited for research. We should, however, keep in mind that linguistics or psycholinguistics can explain only a small portion of the symptoms and symptom complexes found in aphasia.

The theory that recovery is based on reorganization of brain functions assumes that when a function cannot be mediated by the part of the brain that normally mediates it, it may be mediated by a part of the brain that normally may not be critically involved in that function. Examples of techniques based on this theory are "Melodic Intonation Therapy" (Sparks, 1981) assumed to take advantage of the right hemisphere capacity to process intonation, and "Visual Action Therapy" (VAT, Helm-Estabrooks, Fitzpatrick, & Barresi, 1982), which attempts to strengthen the ability to use referential gesture through completely nonverbal training. VAT, thus, uses a nonverbal subsystem to mediate a symbolic function.

Alternative Strategies
to Circumvent the Loss of Language

Experience with global aphasics led to the view that it is not possible to retrain or stimulate language in these patients. For such cases, alternative strategies using nonspeech symbolic communication are suggested and practiced (Collins, 1983; Gardner, Zurif, Berry, & Baker, 1976; Glass, Gazzaniga, & Premack, 1973; Helm-Estabrooks, Fitzpatrick, & Barresi, 1982; Johannsen-Horbach, Cegla, Mager, Schempp, & Wallesch, 1985; Moody, 1982; Rowley, 1983).

BASIC PROBLEMS
IN RESEARCH ON THERAPY

A program of therapy—no matter what model is applied—begins and ends with testing. The following is a discussion of issues concerning testing in aphasia therapy: test construction, comparability of tests, explanatory force of test results and, finally test sensitivity to changes in performances.

Testing

From a therapist's point of view, tests of language and/or communicative ability in an aphasic individual should be sensitive, comprehensive, and reliable. Tests should allow for an objective scoring of the degree of expressive/receptive disturbance in all modalities.

The tests also should permit the identification of patients with similar problems. This is especially important if therapeutic procedures are tested with matched groups of patients. Moreover, test batteries should contain functionally independent subtests that are based on a fundamental language process. In addition, subtests should gradually increase in difficulty and be sensitive enough to demonstrate even small changes in language performances. Most important, tests should allow for predicting language/communicative performances in "natural situations." (For a detailed description of requirements for test construction see Kertesz, this volume.) In reality therapists are confronted with a rather frustrating situation. Each of the test batteries used today covers different and limited areas of language and/or communicative abilities; and, given the different approaches to aphasia in general, different tests stress different aspects of the entire complex of disturbances. Even if each of the batteries did meet all methodological requirements of test construction, the results of different tests can hardly be compared.

A comparison between the "Aachen Aphasia Test" (AAT) (Huber, Po-eck, & Willmes, 1984) and the "Porch Index of Communicative Ability" (PICA) (Porch, 1967/1971) may serve to illustrate these serious differences. (Compare also the Western Aphasia Battery (WAB), Kertesz this volume.) The AAT is now widely used by German researchers and therapists, whereas the PICA is very often used in therapy studies in Great Britain.

The AAT focuses predominantly on linguistic aspects of aphasia, including all levels and all modalities of language. But even though each of the subtests is related to independent language functions, the number of items for each subtest is too small to detect slight performance changes. In addition, the scoring system is not sensitive enough to demonstrate slight improvement on tasks and does not take into account alternative strategies for solving tasks.

In contrast, the PICA does allow for documentation and scoring of small incremental changes in task performance. But the subtests do not meet linguistic requirements for a full evaluation of the disturbances in terms of different linguistic levels. In addition to the aforementioned problems, each of the tests used today, raises questions related to test construction. Assuming that subtests are indeed measuring independent language functions, are those subtests of equal sensitivity? Only if subtests are equally sensitive are they comparable in terms of the validity with which they measure rate of progress.

The Role of Linguistics in Testing

A great deal of current research as well as clinical practice in aphasia is based on linguistic notions. We might, therefore, ask: what is the explanatory value of linguistics in aphasia? It is easy to demonstrate that linguistic explanations are relevant only to a few aphasic symptoms. According to Poeck (1983) there are eleven symptoms, the specific combinations of which constitute the classical syndromes. These symptoms refer exclusively to language production, and only four of them are linguistic in nature: agrammatism, paragrammatism, phonemic paraphasia, and semantic or verbal paraphasia. The interpretation of these symptoms is currently a rather controversial issue.

According to Poeck, language comprehension is independent of the linguistic components that are fundamental to a definition of a syndrome, because language comprehension involves structural linguistic knowledge, pragmatic knowledge, and cognitive factors as well. (Compare, e.g., Brookshire & Nicholas, 1984; Clark & Lucy, 1975; Haviland & Clark, 1974; Pierce & Beekman, 1985; Rees & Shulman, 1978; Wilcox, Davis, & Leonard, 1978.) Nevertheless, assessment of comprehension is an essential part of the Aachen Aphasia Test.

Additional problems concerning test construction, comparability of tasks, and interpretation of the patient's performances on each task are discussed thoroughly by Parisi (1985). Parisi argued that linguistic concepts and models of aphasia cannot explain the association and dissociation of symptoms in different patients. According to Parisi we should distinguish between two types of associations/dissociations that occur within a single task or modality (intratask) and those that occur among tasks or modalities (intertasks). Although linguistic notions/models may explain intratask associations/dissociations (e.g., difference between processing of content words and function words in spontaneous speech) it seems to be beyond the explanatory power of linguistics to interpret or to predict patterns of intertask associations or dissociations. Thus, Parisi argued, it is beyond the scope of linguistics to explain differences in judgments of acceptability of aural versus written sentences or in comprehension versus production of sentences. These methodological problems are especially relevant in the interpretation of "agrammatism" (e.g., Kean, 1985; Parisi, 1985, 1987), but should also be kept in mind when designing therapy programs on the basis of purely linguistic considerations.

Formal Testing and Communication in Everyday Situations

In their study of recovery from aphasia, Prins, Snow, & Wagenaar (1978) investigated the parameters of speech production. The same parameters were also analyzed in the speech of a non-brain-damaged control group. Their results show that control subjects frequently make mistakes that are typical in an aphasic population (including semantic paraphasias), thus, supporting the view that the everyday speech of normals does not typically conform strictly to formal linguistic constraints. Yet evaluation of spontaneous speech is only one part of the testing procedure. Inspection of typical tasks in a test battery reveals that the tasks are rather artificial as compared to natural communication. It is questionable, for example, how confrontation naming, sentence production stimulated by pictures, and object identification are related to spontaneous linguistic communication in natural settings. Opinions about this problem differ. Helm-Estabrooks and Ramsberger (1986) reported a study that found no qualitative differences between picture description on the Boston Diagnostic Aphasia Examination and spontaneous conversation in terms of range and form of grammatical structures. On the other hand, Ahlsen (1986) found no correlation between a picture-naming test and wordfinding problems in conversational speech where various compensation techniques enter into play.

The questionable relation between formal testing and spontaneous multidimensional communication in everyday settings has led to the development of alternative approaches (e.g., Davis & Wilcox, 1985; Foldi, Cicone, & Gardner, 1983) to the evaluation of an aphasic's communication (verbal/ nonverbal) skills.

Formal Testing in Mild and Severe Cases

The shortcomings of most test batteries (especially those based on a one-dimensional, e.g., purely linguistic, approach) are apparent in very severe as well as mild cases. Therapists are also well aware of the problem of evaluating highly educated patients, who are classified as nonaphasic but nevertheless feel (and are indeed) handicapped in their verbal skills. (Compare also Shewan & Kertesz, 1984.) This problem stems not only from the limitations of aphasia tests but also from a poor definition of the aims of therapy in relation to a patient's language performance and individual needs.

The limitations of formal testing are even more obvious in severe cases. Because global aphasics constitute a rather large percentage of the aphasic population, they demand special attention. As is often described, global aphasics do not improve much on formal testing. Yet everyday experience as well as careful long-term observations (e.g., over 1 year in the study of Sarno and Levita, 1981) reveal behavior changes that can be interpreted as better adaptation to verbal as well as nonverbal means of communication. Alternative methods for training nonverbal skills should be accompanied by alternative means of testing both expressive and receptive performances. Edelman (1984) suggested that language comprehension should be assessed in different contexts using different types of cueing. Improvement of speech comprehension in global aphasics might thus be measured in terms of reduced cues. The use of different cues and gradual reduction of cues might also be informative in evaluating speech production. Nevertheless, the problem remains, that globals do not recover the capacity for spontaneous speech production which varies according to the differing communication situations. To summarize: global aphasics form a heterogeneous group with unique problems which require special strategies and procedures in training and testing. They should therefore be excluded from group studies of training methods.

Spontaneous Recovery and Prognosis

To fully evaluate the success of training procedures we should be able to distinguish between spontaneous and therapy-related improvement.

There are several recent studies that investigate the time course and pattern of recovery in different aphasic groups (e.g., Basso et al., 1979; Demeurisse, Demol, Derouck, de Beuckelaer, 1980; Hanson & Cicciarelli, 1978; Keenan & Brassel, 1974; Kertesz, 1979, 1984; Kertesz & McCabe, 1977; Prins et al., 1978; Willmes & Poeck, 1984; Kenin & Swisher, 1972; Lomas & Kertesz, 1978). A comparison of these studies is difficult because they differ with respect to procedures for evaluation as well as variables thought to influence the process of recovery. I will therefore deal primarily with the most recent of these studies which was based on the Aachen Aphasia Test.

Willmes and Poeck (1984) studied a group of 96 vascular cases which included aphasics of all types and 12 cases with nonclassifiable aphasias. The first assessment was about 4–6 weeks postonset, the second and third followed after 4 and 7 months, respectively. To insure that the recovery pattern was not influenced by speech therapy, the study was conducted at hospitals that could not offer any language training, thus none of the patients received systematic therapy.

The following results are of particular interest. Performance changes, including a change in the aphasia classification, were greatest between the 1st and the 4th month postonset. This is consistent with other studies. Patients who demonstrated no change were typically the most severely impaired of each subgroup. Within each group an unpredicted variability of performances was found, and the rate of improvement differed for each subtest. The commonly cited finding that auditory comprehension improves most was not confirmed by the data, perhaps because, as the authors argue, most tests contained comprehension tasks that were too simple. With respect to the prognosis in individual cases, Willmes and Poeck concluded from their data that patients who were above the median of their subgroup in initial testing also showed the greatest improvement in subsequent testing. Thus, we can assume that it is not severity of aphasia as such which influences recovery but rather severity within a single syndrome. Yet, the results also show that poor performance does not automatically indicate a bad prognosis for an individual aphasic.

The results of this and other investigations indicate once more, that an individual prognosis cannot be given and, that as a consequence of the great variability in courses of spontaneous recovery, effects of therapy cannot be separated from spontaneous improvement within the first 4 months post onset of aphasia. Nevertheless, it seems reasonable to begin therapy as early as possible.

Concerning the evaluation of specific therapeutic procedures, it therefore seems appropriate to examine therapy-related changes after the period of spontaneous recovery. Yet, in doing so, we neglect another problem. Most studies demonstrate spontaneous improvement in the first few months and up to 1 year. Yet there is evidence that in individual cases the time course is prolonged (Kertesz, 1979) beyond 1 year. Indeed Sarno and Levita (1981) found that rate of improvement accelerated in their group of globals from the 6th–12th month post stroke. Thus, even in treatment studies with patients whose aphasia is of remote onset, spontaneous recovery cannot be easily distinguished from therapy-related improvement.

The Matching Problem

Most studies of aphasia therapy attempt to match patients in terms of their behavior. Yet therapists' verbal and nonverbal behavior is equally important. This holds true especially for the varying stimulation and facilitation techniques in the so-called traditional therapy approaches.

Typically, the most structured and hierarchically organized therapy models (e.g., Melodic Intonation Therapy, Sparks, 1981, or Visual Action Therapy, Helm-Estabrooks et al., 1982) do more than define the patients who will succeed with this sort of training. In those models special attention is given to the way in which therapists correct or reinforce a patient's response. Narrowly defined verbal/nonverbal reinforcement techniques are a part of all operant-conditioning models of aphasia therapy. On the other hand, the classical stimulation approach recommends against correcting a wrong answer and instead encourages restimulation. As a consequence, the therapist might change his verbal/nonverbal behavior without even being aware of it. Thus, in studies of the effects of traditional stimulation therapy, we must take into account the problem of matching therapists as well as matching patients.

Interaction in a Changing Dyad

The changing interaction between patient and therapist within the "same" task was carefully analyzed by Crystal (1984). His example illustrates how in a series of therapy sessions an individual therapist varied her stimuli in presenting the "identical task" (e.g., pointing to pictures) to the same patient. Crystal demonstrated that there is a strong interrelation between the patient's performance difficulties and the spontaneous variations in stimulus presentation; that is, the patient's performances determine the therapist's verbal and nonverbal behavior.

As Crystal suggested, a full description of all relevant input variables should include linguistic structure and language use. The latter refers not only to pragmatics in general but also to a rather large set of factors relating to the extralinguistic setting of the communication situation, including its participants. Consequently, we are left with the additional problem of comparing therapeutic procedures, which allow for creative and individualized strategies (e.g., the stimulation approach and the communication-related model of PACE (Promoting Aphasic's Communicative Effectiveness, Davis & Wilcox, 1981, 1985). Yet, even though the "human factor" creates additional problems in therapy research, it is essential to the therapy process.

APPROACHES TO THE STUDY OF THE EFFECTS OF THERAPY

Single Case Studies

The basic advantage of the single-case method of investigation seems to be that in comparing an individual to himself one avoids the matching problem inherent in group studies. The single-case method allows for a wide range of different research designs (e.g., Byng & Coltheart, 1986; Coltheart, 1983; Hesketh, 1986; Howard, 1986; Pring, 1986).

Even when we can be confident that a methodologically exact study has demonstrated the efficacy of a particular training method in an individual patient, the question will remain, whether this method will meet with equal success in training another patient with similar problems. Yet precise duplication of procedures is critical in proving the success or failure of a particular method of treatment for an aphasic symptom. Consequently, we are again faced with the crucial problem of matching patients and therapists.

Patient Description, Isolation of Functions, and Measurement

The description of a patient's language performance should be sufficiently detailed to allow for hypotheses concerning those processes that underly the deviant language behavior in this individual aphasic. If the aim of therapy is to prove that an isolated function (or underlying process) can be influenced by certain therapeutic procedures, the therapist must be sure that that function is not related to untrained ones serving as controls. In neglecting this basic problem, results of therapy become uninterpretable, because apparently unrelated functions may interact with one another in an uncontrolled way. Moreover, the interaction of functions may vary according to the different symptoms (or symptom combinations) in individual cases. For example, it seems reasonable to assume a relation between naming problems and reading performance in some deep dyslexics but not in phonological dyslexic patients. If we can assume that a thorough description of the patient's language allows for reasonable isolation of functions, then the next step must be to construct an evaluation metric that is sensitive enough to measure degree of impairment and degree of progress after training. As was argued before, none of the available test batteries meet this requirement, and one is forced to develop case-by-case "ad hoc" tests (Byng & Coltheart, 1986; Coltheart, 1983), which do not allow for standardization. According to Coltheart (1983), standardization is not relevant in single-case studies that are based on pre- and posttraining measurements.

Selection of Functions

As suggested by Coltheart (1983), the functions to be trained should be defined neither too broadly (e.g., speech production) nor too narrowly (e.g., producing stop consonants). Coltheart suggested training "functions" at different levels in the language system and also possible communication strategies (e.g., nonverbal behavior assisting conversational speech). We are, therefore, faced initially with deciding upon a general approach, for example, whether to train speech behavior, linguistic functions, or their underlying processes.

In deciding to train a certain linguistically definable function, we must deal with problems like constructing hypotheses about the normal processes that underly this function and then testing these hypotheses on the individual patient (compare Seron, 1984). A task like this is to be solved only against the background of a more or less elaborate model of language processing. Only if we can locate a certain (normal or deviant) language performance at a distinct point in the model, can we motivate specified training procedures and training tasks.

Different Approaches to Selection of Functions

To my knowledge, there are two approaches to aphasiology and therapy based on models of language processing detailed enough to allow for "locating" a deviant language process. The two approaches are based on divergent theoretical positions, yet both allow for developing training procedures thought to influence the changed function or process. The older functional model is based on Luria's interpretation of aphasia (for an overview, see Luria, 1977).

Therapy, according to this approach, is based on an elaborate model of functional subsystems that are related to each other in a rather complex way. The therapeutic aim of this approach can be described as follows: reorganization of functions in terms of functional subsystems, which are not normally constituent parts of the impaired system. (This approach is strongly related to the procedures of deblocking, described in an earlier section of this chapter.)

An instructive example of a single case study using this approach was given by Ulatowska and Richardson (1974). However, because they used a combination of methods and began training during the presumed period of spontaneous recovery, it is difficult to determine which of them is most effective. This problem of interpretation is critical in all forms of therapy (including Schuell's (1974) traditional stimulation approach (Duffy, 1981), in view of the possible interrelation of functional subsystems.

The second approach is based on processing models of modern psycholinguistics. Process models are concerned primarily with two issues: (a) interpretation of the different symptoms of reading and writing disturbances, a topic which I disregard here, and, (b) interpretation of the processes that lead to different symptoms (symptom-combinations) in agrammatic speech production and sentence comprehension. As is well known, the underlying processes have been interpreted quite differently by various authors (e.g., compare Kean, 1985; Berndt, 1987; Parisi, 1985, 1987; Schwartz, 1987). Very few studies of therapy are based on a processing model. The therapeutic aim of this approach is direct training of the impaired process, even if this process is only a small part of the combined processes that may constitute a "symptom."

The "Nature" of Process-Related Training Methods

Process-related methods are rather "artificial." Yet, most methods applied in training surface structure of sentences are also artificial. This holds true not only for describing pictures or building sentences from given words or answering questions in formalized dialogues (e.g., Engl et al., 1982) but also for completing short texts that refer to commonplace situations, using everyday phrases according to a hierarchy of difficulties in sentence construction (Helm-Estabrooks & Ramsberger, 1986). Followers of a pragmatic approach (e.g., Davis & Wilcox, 1981, 1985) who aim to reflect everyday communication strategies in therapy will probably reject these methods.

Moreover, process related methods seek to locate the point where sentence comprehension breaks down by testing the interpretation of syntactic (or thematic) roles independent of pragmatic knowledge. Yet, even if further research demonstrates the advantage of process-related procedures, especially in chronic patients who have failed with conventional methods, one must keep in mind that tasks and training procedures have to be constructed according to the needs of the individual patient. Process-related procedures do not allow for a therapeutic model with cookbook instructions. Therefore, applying this approach in an everyday clinical setting may not be possible for the typical aphasia therapist.

The Single Case Approach in Training Agrammatic Patients

Three recently published studies illustrate individual therapy procedures that directly try to influence processes underlying syntactic deficits in chronic agrammatic patients (Byng & Coltheart, 1986; Jones, 1986; Kotten, 1985b). The studies differ with respect to their "ad hoc" tests and their treatment procedures, yet they have a basic idea in common. If an underlying deficit in analyzing syntactic relations leads to comparable mistakes in sentence production and comprehension, then basic components of sentence analysis should be built up first. To avoid additional problems in speech production, the training of sentence analysis is best performed by receptive tasks. In defining the point at which sentence analysis breaks down, three components should be investigated (Byng & Coltheart, 1986).

1. the parsing component that carries out the syntactic analysis, resulting in a hierarchical representation of the syntactic structure;
2. the component that assigns the thematic roles of the verb used in the sentence;
3. the component that maps syntactic functions (subject–object) onto thematic roles.

To demonstrate the therapeutic procedure in detail, I rely predominantly on the study of Byng and Coltheart.

The (chronic) agrammatic patient, investigated by Byng and Coltheart, had serious difficulty understanding reversible, active, declarative sentences and reversible locative sentences. Testing revealed that the patient could detect syntactic "illegalities" (i.e., the parsing component worked) yet was unable to map thematic roles of a given verb onto a visual representation. Similar problems in mapping thematic roles of verbs and syntactic functions were found in his spontaneous speech. (Only a few instances of combined arguments and functions were found.) For treatment, reversible locative sentences were selected. The procedure was designed to teach the thematic role of each of the noun phrases in a particular position in the sentence.

Training Steps

The tasks were constructed to allow the patient to control his or her own performance. For each of 20 reversible locative (written) sentences, the patient had to choose between a correct picture and one with the reverse relationship. The training included four locative prepositions. Visual clues were prepared to aid performance.

Clues

- A "meaning" card, diagrammatically depicting the relationship between the two noun phrases (different colors for the first and the second noun phrases)
- A structural clue like "1" (noun phrase) is *in* "2" (noun phrase), whereby "1" and "2" were written in the same colors as in the diagram.
- "Practice cards" containing the sentences to be trained, but written in colors corresponding to the meaning card
- The correct pictures also correspond to the colored cueing of the noun phrases. The incorrect pictures showed the reverse colors.

This color matching thus serves as a means of monitoring ones own performance, allowing the patient to detect his or her mistakes in matching without assistance.

The final step of the procedure was training patients to match sentences and pictures without the help of colors. It was expected that if the patient improved on the original tasks because he or she had learned to map thematic roles onto syntactic structures, the effect should generalize. This hypothesis was tested by auditory comprehension tasks using nonlocative passive sentences. In processing these sentences 100% improvement was found. To summarize, post-training tests demonstrated that the patient now performed perfectly on those comprehension tasks involving mapping of thematic roles onto syntactic structures.

To guarantee that the improvement was a result of the training procedure, Byng and Coltheart applied a crossover design which showed that existing deficits (e.g., understanding of abstract words) were unimproved in the first phase. After completing the first phase, the next deficit to be trained (reduced understanding of abstract words) was selected.

The outcome of this second phase reveals that processing of previously trained sentence comprehension remained perfect and that there was improvement in the deficit currently being trained. The study not only demonstrates how careful design of a training program allows for objective measurement of the effects of therapy, it also illustrates how research findings can be transformed into practicable procedures in aphasia therapy.

Nevertheless, there remains the problem that training methods (and tasks) cannot be generally applied to an entire population of agrammatic patients, because agrammatic patients may differ considerably in their symptom combinations (cf., S. G. LaPointe, 1985; Miceli, Silveri, Villa, & Caramazza, 1984).

Group Studies

In discussing the methodological problems of group studies, several authors suggested using a rather limited approach called "item-specific improvement," where one examines the effects of one or several narrowly defined training procedures on the processing of a specific set of items (Howard, 1986; Howard et al., 1985b; Patterson, Purell, & Morton, 1983). As is argued by Howard et al. (1985b), multimodal treatment approaches that stimulate language through different channels simultaneously (e.g., spoken + written word + picture, to elicit naming) seem to be appropriate in general treatment plans. But they are inappropriate for testing the efficacy of different training procedures. The same argument holds true for the deblocking method, which uses stimulation through the best channel to yield better processing in a more disturbed channel (e.g., deblocking comprehension of a spoken item by first presenting this item in a set of written words). Thus, in discussing the well-known deblocking experiments of Wiegel-Crump and Koenigsknecht (1973) demonstrating improved naming in both trained and untrained items, Howard et al. (1985b) pointed out that given the research design used in those experiments, it is not clear which of the manifold techniques actually caused the improvement in naming. We are therefore left wondering whether results will necessarily be limited if each of the treatment techniques is applied in isolation, though the combination of all techniques is highly effective. But how do we test this?

Item-Specific Group Studies: Naming Experiments

Several studies (Howard et al., 1985a, 1985b; Patterson et al., (1983) have investigated the effects of different facilitation techniques on word retrieval. Howard (1986) avoided the matching problem in selecting patients, by using a design in which the target items for each patient are randomly allocated to different training procedures. The selection of items to be trained differs from patient to patient according to their individual difficulties in naming on one or more pretests. (The consistency of naming performance for individual aphasics in repeated tests was demonstrated in a study by Howard et al. (1984). Patterson et al. (1983) used the same design to test general effects and the stability of facilitation techniques. In this study, however, the target items for each facilitation method were equated for frequency. The experiment investigated widely used facilitation techniques: repetition and phonemic cueing. Different methods of repetition were compared, including immediate and delayed naming after one or more repetitions. The results clearly demonstrate immediate facilitation but no long-term effects, and the results of delayed naming were not much better than in the control condition. With respect to phonemic cueing (initial sound/ or up to 3 sounds), strong facilitation effects for word retrieval were also demonstrated though these effects were short term and there was no evidence for longer-term efficacy.

In comparing their findings with the crossmodal methods of deblocking, which yielded a generalized improvement of naming, Patterson et al. (1983) pointed out that though crossmodal deblocking mainly aims at the facilitation of access to semantics, repetition or phonemic cueing only facilitates access to the phonetic structure of an object's name.

To demonstrate the effects of semantic facilitation in comparison with phonological techniques further experiments were carried out by Howard et al. (1985a). The experimental design was similar to the aforementioned study. In testing semantic facilitation the authors used three different techniques typical in conventional therapy for word-finding impairments: (a) matching a spoken word to (one of four) picture(s) (b) matching a written word to (one of four) picture(s) (c) yes/no judgments concerning category/property of objects. In testing phonological facilitation, phonemic cueing, repetition, and judging rhymes were used. Each of these techniques was applied to a separate set of items, and each set was matched with a control set.

Howard et al. (1985a,b) demonstrated the expected superiority of semantic strategies over phonological ones. The phonological techniques yielded effects that lasted only a few minutes, whereas the effects of the semantic methods were still evident after 24 hours. As suggested by the authors, this difference may reflect the properties of the two levels of lexical representation.

Because of the rather small number of therapy sessions, overall improvement was rather limited, and evidence of improvement disappeared after 6 weeks. One might therefore argue that a minimum amount of therapy is necessary to gain stable improvement (compare Howard et al., 1985b) especially in training chronic aphasics. In addition to the differing stability of semantic and phonological facilitation effects, a slight improvement for untrained items, too, could be demonstrated.

Theoretical Implications of Naming Experiments

We have seen that improvement in naming is not item specific. This result, together with Wiegel-Crump and Koenigsknecht's demonstration of a generalization effect, raises certain questions as to the nature of naming disturbances. Does a naming impairment result when the transmission of information from the semantic system to the output system is impeded or have the thresholds for output devices been raised (Patterson et al. 1983)? Both assumptions allow for nonspecific training effects resulting from a general improvement in the retrieval process(es). But further research is needed to elucidate the mechanism underlying that improvement.

Learning Locative Prepositions: Two Methods Compared

A pilot study was carried out by Kotten, Stachowiak, & Willeke (1985) to compare the effects of two methods for training in the use of locative prepositions. Both methods involved inserting the correct preposition (out of a set of four) into a given sentence frame, but they differed greatly in the degree to which the relation indicated by a preposition could be visualized.

The first method was nonvisual and completely avoided the use of gesture. A short text was read to the patient, who was then asked to answer a set of questions in which the preposition had to be filled in. For each patient, the story was read by the same therapist, who carefully avoided representational gestures. The second method was highly visual, using a special computer program, which presented pictures (even moving pictures) and written and spoken language at the same time.

Both methods involved sentence completion with a preposition in a multiple choice paradigm, to complete the final sentence, and trials were repeated until the patient responded correctly. Participants in the study were chronic aphasics, who could be unambiguously labelled as either a Broca or Wernicke aphasic on the basis of the Aachen Aphasia Test.

Selection of items and training conditions. The same locative prepositions can be used dynamically and statically, and the distinction is marked only by morphology. Both applications of prepositions were trained with both methods. Patients were randomly assigned to the two training conditions. If static usage was trained by the nonvisual text then the dynamic use was trained with the visualized computer program and vice versa.

Before training, subjects were given a pretest in which they had to fill in the correct preposition in sentences corresponding to pictures. A multiple-choice method for selecting the correct preposition was used. To avoid the issue of reading, the sentences as well as the prepositions were read to all patients. The sentences included prepositions to be trained and those that were not trained. After training, a posttest (same sentences as in the pretest) was administered. The criterion level for success was a reduction by one half in the error rate demonstrated on the pretest (i.e., the number of failures varied from patient to patient).

As the results illustrate, the respective procedures had different effects for Broca and Wernicke aphasics. Brocas succeeded with both methods, and showed a slight tendency to generalize on untrained items. In contrast, the Wernicke patients were found to be a rather heterogeneous group. Consequently, each individual Wernicke patient must be studied very carefully before applying an individual case-related training program. In comparing both methods, the computer-based visualized training is preferable for Broca's aphasics because it does not involve time constants and gives the patient more control. It thereby allows him or her to become an independent and self-sufficient person.

It is also obvious that only a small group of Broca's (predominantly those without a receptive agrammatism) will succeed in using training methods that deal exclusively with surface structure of sentences. Therefore we must develop alternative procedures for these patients, who exhibit problems in processing deep structure relations in sentence production as well as sentence comprehension.

SUMMARY

It should be apparent from this discussion of research problems and from the promising examples of research on the efficacy of aphasia therapy that our initial question about the efficacy of aphasia therapy cannot be answered simply by "yes" or "no." Indeed, if we are to answer the question, we must rephrase it: "What sort of therapeutic model/program/procedure will yield the best results for a given patient's individual problems?" Future research will likely show both that rather different methods may yield similar results and that methods used successfully with some patients will fail with others.

ACKNOWLEDGMENTS

Many thanks to Ellen Perecman for her friendship and her patience in editing the manuscript.

REFERENCES

Ahlsen, E. (1986). Possibilities of spontaneous compensation for aphasic symptoms. In E. Hjelmquist, L. G. Nilson (Eds.), *Communication and handicap: aspects of psychological compensation and technical aids* (pp. 215–233). North-Holland: Elsevier Science Publishers B.V.

Aten, J. L., Caligiuri, M. P., & Holland, A. E. (1982). The efficacy of functional communication therapy for chronic aphasic patients. *Journal of Speech and Hearing Disorders, 47,* 93–96.

Basso, A., Capitani, E., & Vignolo, L. A. (1979). Influence of rehabilitation on language skills in aphasic patients: A controlled study. Archives of Neurology, 36, 190–196.

Berndt, R. S. (1987). Symptom co-occurrence and dissociation in the interpretation of agrammatism. In M. Coltheart, G. Sartori, R. Job (Eds.), *The cognitive neuropsychology of language* (pp. 221–233). Hillsdale, NJ: Lawrence Erlbaum Associates Publishers.

Brookshire, R. H., & Nicholas, L. E. (1984). Comprehension of directly and indirectly stated main ideas and details in discourse by brain-damaged and non-brain-damaged listeners. *Brain and Language, 21,* 21–36.

Byng, S., & Coltheart, M. (1986). Aphasia therapy research: Methodological requirements and illustrative results. In E. Hjelmquist, L. G. Nilson (Eds.), *Communication and handicap: Aspects of psychological compensation and technical aids* (pp. 191–215). North-Holland, Elsevier Science Publishers B.V.

Chapey, R. (Ed.) (1981). *Language intervention strategies in adult aphasia.* Baltimore: Williams & Wilkins.

Clark, H. H., & Lucy, P. (1975). Understanding what is meant from what is said: A study in conversationally conveyed requests. *Journal of Verbal Learning and Verbal Behavior, 14,* 56–76.

Code, C., & Müller, D. J. (Ed.) (1983). *Aphasia therapy. Studies in language disability and remediation* (Vol. 6). London: E. Arnold.

Collins, M. (1983). Treatment of global aphasia. In W. H. Perkins (Ed.), *Language handicaps in adults* (pp. 25–35). New York: Thieme & Stratton.

Coltheart, M. (1983). Aphasia therapy research: A single case study approach. In C. Code & D. J. Müller (Eds.), *Aphasia therapy. Studies in language disability and remediation* (Vol. 6, pp. 193–203). London: E. Arnold.

Crystal, D. (1984). Language input variables in aphasia. In P. C. Rose (Ed.), *Progress in aphasiology* (pp. 145–158). *Advances in neurology, 42,* New York: Raven Press.

David, R., Enderby, P., & Bainton, D. (1982). Treatment of acquired aphasia—speech therapists and volunteers compared. *Journal of Neurology, Neurosurgery, & Psychiatry, 45,* 957–961.

Davis, G. A., & Wilcox, M. J. (1981). Incorporating parameters of natural conversation in aphasia treatment. In R. Chapey (Ed.), *Language intervention strategies in adult aphasia* (pp. 169–190). Baltimore: Williams & Wilkins.

Davis, A. G., & Wilcox, M. J. (1985). *Adult aphasia rehabilitation. Applied pragmatics.* San Diego: College-Hill Press.

Demeurisse, G., Demol, O., Derouck, M., de Beuckelaer, R., Coekaerts, M.-J., & Capon, A. (1980). Quantitative study of the rate of recovery from aphasia due to ischemic stroke. *Stroke, 11,* 455–458.

Duffy, J. R. (1981). Schuell's stimulation approach to rehabilitation. In R. Chapey (Ed.), *Language intervention strategies in adult aphasia* (pp. 105–141). Baltimore: Williams & Wilkins.

Edelman, G. M. (1984). Assessment of understanding in global aphasia. In C. F. Rose (Ed.), *Progress in aphasiology. Advances in neurology* (Vol. 42, pp. 277–291). New York: Raven Press.

Engl, E. M., Kotten, A., Ohlendorf, I, & Poser, E. (1982). *Sprachübungen zur Aphasiebehandlung. Ein linguistisches Übungsprogramm mit Bildern* [Language exercises for aphasia therapy. A linguistic training program with pictures.] Berlin: Marhold.

Fitzgibbon, C. T. (1986). In defense of randomized controlled trials, with suggestions about the possible use of meta-analysis. *British Journal of Disord of Communication, 21,* 117–125.

Foldi, N. S., Cicone, M., & Gardner, H. (1983). Pragmatic aspects of communication in brain-damaged patients. In S. Segalowitz (Ed.), *Language functions and brain organization* (pp. 51–87). New York: Academic Press.

Gardner, H., Zurif, E. B., Berry, T., & Baker, E. (1976). Visual communication in aphasia. *Neuropsychologia, 14,* 275–292.

Glass, A. V., Gazzaniga, M. S., & Premack, D. (1973). Artificial language training in global aphasia. *Neuropsychologia, 11,* 95–163.

Hanson, W. R., & Cicciarelli, A. W. (1978). The time, amount and pattern of language improvement in adult aphasics. *Brit. Journ. of Disord. of Communic., 13,* 59–63.

Hatfield, F. M. (1979). Aphasiebehandlung: Methoden und Ansichten [Aphasia therapy: Methods and opinions]. In G. Peuser (Ed.), *Studien zur Sprachtherapie* (pp. 395–428). München: Fink.

Hatfield, F. M., & Shewell, C. (1983). Some applications of linguistics to aphasia therapy. In C. Code & D. J. Müller (Eds.), Aphasia therapy. *Studies in language disability and remediation* (Vol. 6, pp. 61–76). London: E. Arnold.

Haviland, S. E., & Clark, H. H. (1974). What's new? Acquiring new information as a process in comprehension. *Journal of Verbal Learning and Verbal Behavior, 13,* 512–521.

Helm-Estabrooks, N., Fitzpatrick, P. M., & Barresi, B. (1982). Visual action therapy for global aphasics. *Journal of Speech and Hearing Disorders, 47,* 385–389.

Helm-Estabrooks, N., & Ramsberger, G. (1986). Treatment of agrammatism in long-term Broca's aphasia. *British Journal of Disord of Communication, 21,* 39–47.

Hesketh, A. (1986). Measuring progress in aphasia therapy: A multiple baseline study. *British Journal of Disord of Communication, 21,* 47–63.

Howard, D. (1986). Beyond randomized controlled trials: The case for effective case studies of the effects of treatment in aphasia. *British Journal of Disord of Communication, 21,* 89–102.

Howard, D., Patterson, K. E., Franklin, S., Morton, J., & Orchard-Lisle, V. M. (1984). Variability and consistency in picture naming by aphasic patients. In F. C. Rose (Ed.), *Progress in aphasiology. Advances in neurology* (Vol. 42., pp. 263–277). New York: Raven Press.

Howard, D., Patterson, K. E., Franklin, S., Orchard-Lisle, V., & Morton, J. (1985a). The facilitation of picture naming in aphasia. *Cognitive Neuropsychology, 2,* 49–80.

Howard, D., Patterson, K. E., Franklin, S., Orchard-Lisle, V. M., & Morton, J. (1985b). Treatment of word retrieval deficits in aphasia: A comparison of two therapy methods. *Brain, 108,* 817–892.

Huber, W., Poeck, K., & Willmes, K. (1984). The Aachen Aphasia Test. In C. F. Rose (Ed.), Progress in aphasiology. Advances in neurology (Vol. 42, pp. 291–305). New York: Raven Press.

Johannsen-Horbach, H., Cegla, B., Mager, U., Schempp, B., & Wallesch, C.-W. (1985). Treatment of chronic global aphasia with a nonverbal communication system. *Brain and Language, 24,* 74–82.

Jones, E. V. (1986). Building the foundations for sentence production in a non-fluent aphasic. *British Journal of Disord of Communication, 21,* 63–83.

Kean, M.-L. (Ed.). (1985). *Agrammatism. Perspectives in neurolinguistics, neuropsychology, and psycholinguistics.* London: Academic Press.

Keenan, J. S., Brassel, E. G. (1974). A study of factors related to prognosis for individual aphasic patients. *Journal of Speech and Hearing Disorders, 39,* 257–268.

Kenin, M., & Swisher, L. P. (1972). A study of pattern of recovery in aphasia. *Cortex, 8,* 56–68.

Kertesz, A. (1979). *Aphasia and associated disorders: Taxonomy, localization and recovery.* New York: Grune & Stratton.

Kertesz, A. (1984). Recovery from aphasia. In F. C. Rose (Ed.), *Progress in aphasiology. Advances in neurology* (Vol. 42, pp. 23–65). New York: Raven Press.

Kertesz, A., & McCabe, P. (1977). Recovery patterns and prognosis in aphasia. *Brain, 100,* 1–18.

Kotten, A. (1981). Aphasietherapie: Linguistisch gesteuerter Wiedererwerb der Muttersprache. [Linguistically directed reacquisition of language.] In G. Peuser & S. Winter (Eds.), *Angewandte Sprachwissenschaft: Grundfragen-Bereiche-Methoden* [Applied linguistics: basic questions-topics-methods] (pp. 361–390). Bonn: Bouvier.

Kotten, A. (1985a). Sprachübungen zur Aphasiebehandlung. [Language exercises for aphasia therapy.] In L. Springer & G. Kattenbeck (Eds.), *Aphasie: Interdisziplinäre Beiträge zur Theorie und Praxis der Logopädie.* [Aphasia: interdisciplinary contributions to the theory and practice of logopaedics.] (pp. 109–141). Munich: tuduv-Verlagsgesellschaft.

Kotten, A. (1985b). Die Behandlung des "rezeptiven Agrammatismus" (Therapy for "receptive agrammatism".) In H. Andresen Redder (Eds.) *Aphasie. Kommunikation von Aphatikern in Therapiesituationen* [Aphasia. Communication of aphasics in therapy-situations.] Osnabrücker Beiträge zur Sprachtheorie. Vol. 32, pp. 85–110.

Kotten, A. (in press). Basisprincipes by het behandeling van aphatische patienten [Basic principles for therapy of aphasic patients]. In E. Visch-Brink, F. van Harskamp & D. de Boer (Eds.). *Afasietherapie.* [Aphasia therapy]. Amsterdam: Swets Zeitlinger.

Kotten, A., Stachowiak, F. J., Willeke, A. (1985). Veranschaulichung als methodisches Prinzip der Sprachtherapie [Illustration as a methodical principle of aphasia therapy]. Paper presented at the annual meeting of the Gesellschaft für Aphasieforschung und -therapie, Rotterdam.

La Pointe, L. L. (1977). Base-10 programmed stimulation: Task specification, scoring and plotting performance in aphasia therapy. *Journal of Speech and Hearing Disorders, 42,* 90–105.

La Pointe, L. L. (1978). Aphasia therapy: Some principles and strategies for treatment. In D. F. Jones (Ed.), *Clinical management of neurogenic communicative disorders* (pp. 129–190). Boston: Little, Brown.

La Pointe, L. L. (1984). Approaches to aphasia treatment. In F. C. Rose (Ed.), *Progress in aphasiology. Advances in neurology* (Vol. 42, pp. 305–317). New York: Raven Press.

La Pointe, S. G. (1985). A theory of verb form use in the speech of agrammatic aphasics. *Brain and Language, 24,* 100–155.

Lesser, A. (1985). Aphasia therapy in the early 1980s. In St. Newman, & R. Epstein (Eds.), *Current perspectives in dysphasia* (pp. 198–217). London: Churchill Livingstone.

Lincoln. N. B. (1985). Recovery from dysphasia. In St. Newman, & R. Epstein (Eds.), Current perspectives in dysphasia (pp. 97–113). London: Churchill Livingstone.

Lincoln, N. B., McGuirk, E., Mulley, G. P., Lendrem, W., Jones, A. C., & Mitchell, J. R. A. (1984). Effectiveness of speech therapy for aphasic stroke patients: A randomized controlled trial. *Lancet, 1,* 1197–1200.

Lomas, J. A., Kertesz, A. (1978). Patterns of spontaneous recovery in aphasic groups: A study of adult stroke patients. *Brain and Language, 5,* 388–401.

Luria, A. (1977). Neuropsychological studies in aphasia. *Neurolinguistics* (Vol. 6). Amsterdam: Swets & Zeitlinger.

Marshall, R. C., Tompkins, C. A., & Phillips, D. S. (1982). Improvement in treated aphasia: Examination of selected prognostic factors. *Folia Phoniat., 3,* 305–315.

Miceli, G., Silveri, M. C., Villa, G., & Caramazza, A. (1984). On the basis for the agrammatic's difficulty in producing main verbs. *Cortex, 20,* 207–220.

Moody, E. J. (1982). Sign language acquisition by a global aphasic. *Journal of Nervous and Mental Diseases, 170,* 113–116.

Parisi, D. (1985). A procedural approach to the study of aphasia. *Brain and Language, 26,* 1–15.

Parisi, D. (1987). Grammatical disturbances of speech production. In M. Coltheart, G. Sartori, & R. Job (Eds.), *The cognitive neuropsychology of language* (pp. 201–215). London: Lawrence Erlbaum Associates.

Patterson, K., Purell, C., & Morton, J. (1983). Facilitation of word retrieval in aphasia. In C. Code & D. J. Müller (Eds.), *Aphasia therapy. Studies in language disability and remediation* (Vol. 6, pp. 76–87). London: E. Arnold.

Pickersgill, M. J., & Lincoln, N. B. (1983). Prognostic indicators and the pattern of recovery of communication in aphasic stroke patients. *Journal of Neurology, Neurosurgery, & Psychiatry, 46,* 130–139.

Pierce, R., Beekman, L. (1985). Effects of linguistic and extralinguistic context on semantic and syntactic processing in aphasia. *Journal of Speech and Hearing Research, 28,* 250–254.

Pring, T. R. (1986). Evaluating the effects of speech therapy for aphasics: Developing the single case methodology. *British Journal of Disord of Communication, 21,* 103–117.

Prins, R. S., Snow, E., & Wagenaar, E. (1978). Recovery from aphasia: Spontaneous speech versus language comprehension. *Brain and Language, 6,* 192–211.

Poeck, K. (1983). What do we mean by "aphasic syndromes"? A neurologist's view. *Brain and Language, 20,* 79–89.

Porch, B. (1967). Porch index of communicative ability; vol. 1: Theory and development. Palo Alto, Ca: Consulting Psychologists' Press.

Porch, B. (1971). Porch index of communicative ability; vol. 2: Administration, scoring and interpretation. Palo Alto, Ca: Consulting Psychologists' Press.

Rees, N. S., Shulman, J. (1978). I don't understand what you mean by comprehension. *Journal of Speech and Hearing Disorders, 43,* 208–219.

Rowley, D. T. (1983). Artificial languages and communication aids in aphasia therapy. In C. Code & D. J. Müller (Eds.), *Aphasia therapy. Studies in language disability and remediation* (Vol. 6, pp. 171–178). London: E. Arnold.

Salonen, L. (1980). The language enriched, individual therapy program for aphasic patients. In M. T. Sarno & O. Höök (Eds.), Aphasia. Assessment and Treatment (pp. 105–116). Stockholm: Almqist & Wiksell.

Sarno, M. T., & Levita, E. (1981). Some observations on the nature of recovery in global aphasia after stroke. *Brain and Language, 13,* 1–12.

Schuell, H. (1974). Aphasia theory and therapy. Selected lectures and papers of Hildred Schuell. L. F. Sies (Ed.). Baltimore: University Park Press.

Schwartz, M. F. (1987). Patterns of speech production deficit within and across aphasia syndromes: Application of a psycholinguistic model. In M. Coltheart, G. Sartori, & R. Job (Eds.), *The cognitive neuropsychology of language* (pp. 163–199). London: Lawrence Erlbaum Associates.

Seron, X. (1984). Reeducation strategies in neuropsychology: Cognitive and pragmatic approaches. In F. C. Rose (Ed.), *Progress in aphasiology. Advances in neurology* (Vol. 42, pp. 317–327). New York: Raven Press.

Shewan, C. M., & Kertesz, A. (1984). Effects of speech and language treatment on recovery from aphasia. *Brain and Language, 23,* 272–299.

Sparks, R. W. (1981). Melodic Intonation Therapy. In R. Chapey (Ed.), *Language intervention strategies in adult aphasia* (pp. 265–282). Baltimore: Williams & Wilkins.

Ulatowska, H. K., & Richardson, S. M. (1974). A longitudinal study of an adult with aphasia: Considerations for research and therapy. *Brain and Language, 1,* 151–166.

Weigl, I. (1979). Neuropsychologische und psycholinguistische Grundlagen eines Programms zur Rehabilitierung aphasischer Störungen [Neuropsychological and psycholinguistic fundamentals of a rehabilitation program for aphasic disturbances]. In G. Peuser (Ed.), *Studien zur Sprachtherapie* (pp. 491–515). München: Fink.

Weniger, D., Huber, W., Stachowiak, F.-J., & Poeck, K. (1980). Treatment of aphasia on a linguistic basis. In M. T. Sarno, & O. Höök (Eds.), Aphasia. Assessment and treatment (pp. 190–207). Stockholm: Almquist & Wiksell.

Wiegel-Crump, C., & Koenigsknecht, R. A. (1973). Tapping the lexical store of the adult aphasic: Analysis of improvement made in word-retrieval skills. *Cortex 9,* 411–418.

Wilcox, M. J., Davis, G. A., & Leonard, L. B. (1978). Aphasic's comprehension of contextually conveyed meaning. *Brain and Language, 6,* 362–377.
Willmes, K., & Poeck, K. (1984). Ergebnisse einer multizentrischen Untersuchung über die Spontanprognose von Aphasien vaskulärer Ätiologie [Results of a multicentre study on the spontaneous recovery of aphasia of vascular aetiology.] *Nervenarzt, 55,* 62–71.

12

Treatment Software for Aphasic Adults

Richard C. Katz

Treatment of the communication problems resulting from aphasia is usually a long and expensive process. As costs of health care continue to rise and the number of chronic aphasic patients increases, many clinicians find it more and more difficult to provide their patients with sufficient treatment that is both effective and cost efficient.

Developments in computer technology have introduced the potential for extensive use of microcomputers in aphasia rehabilitation at a reasonable cost. Carefully planned administrative and diagnostic computer programs can reduce both the time required by many essential activities and the probability of recording and calculation errors. An even greater contribution, however, is the ability of the microcomputer to provide treatment activities directly to patients with minimal on-site supervision from a clinician. Treatment for aphasia, however, can be far more complex and individualized than most computer programs.

Schuell (1974) maintained that certain principles of aphasia treatment should serve as the foundation of new treatment procedures. New clinical tools, whether treatment approaches, forms, or devices, develop as a consequence of many factors. Most represent principles that are consistent with what is known or believed to be known about treatment. In addition, the effectiveness of each tool should be demonstrated experimentally and documented in the literature. The clinician should assess treatment tools used in therapy with each patient. As a treatment tool, a microcomputer is only as good as its software. Treatment software is limited less by hardware than by the abilities and imagination of clinicians and researchers.

The purpose of this chapter is to examine the relationship between aphasia therapy and treatment software. Efficacy of treatment, not cost, should be our primary focus. The mechanics and logistics of using microcomputers and software when treating aphasic adults are described in detail elsewhere (e.g., Katz, 1986). Issues such as "cost effectiveness" and

317

"compatibility" are relevant, but are not central to determining the real value of aphasia treatment software. Clinicians and researchers share the responsibility to see that the aphasia therapy principles referred to by Schuell are incorporated into treatment software and tested appropriately. Creating treatment software in the image of computer programs is most likely the wrong approach. Most commercial software is designed for normal, non-brain-damaged people who are motivated to work with computers. Rather, aphasia treatment software, like other forms of treatment, should be consistent with what we know about brain function, its disruption and rehabilitation. Clinicians and researchers have been attempting to build a solid foundation for treating aphasic patients. Though some may feel this foundation more closely resembles the Tower of Babel, several areas basic to aphasia treatment are also relevant when considering computer programs as treatment.

MODELS OF REHABILITATION

Wolfe (1987) encouraged the use of explicit models of rehabilitation in the development of treatment software. Models can be used (a) to improve communication between clinicians, researchers, and software developers; (b) to aid clinicians in selecting appropriate treatment software; (c) to develop assessment procedures to measure efficacy; and (d) to systematically develop new treatment approaches. Wolfe reviewed the literature and identified three categories for models of rehabilitation. *Brain-behavior relationships* includes neuropsychological models of brain functioning, for example, retraining (Luria, 1973). *Behavior modification* includes operant procedures and components, such as cues and reinforcers. *Education* includes individual drill and practice, educational games, and "simulations" (Lepper, 1985).

The brain-behavior model is represented in many programs designed for "cognitive rehabilitation" for head trauma patients (e.g., Bracy, 1986; Gianutsos, 1980). Most commercially available language treatment software designed for aphasic patients simply replicates general treatment exercises from workbooks and similar sources of supplementary treatment. This nonspecific form of treatment usually represents behavior modification and educational models of rehabilitation. Simulations, also called "artificial realities," are becoming increasingly sophisticated and gaining a more prominent role in training, especially for those in high-risk situations, such as pilots, physicians, police, and the military. Enhanced by microcomputers controlling high quality graphics and sound, these simulations are highly interactive, placing the participant in a role-playing situation that would be too costly or dangerous in real life. In rehabilitation, simulations such as "microworlds" represent excellent creative use of models on microcomputers. Currently, videotape and film have been used (without computer support) in a similar fashion to heighten realism in interview training and stuttering therapy. As "interactive video" becomes more available, the potential benefit of microworld tasks will increase greatly. Wolfe (1987) indicated that software developers should provide greater detail of the rationale behind their treatment programs in much the same way as provided by many researchers (e.g., Loverso, Selinger, & Prescott, 1985). In this way, models will help commercial developers become more responsive to the needs of clinicians, and thus produce software that becomes a valuable part of therapy.

TREATMENT APPROACHES

Good theory is always clinically relevant. Models of rehabilitation should imply approaches to treatment. Two major treatment approaches are stimulation and programmed learning. Though many view these two approaches as mutually incompatible techniques, LaPointe (1977) placed them at opposite ends of a continuum, where features of the two approaches could be combined as indicated by the needs of the patient.

At one end of the continuum is the stimulation approach, in which the goal is to "activate the language system." Rather than teach specific responses to stimuli, the stimulation approach assumes that a patient's impaired language system requires ample opportunity to respond appropriately if improvement is to occur. Much of this approach is based on Schuell (1974) who wrote that frequent and repeated sensory stimulation is necessary for the organization, storage, and retrieval of language behavior. Porch (1981) also supported this view when he stated that aphasic patients should interact within a reasonably stimulating language environment in order to achieve their potential for language recovery.

To many, the programmed–learning approach represents the antithesis of stimulation therapy. Patients work in a linear fashion toward eliciting specific responses to specific stimuli. Educators and clinicians have known the benefits of the programmed–learning approach for years (e.g., Costello, 1977). Early work by Holland (1970) provided a description of the advantages of the programmed–operant learning approach to aphasia treatment. She wrote that the approach allows the clinician (a) to carefully control the amount of stimulation a patient receives, (b) to require the patient to respond many times, (c) to automatically restimulate the patient following a response, and (d) to constantly evaluate the patient's performance. Other principles, such as changing criterion, shaping behavior, and adjusting schedules of reinforcement, are frequently incorporated into this approach to increase the rate of learning.

Many currently used treatment approaches can be found along this treatment continuum, including cognitive retraining (Wepman, 1972), hierarchical task continuum (Rosenbek, Lemme, Ahern, Harris, & Wertz, 1973), Melodic Intonation Therapy (Sparks, Helm, & Albert, 1974), and Matrix Training (Salvatore, 1982; Thompson, McReynolds, & Vance, 1982; Tonkovich & Loverso, 1982). In a similar fashion, computerized treatment programs can also be located on the continuum. Elements of the stimulation approach are evident in treatment software that provides patients with the opportunity for hundreds of stimulus presentations over relatively short periods of time and with minimal on-site supervision from a clinician. Principles from the programmed-learning approach are illustrated in the branching techniques and evaluation procedures that are a part of highly interactive computerized treatment programs that continuously modify stimuli as a function of the patient's responses.

EVOLUTION OF RECOVERY

Recovery from aphasia appears to follow a basic pattern, subject to a number of different physical, psychological, and environmental factors. Most often, recovery occurs in two stages. During the acute stage, language ability usually improves relatively quickly, perhaps reflecting rapid changes in physiology (e.g., reduced cerebral edema). Attempts to communicate become increasingly successful for most aphasic patients. This early change is referred to as the period of spontaneous recovery and is assumed to last from 1 month (Culton, 1969) to 6 months (Luria, 1965; Vignolo, 1964) in patients following cerebral vascular accidents.

The second, chronic, phase of recovery represents a slowing down in the rate of improvement. Porch (1981) described the language recovery process in aphasia as following a "negatively accelerating curve," during which the rate of recovery decreases as the period of time post onset increases (Fig. 12.1). Chronic aphasia is this language plateau, for the most part the result of physiologic stability and adaptation of the patient and others to his communication limitations. Treatment of chronic aphasic patients can be a long and expensive process. When resources are limited, it is not uncommon for relatively stable chronic aphasic patients to be passed over in favor of acute patients in whom greater change can usually be affected. Experience demonstrates, however, that even small changes in a patient's behavior can improve quality of life for the patient and family by increasing independence, developing a sense of well-being, and reducing the cost of providing care. The microcomputer can make its greatest

HYPOTHETICAL RECOVERY CURVE

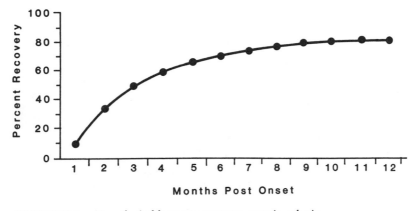

FIGURE 12.1. Hypothetical language recovery curve in aphasia.

contribution to rehabilitation during this phase of recovery by providing unlimited opportunity for interactive language focused activities in an emotionally neutral environment.

TASK STRUCTURE

Task structure determines the extent to which treatment will influence a given patient's ability to use language. No one paradigm is appropriate for all patients and conditions. At one extreme, highly unstructured tasks are similar to daily spontaneous conversational conditions, but provide patients with little systematic intervention to develop compensatory techniques. Highly structured tasks with multiple levels of cuing support the efforts of patients, but offer little opportunity for independent and realistic behavior. Regardless of these differences, treatment activities generally share some common features or components that are useful for describing and developing tasks (Fig. 12.2).

The structure of treatment software varies along a continuum, ranging in complexity from simple, repetitive drills that only evaluate accuracy of individual responses to active treatment tasks that select different cues or levels of intervention. Ideally, treatment software should automatically adjust task complexity according to performance at any level, thus, creating an interactive learning environment for the patient by imitating the decision process made by a clinician. This would require a program that monitors performance, identifies error patterns, generates a hypothesis,

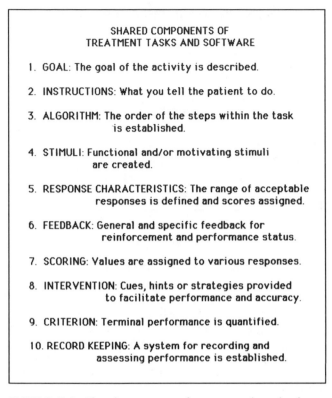

FIGURE 12.2   Shared components of treatment tasks and software.

modifies feedback, and evaluates the effect of the change on patient performance. The cycle is repeated by the program until criterion is achieved (Fig. 12.3). The relatively small capacity of microcomputer hardware limits the size and power of programs, but this problem is quickly diminishing. Since first developed in the late 1970s, more powerful and less expensive microcomputers are introduced each year.

TASK CONTENT

Treatment of communication problems in aphasia is complex and multifaceted. Language, the primary focus of treatment, is a communicative behavior and though responsive to the rules of the general language community, also reflects unique elements of each interlocutor. According to the most recent figures, there are approximately 1 million chronically aphasic people in the United States (Howell, 1978). A random sample of these patients would reveal all types and severities of aphasia with each patient representing a unique combination of biological, psychological, and environmental factors. Clinicians designing treatment software cannot anticipate all possible patient behaviors, and programmers can code only a limited number of contingencies.

Most commercial software replicates stimuli and tasks from workbooks and other sources of supplementary treatment activities. The resulting software is thus useful as supplemental, general language stimulation (in the form of drills) for many patients, but can lack functional relevance and specific intervention strategies that are the real value of treatment. Publishers rarely claim their software is effective. The warranty that accompanies commercial software is actually a disclaimer and usually contains statements, such as "the publisher makes no warranty or claims of any kind with regard to this material including . . . the fitness for a particular purpose," and "it is the responsibility of the purchaser to determine the suitability of the product . . . ." It is unlikely that any

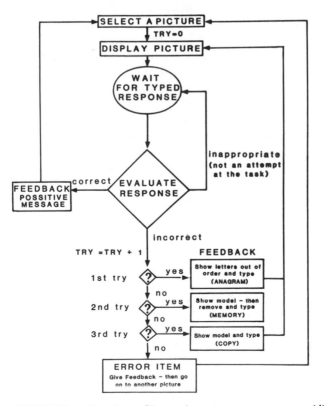

FIGURE 12.3 Flowchart of interactive treatment program providing multi-level cuing.

clinician treating aphasic patients would characterize a treatment protocol in this manner.

The microcomputer is basically a graphic machine. Information is usually entered by the user by typing on a keyboard; the computed results are read by the user from a monitor screen. This makes the computer well-suited for presenting reading and writing (typing) tasks. Reading and writing skills appear to be an appropriate focus for computerized language treatment. Most aphasic patients have reading and writing problems. Reading requires minimal responses from the patient. Programs for treating reading can run on the standard configuration of a microcomputer, without expensive modifications or special peripheral devices. Also, reading and writing as communicative acts are usually done alone and in many ways are less direct and responsive (i.e., have greater interpersonal distance) than speaking and listening. Computerized reading and writing treatment tasks can free up valuable time in therapy so that face-to-face, individual work can emphasize auditory comprehension and verbal output skills. Additional noncomputerized reading or writing tasks can be scheduled as indicated by patient performance. As improvements in sound are achieved and standardized, auditory comprehension tasks will become increasingly available on microcomputers. Coupled with improved graphics and speech recognition, microcomputers will eventually provide treatment activities in all language modalities.

The content of software cannot be cast in stone. Flexibility increases the value of a program as a treatment tool. Clinicians, ultimately responsible for the quality of treatment, should be able to modify the content of treatment programs to meet the individual needs of each patient. Modifications can be achieved in two ways. Programs written in general-purpose programming languages (such as BASIC) or languages specifically designed for creating treatment lessons (such as PILOT) on non-copy-protected disks can be modified by clinicians with little programming experience. This approach offers the greatest clinician control over the direction of treatment software. Many other programs allow modification of stimuli and target responses without programming skills through special options for the clinician.

Treatment software may eventually be organized much like treatment plans and lesson plans, consisting of task paradigms or "shells." Clinicians will be able to select a shell, modify its structure according to the needs of the patient (e.g., total number of stimuli, conditions for presenting intervention routine, etc.), and enter the actual content (e.g., stimuli, target responses, specific cues, and general feedback). The process for the clinician could be similar to using a word processor to write a report from an existing template. This kind of flexibility is necessary if software is truly to become an effective treatment tool for clinicians.

ASSESSING EFFICACY OF TREATMENT

Once a patient is physiologically stable, our greatest influence on recovery is treatment. Wepman (1970, p. 128) wrote "too many patients get better and too many fail to do so without our knowing why. If we knew why or even if we knew only the stages through which they recovered when they do perhaps we could begin to understand why others do not get better." When treating aphasic patients, clinicians are guided by their training and experience, objective clinical measures, and research documented in the literature. Theory, observation, and research are our tools to identify the salient parameters of efficacious treatment. A considerable amount of treatment can be provided by microcomputers.

Effective treatment for aphasic patients, however, is not simply an issue of what works. Darley (1972) wrote that the question we should ask is not "Does therapy work?" but (a) For whom does it work? (b) What does the treatment consist of? (c) When should treatment begin and end? and (d) How frequently should treatment be provided? The "Base-10" design (LaPointe, 1977), statistical prognostic indicators (Matthews & LaPointe, 1981, 1983), and single-subject design (McReynolds & Kearns, 1983) are examples of procedures designed to help clinicians measure the effectiveness of all forms of treatment activities for each aphasic patient.

Measuring the degree to which treatment tasks are successful is an essential part of any therapy program (Prescott & McNeil, 1973). The relative effects of linguistic, physical, and psychological variables are compared in order to determine their value for the patient. The computer can provide treatment in a standard manner and routinely store and display performance data for frequent analysis of task effectiveness. Valuable descriptive statistics can be obtained quickly, easily, and frequently. This can help answer the efficacy question posed earlier by Darley (1972). Eventually, it may be said with confidence that a 55-year-old Broca's aphasic adult who is 1-year post onset and at the 50th percentile on the PICA should require between 125 and 150 trials to learn to write or print 10 words at the third-grade level (LaPointe, 1977). Such prognostic ability is a valuable clinical yardstick against which treatment and recovery can be measured (Matthews & LaPointe, 1981, 1983).

ROLE OF THE CLINICIAN

The clinician is responsible for treatment efficacy, not the microcomputer, software, programmer, designer, or publisher. Software simply cannot do everything clinicians do. The format of computer-aided therapy is restricted to presenting and receiving very specific and concrete information. Some fundamental components of treatment such as verbal training and practice in interpersonal communication (Egolf & Chester, 1973) cannot be adequately addressed with computer resources. Verbal and other communicative exercises must be flexible and adaptive to meet the individual needs of patients, requiring the involvement of a clinician and other significant persons. Most importantly, individualized, comprehensive treatment plans requiring the knowledge and skill of a trained clinician should be developed for each patient. Additionally, the clinician communicates empathy, honesty, and genuine concern to the patient, and offers appropriate patient education and counseling—services a microcomputer cannot provide. Microcomputers and treatment software, like all tools, should extend the abilities of the clinician, so that treatment is provided more quickly, more often, and more accurately. It is unreasonable, unethical, and certainly misrepresents the complexity of the job to assume that at this time a machine can perform the functions of a clinician. Microcomputers cannot be trusted to make critical treatment decisions independently until software is developed that can react to a greater variety of treatment-related events.

ADDITIONAL FACTORS

In addition to language, many other factors should be considered when providing treatment for aphasic patients. Treatment must respond to the patient's sensory (e.g., LaPointe & Culton, 1969) and motor (e.g., Stanton, Yorkston, Kenyon, & Beukelman, 1981) limitations. Cognitive impairments also must be addressed, for example, problems in reaction time (Loverso & Prescott, 1981), attention (McNeil, Darley, Rose, & Olsen, 1979), memory (Loverso & Craft, 1982), and abstraction and reasoning skills (Bracy, 1983; Prescott, Loverso, & Selinger, 1984). Clinicians determine the degree to which these factors can interfere with communication, treatment, and generalization. Psychological factors, such as motivation, dependency, and quality of life, are also concerns that become increasingly important as recovery slows and the degree of disability and its subsequent effect on life become more apparent. Decision making and expression of personal preferences by each patient should be a basic part of patient management whenever possible (Bengston, 1973; Wertz, 1981).

RESEARCH

The use of microcomputers and treatment software is a recent development in aphasia rehabilitation. The following studies investigated the efficacy of various computerized treatment program written specifically for adult aphasic subjects using microcomputers.

Auditory Comprehension

Mills and Thomas (1981) and Mills (1982) used a microcomputer to provide auditory comprehension practice for an aphasic adult 2 months after he suffered a single occlusive left CVA. The microcomputer displayed on the screen line drawings of four objects and simultaneously presented auditory commands (e.g., "Find the cat.") via a speech digitizer (4Kbyte sampling rate). The quality of speech was very good, similar to that produced by a high-quality cassette tape recorder. The subject responded by pressing the number key (1, 2, 3, or 4) corresponding to the target picture. Feedback was provided for all responses. If the response was correct, the next stimulus was presented. The subject was prompted to "try again" in response to the first error made in response to each stimulus; the correct answer was displayed if an error was made on the second attempt.

The subject could request an unlimited number of repetitions of the auditory stimulus prior to responding. No other intervention was provided. The effects of the program might be enhanced if the option to hear the word again were available after the second error. Nevertheless, the performance of the aphasic subject improved over 5 months both on the specific task and on the Porch Index of Communicative Ability (PICA) (Porch, 1981).

Verbal Output

Colby, Christinaz, Parkison, Graham, and Karpf (1981) built a microcomputer to facilitate word finding for aphasic subjects whose major deficit was dysnomia. The small, portable microcomputer was carried by subjects on a sling/shoulder strap combination, allowing the device to function during actual communicative situations. The patient pushed a key when experiencing difficulty remembering a word. In response, the microcomputer displayed a series of questions designed to help identify (i.e., predict) the forgotten word, "Do you remember the first letter of the word?, . . . the last letter, . . . any other letters, . . . any other words that go with the forgotten word?" The subject typed single-key answers that were then applied according to a sequence of steps controlled by the program, resulting in a list of possible words that was displayed across the computer screen beginning with the most "probable" words. This type of cue is appropriate for dysnomic patients, who typically can recognize the correct word and say it after a visual or auditory model. When the subject recognized the forgotten word, he or she pressed a key and the word was produced via synthesized speech.

Although intended as a compensatory device, the most significant finding was the generalization of the cuing algorithm to noncomputer settings. After several weeks of using the microcomputer, subjects reported that they no longer used the portable microcomputer. When they forgot a word and did not have the microcomputer immediately available, they simply began to ask themselves the same series of questions displayed by the computer. The subjects, it appeared, had learned to initiate and utilize the cuing algorithm without the need to be prompted by the microcomputer. They had *internalized the algorithm*. Portable microcomputers have the potential to model for and cue patients during actual communication situations, providing both compensatory and therapeutic functions for patients.

Reading Comprehension

Katz and Nagy (1982, 1983, 1985) conducted three studies assessing the ability of microcomputers to improve reading comprehension in aphasic adults. The purpose of the first study was to assess the feasibility and effectiveness of microcomputers for testing and treating five mildly and moderately impaired chronic aphasic subjects (Katz & Nagy, 1982). The disk, Computerized Aphasia Treatment Systems (CATS), incorporated six reading activities into a consistent computer format that could be operated by aphasic subjects with little or no assistance by the clinician. CATS also consists of a diagnostic reading test and a program that enables the experimenter to retrieve subject-performance data. Subjects selected treatment tasks via an on-screen menu and were prompted to enter their names, the number of items they wished to attempt, and other options. Tests were administered before and after the 8-to-12 week treatment period to measure the effects of the computer programs. Scores increased on the computerized test (CATS), though standard (e.g., PICA) and non-standard tests administered through traditional "paper and pencil" procedures did not show change. Nevertheless, subjects in this study demonstrated the ability to independently operate microcomputers using treatment programs that were organized in logical, predictable sequences, were menu driven, and trapped commonly occurring errors. The program provided subjects with language-stimulation activities that were structured and accountable. At the same time, the program allowed the subjects to take on more active roles in their treatment by encouraging independent behavior, judgment, and decision making.

A second study (Katz & Nagy, 1983) measured the effects of frequent and brief exposure of single words on word recognition ability in aphasic subjects. The program *Flash* is a tachistoscopic word-recognition task containing sight vocabulary words. Single words were initially exposed for approximately .01 second. Duration of exposure time increased (by .2 second) when the stimulus was repeated following errors in matching and typing words from memory. All subjects improved on the task; improvement, however, did not generalize to oral reading tests and writing-to-dictation tasks, which were presented before and following the treatment phase. This study demonstrates that the computer can continually modify elements within a task with a high degree of precision. Intervention that requires little or no linguistic processing, however, may be of limited benefit to aphasic adults outside of the task. Computerized treatment could become more effective if programs were developed that could provide linguistically relevant cues when performance indicated the need.

The objective of a third reading study (Katz & Nagy, 1985) was to improve functional reading in severely impaired aphasic adults. Five aphasic subjects (average PICA overall percentile of 35) were shown computer line drawings of 12 semantically related objects (e.g., spoon, fork, knife) and required to match the correct word to the picture. The program began as a simple word discrimination task and became more difficult as the number and type of foils were increased. Two choices were presented per drawing for the first session. Criterion was 83% or better over three consecutive sessions with six choices displayed per drawing in sessions two and three. The level of difficulty was automatically adjusted by the program within the session and from session to session in response to the subject's performance. In this way, subjects could maintain a high level of accuracy, whereas the task remained challenging. Also, the program generated and printed out at the end of each session four different writing activities to be practiced outside of the treatment session.

Three out of the five subjects (average PICA overall 36th percentile) demonstrated improvement between pre- and posttreatment reading tests (average 39% improvement). These subjects maintained good performance during the task for most sessions, demonstrating steady increases in the number of foils from session to session. Two subjects (average PICA overall 33rd percentile) did not show improvement beyond the first level. The computer-administered intervention was not effective for these two subjects. The study indicated that even computer programs designed specifically for certain types of patients should include a wide range of contingencies for various possible responses. In this case, the program could have included more fundamental information and offered alternative cues when a single approach failed to improve performance.

Writing: Typing/Spelling Words

Scron, Deloche, Moulard, and Rouselle (1980) reported the effectiveness of a computerized treatment program designed to improve spelling and writing (typing) for five aphasic subjects. Words were presented verbally by a clinician and the subjects typed their responses on a computer terminal keyboard. A horizontal sequence of boxes was drawn on the screen to represent letters in the target word. The computer program evaluated each subject's response and provided appropriate cues to aid spelling. If the chosen letter was in the word and in the correct position, then the letter was printed on the screen. If the letter typed was in the target word, but not in the correct position, then the letter was placed in the correct position automatically and accompanied by auditory feedback. If the letter was not in the word, no letter was printed and auditory feedback was provided. Results showed a significant reduction in the number of misspelled words as well as in the selection and sequencing of letters. Later, Deloche (1983, personal communication) modified the task for the Apple II microcomputer using high-resolution drawings instead of a clinician to present the stimuli. Thus, subjects were required to first recall the name of the stimulus and then spell the word.

Katz and Nagy (1984) developed and evaluated a computer program designed to teach subjects to write the names of seven objects (confrontation naming). Drawings were displayed on the computer monitor and subjects were required to type the name of the object shown. The program evaluated subject responses and provided appropriate feedback. The program incorporated conditional branching algorithms in response to errors to display one of six hierarchically arranged cues (Fig. 12.4), depending on the number of previous (erroneous) attempts at the target word.

Attempt	Score If Correct	Cue If Error
1	7	Repeat stimulus picture only
2	6	Anagram without feedback
3	5	Copying words from memory
4	4	Anagram with selection feedback
5	3	Multiple choice cues
6	2	Copying from printed word
7	1	ERROR / score equals 0 / next word

FIGURE 12.4   Hierarchy of computer-generated cues (Katz & Nagy, 1984).

If a response was correct on the first attempt, feedback was provided and the next stimulus picture and prompt was displayed. If the subject response was inaccurate, the aforementioned hierarchy was invoked. Successive cues were provided until the response was correct. Once an accurate response was produced, feedback was provided and the successful cue was repeated. If the subject responded correctly a second time, the cue from the level previously failed (next higher in the hierarchy) was repeated. In addition, copying homework consisting of only the erroneous items was generated by the printer at the end of each session. The task structured in this way more closely approximated the procedure used by speech clinicians to modify the task as the abilities of their patients change during the course of treatment.

The average performance of the eight subjects for reading and writing, and overall score was at the 50th percentile on the PICA. Four severely impaired Broca aphasic subjects and two mild dysnomic aphasic subjects demonstrated improvement on the task over 15 sessions (by over four points) and on comparison of a writing to dictation task administered before and after the treatment period ($p < .01$). Two severely impaired subjects, one global and one Wernicke's aphasic subject, did not show improvement. The global subject improved when stimulus items were personalized and reduced from seven to three. The Wernicke's subject was initially a poor candidate for therapy, due to family and alcohol problems. He dropped out of the study after only four sessions and soon after discontinued treatment altogether.

Improvement in written confrontation naming for the seven remaining subjects represents a gain in the ability to actually write the target words correctly from memory, not simply type the words. A major part of the transition from typing to writing may have been facilitated by the copying homework following the task.

Loverso, Prescott, Selinger, Wheeler, and Smith (1985) compared the effects of a treatment approach provided by a clinician with a similar treatment program presented on a microcomputer. Verbs were paired with WH-words (question words) to develop cues to elicit sentences in aphasic subjects (Loverso, Selinger, & Prescott, 1979). Stimuli were presented visually (printed text) and auditorially (digitized speech). Table 12.1 displays the number of sessions for clinician- and computer-provided treatment conditions needed to reach criteria for each level in the treatment hierarchy.

An alternating treatment design with multiple probes (McReynolds & Kearns, 1983) was used in this well-designed single-case study to compare treatment presented by the clinician with treatment presented by the microcomputer. Treatment conditions (clinician and microcomputer) were randomly assigned to morning and afternoon sessions, 5 days a week,

TABLE 12.1

Level	Description	Clinician	Computer
IA	Copy/repeat actor and action	8	14
IB	Select correct actor and object from array	7	20+
I	Supply self-generated actor and action	4	3
IIA	Same as IA but with direct object required	4	3
IIB	Same as IB but with direct object required	3	20+
II	Same as I but with direct object required	10	7

Number of Clinician and Computer Sessions to Reach Criteria for each Level

over a 5 month period. Internal probes (untreated but similar items) were periodically administered to measure the subject's ability to maintain performance of all completed levels. External probes (the PICA) were administered after each level to assess generalization.

The authors reported that 36 visits with the clinician and 67 visits with the computer were needed to complete the treatment program. Improved performance was measured on the basis of performance on internal probes (similar, but nontreated items) at most levels. More importantly, external probes showed a significant increase ($p < .01$) in *PICA* performance from baseline to completion of the program and these gains were maintained 3 months following completion of the study. Results indicated that the clinician was more efficient in bringing these subjects to criteria than was the microcomputer. The authors concluded that the microcomputer can be an effective, but slower means of providing treatment.

SUMMARY

The preceding studies show the feasibility and effectiveness of using microcomputers in the treatment of aphasic adults. Experimental treatment programs stimulated independent decision making and behavior; provided considerable opportunity for language stimulation; modeled compensatory strategies for the patient in realistic and functional settings; determined the appropriate level of difficulty for optimal learning to occur; and individualized the intervention for each patient using performance data and advanced branching techniques. They also demonstrate some limitations that help illustrate the importance of the eight factors described earlier for the development of effective treatment software.

As computer technology improves, microcomputers will evolve. Faster microprocessors and increases in computer memory result in programs that are more responsive, flexible, and "intelligent." Portability and a standardized, familiar mode of operation increase the likelihood that many patients will not only accept, but expect microcomputers in treatment.

The latest, currently available features, such as high-quality speech production, photographic-quality color graphics and animation, and telecommunications will certainly lead to the development of software that can offer most patients treatment opportunities otherv ise impossible or impractical.

Patients must interact in a world of people, not computers. The technological advances described here are new means to achieve an old goal, to improve the ability of aphasic patients to communicate. If all the intervening variables are known, the value of treatment could be the same whether delivered by a clinician or a machine; the therapy is the same. Though expensive, exotic treatment prototypes can be constructed, our goal can best be accomplished by improving the quality of treatment provided for all patients, not a select few. Powerful treatment programs are needed to allow clinicians to easily control task parameters and content for each patient. As these programs are evaluated for each patient, a data base will steadily grow that contains what we know about aphasia, communication, behavior, learning, and therapy. That information will be used in other aspects of treatment and patient management, and ultimately improve the quality of life for all patients.

REFERENCES

Bengston, V. L. (1973). Self-determination: A social-psychologic perspective on helping the aged. *Geriatrics, 28*(12), 118–130.

Bracy, O. L. (1983). Computer based cognitive rehabilitation. *Cognitive Rehabilitation, 1*(1), 7–8, 18–19.

Bracy, O. L. (1986). Cognitive rehabilitation: A process approach. *Cognitive Rehabilitation, 4*(3), 10–17.

Colby, K. M., Christinaz, D., Parkison, R. C., Graham, S., & Karpf, C. (1981). A word-finding computer program with a dynamic lexical-semantic memory for patients with anomia using an intelligent speech prosthesis. *Brain and Language, 14,* 272–281.

Costello, J. M. (1977). Programmed Instruction. *Journal of Speech and Hearing Disorders, 42*(1), 3–28.

Culton, G. L. (1969). Spontaneous recovery from aphasia. *Journal of Speech and Hearing Research, 12,* 825–832.

Darley, F. L. (1972). The efficacy of language rehabilitation in aphasia. *Journal of Speech and Hearing Research, 37,* 3–21.

Egolf, D. B., & Chester, S. L. (1973). Nonverbal communication and the disorders of speech and language. *ASHA, 15,* 511–518.

Gianutsos, R. (1980). What is cognitive rehabilitation? *Journal of Rehabilitation,* July-September, 161–164.

Holland, A. L. (1970). Case studies in aphasia rehabilitation using programmed instruction. *Journal of Speech and Hearing Disorders, 35,* 377–390.

Howell, L. (1978). Stroke. In Goldenson, R. M., Dunham, J. R., & Dunham, C. S. (Eds.), *Disability and rehabilitation handbook* (pp. 573–580). New York: McGraw-Hill.

Katz, R. C. (1986). *Aphasia treatment and microcomputers.* College-Hill Press.

Katz, R. C., & Nagy, V. Tong. (1982). A computerized treatment system for chronic aphasic patients. In R. H. Brookshire (Ed.), *Clinical aphasiology: Conference proceedings* (pp. 153–160). Minneapolis: BRK Publishers.

Katz, R. C., & Nagy, V. (1983). A computerized approach for improving word recognition in chronic aphasic patients. In R. H. Brookshire (Ed.), *Clinical Aphasiology: Conference Proceedings* (pp. 65–72). Minneapolis: BRK Publishers.

Katz, R. C., & Nagy, V. (1984). An intelligent computer-based spelling task for chronic aphasic patients. In R. H. Brookshire (Ed.), *Clinical aphasiology: Conference proceedings* (pp. 65–72). Minneapolis: BRK Publishers.

Katz, R. C., & Nagy, V. (1985). A self-modifying computerized reading program for severely-impaired aphasic adults. In R. H. Brookshire (Ed.), *Clinical Aphasiology Conference* (pp. 184–188). Minneapolis: BRK Publishers.

LaPointe, L. L. (1977). Base-10 programmed stimulation: Task specification, scoring and plotting performance in aphasia therapy. *Journal of Speech and Hearing Disorders, 42,* 90–105.

LaPointe, L. L., & Culton, G. L. (1969). Visual-spatial neglect subsequent to brain-injury. *Journal of Speech and Hearing Disorders, 34,* 82–86.

Lepper, M. R. (1985). Microcomputers in education: motivational and social issues. *American Psychologist, 40,* 1–18.

Loverso, F. L., & Craft, R. (1982). Memory performance as a function of stimulus characteristics for aphasic and normal adults. In R. H. Brookshire (Ed.), *Clinical Aphasiology: Conference Proceedings* (pp. 192–199). Minneapolis: BRK Publishers.

Loverso, F. L., & Prescott, T. E. (1981). The effects of alerting signals on left brain damaged (aphasic) and normal subjects' accuracy and response time to visual stimuli. In R. H. Brookshire (Ed.), *Clinical Aphasiology: Conference Proceedings* (pp. 55–67). Minneapolis: BRK Publishers.

Loverso, F. L., Prescott, T. E., Selinger, M., Wheeler, K. M., & Smith, R. D. (1985). The application of microcomputers for the treatment of aphasic adults. In R. H. Brookshire (Ed.), *Clinical Aphasiology: Conference Proceedings* (pp. 189–195). Minneapolis: BRK Publishers.

Loverso, F. L., Selinger, M., & Prescott, T. E. (1979). Application of verbing strategies to aphasia treatment. In R. H. Brookshire (Ed.), *Clinical Aphasiology: Conference Proceedings* (pp. 229–238). Minneapolis: BRK Publishers.

Luria, A. R. (1965). *Human brain and psychological processes.* New York: Harper & Row.

Luria, A. R. (1973). *The working brain.* New York: Basic Books.

Matthews, B. A. J., & LaPointe, L. L. (1981). Determining rate of change and predicting performance levels in aphasia therapy. In R. H. Brookshire (Ed.), *Clinical Aphasiology: Conference Proceedings* (pp. 17–25). Minneapolis: BRK Publishers.

Matthews, B. A. J., & LaPointe, L. L. (1983). Slope and variability of performance on selected aphasia treatment tasks. In R. H. Brookshire (Ed.), *Clinical Aphasiology: Conference Proceedings* (pp. 113–120). Minneapolis: BRK Publishers.

McNeil, M., Darley, F. L., Rose, D. E., & Olsen, W. O. (1979). *Effects of selective binary intensity variations on auditory processing in aphasia.* Paper presented at the 9th Clinical Aphasiology Conference, Phoenix.

McReynolds, L. V., & Kearns, K. P. (1983). *Single-subject experimental designs in communicative disorders.* Baltimore: University Park Press.

Mills, R. H. (1982). Microcomputerized auditory comprehension training. In R. H. Brookshire (Ed.), *Clinical Aphasiology: Conference Proceedings* (pp. 147–152). Minneapolis: BRK Publishers.

Mills, R. H., & Thomas, R. P. (1981). Microcomputerized language therapy for the aphasic patient. *I.E.E.E. Proceedings of the John Hopkins First National Search for Personal Computing to Aid the Handicapped,* 45–46.

Porch, B. E. (1981). *Porch Index of Communicative Ability: Vol. 1; Administration, scoring and interpretation* (3rd ed). Palo Alto, CA: Consulting Psychologists Press.

Prescott, T. E., & McNeil, M. R. (1973). *Measuring the effects of treatment of aphasia.* Paper presented at the Third Conference on Clinical Aphasiology, Albuquerque.

Prescott, T. E., Loverso, F. L., & Selinger, M. (1984). Differences between normals and left brain damaged (aphasic) subjects on a nonverbal problem solving task. In R. H. Brookshire (Ed.), *Clinical Aphasiology: Conference Proceedings* (pp. 235–240). Minneapolis: BRK Publishers.

Rosenbek, J. C., Lemme, M. L., Ahern, M. B., Harris, E. H., & Wertz, R. T. (1973). A treatment for apraxia of speech in adults. *Journal of Speech and Hearing Disorders, 38,* 462–472.

Salvatore, A. (1982). Artificial language learning in brain damaged adults using a matrix training procedure. In R. H. Brookshire (Ed.), *Clinical Aphasiology: Conference Proceedings* (pp. 298–307). Minneapolis: BRK Publishers.

Schuell, H. (1974). *Aphasia theory and therapy: Selected lectures and papers of Hildred Schuell.* Baltimore: University Park Press.

Schuell, H., Jenkins, J. J., & Jimenez-Pabon, E. (1964). *Aphasia in adults.* New York: Harper & Row.

Seron, X., Deloche, G., Moulard, G., & Rouselle, M. (1980). A computer-based therapy for the treatment of aphasic subjects with writing disorders. *Journal of Speech and Hearing Disorders, 45,* 45–58.

Sparks, R., Helm, N., & Albert, M. (1974). Aphasia rehabilitation resulting from melodic intonation therapy. *Cortex, 11,* 303–316.

Stanton, K., Yorkston, V. T., Kenyon, D. R., & Beukelman. (1981). Language utilitation in teaching reading to left neglect patients. In R. H. Brookshire (Ed.), *Clinical Aphasiology: Conference Proceedings* (pp. 262–271). Minneapolis: BRK Publishers.

Thompson, C., McReynolds, L., & Vance, C. (1982). Generative use of locatives in multi-word utterances in agrammatism: A matrix training approach. In R. H. Brookshire (Ed.), *Clinical Aphasiology: Conference Proceedings* (pp. 289–297). Minneapolis: BRK Publishers.

Tonkovich, J., & Loverso, F. L. (1982). A training matrix approach for gestural acquisition by the agrammatic patient. In R. H. Brookshire (Ed.), *Clinical Aphasiology: Conference Proceedings* (pp. 283–288). Minneapolis: BRK Publishers.

Vignolo, L. A. (1964). Evolution of aphasia and language rehabilitation: A retrospective exploratory study. *Cortex, 1,* 344–369.

Wepman, J. M. (1970). Approaches to the analyses of aphasia. In Carhart, R. (Ed.), *Human Communication and Its Disorders.* NINDS Monograph No. 10. Washington, D.C., U.S. Department of Health, Education and Welfare, National Institute of Health.

Wepman, J. (1972). Aphasia therapy: A new look. *Journal of Speech and Hearing Disorders, 37,* 203–214.

Wertz, R. T. (1981). Aphasia management: The speech pathologist's role. *Seminars in Speech, Language and Hearing, 2,* 315–331.

Wolfe, G. R. (1987). Microcomputers and treatment of aphasia. *Aphasiology, 1*(2), 165–170.

Yorkston, K. M., Stanton, K. M., & Beukelman, D. R. (1981). Language-based compensatory training for chronic head injured patients. In R. H. Brookshire (Ed.), *Clinical Aphasiology: Conference Proceedings* (pp. 293–300). Minneapolis: BRK Publishers.

13

Management of Neuropsychological Impairment after Severe Head Injury

J. M. Mazaux
M. Gagnon
M. Barat

Head injury represents the primary cause of death in adults under 45 years of age. It is also a major cause of disability in industrialized countries and 180/100,000 people die and/or are hospitalized every year as a result of head injury (Jennett & McMillan, 1981; Kraus et al., 1984; Mazaux, 1985). This situation has led to staggering human and social costs. Although the progress of medical imagery, emergency techniques, and neurosurgical procedures allow for an increasing number of survivors, the benefits of rehabilitation should not be ignored. For many patients rehabilitation represents the only hope for an acceptable quality of life.

In cases of severe head injury, the aims of rehabilitation may be outlined as follows: In the early stages of recovery, the functional status of the patient should be preserved and attention should be given to avoiding complications following coma and lengthy emergency care. Later, when the patient has reached a sufficient level of arousal, motor and cognitive abilities should be addressed while trying to restore the patient's psychological identity. Finally, social and vocational adjustment should be optimized.

The successful completion of such goals raises a number of difficulties. Theoretically, in order to provide adequate assessment and remediation, we must know the nature and extent of the traumatic brain lesions and have specific hypotheses about the way cerebral functions are reorganized after the insult. Practically, successful rehabilitation procedures can be achieved only if they are included in an extensive therapeutic framework, in which all pathological events and loss of adaptability are taken into account. Thus, first aid and emergency care, neurosurgical procedures, rehabilitation of motor and cognitive functioning, reorganization of the patient's self-image, and late social adjustments should all be closely linked in order to optimize the efficacy of the rehabilitation program.

Neuropsychological impairment is the most important sequelae after severe head injury. Despite the fact that rehabilitation has been carried out since World War II, much more has been written on the clinical features and assessment strategies than on the practical management of head injury. This tendency reflects, in our opinion, the historical consequence of the fact that a notably large number of war wounds had to be treated before strong theoretical and methodological support was available. In spite of the pioneering work of Luria, Teuber, Weisenburg, and McBride, and others, rehabilitation techniques have been, until recent years, a set of insufficiently organized empirical procedures. In addition, there remains a lack of objective evidence for the efficacy of rehabilitation. Standard neuropsychological batteries were not designed specifically for the assessment of head injury patients, and the highly sensitive and widely used Glasgow Coma Outcome Scale (Jennett & Bond, 1975) lacks specificity in that it provides only a rough categorization of outcome. Substantial progress in assessment was achieved with the development of scales designed especially for this population, such as Levin's simple and valid Neuro-Behavioral Rating Scale (Levin et al., 1987). The progress of therapeutic intervention depends on the development of objective assessment methods.

Our Neurological Rehabilitation Unit is located in the Academic Hospital of Bordeaux (France) and has been receiving head injury patients for the past 15 years. Every year, about 40 patients with severe injuries are admitted at the stage of arousal from coma. These patients are provided with neuromotor and neuropsychological therapy and are followed up after discharge for long-term outcome assessment and assistance with social readjustment. We believe that the patient will benefit from having the same team of therapists working with him throughout the course of rehabilitation, given the unique problems engendered by head injury. The next section deals with practical management of the successive stages of cognitive rehabilitation primarily in adults.

CAN AROUSAL FROM TRAUMATIC COMA BE IMPROVED?

The Impact of Comforting Nursing During Coma

As a general rule, emergency care is delivered for patients in acute phases, whereas rehabilitation is given subsequently in subacute phases. However, when considering head injury patients, rehabilitative prevention care must be undertaken in the emergency context of coma, that is, in the absence of a functional prognosis and without even knowing if a patient will survive. Moreover, the affective dimension of procedures such as nursing, orthopedic, and respiratory care should not be underestimated because, although consciousness is suppressed by deep coma, relations between sensorial information and vegetative functions probably remain. Thus, the comatose patient may "feel" something from his surroundings and, possibly, nontraumatic arousal should be prepared as early as the stage of coma.

In our practice, we frequently observe vegetative reactions such as sweating, variations in pupil size or cardiac and respiratory rhythms, which are not simply related to brain-stem automatisms, but rather, are a consequence of the presence of family members or of empathetic nursing care. Perhaps affective components of the human voice are perceived by comatose patients. Let us relate a personal observation (Barat & Mazaux, 1986). A 6-year-old child suffering an apallic state had great spontaneous variations of cardiac rhythm on 24 hour Holter registration. Periodically the child was presented via headphones with a 10 minute tape-recorded message from his mother. Interestingly, the cardiac rhythm became slower and more regular only when these affective messages were delivered. Prosody of the mother's voice, and not verbal content, seemed to be the factor involved as the same message recorded by a neutral voice (nurse) had no effect on the child's cardiac rhythm. Though more research is needed on this topic, it appears that comatose patients may be able to perceive the affective components of the human voice, but sensitive nursing is therefore helpful in preparing a favorable arousal from coma.

During the emergence from coma, the patient's arousal in the emergency ward is usually a tremendously hallucinatory moment that resembles a transient dissociative psychosis accompanied by major anxiety. Reasoning and perception of the patient's self and surroundings are impaired by a global failure of cognitive processing. In closed-head injury, this failure is related to the diffuse character of traumatic brain lesions. Compressive disturbances of mesodiencephalic reticular systems and projections, diffuse torsional lesions of hemispheric white matter, and diffuse superficial cortical contusions are of major importance in the failure of such functions as memory, attention, analysis and synthesis. Because both exteroceptive and interoceptive information are no longer processed, adjustment strategies in response to the changes of the external world are no longer possible. Memory disorders deprive the patient of the awareness of time and chronology. The patient's attention span is also greatly reduced. When focal lesions are present, as in penetrating head injuries, these general disorders are supplemented by focal syndromes that involve language, organization of gesture, and perception. Motor behaviors are sparse, economical, and oriented toward satisfaction of archaïc compulsions; they do not allow for effective control of the patient's surroundings. Especially frequent are behavioral consequences related to frontal and temporal lobe lesions, which are involved to a great extent in the course of the brain's linear accelerations and translations. For example, some patients suffering from frontotemporal lobe syndromes also experience states resembling a Korsakoff psychosis or Klüver and Bucy's syndrome.

Strategies upon Arousal

Relatively few investigations have focused on trying to improve or accelerate the arousal process. Very few controlled studies have provided evidence for the efficacy of treatments involving dextroamphetamines, dopamine, acetylcholine, or antidepressant tricyclic agents. Stern (1978), however, obtained promising results in a sample of 11 patients treated with dextroamphetamines. Based on the theoretical evidence of the noradrenergic and dopaminergic mediation in active reticular systems (Jouvet & Pujol, 1972; Plum & Posner, 1983; Schott et al., 1972) 500 to 1,000 mg of levodopa with benserazide are still being administered by our unit at the early stages of arousal. However, as the patient's reactions to neurochemical intervention are heterogeneous, generalization of these results is difficult. Nevertheless, a neurochemical approach to arousal remains a hopeful direction for future research.

Similar methodological obstacles are present when rehabilitation procedures upon arousal are considered. In our rehabilitation unit patients are admitted once tracheotomy and respiratory assistance are terminated. Subsequently, the rehabilitation team gets valuable medical information on the newly admitted patient from family members. For instance, the social worker focuses mainly on information about the family structure and on the patient's previous social support and social networks; the nurses record the patient's first behavioral reactions, while the neurologists develop an adequate rehabilitation program. Major aims of the program are to improve the patient's perception of his own body and surroundings, as well as to create optimal conditions for recovery of motor and neuropsychological functions. Of course, specific cognitive remediation is not possible at this stage. There is, however, the possibility that positive sensory stimulation in peaceful, secure, and comforting surroundings are helpful in optimizing the conditions for the patient's arousal. Neuromotor therapy is then undertaken with global moving exercises and Bobath's procedure (Barat & Mazaux, 1986).

In order to allow for a confused and agitated patient to move freely without any risk of falling, the bed is substituted by two mattresses placed on the floor side by side. Some of the patient's personal belongings (photographs, radio) are also placed in the bedroom. Walls (and in some units such as Nantes' Hospital, even the ceiling) are brightly decorated, as neutral colors of hospital walls do not stimulate the patient's senses (Mathè, 1987). Venous catheters and bladder probes are removed precociously; feeding probes are also removed early, as a meal provides a good circadian synchronizer and also a good opportunity for the staff to "mother" the patients. The nursing care thus provides comforting tactile and proprioceptive stimuli. Similarly, bathing and washing enhances the patient's well-being and improves body-schema reconstruction. Auditory and visual stimulation are provided by periodic contact with radio and television, and occupational therapists provide for other sensory stimulation. Such stimulation is organized hierarchically; stimuli range from light flashes and brightly colored shapes, to motionless and moving targets where the patient is invited to either look at or follow the target with his or her eyes. Meals, bathing, grooming, therapy sessions, family visits, and leisure time are alternated regularly in order to improve the patient's notion of time and circadian rhythms.

Family plays a major role in the patient's arousal. The team first meets with family members upon admission and then weekly. The goal of these meetings is to explain in detail the major objectives and various phases of rehabilitation and to keep family members informed regarding the patient's well-being and progress. Family members are often disconcerted by the team's patience and reserve regarding the patient's state. They saw the coma as a potentially lethal experience for the patient and believed that immediate and complete recovery would follow upon arousal. Short but regular visits are advised, and as several authors suggest some relatives (usually mothers) can also help with the nursing care (Brooks, 1984; Najenson, Grosswasser, Mendelson, & Hacken, 1980; Romano, 1974; Stern, 1978). Discussions with the psychologist help family members to cope more adequately with the traumatic experience.

Much effort and devotion are required from the therapists, especially nurses, to provide supportive arousal procedures to patients. Because arousal stimulation and nurturing can be carried out only by highly motivated staff, no more than six or eight patients are managed simultaneously. The patient's rehabilitation program is revised weekly in staff meetings; the nurses' feelings and opinions about a particular case still provide the best assessment for modifying a rehabilitation program (an objective test is not yet available). Tremendous efforts are required on the staff's part in extremely severe states such as Cairns' akinetic mutism, Gerstenbrand's apallic state, or more rarely, Plum and Posner's locked-in syndrome. In such states, in order to establish a valuable prognosis, procedures such as polygraphy, evoked potentials and magnetic resonance imaging are undertaken. Of course, the possibility always remains that the severity of the cerebral lesions will prevent the patient from improving—the only possible evolution being a persistent vegetative state. In the case of misdiagnosis of the severity of the lesions, considerable time and effort on the part of therapists and nurses is lost, resulting in a decrease in the team's motivation.

Although rehabilitation procedures are now carried out in most specialized units, objective evidence of the efficiency of such procedures is unfortunately lacking. Data derived from sensory stimulation experiments in animals suggest that recovery of visual and motor functions is greatly improved in animals living in groups and in surroundings that provide rich sensory stimulation (Chow, & Stewart, 1972; Rosenzweig, 1980; Will, Rosenzweig, Bennett, Hebert, & Morimoto, 1977). Research on human sensory deprivation experiments provides similar conclusions. Clinical reports of patients suffering from anxious delirium with persecution ideation in cardiac intensive care units suggest the phase of emergence from coma in head-injury patients.

Daily clinical observations in specialized units indicate that rehabilitation techniques coupled with enhanced extraneous stimulation provides considerable benefits over a natural course of recovery. However, because of the scarcity of experimental evidence on this topic, one can merely suggest that such conditions are optimal for recovery.

NEUROPSYCHOLOGICAL MANAGEMENT IN THE ACTIVE PHASE OF REHABILITATION

After complete arousal, the patient progressively enters into a more active phase of rehabilitation. The patient is now emotionally and physically stronger and can cope more adequately with efforts and frustration. The patient also becomes more aware of the necessity for and beneficial aspects of therapeutic intervention. Neuromotor and neuropsychological management can then actively begin; up to this phase, the focus of rehabilitation had been on general environmental stimulation and on the nurses' supportive and comforting intervention. Throughout the second and more active phase of the rehabilitation program, technical remediation therapy will be provided by specialized therapists.

Neuropsychological management is the most important aspect of rehabilitation after severe head injury. The development of a neuropsychological remediation program requires strong theoretical bases regarding the pathological phenomenon considered, as well as adequate assessment techniques. It is then of critical importance to keep in mind the uniqueness of head injury in establishing a rehabilitation management program.

First, the uniqueness of head injury can be illustrated from an anatomical and pathophysiological point of view. Penetrating missile wounds and some closed-head injuries involving mainly focal contusions or hematomas induce well-defined neuropsychological syndromes that are similar in evolution to stroke pathology. However, in comparison to strokes, closed-head injuries result in quite diffuse lesions involving nearly every aspect of the cerebral structures associated with cognition and higher symbolic activities. Several disorders of language, memory, and attention can be distinguished on the basis of neuropsychological assessment, but the development of remediation exercises must always take into account the intricacy of the disorders. The connections between these disorders increase the difficulty of a precise diagnosis.

Because recovery from traumatic brain damage represents a specific process, comparisons cannot be made with diffuse cortical lesions that appear in dementia. However, even if the underlying processes involved in cerebral restoration and reorganization still remain largely unknown, careful observation of long-term social and vocational therapies provide evidence for the improvement of neuropsychological functioning, (Katz, Galatzer, & Kravetz, 1978). Therefore, the diffuse nature of the anatomical lesion stemming from a traumatic brain lesion and the large capacity for recovery of functions both result in a neuropsychological syndrome considerably distinct from syndromes that are the consequence of cerebral lesions involved in strokes or dementia.

Reconstruction of the head injury patient's personality is another major element to consider in rehabilitation. The uniqueness of head injury is again apparent because it is one of the most highly emotional traumas. The unpredictability and sudden onset of head injury, as well as the loss of consciousness are described by some patients as a symbolic experience of death. In addition, because the head represents the body's most affectively invested part, the injury often leads to self-deprecation and low self-esteem. The patient's personality, especially the self, seems deeply affected by the traumatic experience of head injury. (Barat & Mazaux, 1986; Cohadon, 1975; Cronholm, 1972; DeAngelis & Morosini, 1983; Stern, 1978).

During the active phase of rehabilitation, important psychological changes are manifested. A new, posttraumatic personality emerges with a tentative reorganization of the self. Regressive childlike behaviors, transient lack of motivation, and sudden changes in cognitive and affective states are all present during this phase of active therapeutic intervention.

Extensive neuropsychological assessment is performed in order to develop an adequate rehabilitation program. The aims of assessment are to evaluate the patient's disorders and to provide a baseline for therapeutic intervention. Neuropsychological testing provides objective data on stages of the patient's evolution and also, hopefully, distinguishes spontaneous recovery from therapeutic effectiveness. Most frequent impairments after head injury involve such lateralized hemispheric functions as language, gestural skills, neurological aspects involved in vision, body and space perception, and general cognitive processing such as memory, attention, intellectual activity, and frontal-lobe strategies. Because projective tests or batteries such as the MMPI focus on personality characteristics as a whole, short sessions with a psychologist appear a more appropriate assessment strategy in obtaining daily information on personality changes and behavior disorders.

Rehabilitation programs must be very precise with respect to the exact strategies to be used, the length of the program, and the expected results. Rehabilitation programs differ depending on the adopted school of thought. For instance in structured group therapy (Gerstenbrand, 1969), the major goal is for the group to reach given levels of neuropsychological processing, each level differing in complexity. Other programs, such as the Israeli School, focus on computer-assisted cognitive therapy, individual psychotherapy, and early vocational oriented therapy (Najenson et al., 1974; Raahmani, Stern, Geva, & Eytran, 1983). Structured behavior therapy is also used for rehabilitation (Evans, 1981; Wood, 1984) but in our opinion one of the best models for approaching the uniqueness of head injury is derived from "homegrown" programs based on workshops set in the hospital itself (Rosenbaum, Lipsitz, Abraham, & Najenson, 1978).

The general consensus among authors is that for such a fast changing pathology as head injury, a rigid and inflexible program would invariably lead to failure. Programs must then be dynamic, adaptable, and modified upon assessment of the patient's evolution.

The cognitive rehabilitation program in Bordeaux classically links speech therapy, occupational therapy, and short therapeutic sessions with the psychologist who supervises the team. Computer-assisted therapy is also used for spatial, memory, and attention impairments. Unfortunately, our structure does not at present allow for early vocational therapy; this remains a future objective.

Targeted therapeutic intervention might be undertaken when the patient presents a few focal symptoms involving relatively minor cognitive impairment and behavioral disorders. On the other hand, a more general and adaptive therapeutic program is required for patients suffering from a global posttraumatic encephalopathy that involves several neuropsychological and behavioral dysfunctions. All of the assessments are carried out at the hospital. Social workers assist the patient in preparing future social adjustment, and private speech therapists are available after discharge for individual speech and cognitive therapy.

Specific Rehabilitation Strategies

Management of language, memory, and attention disorders as well as computer-assisted therapy are discussed extensively in other chapters of this book (see chaps. by Kotten, Wilson, Mirsky, and Katz). Previous results of our team's neuropsychological remediation programs in head injury patients have been reported elsewhere (Arné, Barat, Giroire, & Lafoy, 1975; Arné, Barat, Mazaux, & Giroire, 1982; Arné, Dartigues, Barat, & Giroire, 1980; Mazaux & Arné, 1978; Mazaux, Barat, Giroire, & Arné, 1982; Mazaux, Barat, Giroire, LeBivic, & Arné, 1982).

Because general cognitive impairment creates the greatest difficulties in a rehabilitation program, an example of specific strategies used in such a case is discussed further. Cognitive strategies such as novel problem-solving abilities, concept formation, and adaptive abilities in general all depend on the brain's integrity and adequate functioning. Cognitive impairment is of special importance in head injury, yet has received considerably less attention than motor, memory, and language deficits (Finlayson, Alfano, & Sullivan, 1987).

Our rehabilitation management program has been inspired by the work of Luria and Tsevetkova (1967) and Derouesné, Séron, and Lhermitte (1975). In the case of damage to frontobasal areas, disinhibition and impulsiveness prevail. Frontal-lobe disorders also deprive the patient of careful planning and accurate decision making (Perecman, 1987). The major goal of therapy in such cases is to have the patient carefully analyze a problem and also refrain from impulsive and thoughtless answers. Exercises are designed that require a patient to examine and then divide a problem into its basic elements (even in writing), resulting in a proposed problem-solving strategy. The proposed plan is then applied to the problem in order to verify that the expected goal has been reached.

Other frontal-lobe syndromes are characterized by apathy, a decrease in motivation and in the dynamics of mental processing. Accordingly, the therapist chooses specific exercises that in the initial stages, will provide external stimulation designed to develop a sequence in reasoning and refrain from poor stereotyped strategies. Progressively, throughout the program, external stimulation is reduced. Finally, once the patient's problem-solving abilities have improved, the generalization of training tasks to concrete activities is assessed with the therapist adapting the program to daily living activities such as cooking, simulations of shopping, cards, puzzles, and videogames.

A series of exercises devoted to cognitive impairment of such functions as categorization, judgment, and classification is also provided by occupational therapists. For instance, certain items must be selected and classified according to a given criteria. Following this procedure, patients have to organize the material based on a logical rule of progression or rehearsal. Finally, patients have to find errors in a set of pictures and then match the pictures correctly. Computer programs assist the occupational therapist throughout the rehabilitation process.

An objective assessment of such cognitive remediation strategies has been provided in a study by Raahmani et al., (1983) in which they compared untreated controls with 37 patients in an information-processing rehabilitation program. The following tasks were included in the program: classifying items on the basis of given criteria, selecting concepts from concrete to abstract, solving problems involving an increasing number of items to memorize, and finally solving problems using either analogic, inductive, or syllogistic strategies. Results showed that patients included in the rehabilitation program, as compared to controls, improved in concentration, mental flexibility, and awareness of situations and events. The time elapsed since the trauma (1 year) suggests that changes in the patient's condition were not a mere consequence of spontaneous recovery, but rather resulted from the therapeutic intervention. Finlayson et al. (1987) related another example of the beneficial effects of rehabilitation in a single-case study of a woman who received a 12-week program based on Reitan's rehabilitation principles consisting of four microcomputer exercises focusing mainly on logical analysis and visuospatial manipulatory skills. Such well-designed studies represent a major interest in providing credibility for cognitive remediation strategies in head injury.

Posttraumatic Global Encephalopathy

Some severe head-injury patients who emerge from a coma of long duration or from apallic states suffer from long-term failure of neuropsychological functions. The resulting disorders are so intricate and are often characterized by such regressive behaviors and inability to relate to immediate social environment that one can only rely on global behavioral assessment scales (Levin et al., 1987). In many cases, the patient's clinical profile will resemble a dementia, which unfortunately, will not be reversible in some patients.

The management of patients who have suffered such a traumatic insult remains very difficult. General cognition and self-identity can be restored in part by providing the patient with a secure therapeutic environment (see case reports in Mazaux et al., 1982). Later, nurses, occupational therapists, and psychologists focus on providing carefully adapted activities tailored to the patient's attentional capacities and motivation. Based on the patient's tolerance for the program, the team will begin to concentrate on improving socially adapted behaviors. To our knowledge, no truly satisfying rehabilitation program exists for head injury patients who suffer severe and enduring intellectual impairments and gross behavioral disorders.

COGNITIVE BEHAVIORAL DISORDERS AND LATE SOCIAL ADJUSTMENT

Studies of long-term outcome of severe head-injury patients demonstrate that these patients suffer more from social isolation than from dependence or motor disabilities. In 1984, our rehabilitation unit studied the outcome of 100 patients divided on the basis of severity of trauma. Half of the patients had suffered from severe head injury (initial Glasgow Coma Scale under 8, coma over 10 days and posttraumatic amnesia over 1 month in 53 patients), and the remaining half had suffered from mild or moderate head injury (Haramburu et al., 1984). Of the total sample, results of 82 subjects were analyzed. Of this sample 90% of the patients were considered independent in performing daily activities and 88% were living at home 1 year after the trauma. However, of the total sample, only 65% had a complete social adjustment; 34% still suffered from persistent memory and/or intellectual impairments, whereas 30% had language or speech disorders. Almost all patients were described by others as having "changed;" they were no longer "the same person." Similar results have been reported in previous studies (Bond, 1979; Brooks, 1984; Brooks & Aughton, 1979; Crahay, 1975; Jennett & Teasdale, 1981; Lezak, 1979; Lundholm, Jepsen, & Thornval, 1975; McKinlay, Brooks, Bond, Martinage, & Marshall, 1981; Oddy & Humphrey, 1980; Panting & Merry, 1972). So the remaining cognitive impairments and personality changes seem to be the major cause of the social difficulties experienced and, as such, represent the main problem to consider when dealing with the social adjustment of head-injured patients. Of foremost importance in the design of a specific rehabilitation plan is the psychoorganic dimension of head injury itself. A realistic outcome of such a plan cannot be undertaken without an extensive assessment of cognitive and behavioral impairment, adequate knowledge of previous familial and social conditions, and good understanding of working and economic realities.

Cognitive and behavioral disorders are to be the first ones considered when the patient leaves the hospital setting for home. When the sequelae are minor, all goes well: The patient, the family and the rehabilitation team agree on an early discharge from the rehabilitation center or the hospital. The decision is more difficult when severe disorders remain and when the family is still hoping for substantial improvement once the patient goes home. This situation will often lead to a decision for further hospital management. The patient's own reactions are often unpredictable: Some patients, aware of their states, will accept long-term out-patient care or speech therapy. However, most patients remain anosognostic, with intellectual impairment and frontal-lobe syndrome depriving them of a realistic view of their condition and prognosis. Most often these patients will imagine that their condition will improve once they return home, or that they will be able to return to their previous occupation without any difficulty. Still other patients remain unsure of their condition and do not make any plans for their future. Memory and learning disorders are often alleged because of an inability to accept new ways of working. Because these cognitive disorders are in fact frontal-lobe disorders of planning and self-anticipation (Perecman, 1987), the patients have a tendency to let the medical team and relatives make all the important decisions. In cases of such severe cognitive impairment, a special rehabilitation program is designed very early and followed step by step. The patient will first be allowed to leave the hospital setting for a few days in order to allow for a progressive reorganization of family and social life. Later, the patient will be discharged and followed up daily through the services of a day hospital. Throughout this stage, the psychologist gets detailed information on the patient's adjustment at home and discusses the benefits of the program in order to prepare the patient for eventual discharge.

Family Life

Following the trauma, in cases of severe head injury, the quality of family life is deeply altered (Brooks, 1984; Lezak, 1978; Thomsen, 1974). Panting and Merry (1972) reported that in 50% of cases, family members use anxiolytic drugs. Family members complain that the patient needs daily care, that because of him/her vacations and trips are reduced, and that the patient is a financial burden. But the family's main complaint is related to the patient's memory disorders and behavioral changes, which characterize posttraumatic personality changes. The patient is described as "very slow, unable to make appropriate decisions, even in babysitting or domestic chores." Affect is also altered. Some patients become irascible, others display a blunt affect, not showing any interest in relatives, children, or previously enjoyed hobbies.

Such difficulties faced by family members provide evidence for a need to broaden the scope of rehabilitation to include family life. During the final phase of rehabilitation, occupational therapists and psychologists try to prepare the patient's return to active social life through collective activities of groups of three to four patients and group therapy. Collective activities consist of music therapy, body expression, pantomime and puppet shows. Rosenbaum et al. (1978) reported extensive programs of sociotherapy in the rehabilitation hospital itself, in which difficulties with which the patient will have to cope in the future are simulated. Romano (1974) further proposed that parents and relatives should join the patient in group therapy. Later, weekend home leaves appear a good preparation for the eventual return to family life.

Another way to help the families is to provide explicit and detailed information about the patient's cognitive and behavioral changes. However, because most relatives are concerned mainly with prognosis, which we cannot provide initially, they have a tendency to complain of a lack of medical information about their relatives' case. Romano (1974) has emphasized that such claims are characteristic of family members with elevated levels of anxiety as well as those who deny the patient's illness. Nevertheless, the same team of therapists meets weekly with family members to inform them about the patient's various psychological changes.

After discharge, an average follow-up of 2 to 3 years is proposed with periodic assessments of cognitive and motor impairments. The rehabilitation team still meets with the family to discuss changes in the patient's condition. If the patient improves gradually, favorable progress is reported; if, on the other hand, the patient's condition is not improving, we help the family cope with this unfortunate reality. Our role is to listen to the disappointments and to reiterate the fact that the family provides psychological support for the patient, and can play an important role in future behavioral improvement.

Constant support from medical teams and family associations undoubtedly represents major advances of the past years in focusing on improving family life of head-injured patients (see chapter 14).

Somewhat less attention has been given in the head-injury literature to sexual problems related to posttraumatic head injury. In some cases hormonal and neuroradiological studies are necessary in the face of persistent unexplained frigidity or impotence. Also, one should consider providing patients with the opportunity to discuss possible sexual difficulties during the rehabilitation program. In our program, when there are persistent sexual problems, counseling or therapeutic intervention with a psychiatrist is undertaken (for a detailed review, see Barat & Mazaux, 1986).

Social Life

Head-injury patients also suffer from social isolation. Friends and acquaintances are no longer available (Brooks, 1984; Lezak, 1978; McKinlay et al., 1971; Oddy & Humphrey, 1980). Often young patients lead a lonely life living with their parents, parent's friends, or with elderly people. In some cases, patients ask for readmission to a medical center or for extension of physical or speech therapy programs. These behaviors are in fact motivated by social isolation and a need for more meaningful relationships with other human beings.

Visits to restaurants and theaters as well as travel, in general, are greatly reduced, whereas solitary leisure activities, such as reading and watching television, are common. Establishments providing nonmedical recreational activities are seriously lacking in France. Several authors have reported that in about 30% of severe head-injury patients who can no longer work, an adequate structure providing outside occupational activities adapted to their cognitive impairment would have been beneficial (Katz et al., 1978; Najenson et al., 1980; Oddy & Humphrey, 1980). Relatively few specialized units exist at present, and the existing ones have psychiatric patients or elderly people as clients. So, again, the neuropsychological uniqueness of head-injury patients is not taken into consideration. Undoubtedly, family associations will eventually play a major role in establishing such specialized structures.

Because most head-injury patients are young adults, the majority were engaged in sports before their trauma. Sports provide precious physical, psychological, and social benefits to cognitively impaired patients by helping them cope more adequately with their new life, personality, and relationships. Of course, patients with severe ataxia, tremor, or hemianopia will not be able to engage in sports, but often a cognitive impairment does not prevent motivated patients from benefiting from practice. Some sports will improve neuromotor rhythm disorders and slowness, and will also improve attention, visuospatial, and judgment abilities. Sports may also enhance verbal communication in some aphasic patients. Therapy using horseback riding has been shown to provide postural-proprioceptive therapy as well as improvement of rhythm, social behaviors, and self-confidence (Mazaux and Larat, 1988). However, to date, an objective assessment of the beneficial effects of sports therapy remains difficult.

Driving ability must also be considered with respect to cognitive impairment. Posttraumatic seizures remain the central problem, but this issue is beyond the scope of this chapter (Steinwall, 1972, provided a pragmatic review of the issue). The patient's attention must be drawn toward the existing danger of slight or transient disorders such as spatial agnosia or increased reaction time. Slight impairments in the peripheral visual field of which the patients are unaware similarly increase the risk of accidents (Johnson & Keltner, 1983). When the decision about allowing a patient to drive remains difficult, Baten's (1982) standardized questionnaire and clinical assessment for cognitively impaired hemiplegic patients has proved useful. The assessment is completed with a driving test on private hospital grounds and, if satisfactory, in city streets. All abilities needed for driving are thereby systematically evaluated.

Return to Work

Return to work generally provides a good indication of adjustment in disabled persons. Note, however, that in several cases, patients will prefer to remain inactive instead of having to face a difficult or dull job. This is an important bias to consider when devising a rehabilitation plan.

Our rehabilitation unit has performed a study where the sample consisted of 70 patients between 17 and 64 years of age (Barat & Mazaux, 1986) forty-two patients had been working at the time of the trauma, and of these, 25 (63%) returned to work within a year. In addition, 13 out of 24 undergraduate university students found jobs, 4 returned to school, whereas 7 failed at vocational adjustment. Four housewives returned home after the trauma. Global rates of adjustment reached 62%. Similar data were found in the literature where 50% to 65% of severe head-injury patients are reported to return to work (Cohadon & Richer, 1983; Humphrey & Oddy, 1980; Najenson et al., 1980; Oddy & Humphrey, 1980) and 30% to 40% of patients are reported to return to their previous jobs, whereas 15% to 35% work at a lower level or find part-time jobs.

Cognitive impairment plays an important role in vocational adjustment. In our study, return to work was correlated with young age, mild severity, and short duration of coma, and less significantly with disorders of memory assessed by Rey's "Profil de Rendement Mnésique." The incidence of memory disorders has been broadly investigated (Brooks, 1984; Levin, Benton, & Grossman, 1982; Lezak, 1979; Oddy & Humphrey, 1980). However, the intellectual impairment is more difficult to assess, and data on pretraumatic intellectual performance are not readily available. Dresser et al. (1973) had the opportunity to examine head-injury veterans from the Korean war who had been tested upon entry in the army. They found that the patients with the highest intelligence quotient (IQ) had the best vocational situations, supposedly because they had good mental flexibility and the ability to face new situations.

The incidence of communication and aphasic disorders may also be outlined especially in jobs involving public contacts (Arné et al., 1975; Levin et al., 1982). In our rehabilitation unit, we observed in 1978 that 17 out of 33 patients suffering from a posttraumatic aphasia adjusted poorly, despite the generally admitted good prognosis of this syndrome (Mazaux & Arné, 1978). Thus, even when the goal is a return to work, patients with language disorders need long-term speech therapy.

Practical Organization

As a general rule, the rehabilitation plan designed especially for head-injury patients who wish to return to work is divided into three different phases: First, an assessment is made of the neuropsychological sequelae and their consequences on the patient's ability to work; of course, local unemployment rates as well as other economic realities are taken into account when establishing the plan. Later, the most effective procedures for optimizing the patient's medico-social environment are identified and implemented. Finally, the patient actually returns to work.

Assessments evaluate such neurological sequelae as hemiparesis and epilepsy, or neuropsychological disorders and their functional consequences for locomotion, grasping, communication, decision-making abilities, and appropriate judgment. Social workers collect data on previous training, jobs, and the patient's financial situation. Physicians from occupational medicine and psychologists are involved in the assessment of the characteristics and aptitudes required in the patient's previous job, and in case of an inability to pursue such employment, the patient is guided in a new direction. Some rehabilitation teams suggest a vocational probationary period ranging from 1 to 3 months in workshops managed by teachers and occupational therapists. Unfortunately, in Bordeaux this procedure cannot be followed systematically, but help for vocational guidance decisions is requested.

Once the assessments are over, the team is faced with a variety of situations. In some cases, pretraumatic social and vocational conditions were good, the patient's neurological sequelae are only minor and do not interfere with previous work, and the patient is highly motivated to work. In such cases, the role of the rehabilitation team is minimal where the only issues discussed are the delay required before the patient can return to work and where suggestions are made on how reintegration in the work structure can be facilitated.

In other cases, the neurological sequelae and their functional consequences are so severe that a patient is obviously unable to return to work. Similarly, a patient's return to a work structure can seem extremely unlikely in light of an unfavorable social and economic context.

A final and more important case to consider arises when neurological assessments show that a patient can carry out some work but that adjustment failures are highly probable if the team does not provide long-term rehabilitation support. In such a case, assessment of general aptitudes, cognitive abilities, and the determination of the patient's underlying motivations in returning to work are all important aspects to consider in devising the rehabilitation program.

Such assessment procedures vary considerably from one country to another, and also, from one hospital administration to another. In some centers, part of occupational therapy is devoted to vocational workshops, whereas in other centers the patient must be transferred to a special vocational guidance center (a process that is, however, very lengthy). Returning to work on a part-time basis for a trial period of 3 to 6 months is often suggested to patients. This strategy is followed in order to prevent the patient's hopelessness in the face of work-related difficulties.

When return to previous work is unrealistic, based on initial assessment, the patient must be guided in a new direction. In the case of patients suffering from sequelae of frontal-lobe disorders, work reorientation is extremely difficult. Patients with minor neuropsychological problems are often admitted to a vocational guidance center to learn new skills. However, the patient's diminished attention and concentration capacities and memory and language disorders may be directly linked to failure in learning a new skill. The development of vocational centers designed specifically for head-injury patients probably represents the most successful alternative in attempting social and economic reintegration of these patients.

Unemployment remains frequent, however, in patients with severe head injury. Najenson observed that two thirds of his patients were either not working at the performance level expected, or were not working at all. However, an attractive alternative to unemployment for patients who are too severely impaired to work in normal conditions is the sheltered workshop. Katz et al. (1978) compared the psychological and social outcome of 13 patients working in a sheltered workshop to controls who had a disability pension, but who were inactive. Working conditions were graduated based on the patient's abilities, and patients were paid according to their productivity. Patients could also participate in conducting workshops. Two years later, all patients felt better and families reported substantial behavioral improvements, in spite of the fact that patients were in a financial situation similar to that of controls. Such alternatives seem beneficial when considering reintegration of head-injury patients into society.

CONCLUDING REMARKS

The most important elements to take into consideration in rehabilitation of head-injury patients remain neuropsychological problems and their effect on eventual social reintegration. The uniqueness of head injury stems from the fact that it involves an interaction among anatomical, physiological, psychopathological, and social factors, and its very uniqueness explains why other therapeutic intervention strategies are not applicable to head injury. Rehabilitation should thus focus on programs that are precise and periodically revised by a specialized team of therapists. Moreover the fact that the same rehabilitation team intervenes from the stage of arousal until the patient's reintegration into society allows for a longitudinal evaluation of the patient's neuropsychological functioning, the progressive transformation of posttraumatic personality, and the dynamic aspects of familial relations.

Although previous studies have provided substantial information on the symptomatology of head injury, future efforts should focus on 1) developing assessment batteries and therapeutic strategies that would take into consideration the specificity of the syndrome, and 2) improving social reintegration procedures for head-injury patients presenting severe behavioral disorders and/or neuropsychological functioning impairment.

ACKNOWLEDGMENTS

We are greatly indebted to Dr. J. W. Brown for his comments and suggestions, to D. Castaing for preparing the manuscript, and Dr. E. Perecman for corrections.

REFERENCES

Arné, L., Barat, M., Giroire, J. M., & Lafoy, M. C. (1975). Comportements linguistiques au cours des traumatismes crâniens [Linguistic behavior in traumatic head injury]. *Annales Médecine Physique, 18,* 448–451.

Arné, L., Barat, M., Mazaux, J. M., & Giroire, J. M. (1982). La réadaptation des traumatisés du crâne [Rehabilitation after head injury]. *VIth Congress of the European Federation of Physical Medicine and Rehabilitation, Proceedings* (pp. 83–85). Gent: EFPMR.

Arné, L., Dartigues, J. F., Barat, M., & Giroire, J. M. (1980). Traumatisme crânien grave de l'enfant Rééducation et pronostic [Severe head injury in childhood and adolescence Rehabilitation and Prognosis]. *IRMA 3rd Congress, Proceedings* (P. 464). Basel: IRMA.

Barat, M., Mazaux, J. M., Giroire, J. M., & Signoret, J. L. (1985). La rééducation des amnésies neurologiques: Méthodes et résultats [Memory therapy after brain damage: Methods and results]. *Annales de Réadaptation et Médecine Physique, 27,* 293–306.

Barat, M., & Mazaux, J. M. (1986). *Rééducation et réadaptation des traumatisés crâniens* [Rehabilitation after head injury]. Paris: Masson.

Baten, G. (1982). L'aptitude à la conduite et le patient hémiplégique. [Driving Aptitude and the Hemiplegic Patient]. *VIth Congress of the European Federation of Physical Medicine and Rehabilitation, Proceedings* (pp. 151–153). Gent: EFPMR.

Bond, M. R. (1979). The stages of recovery from severe head injury with special references to late outcome. *International Rehabilitation Medicine, 1,* (4), 155–159.

Brooks, D. N. (1984). *Closed head injury: Psychological, social and family consequences.* Oxford: Oxford University Press.

Brooks, D. N., & Aughton, M. E. (1979). Psychological consequences of blunt head injury. *International Rehabilitation Medicine, 1,* 160–165.

Chow, K. L., Stewart, D. L. (1972). Reversal of structural and functional effects of long term visual deprivation in cats. *Experimental Neurology, 34*, 409–433.

Cohadon, F. (1975). Possibilités et limites de la réadaptation des traumatisés crâniens dans la prévention du syndrome subjectif post-traumatique [Success and limits of a rehabilitative prevention of post concussional syndrome]. *Annales de Médecine Physique, 18*, 369–410.

Cohadon, F., & Richer, E. (1983). Evolution et devenir des comas traumatiques graves. *Neurochirurgie, 29*, 303–325.

Crahay, S. (1975). Suites des traumatismes crâniens sévères: Analyse psycho-pathologique et bilan de la réadaptation [Outcome after severe head injury: Psychopathological study and results of rehabilitation]. *Annales de Médecine Physique, 18*, 3, 361–368.

Cronholm, B. (1972). Evaluation of mental disturbances after head injury. *Scandinavian Journal of Rehabilitation Medicine, 4*(1), 35–38.

De Angelis, R., & Morosini, C. (1983). Aspetti psicodinamici dell'emergence della conscienza [Psychodynamical features of arousal from a coma]. *Associazione Riabilitazione Comatosi, 1° Conveqno* (pp. 187–196). Milano: ARICO.

Derouesne, J., Séron, X., & Lhermitte, F. (1975). Rééducation des patients atteints de lésions frontales [Rehabilitation after frontal lobes damage]. *Revue Neurologique, 131*(10), 677–689.

Dresser, A. C., Meirowsky, A. M., Weiss, G. H., McNeel, M. L., Simon, A. G., & Caveness, W. F. (1973). Gainful employment following head injury. *Archives of Neurology, 29*, 111–116.

Evans, C. D. (1981). *Rehabilitation after severe head injury.* Edinburgh: Churchill Livingstone.

Finlayson, A. J., Alfano, D. P., & Sullivan, J. F. (1987). A neuropsychological approach to cognitive remediation: Microcomputer applications. *Canadian Journal of Psychology, 28*(2), 180–190.

Gerstenbrand, F. (1969). Rehabilitation of the head injury. In A. E. Walker, W. F. Caveness, & M. D. Critchley (Eds.), *The late effects of head injury* (pp. 340–350). Thomas.

Haramburu, P., Dartigues, J. F., Giroire, J. M., Mazaux, J. M., Barat, M., & Arné, L. (1984). Troubles mnésiques, réinsertion sociale et professionnelle chez les traumatisés crânio-encêphaliques graves [Evidence for a role of memory disorders in social and vocational adjustment after severe head injury]. *Annales de Réadaptation et Médecine Physique, 26*, 271–284.

Humphrey, M., & Oddy, M. (1980). Return to work after head injury: A review of post war studies. *Injury, 12*(2), 107–114.

Jennett, B., & Bond, M. (1975). Assessment of outcome after severe brain damage. A practical scale. *Lancet, 1*, 480–484.

Jennett, B., & McMillan, R. (1981). Epidemiology of head injury. *British Medical Journal, 282*, 101–106.

Jennett, B., & Teasdale, G. (Eds.) (1981). Management of head injuries. *Contemporary neurology series.* Philadelphia: F. A. Davis Company.

Johnson, C. A., & Keltner, J. L. (1983). Incidence of visual field pass in 20,000 eyes and its relationship to driving performance. *Archives of Ophtalmology, 101,*(3), 371–375.

Jouvet, M., & Pujol, M. F. (1972). Rôle des monoamines dans la régulation de la vigilance: Étude neurophysiologique et biochimique [Neurophysiological and biochemical studies of monoamines in reticular systems]. *Revue Neurologique, 127*, 115.

Katz, S., Galatzer, A., & Kravetz, S. (1978). The physical, psychosocial and vocational effectiveness of a sheltered workshop for brain damaged war veterans. *Scandinavian Journal of Rehabilitation Medicine, 10*(2), 51–57.

Kraus, J. F., Black, M. A., Hessol, N., Ley, P., Rokaw, W., Sullivan, C., Bowers, S., Knowlton, S., & Marshall, L. (1984). The incidence of acute brain injury. *American Journal of Epidemiology, 119*(2), 186–201.

Levin, H. S., Benton, A. L., & Grossman, R. G. (1982). *Neurobehavioral consequences of closed head injury.* Oxford: Oxford University Press.

Levin, H., High, W., Goethe, K., Sisson, R., Overall, J., Rhoades, H., Eisenberg, H., Kalisky, Z., & Gary H. (1987). The neurobehavioral rating scale: Assessment of the behavioral sequelae of head injury by the clinician. *Journal of Neurology, Neurosurgery and Psychiatry, 50,* 183–193.

Lezak, M. (1978). Living with the characterologically altered brain injured patient. *Journal of Clinical Psychiatry, 39,* 592–598.

Lezak, M. (1979). Recovery of memory and learning functions following traumatic brain damage. *Cortex, 15,* 63–72.

Lundholm, J., Jepsen, B. N., & Thornval, G. (1975). The late neurological, psychological and social aspects of severe traumatic coma. *Scandinavian Journal of Rehabilitation Medicine, 7,* 97–100.

Luria, A. R., & Tsvetkova, L. S. (1967). *Les troubles de la résolution des problèmes [Disturbances of problem-solving strategies].* Paris: Gauthier-Villars.

McKinlay, W. W., Brooks, D. N., Bond, M. R., Martinage, D. P., & Marshall, M. M. (1981). The short term outcome of severe blunt head injury as reported by the relatives of the injured person. *Journal of Neurology, Neurosurgery and Psychiatry, 44,* 527–533.

Mathe, J. F. (1987). Coma chronique, conscience et vigilance [Long-lasting coma, consciousness, and vigilance]. *Workshop of Neuropsychology,* Lyon, France.

Mazaux, J. M. (1985). Approche épidémiologique des traumatismes crâniens [Epidemiology of head injury]. *Journal de Réadaptation Médicale, 5,* 185–189.

Mazaux, J. M., & Arné, L. (1978). Aspects évolutifs et devenir à long terme des aphasies traumatiques. *Revue Réadaptation Fonctionnelle, Professionnelle et Sociale, 3,* 35–39.

Mazaux, J. M., Barat, M., Giroire, J. M., & Arné, L. (1982). Les troubles de la mémoire chez les traumatisés crâniens: Intérêt et limites de la rééducation [Success and failure of memory therapy after severe head injury]. *VIth Congress of the European Federation of Physical Medicine and Rehabilitation, Proceedings* (pp. 115–121). Gent: EFPMR.

Mazaux, J. M., Barat, M., Giroire, J. M., Le Bivic, A., & Arné, L. (1982). Place de la rééducation des troubles des fonctions symboliques dans la prise en charge des traumatisés crâniens graves [Management of neuropsychological impairment after severe head injury]. *Annales de Médecine Physique, 25,* 177–188.

Mazaux, J. M., & Larat, M. (in press). Rééducation par l'equitation et traumatisme cránién. Handisoft.

Najenson, T., Grosswasser, Z., Mendelson, L., & Hacken, P. (1980). Rehabilitation outcome of brain damaged patients after severe head injury. *International Rehabilitation Medicine, 2,* 17–22.

Najenson, T., Mendelson, L., Schechter, I., David, C., Mintz, H., & Grosswasser, Z. (1974). Rehabilitation after severe head injury. *Scandinavian Journal of Rehabilitation Medicine, 6,* 5–14.

Oddy, M., & Humphrey, M. E. (1980). Social recovery during the year following severe head injury. *Journal of Neurology and Psychiatry, 43*(9), 798–802.

Panting, A., & Merry, P. (1972). The long term rehabilitation of severe head injuries with particular reference to the need for social and medical support for the patient's family. *Rehabilitation, 38,* 33–37.

Perecman, E. (Ed.) (1987). *The frontal lobes revisited.* New York: IRBN Press.

Plum, F., & Posner, J. B. (1983). *Diagnostic de la stupeur et des comas.* [Diagnosis of stupor and coma]. (2nd ed.) Paris: Masson.

Raahmani, L., Stern, A., Geva, N., & Eytran, R. (1983). The intellectual rehabilitation of the cranio-cerebral injured patient. *Proceedings of Associazione Riabilitazione Comatosi, 1° Convegno,* (pp. 181–185). Milano: ARICO.

Romano, M. D. (1974). Family response to traumatic head injury. *Scandinavian Journal of Rehabilitation Medicine, 6*(1), 1–4.

Rosenbaum, M., Lipsitz, N., Abraham, J., & Najenson, T. (1978). A description of an intensive treatment project for the rehabilitation of severely brain injured patients. *Scandinavian Journal of Rehabilitation Medicine, 10,* 1–6.

Rosenzweig, M. R. (1980). Animal models for effects of brain lesions and for rehabilitation. In P. Bach-y-Rita (Ed.), *Recovery of function: Theoretical considerations for brain injury rehabilitation* (pp. 127–173). Bern: Hans Huber Publisher.

Schott, B., Michel, D., Mouret, J. R., Renaud, B., Quenin, P., & Tommasi, M. (1972). Monoamines et régulations de la vigilance: Syndromes lésionnels du système nerveux central [Monoamines mediated systems and vigilance processing after brain damage]. *Revue Neurologique, 127,* 157.

Steinwall, O. (1972). Epilepsy and driver's licence. Some comments. *Scandinavian Journal of Rehabilitation Medicine, 4,* 123–125.

Stern, J. M. (1978). Cranio-cerebral injured patients: A psychiatric clinical description. *Scandinavian Journal of Rehabilitation Medicine, 10,* 7–10.

Thomsen, I. V. (1974). The patient with severe head injury and his family: A follow up study of 50 patients. *Scandinavian Journal of Rehabilitation Medicine, 6,* 180–183.

Will, B. E., Rosenzweig, M. R., Bennett, E. L., Hebert, M., & Morimoto, H. (1977). Relatively brief environmental enrichment aids recovery of learning capacity and alters brain measures after post weaning brain lesions in rats. *Journal of Comparative Physiological Psychology, 91,* 33–50.

Wood, R. L. (1984). Behavior disorders following severe brain injury: Their presentation and psychological management. In D. N. Brooks (Ed.), *Closed head injury. Psychological, social and family consequences* (pp. 195–219). Oxford: Oxford University Press.

14

Staying in the Community After a Head Injury

Noemi F. Cohen

Head injury rehabilitation has become a major concern of the professional community because of the high incidence of traumatic brain injury each year. The National Head Injury Foundation and the National Institute of Neurological and Communicative Disorders and Strokes (Frankowski et al. 1985) have reported that since 1975 there have been approximately 700,000 head injuries per year in the United States and that the victims are mainly adolescents and young adults. At present there are in this country at least 7 million head-injured individuals, many of whom are in the prime of their lives.

An increased concern for the welfare of this population has yielded an enormous upsurge in programs and facilities available for treatment (Cope, 1986). Of the 12 classifications of rehabilitation settings at least 5 deal with community reentry. This reflects the ultimate goal of the head-injured person and his family, as well as health care professionals—to return the head-injured person to society.

The problem with head injury rehabilitation, to date, is that it is long and costly (NHIF, 1986) and that its rate of success is unclear. Clinicians, head-injured patients, and above all, families know that even after numerous attempts at rehabilitation, head-injured patients usually remain dependent on their significant others or society to some extent.

Part of the problem is clearly related to the residual impairments of the head injured. Levin, Grossman, Rose, & Teasdale (1979) indicated that neuropsychological and psychiatric deficits are characteristic of severely and moderately impaired head-injured patients. Specific deficits were found in performance IQ, memory, retrieval of names, and behavior even in patients with good recovery. Bond (1976) found that patients who were 2 years post injury demonstrated daily living impairments due primarily to intellectual and personality deficits and, to a lesser extent, to physical incapacity. Lezak (1987) concluded from a long-term study that traumatically brain-injured patients are more handicapped by emotional and personality disturbances than by their residual cognitive and physical disabilities. Out of 39 patients in their third postaccident year, only 18 were working, and only 6 were in school or work situations equivalent to their premorbid level. Furthermore, at 5 years post injury, 12 of those patients appeared to deteriorate, requiring institutionalization either in care facilities or psychiatric hospitals.

Lezak (1987) and Jacobs (1984) have both reported that the great majority of patients do not resume self-fulfilling activities of leisure. Transportation is problematic and work or school related problems are prevalent. The Jacobs study, later known as the Los Angeles Head Injury Survey (Jacobs, 1987) evaluated over 700 discrete daily behaviors. As a whole, patients displayed deficits that were sufficiently significant to require dependence on families for activities of daily living (ADL), social, and economic needs. Similar results were reported by Brooks and Aughton (1979). Long-term sequela have been reported by Thorp (1956, 1983) and Todd and Satz (1980).

It seems that if the head-injured person is to remain a viable member of the community, both the family and society should be given sufficient education and support to cope with the injured person's needs. Conversely, for the injured person there should be channels for outreach to maintain a relatively acceptable quality of life.

The family of the injured person is clearly thrust into a turmoil of intense emotions. Lezak has described the fluctuation of feelings from puzzlement to sadness and hostility over the person's behavior. Rosenbaum and Najenson (1976) indicated that the spouse is especially victimized because of the sudden change in roles. Families go through a peculiar mourning process for the loss of a soul in a body that is still familiar.

Many families feel that the behavior changes in the head-injured person have robbed him or her of the positive human qualities that were respected and admired in his social milieu. They feel that the head-injured person violates their concepts of right and wrong and they are uncertain about how to treat outbursts or exaggerations. Other families complain that their relative demonstrates Jeckle-and-Hyde qualities and that the unpredictable behavior is the most difficult problem with which they must deal. Head injury is often reported to exaggerate premorbid tendencies.

The professional community has advocated family counselling and education (Rollin, 1987) and the National Head Injury Foundation has provided a sophisticated network of support. However, it is clear that many families struggle on a daily basis with catastrophic outbursts, numerous responsibilities, and various untold situations that challenge their creativity and their peace of mind.

It is obvious, therefore, that families alone cannot assume total responsibility for their injured relatives. It is possible, however, that maintaining the injured person in society would become more feasible if the professional community and society at large were to provide assistance on a regular basis.

Unfortunately, society is ill prepared, at present, to serve the disabled and the head-injured person in particular. Carol Sigelman (1983), who has conducted an extensive review of the professional literature on the topic of community integration of disabled people, found that there was a substantial difference between verbal support and actual support by educators and citizens. For example, educators appeared to be supportive of the concept of mainstreaming, but voiced reservations about being able and willing to integrate disabled children into their own classrooms. This study is consistent with Savage and Carter's (1984) report summarizing the work by the Head Injury/Stroke Independence Project, Inc. on the reentry of head-injured children and young adults into their former school systems. It was found "that the majority of teachers never received training specifically about head-injured youngsters."

Community residential living (Sigleman, 1983) for the disabled, even if achieved, does not insure social integration into the mainstream. Moreover, Rehab Brief has reported in its nationwide survey on disabled Americans that "Exclusionary employer attitudes and nonexistent transportation resources continue to bar people with disabilities from working and socializing. . . . The majority of disabled people are still not familiar with the most common service available to them." Many head-injured patients have transportation difficulties as a result of cognitive and perceptual problems (Sivak, Olson, Kewman, Won, & Henson, 1981). Though it may not be immediately apparent, the head-injured population is at least as much in need of transportation services as other disabled groups.

In conclusion, the literature on head injury indicates that head-injured patients demonstrate significant impairments for some time after the injury that dramatically alters the quality of their own lives as well as that of their significant others.

Successful community reentry depends on a number of interrelated factors. Not only is skills retraining necessary but patient, family, and society should have available the resources and mechanisms to help them accept and adjust to the patient's residual problems. This requires a rehabilitation process, which directs its attention to the patient, as well as to the family and society. Though it seems to be a much more complex task, it may be necessary to close those gaps that interfere with successful placement in the community.

The purpose of this chapter is to describe preliminary results of a home- and community-based rehabilitation program designed to encourage patients to remain in society and which attempts to address the needs of the patient, family, and community.

The program's philosophy is based on a number of assumptions:

1. Cognitive skills can be learned more easily if cognitive retraining tasks were more functional (e.g., involved self-care, housekeeping, social situation, etc.)

2. Head injured patients continue to demonstrate a dependence on others due to a number of cognitive deficits:

   a. They do not generalize information learned in one setting to another (Thomas & Trexler, 1982; Strum, Dahmen, Hartje, & Williams, 1983). Thus, upon returning home, a good percentage of the patients would not automatically apply principles learned in a therapy session to tasks in a different environment.

   b. Poor initiative and residual memory problems must be compensated for with individually taylored supports. The failure to complete assignments as a result of these problems may partially account for the frequently noted deterioration of skills following discharge from facilities.

   c. The patient needs assistance in carrying or monitoring elementary activities. For example, unless a patient has someone to manage his finances, he may not have money for basic needs.

3. Dependency may also occur as a result of a patient's poor insight, which interferes with his ability to live up to his own potential. From clinical observations and research, it has often been apparent that patients' poor insight and concrete thinking stand in the way of their progress.

Goldstein (1942) and Tyerman and Humphrey (1984) have reported that the head-injured person denies his or her problems and avoids situations in which deficits would be apparent. Thus, head-injured people usually do not take advantage of their educational settings to gather information as a normal student might. Rather, time is frequently spent disproving the therapist's claim that the patient has a problem. It has also been observed that patients demonstrate greater interest in treatment that involves activities familiar to the patients. It was, therefore, assumed that practical situations relevant to day-to-day life or to one's previous lifestyle would mean much more to the patient and would motivate him or her to learn.

4. Some of the behavior problems of the head-injured originate in the individual's difficulty in handling pressure because of his or her deficits in problem solving and conflict resolution.

Specifically, it appears to be necessary to focus more on the meaning of the acquired injury in the context of the patient's own life. Clinical observations have suggested that head-injured patients are frequently as aware of their age role system (Neugarten, 1970) as noninjured people are. It was noticed that even patients disoriented in time and place may vividly recall their premorbid life. Moreover, even if that past becomes vague, the patients still have a notion of what they should do or should have done with their life. The adolescent struggles with different issues (Carberry, 1985; Goldbert, 1980) than the young man or woman or the older person (Gogstad & Kjellman, 1976), but their frustration, sadness, or anger may be regarded equally intolerable by the community at large.

5. The head-injured person's problems are so complex and unique to each individual, that each care plan must be individually designed.
6. The head-injured person's future in the community depends largely on the family's readiness to live with an injured relative.
7. The family's burden is so extensive because the family has insufficient support from the community, and because its members are torn between their wish to resume a normal lifestyle and their fears that the patient will remain helpless without them. This fear could be further aggravated by the perception that there will be little community support for the head-injured person after members of the family have passed away.

PROGRAM GOALS

The program goals were to:

1. Improve functional ADL, communication, behavioral, social, community, educational, and additional potential by using a functional cognitive retraining approach and applying cognitive training principals directly to the activity.
2. Enhance motivation and interest by providing tasks that the patient would consider relevant and important for him or her to perform.
3. Increase patient's insight by allowing people and experiences having particular relevance for the patient to provide feedback and demonstrate the patient's deficits or strengths.

4. Maximize community interaction to facilitate early identification of resources within the person's own community.

5. Establish a working relation among community, family, patient, and therapists so that family members can live more productively with the injured person and so that therapists and family find working together an enriching experience.

PROGRAM PROCEDURES

The program is staffed by an interdisciplinary team of physicians and therapists. The team has been coordinated by a specialist in the area of head injury.

PROCEDURES

The following treatment policies were adopted:

1. Therapists treat patients in the patients' home, but are also responsible for taking them out into the community for various functions.

2. Therapists provide all cognitive retraining as well as training in the use of a computer. The patients' skills, environment, and family habits are all major considerations in the formulation of the care plan.

3. An individualized care plan is designed that is considered relevant, exciting, and image enhancing for a particular patient. Therapy techniques addressing initiation, organization, problem solving, communication, and social skills are applied to a global project. Writing to a movie star, painting a picture, cooking for two, volunteering at a print shop, setting up a photography exhibit can all be therapeutic, given a sound cognitive and behavioral management approach.

4. The community at large is used as a treatment center. Trips to a nearby mall, bank, library, concert, and so on, by bus or cab are used to teach community survival and management skills.

5. Insight training is provided through projects and formal as well as informal interactions with friends and coworkers.

6. Social skills are trained directly during patient's interactions with families, friends, former colleagues, or neighbors. Although many of the tasks are preplanned, there are opportunities for spontaneous interactions.

7. Social skills within the community are also trained through interactions with shop keepers, supermarket stockpersons, receptionists, bankers, and so forth. Emphasis is placed on establishing a good

rapport with people in places that the patient would have occasion to visit most frequently.

8. On-site training at school, prevocational, or even vocational training is offered to every patient until the network of props and supervisors in the community is in place and functioning.

9. Program goals and procedures are taught to the home health staff to increase consistency and enhance work hours during the patients' periods of good concentration. The program trains companions where necessary.

10. Families are regularly informed of the progress of the care plan and their opinion is always considered. Unless the family agrees to a particular plan, that plan will be abandoned.

11. Follow up of the home and community system extends for as long as needed.

PROGRAM PARTICIPANTS

At first, the program was restricted to individuals who were medically stable and whose behavior was fair. Destructive patients were not considered good candidates. There were no exclusionary criteria for families.

Sixteen head-injured patients and their families have been treated in the program. All the patients already lived in the community when the admission was made. All but one lived with a family member.

Fourteen of the 16 were males. Upon admission three were in their early 50s; one was in his 30s; eight were in their 20s and one was 10 years old. There were only two women, one 17, the other 27. Six patients were within 1 year post trauma, one was 3 months post, four were a year and a half post, and one was 1 year post injury. The others ranged from 2 to 8 years post injury.

Length of coma varied considerably, ranging from 1 week to 7 months. Thirteen had been in previous treatment. Programs ranged from intensive long-term hospitalizations to private therapy over a 4- and 5-year period. Reportedly, patients' reasons for discharge varied from failure to comply with a program to having reached maximum potential. Patients were referred to the program because they were either impossible to live with, too dependent, or too lonely and depressed. It was usually the families that sought out additional help and novel approaches.

To our surprise we have found patients in the community with serious medical, physical, and behavioral difficulties. Thirty-seven percent had serious ambulation problems, four were wheelchair bound, and three needed special assistance in feeding because of dysphagia. Five had consistent incontinence problems, and two were unpredictably incontinent during the night.

Behaviorally, 43% were considered by the family to be severely destructive. Three were actually physically abusive to family members, staff, or their homes. For example, one would bite, the other would run over a person with his wheelchair if his wishes were not met, and another would clog sinks and toilets, pour liquids down the drain, or destroy family pictures.

Fifteen of the patients demonstrated very difficult behavior. Families described their relative as humiliating, embarrassing, intolerant, domineering. One patient would shout if he disliked the family's comments. He would come and go at any time, sleep all day and be up all night. Others were prone to criticizing and shaming their family members in front of strangers. For one patient, this criticism almost cost him his marriage, and another almost lost his job at the family-owned business.

Thirteen of the patients could be considered dependent for major ADL activities. Although some could clearly do some things for themselves, such as cooking a meal, dressing, and washing, they rarely did so without coaxing. Primarily, ADL related difficulties occurred because the head-injured patients did not initiate, organize, or remember specific instructions. Higher-level functioning such as planning activities—researching information, starting, and pursuing them—were found in only three patients.

Fourteen patients were completely dependent on their family for social outlets, for transportation, and any scheduled appointments. Only one person worked but he was so disruptive that he would have probably lost his job had he not been a partner in the business.

Seven families had various degrees of help. Caregivers ranged from companions to RNs, serving usually from 8 to 24 hours a day. Most received 16 hours of assistance a day.

FAMILIES

Two types of families were drawn into this program: those who believed that it was their responsibility to care for their disabled family member at home regardless of the burden and those who lived with the injured party but could not tolerate the difficulties.

The families who decided to stick the problems out, did so regardless of the difficulty they encountered. They either fought to receive assistance or decided to confront the problems on their own. These families wanted decision-making power in every stage of the rehabilitation. In many instances they felt that they were best equipped to handle the patient, based on their past knowledge of him or her.

All of those families also shared the hope that their relative would improve. They were able to use the slightest indication of improvement as a source of energy and motivation to continue their efforts. For some it was the patient's improved physical skill, for others it was speech or the ability to interact more adequately with strangers that made the difference. Above all they shared a major concern for the future of their relative when they themselves pass on. Usually they translated this concern by demanding that their relative improve to maximum potential.

If the families were convinced that a decent dignified living arrangement could be found for their relative, they might have pressed their relative less in the struggle for improvement.

The families who, on the other hand, perceived themselves as unable to carry the burden, were found to generate more conflicts between themselves, their relative, and the therapists. For these family members, it appeared that preservation of emotional, economical, and social life was of primary concern.

It was felt that such family members had difficulty absorbing educational material, following instructions, and acting on suggestions. They were rarely at home and were unavailable for team conferences or informal discussions.

RESULTS

The results of rehabilitation in a community based program must naturally be measured by the duration of the patient's stay in the community and by the quality of life that the patients and significant others believe has been achieved. Of the 16 patients in our program, 2 are working. One is able to work but is not eager to do so because of litigation-related issues, one is offering his services on a volunteer basis independently at a hospital and a library. Another patient is doing volunteer work with minimum assistance from a companion. The child returned to school under special supervision. In terms of patient and family quality of life, 7 patients now interact regularly in various social and entertainment activities in the community. These include participation in bowling and volleyball groups, social programs for the handicapped and nonhandicapped, church activities, visits to movies, concerts, and community shows. Eight are able to help at home in household activities.

One patient with serious swallowing and drooling problems has become a more functional eater, thus opening the road to further interactions in the community. Two patients who were operating at a low cognitive level have not changed dramatically. One patient deteriorated as a result of substance abuse. Contact with the two remaining patients was eventually lost. Behavioral problems for all the preceding patients subsided, although they did not disappear.

CASE HISTORIES

Examples of a Functional Cognitive Approach

The following treatment procedures use a variety of cognitive strategies to improve function.

Case 1: Profound Initiative Problems and Effects on ADL

The patient was capable of performing household duties but sat in his easy chair virtually from morning until night.

Patient's preferences with respect to household responsibilities were analyzed and a list of priorities was established for him and his wife. Patient chose to make the beds and prepare his wife's coffee before she went to work and had no difficulty initiating these activities. However, becoming a househusband negatively affected his self-image. After discussing this with his wife and therapist, he eventually came to believe that vacuuming could be considered chivalrous, as it decreased her work load. Dusting was less accepted, but cooking was fine. A set of home-related activities was constructed, which was acceptable to the patient and his wife. Despite the agreement, patient failed to perform his duties; because of initiation problems, patient forgot to remember his tasks. Consequently, a timer was rigged to a taped message that reminded patient at designated times to get up and perform his house duties. The gadget helped the patient get started. Patient and wife now feel better about each other, and patient feels that he is contributing to the household.

Case 2: Memory and Effects on ADL

In at least three instances, patients had serious difficulties remembering information. When these patients were cooking, for example, they could not remember whether they had placed ingredients in the dish or not. In two of the three cases, it was found that immediate, visual feedback could be helpful. Thus, recipes were rewritten in a clearly organized fashion on an index card. A transparent plastic cover was placed over the index card and a wax pen was supplied. Patients were taught to cross out the ingredients as they were used. This method helped reduce patients' frustrations and raised their esteem in the eyes of their family members.

Case 3: Multiple Processing Difficulties and Effects on Household Business

A young man who had cooked premorbidly and still loved cooking, had to cook for himself. He was unable to make up a menu without significant assistance and was unable to predict his weekly supermarket expenses.

He was taught to cook several different meals. These recipes were organized in a sequence that repeated itself each month. The cost of the groceries was calculated for each recipe so he could predict this expense routinely. Finally he was able to learn the location of necessary items in his nearby supermarket. Although this man is not a comparison shopper or a terribly creative cook, he can now shop and cook for himself. With the assistance of his companion, he is learning to use those strategies more independently.

Case 4: Multiple Processing Problems and Effects on Communication Within the Community

A patient with information-processing, memory, organizational, and hand-coordination problems was unable to obtain information over the phone, especially when it was presented by a tape recorder. This made life difficult when he wanted to obtain a movie or baseball game schedule. It was also problematic during interactions with salesmen or shopowners.

The problem was alleviated when he purchased a small tape recorder and learned to record the messages, then rewind the recording, listen to the message and write it down if necessary. His neighborhood is tolerant of these habits as the patient's needs were curtiously explained to the appropriate personnel.

Case 5: Multiple Processing Skills and Vocation

Multiple-processing difficulties can also be self-evident at a work site. A young woman, age 27, who had been connected with a library on a volunteer basis, was given two sets of books to shelve on two different shelves. Although she started out well, she soon lost track of her purpose and began to shelve all the books on the same shelf.

The patient was removed from the job but was reinstated when her therapist accompanied her to the library to teach her the task. Once the patient mastered each part of the shelving task separately, she was able to put books on both shelves simultaneously and accomplish her job.

The problem resurfaced when the patient began categorizing plants in a greenhouse; she once again repeated the mistake. Because the problem was so blatant, familiar retraining went more quickly. After providing her with enough examples, at different work sites, a strategy was developed to help her identify whether she was dealing with a sequential or a multiprocessing activity.

Case 6: Inductive/Deductive Thought Principals

A young woman, age 27, had severe analytical and problem-solving deficits. Attempts to teach her inductive and deductive principles of thought through exercises on a computer and a videotape demonstration of such processes totally failed.

The patient was taken to a gift shop to examine the window display and asked to identify the function of a pair of small china figurines. After spending 20 minutes analyzing possible functions of these figurines, the patient was convinced that the items were salt and pepper shakers. She recognized that it took her an exceptionally long time to identify such simple and common items. This practical example convinced the patient for the first time of the importance of collecting enough information to draw the proper conclusion.

Case 7: Relevancy

Finding activities that head-injured patients enjoy is the key to cooperation. The advantage of incorporating former interests into a cognitive program is that they help the learning process through the "old memory banks."

In the case of a young man with poor conversational skills, analyzing Star Trek movies helped considerably. Having been a "Trecky" premorbidly, the patient agreed to watch the movies on the VCR and discuss them. Using the remote control as a mechanism to control the flow of information yielded noticeable progress in his turn-taking skills, presumably because the material was interesting and familiar to him.

Case 8: Relevancy

In another case, a young man with minimal motivation was found to have great interest in photography. He enjoyed organizational tasks such as selecting good from bad photos, and choosing frames. Eventually he consented to an exhibit of his photographs at a local library. The event required him to make decisions on matters such as frame color and display arrangement and also highlighted the need to dress appropriately for different occasions.

Case 9: Insight

A 48-year-old man had been declaring for 5 years that he could still be a top mechanic. His wife and daughters were totally frustrated with his denial, tactlessness, and rudeness.

An evaluation revealed that this individual, who had entered various treatment programs, and who was later rejected by a few, was completely out of touch with his condition.

Two procedures were followed. At first, the patient's problems and symptoms were described to him and tape-recorded. As the patient has serious initiation problems as well as visual problems, his wife turned on the recorder for her husband each day. It was noted that although the patient was able to repeat the taped message, he did not believe it.

The patient's former supervisor and friend agreed to engage in several projects with the patient, which helped identify the patient's skills and ability for follow through. The patient's tasks were similar to those he had carried out premorbidly, except that the supervisor now performed the visual aspects of the task.

The supervisor gradually recognized the patient's specific problems. When he felt ready to communicate them to the patient, in the presence of the patient's wife and therapist, the conversation was tape-recorded.

Eventually, the patient conceded that his problems did exist because his old friend, whom he trusted, saw them as well. Although he still does not fully understand the consequences of his injury, the patient has agreed to cooperate and participate in a program. At present he is minimally supervised in his job stocking central-supply carts at a major hospital.

This particular case illustrated that insight therapy may often be more effective with the help of previously trusted friends and supervisors. Furthermore, frequently there are advantages to conducting insight therapy in a relaxed atmosphere, for example, sitting in a car watching the rain or munching on a pizza at a quiet restaurant, as opposed to a formal setting.

BEHAVIOR PROBLEMS

Behavior therapy techniques can also be implemented at home. In fact, it is a natural place to provide discipline, because the home is where discipline is first introduced.

A 20-year-old male, who was discharged from a facility because of uncontrollable physical outbursts, was noted to demonstrate more appropriate behavior at home. Not only did he calm down once he returned to his familiar surrounding, but he behaved as though he simply did not dare lose complete control in his parents' presence.

The disciplinary action, however, cannot usually be left to the parents or spouses alone, because patients, a number of years post injury, often develop bad habits and negative feelings toward their families.

We found that these patients respond to a reward and penalty system. The strength of the program is in the ability to address meaningful adult experiences. However, the success of such a program lies with the family and the caregivers. If any team member disagrees even with the minutest detail, the program will fail. We found that families take a long time to accept a stranger's assistance in providing discipline. Families frequently perceive disciplinary activity as the role of the parent. Wives regard such interference as involvement in the couple's intimate relationship. It is important that the therapists remain patient and understanding. When the family finally does request assistance and sees the changes, improvement tends to last longer.

In contrast to the physically destructive individuals, we have found that many of the verbally abusive patients begin to behave more appropriately as their lives become more satisfying. Behavioral therapy programs are usually not necessary if the therapist assumes the role more of a mentor than a supervisor. Moreover, as their hopes for improvement grow and as families' styles of interaction improve, the patients appear to become friendlier.

Behavior also improves more when friends or colleagues continue to visit. A home program facilitates the maintenance of old contacts. When friends are willing to serve as role models and to provide opportunities for normal social activities, the patient's behavior will be more acceptable.

THE FAMILY

Successful interaction with the family requires the most sensitive and sophisticated approach. Families in a home program often seem to expect the therapists to solve all of the patient's and family's problems. On the other hand, the family appears to have an underlying need to be in control of the rehabilitation program.

In addition, families frequently struggle with issues of privacy, for home programs interfere in some ways with the family's lifestyle. Some families permit the therapists to work in their home but not within the community. Others, permit only select community interactions. We have found that a few parents are especially sensitive about the issue of supervising a patient at a school setting. Two such families could not overcome their personal embarrassment and insisted that the patient go to school on his own. Needless to say, the experience was most negative to all concerned.

Therapists must take their time to learn the family's true concerns. Suggestions can be made but not enforced. Maximum tact and politeness rather than a power struggle must mark the interaction. When families feel comfortable and trusting they are more able to accept challenges.

Even after several years of living with the patient, families often do not really understand the problems. Ongoing education under informal conditions serves well to provide family members with the correct language and thinking style. Specifically, families must be helped to see not only the patient's deficits, but also his or her strengths, and particularly, the ways in which the patient is the same person he or she always was. When they recognize that the patient has something to offer, they can begin to adjust to this changed person in their midst.

Families, patients, and therapists are each a part of one concerned team. In fact, once improvements begin to take place, families are more willing to assist with the therapy. Their purpose and function become clearer and they can see their importance in the recovery process. The therapist who can design a care plan and chart short- and long-term goals along with the family will have done more for the patient and family than all of the therapies combined.

Our experience leads us to believe that the patient's fate usually depends upon the family. If families can learn to differentiate between positive and negative involvement, if they can feel good about helping their relative then their own and their relative's quality of life will improve.

Case 1

The program evaluated a 30-year-old man who was 5 years post injury. He had been seen by a psychologist for 5 years but the family was at wits end. The patient was a partner in a family-owned business. The family could not tolerate his outbursts, humiliations, and poor planning skills. He was a burden and they wanted to buy him out.

The evaluation revealed that the patient was unable to shift sets easily and that he needed clear-cut directions. He was aware of his problems at work and assumed a rigid confrontational stance.

The family members were called in and allowed to express their anger and pain. After a few sessions they were advised of the nature of the patient's problems, and expressed amazement that no one had ever explained his problems to them before. They were now willing to give him a few more months at work provided he agreed to receive therapy. The therapist requested permission to go into the workplace and evaluate the patient's problems on the job. To maintain confidentiality, the therapist was introduced as a business consultant and spent a number of hours in the patient's plant.

A care plan for the family was drawn up following several meetings with the partner, patient, and therapist. This family was willing to follow suggestions, despite initial feelings of anger and humiliation. The patient and family continue to work together. He now has added responsibilities and is seen by the program for follow-up purposes only.

THE COMMUNITY

A home- and community-based program needs to identify each person's community boundaries in terms of the person's needs and interests. As with unrestricted people, the number of contacts at various distances may create an individual's community.

In our experience, because the patient lacks problem-solving skills the therapist must help him or her identify interests, assist in making contacts in the community, and facilitate the conditions for maintaining these contacts. Clearly, establishing the mechanisms to maintain the contacts is the hardest and most crucial aspect of all. Head-injured patients may find it difficult to maintain contact, unless there are sufficient props and safeguards implanted into the situation. Typically, head-injured families are unable to provide continuity and the program should not rely on them for such purposes. There is a select group of people who are willing to provide such assistance. These are usually volunteers at hospitals and nursing homes. Librarians are also frequently helpful, as well as vendors, who are interested in the patient as a customer. In general, however, the entire process is slow, and therapists play a major role in developing trust, in clarifying the situation, and in providing back-up systems. The community is not easily prepared to compromise work flow or productivity.

Case 1

The patient had been a steady customer at a bank and supermarket premorbidly. Following his injury his wife took him along on errands but conducted the business herself. Eventually the patient refused to go along.

The wife and husband agreed, however, that the therapist should reintroduce those skills. Gradually he learned to identify items on supermarket shelves and to purchase most of the items. A problem remained with the items that he could not locate. He could not figure out how to approach the problem. Finally it was decided to introduce the patient to the store manager. An arrangement was worked out where if the patient felt stuck he could count on the staff's help. The same procedure was adopted at the patient's bank.

At present the patient is able to shop from his wife's list. She drops him off at the supermarket, goes on to run her own errands, then picks him up. When he goes to the bank, he is usually greeted by one of the tellers who knows to direct him discretely to complete the transactions.

Case 2

This patient has shown good progress and is working as a volunteer. She was evaluated over a period of 2 months at six different job sites at a neighboring hospital. A therapist had been with her at all times to educate and supervise. Eventually, the patient opted for a job in the Public Relations Department mailing bulk mail. She was trained and the director of volunteers was advised of strategies for future learning tasks.

A transportation plan was then developed for the patient so that she could travel on her own. The therapist discontinued the patient's on-site supervision and began to develop volunteering skills with her at a different site. Eventually, the patient developed three discrete skills, which are practiced in three different places.

The patient benefits from a variety of activities, but cannot handle variety at one work site. Part-time arrangements at three sites actually provide her with a full-time occupation. Eventually she will be able to develop the stamina and speed necessary to hold a paying job.

CONCLUSION

Head-injured patients have been reported to have residual problems that impair their independent functioning. Self-care, household business, housework, communication, behavioral, educational, community, and employment problems have been found to persist years after the injury and despite previous rehabilitation efforts (Jacobs, 1984).

Staying in the community following an accident usually entails a considerable reduction in quality of life for the head-injured person (Karpman, et al. 1986). Often further deterioration occurs with time and patients require reinstitutionalization (Lezak, 1987).

Several writers have promoted the need to functionalize and individualize various aspects of a treatment program. Fowler, Hart, & Sheehan (1972) highlighted the value of a prosthetic memory device for use in the environment. McCann and Detweiler (1985) suggested a functional cognitive training approach. Ben-Yishay, Silver, Piasetsky, & Rattok (1987) promoted the idea of on-site training.

A head-injury rehabilitation program can be offered within the person's own environment (i.e., home and community). As others have noted, making the transition from a facility to home is extremely difficult because of patients' integration problems, families' and communitys' in-experience and insufficient community services. A community-based program can address all of those problems directly and more efficiently.

A model program presented here focused its attention equally on the patient, the family, and the community. It has worked with 16 patients 3 months to 8 years post injury. These patients were dependent, isolated, and problematic. They were maintained at home despite the burden that they imposed on their families, and in essence, they have all been in danger of reinstitutionalization. It appeared that once the family was "burned out" the patient's chances of survival in the community diminished.

The communities were found to be almost barren for the head-injured person's needs. Lack of education and lack of resources have been apparent everywhere. Transportation has been virtually absent for community interaction purposes, although more available for periodic trips to a physician. Most families and patients had little idea of what was available for their relatives.

Clearly, stepping onto untrodden ground, and with much to learn, the program began to gently pull patients and families along, gradually returning both to the main stream of life. The preliminary results indicate that even misdirected nonoperative individuals can improve up to 8 years post onset. It seems that this improvement may be explained on the basis that even the most impaired patients must have a sense of direction and goals. By surrounding each patient with tasks that are relevant and meaningful to him or her in a normal and familiar environment, he becomes more motivated. It was found that many of these patients felt derailed but that they did not know how to return to the main track. It was also noted that the longer they felt out of control, the worse their habits were. The individuals with the fresher injuries could be returned to their familiar schools and work environments sooner. Perhaps they retained their desire to resume a normal lifestyle because they had fewer institutional experiences.

There appears to be justification for returning patients to their former settings as soon as possible. School children and adolescents, in particular, were found to benefit from early, selective and controlled reintroduction into the community of teachers and friends. Although their first few weeks exhausted them and they may have gone through some confusion, these patients made quantum leaps and were better integrated with their schoolmates because of shorter absences.

A home-based rehabilitation program does not appear to be enough. Even if the patient is too confused to plan an outing, community interaction must be maintained. Patients may otherwise become institutionalized in their own home and all involved will suffer.

We have found that mothers usually give up their jobs to stay with their head-injured children. After a few months, without much assistance from the outside, both mother and child are at each others throats in perpetual conflict similar to the situation of the healthy adolescent.

It is not so much the therapist's confrontation, but rather the feedback from society and the environment that provides the patient with insights. One sharp glance from a police officer or guard at the printing department of a state-wide newspaper stopped a patient from smoking much faster than any therapist's request. Conversely, a quiet discussion over one's future goals at a restaurant or while watching sailboats on a river seems to be retained easily and have profound effects. It is true that head-injured patients have multiple processing problems, but when a cognitive activity is attached to an emotionally pleasing experience, the cognitive task is learned decidedly more easily.

We were impressed by the successful reintegration of patients into volunteer or paid work situations after on-site training. Sherril, Goodall, Barcus, & Brooke (1985) reported good results with an otherwise handicapped population. It may be that such procedures should be applied to the head-injured population on a larger scale.

The home program component, which is clearly important, is the one that helps place the patient in a better standing with the family. If cooking meals or cleaning or being a gardener provides some happiness to the household, then this is an important goal to aim for. From the family's point of view, the availability of the therapist at home serves as a golden opportunity to learn about their and the patient's needs. Informal discussions in the kitchen, laundry room, or exercise room are more effective than formal family conferences. The family members are less intimidated on their own territory. Families who are truly involved with the program from the start see the progress they have helped achieve, and they seem to burn out less frequently or rapidly. But not all families can tolerate a home-based program for very long. Professionals might use this as a yardstick to plan for the patient's future away from home.

Society as a whole is biased against the disabled. For this reason therapists must use their charm, creativity, and patience to handpick the environment, people, activity, and transportation. As a rule, it is much harder to rekindle old contacts, but it is possible if conditions are orchestrated properly. Nonprofit health organizations are more tolerant than pure business-oriented environments, unless the patient is a customer.

Although communities at large are not terribly helpful, there are encouraging new trends in society with respect to the patient with an acquired injury. The fact that our society allows for greater diversity of lifestyles helps the individual whose life may be out of the ordinary. For example, if the head-injured person returns to school after a considerable period of time he may feel more accepted because there are likely to be other older students as well. The concept of the househusband is less foreign today and can also be taught. The therapists must capitalize on these social developments as they clearly assist in patients' adjustment processes.

The community-based program is not likely to improve all of the patient's deficits. It is hoped, however, that such a program would increase the patient's actual level of functioning in two ways: one, by providing all the individual attention and repetition required to function effectively within the home and community; and second, by structuring the environment to compensate for the patient's residual deficits. The latter will be more easily achieved on a larger scale when more sources of work and entertainment are available to the head-injured patient and family.

It is possible that the head-injured patients will always need some follow-up by a home program to facilitate adjustment to changes which occur during the normal course of life. Such mechanisms might help prevent catastrophic deterioration that occurs when problems accumulate beyond family and patient control. To satisfy the family's concern over their relative's future one might consider long-term planning strategies created and managed by a team of health professionals, lawyers, and family members that would ensure a safe and dignified quality of life for the injured person.

Not all patients are appropriate for such a program. Those who cannot be controlled through behavioral therapy and who continue to evidence grave destructive behaviors are probably not good candidates. However, many head-injured patients who originally appear uncontrollable do calm down within their home environment. For this reason even such patients should be given a home trial.

The future of a home- and community-based program will, like all other programs, have to withstand the test of time. However, the ingredients are there to facilitate a worthwhile stay within the community after a head injury.

REFERENCES

Ben-Yishay, Y., Silver, S., Piasetsky, E., & Rattok, J. (1987). Relationship between employability and vocational outcome after intensive holistic cognitive rehabilitation. *Journal of Head Trauma Rehabilitation, 2*(1) 35–48.

Bond, M. S. (1976). Assessment of the psychological outcome of severe head injury. *Acta Neurochicurgicia, 34*, 57–70.

Brooks, D. N., & Aughton, M. E. (1979). Psychological consequences of blunt head injury. *International Rehabilitation Medicine, 1*, 160–165.

Carberry, H. (1985, March). Psychological methods of helping the adolescent rehabilitation patient. *Cognitive Rehabilitation*, 24–25.

Cope, N. D. (1986). Brain injury rehabilitation. *Rehabilitation Report, 2*(3), 1–2.

Fowler, R. S., Hart, J., & Sheehan, M. (1972, December). A prosthetic memory: An application of the prosthetic environment concept. *Rehabilitation Counselling Bulletin,* pp. 80–85.

Frankowski, R. F., Annegers, J. F., & Whitman, S. (1985). Epidemiological and descriptive studies: Part I, The descriptive epidemiology of head trauma in the United States. In D. P. Becker & J. T. Povlishock (Eds.), *Central Nervous System Trauma Status Report* (pp. 33–50). National Institute of Neurological and Communicative Disorders and Stroke, National Institutes of Health.

Gogstad, A. C., & Kjellman, A. M. (1976). Rehabilitation prognosis related to clinical and social factors in brain injured of different etilogy. *Social Science and Medicine, 10,* 283–288.

Goldberg, R. T. (1981). Toward an understanding of the rehabilitation of the disabled adolescent. *Rehabilitation Literature, 42,* (3–4), 66–74.

Goldstein, K. (1942). *Affects of brain injury in war.* New York: Grune & Stratton.

Jacobs, H. E. (1984). The family as a therapeutic agent: Long term recovery of severe head trauma survivors (pp. 1–83). Los Angeles, UCLA School of Medicine.

Jacobs, H. E. (1987). The Los Angeles Head Injury Survey: Project rationale and design implications. *Journal of Head Trauma Rehabilitation 2*(3), 37–50.

Karpman, T., Wolfe, S., & Vargo, J. W. (1986). The psychological adjustment of adult clients and their parents following closed head injury. *Journal of Applied Rehabilitation Counseling, 17* (1).

Levin, H., Grossman, R. G., Rose, J. E., & Teasdale, G. (1979). Long term neuropsychological outcome of closed head injury. *Journal of Neurosurgery, 50*(4), 412–422.

Lezak, M. D. (1978). Living with the characterologically altered brain injured patient. *Journal of Clinical Psychiatry, 39,* 592–598.

Lezak, M. D. (1987). Relationships between personality disorders, social disturbances and physical disability following traumatic brain injury. *Journal of Head Trauma Rehabilitation, 2*(1), 57–69.

McCann, L., & Detweiler, E. (1985, May/June). Functional cognitive training: A philosophical and realistic approach to rehabilitation. *Cognitive Rehabilitation,* 22–26.

Neugarten, B. L., & Moore, J. W. (1970). The changing age-status system. In B. L. Neugarten (Ed.), *Middle age and aging* (pp. 5–21). Chicago: Chicago Press.

Rollin, Walter, J. (1987). Psychological considerations of the traumatically head injured and their families. The psychology of communication disorders in individuals and their families (pp. 74–95). Englewood Cliffs, NJ: Prentice Hall.

Rosenbaum, M., & Najenson, T. (1976). Changes in life patterns and symptoms of low mood as reported by wives of severely brain injured soldiers. *Journal of Consulting Clinical Psychology, 44,* 881–886.

Savage, R., & Carter, R. (1984). Re-entry: The head injured student returns to school. *Cognitive Rehabilitation, 12*(6), 28–33.

Sherril, M., Goodall, P., Barcus, M., & Brooke, V. (1985). The supported work model of competitive employment for citizens with severe handicaps. Richmond, VA: Virginia Commonwealth University, Rehabilitation Research and Training Center.

Sigelman, C. K. (1983). Community integration of disabled people: Attitudinal and behavioral reactions of the nondisabled. The National Information Center, Rehab Brief, Vol. IX, No. 8 (pp. 1–83). National Institute of Handicapped Research Office of Special Education and Rehabilitative Services, Department of Education, Washington, DC 20202.

Sivak, M., Olson, P. L., Kewman, D. G., Won, H., & Henson, D. L. (1981). Driving and Perceptual/Cognitive Skills: Behavioral consequences of brain damage. *Archives of Physical Medicine and Rehabilitation, 62*(10), 476–483.

Strum, W., Dahmen, W., Hartje, W., & Williams, K. (1983). Ergebnisse eines Trainings-programms zur Verbesserung der visuellen Auffassungsschnelligkeit und Konzentra-tionsfahigkeit bei Hirngeschadingten [Results of a program for the training of perceptual speed and attention in brain damaged patients]. *Archives Für Psychiatrie und Nervenk-rankheiten, 233*(1), 9–22.

Thomas, J. D., & Trexler, L. E. (1982). Behavioral and cognitive deficits in cerebrovascular accident and closed head injury. Implications for cognitive rehabilitation. In L. E. Traxler (Ed.), *Cognitive rehabilitation* (pp. 27–62). New York: Plenum Press.

Thorp, M. J. (1956). An exercise program for the brain injured. *Physical Therapy Review, 36,* 664–675.

Thorp, M. J. (1983). *Thirty year brain trauma follow up*. Los Angeles: American Congress of Rehabilitation Medicine.

Todd, J., & Staz, P. (1980). The effects of long term verbal memory deficits. A case study of an adolescent and his family. *Journal of Marital and Family Therapy, 6,* 431–438.

Tyerman, A., & Humphrey, M. (1984). Changes in self-concept following severe head injury. *International Journal Rehabilitation Research, 7*(1), 11–23.

15

Assessment of Cognitive Disorders in the Elderly

Wilma G. Rosen

The paucity of theory presents no deterrent to the abundance of practice in the assessment of cognitive disorders in the elderly. Whether in the presence or absence of theory, the basic tenet of neuropsychological assessment is that differential patterns of performance on neuropsychological tests are assumed to accompany different psychiatric and neurological disorders. This assumption is based upon either empirical derivation of performance patterns for different diagnostic groups or from clinical experience. Expectations based upon these patterns guide the assessment process, and the interpretation of findings. Thus, a set of impaired cognitive functions is considered to be a manifestation of a specific disorder. The presence of the symptoms signifies a positive identification of the disorder, whereas absence of a symptom or symptoms may be sufficient to rule out the disorder. The positive or negative detection of symptoms often marks the conclusion of the neuropsychological assessment in the elderly, at which point one confidently offers a statement about the presence or absence of a dementing disorder, depression, and so on. No theory guides these kinds of binary diagnostic decisions, which are most useful and likely to be highly accurate in unambiguous cases. By their very nature though, the straightforward cases are least likely to be referred for neuropsychological evaluation. Instead, we assess the "difficult" cases that fail to satisfy all criteria of the presence-absence differential, or where the overlap in symptoms shared by different disorders is too extensive to determine which disorder is present. Consequently, this atheoretical approach fails to apply to the more ambiguous cases, and we must use a model or theory to guide our interpretations.

USING THEORY
IN THE ASSESSMENT PROCESS

In the assessment of cognitive functioning in the elderly, there are at least four ways in which a model or theoretical approach is useful for differentiating among the disorders affecting the elderly. Three ways are reviewed, with the major focus placed on the fourth approach, predictive changes over time.

Statistical Approach

One approach, based completely upon empirically derived statistical relationships between test performances and biological characteristics of the cerebral cortex, is best exemplified by the Halstead-Reitan Neuropsychological Test Battery (HRB) (Reitan, 1986). Performances by thousands of persons with documented focal or diffuse brain damage on the several tests comprising the HRB were analyzed according to patterns and relationships among scores, pathognomonic signs, and right- versus left-hemisphere comparisons in order to determine specific indicators of the functional condition of different areas of the cerebral cortex. Subsequently, these indicators have formed the basis for inferential analysis of the biological characteristics of the brain of an individual. Analysis of a person's test scores according to the specific indicators permits inferences about the presence or absence of cerebral damage, the type of lesion, and the etiology.

Unfortunately, applicability of the HRB to assessment of the elderly is questionable in view of the fact that in studies of persons aged 60 and above, who showed no evidence of brain damage, many subjects scored in the impaired range on several measures of the battery. On the Tactual Performance Test approximately 50% of a sample of 47 retired teachers with a mean age of 72 years scored in the brain-damaged range on all dependent measures but one, memory for shapes (Price, Fein, & Feinberg, 1980). Approximately 90% of this sample was significantly impaired on three measures of timed performance. In addition, approximately 47% of this presumed normal elderly group scored in the brain-damaged range on Trails B.

In a more recent study of the relationship of age and education level to performance on the HRB (Heaton, Grant, & Matthews, 1986), less than 50% of persons aged 60 and above with 16 or more years of education were classified as normal according to the Impairment Index, which is the proportion of tests failed on the HRB. Thus, these investigators suggested that the standard cutoff scores on individual HRB tests established for young normals are inappropriate for older persons. Although the HRB, as it currently stands, appears to overdiagnose the presence of brain damage in the elderly, its inadequacies do not invalidate the theoretical method on which it is based.

Relative Levels of Performance

A second approach goes beyond the confirmation of symptoms to the examination of relative levels of performance. One examines patterns of deficits and spared functions and the relative levels of severity of dysfunction among the affected abilities. This approach presumes either knowledge of or a theory about the patterns of deficits that accompany various disorders. This method can be useful in both the differentiation among the types of dementias and between dementia and normal aging, although its speculative nature must be recognized.

Differentiation between an early dementia and normal aging is problematic primarily in persons who are quite intelligent and have or had a high level of occupational functioning. Some of their test scores remain well within normal limits, that is, outside the impaired range. The problem lies in making a clinical judgment about whether this "normal" test score actually reflects the patient's premorbid abilities or a decline from a higher level of functioning. The procedure recommended in this case is to use as a guide the expected set of symptoms of a progressive dementia (Diagnostic and Statistical Manual of Mental Disorders–Third Edition [DSM–III], 1986) and then to attempt to determine if the specified abilities (e.g., intellectual functioning, memory, etc.) deviate from expectations based upon an estimated premorbid level of functioning. Such an estimate can be derived from a formula (Wilson, Rosenbaum, & Brown, 1979), educational and occupational history, and information obtained from reliable informants (usually family members). This approach may be hazardous (Reitan, 1986) because one is dealing with performances that are distributed within the low-average to high-average range rather than with clearly deviant, low scores. Diagnostic errors may occur either as false positives (i.e., diagnosis of a disorder is made when no disorder exists) or false negatives (i.e., no disorder is diagnosed although the disorder is present). These sorts of judgments can be made conservatively by clinicians who have had much experience with dementing and normal elderly. Nevertheless, report of the evaluation should include the caveat of the need for a reexamination after approximately 6–12 months have elapsed, a stipulation that is discussed below.

Before illustrating the use of this method in differentiating normal aging from dementia, the typical set of neuropsychological diagnostic criteria for dementia and Alzheimer's disease, in particular, are briefly presented. First, the DSM–III diagnostic criteria stipulate the broadest range of cognitive deficits necessary for a diagnosis of dementia, and include impairment in intellectual, occupational or social functioning, memory impairment, and a deficit in another higher cortical function, such as language. Second, as suggested previously (Rosen, 1983), more specific cognitive deficits can be expected in Alzheimer's disease (Table 15.1). As it turns out, this set of dysfunctions is consistent with the recommendation of a work group in the diagnosis of Alzheimer's disease, which, in addition, suggested evaluation for deficits in attention, visual perception, and problem-solving skills (McKhann et al., 1984).

TABLE 15.1
Primary Changes in Cognitive Functioning
in Alzheimer's Disease

Decline in overall level of intellectual functioning
Significant Verbal IQ—Performance IQ difference with a greater Verbal IQ
Memory impairment
Constructional apraxia
Decreased verbal fluency
Anomia

In a case I evaluated, a 68-year-old lawyer, who graduated Phi Beta Kappa from an Ivy League university, obtained a Full Scale IQ score of 118 on the Wechsler Adult Intelligence Scale (Wechsler, 1955), which was judged to represent a decline from a higher premorbid level of functioning. He achieved a Verbal IQ score of 124 and a Performance IQ score of 107, which confirmed the expected Verbal IQ—Performance IQ discrepancy. Significant verbal and visual memory deficits were apparent on subtests of the Wechsler Memory Scale (Wechsler, 1945). None of the scores on the additional neuropsychological tests administered (Table 15.2) were in the impaired range. On two verbal fluency tasks he retrieved only 14 animal names in 1 minute and scored at the 38th percentile in retrieval of words that began with particular letters within a specified time period (Benton & Hamsher, 1977). Although neither of these scores was in the impaired range, they were judged to be below the expected level of performance given his high levels of verbal and occupational functioning.

Clinical judgments of decline in intellectual functioning and decreased verbal fluency skills illustrate the use of relative levels of performance in determining the likelihood of a deficit in higher cortical functioning. Having met the DSM–III criteria for cognitive dysfunction as well as the other specified criteria, the patient was diagnosed as suffering from a dementia. In addition, a further step was taken to differentiate among

TABLE 15.2
Neuropsychological Test Battery for Dementia

Information-Memory-Concentration Test (IMC) (Blessed, Tomlinson, & Roth, 1968)

Wechsler Adult Intelligence Scale—Revised (WAIS-R) Wechsler, 1981)

Wechsler Memory Scale (WMS) (Wechsler, 1945)

Boston Naming Test (Kaplan, Goodglass, & Weintraub, 1983)

Boston Diagnostic Aphasia Examination—selected subtests (Goodglass & Kaplan, 1983)

Controlled Oral Word Association Test (Benton & Hamsher, 1977)

Rosen Drawing Test (RDT) (Rosen, 1984)

Tests of Motor and "Executive" Functioning (Christiansen, 1979)

---

types of dementia. Review of the inclusion and exclusion criteria for Alzheimer's disease, as they were specified in a later article by McKhann et al. (1984), led to the speculation that the patient was in the early stages of Alzheimer's disease. Follow-up of this patient revealed a progressive decline in functioning over several years. The analysis of this case represents the use of deviations from expected levels of performance to confirm the presence of dementia and then determine the possible etiology.

Differentiation among the types of dementias can be achieved via both theoretical and atheoretical approaches. In the latter approach, the presence–absence differential can be used, as in the diagnosis of multi-infarct dementia, where the presence of several clinical features of this disorder is determined and summed to yield an Ischemic Score (Hachinski et al., 1975; Rosen, Terry, Fuld, Katzman, & Peck, 1980). At the level of a model or theory, the presumption is that for certain abilities, patients with a specific type of dementia exhibit a particular pattern of performance depending on the severity of dysfunction. Although the types of deficits one encounters in a patient with Alzheimer's disease have been presented (Table 15.1), the relative degrees of severity among the dysfunctions have not been specified. When this deficit pattern was first identified (Rosen, 1983), a case with a peculiarly deviant pattern in severity among the impaired functions was also presented in which Performance IQ was greater than Verbal IQ, there was severe memory impairment, intact constructional ability, and good naming. Although the presence of a dementing disorder was unquestionable, the deficit pattern, considered in conjunction with the medical and psychiatric history and test-taking behaviors, was not characteristic of Alzheimer's disease. The memory disorder was disproportionate to intact functioning in other ability areas. The medical and psychiatric history included marked anxiety presenting early and consistently in the disorder, outstanding memory disorder with the eventual development of a dementia, seizures, abnormal EEG, and a secondary carcinoma in the lung. Unusual test-taking behaviors included lack of equivocation on time orientation despite gross errors, nonchalance about poor performances, and no confusion in understanding the requirements of complex tasks. The course of the disorder and the medical and psychiatric history were most consistent with a diagnosis of limbic encephalopathy.

The problem with this approach, which is based on expected relative levels of severity of dysfunction, is that it leads to incorrect diagnosis. With respect to Alzheimer's disease, several investigators (Albert, 1981; Katzman, 1985; Rosen, 1983) have suggested that all patients do not initially show an entire expected pattern of deficits, nor do all cognitive abilities show the same pattern of decline across patients (Rosen, Mohs, & Davis, 1986). There are rare patients with unusual clinical presentations that are highly suggestive of the presence of a focal lesion (Crystal, Horoupian, Katzman, & Jotkowitz, 1982; Katzman, 1985). A recent study identified two subgroups within a group of mild to severely impaired Alzheimer's disease patients: One exhibited profound deficits in word-finding ability but mild visuoconstructional deficits, and the other group showed intact word-finding ability but a severe constructional deficit (Martin et al., 1986). These studies suggest that despite our expectations about the pattern of deficits in a "protypical" Alzheimer's disease patient, there appear to be clinical variants of the disorder.

Stage Model

A third theoretical approach useful in assessment is a stage model of the dissolution of functions in a progressive, degenerative dementia. The major proponents of such a model based their analysis of the disintegration of functions on Piaget's theory of cognitive development (Piaget & Inhelder, 1956). Their several cross-sectional and longitudinal studies of dementia patients revealed the dissolution of functions (apraxia, aphasia) in a progression opposite the stages of development of these functions (Ajuriaguerra & Tissot, 1968; Constantinidis, Richard, & de Ajuriaguerra, 1978). In a longitudinal study of the disintegration of constructional praxis for drawing, Alzheimer's disease patients also showed a pattern opposite the developmental sequence (Rosen, 1984). In addition, these patients exhibited drawing behaviors completely uncharacteristic of children, such as "closing in" on the model, an unexpected finding that underscores the notion that the loss of function is not necessarily the mirror image of the development of function.

The utility of a stage model lies in its predictability. Given the particular stage at which the Alzheimer's disease patient is functioning, the model predicts that with the passage of time the patient will regress to the next stage, which is characterized by complete or partial loss of additional components of functions. The stage model has the potential for confirming or disconfirming a diagnosis because deviations from the predicted pattern of regression would signify that a different disorder is present.

Although little research has been carried out in this area recently, it has been shown that all Alzheimer's disease patients do not exhibit the same rate of deterioration in all functions (Rosen et al., 1986). Reisberg and his collaborators (Reisberg, Ferris, & de Leon, 1985) developed several scales that are purported to reflect different stages in the global loss of function as well as individual functions. The only independent validation of the presumed order of their stages is a longitudinal study showing that the global scale reflects increasing functional deterioration (Reisberg, Shulman, Ferris, de Leon, & Geibel, 1983).

Predictive Changes in Different Disorders

As can be discerned from the preceding approaches, there are no simple formulas for evaluating the outcome of a cognitive assessment in the elderly person. Despite expected patterns of performance for normal elderly, people with dementia, and people with Alzheimer's disease, there is sometimes equivocation in diagnosis because the findings are too tentative to confidently support any particular diagnosis. Nonetheless, I propose that all of these disorders in the elderly share the common characteristic of being "time-locked," that is, particular changes in cognitive functioning are expected to occur in each disorder with the passage of time, and that this feature has the potential to be the most useful in the resolution of a diagnostic dilemma in an elderly individual.

The presence of a dementing disorder (unspecified etiology) is signified by the continued presence of scores in the impaired range or below expectations. Further decline in these scores is predictive of the presence of a progressive, degenerative dementia, such as Alzheimer's disease. After remission of a depressive episode, an improvement in cognitive functioning is expected (Caine, 1986; Johnson & Magaro, 1987). Thus, the model predicts changes over time in cognitive functions accompanying different disorders in the elderly. Consequently, it requires a test–retest comparison between a baseline performance obtained at the initial test session and that obtained at a second session. Three cases are presented in which the inconclusive test findings at the first session necessitated a second test session, whose findings led to clarification of the initial diagnostic impression.

Case 1: Early Progressive Degenerative
Dementia—Probable Alzheimer's Disease

This 76-year-old, right-handed female, who was a college graduate and artist, was referred for evaluation because of complaints of forgetfulness and word-finding difficulty. The scores obtained at baseline and 6-month retest are shown in Table 15.3. All WAIS or WAIS-R subtest scores are age-corrected, scaled scores.

At the first evaluation, this woman exhibited a higher Performance IQ than Verbal IQ, which is a reversal of the expected discrepancy, and significant deficits in verbal learning, delayed verbal memory, and delayed visual memory. Verbal fluency, naming, and constructional praxis were all in the superior range. Other than the prominent memory deficit, the performance pattern did not resemble a dementing disorder, nor was there any evidence from the neurological exam, laboratory tests, or history to suggest a particular etiology for the memory problems. Consequently, the patient was recommended for reevaluation. When the 6-month retest results are examined without reference to the baseline scores, the only prominent finding remains the significant memory deficit. However, comparison of the baseline and retest scores reveals changes in perfor-

TABLE 15.3
Baseline and 6-Month Retest Scores Obtained by a
Patient with the Diagnosis of Probable Early
Alzheimer's Disease

	Baseline		6-Mo. Retest	
Mental Status Exam				
IMC (Errors)	9		7	
WAIS				
Verbal IQ	120		128	
Performance IQ	129		123	
Full scale IQ	125		127	
WMS	*Immediate Recall*	*10-Min Recall*	*Immediate Recall*	*10-Min Recall*
Logical memory	7	0	6	0
P–A learning	9	—	10	—
Visual reprod.	6	2	8	1
Constructional Praxis				
Block design	14 (Superior)		14 (Superior)	
RDT	All correct		All correct	
Language				
Controlled word assoc.	97%		83%	
Animal naming	$\frac{14}{1}$ min		$\frac{11}{1}$ min	
Object naming	Intact		Intact	

mances that are consistent with a diagnosis of Alzheimer's disease. The VIQ-PIQ differential, though different only by a nonsignificant 5-points at retest, has shifted in the direction of a higher VIQ with an actual change in 14 points between the two scores. A subtle decline in verbal fluency was also noted on both the Controlled Word Association Test and the Animal Naming task. Thus, examinations of the retest findings in relation to the baseline results revealed shifts in performance consistent with the predicted changes for probable Alzheimer's disease, which was the suggested diagnosis. Clinically, the patient still complained of memory problems, and the word-finding difficulty in spontaneous speech was more apparent. Over the years, this patient has continued to show a decline in cognitive and social functioning.

Case 2: "Mixed" Dementia— Multiinfarct Dementia and Alzheimer's Disease

This 67-year-old, right-handed male, who was a high school graduate and retired diamond assorter, had sustained a right-temporal infarct approximately 1½ years prior to the initial evaluation. He had a history of hypertension and abrupt onset of confusion. He experienced topographic memory problems, dyscalculia, but no reported further decline in function after the effects of the cerebrovascular accident (CVA) were noted.

As shown in Table 15.4, the patient was evaluated at baseline and after a 5-month interval because of the initial test performances that were inconsistent with the lesion locus and the overlap in symptoms accompanying a right-temporal infarct and Alzheimer's disease. With respect to the latter point, both disorders share visuospatial and visuoconstructional deficits. Thus, the lower Performance IQ, visual memory deficit, and constructional apraxia found in this case are consistent with both disorders, and therefore do not contribute to the differential diagnosis. The performances inconsistent with a right-temporal infarct were the impaired verbal fluency and the mild verbal learning and recall deficits. Therefore, a reevaluation was recommended in order to determine the stability of these unexpected deficits in language.

At the second evaluation, the tests administered pertained primarily to language functioning. On the two spatial tasks readministered, the patient actually showed some improvement, which may have represented partial recovery of function following the CVA. Because he continued to exhibit significant deficits in three language areas (learning, memory, fluency), left-hemisphere functioning was also thought to be compromised. The patient had, therefore, not only an infarct, but was presumed to have a degenerative dementia (most likely Alzheimer's disease), and the diagnosis

TABLE 15.4
Baseline and 5-Month Retest Scores Obtained by a
Patient with the Diagnosis of Mixed Dementia

	Baseline		5-Mo. Retest	
Mental Status Exam				
IMC (Errors)	2		3	
WAIS				
Verbal IQ	100		—	
Performance IQ	77		—	
Full scale IQ	90		—	
WMS	*Immediate Recall*	*10-Min. Recall*	*Immediate Recall*	*10-Min Recall*
Logical memory	6	—	3	—
P–A learning	8.5	—	5.5	—
Visual reprod.	0	—	5	—
Constructional Praxis				
Block design	6 (Borderline)		—	
RDT	Moderate impairment		Moderate impairment	
Language				
Controlled word assoc.	1%		2%	
Animal naming	$\frac{9}{1}$ min		$\frac{6}{1}$ min	
Object naming	Intact		Intact	

of mixed dementia was suggested. The patient showed progressive decline in functioning and died 5 years later.

Case 3: Major Depressive Disorder

This 72-year-old, right-handed female, who graduated college and did volunteer work, had become a widow approximately 1½ years prior to the baseline evaluation. She had a history of multiple episodes of depression and had been treated with antidepressants and electroconvulsive therapy (ECT) previously. Approximately 1 month prior to the baseline evaluation, she experienced an acute onset of mental and physical fatigue with confused thinking and disorientation to time. She was hospitalized for evaluation, and the neuropsychological assessment occurred prior to treatment.

As shown in Table 15.5, at baseline testing she exhibited a decline in overall intellectual functioning, the expected Verbal IQ-Performance IQ differential, decreased verbal fluency, constructional apraxia for drawing, and an anomia, but she showed no significant memory impairment. There was evidence of average verbal learning abilities for her age and no decline in delayed recall of both verbal and visual material.

Despite several deficits in cognitive functioning, which would be consistent with a diagnosis of dementia, this patient did not exhibit the necessary memory impairment. Given her history of unipolar depression, widowhood of rather recent onset, and lack of memory deficits, she was most likely not suffering from a dementia, but rather from depression. This impression was confirmed when we evaluated her 10 days after she had received four or five ECT treatments. Most significant were the improvements in verbal fluency, verbal learning, immediate verbal recall, and immediate visual memory (Table 15.5). However, she now showed a deficit in delayed verbal and visual memory where none had existed previously, which may reflect the effects of ECT.

In all three cases, complicating factors in the patient's history and ambiguities in the test findings made it somewhat difficult to be reasonably confident of the proposed diagnosis, and the test–retest comparison permitted an analysis based upon expected changes. Thus, the model of predictive changes in cognitive functioning that accompany particular disorders has pragmatic value in the clinical setting.

TABLE 15.5
Baseline and 1-Month Retest Scores Obtained by a Patient
with the Diagnosis of Major Depressive Disorder

	Baseline		*1-Mo. Retest*	
WAIS			—	
Verbal IQ	94			
Performance IQ	76		—	
Full scale IQ	85		—	
WMS	*Immediate Recall*	*10-Min Recall*	*Immediate Recall*	*10-Min Recall*
Logical memory	6	5	8	4
P–A learning	11	—	7.5	—
Visual reprod.	4	3	7	3
Memory quotient	89		94	
Rey auditory-verbal	6, 7, 8, 10, 10		5, 8, 8, 13, 13	
learning test (5 trials—number of words recalled)				
Constructional Praxis				
Block design	7 (Low Average)		8 (Low Average)	
RDT	Mild-moderate impairment		—	
Language				
Controlled word assoc.	15%ile		47%ile	
Animal naming	$\frac{18}{1}$ min		$\frac{20}{1}$ min	
Object naming	Moderate impairment		—	

CONCLUSION

In each of these cases, additional factors were important to the evaluation, including the history of the current episode and the patient's previous history. Unlike the statistical approach to assessment, which ignores the patient's case history, the method advocated here places the results of the baseline evaluation within that context. Without a case history, the only theoretical approach of the four discussed that could be employed completely is the statistical one. However, this approach has not yet provided a sufficiently broad range of acceptable normative data on the elderly that bears on the issue of differential diagnosis. As indicated, the data available from the administration of the HRB to normal elderly would suggest that a sizable proportion (up to 50%) were neurologically impaired. There is very little useful data available on persons above 75 years of age that can serve as a "normative" guide for evaluating performances on any neuropsychological tests. There are no studies with a sufficiently large subject pool that have simultaneously compared normal elderly, Alzheimer disease patients, and depressed elderly on several different measures (e.g., IQ, memory, language, praxis).

Neuropsychology currently plays an especially important role in the diagnosis of disorders in the elderly whenever cognitive functioning has been compromised. Because there are no definitive tests to establish a diagnosis of Alzheimer's disease short of cerebral biopsy, evaluation of the patient's mental status is an essential part of the entire work-up. In any case in which dementia or Alzheimer's disease, in particular, forms a component of the differential diagnosis, cognitive functioning must be assessed. Once the different patterns of performance representative of normal, neurologically impaired, and psychiatrically compromised individuals are familiar to the clinical neuropsychologist, the likelihood of diagnostic error will decrease. Only then can the neuropsychologist select the most appropriate of the theoretical approaches discussed here in order to make a valuable contribution to the entire evaluation of the patient.

ACKNOWLEDGMENTS

The author gratefully acknowledges the discussions with Jeffrey J. Rosen about some ideas advanced in this chapter.

REFERENCES

Albert, M. S. (1981). Geriatric neuropsychology. *Journal of Consulting and Clinical Psychology, 49,* 835–850.

Benton, A. L., & Hamsher, K. (1977). *Multilingual aphasia examination.* Iowa City: University of Iowa.

Blessed, G., Tomlinson, B. E., & Roth, M. (1968). The association between quantitative measures and degenerative changes in the cerebral gray matter of elderly patients. *British Journal of Psychiatry, 114,* 797–811.

Caine, E. D. (1986). The neuropsychology of depression: The pseudodementia syndrome. In I. Grant & K. M. Adams (Eds.), *Neuropsychological assessment of neuropsychiatric disorders* (pp. 221–243). New York: Oxford University Press.

Christiansen, A. -L. (1979). *Luria's neuropsychological investigation. Manual.* Copenhagen: Munksgaard.

Constantinidis, J., Richard, J., & de Ajuriaguerra, J. (1978). Dementias with senile plaques and neurofibrillary tangles. In A. D. Isaacs & F. Post (Eds.), *Studies in geriatric psychiatry* (pp. 119–152). Chicester: Wiley.

Crystal, H. A., Horoupian, D. S., Katzman, R., & Jotkowitz, S. (1982). Biopsy-proved Alzheimer disease presenting as a right parietal lobe syndrome. *Annals of Neurology, 12,* 186–188.

de Ajuriaguerra, J., & Tissot, R. (1968). Some aspects of psycho-neurologic disintegration in senile dementia. In C. Muller & L. Ciompi (Eds.), *Senile dementia* (pp. 69–79). Switzerland: Huber.

Diagnostic and Statistical Manual of Mental Disorders. (1980). Washington, DC: American Psychiatric Association.

Goodglass, H., & Kaplan, E. (1983). *The Assessment of aphasia and related disorders* (2nd ed.). Philadelphia: Lea & Febiger.

Hachinski, V. C., Illiff, L. D., Ziklha, E., duBoulay, G. H., McAllister, V. C., Marshall, T., Russell, R. W. R., & Symon, L. (1975). Cerebral blood flow in dementia. *Archives of Neurology, 32,* 632–637.

Heaton, R. K., Grant, I., & Matthews, C. G. (1986). Differences in neuropsychological test performance associated with age, education, and sex. In I. Grant & K. M. Adams (Eds.), *Neuropsychological assessment of neuropsychiatric disorders* (pp. 100–120). New York: Oxford University Press.

Johnson, M. H., & Magaro, P. A. (1987). Effects of mood and severity on memory processes in depression and mania. *Psychological Bulletin, 101,* 28–40.

Kaplan, E., Goodglass, H., & Weintraub, S. (1983). *The Boston naming test.* Philadelphia: Lea & Febiger.

Katzman, R. (1985). Clinical presentation of the course of Alzheimer's disease: The atypical patient. In F. C. Rose (Ed.), *Modern approaches to the dementias. Part II: Clinical and therapeutic aspects* (pp. 12–18). Basel: Karger.

Martin, A., Brouwers, P., Lalonde, F., Cox, C., Teleska, P., & Fedio, P. (1986). Towards a behavioral typology of Alzheimer's patients. *Journal of Clinical and Experimental Neuropsychology, 8,* 594–610.

McKhann, G., Drachman, D., Folstein, M., Katzman, R., Price, D., & Stadlan, E. M. (1984). *Clinical diagnosis of Alzheimer's disease.* Report of the NINCDS-ADRDA work group under the auspices of Department of Health and Human Services Task Force on Alzheimer's disease. *Neurology, 34,* 939–944.

Piaget, J., & Inhelder, B. (1956). *The child's conception of space.* London: Routledge.

Price, L. J., Fein, G., & Feinberg, L. (1980). Neuropsychological assessment of cognitive functioning in the elderly. In L. W. Poon (Ed.), *Aging in the 1980's* (pp. 78–85). Washington, DC: American Psychological Association.

Reisberg, B., Ferris, S. H., & de Leon, M. J. (1985). Senile dementia of the Alzheimer type: Diagnostic and differential diagnostic features with special reference to functional assessment staging. In J. Traber & W. H. Gispen (Eds.), *Senile dementia of the Alzheimer type. Early diagnosis, neuropathology and animal models* (pp. 18–37). Berlin: Springer-Verlag.

Reisberg, B., Shulman, E., Ferris, S. H., de Leon, M. J., & Geibel, V. (1983). Clinical assessment of age-associated cognitive decline and primary degenerative dementia: Prognostic concomitants. *Psychopharmacology Bulletin, 19,* 734–739.

Reitan, R. M. (1986). Theoretical and methodological bases of the Halstead-Reitan neuropsychological test battery. In I. Grant & K. M. Adams (Eds.), *Neuropsychological assessment of neuropsychiatric disorders* (pp. 3–30). New York: Oxford University Press.

Rosen, W. G. (1983). Clinical and neuropsychological assessment of Alzheimer disease. In R. Mayeux & W. G. Rosen (Eds.), *The Dementias. Advances in neurology* (Vol., 38, pp. 51–64). New York: Raven Press.

Rosen, W. G. (1984, February). Neuropsychological patterns with focus on constructional praxis. In S. Brinkman & J. Largen (Chair), *Longitudinal studies of dementia of the Alzheimer type: Neuropsychological and neurophysiological patterns.* Symposium conducted at the meeting of the International Neuropsychological Society, Houston, TX.

Rosen, W. G., Mohs, R. C., & Davis, K. L. (1986). Longitudinal changes: Cognitive, behavioral, and affective patterns in Alzheimer's disease. In L. Poon (Ed.), *The handbook of clinical memory assessment of older adults* (pp. 294–301). Washington, DC: American Psychological Association.

Rosen, W. G., Terry, R. D., Fuld, P. A., Katzman, R., & Peck, A. (1980). Pathological verification of ischemic score in differentiation of dementias. *Annals of Neurology, 7,* 486–488.

Wechsler, D. (1945). A standardized memory scale for clinical use. *Journal of Psychology, 19,* 87–95.

Wechsler, D. (1955). *Manual for the Wechsler Adult Intelligence Scale.* New York: The Psychological Corporation.

Wechsler, D. (1981). *Manual for the Wechsler Adult Intelligence Scale* (Rev. ed.). New York: The Psychological Corporation.

Wilson, R. S., Rosenbaum, G., & Brown, G. (1979). The problem of premorbid intelligence in neuropsychological assessment. *Journal of Clinical Neuropsychology, 1,* 49–53.

16

Cognitive Rehabilitation in the Elderly: A Computer-Based Memory Training Program

Georgine Vroman
Lucia Kellar
Ilene Cohen

This chapter is based on the Computer Memory Project of the Bellevue Hospital Center's Geriatric Outpatient clinic (New York, NY). We begin with a general discussion of cognitive rehabilitation in the elderly, then describe the Bellevue Project, and finally present some case material taken from patients in the program.

BACKGROUND

Cognitive rehabilitation attempts to restore, alleviate, or compensate for losses in cognitive functioning. Cognitive functions can be defined as all processes that make it possible for persons to obtain, retain, and integrate information about themselves, other people, and the environment, and that enable them to share this information and act upon it. This definition, which derives from information theory and computer processing, may sound simplistic and reductionist, but has shown itself to be a useful working definition, especially within the context of cognitive rehabilitation (Gianutsos, 1980).

In accordance with this definition we can distinguish the following aspects of cognitive function: INPUT, PROCESSING, and OUTPUT. These steps should not, however, be seen as sequential and one-directional only. We must assume that there exists a continuous feedback between them, which determines the outcome of the cognitive process. In the following discussion this proviso should be kept in mind.

Among cognitive functions, perception is part of *input*; the integration and storage of information in an accessible manner are part of *processing*; and *output* includes language and the execution of decisions. Expressed in noncomputer terms, we can distinguish the following important cognitive functions: accurate observation, attention, concentration, language ability, the ability to think logically and make comparisons, categorization, and making use of previous knowledge (memory). A serious shortcoming in any of these functions is likely to influence the process of cognition as a whole. Effective cognitive rehabilitation should attempt to evaluate and address all these functions.

In addition, more peripheral factors may indirectly affect adequate cognitive processing. For example, defective visual perception (poor visual acuity or visual field deficits) and hearing problems reduce both quality and quantity of incoming information. Also, any condition that hampers a person's ability to speak clearly will make communication less effective. Conditions such as depression, confusion, or psychopathological states, whatever the underlying cause, may affect all three steps in the cognitive process. Physical illness (and this can be as minor as a toothache or stomachache) can often cause a decline in concentration, attention, or judgment. Thus, a great many factors have to be taken into account if a person's cognitive functions are to be accurately evaluated, and any subsequent cognitive rehabilitation must reflect the findings of such an assessment.

Although the elderly are not the only group for whom cognitive rehabilitation has been considered as a way of dealing with a decline in cognitive functioning, they appear to form a population that is particularly at risk for such a decline. The incidence of all forms of dementia increases with aging. Deterioration of sensory functions and physical illness are encountered more frequently in an elderly population as is the social isolation many elderly suffer with loss of regular work, income, and the people they were close to. Frequently these conditions can result in a depression that may mimic dementia or complicate a genuine one. Furthermore, research suggests that the elderly may not be capable of handling several forms of input at once or of making fast and accurate decisions, resulting in decreased effectiveness (Willis, 1985). Thus, cognitive decline in the elderly may present a particularly complicated picture with regard to causative factors.

Most cognitive rehabilitation has been developed for the treatment of young patients, specifically for survivors of traumatic brain injury (TBI). Cognitive rehabilitation for this group of patients differs in several significant ways from that for an elderly population. In the first place, although the trauma may have been massive, the surrounding brain tissue in younger patients is usually in reasonably good condition. The elderly are much more likely to show underlying deterioration of the brain itself. The effect of aging on the brain and its functions remains an area of some uncertainty and speculation. However, there is evidence that age influences the rate and extent of recovery after brain injury (Miller, 1984). The second difference between younger and older populations is that the available resources, support systems, and attitudes of health care providers are not the same for these groups. Although there is general agreement that a younger person "deserves" a chance at rehabilitation, this is not always the case for older patients. Cognitive rehabilitation, as all forms of rehabilitation, seeks to return the patient to a maximal possible independence and a useful life in the community, but the definition of these conditions is not the same for different age groups. Thus, the goals set for a rehabilitation process will vary for these age groups and so will the strategies used.

Any cognitive rehabilitation program needs to address the issues of ecological validity, length of treatment, and expectations of change.

Ecological validity is the term used to define the usefulness of performance scores on tests for predicting the level of performance in daily life and the need to make the course of treatment relevant to the problems of daily living (Hart & Hayden, 1986). Mayer, Keating, and Rapp (1986) described a cognitive rehabilitation program for head–injury survivors that includes simulations of daily life situations and observations of performance at home. The Bellevue program, at present, does not take this approach. However, our patients are taught to practice memory-enhancing strategies for the different computer memory tasks that can be transferred to daily life situations.

Cognitive rehabilitation is likely to be a long-term process. This is especially true for head–injury survivors. Many of our patients also continue working with the computer program on an ongoing basis for periods ranging from several months to over a year beyond the original treatment period (our "graduate" program). Some cognitive rehabilitation specialists may have to assume a mediating role between persons, groups, and institutions on their patients' behalf, in order to ensure continuity of treatment and maintenance of gains.

It has been argued (Schacter & Glisky, 1986) that cognitive rehabilitation, or "neuropsychological intervention," must be understood from the goals that its practitioners set themselves. These authors doubt whether it is realistic to speak of retraining memory. They consider it much more likely that patients are taught to compensate for cognitive losses by making use of preserved learning skills that can be applied to specific tasks. Gianutsos (1986), quoting extensively from the literature, challenged this position. Change and improvement in performance have been documented. Furthermore, Gianutsos considers it counterproductive to start on a course of cognitive rehabilitation from this general premise of limited expectations. Though remaining realistic, one must never set one's aims too low.

Cicerone and Tupper (1986) discussed "metacognition," which includes the ability of a patient to reflect consciously on his or her cognitive abilities and the existence and further development of that patient's self-regulatory mechanisms that help in learning and in solving problems. We have found that the use of the personal computer in a series of cognitive exercises lends itself particularly well to the development of this metacognitive capability. Not only can computer exercises be given in countless variations on the same theme, but they can be narrowly focused on a task and allow the introduction of specific facilitating strategies. Patients can experience and observe the strengths and weaknesses of their own memory systems and learn what works to make the best of what they have available. This in turn may result in increased independence (if necessary with the help of appropriate support groups or persons), increased self-confidence to pursue existing or new interests without fear of immediate failure, knowing strategies to overcome persisting cognitive shortcomings and replacing poor strategies with more effective ones.

Finally, even in a geriatric population it may be important to distinguish between goals and expectations for different age groups. For example, we have observed significant differences between "normal" 65-year-olds and "normal" 85-year-olds (see also Willis, 1985). Certain neuropsychological tests give norms by decade, which go beyond age 90, supporting our own observation. The Randt Memory test (Randt & Brown, 1983) is an example. We use this test in our neuropsychological test battery for the project.

Using Computers in Cognitive Rehabilitation of the Elderly

As mentioned, cognitive rehabilitation has had its greatest development in the treatment of younger patients, specifically head-injury survivors. Although the causes of cognitive failure, the circumstances of the patients and the goals set for their rehabilitation are all likely to be different for the elderly, many of the techniques developed for the younger population can be modified for use with the older age group. A survey of the literature indicates that there is a great variety of methods in use, ranging from the highly sophisticated and instrumentalized rehabilitation of visual perceptual deficits (see for instance Piasetsky, Ben-Yishay, Weinberg, & Diller, 1982) to the almost homespun methods used by Griffith (1979) in her treatment of the actress Patricia Neal's aphasia. Gross and Schutz (1986) presented a useful discussion of the models of intervention in neuropsychology. These authors argued that the best results are obtained when these models are applied in a flexible manner. Strategies, such as environmental control, stimulus–response conditioning, training in specific skills, as well as focusing on the steps in the cognitive process in general, each have their specific application. The literature stresses the need for setting specific long- and short-term goals and establishing transfer of the patients' accomplishments in the rehabilitation setting to the situations and demands of daily life. Thus, the best approach in cognitive rehabilitation may well be one that is eclectic and opportunistic, at least from the point of view of the patient.

In view of the fact that cognitive rehabilitation is likely to be a long-term process and that the available resources (specifically, financial and professional) may be limited or may change during the period of treatment, it is important to consider ways to reduce these demands. One solution that shows considerable promise is the introduction of personal computers into the field. This can range from using computer games in geriatric settings (Lynch, 1982) to the administration of specifically designed cognitive exercises as Gianutsos has done. Many such programs by a number of authors have now become available. Schacter and Glisky (1986) wrote somewhat disdainfully about a "virtual cottage industry" of "so-called remedial software" (p. 264) that makes allegedly unsubstantiated claims for promoting the restoration of memory. These authors do, however, see some value in teaching patients with memory loss the skills and vocabulary needed to deal with microcomputers as a new domain of knowledge. Gianutsos & Gianutsos (1979) demonstrated the efficacy of memory training in an amnesic by applying the single-case experimental design as described by Hersen and Barlow (1976). Gianutsos and Gianutsos (1987) have since described the use of this method to prove the microcomputer's worth as an instrument for cognitive rehabilitation.[1] Miller (1984), though remaining cautious, considered microcomputers a potentially valuable tool. He analyzed the difficulties in proving the effectiveness of any method of intervention for the many individually varied manifestations of cognitive dysfunctioning and warned that this will remain a difficult task, possibly because it is a matter of the "cumulative effects of many small advances on a number of fronts" (p. 143). Another problem concerns the understanding and evaluation of the processes of recovery of function, with or without intervention. Of course, this problem is most relevant in cases of cognitive dysfunction resulting from acute brain injury. Kramer and Smith (1986) addressed the issue of evaluating treatment through the use of meta-analysis. With this method, standards of

---

[1]In a different context, Wilson (1986) showed that the single case experimental design is useful in evaluating a multidisciplinary course of memory rehabilitation.

effectiveness are applied to the data from all available controlled assessment studies. Their findings suggest that, in general, cognitive rehabilitation is an effective treatment modality for older patients.

THE PROJECT

The data in this chapter are based on a pilot project in which microcomputer programs have been used in treating geriatric patients with memory complaints. Both practical aspects of the use of microcomputers and some theoretical insights gained will be discussed.

The Geriatric Clinic of Bellevue Hospital Center, New York City, provides comprehensive medical and mental health services for patients over 65 years of age. Memory loss, whether self-reported or observed by family members or caretakers, is a frequent complaint among the clinic's clientele. Many of the patients treated in the clinic are diagnosed as suffering from some variant of dementia. However, even when neuropsychological tests do not show an appreciable impairment in memory functions, the fear of memory loss appears to be so prevalent in this age group, that even minor lapses cause serious apprehension.

Two questions often asked, not least by the patients themselves are: (a) Can elderly people learn new skills? and (b) Can people with memory loss learn new skills? The underlying assumption is, of course, that without an affirmative answer, cognitive rehabilitation will not make sense. It has been shown (Miller, 1984; Squire, 1986) that advanced age does not preclude new learning, and that even amnesics can learn. Schacter and Glisky (1986) qualified the latter finding by adding that, in therapy, learning should be directed toward specific practical tasks. In our project it was found that even people diagnosed as being significantly impaired were able to learn and maintain new skills and to improve on certain computer-presented tasks. It might be added that the level of education plays a role—the more highly educated patients are able to make better use of cognitive rehabilitation, possibly due to a greater potential for metacognition.[2]

The Bellevue Geriatric Computer Memory-Retraining Project was initiated in late 1984. Its aim was to provide short-term (15 weeks) cognitive rehabilitation to geriatric patients presenting with memory problems of

---

[2]Our less well-educated patients sometimes misinterpreted a verbal memory task as a test for spelling and vocabulary and rejected it for this reason. Also, in contrast to most of our female patients, especially the career women, the majority of our male patients had great difficulty finding their way on the keyboard. This may well have reflected a division of labor by gender, not unusual for this age group.

various etiologies. The patients participated in weekly sessions, using personal computers and assisted by a trained volunteer. The project has developed into an integral part of the Bellevue Geriatric Clinic, providing a much needed service for this pervasive problem among the geriatric population. The initial project has been expanded to allow those patients who are interested in continuing beyond the initial 15 weeks (the so-called graduate program). Extensive neuropsychological testing is carried out routinely to document changes and to provide guidelines for treatment.

The decision to use the personal computer was based on the following considerations:

1. The computer requires direct and active participation of the patient in the rehabilitation program.
2. Patients report a sense of satisfaction in being able to master an aspect of modern technology.
3. Cost- and time-effectiveness. The structured material requires little preparation. It can be mastered and administered by relatively inexperienced volunteers working under supervision of a specialist after a short training period.
4. Computer programs can be designed to keep performance records and thus allow for the compilation of comparable data.

The Programs

The computer programs that make up the core of the project repertoire were taken from software (Gianutsos, Blouin & Cochran, 1984) that had already proven its effectiveness in the cognitive rehabilitation of stroke patients and (young) survivors of head injury. These programs could be easily adapted for use with memory-impaired elderly. In addition, some programs derived from commercially available games and learning software were selected. The following criteria determined the selection:

1. Programs were chosen that focus on a specific aspect of cognitive functioning. For instance, the project contains programs focusing on verbal memory (word memory span and memory for association of paired, unrelated words), visual memory, concentration, attention, processing speed, logical reasoning, problem solving and the ability to follow instructions toward the completion of multiple-step and unfamiliar tasks. Learning programs (for math and vocabulary) were also included. The latter programs, though still challenging, were often easier for patients to perform, providing a sense of accomplishment.

2. Programs were chosen that were capable of being administered in a flexible manner, that is, ones that could be varied in level of difficulty to accommodate a patient's initial level of functioning and changes over time. The aim in program selection is to provide focused exercises at a level where success, although a challenge, remains possible. We may have to provide help to the patient, in the initial stages, but we aim for standardized administration of the tasks, as soon as this is feasible. Careful notes are kept of any deviation from standard procedures.

3. Programs were selected where the basic instructions are relatively easy to master and a programmed set-up procedure was adopted that requires minimal manipulation of the keyboard in order to select specific programs. This allows the patients to learn the necessary computer procedures quickly and facilitates the training of the volunteer staff.

Mastery of the tasks is the goal. In order to obtain this, it may be necessary to focus on enhancing the ability to concentrate and to counteract frustration. In this regard, Taylor and Yesavage (1984) found memory exercises to be most effective if preceded by a series of relaxation and concentration exercises.

Furthermore, we introduce memory-enhancing strategies, in order to demonstrate to the patient that there are ways of facilitating the tasks they are asked to perform. Some of these strategies are discussed by Miller (1984) and by Wilson and Moffat (1984).[3]

The Volunteers

Originally the pilot project proposed using both young volunteers and age peers of the patients as two distinct categories. In practice, we have been using almost exclusively young volunteers, mostly undergraduates and occasionally graduate students. Older volunteers proved to have more difficulty mastering the computer skills sufficiently well to teach and assist the patients, although there were some exceptions. In addition, patients

---

[3]Among the strategies we suggested to our patients the following were found to be the most useful: repetition of words, reading out loud; making use of alliteration; lumping words together ("compound word" strategy); using visual imagery; forming associations between words. For visual memory tasks, verbalizing the image or analyzing it into patterns and relationships were the most useful strategies. It is most important to keep an open mind and to find out for oneself what is useful. Active, rather than passive observation of the presented task appears to be essential.

A measure of success is very important to people who interpret their memory lapses as indicative of oncoming dementia. The strategies we help our patients develop are an integral part of the treatment because they make success possible.

generally felt more comfortable working with young volunteers. In part this could be because the patients' comparison of their own abilities with those of a less impaired person of similar age was disturbing to them. The older volunteers themselves were not always comfortable with impaired age mates. Another reason may have been the obvious delight that the elderly patients derived from direct contact with young people.

Intensive initial training in the use of the computer was provided to volunteers, followed by supervised work with individual patients. Volunteers worked independently, although ongoing supervision dealt with developing appropriate strategies for patients and help with problems that arose during the sessions. The latter could be advice on the proper help to give a particular patient or on how to deal appropriately with changes in a patient's behavior. Volunteers are instructed to report such changes because these may indicate the need for intervention by clinic staff, and the volunteers' regular contact with the patient provides a unique opportunity for monitoring such changes.

The Patients

Participating patients were drawn from the Bellevue Geriatric Clinic. They ranged in age from 62 to 89, with 30% of them men and 70% women. (Thirteen men and 30 women completed the course of treatment.) Prior to retirement, most of the patients were employed in intellectually demanding occupations (e.g., lawyers, administrators, executive secretaries). Although all participants presented with a primary complaint of memory loss, the underlying causes were quite varied. An initial screening interview excluded patients who demonstrated severe impairment. This was done because pilot work had indicated that in order to benefit from the program it was important for patients to be able to understand and maintain a simple instructional set within a session. Furthermore, severely impaired patients often lacked the motivation to participate in an ongoing rehabilitation program and might have difficulty tolerating the frustration involved.

As part of the prescreening interview, patients were assessed using the Global Dementia Scale (Reisberg, Ferris, deLeon, & Crook, 1982). All patients scored between a scale score 2 (forgetfulness, mild cognitive decline) and scale score 4 (late confusional state, moderate cognitive decline). In addition, patients had to be assessed as sufficiently physically intact to be able to participate in weekly sessions over the 15-week initial program. All patients were independently assessed by clinic physicians and psychologists and were diagnostically assigned to one of three general categories as follows:

1. *Organic dementias such as Alzheimer's disease, Multiple Infarct Dementia, Parkinson's Disease, and so on.* Patients in this category demonstrated impairments on objective neuropsychological testing and mental status evaluations, with medical and/or neurological examinations supporting these indications. Among the patients in our program 17 fell into this group (40%).

2. *Psychiatric illness without objective evidence of organicity, but presenting with primary complaints involving memory loss.* Neuropsychological test data and mental status determinations were within normal limits, but with a suggestion that cognitive functioning was below optimum for the individual. Patients in this category were independently diagnosed as suffering from a psychiatric disorder. In general, pathological conditions included dysthymia, character disorders, and neuroses. Almost all patients in this group had at one time been depressed or were currently assessed as such. Many of these patients had received long-term treatment with antidepressant medications. Among the patients in our program 7 fell into this category (16%).

3. *Subjective complaints of memory loss in the absence of either diagnosed organic pathology or primary psychiatric disorder.* Neuropsychological test data and mental status determinations were within normal limits, but as with category 2 there was the suggestion of below optimal performance. These patients were independently assessed as suffering from an adjustment disorder with depressive and anxious features. Among the patients in our program 19 belonged to this group (44%).

It is of interest to note that depression, although primarily evident in the psychiatric group, was to some extent a contributing factor in the presentation of many of the patients in the program. The patients with adjustment disorders in category 3 often demonstrated depressive features, whereas the organic patients were often depressed secondary to their dementia. It is likely that one cause of depression in a cohort of elderly patients with memory loss is the patient's increasing awareness of the changes in his or her ability to function as before. The relationship between depression, self esteem, sense of hopelessness, and feelings of loss of control over one's environment may be particularly relevant to the efficacy of cognitive rehabilitation in a geriatric population. This point is addressed more fully later in this chapter.

CASE MATERIAL

In this section some observations from this ongoing project are presented with illustrative case material. In general, patients were easily able to accommodate to working with the computer, finding the experience challenging and rewarding. Patients were given the choice of continuing after the initial 15 weeks (which many opted to do) or were allowed to return for "refresher" sessions after a period of time. Data from patients returning after periods of up to 1 year indicate that there was a consistent maintenance of the gains made during the initial program, suggesting that they were able to utilize learned strategies in an ongoing manner.

Case 1

Ms. B. is a 68-year-old woman who requested evaluation and treatment of her memory problems. She had been receiving medication for a neurological condition for many years, and her physician had increased her dosage of medication several weeks prior to initial contact with the program. The patient reported that she was having problems remembering names and appointments and was misplacing objects. She was quite distressed about this, fearing it was the beginning of Alzheimer's disease. Baseline neuropsychological test scores were in general within normal limits for her age. There was some lowering of scores on abstract reasoning for both visual and verbal modalities, but the profile was of someone without objective signs of cognitive decline (group 3).

Ms. B. completed the initial 15-week series, showing improvement on most tasks. Then she chose not to continue as she was planning to find a part-time job. After 11 months she returned to the program for additional sessions because she was again concerned about her memory.

Figure 16.1 is a graphic presentation of her performance on the Concentration task (Levin, 1978). This task is similar to the game Concentration, which uses conventional playing cards. It involves a computer display of a 4 × 5 grid of 20 numbered boxes. Each numbered box contains the name of an item (object or animal), which is only displayed when called up by number during one of the turns. The patient's task is to match the pairs in the least number of turns by exposing two boxes per turn. Mismatches are covered up again, and correct pairs are eliminated from the grid. Thus lower scores reflect better performance (fewer turns to match all 10 pairs) with 15 or 16 the best possible score. Performance on this particular task is quite sensitive to the use of different strategies and easily affected by deficits in attention or concentration.

Examination of Fig. 16.1 reveals a gradual improvement of performance in Sessions 1 through 11. Her performance in Session 1 (training) reflects greater assistance from the volunteer. On her own (from Session 2 on) performance declined, and then improved, achieving an optimal level in Session 11. The general increase in scores (and decline in performance) in Sessions 12–15 reflects what may be fatigue or boredom, as this task can become tedious for patients once they feel they have mastered it.

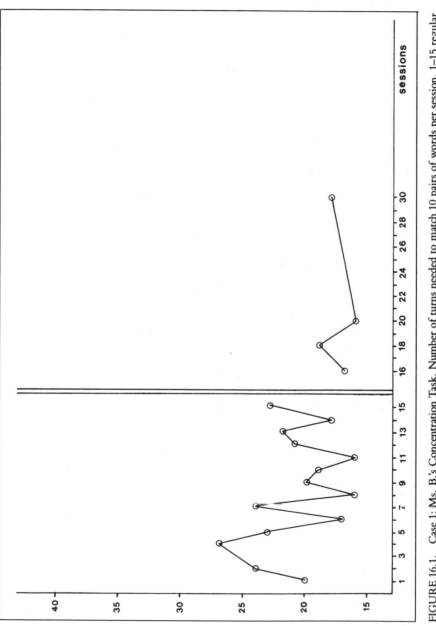

FIGURE 16.1. Case 1: Ms. B.'s Concentration Task. Number of turns needed to match 10 pairs of words per session. 1–15 regular sessions; 16–30 graduate sessions. Interval: 11 months.

What is noteworthy, however, is that after 11 months, Ms. B. was able to resume her optimal level of performance (Sessions 16, 18, 20, and 30). The impression is that Ms. B. had learned and maintained the appropriate strategies and was able to apply these to the task at hand in an effective manner.

Poor performance on memory tasks was frequently associated with maladaptive emotional responses to failure. This may be the situation particularly with individuals who have relied heavily upon their intellectual capacities throughout their lives as a means of coping with emotional demands. These patients are often acutely aware of changes in functioning and may respond with overwhelming anxiety and frustration. Rehabilitation focuses on assisting such patients in moderating interfering negative emotions. They are taught to reflect on how their responses affect outcome and are trained to develop more adaptive strategies for approaching the task at hand. The immediate feedback provided by the computer reinforces appropriate responses.

Case 2

Ms. S., age 75, had been a patient at the clinic for several years prior to beginning the computer program. She was being treated medically for a systemic disease and was seen for weekly psychotherapy. An accomplished musician, she was struggling with increasing physical disability and had begun to experience symptoms of memory impairment, which had grown worse during and after an acute medical hospitalization. Her therapist had noted that although there was probably an organic component to her symptoms, her memory problems were also linked to her depression and sense of helplessness in the face of aging and illness (group 2).

Her medical history revealed objective neurological findings including an abnormal EEG, a history of seizure activity, and acute episodes of disorientation. In addition, it was noted that her systemic disease was frequently associated with encephalopathy. Neuropsychological test scores, although generally within normal limits for her age, were probably lower relative to her previous level of functioning, which was assessed to be in the superior range.

Figure 16.2 is a graphic representation of performance on the Concentration task.

Initially Ms. S. was unable to cary out the task at all due to extreme anxiety, frustration, and a sense of helplessness. This performance was extremely at odds with her premorbid intellectual functioning and current cognitive capacity as measured by baseline testing.

By Session 8 she could complete the task with a great deal of help from the volunteer, and showed improvement (Sessions 9–11). Working more

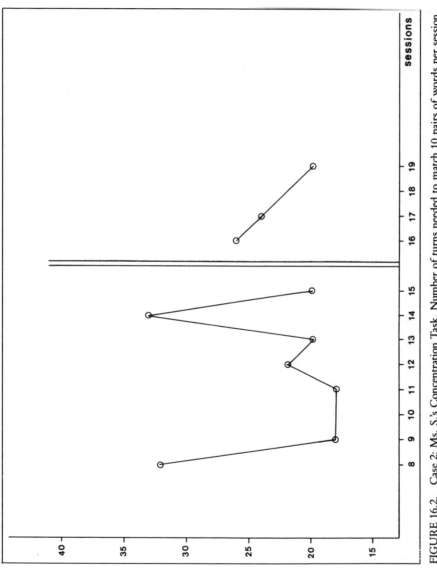

FIGURE 16.2. Case 2: Ms. S.'s Concentration Task. Number of turns needed to match 10 pairs of words per session. 1–15 regular sessions; 16–19 graduate sessions. Interval: 3 weeks.

independently, her scores started to level off indicating improvement (Sessions 12–15). However, there was a marked deterioration during Session 14. Interestingly, this session coincided with behavioral observations indicating a high level of anxiety and frustration.

As was the case with Ms. B., following a brief (3 week) interruption, the patient was able to maintain her gains.

As noted, about 40% of the patients in the program carry a diagnosis of organic dementia. Typically, the course of dementia is chronic and deteriorating, although periods of stable functioning have been observed. One issue relevant to work with demented patients concerns the capacity to learn in a systematic manner.

Case 3

Ms. F., 80 years old, was referred to the clinic by her private physician for treatment of cardiac problems and memory loss. The patient was aware of some of her difficulties, reporting that she misplaced objects and missed appointments. However, she was unaware of the extent of her impairment. Her husband, who was younger than she, reported that he had to select her clothes, and remind her to eat, although she was able to maintain her personal care. Her score on the GDS (Global Dementia Scale) was 4 (moderate impairment). Initial evaluation revealed significant impairments on tests of verbal and spatial memory, significant word-finding problems (possibly due in part to the fact that English was not her native language, although she spoke it fluently), and evidence of mild depression. Her abstract reasoning skills were within normal limits. The general impression was of a Multiple Infarct Dementia with depression secondary to the dementia (group 1). Cases 1 and 2 present data from the memory program Concentration. Our experience with patients with moderate organic pathology reveals that this program is too difficult for them to master, requiring more complex memory and concentration skills than are available to them. For these patients a simpler memory task was chosen that had more structure and could be adjusted to their level of functioning. This task, Word Memory Span (Gianutsos et al., 1984), presents patients with lists of words varying in length from one to seven words and with an adjustable exposure time. The patient's task was to recall as many of these words as possible in the correct order.

Figure 16.3 is a graphic presentation of Ms. F.'s performance on the Word Memory Span task. Scores reflect total number of words recalled per session divided by the number of lists of words presented in that session. As can be readily seen, learning occurred over a period of about 1 year with a gradual but steady increase in score. It is interesting to note

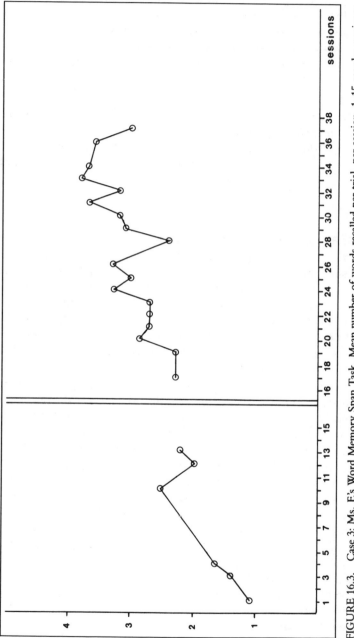

FIGURE 16.3. Case 3: Ms. F.'s Word Memory Span Task. Mean number of words recalled per trial, per session. 1–15 regular sessions; 16–40 graduate sessions. No interval.

that there was a period of five sessions during which this program was not presented, yet the patient was able to maintain the earlier level of learning. Ms. F. is one of the patients who chose to continue without interruption after the initial series of computer sessions. As the data indicate, there was continued improvement in her verbal recall over a period of 6 months. These gains are particularly striking in view of the fact that her diagnosis was one of progressive dementia. In her daily life over this period her emotional state improved, in part due to an easing of family pressure on her to perform at her premorbid level. One might speculate that her sense of mastery contributed to her ability to learn and to her improved emotional state.

DISCUSSION

Metacognition is a term used to describe an individual's awareness of how his or her cognitive processes function. Under normal circumstances, individuals are not consciously aware of metacognitive strategies. Perception, organization of material, memory strategies, and coding of information occur without a second thought. Sometimes when under pressure—for example, a college student studying for an exam—metacognitive strategies may become more apparent, but generally this is not the case. It is when cognitive processes fail to operate smoothly that individuals may become acutely aware of dysfunction and that it becomes useful to pay closer attention to the manner in which cognition operates. Recent studies (Smith & Kramer, 1987) have demonstrated that development of metacognition can increase cognitive abilities. In a rehabilitation program this is accomplished through the learning of specific facilitating strategies and through discussion. In the present situation, although there are general guidelines, strategies are developed on an individualized basis. For example, when a new task is presented and explained to a patient and things go well, the volunteer (worker) might say: "How did you do that?" In this way the patient is encouraged to reflect upon his or her behavior and helpful strategies can spontaneously be brought to awareness. If necessary the worker may suggest a strategy that has been found helpful. The patients are then able to develop and practice these strategies in a non-threatening environment and eventually experience success. During the rehabilitation session the patients are asked to reflect upon the demands of a particular task and develop appropriate strategies. This process requires conscious and systematic effort that trains the ability to pay attention and concentrate. Shortcomings in these areas may well have been responsible at least in part for the apparent memory failures. Gradually such strategies may generalize to other tasks in daily life. Similarly, patients are helped to identify intact areas of functioning and to rely more heavily upon these areas when approaching a task. The use of computers enhances the development of metacognition through strategies. Because feedback is immediate, it provides a patient with an opportunity for quick assessment of their usefulness, and so reinforces successful behavior. For example, Ms. S. eventually understood that her global sense of loss of control led to poor performance, and that a steady focus on the task could lead to success.

Learned helplessness (LH) as identified by Seligman (1974) is another concept that may be particularly relevant to cognitive rehabilitation. Seligman demonstrated in a wide variety of experimental and natural situations that LH, a sense of loss of control over one's environment, is closely connected to, or as he suggests, a significant cause of depression. Clearly, even minor lapses in memory can result in a sense of helplessness and more significant losses can be devastating to one's sense of control. The world becomes unpredictable: wallets disappear, well-known places and people are suddenly unfamiliar, once-dependable skills are gone. In this context it is not surprising that many demented patients develop "paranoid" delusions, such as that people are stealing their money and taking their possessions. These delusions at least seem to help in organizing and explaining a chaotic world. In the less extreme cases there may be a sense of depression related to the inability to maintain control over one's experience. Cognitive rehabilitation, specifically with the use of computers, returns the sense of control to the individual. Reinforcement is immediate and contingent upon performance rather than unsystematic and unpredictable. During the sessions patients feel more in control over their environment, especially because the tasks can be adapted to a patient's level of capability, and mastery is the goal. One can speculate that this experience of control may generalize to other areas of life, thus alleviating some of the secondary depression associated with cognitive dysfunction.

Finally, for many of our geriatric patients the opportunity to work with younger volunteers has proved very rewarding. The volunteers are trained to be flexible and supportive, providing patients with an added sense of value and self worth. As mentioned earlier, it is interesting to note that although we originally planned to have age peer volunteers as well, this did not work out well for either patients or volunteers. Some of the patients may have felt threatened by being assisted by older individuals who were "intact" and some of our older volunteers reported emotional stress because they either identified with the patients or were reminded of loved ones with similar impairments.

Given these psychological issues one may ask why the same results could not be achieved by psychotherapy. Several answers suggest themselves. First these patients are not asking for psychotherapy and many-would be resistant to the suggestion. In a geriatric population especially, the need for a psychologist's or psychiatrist's care carries a certain stigma. These patients are not asking for help with "emotional" problems. Thus, many in our geriatric program would not accept the suggestion that they need psychotherapy. Secondly, cognitive rehabilitation is symptom-specific and directly addresses the patients' concerns. It requires active participation by the patient. The emphasis is on developing strategies to cope with memory problems and these problems are taken quite seriously. This is particularly important for patients with minimal impairment who are nevertheless quite disturbed about it, and who may have already heard: "Don't worry, you are fine," or "It's just part of getting old." They know they are not fine and these global reassurances will usually make them feel worse, because their symptoms persist and yet they are being told that there is something wrong with their concern.

Finally, the immediate, response contingent, and nonjudgmental reinforcement provided by the computer may specifically counteract the experience of helplessness and loss of control.

In a geriatric population, assessing the effectiveness of a cognitive rehabilitation program presents a number of difficulties. The programs are individualized and often administered in the context of a prognosis of persistent cognitive decline on an organic basis (patients with Primary Degenerative Dementia, PDD). Thus, for many patients, just remaining stable may be the best criterion of success. In spite of this difficulty, Kramer and Smith (1986), using a meta-analytic approach, demonstrated the general efficacy of cognitive rehabilitation in a geriatric population. The focus of the present program is primarily clinical, offering treatment for a uniquely underserved population. The main indication of success, under these circumstances, may well be the fact that, in spite of practical hardships, patients return for their computer sessions, week after week. Gianutsos (1986) suggested that one measure of success of a particular treatment program can be found in the amount of use it gets and in the subjective feelings the patients express about it. Furthermore, as in the case of Ms. F., almost all of our patients improved in performance scores, for at least some of the programs, indicating that learning did take place.

ACKNOWLEDGMENTS

The Bellevue Computer Memory Project was started in 1984 with a seed grant from the United Hospital Fund of New York, and has since been supported in part by a grant from the Metropolitan Jewish Geriatric Center.

We thank Dr. Rosamond Gianutsos, Cognitive Rehabilitation Services, Sunnyside, N.Y., for her invaluable help and advice in starting the Project. The Department of Volunteer Services of Bellevue Hospital Center, Ms. Joan Dumont, Director, provided us with our staff of excellent volunteers, who formed an integral part of the Project.

REFERENCES

Cicerone, K. D., & Tupper, D. E. (1986). Cognitive assessment in the neuropsychological rehabilitation of head-injured adults. In B. P. Uzzell & Y. Gross (Eds.), *Clinical neuropsychology of intervention* (pp. 59–83). Boston: Martinus Nijhoff Publishing.

Gianutsos, R. (1980, August/September). What is cognitive rehabilitation? *Journal of Rehabilitation,* 36–40.

Gianutsos, R. (1986). *"Conversation Hour"* with D. Schacter, American Psychological Association meeting, Division 40 (Clinical Neuropsychology), Washington, DC.

Gianutsos, R., Blouin, M., & Cochran, E. L. (1984). *Manual and software, Cogrehab* (Vol. 3). Bayport, NY. Life Science Associates.

Gianutsos, J., & Gianutsos, R. (1979). Rehabilitating the verbal recall of brain-injured patients by mnemonic training: An experimental demonstration using single-case methodology. *Journal of Clinical Neuropsychology, 2,* 117–135.

Gianutsos, J., & Gianutsos, R. (1987). Single-case experimental approaches to the assessment of interventions in rehabilitation psychology. In B. Kaplan (Ed.), *Rehabilitation psychology desk reference* (pp. 453–470). Rockville, MD: Aspen.

Griffith, V. E. (1979). *A stroke in the family.* London, England: Wildwood House.

Gross, Y., & Schutz, L. E. (1986). Intervention models in neuropsychology. In B. P. Uzzell & Y. Gross (Eds.), *Clinical neuropsychology of intervention* (pp. 179–204). Boston: Martinus Nijhoff Publishing.

Hart, T., & Hayden, M. E. (1986). The ecological validity of neuropsychological assessment and remediation. In B. P. Uzzell & Y. Gross (Eds.), *Clinical neuropsychology of intervention* (pp. 21–50). Boston: Martinus Nijhoff Publishing.

Hersen, M., & Barlow, D. H. (1976). *Single case experimental designs: Strategies for studying behavior change.* New York: Pergamon Press.

Kramer, N. A., & Smith, M. C. (1986). Cognitive training of older subjects: Factors influencing effectiveness. Gerontological Society of America meeting, Chicago.

Levin, E. (1978). Memorybuilder. Program Design, Inc. [computer software].

Lynch, W. J. (1982). The use of electronic games in cognitive rehabilitation. In L. E. Trexler (Ed.), *Cognitive rehabilitation: Conceptualization and intervention* (pp. 263–274). New York, Plenum Press.

Mayer, N. H., Keating, D. J., & Rapp, D. (1986). Skills, routines, and activity patterns of daily living: a functional nested approach. In B. P. Uzzell & Y. Gross (Eds.), *Clinical neuropsychology of intervention* (pp. 205–222). Boston: Martinus Nijhoff Publishing.

Miller, E. (1984). *Recovery and management of neuropsychological impairments.* New York: Wiley.

Piasetsky, E. B., Ben-Yishay, Y., Weinberg, J., & Diller, L. (1982). The systematic remediation of specific disorders: Selected application of methods derived in a clinical research setting. In L. E. Trexler (Ed.), *Cognitive rehabilitation: Conceptualization and intervention* pp. 205–222. New York: Plenum Press.

Randt, C. T., & Brown, E. R. (1983). *The Randt Memory Test.* Bayport, NY: Life Sciences Associates.

Reisberg, B., Ferris, S. H., de Leon, M. J., & Crook, T. (1982). Global Deterioration Scale (GDS) for age-associated cognitive decline and Alzheimer's disease. *American Journal of Psychiatry, 139,* 1136–1139.

Schacter, D. L., & Glisky, E. L. (1986). Memory remediation: Restoration, alleviation and the acquisition of domain-specific knowledge. In B. P. Uzzell & Y. Gross (Eds.), *Clinical neuropsychology of intervention* (pp. 257–282). Boston: Martinus Nijhoff Publishing.

Seligman, M. E. P. (1974). Depression and learned helplessness. In R. J. Freedman & M. M. Katz (Eds.), *The psychology of depression. Contemporary theory and research.* (pp. 83–125). New York: Wiley.

Smith, M. C., & Kramer, N. A. (1987). Workshop session in *Teaching reasoning and memory strategies to older adults,* sponsored by the Program in Counseling Psychology, Teachers College, Columbia University, New York.

Squire, L. R. (1986). Mechanisms of memory. *Science, 232,* 1612–1619.

Taylor, L. L., & Yesavage, J. A. (1984). Cognitive retraining programs for the elderly: A case study of cost/benefit issues. *Clinical Gerontology, 2*(4), 51–63.

Willis, S. L. (1985). Toward an educational psychology of the adult learner: Cognitive and intellectual bases. In J. E. Birren & K. W. Schaie (Eds.), *Handbook of the psychology of aging* (2nd ed., pp. 818–844). New York: van Nostrand Reinhold.

Wilson, B. A. (1986). *Rehabilitation of memory.* New York: Guilford Publications.

Wilson, B., & Moffat, N. (1984). Rehabilitation of memory for everyday life. In J. E. Harris & P. E. Morris (Eds.), *Everyday memory. Actions and absent-mindedness* (pp. 207–233). Orlando: Academic.

Author Index

Subject Index